Lecture Notes in Computer Science　　　10942

Commenced Publication in 1973
Founding and Former Series Editors:
Gerhard Goos, Juris Hartmanis, and Jan van Leeuwen

More information about this series at http://www.springer.com/series/7407

Ying Tan · Yuhui Shi
Qirong Tang (Eds.)

Advances
in Swarm Intelligence

9th International Conference, ICSI 2018
Shanghai, China, June 17–22, 2018
Proceedings, Part II

 Springer

Editors
Ying Tan
Peking University
Beijing
China

Qirong Tang
Tongji University
Shanghai
China

Yuhui Shi
Southern University of Science
  and Technology
Shenzhen
China

ISSN 0302-9743   ISSN 1611-3349 (electronic)
Lecture Notes in Computer Science
ISBN 978-3-319-93817-2   ISBN 978-3-319-93818-9 (eBook)
https://doi.org/10.1007/978-3-319-93818-9

Library of Congress Control Number: 2018947347

LNCS Sublibrary: SL1 – Theoretical Computer Science and General Issues

Printed on acid-free paper

This Springer imprint is published by the registered company Springer International Publishing AG part of Springer Nature
The registered company address is: Gewerbestrasse 11, 6330 Cham, Switzerland

Preface

This book and its companion volumes, LNCS vols. 10941 and 10942, constitute the proceedings of the 9th International Conference on Swarm Intelligence (ICSI 2018) held during June 17–22, 2018, in Shanghai, China.

The theme of ICSI 2018 was "Serving Life with Intelligence Science." ICSI 2018 provided an excellent opportunity and/or an academic forum for academics and practitioners to present and discuss the latest scientific results and methods, innovative ideas, and advantages in theories, technologies, and applications in swarm intelligence. The technical program covered most aspects of swarm intelligence and its related areas.

ICSI 2018 was the ninth international gathering in the world for researchers working on swarm intelligence, following successful events in Fukuoka (ICSI 2017), Bali (ICSI 2016), Beijing (ICSI-CCI 2015), Hefei (ICSI 2014), Harbin (ICSI 2013), Shenzhen (ICSI 2012), Chongqing (ICSI 2011), and Beijing (ICSI 2010). The conference provided a high-level academic forum for participants to disseminate their new research findings and discuss emerging areas of research. It also created a stimulating environment for participants to interact and exchange information on future challenges and opportunities in the field of swarm intelligence research. ICSI 2018 was held in conjunction with the Third International Conference on Data Mining and Big Data (DMBD 2018) at Shanghai, China, with the aim of sharing common mutual ideas, promoting transverse fusion, and stimulating innovation.

ICSI 2018 took place at the Anting Crowne Plaza Holiday Hotel in Shanghai, which is the first five-star international hotel in the Jiading District of Grand Shanghai. Shanghai, Hu for short, also known as Shen, is the largest and the most developed metropolis with both modern and traditional Chinese features in China. It is also a global financial center and transport hub. Shanghai offers many spectacular views and different perspectives. It is a popular travel destination for visitors to sense the pulsating development of China. The participants of ICSI 2018 had the opportunity to enjoy traditional Hu operas, beautiful landscapes, and the hospitality of the Chinese people, Chinese cuisine, and modern Shanghai.

We received 197 submissions and invited submissions from about 488 authors in 38 countries and regions (Algeria, Argentina, Aruba, Australia, Austria, Bangladesh, Brazil, China, Colombia, Cuba, Czech Republic, Ecuador, Fiji, Finland, Germany, Hong Kong, India, Iran, Iraq, Italy, Japan, Malaysia, Mexico, New Zealand, Norway, Portugal, Romania, Russia, Serbia, Singapore, South Africa, Spain, Sweden, Chinese Taiwan, Thailand, UK, USA, Venezuela) across six continents (Asia, Europe, North America, South America, Africa, and Oceania). Each submission was reviewed by at least two reviewers, and on average 2.7 reviewers. Based on rigorous reviews by the Program Committee members and reviewers, 113 high-quality papers were selected for publication in this proceedings volume, with an acceptance rate of 57.36%. The papers are organized in 24 cohesive sections covering major topics of swarm intelligence, computational intelligence, and data science research and development.

On behalf of the Organizing Committee of ICSI 2018, we would like to express our sincere thanks to Tongji University, Peking University, and Southern University of Science and Technology for their sponsorship, and to the Robotics and Multi-body System Laboratory at the School of Mechanical Engineering of Tongji University, the Computational Intelligence Laboratory of Peking University, and the IEEE Beijing Chapter for its technical cosponsorship, as well as to our supporters: International Neural Network Society, World Federation on Soft Computing, Beijing Xinghui Hi-Tech Co., Bulinge, and Springer.

We would also like to thank the members of the Advisory Committee for their guidance, the members of the international Program Committee and additional reviewers for reviewing the papers, and the members of the Publications Committee for checking the accepted papers in a short period of time. We are particularly grateful to Springer for publishing the proceedings in the prestigious series of *Lecture Notes in Computer Science*. Moreover, we wish to express our heartfelt appreciation to the plenary speakers, session chairs, and student helpers. In addition, there are still many more colleagues, associates, friends, and supporters who helped us in immeasurable ways; we express our sincere gratitude to them all. Last but not the least, we would like to thank all the speakers, authors, and participants for their great contributions that made ICSI 2018 successful and all the hard work worthwhile.

May 2018   Ying Tan
                                                                         Yuhui Shi
                                                                        Qirong Tang

Organization

General Co-chairs

Ying Tan	Peking University, China
Russell C. Eberhart	IUPUI, USA

Program Committee Chair

Yuhui Shi	Southern University of Science and Technology, China

Organizing Committee Chair

Qirong Tang	Tongji University, China

Advisory Committee Chairs

Gary G. Yen	Oklahoma State University, USA
Qidi Wu	Ministry of Education, China

Technical Committee Co-chairs

Haibo He	University of Rhode Island Kingston, USA
Kay Chen Tan	City University of Hong Kong, SAR China
Nikola Kasabov	Aukland University of Technology, New Zealand
Ponnuthurai N. Suganthan	Nanyang Technological University, Singapore
Xiaodong Li	RMIT University, Australia
Hideyuki Takagi	Kyushu University, Japan
M.Middendorf	University of Leipzig, Germany
Mengjie Zhang	Victoria University of Wellington, New Zealand
Lei Wang	Tongji University, China

Plenary Session Co-chairs

Andreas Engelbrecht	University of Pretoria, South Africa
Chaoming Luo	University of Detroit Mercy, USA

Invited Session Co-chairs

Maoguo Gong	Northwest Polytechnic University, China
Weian Guo	Tongji University, China

Special Sessions Chairs

Ben Niu   Shenzhen University, China
Yinan Guo   China University of Mining and Technology, China

Tutorial Co-chairs

Milan Tuba   John Naisbitt University, Serbia
Hongtao Lu   Shanghai Jiaotong University, China

Publications Co-chairs

Swagatam Das   Indian Statistical Institute, India
Radu-Emil Precup   Politehnica University of Timisoara, Romania

Publicity Co-chairs

Yew-Soon Ong   Nanyang Technological University, Singapore
Carlos Coello   CINVESTAV-IPN, Mexico
Yaochu Jin   University of Surrey, UK

Finance and Registration Chairs

Andreas Janecek   University of Vienna, Austria
Suicheng Gu   Google Corporation, USA

Local Arrangements Co-chairs

Changhong Fu   Tongji University, China
Lulu Gong   Tongji University, China

Conference Secretariat

Jie Lee   Peking University, China

Program Committee

Kouzou Abdellah   University of Djelfa, Algeria
Peter Andras   Keele University, UK
Esther Andrés   INTA, Spain
Sz Apotecas   UAM-Cuajimalpa, Mexico
Carmelo J. A. Bastos Filho University of Pernambuco, Brazil
Salim Bouzerdoum   University of Wollongong, Australia
Xinye Cai   Nanjing University of Aeronautics and Astronautics,
                             China
David Camacho   Universidad Autonoma de Madrid, Spain

Bin Cao	Tsinghua University, China
Josu Ceberio	University of the Basque Country, Spain
Kit Yan Chan	DEBII, Australia
Junfeng Chen	Hohai University, China
Mu-Song Chen	Da-Yeh University, Taiwan, China
Walter Chen	National Taipei University of Technology, Taiwan, China
Xu Chen	Jiangsu University, China
Yiqiang Chen	Institute of Computing Technology, Chinese Academy of Sciences, China
Hui Cheng	Liverpool John Moores University, UK
Ran Cheng	University of Surrey, UK
Shi Cheng	Shaanxi Normal University, China
Prithviraj Dasgupta	University of Nebraska, USA
Kusum Deep	Indian Institute of Technology Roorkee, India
Mingcong Deng	Tokyo University of Agriculture and Technology, Japan
Bei Dong	Shaanxi Nomal University, China
Wei Du	East China University of Science and Technology, China
Mark Embrechts	RPI, USA
Andries Engelbrecht	University of Pretoria, South Africa
Zhun Fan	Technical University of Denmark, Denmark
Jianwu Fang	Xi'an Institute of Optics and Precision Mechanics of CAS, China
Wei Fang	Jiangnan University, China
Liang Feng	Chongqing University, China
A. H. Gandomi	Stevens Institute of Technology, USA
Kaizhou Gao	Liaocheng University, China
Liang Gao	Huazhong University of Science and Technology, China
Shangce Gao	University of Toyama, Japan
Ying Gao	Guangzhou University, China
Shenshen Gu	Shanghai University, China
Ping Guo	Beijing Normal University, China
Weian Guo	Tongji University, China
Ahmed Hafaifa	University of Djelfa, Algeria
Ran He	National Laboratory of Pattern Recognition, China
Jun Hu	Chinese Academy of Sciences, China
Xiaohui Hu	GE Digital, Inc., USA
Andreas Janecek	University of Vienna, Austria
Changan Jiang	Ritsumeikan University, Japan
Mingyan Jiang	Shandong University, China
Qiaoyong Jiang	Xi'an University of Technology, China
Colin Johnson	University of Kent, UK
Arun Khosla	National Institute of Technology Jalandhar, India

Pavel Kromer   VSB Technical University, Ostrava, Czech Republic
Germano Lambert-Torres   PS Solutions, USA
Xiujuan Lei   Shaanxi Normal University, China
Bin Li   University of Science and Technology of China, China
Xiaodong Li   RMIT University, Australia
Xuelong Li   Chinese Academy of Sciences, China
Yangyang Li   Xidian University, China
Jing Liang   Zhengzhou University, China
Andrei Lihu   Politehnica University of Timisoara, Romania
Jialin Liu   Queen Mary University of London, UK
Ju Liu   Shandong University, China
Qunfeng Liu   Dongguan University of Technology, China
Hui Lu   Beihang University, China
Wenlian Lu   Fudan University, China
Wenjian Luo   University of Science and Technology of China, China
Jinwen Ma   Peking University, China
Lianbo Ma   Northeastern University, USA
Katherine Malan   University of South Africa, South Africa
Chengying Mao   Jiangxi University of Finance and Economics, China
Michalis Mavrovouniotis   Nottingham Trent University, UK
Yi Mei   Victoria University of Wellington, New Zealand
Bernd Meyer   Monash University, Australia
Efrén Mezura-Montes   University of Veracruz, Mexico
Martin Middendorf   University of Leipzig, Germany
Renan Moioli   Santos Dumont Institute, Edmond and Lily Safra
                                International Institute of Neuroscience, Brazil
Daniel Molina Cabrera   Universidad de Cádiz, Spain
Sanaz Mostaghim   Institute IWS, Germany
Carsten Mueller   University of Economics, Czech Republic
Ben Niu   Shenzhen University, China
Linqiang Pan   Huazhong University of Science and Technology,
                                China
Quan-Ke Pan   Huazhong University of Science and Technology,
                                China
Bijaya Ketan Panigrahi   IIT Delhi, India
Mario Pavone   University of Catania, Italy
Yan Pei   University of Aizu, Japan
Thomas Potok   ORNL, USA
Mukesh Prasad   University of Technology, Sydney, Australia
Radu-Emil Precup   Politehnica University of Timisoara, Romania
Kai Qin   Swinburne University of Technology, Australia
Quande Qin   Shenzhen University, China
Boyang Qu   Zhongyuan University of Technology, China
Robert Reynolds   Wayne State University, USA
Guangchen Ruan   Indiana University Bloomington, USA
Helem Sabina Sanchez   Universitat Politècnica de Catalunya, Spain

Yuji Sato	Hosei University, Japan
Carlos Segura	Centro de Investigación en Matemáticas, A.C. (CIMAT), Mexico
Zhongzhi Shi	Institute of Computing Technology Chinese Academy of Sciences, China
Joao Soares	GECAD, Germany
Ponnuthurai Suganthan	Nanyang Technological University, Singapore
Jianyong Sun	University of Nottingham, UK
Yifei Sun	Shaanxi Normal University, China
Hideyuki Takagi	Kyushu University, Japan
Ying Tan	Peking University, China
Qirong Tang	Tongji University, China
Qu Tianshu	Peking University, China
Mario Ventresca	Purdue University, USA
Cong Wang	Northeastern University, USA
Gai-Ge Wang	Chinese Ocean University, China
Handing Wang	University of Surrey, UK
Hong Wang	Shenzhen University, China
Lei Wang	Tongji University, China
Lipo Wang	Nanyang Technological University, Singapore
Qi Wang	Northwestern Polytechnical University, China
Rui Wang	National University of Defense Technology, China
Yuping Wang	Xidian University, China
Zhenzhen Wang	Jinling Institute of Technology, China
Ka-Chun Wong	City University of Hong Kong, SAR China
Man Leung Wong	Lingnan University, Hong Kong, SAR China
Guohua Wu	National University of Defense Technology, China
Zhou Wu	Chonqing University, China
Shunren Xia	Zhejiang University, China
Ning Xiong	Mälardalen University, Sweden
Benlian Xu	Changshu Institute of Technology, China
Rui Xu	Hohai University, China
Xuesong Yan	China University of Geosciences, China
Shengxiang Yang	De Montfort University, UK
Yingjie Yang	De Montfort University, UK
Zl Yang	Shenzhen Institute of Advanced Technology, Chinese Academy of Sciences, China
Wei-Chang Yeh	National Tsinghua University, Taiwan, China
Guo Yi-Nan	China University of Mining and Technology, China
Peng-Yeng Yin	National Chi Nan University, Taiwan, China
Jie Zhang	Newcastle University, UK
Junqi Zhang	Tongji University, China
Lifeng Zhang	Renmin University, China
Qieshi Zhang	Shenzhen Institutes of Advanced Technology, Chinese Academy of Sciences, China
Tao Zhang	Tianjin University, China

Xingyi Zhang   Anhui University, China
Zhenya Zhang   Anhui Jianzhu University, China
Zili Zhang   Deakin University, Australia
Jianjun Zhao   Kyushu University, Japan
Xinchao Zhao   Beijing University of Posts and Telecommunications,
                               China
Wenming Zheng   Southeast University, China
Yujun Zheng   Zhejiang University, China
Zexuan Zhu   Shenzhen University, China
Xingquan Zuo   Beijing University of Posts and Telecommunications,
                               China

Additional Reviewers

Cheng, Tingli   Tang, Chuangao
Ding, Jingyi   Tian, Yanling
Dominguez, Saul   Wang, Shusen
Gao, Chao   Xie, Yong
Jin, Xin   Xu, Gang
Lezama, Fernando   Yu, Jun
Li, Xiangtao   Zhang, Mengxuan
Lu, Cheng   Zhang, Peng
Pan, Zhiwen   Zhang, Shixiong
Song, Tengfei   Zhang, Yuxin
Srivastava, Ankur   Zuo, Lulu
Su, Housheng

Contents – Part II

Fuzzy Logic Approaches

Planning and Routing Problems

Recommendation in Social Media

Image Enhancement

Deep Learning

Contents – Part I

Differential Evolution

Fireworks Algorithm

Bacterial Foraging Optimization

Hybrid Optimization Algorithms

Multi-Objective Optimization

Multi-Agent Systems

Path Following of Autonomous Agents Under the Effect of Noise

Krishna Raghuwaiya[1,2]($\boxtimes$), Bibhya Sharma[1,2], Jito Vanualailai[1], and Parma Nand[2]

[1] The University of the South Pacific, Suva, Fiji
raghuwaiya_k@usp.ac.fj
[2] Auckland University of Technology, Auckland, New Zealand

Abstract. In this paper, we adopt the architecture of the Lyapunov-based Control Scheme (LbCS) and integrate a leader-follower approach to propose a collision-free path following strategy of a group of mobile car-like robots. A robot is assigned the responsibility of a leader, while the follower robots position themselves relative to the leader so that the path of the leader robot is followed with arbitrary desired clearance by the follower robot, avoiding any inter-robot collision while navigating in a terrain with obstacles under the influence of noise. A set of artificial potential field functions is proposed using the control scheme for the avoidance of obstacles and attraction to their designated targets. The effectiveness of the proposed nonlinear acceleration control laws is demonstrated through computer simulations which prove the efficiency of the control technique and also demonstrates its scalability for larger groups.

Keywords: Lyapunov · Nonholonomic mobile robots
Path following · Leader-follower

1 Introduction

Motion control problems with mechanical systems with nonholonomic constraints, widely addressed in literature, can be roughly classified into three groups: point stabilization, trajectory tracking and path following [1]. Formation control algorithms that enable groups of autonomous agents to follow designated paths can be useful in the planning and execution of various assignments and problem domains such as search and rescue, space exploration, environmental surveillance to name a few [2].

From a control science point of view, the accuracy and performance of wheeled mobile robots trajectory tracking are subject to nonholonomic constraints, and it is usually difficult to achieve stabilized tracking of trajectory points using linear feedback laws [3]. To deal with these, many researchers have proposed controllers that utilized discontinuous control laws, piecewise continuous control laws, smooth time varying control laws or hybrid controllers [4].

© Springer International Publishing AG, part of Springer Nature 2018
Y. Tan et al. (Eds.): ICSI 2018, LNCS 10942, pp. 3–14, 2018.
https://doi.org/10.1007/978-3-319-93818-9_1

Path following problems are more flexible than trajectory tracking, and are primarily concerned with the design of control laws when manoeuvring objects (robot arm, mobile robots, ships, aircraft etc.) to reach and follow a geometric path without strict temporal specifications [5,6]. In path following, the control laws consider the distance from the vehicle to the reference path and the angle between the vehicle's velocity vector and the tangent to the path [7]. For multi robot systems, coordinated path following entails making each robot approach a preassigned path and once on the path, the robots are required to coordinate. This could mean getting into prescribed formation, maintaining a desired intervehicle formation, or getting its path variables [8].

In this paper, we adopt the architecture of the LbCS in [9] and integrate a leader-follower approach to propose a collision-free path following strategy of a group of mobile car-like robots. A robot is assigned the responsibility of a leader, while the follower robots position itself relative to the leader so that the leader robot is followed with arbitrary desired clearance by the follower robot under the influence of noise. The scheme uses Cartesian coordinate's representation as proposed in [10]. Based on artificial potential fields, the LbCS is then used to derive continuous acceleration-based controllers, which render our system stable. The control algorithm used merges together the problems of path following, and obstacle and collision avoidances as a single motion control algorithm.

The remainder of this chapter is structured as follows: in Sect. 2, the robot model is defined; in Sect. 3, the artificial potential field functions are defined under the influence of kinodynamic constraints; in Sect. 4, the acceleration-based control laws are derived and stability analysis of the robotic system is also carried out; in Sect. 6, we demonstrate the effectiveness of the proposed controllers via computer simulations which guide the follower robot to follow the leaders reference path with an error; and finally, Sect. 7 closes with a discussion on its contributions.

2   Vehicle Model

Consider the vehicle model of $\mathcal{N}_i$ for $i = 1, \ldots, n$ in the Euclidean plane. Without loss of generalization, we let $\mathcal{N}_1$ represent the leader and $\mathcal{N}_i$, for $i = 2, \ldots, n$ take the role of followers. With reference to Fig. 1, adopted from [10], and for $i = 1, \ldots, n$, (x_i, y_i) represents the Cartesian coordinates and gives the reference point of each mobile robot, θ_i gives the orientation of the ith car with respect to the z_1-axis of the $z_1 z_2$-plane.

The kinodynamic model of the system is described as

$$\left.\begin{aligned}
\dot{x}_i &= v_i \cos \theta_i - \tfrac{L_i}{2} \omega_i \sin \theta_i, & \dot{y}_i &= v_i \sin \theta_i + \tfrac{L_i}{2} \omega_i \cos \theta_i, \\
\dot{\theta}_i &= \tfrac{v_i}{L_i} \tan \phi_i =: \omega_i, & \dot{v}_i &:= \sigma_{i1}, & \dot{\omega}_i &:= \sigma_{i2},
\end{aligned}\right\} \tag{1}$$

for $i = 1, \ldots, n$. Here, v_i and ω_i are, respectively, the instantaneous translational and rotational velocities, while σ_{i1} and σ_{i2} are the instantaneous translational and rotational accelerations of the ith robot. Without any loss of generality, we assume that $\phi_i = \theta_i$. Moreover, ϕ_i gives the ith robots steering angle with respect to its longitudinal axis. L_i represents the distance between the centers of the front and rear axles of the ith robot, and l_i is the length of each axle.

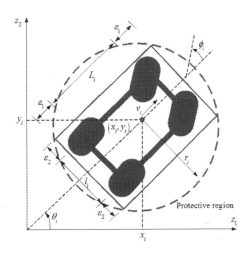

Fig. 1. Kinematic model of the car-like mobile robot.

Next, to ensure that each robot safely steers past an obstacle, we adopt the nomenclature of [9] and construct circular regions that protect the robot. Furthermore, we assume no slippage (i.e., $\dot{x}_i \sin\theta_i - \dot{y}_i \cos\theta_i = 0$) and pure rolling (i.e., $\dot{x}_i \cos\theta_i + \dot{y}_i \sin\theta_i = v_i$) of the car-like mobile robots. These conditions are captured within the form of the kinodynamic model governed by (1).

2.1   Proposed Scheme

Next we define two reference frames as seen in Fig. 2, adopted from [10]: the body frame which is fixed with the rotating body of the leader, $\mathcal{N}_1$, and a space frame, the inertial frame similar to one proposed in [11]. We assign a Cartesian coordinate system $(X - Y)$ fixed on the leaders body based on the concept of an instantaneous co-rotating frame of reference. Thus, when the leader, $\mathcal{N}_1$ rotates, we have a rotation of the $X - Y$ axes.

To avoid any singular points, we consider the position of the kth follower by considering the relative distances of the kth follower from the leader, $\mathcal{N}_1$ along the given X and Y directions:

$$A_k = -(x_1 - x_k)\cos\theta_1 - (y_1 - y_k)\sin\theta_1,$$
$$B_k = (x_1 - x_k)\sin\theta_1 - (y_1 - y_k)\cos\theta_1,$$
$$\tag{2}$$

for $k \in \{2, \ldots, n\}$ and A_k and B_k are the kth followers relative position with respect to the X-Y coordinate system. If A_k and B_k are known and fixed, the follower's position will be distinctive. Thus, to obtain a desired formation, one needs to know distances a_k and b_k, the desired relative positions along the X-Y directions, such that the control objective would be to achieve $A_k \longrightarrow a_k$ and $B_k \longrightarrow b_k$, i.e., $r_{1k} \longrightarrow r_{1k}^d$ and $\alpha_{1k} \longrightarrow \alpha_{1k}^d$, where $r_{1k}^d = \sqrt{a_k^2 + b_k^2}$ and $\alpha_{1k}^d = \tan\left(\frac{a_k}{b_k}\right)$.

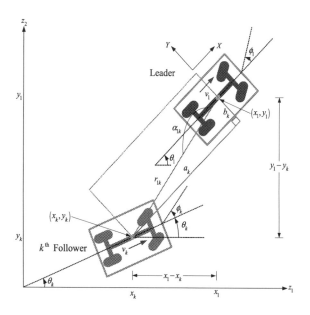

Fig. 2. The proposed scheme utilizing a rotation of axes fixed at the leader robot.

3 Artificial Potential Field Functions

This section formulates collision free trajectories of the robot system under kinodynamic constraints in a fixed and bounded workspace. We want to design the acceleration controllers, σ_{i1} and σ_{i2}, such that a follower robot is able to follow the leader robot, while the leader robot moves towards its predefined target in an obstacle cluttered environment. The attractive potential field functions establish and translate the formation enroute the journey. The repulsive potential field functions, on the other hand, ensure collision and obstacle avoidances in the workspace.

In the following subsections, we will design these attractive and repulsive potential field functions.

3.1 Attraction to Target

A target is assigned to the leader, $\mathcal{N}_1$. When the leader moves towards its defined target the follower robots move with the leader. We want the leader $\mathcal{N}_1$ to start from an initial position, move towards a target and finally converge at the center of the target.

For the attraction of the leader, $\mathcal{N}_1$ to its designated target, we consider an attractive potential function

$$V_1(\mathbf{x}) = \frac{1}{2} \left[(x_1 - p_{11})^2 + (y_1 - p_{12})^2 + v_1^2 + \omega_1^2 \right]. \tag{3}$$

The above function is not only a measure of the Euclidean distance between the center of the leader, $\mathcal{N}_1$ and its target but also a measure of its convergence to the target with the inclusion of the velocity components [9]. For the follower robot, $\mathcal{N}_i$ for $i = 2, \ldots, n$ to maintain its desired relative position with respect to the leader, $\mathcal{N}_1$, we utilize:

$$V_i(\mathbf{x}) = \frac{1}{2} \left[(A_i - a_i)^2 + (B_i - b_i)^2 + v_i^2 + \omega_i^2 \right], \tag{4}$$

for $i = 2, \ldots, n$.

3.2 Auxiliary Function

To guarantee the convergence of the mobile robots to their designated targets, we design an auxiliary function as

$$G_1(\mathbf{x}) = \frac{1}{2} \left[(x_1 - p_{11})^2 + (y_1 - p_{12})^2 + \rho_1 (\theta_1 - p_{13})^2 \right], \tag{5}$$

where p_{13} is the prescribed final orientation of the leader robot, $\mathcal{N}_1$ and

$$G_i(\mathbf{x}) = \frac{1}{2} \left[(A_i - a_i)^2 + (B_i - b_i)^2 + \rho_i (\theta_i - \theta_1)^2 \right], \tag{6}$$

for $i = 2, \ldots, n$. The constant ρ_i is a binary constant denoted in (5) and (6) as the *angle-gain parameter* for $\theta_i, i = 1, \ldots, n$. This auxiliary function is then multiplied to the repulsive potential field functions.

3.3 Fixed Obstacles in the Workspace

Let us fix q solid obstacles within the boundaries of the workspace. We assume that the lth obstacle is a circular disk with center (o_{l1}, o_{l2}) and radius ro_l. For the ith mobile robot to avoid the lth obstacle, we consider

$$FO_{il}(\mathbf{x}) = \frac{1}{2} \left[(x_i - o_{l1})^2 + (y_i - o_{l2})^2 - (ro_l + r_i)^2 \right], \tag{7}$$

as an avoidance function, where $i = 1, \ldots, n$, and $l = 1, \ldots, q$.

3.4   Workspace Limitations

We desire to setup a definite framework of dimension η_1 by η_2 for the workspace of our robots. In our Lyapunov-based control scheme, these boundaries are considered as *fixed obstacles*. For the ith robot to avoid these, we define the following potential functions for the left, upper, right and lower boundaries, respectively:

$$W_{i1}(\mathbf{x}) = x_i - r_i \tag{8}$$

$$W_{i2}(\mathbf{x}) = \eta_2 - (y_i + r_i), \tag{9}$$

$$W_{i3}(\mathbf{x}) = \eta_1 - (x_i + r_i), \tag{10}$$

$$W_{i4}(\mathbf{x}) = y_i - r_i. \tag{11}$$

Embedding these functions into the control laws will contain the motions of the robots to within the specified boundaries of the workspace. These obstacle avoidance functions will be combined with appropriate tuning parameters to generate repulsive potential field functions in the workspace. The same will be applicable for all avoidance functions designed later in the paper.

3.5   Moving Obstacles

To generate feasible trajectories, we consider moving obstacles of which the system has prior knowledge. Here, each mobile robot has to be treated as a moving obstacle for all other mobile robots in the workspace. The follower robots will then have to travel towards their desired positions while avoiding other mobile robots in their paths. This also helps to maintain a minimum separation distance between any two mobile robots.

For the robot, $\mathcal{N}_i$, to avoid the robot, $\mathcal{N}_j$, we adopt an avoidance function

$$MO_{ij}(\mathbf{x}) = \frac{1}{2}\left[(x_i - x_j)^2 + (y_i - y_j)^2 - (r_i + r_j)^2\right], \tag{12}$$

for $i, j = 1, \ldots, n$ with $i \neq j$.

3.6   Dynamic Constraints

Practically, the steering angle of the ith mobile robot are limited due to mechanical singularities while the translational speed is restricted due to safety reasons. Let $v_{\max}$ be the maximal achievable speed of the ith robot and $\rho_{\min} := \frac{L_i}{\tan(\phi_{\max})}$ where $\phi_{\max}$ is the maximal steering angle. We then consider the following avoidance functions:

$$U_{i1}(\mathbf{x}) = \frac{1}{2}\left(v_{\max} - v_i\right)\left(v_{\max} + v_i\right), \tag{13}$$

$$U_{i2}(\mathbf{x}) = \frac{1}{2}\left(\frac{v_{\max}}{|\rho_{\min}|} - \omega_i\right)\left(\frac{v_{\max}}{|\rho_{\min}|} + \omega_i\right), \tag{14}$$

for $i = 1, \ldots, n$. These positive functions would guarantee the adherence to the limitations imposed upon the steering angle and the velocities of $\mathcal{N}_i$ when encoded appropriately into the repulsive potential field functions.

4   Design of Acceleration Controllers

The nonlinear acceleration control laws for system (1), will be designed using the LbCS.

4.1   Lyapunov Function

We now construct the total potentials, that is, a Lyapunov function for system (1). First, for $i = 1, \ldots, n$, we introduce the following *control parameters* that we will use in the repulsive potential functions:

(i) $\alpha_{il} > 0$, $l = 1, \ldots, q$, for the collision avoidance of q disk-shaped obstacles.
(ii) $\beta_{is} > 0$, $s = 1, 2$, for the avoidance of the artificial obstacles from dynamic constraints.
(iii) $\eta_{ij} > 0$, $j = 1, \ldots, n$, $i \neq j$, for the collision avoidance between any two robots.
(iv) $\kappa_{ip} > 0$, $p = 1, \ldots, 4$, for the avoidance of the workspace boundaries.

Using these, we now propose the following Lyapunov function for system (1):

$$L_{(1)}(\mathbf{x}) = \sum_{i=1}^{n} \{V_i(\mathbf{x}) + G_i(\mathbf{x})H_i(\mathbf{x})\} \tag{15}$$

where

$$H_i(\mathbf{x}) = \sum_{l=1}^{q} \frac{\alpha_{il}}{FO_{il}(\mathbf{x})} + \sum_{s=1}^{2} \frac{\beta_{is}}{U_{is}(\mathbf{x})} + \sum_{p=1}^{4} \frac{\kappa_{ip}}{W_{ip}(\mathbf{x})} + \sum_{\substack{j=1 \\ j \neq i}}^{n} \frac{\eta_{ij}}{MO_{ij}(\mathbf{x})},$$

4.2   Nonlinear Acceleration Controllers

The process of designing the feedback controllers begins by noting that the functions f_{ik} to g_{ij} for $i = 1, \ldots, n, j = 1, 2$ and $k = 1, 2, 3$, are defined as (on suppressing $\mathbf{x}$):

$$f_{11} = [1 + H_1](x_1 - p_1) + \frac{\kappa_{11}}{W_{11}^2} - \frac{\kappa_{13}}{W_{13}^2} + \sum_{r=2}^{n} H_1 [(B_r - b_r) \sin \theta_1 - (A_r - a_r) \cos \theta_1]$$

$$- \sum_{l=1}^{q} \frac{\alpha_{1l}G_1}{FO_{1l}^2}(x_1 - o_{l1}) - \sum_{\substack{j=1 \\ j \neq i}}^{n} \frac{2\eta_{1j}G_1}{MO_{1j}^2}(x_1 - x_j),$$

$$f_{12} = [1 + H_1](y_1 - p_2) - \frac{\kappa_{12}}{W_{12}^2} + \frac{\kappa_{14}}{W_{14}^2} - \sum_{r=2}^{n} H_1 [(A_r - a_r) \sin \theta_1 + (B_r - b_r) \cos \theta_1]$$

$$- \sum_{l=1}^{q} \frac{\alpha_{1l}G_1}{FO_{1l}^2}(y_1 - o_{l2}) - \sum_{\substack{j=1 \\ j \neq i}}^{n} \frac{2\eta_{1j}G_1}{MO_{1j}^2}(y_1 - y_j),$$

$$f_{13} = \rho_1(\theta_1 - p_{13})H_1 - \sum_{i=2}^{n} \rho_i(\theta_i - \theta_1)H_i, \quad g_{11} = 1 + G_1 \frac{\beta_{11}}{U_{11}^2}, \quad g_{12} = 1 + G_1 \frac{\beta_{12}}{U_{12}^2},$$

and for $i = 2, \ldots, n$

$$f_{i1} = [1 + H_i]\left[(A_i - a_i)\cos\theta_1 - (B_i - b_i)\sin\theta_1\right] + \frac{\kappa_{i1}}{W_{i1}^2} - \frac{\kappa_{i3}}{W_{i3}^2},$$

$$-\sum_{l=1}^{q} \frac{\alpha_{il}G_i}{FO_{il}^2}(x_i - o_{l1}) - \sum_{\substack{j=1 \\ j \neq i}}^{n} \frac{2\eta_{ij}G_i}{MO_{ij}^2}(x_i - x_j)$$

$$f_{i2} = [1 + H_i]\left[(A_i - a_i)\sin\theta_1 + (B_i - b_i)\cos\theta_1\right] + \frac{\kappa_{i2}}{W_{i2}^2} - \frac{\kappa_{i4}}{W_{i4}^2},$$

$$-\sum_{l=1}^{q} \frac{\alpha_{il}G_i}{FO_{il}^2}(y_i - o_{l2}) - \sum_{\substack{j=1 \\ j \neq i}}^{n} \frac{2\eta_{ij}G_i}{MO_{ij}^2}(y_i - y_j)$$

$$f_{i3} = \rho_i(\theta_i - \theta_1)H_i, \quad g_{i1} = 1 + G_i\frac{\beta_{i1}}{U_{i1}^2}, \quad g_{i2} = 1 + G_i\frac{\beta_{i2}}{U_{i2}^2}.$$

Remark 1. With the inter-robot bounds in place, it is assumed that the robots re-establish the pre-determined formation, if the robot positions are slightly distorted with the encounter of obstacle(s), soon after the avoidance and before reaching the target. Thus, we state the following theorem:

Theorem 1. Consider n car-like mobile robots whose motion is governed by the ODEs described in system (1). The principal goal is to establish and control the follower robots to follow a designated leader, facilitate maneuvers within a constrained environment and reach the target configuration. The subtasks include; restrictions placed on the workspace, convergence to predefined targets, and consideration of kinodynamic constraints. Utilizing the attractive and repulsive potential field functions, the following continuous time-invariant acceleration control laws can be generated, in accordance to the LbCS, of system (1):

$$\sigma_{i1} = -[\delta_{i1}v_i + f_{i1}\cos\theta_i + f_{i2}\sin\theta_i]/g_{i1},$$

$$\sigma_{i2} = -\left[\delta_{i2}\omega_i + \frac{L_i}{2}(f_{i2}\cos\theta_i - f_{i1}\sin\theta_i) + f_{i3}\right]/g_{i2},$$

for $i = 1, \ldots, n$, where $\delta_{i1} > 0$, and $\delta_{i2} > 0$ are constants commonly known as convergence parameters.

5   Stability Analysis

We utilize Lyapunov's Direct Method to provide a mathematical proof of stability of the kinodynamic system (1).

Theorem 2. Let (p_{11}, p_{12}) be the position of the target of the leader, and p_{i3} for $i = 1, \ldots, n$, be the desired final orientations of the robots. Let p_{i1} and p_{i2} satisfy

$$a_i = -(p_{11} - p_{i1})\cos\theta_1 - (p_{12} - p_{i2})\sin\theta_1,$$

$$b_i = (p_{11} - p_{i1})\sin\theta_1 - (p_{12} - p_{i2})\cos\theta_1,$$

for any given a_i and b_i, for $i = 2, \ldots, n$. If $\mathbf{x}^* \in \mathbf{R}^{5n}$ is an equilibrium point for (1), then $\mathbf{x}^* \in D(L_{(1)}(\mathbf{x}))$ is a stable equilibrium point of system (1).

Proof. One can easily verify the following, for $i \in \{1, \ldots, n\}$:

1. $L_{(1)}(\mathbf{x})$ is defined, continuous and positive over the domain $D(L_{(1)}(\mathbf{x})) = \{\mathbf{x} \in \mathbf{R}^{5n} : FO_{il}(\mathbf{x}) > 0, l = 1, \ldots, q; MO_{ij}(\mathbf{x}) > 0, j = 1, \ldots, n, j \neq i; W_{ip}(\mathbf{x}) > 0, p = 1, \ldots, 4; U_{is}(\mathbf{x}) > 0, s = 1, 2\}$;
2. $L_{(1)}(\mathbf{x}^*) = 0$;
3. $L_{(1)}(\mathbf{x}) > 0 \ \forall \mathbf{x} \in D(L_{(1)}(\mathbf{x}))/\mathbf{x}^*$.
4. $\dot{L}_{(1)}(\mathbf{x}) = -\sum_{i=1}^{n} \left(\delta_{i1} v_i^2 + \delta_{i2} \omega_i^2 \right) \leq 0$.

Thus, $\dot{L}_{(1)}(\mathbf{x}) \leq 0 \ \forall \mathbf{x} \in D(L_{(1)}(\mathbf{x}))$ and $\dot{L}_{(1)}(\mathbf{x}^*) = 0$. Finally, it can be easily verified that $L_{(1)}(\mathbf{x}) \in C^1 \left(D(L_{(1)}(\mathbf{x})) \right)$, which makes up the fifth and final criterion of a Lyapunov function. Hence, $L_{(1)}(\mathbf{x})$ is classified as a Lyapunov function for system (1) and $\mathbf{x}^*$ is a stable equilibrium point in the sense of Lyapunov. ∎

Remark 2. This result is in no contradiction with Brockett's Theorem [3] as we have not proven asymptotic stability. Because the system attains stability, which suffices for practical situations.

6   Simulation Results

In this section, we illustrate the effectiveness of the proposed continuous time-invariant controllers within the framework of the LbCS by simulating virtual scenarios. We consider the motion of 2 cars in a two dimensional space in the presence of randomly generated fixed obstacles and a randomly generated target for the leader robot. To evaluate the robustness of the proposed scheme, we look at the effect of noise on the formation of the mobile robots. It is sufficient to include the noise parameters in the components A_k and B_k which define the followers relative position to the leader with respect to the $X - Y$ coordinate system similar to one proposed in [12]. Thus we have

$$A_k = -(x_1 - x_k)\cos\theta_1 - (y_1 - y_k)\sin\theta_1 + \xi\gamma_k(t),$$
$$B_k = (x_1 - x_k)\sin\theta_1 - (y_1 - y_k)\cos\theta_1 + \xi\nu_k(t). \tag{16}$$

The terms $\xi\gamma_k(t)$ and $\xi\nu_k(t)$ are the small disturbances where $\xi \in [0, 1]$ is the noise level while $\gamma_k(t)$ and $\nu_k(t)$ are randomized time dependent variables such that $\gamma_k(t) \in [-1, 1]$ and $\nu_k(t) \in [-1, 1]$. Figures 3 and 4 show the trajectories under the influence of small disturbances, $\xi \in [0, 1]$. There are slight distortions in the desired positions of the follower as seen in Figs. 5 and 6 when the two robots encounter an obstacle but as seen the figures, these distortions are temporary.

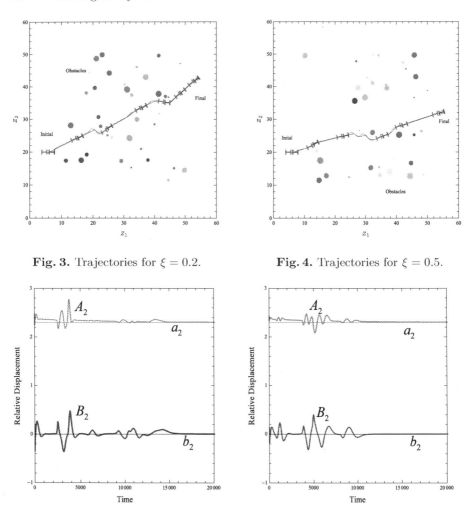

Fig. 3. Trajectories for $\xi = 0.2$.   **Fig. 4.** Trajectories for $\xi = 0.5$.

Fig. 5. Relative distance error for $\xi = 0.2$.   **Fig. 6.** Relative distance error for $\xi = 0.5$.

Assuming that the appropriate units have been accounted for, Table 1 provides the corresponding initial and final configurations of the two robots and other necessary parameters required to simulate the scenario.

Table 1. Numerical values of initial and final states, constraints and parameters

	Initial Configuration
Rectangular positions	$(x_1, y_1) = (7, 20), (x_2, y_2) = (4, 20)$
Translational velocity	$v_i = 0.5$ for $i = 1, 2$
Rotational velocities	$\omega_i = 0$, for $i = 1, 2$
Angular positions	$\theta_i = 0$, for $i = 1, 2$
	Constraints and Parameters
Dimensions of robots	$L_i = 1.6, l_i = 1.2$ for $i = 1, 2$
Final orientations	$\rho_1 = \rho_2 = 0$
Max. translational velocity	$v_{\max} = 5$
Max. steering angle	$\phi_{\max} = \pi/2$
Clearance parameters	$\epsilon_1 = 0.1, \epsilon_2 = 0.05$
	Control and Convergence Parameters
Collision avoidance	$\eta_{ij} = 0.001$, for $i, j - 1, 2, j \neq i$,
	$\kappa_{ik} = 0.1$, for $i = 1, 2, k = 1, \ldots, 4$
	$\alpha_{il} = 0.1$, for $i = 1, 2, l = 1, \ldots, 50$
Dynamics constraints	$\beta_{is} = 0.01$, for $i, s = 1, 2$,
Convergence	$\delta_{11} = 3000, \delta_{12} = 100, \delta_{21} = 10$,
	$\delta_{22} = 100$

7   Concluding Remarks

A leader-follower based path following control of mobile robots is proposed for a group of robots which navigates in a constrained environment with external influence of noise. A set of nonlinear control laws are extracted using the LbCS. The proposed leader-follower scheme uses a Cartesian coordinate system fixed on the leader's body based on the concept of an instantaneous co-rotating frame of reference to uniquely assign a position to each follower. The approach considers nonholonomic constraints of the system, inter-robot collisions and collisions with fixed obstacles are taken into account. The derived controllers produced feasible trajectories and ensured a nice convergence of the system to its equilibrium state while satisfying the necessary kinematic and dynamic constraints.

The effectiveness of the proposed control laws were demonstrated via computer simulations using different traffic situations. The presented algorithm, which is scalable to multiple robots, again performs very well even under severe disturbances indicating the robustness of the system.

References

1. Morin, P., Samson, C.: Motion Control of Wheeled Mobile Robots. Springer, Heidelberg (2008)
2. Reyes, L.A.V., Tanner, H.G.: Flocking, formation control and path following for a group of mobile robots. IEEE Trans. Control Syst. Technol. **23**(4), 1268–1282 (2015)
3. Brockett, R.W.: Asymptotic Stability and Feedback Stabilisation. In: Differential Geometry Control Theory, pp. 181–191. Springer (1983)
4. Dixon, W., Dawson, D., Zergerogulu, E., Jiang, Z.: Robust tracking and regulation control of mobile robots. Int. J. Robust Nonlinear Control **10**, 199–216 (2000)
5. Aquiar, A.P., Hespanha, J.P., Kokotovic, P.V.: Path following for nonminimal phase systems removes performance limitations. IEEE Trans. Autom. Control **50**(2), 234–239 (2005)
6. Xiang, X., Lapierre, L., Jouvencel, B., Parodi, O.: Coordinated path following control of multiple nonholonomic vehicles. In: Oceans 2009-EUROPE, pp. 1–7. Bremen (2009)
7. Kanjanawanishkul, M., Hofmeister, K., Zell, A.: Smooth reference tracking of a mobile robot using nonlinear model predictive control. In: Proceedings of the 4th European Conference on Mobile Robots, pp. 161–166. Croatia (2009)
8. Li, Y., Nielsen, C.: Synchronized closed path following for a differential drive and manipulator robot. IEEE Trans. Control Syst. Technol. **25**(2), 704–711 (2017)
9. Sharma, B.: New Directions in the Applications of the Lyapunov-based Control Scheme to the Findpath Problem. Ph.D. thesis, The University of the South Pacific, Fiji Islands (2008)
10. Raghuwaiya, K., Sharma, B., Vanualailai, J.: Cooperative control of multi-robot systems with a low-degree formation. In: Sulaiman, H.A., Othman, M.A., Othman, M.F.I., Rahim, Y.A., Pee, N.C. (eds.) Advanced Computer and Communication Engineering Technology. LNEE, vol. 362, pp. 233–249. Springer, Cham (2016). https://doi.org/10.1007/978-3-319-24584-3_20
11. Kang, W., Xi, N., Tan, J., Wang, Y.: Formation control of multiple autonomous robots: theory and experimentation. Intell. Autom. Soft Comput. **10**(2), 1–17 (2004)
12. Prasad, A., Sharma, B., Vanualailai, J.: A new stabilizing solution for motion planning and control of multiple robots. Robotica, 1–19 (2014)

Development of Adaptive Force-Following Impedance Control for Interactive Robot

Huang Jianbin[1(✉)], Li Zhi[1], and Liu Hong[2]

[1] Qian Xuesen Laboratory of Space Technology, China Academy of Space Technology, Beijing 100094, People's Republic of China
huangjianbin@qxslab.cn
[2] State Key Laboratory of Robotics and System, Harbin Institute of Technology, Harbin 150001, People's Republic of China

Abstract. This paper presented a safety approach for the interactive manipulator. At first, the basic compliance control of the manipulator is realized by using the Cartesian impedance control, which inter-related the external force and the end position. In this way, the manipulator could work as an external force sensor. A novel force-limited trajectory was then generated in a high dynamics interactive manner, keeping the interaction force within acceptable tolerance. The proposed approach also proved that the manipulator was able to contact the environment compliantly, and reduce the instantaneous impact when collision occurs. Furthermore, adaptive dynamics joint controller was extended to all the joints for complementing the biggish friction. Experiments were performed on a 5-DOF flexible joint manipulator. The experiment results of taping the obstacle, illustrate that the interactive robot could keep the desired path precisely in free space, and follow the demand force in good condition.

Keywords: Interactive robot · Cartesian impedance control
Collision detection

1 Introduction

Imitation of the human arm and its safe operation is an exciting and challenging frontier for robotics. Interactive robot which is designed for intimate physical operation in unstructured and dynamic environment should be paid more attention on safety and controllable physical interaction [1]. Especially as the robot collides with the environment, too high energy/power may be transferred by the robot. Thus, the robot should be enhanced in terms of the designs of mechanics, perception and control to restrain the interactive force, while preserving accuracy and performance in free space [2].

Mechanical designs can reduce the instantaneous severity of impacts. These designs include the reduction of inertia and weight and the introduction of compliant components such as the viscoelastic material cover, flexible joint [3], tendons [4], distributed macro-mini actuation with elastic coupling, variable stiffness actuator [5], compliant shoulders, the mechanical impedance adjuster, and viscoelastic passive trunks [6]. However, just the flexible mechanism without instantaneous action, the contact force will also increase rapidly resulting in excessive impact for instantaneous

© Springer International Publishing AG, part of Springer Nature 2018
Y. Tan et al. (Eds.): ICSI 2018, LNCS 10942, pp. 15–24, 2018.
https://doi.org/10.1007/978-3-319-93818-9_2

impact. Furthermore, highly flexible hardware design may decrease the precision and system control bandwidth.

Since the torque sensor is introduced, it allows a fast detection of the force state of robot and the interaction control between the end-effector of manipulator and environment [7]. Interaction control strategies based on torque sensors can be grouped in two categories: direct and indirect force control. Direct force control offers the possibility of controlling the contact force to a desired value, due to the closure of a force feedback loop [8]. Impedance control is one of the most intuitive approaches of indirect force controls, which provides a unified framework for achieving compliant behavior when robot contacts with an unknown environment. It was extensively theorized by Hogan [9] and experimentally applied by Kazerooni et al. [10]. Albu-Schaffer [5] investigated in Cartesian impedance control for the DLR (The German Aerospace Center) light weight arms with completely static states feedback, and used PD (Proportion Differentiation) control with gravity compensation to compensate the dynamics uncertainties.

Interactive path generation, coupled with the identification of estimated hazardous situations, has received less attention than the mechanical and control-based techniques as a means of protecting robot and environment. However, safe planning is important for any interaction that involves motion in unstructured environment. Brock and Khatib [11] proposed an elastic strips framework, where the local modification of motion is performed in a task-consistent manner, leaving globally planned motion execution possibly unaffected by obstacle avoidance. But the method should get the region of obstacle in advance and is efficient for redundant robot.

In nature, if the whole robot could behave as a force sensor, the robot can sense the environment and prevent collision accident with appropriate control strategy. The paper is aiming at developing a new safe-operated system by using joint torque sensors for the flexible joint manipulator. First, Cartesian impedance control is introduced not only to realize the compliance contact with environment, but also act as a sensor which comes the external force and the end position into mutual relationship. Then, thanks to "the external force sensor", a force-limited interactive path generation is implemented into the control loop to keep the Cartesian force to the desired value when collision occurs. Furthermore, adaptive dynamics control law is introduced to improve the control precision.

2   Design of the Cartesian Force Sensor System

2.1   Cartesian Force Sensor Design Based on the Impedance Control

Consider a n-DOF (Degree Of Freedom) non-redundant manipulator with joint coordinates q_i, $i = 1, 2, \ldots, n$, and a Cartesian coordinate $x \in R^n$. With respect to n joint coordinates $q = [q_1, q_2, \ldots, q_n]^T \in R^n$ and its velocities $\dot{q}$ and accelerations $\ddot{q}$, the joint torques $\tau \in R^n$ of the manipulator can be given in a well-known form as follows

$$M(q)\ddot{q} + C(q, \dot{q})\dot{q} + g(q) = \tau + \tau_{ext}, \tag{1}$$

where $M(q)$ represents the inertia matrix; $C(q, \dot{q})$ is the centrifugal/Coriolis term; and $g(q)$ and τ_{ext} are the vectors of gravity force and external force, respectively.

The dynamic of the manipulator could be translated from joint space to Cartesian space by the following equations

$$
\begin{aligned}
x &= f(q) \\
\dot{x} &= J(q)\dot{q} \\
\ddot{x} &= J(q)\ddot{q} + \dot{J}(q, \dot{q})\dot{q} \\
F_{ext} &= J(q)^{-T}\tau_{ext},
\end{aligned}
\tag{2}
$$

where $\dot{x}$, $\ddot{x}$ and F_{ext} are n-dimensional velocities, accelerations and external force in Cartesian space; $f \in R^n$ represents direct kinematics; $J \in R^{n \times n}$ is the Jacobian matrix, and $\dot{J}$ is its time derivative.

Thus, the dynamics of a manipulator are described by

$$
\Lambda(x)\ddot{x} + \mu(x, \dot{x})\dot{x} + J(q)^{-T}g(q) = J(q)^{-T}\tau + F_{ext}.
\tag{3}
$$

The matrices $\Lambda(x)$ and $\mu(x, \dot{x})$ are given by

$$
\Lambda(x) = J(q)^{-T}M(q)J(q)^{-1}
\tag{4}
$$

$$
\mu(x, \dot{x}) = J(q)^{-T}(C(q, \dot{q}) - M(q)J(q)^{-1}\dot{J}(q))J(q)^{-1}.
\tag{5}
$$

The Cartesian impedance behavior of the manipulator is usually given by a differential equation of second order representing a mass-damper-spring system

$$
\Lambda_d\ddot{\tilde{x}} + D_d\dot{\tilde{x}} + K_d\tilde{x} = F_{ext}.
\tag{6}
$$

In this equation, $\tilde{x} \in R^n$ is defined as Cartesian position error $\tilde{x} = x - x_d$, which is between real endpoint position x and reference trajectory vector of the endpoint x_d. Λ_d, D_d and K_d are the symmetric and positive definite matrices of the desired inertia, damping and stiffness, respectively

The Cartesian impedance control law can be directly computed from Eq. (3). The control input $F_\tau = J(q)^{-T}\tau$ which leads to the desired closed loop system Eq. (6). And the feedback of external forces F_{ext} can be avoided when the desired inertia Λ_d is identical to the inertia $\Lambda(x)$ of robot. The Classical Cartesian impedance control law can be written as

$$
F_\tau = \Lambda(x)\ddot{x}_d + \mu(x, \dot{x})\dot{x} + J(q)^{-T}g(q) - D_d\dot{\tilde{x}} - K_d\tilde{x}.
\tag{7}
$$

Using the Cartesian impedance control above, the manipulator can be considered as a force sensor. The external force can be measured by the Cartesian errors of position, velocity and acceleration from Eq. (6) (Fig. 1).

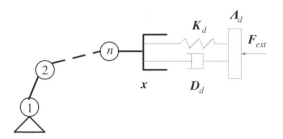

Fig. 1. Cartesian impedance control

2.2 Load Measurement with the Force Sensor

Generally, the manipulator will take the load (or tool) to do some work. If we don't consider the load, the manipulator will get some bias while using the proposed Cartesian impedance control. Thus, it is essential that the controller should measure the load at first.

Intuitively, the external force F_{ext} is split up to two parts: the load-based force F_{load} and the disturbing force F_{dis}.

$$F_{ext} = F_{load} + F_{dis}. \tag{8}$$

While there is no disturbance, the load-based external force could be measured by the Cartesian force sensor in advance

$$F_{load} = \Lambda_d(\ddot{x}_{load} - \ddot{x}_d) + D_d(\dot{x}_{load} - \dot{x}_d) + K_d(x_{load} - x_d). \tag{9}$$

Therefore, just like the human arm handing the load by pre-estimating the external force, the manipulator could feed forward the load force by the measured Cartesian force. And the Cartesian impedance control could be rewritten as

$$F_{\tau} = \Lambda(x)\ddot{x}_d + \mu(x,\dot{x})\dot{x} + J(q)^{-T}g(q) - F_{load} - D_d\dot{\tilde{x}} - K_d\tilde{x}. \tag{10}$$

In the equation, the terms in the pane are the feed-forward terms. As a result, the Cartesian impedance behavior has the form of

$$\Lambda_d\ddot{\tilde{x}} + D_d\dot{\tilde{x}} + K_d\tilde{x} = F_{dis}. \tag{11}$$

Consequently, the manipulator can handle the different loads (not varied) to track the desired trajectory.

3   Adaptive Force Limited Control

3.1   Path Generation Based on the Real-Time Force Feedback

Conventional robot path generation is an off-line path on presuming that the environment is completely known. For the complex and time-varying environment, the search for a feasible off-line way seems time-consuming and impractical. Therefore, the additional features of intelligibility and acceptability of robot motion should be considered. Apply the Cartesian impedance control individually can improve the compliance characteristic of the manipulator. However, the force will be increased as the motion is restricted. So the new path generation which we named force-following path x_{pg} should be established to detect the possible collision and to control the contact force.

With the advantages of Cartesian impedance control, the manipulator can be acted as a Cartesian force sensor, and the estimated external force $\hat{f}$ of off-line planning can be calculated as

$$\hat{f} = \Lambda_d \ddot{\tilde{x}} + D_d \dot{\tilde{x}} + K_d \tilde{x}. \tag{12}$$

A threshold of the contact force F_{cd} is used to check if collision occurs. For a certain detection period Δt, collision occurs when

$$\int_T^{T+\Delta t} |\hat{f}| dt \geq \int_T^{T+\Delta t} |F_{cd}| dt \tag{13}$$

and the real external force equals to F_{cd} at the same time

$$F_{cd} = \Lambda_d(\ddot{x} - \ddot{x}_{pg}|_{T+\Delta t}) + D_d(\dot{x} - \dot{x}_{pg}|_{T+\Delta t}) + K_d(x - x_{pg}|_{T+\Delta t}). \tag{14}$$

Choosing $C_1(\hat{f})$ and $C_1(\hat{f})$ is the coefficient of off-line path planner x_d and the force feedback path planner, respectively. The force-following path generation has the form of

$$x_{pg} = C_1(\hat{f})x_d + C_2(\hat{f})(\hat{f} - F_{cd}). \tag{15}$$

And the path generation should meet the following requirements:

(1)   When the collision isn't happen, there is $x_{pg} = x_d$, so $C_1(\hat{f}) = 1$ and $C_2(\hat{f}) = 0$;
(2) $C_2(\hat{f})$ are the function of estimated external force, and increases while the $\hat{f}$ is growing;
(3) $C_1(\hat{f}) \in (0, 1]$, $C_2(\hat{f}) \in [0, 1)$, and $x_{pg}, \dot{x}_{pg}, \ddot{x}_{pg}$ are all continuous and bounded.
(4) $C_1(\hat{f}) + C_2(\hat{f}) = 1$

Then applying Eq. (15) to Eq. (14), the coefficient of force-feedback path planner $C_2(\hat{f})$ has the form of

$$C_2(\hat{f}) = \begin{cases} \dfrac{F_{cd}-\hat{f}}{K_d(x_d-\hat{f}+F_{cd})+D_d(\dot{\hat{f}}-\dot{x}_d)+A_d(\ddot{x}_d-\hat{f})} & \text{Collision} \\ 0 & \text{Others} \end{cases}.$$

Replacing the off-line path x_d by the Cartesian force-feedback path generation x_{pg} in Eq. (11), the real external force has the following form

$$F_{dis} = \begin{cases} A_d\ddot{\tilde{x}}+D_d\dot{\tilde{x}}+K_d\tilde{x} & |\hat{f}|<F_{cd} \\ F_{cd} & \text{others} \end{cases} \tag{16}$$

Thus, when the collision happens, we can easily control the contact force within the expected force F_{cd}.

3.2   Adaptive Dynamics Control of the Flexible Joint

The controllers above are based on the rigid joint manipulator, and not consider the motor dynamics. To put the controllers into practical use, the dynamics of the motor and the flexible joint are considered

$$B\ddot{\theta} + \tau + \tau_F = \tau_m \tag{17}$$

$$\tau = K(\theta - q), \tag{18}$$

where θ, q indicate the vector of the motor angle divided by the gear ratio and the joint angle respectively; K and B are diagonal matrices which contain the joint stiffness and the motor inertias multiplied by the gear ratio squared; τ_F is the friction; and τ_m is the generalized motor torques vector which is regarded as input variables.

In servo systems, steady-state errors and tracking errors are mainly caused by static friction, which depends on the velocity's direction, payload and motor position. The friction model from the LuGre steady-state friction [12], payload-dependent friction [13] and motor position based friction, is expressed as

$$\tau_F = g_\tau(\tau)(\alpha_0 + \alpha_1 e^{-(\dot{\theta}/v_s)^2})\operatorname{sgn}(\dot{\theta}) + a_2\dot{\theta} + H(\theta) \overset{def}{=} Y(\tau,\dot{\theta})K_F \tag{19}$$

$$g_\tau(\tau) \overset{def}{=} (1 + g_1|\tau| + g_2|\tau|^2). \tag{20}$$

It covers Stribeck velocity v_s, static friction at zero payload $(\alpha_0 + \alpha_1)$, viscous friction a_2 and position-based friction $H(\theta)$. Additionally, with $g_1 > 0$ and $g_2 > 0$, $g_\tau(\tau)$ is used to emulate the load-dependent static friction effect. The complete friction model is characterized by four uncertain parameter vectors

$$K_F = [\,\alpha_0 \quad \alpha_1 \quad a_2 \quad H(\theta)\,]^T \in R^{4 \times n} \tag{21}$$

and a corresponding regression matrix $Y(\tau,\dot{\theta}) \in R^{1 \times 4}$.

By using the adaptive control law in the consideration of the lower and upper bounds of the K_F elements, Eq. (19) can be written as

$$\hat{\tau}_F = Y(\tau, \dot{\theta})\hat{K}_F. \tag{22}$$

Considering the joint flexibility, the joint position is updated by

$$\hat{q} = \theta - \frac{1}{K}\tau. \tag{23}$$

Finally, incorporating the motor dynamics (Eq. (17)), the control torque at the ith motor to achieve the Cartesian impedance is computed as

$$\tau_m = B\ddot{\theta}_{pg} + \hat{\tau}_F(\dot{\theta}, \tau) + \tau_r + k_\tau(\tau_r - \tau) + k_\theta(\theta_{pg} - \theta), \tag{24}$$

where, k_τ, k_θ are diagonal gain matrices, which are used as the state feedback to compensate the variation of centripetal and Coriolis terms as well as inertial couplings to implement variable joint stiffness and damping.

4   Experiments

4.1   Experimental Manipulator

The proposed control scheme has been implemented on a 5-DOF manipulator (Fig. 3). The mass of the arm is 3.9 kg and the payload is up to 3 kg, while the length with full stretch is 1200 mm. The joints are actuated by brushless motors via gear trains and harmonic drive gears. A potentiometer and a magnetic encoder are equipped to measure the absolute angular position of the joint and the motor respectively. The joint torque sensor is designed basing on shear strain theory. Eight strain gauges are fixed crossly to the output shaft of the harmonic drive gear to construct two full-bridges which measure the joint torque. The robot is controlled by DSP/FPGA hardware architecture. The Cartesian impedance control and online trajectory generation are implemented in the floating point DSP, and the adaptive dynamics joint controller (Eq. (24)) together with the sensors detector and transformation are performed in FPGA. Two controllers are connected to 25 Mbps LVDS serial data bus with the cycle time less than 200 μs. Furthermore, the control frequency of the Cartesian and joint controller can be up to 5 kHz and 20 kHz, respectively [14] (Fig. 2).

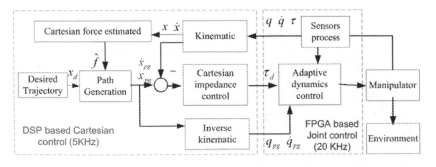

Fig. 2. Internal architecture of the robot controller

Table 1. Cartesian impedance parameters

Coordinates	X	Y	Z
Stiffness	1300 N/m	1300 N/m	5000 N/m
Damping	10 Ns/m	10 Ns/m	10 Ns/m

A major practical step for the implementation of the proposed controller structure is the parameter identification. The robot parameters of kinematics and dynamics are very precisely computed by using 3D mechanical CAD (Computer Aided Design) programs. By using Field-oriented control and off-line experiment estimate, we can get the bounds of the fiction parameters (Eq. (21)). In the experiment of the joint impedance control, the joint can be kept to contact a rigid environment and the joint torque and the bias of motor position are measured. Then, K can be calculated by Eq. (18). The manipulator parameters are listed in Table 1.

Table 2. Manipulator parameters

Parameters	{L1}	{L2}	{L3}	{L4}	{L 5}
a_i (mm)	0	530	470	0	200
α_i	$-90°$	$0°$	$0°$	$90°$	$0°$
d_i	0	0	0	-135.66	0
θ_i	$0°$	$0°$	$0°$	$0°$	$0°$
Mass (kg)	0.7	0.92	0.88	0.7	0.7
$B_i(\text{kgm}^2)$	0.2	0.2	0.2	0.2	0.2
v_{si} (rad/s)	0.004	0.004	0.004	0.004	0.004
K_i (Nm/rad)	12	12	12	12	12

4.2   Experiment of the Load Measurement and Position/Force Tracing

The performance of the "Cartesian force sensor" is tested by the experiment which the end-effector of the manipulator taps on rubbers without and with load. The end-effector is required to move in the Z-axis and contact the rubbers at the velocity of 150 mm/s. Furthermore, while the manipulator contacts the rubbers, the desired force should be followed. The stiffness and damping parameters of the manipulator are set as Table 2 shows.

As the Fig. 4 shows, the end-effector is required to track a desired off-line path, which has a vertical displacement of 200 mm along the Z-axis of the base frame with the velocity ranged from -150 mm/s to 150 mm/s. Furthermore, while the manipulator contacts the rubbers, the desired vary sine force should be followed. Figure 4(a) illustrates the result of Z-axis trajectory tracing, in which the dotted, dash and solid line represents desired (Xz_d), force-following (Xz_{pg}) and real (Xz) trajectory, respectively. Figure 4(b) represents the velocity tracing of the manipulator, in which the dotted and solid line represents desired (Vz_d) and real velocity (Vz), respectively. Figure 4(c) shows the Z-axis force tracing when the manipulator taped on the rubber, in which the dotted and solid line represents desired (Fz_d) and real force (Fz), respectively.

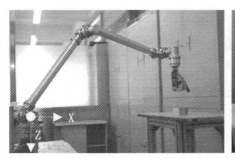

Fig. 3. Experiment of tapping on an egg

In fact, the manipulator is tracking the force-following path Xz_{pg}. When there is no contact, the force-following path is the same as the desired trajectory because the estimated force is less than the desired force Fz_d. When the manipulator contacts with the rubbers, the manipulator continuously departs from the desired trajectory and the estimated force increases to exceed the desired force. Then the force-following path is adjusted to keep the real contact force within the expected force. In the experiment, when the manipulator taped at the rubbers, no real trajectory dithering and large force oscillation is presented. It can be concluded that the operation object can stay in good condition under manipulator's operated region.

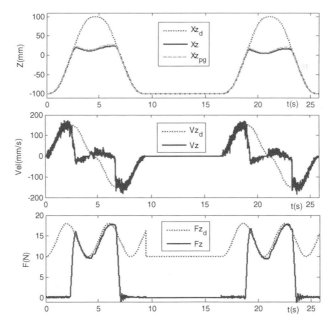

Fig. 4. Cartesian position (a, b), velocity (c) and force (d) in Z-axis versus time when the end-effector taps on an rubber at vary sine velocity.

5 Conclusions

In this paper, a safety reaction approach by using joint torque sensors was developed. By using the Cartesian impedance control, the manipulator behaved as a Cartesian force sensor, and presented compliantly to environment in nature. Adopting the estimated external force to the online trajectory plan, the manipulator performed the global planned motion, avoided the collision reactively, and ensured the contact force within expected value. Additionally, adaptive dynamics joint control could compensate the joint friction efficiently. The efficacy of the method was validated by the experiments of 5-DOF flexible robot to contact an obstacle and follow the pre-desired interactive force. With the proposed adaptive Cartesian impedance control and online path planner, the robot will be manipulation-friendly in an unstructured environment.

References

1. Mühlig, M., Gienger, M., Steil, J.J.: Interactive imitation learning of object movement skills. Auton. Robot. **32**(2), 97–114 (2012)
2. Haddadin, S., Albu-Schäffer, A., Hirzinger, G.: Safe physical human-robot interaction: measurements analysis and new insights. In: Kaneko, M., Nakamura, Y. (eds.) Robotics Research. Springer Tracts in Advanced Robotics, vol. 66. Springer, Heidelberg (2010). https://doi.org/10.1007/978-3-642-14743-2_33
3. Huang, J.B., et al.: DSP/FPGA-based controller architecture for flexible joint robot with enhanced impedance performance. J. Intell. Robot. Syst. **53**(3), 247 (2008)
4. Doggett, W.R., et al.: Development of a Tendon-Actuated Lightweight In-Space MANipulator (TALISMAN) (2014)
5. Albu-Schäffer, A., Bicchi, A.: Actuators for Soft Robotics. In: Siciliano, B., Khatib, O. (eds.) Springer Handbook of Robotics. Springer, Cham (2016). https://doi.org/10.1007/978-3-319-32552-1_21
6. Olson, M.W.: Passive trunk loading influences muscle activation during dynamic activity. Muscle Nerve **44**(5), 749 (2011)
7. Hongwei, Z., Ahmad, S., Liu, G.: Torque estimation for robotic joint with harmonic drive transmission based on position measurements. IEEE Trans. Robot. **31**(2), 322–330 (2017)
8. Kulić, D., Croft, E.: Pre-collision safety strategies for human-robot interaction. Auton. Robot. **22**(2), 149–164 (2007)
9. Hogan, N.: Impedance control: an approach to manipulation: theory (part 1); implementation (part 2); applications (part 3). ASME J. Dyn. Syst. Measur. Contr. **107**, 1–24 (1985)
10. Kazerooni, H., Sheridan, T.B., Houpt, P.K.: Robust compliant motion for manipulators: the fundamental concepts of compliant motion (part I); design method (part II). IEEE J. Robot. Autom. **2**(2), 83–105 (1986)
11. Brock, O., Khatib, O.: Elastic strips: a framework for motion generation in human environments. Int. J. Robot. Res. **21**(12), 1031–1052 (2002)
12. Wu, X.D., et al.: Parameter identification for a LuGre model based on steady-state tire conditions. Int. J. Automot. Technol. **12**(5), 671 (2011)
13. Hamon, P., et al.: Dynamic identification of robot with a load-dependent joint friction model, pp. 129–135 (2015)
14. Huang, J.B., et al.: Adaptive cartesian impedance control system for flexible joint robot by using DSP/FPGA architecture. Int. J. Robot. Autom. **23**(4), 251–258 (2008)

A Space Tendon-Driven Continuum Robot

Shineng Geng[1], Youyu Wang[2], Cong Wang[1], and Rongjie Kang[1(✉)]

[1] Key Laboratory of Mechanism Theory and Equipment Design,
Ministry of Education, School of Mechanical Engineering, Tianjin University,
Tianjin 300072, China
rjkang@tju.edu.cn
[2] Beijing Institute of Spacecraft System Engineering CAST,
Beijing 100086, China

Abstract. In order to avoid the collision of space manipulation, a space continuum robot with passive structural flexibility is proposed. This robot is composed of two continuum joints with elastic backbone and driving tendons made of NiTi alloy. The kinematic mapping and the Jacobian matrix are obtained through the kinematic analysis. Moreover, an inverse kinematics based closed-loop controller is designed to achieve position tracking. Finally, a simulation and an experiment is carried out to validate the workspace and control algorithm respectively. The results show that this robot can follow a given trajectory with satisfactory accuracy.

Keywords: Space manipulation · Continuum robot · Kinematics

1 Introduction

The exploration of outer space is important for the national communications, defense and technology development. Establishing stable space service systems on the orbit is required for the utilization of space resources. In order to make these systems keep healthy status in long-term service, it is necessary to carry out regular maintenance and upgrade operations. On the other hand, these systems should also have some capabilities of defensing the attack from enemy or space junk. In the harsh space environment, using various space robots to accomplish the above tasks has attracted more and more attention from many countries.

At present, many achievements have been made in the application of the rigid robot in the space. For example, the Canada-arm developed by Canadian Spar Company in the 1980s was used in the construction, maintenance and replenishment of the International Space Station [1]. At the end of the last century, Germany and Japan developed and launched their 6-DOF space robotic systems respectively [1, 2]. In 2007, the "Orbit Express" satellite launched by the United States was equipped with automatic robotic arms with high operability and repeatability [1]. Since 2005, China has made some achievements in the development of the multi-freedom space manipulator [3]. However, rigid space robots often suffer from unpredictable impacts during the capture and operation, especially for the non-cooperative targets [4–6], although the techniques of rigid robotic arms are relatively mature. Therefore, how to overcome the impact

© Springer International Publishing AG, part of Springer Nature 2018
Y. Tan et al. (Eds.): ICSI 2018, LNCS 10942, pp. 25–35, 2018.
https://doi.org/10.1007/978-3-319-93818-9_3

during operation has been a key issue in space manipulation. The above problem can be solved if a flexible operation or flexible connection is established between the base and the target [7].

Continuum robot is a new generation of bionic robot with good flexibility, and its structure does not have discrete joints and rigid links [8]. Since this concept of continuum robot was proposed by Robinson in the UK Heriot-Watt University in 1999 [9], numerous research has been made in the field of continuum robots. Walker from Clemson University firstly studied the Elephant trunk and Tentacle with good bending and grasping properties [10]. Then his team developed the Oct-Arm which has an excellent adaptability to the complex environment driven by pneumatic artificial muscles [11]. In addition, his team also cooperated with NASA to develop the Tendril, a winding slender continuum robot that was used to detect on-orbit targets [12, 13]. Simaan has developed a series of continuum manipulators with the capability of bending and operation in narrow space using a hyper-elastic NiTi alloy as backbone, which was mainly used in minimally invasive surgery [14, 15]. Xu developed a two-arm continuum robot successfully used in minimally invasive surgery [16]. Kang presented a pneumatically actuated manipulator inspired by biological continuum structure [17].

After years of developments, a considerable amount of technical experience has been accumulated in the field of continuum robots. The continuum robots can not only be equipped with end-effector to manipulate, but also can passively absorb the impact of shock with its flexible structure. Therefore, continuum robots can be applied to perform many space tasks with high safety.

In this paper, a space continuum robot driven by elastic tendons is proposed to accomplish flexible operations. The kinematics of the robot and its Jacobian matrix with respect to the joint parameters are formulated. Based on which, a closed-loop controller is designed to improve the accuracy of position tracking.

The rest of the paper is organized as follows: Sect. 2 describes the mechanical design of the continuum robot. Section 3 establishes the kinematic model. In Sect. 4, a closed-loop controller is proposed to achieve position tracking. The simulated and experimental results are shown in Sect. 5, and the conclusion are given in Sect. 6.

2 Design of the Continuum Robot

As mentioned above, the robot is required to have good flexibility to deal with impact during operations. In addition, a versatile mechanical interface at the end is also needed to assemble different end effectors for various tasks. Figure 1(a) shows a scenario of the continuum robot performing maintenance task. As shown in Fig. 1(b), our prototype includes a driving box, a continuum arm and an interchangeable end effector.

2.1 The Continuum Arm

As shown in Fig. 2, there are two joints in the continuum arm. The length of each joint is 480 mm, and the outside diameter is 38 mm. The structure of each continuum joint is composed of a backbone, three driving tendons evenly distributed in a circle, and connecting disks. The backbone and tendons are made of a super elastic NiTi alloy. All the connecting disks are equidistantly spaced on the backbone, and the tendons are fixed to the end disk of corresponding joint and go through other disks allowing for relative sliding. Because the length of the backbone is constant, when the tendons are pushed or pulled with different displacement, the continuum joint will bend under the constraints of connecting disks. We assume L *is* a vector whose elements describe the lengths of tendons. Different selections of L will result in different curved configuration.

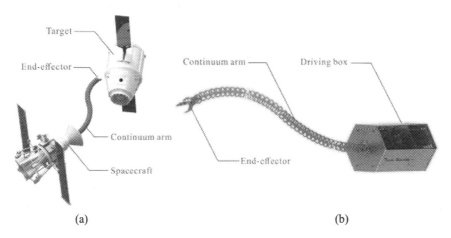

(a)   (b)

Fig. 1. Overall structure of the continuum robot: (a) work situation of space continuum robot; (b) structure of initial ground-based prototype.

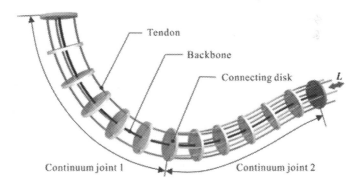

Fig. 2. Structure of the continuum arm.

2.2   The Driving Box

According to the design of the continuum arm, there are totally six tendons which belong to two continuum joints. Therefore, six transmission units are included in the driving box, and each tendon is fixed on corresponding transmission unit. The linear movement of a tendon is realized by the screw-rod sliding mechanism. As shown in

Fig. 3(a), a group of screw, slider and rail compose a transmission unit. As seen in Fig. 3(b), the entire driving box can be divided into two parts, the left half part installs the transmission units, while the right half used to lay out the motors and drivers. The ball screw of the transmission unit and motor is connected via a coupling.

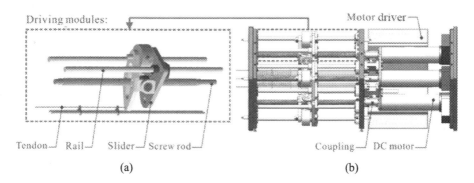

(a)   (b)

Fig. 3. Driving box: (a) the transmission unit; (b) overview of the driving box.

3   Kinematics Analysis

3.1   Kinematic Mapping

Based on the assumption that the bending curvature of each single joint is equal, the relative kinematic parameters are divided into three spaces: the joint space L, the configuration space Ψ and the workspace Q [16, 18]. The joint space is defined as $L = [l_{1,1} \; l_{1,2} \; l_{1,3} \; l_{2,1} \; l_{2,2} \; l_{2,3}]^{\perp}$ which reflects the length of the driving tendons. The configuration space is defined as $\Psi = [\theta_1 \; \varphi_1 \; \theta_2 \; \varphi_2]^{\perp}$, which describes the shape of the continuum arm. The workspace is defined as $Q = [x \; y \; z]^{\perp}$, which shows the absolute coordinates of the end point. In the joint space, $l_{i,k}$ denotes the total length of the kth driving tendon of the ith joint ($i = 1, 2; k = 1, 2, 3$), and the numbering ruler of all tendons is shown in Fig. 4(a), R is distribution radius of all tendons. Base coordinate system {0} and two local coordinate systems {i} ($i = 1, 2$) are established as shown in Fig. 4(b), where θ_i is the bending angle of the ith joint in the bending plane i. The bending plane is the plane where the arc lies. φ_i is the angle between the bending plane and the x_{i-1} axis of {$i - 1$}. In addition, it is known that the length of the backbone of each joint is $l_{\text{ba},i}$ ($i = 1, 2$), and $\omega_{i,k}$ is initial angle between the numbered tendon and the x_{i-1} axis, such as $\omega_{2,1}$ in Fig. 4(b).

As shown in Fig. 4(b), the mapping relationship between the joint space and the configuration space can be obtained according to the geometric relationship between the driving tendons and the backbone.

$$l_{i,k} = \sum_{g=1}^{i} [l_{\text{ba},g} + R\theta_g \cos(\omega_{i,k} - \varphi_g)] \tag{1}$$

Based on the geometric relationship of the coordinate system, the transformation matrix T_i ($i = 1, 2$) from frame $\{i - 1\}$ to $\{i\}$ can be obtained as Eq. (2), where Rot represents the rotation transformation and Tr represents the translation transformation.

$$T_i = Rot_z(\varphi_i)Tr_x(\frac{l_{ba,i}}{\theta_i})Rot_y(\theta_i)Tr_x(\frac{-l_{ba,i}}{\theta_i})Rot_z(-\varphi_i) \tag{2}$$

$$T = T_1 \cdot T_2 = \begin{bmatrix} R & P \\ 0 & 1 \end{bmatrix} \tag{3}$$

In Eq. (3), T represents the transformation matrix from frame $\{0\}$ to frame $\{2\}$, where P is the multivariate function vector of θ_1 φ_1 θ_2 φ_2, which reflects the absolute coordinates in basic frame $\{0\}$. That is, $P = [P_x \ P_y \ P_z]^{\top}$ reflects the mapping relationship between the configuration space Ψ and the workspace Q.

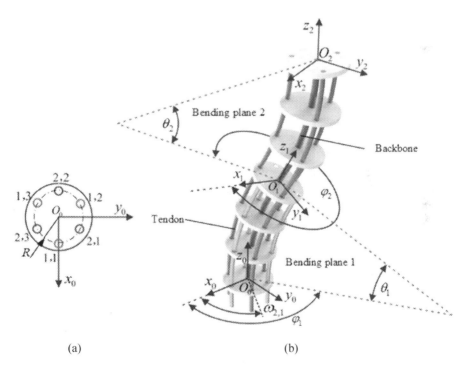

(a)   (b)

Fig. 4. Geometric description of continuum arm: (a) numbering ruler of tendons; (b) coordinate system definition

3.2 Jacobian Matrix

The Jacobian matrix reveals the velocity relationship between workspace, configuration space and joint space. It is the basis for velocity control of configuration or end position point. In the kinematics, two velocity Jacobian matrixes $J_{\Psi L}$ and $J_{\Psi Q}$ are included, which represent the velocity mappings from the configuration space to the joint space and from the configuration space to the workspace.

The velocity mapping from the configuration space to the joint space is expressed as Eq. (4):

$$\dot{L} = J_{\Psi L}\dot{\Psi} \tag{4}$$

According to Eq. (1), the Jacobian matrix from the configuration space to the joint space can be expressed as Eq. (5) by solving the derivative of L to Ψ.

$$J_{\Psi L} = \begin{bmatrix} \frac{\partial L}{\partial \theta_1} & \frac{\partial L}{\partial \varphi_1} & \frac{\partial L}{\partial \theta_2} & \frac{\partial L}{\partial \varphi_2} \end{bmatrix} \tag{5}$$

$$\dot{L} = J_{\Psi L}\dot{\Psi} = \begin{bmatrix} J_1 & 0 \\ J_{21} & J_2 \end{bmatrix} \begin{bmatrix} \dot{\theta}_1 \\ \dot{\varphi}_1 \\ \dot{\theta}_2 \\ \dot{\varphi}_2 \end{bmatrix} \tag{6}$$

In the Eq. (6), J_{21} shows the influence of the configuration of first joint on the second joint. The velocity mapping from the configuration space to the workspace is shown in Eq. (7):

$$\dot{Q} = J_{\Psi Q}\dot{\Psi} \tag{7}$$

Based on Eq. (3), the partial derivative of P to each element of Ψ make up the Jacobian matrix from configuration space to the workspace as Eq. (8):

$$J_{\Psi Q} = \begin{bmatrix} \frac{\partial P}{\partial \theta_1} & \frac{\partial P}{\partial \varphi_1} & \frac{\partial P}{\partial \theta_2} & \frac{\partial P}{\partial \varphi_2} \end{bmatrix} \tag{8}$$

In order to track the trajectory, the inverse kinematics from the workspace to the configuration space is required. The relationship between the inverse velocity of the redundantly actuated robot is shown in Eq. (9) [19]:

$$\dot{\Psi} = J_{\Psi Q}^{+}\dot{Q} + (I - J_{\Psi Q}J_{\Psi Q}^{+})w \tag{9}$$

$J_{\Psi Q}^{+}$ is the generalized inverse matrix of $J_{\Psi Q}$, the Jacobian matrix $J_{\Psi Q}$ is a numerical matrix at each moment. Therefore, $J_{\Psi L}^{+}$ can be solved numerically without solving the complicated nonlinear equations. $(I - J_{\Psi Q}J_{\Psi Q}^{+})w$ is the projection of w on the null space of matrix $J_{\Psi Q}$, which is an additional item caused by the redundant degree of freedom of the continuum arm, making the continuum arm can reach a same point in several poses. w can be any vector, if $w = 0$, a minimal norm solution of $\dot{\Psi}$ can be obtained [19, 20].

In order to control the movement of the end, we need to control the velocity of the driving tendon. Therefore, using Eqs. (4) and (9), and considering the minimal norm solution of the configuration velocity, the velocity mapping relationship between the workspace and the joint space can be obtained by the Eq. (10).

$$\dot{L} = J_{\Psi L} J^{+}_{\Psi Q} \dot{Q} \tag{10}$$

4   Control System

4.1   Control Architecture

As shown in Fig. 5, the control hardware consists of a PC, CAN bus and various control objects. The control objects include six DC brushed motors, the driver of the end-effector and the data acquisition card with analog input and output, which is used to collect feedback signals from end position sensors. Based on the kinematics and control algorithm, the MFC application program is written in the VC++ compilation environment to be used as a control interface. The instructions generated in this control software control all devices through the CAN bus which provides a serial high-speed communication. Different equipment can easily be added to the CAN bus to expand the control system.

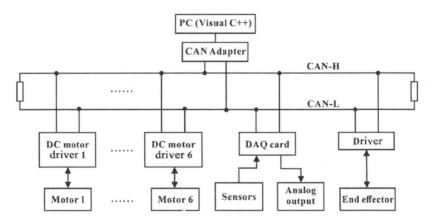

Fig. 5. Block diagram of control architecture

4.2   Closed-Loop Control Algorithm

Due to the high flexibility of the continuum robot, this structure is more sensitive to external disturbances. In addition, the kinematics model is not accurate enough based on the assumption of the constant curvature. Therefore, if only the open-loop control based on inverse kinematics is carried out, the deviation of end position is easy to occur. In particular, the error of continuous trajectory tracking is gradually being accumulated during the tracking procedure, resulting in a large deviation. Adding a position sensor at the end of the arm to establish closed-loop controller can eliminate errors timely, tracking the target trajectory better.

If the error of end is e one moment, it is the D-value between the target position Q_d and the actual position Q as shown in Eq. (11):

$$e = Q_d - Q \tag{11}$$

Using the above error e as the speed compensation and combining the Eq. (10) where the $w = 0$, the closed-loop control algorithm is established as Eq. (12):

$$\dot{L} = J_{\Psi L} J_{\Psi Q}^{+} [\dot{Q}_d + K_p(Q_d - Q)] \tag{12}$$

According to modern control theory [21], as long as the matrix K_p is positive definite, error e approaches 0 and the system is stable. The diagonal matrix is always chosen as K_p. Generally, the larger the value of the diagonal element, the faster the convergence rate and the higher the tracking accuracy.

The structure of closed-loop controller is described in Fig. 6. Firstly, the target trajectory Q_d (t) is given, and the input speed $\dot{Q}$ is obtained by adding up the differential of Q_d (t) and the gain of feedback of position error. According to Eq. (12), the real-time speed $\dot{L}$ of all of the tendons is obtained. $\dot{L}$ integrates over time to get the current length vector L. Based on the Eq. (1), there is a unique configuration mapping it, and the solution of end position of arm is unique too. Taking the disturbance into account, the actual value of end position is Q.

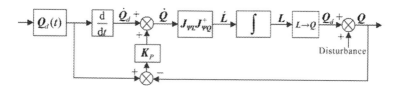

Fig. 6. Flow chart of closed loop inverse kinematics control

5   Simulation and Experiment

5.1   Workspace Simulation

The workspace of the continuum robot is plotted in Fig. 7, which is calculated using Eq. (3) within the allowable configuration. In such simulation, the length of each joint is 480 mm, the range of the bending angle θ_i (i = 1, 2) is [0, π] while the range of the rotation angle φ_i (i = 1, 2) is [0, 2π]. The simulation result shows that this robot has a sufficient and polydirectional workspace nearly 1.3 m^3.

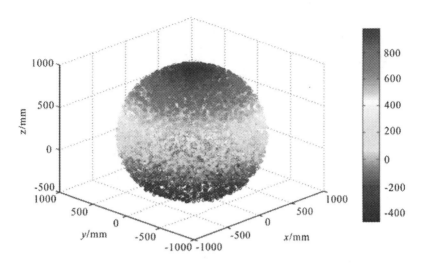

Fig. 7. Workspace of end effector

5.2 Control Experiment

To verify the analysis of kinematics and the design of the closed-loop controller, an experiment making the end of arm track a trajectory is carried out. The desired spatial trajectory is a circle and given by Eq. (13). In order to make the motion smoother, the change of $\alpha(t)$ over time is shown in (14), so that the initial and final velocity and acceleration in all directions are zero, $T = 15$ s.

$$
\begin{cases}
x_d = 0.42 \cos \alpha(t) \\
y_d = 0.42 \sin \alpha(t) \ (0 < \alpha(t) < 2\pi) \\
z_d = 0.7
\end{cases}
\tag{13}
$$

$$
\alpha(t) = \sin(\frac{2\pi}{T}t - \pi) + \frac{2\pi}{T}t \ (0 \le t \le T)
\tag{14}
$$

According to the data acquired by position sensor (*3D Guidance tranSTAR* manufactured by *Ascension Technology Corporation* with a measurement error 0.5 mm) placed on the end of the arm, Fig. 8(a) and (b) compares the tracking effects of the open-loop and closed-loop controller in the directions x and y respectively. The experimental result shows that if the open-loop controller is used, the position error will gradually accumulate, and the final error reached about 20 mm. In contrast, the closed-loop control can reduce the position error in time and track the target trajectory very well. It was found that $K_p = 10I$ results in a better tracking accuracy with a deviation below 2 mm compared with $K_p = I$, which shows the effectiveness of the closed-loop control algorithm.

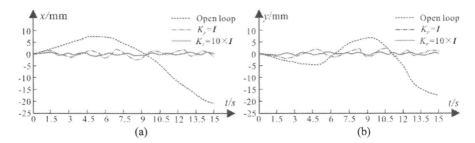

Fig. 8. Tracking effects of open loop and closed loop control: (a) tracking error of direction x; (b) tracking error of direction y

6 Conclusion

In this paper, a two joint tendon-driven continuum robot with passive flexibility is presented. This continuum robot is made up by two continuum joints with elastic NiTi backbone. Based on the prototype physical structure, the kinematic mapping and the Jacobian matrix are obtained through the kinematics analysis. Then, a position feedback kinematic controller is developed to improve the accuracy of movement and operation. Experiments show that the continuum robot is able to track a desired trajectory with errors less than 2 mm under this control algorithm.

Acknowledgments. This work was supported by the National Natural Science Foundation of China (Grant No. 51721003 and 51535008).

References

1. Yoshida, K.: Achievements in space robotics. IEEE Robot. Autom. Mag. **16**(4), 20–28 (2009)
2. Boumans, R., Heemskerk, C.: The European robotic arm for the international space station. Robot. Auton. Syst. **23**(1–2), 17–27 (1998)
3. Li, D.M., Rao, W., Hu, C.W., Wang, Y.B., Tang, Z.X., Wang, Y.Y.: Overview of the Chinese space station manipulator. In: AIAA SPACE 2015 Conference and Exposition 2015, Pasadena, USA (2015)
4. Liu, S.P., et al.: Impact dynamics and control of a flexible dual-arm space robot capturing an object. Appl. Math. Comput. **185**(2), 1149–1159 (2007)
5. Jiao, C., Liang, B., Wang, X.: Adaptive reaction null-space control of dual-arm space robot for post-capture of non-cooperative target. In: Control and Decision Conference 2017, Chongqing, China, pp. 531–537 (2017)
6. Wu, H., et al.: Optimal trajectory planning of a flexible dual-arm space robot with vibration reduction. J. Intell. Robot. Syst. **40**(2), 147–163 (2004)
7. Huang, P., Xu, Y., Liang, B.: Dynamic balance control of multi-arm free-floating space robots. Int. J. Adv. Robot. Syst. **2**(2), 398–403 (2008)
8. Tonapi, M.M., et al.: Next generation rope-like robot for in-space inspection. In: IEEE Aerospace Conference 2014, Big Sky, MT, USA, pp. 1–13 (2014)

9. Robinson, G., et al.: Continuum robots-a state of the art. In: International Conference on Robotics and Automation 1999, Detroit, Michigan, vol. 4, no. 7, pp. 2849–2854 (1999)
10. Jones, B.A., Walker, I.D.: Kinematics for multi-section continuum robots. IEEE Trans. Robot. 22(1), 43–55 (2006)
11. McMahan, W., et al.: Field trials and testing of the oct-arm continuum manipulator. In: IEEE International Conference on Robotics and Automation 2006, Orlando, Florida, pp. 2336–2341 (2006)
12. Mehling, L.S., Diftler, M.A., Chu, M., et al.: A minimally invasive tendril robot for in-space inspection. In: IEEE BioRobotics Conference 2006, pp. 690–695 (2006)
13. Walker, I.D.: Robot strings: long, thin continuum robots. In: IEEE Aerospace Conference, pp. 1–12 (2013)
14. Simaan, N., Taylor, R., Flint, P.: High dexterity snake-like robotic slaves for minimally invasive telesurgery of the upper airway. In: Barillot, C., Haynor, D.R., Hellier, P. (eds.) Medical Image Computing and Computer-Assisted Intervention – MICCAI 2004. Lecture Notes in Computer Science, vol. 3217. Springer, Heidelberg (2004). https://doi.org/10.1007/978-3-540-30136-3_3
15. Simaan, N.: Snake-like units using flexible backbones and actuation redundancy for enhanced miniaturization. In: IEEE International Conference on Robotics and Automation 2005, Piscataway, NJ, USA, pp. 3012–3017 (2005)
16. Xu, K., Simaan, N., et al.: An investigation of the intrinsic force sensing capabilities of continuum robots. IEEE Trans. Robot. 24, 576–587 (2008)
17. Kang, R., Branson, D.T., Zheng, T., et al.: Design, modeling and control of a pneumatically actuated manipulator inspired by biological continuum structures. Bioinspiration Biomim. 8(3), 036008 (2013)
18. Camarillo, D.B., Milne, C.F., Carlson, C.R.: Mechanics modeling of tendon-driven continuum manipulators. IEEE Trans. Robot. 24(6), 1262–1273 (2008)
19. Li, M., Kang, R., Geng, S., Guglielmino, E.: Design and control of a tendon-driven continuum robot. Trans. Inst. Meas. Control (2017). https://doi.org/10.1177/0142331216685607
20. Li, M., Kang, R., et al.: Model-free control for continuum robots based on an adaptive Kalman filter. IEEE/ASME Trans. Mechatron. 23(1), 286–297 (2018)
21. Hammond, P.H.: Modern Control Theory. Prentice-Hall, New York (1985)

A Real-Time Multiagent Strategy Learning Environment and Experimental Framework

Hongda Zhang[1,2(✉)], Decai Li[2], Liying Yang[2], Feng Gu[2], and Yuqing He[2]

[1] University of Chinese Academy of Sciences, Beijing, China
[2] Shenyang Institute of Automation Chinese Academy of Sciences, Shenyang, China
zhanghongda@sia.cn

Abstract. Many problems in the real world can be attributed to the problem of multiagent. The study on the issue of multiagent is of great significance to solve these social problems. This paper reviews the research on multiagent based real-time strategy game environments, and introduces the multiagent learning environment and related resources. We choose a deep learning environment based on the *StarCraft* game as a research environment for multiagent collaboration and decision-making, and form a research mentality focusing mainly on reinforcement learning. On this basis, we design a verification platform for the related theoretical research results and finally form a set of multiagent research system from the theoretical method to the actual platform verification. Our research system has reference value for multiagent related research.

Keywords: Multiagent · Reinforcement learning · Real-time strategy

1 Introduction

In recent years, artificial intelligence research and applications made many breakthroughs. Artificial intelligence in a single aspect of the ability to show close to humans such as intelligent speech recognition, object recognition, and some aspects even more than humans such as Go. However, social animals, such as bees and wolves, know how to cooperate and learn from each other, so they can give full play to the superiority of each individual. Humans, as a social living, know how to cooperate and play far beyond the limits of individual capabilities.

Real-time multiagent system is a kind of complex real-time dynamic system, which not only has a huge state space, but also often accompanied by incomplete information in practical problems. Such complex dynamic environments that have neither perfect information nor complete information available for the current state or dynamic changes in the environment present significant challenges to AI research [1]. Many large and complex dynamic environmental problems in the real world, such as road traffic system, weather forecast, economic forecast, smart city management and military decision-making are all real-time multiagent systems. There are many research methods in this field. Among them, many artificial intelligence researchers adopt the real-time multiagent strategy research mode that uses real-time strategy game of multiagent as

© Springer International Publishing AG, part of Springer Nature 2018
Y. Tan et al. (Eds.): ICSI 2018, LNCS 10942, pp. 36–42, 2018.
https://doi.org/10.1007/978-3-319-93818-9_4

learning environment. Real-time strategy games provide an excellent research platform for such issues. A series of real-time strategy games provide a simulation environment that is complex, imperfect and incomplete information, long-term global planning, and complex decision making it similar to the real environment. Among numerous research platforms, *StarCraft* has become a platform for theoretical research and methodological verification with its most abundant environmental information and realistic environmental scenarios.

Real-time Strategy (RTS) game *StarCraft* puts forward huge challenge for the research field of artificial intelligence with the characteristics of real-time confrontation, huge search space, incomplete information game, multi-heterogeneous agent collaboration, spatiotemporal reasoning, multiple complex tasks. Because of its rich environment and close to the real scene, the platform iterates rapidly and is stable and reliable, which becomes an excellent research and verification platform for artificial intelligence. A series of artificial intelligence research based on *StarCraft* has greatly promoted the development of multiagent systems and machine learning, deep learning and game theory.

The article is organized as follows. The second part reviews the multiagent system research methods and achievements based on real-time strategy game environment. The third part introduces real-time multiagent strategy research environment and related research resources. The fourth part introduces the theoretical ideas of real-time multiagent strategy based on deep reinforcement learning. The fifth part introduces real-time multiagent strategy experiment and application platform. Finally, the article is discussed and summarized.

2   Related Work

Real-time multiagent systems pose great challenges to the field of artificial intelligence with real-time confrontation, huge search space, incomplete information game, multi-heterogeneous agent collaboration, space-time reasoning, multi-complex tasks, long-time planning. Based on a variety of multiagent real-time strategy game environment, many researchers use a variety of methods to solve these difficulties. The main research methods can be divided into five categories as rule-based, classical machine learning, deep learning, (deep) reinforcement learning and others.

In these methods, reinforcement learning (RL) is seen as a very effective way to solve real-time multiagent problems. Thanks to the rapid development of deep learning, deep reinforcement learning (DRL) shows great ability to solve these problems. With the method of DRL, a learning platform has been designed [2]; The learning methods includes Q learning and Sarsa variants [3], deep Q network for end-to-end RL [4], depth-enhanced learning algorithms [5], deep neural networks in conjunction with heuristic reinforcement learning [6], a strategy of interacting and cooperating multi-heterogeneous agents against enemies with DRL [7], a method uses a centralized critic to estimate the Q function and decentralized participants to optimize the agent's strategy [8]. In a *StarCraft II* learning environment, deep learning is used to extract game information and then based on the A3C algorithm, learning decision-making network so that multiagent can complete different minigame micro-tasks [9]. To quantify the interplay between strategies, compute the meta-strategy of strategy selection based on the approximate best response to the strategy mixture generated by the DRL and empirical game analysis [10].

3 Multiagent Strategy Learning Environment Based on *StarCraft*

In many real-time multiagent strategy game AI research environments, the learning environment based on StarCraft games is more challenging than most previous work. StarCraft is a multiagent interaction problem. Due to the partial observation of maps, there is imperfect information. It has a large movement space that involves the selection and control of hundreds of units. It has a large state space. It can be observed from the original input feature plane. It delays credit distribution and requires long-term strategies up to thousands of steps [9]. Facebook developed a learning environment combining *Starcraft I* with Torch, a learning tool called *Torchcraft* and then with the Oculus, a light research platform named ELF for reinforcement learning was made. In August 2017, Deepmind and Bllizard jointly launched the SC2LE (see Fig. 1), a deep learning research environment based on *StarCraft II* [9]. The learning environment provides a free science computing interface and a stable learning environment, allowing researchers the freedom to choose the scientific computing tools they need to learn and simply access the learning environment. Our research is based on this learning environment.

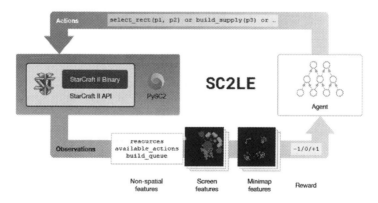

Fig. 1. The StarCraft II learning environment, SC2LE [9].

3.1 Real-Time Strategy Game *StarCraft*

StarCraft offers three types of characters for players to choose from: Terran, Zerg, Protoss.

Players need to choose a role in the game. The game offers two modes, single-player game exploration and multi-player confrontation. In solo exploration mode, individual gamers need to complete various game tasks, break through multiple levels to learn various skills and understand the game better. At the same time can also carry out a variety of skills training or custom game environment. In multiplayer mode, after players choose a character, they need to collect as much mineral, natural gas, or scattered rewards resources as possible to build more functional, training, defensive structures and produce more soldiers, weapons, battleships and other combat units and enhance the building unit and combat unit skill level, and in the shortest possible time destroy the enemy's combat units and buildings to win. Different players choose the role of the same type can also be different. The game offers as little as one player up to eight, while players can also customize the environment and the number of confrontation.

3.2 StarCraft Challenge for AI Research

After several years of research, some achievements have been made in this field, but many problems still have not been solved yet. In conclusion, the current issues of concern are mainly in the following aspects.

Multi-heterogeneous Agent Collaboration. In a two-player game, the number of agents controlled by game player can be as many as 200. Similarly, the number of enemy-controlled agents can be as many as 200. If more than one player confrontation, the number of agents controlled by each player can reach to 200. Importantly, each of these agents are not the same type of agent. They are many types of agents with different kinds, attributes, combat and defensive capabilities, functions, health values, and ways of cooperation. How these so many heterogeneous agents work together is a challenging problem.

Large Search Space and Numerous Complex Tasks. The size of the state space and the choice of action sequences for each decision-making session are enormous. For example, in the case of state space, the average state space for chess games is around 10^{50}, Texas Hold'em is 10^{80} and Go state space is 10^{170}. The state space on a typical map of StarCraft is several orders of magnitude larger than the state space of all these classes. Take a typical 128×128 pixels map as an example. At any time, there may be 50 to 400 units on the map. Each unit may have a complex internal state (remaining energy and beating values, pending action, etc.). These factors will lead to a great possible state. Even if only consider the possible location of each unit on the map, 400 units that is $(128 \times 128)^{400} = 16384^{400} \approx 10^{1685}$ states. If consider other factors of different units, then will get greater value. Another way to calculate complexity is to calculate the complexity of the game using b^d, where chess $b \approx 35$, $d \approx 80$, Go $b \approx 30 \sim 300$, $d \approx 150 \sim 200$, and *Starcraft* $b \in [10^{50}, 10^{200}]$, $d \approx 36000$ (25 min $\times$ 60 s $\times$ 24 frames/s) [1].

Incomplete Information Game. Because of the fog of war, players can only see the environment where the unit they controlled is, other environmental information can't be known. This is a game of incomplete or imperfect information.

Long-Term Overall Planning. In the game of confrontation, different strategies are needed at different times, and these strategies need to consider the overall planning. Early strategies may not be decisive until the very end.

Time and Space Reasoning. The multiagent against the environment not only need to make decisions in accordance with the time, but also need to consider the space for a variety of situations. Such as combat units in the high and low terrain have different attack abilities.

Real-Time Multi-player Confrontation. The game environment of *StarCraft* changes with a speed of 24 fps, it means players can act in less than 42 ms. If the environment changes the average of per 8 frames, the player still needs to play at a rate of 3 moves per second. Moreover, different players in the game can perform actions at the same time, it is different from chess which actions are alternately performed by the two players. Not only that, real-time strategy game with the ongoing action has a certain degree of continuity, need to perform some time, rather than chess game player's action is intermittent, sudden, instantaneous.

4   Real-Time Multiagent Strategy Training Based on Deep Reinforcement Learning

We learned the multiagent collaborative confrontation strategy based on the SC2LE learning environment. As shown in the picture (see Fig. 2), the AI is the game's built-in AI and the Terran soldiers are the combat units under we controlled. In each confrontation, the total confrontation time is set. The one side will win the final victory by eliminating the opponent. When the battle is completely eliminated, the next round of confrontation will begin until the upper limit of the confrontation time is reached. If the soldier is eliminated, the confrontation will be terminated directly. During the confrontation process, the soldier can get a score for each enemy's annihilation and receive a score as a reward. At the same time, if one soldier is eliminated and the corresponding score is deducted. This means that the more scores, the better of the confrontation effect. After a period of training, we pick the best decision network. Based on this, the experimental framework is designed to further apply these collaborative countermeasures to the physical platform.

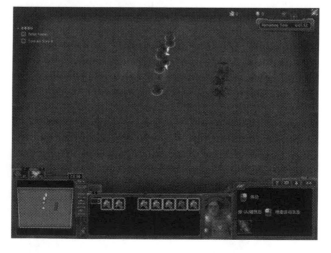

Fig. 2. 9 marines defeat 4 roaches.

5   Real-Time Multiagent Strategy Experiment and Application Platform

In order to verify and apply the multiagent cooperation strategy, we initially built a physical experiment and application platform (see Fig. 3). The platform is mainly composed of multiple unmanned systems in both air and ground. We plan to build a multiplayer unmanned coordination system with open space cooperation capability consisting of multiple drones and multiple unmanned vehicles. The learned multiagent collaboration strategy was deployed on the experimental platform to verify its actual application effect.

Fig. 3. Air-ground cooperation system.

6   Conclusion

In this paper, we reviewed the research on multiagent based on real-time strategy game environments, and introduced the multiagent learning environment and related resources. We chose a deep learning environment based on the *StarCraft* game as a research environment for multiagent collaboration and decision-making, formed a research mentality focusing mainly on reinforcement learning. On this basis, we designed a verification platform for the related theoretical research results and finally formed a set of multiagent research system from the theoretical method to the actual platform verification. Our research system has reference value for multiagent related research.

At present, more and more researchers are focusing on multiagent distributed decision-making. Stratification and sub-task decisions may be a development direction for *StarCraft*. Some researchers use game theory to analyze the game problem in *StarCraft*. Imitative learning, transfer learning, and incremental learning may all show effects in this field.

In the future, we will further study and improve our current learning strategies and apply these strategies to the verification system we have designed.

Acknowledgment. The authors acknowledge the support of the National Natural Science Foundation of China (grant U1608253, grant 61473282), Natural Science Foundation of Guangdong Province (2017B010116002) and this work was supported by the Youth Innovation Promotion Association, CAS. Any opinions, findings, conclusions, or recommendations expressed in this paper are those of the authors, and do not necessarily reflect the views of the funding organizations.

References

1. Santiago, O., Gabriel, S., Alberto, U.: A survey of real-time strategy game AI research and competition in *StarCraft*. IEEE Trans. Comput. Intell. AI Games **5**(4), 293–309 (2013)
2. Marc, G.B., Yavar, N., Joel, V., Michael, B.: The arcade learning environment: an evaluation platform for general agents. In: 24th International Joint Conference on Artificial Intelligence, pp. 4148–4152 (2015)
3. Stefan, W., Ian, W.: Applying reinforcement learning to small scale combat in the real-time strategy game StarCraft: Broodwar. In: 2012 IEEE Conference on Computational Intelligence and Games (CIG 2012), pp. 402–408 (2012)
4. Mnih, V., Kavukcuoglu, K., Silver, D.: Human-level control through deep reinforcement learning. Nature **518**(5740), 529–533 (2015)
5. Sainbayar, S., Arthur, S., Gabriel, S., Soumith, C., Rob, F.: Mazebase: a sandbox for learning from games. https://arxiv.org/abs/1511.07401
6. Nicolas, U., Gabriel, S., Zeming, L., Soumith, C.: Episodic exploration for deep deterministic policies: an application to StarCraft micromanagement tasks. https://arxiv.org/abs/1609.02993
7. Peng, P., Ying, W., Yaodong, Y.: Multiagent bidirectionally-coordinated nets emergence of human-level coordination in learning to play StarCraft combat games. https://arxiv.org/abs/1703.10069
8. Jakob, N.F., Gregory, F., Triantafyllos, A.: Counterfactual multi-agent policy gradients. In: The Thirty-Second AAAI Conference on Artificial Intelligence (AAAI 2018), New Orleans (2018)
9. Oriol, V., Timo, E., Kevin, C.: StarCraft II: a new challenge for reinforcement learning. https://arxiv.org/abs/1708.04782
10. Marc, L., Vinicius, Z., Audrunas, G.: A unified game-theoretic approach to multiagent reinforcement learning. https://arxiv.org/abs/1711.00832

Transaction Flows in Multi-agent Swarm Systems

Eugene Larkin[✉], Alexey Ivutin, Alexander Novikov, and Anna Troshina

Tula State University, Tula, Russia
elarkin@mail.ru, alexey.ivutin@gmail.com, alsnovikov@yandex.ru,
atroshina@mail.ru

Abstract. The article presents a mathematical model of transaction flows between individual intelligent agents in swarm systems. Assuming that transaction flows are Poisson ones, the approach is proposed to the analytical modeling of such systems. Methods for estimating the degree of approximation of real transaction flows to Poisson flows based on Pearson's criterion, regression, correlation and parametric criteria are proposed. Estimates of the computational complexity of determining the parameters of transaction flows by using the specified criteria are shown. The new criterion based on waiting functions is proposed, which allows obtaining a good degree of approximation of an investigated flow to Poisson flow with minimal costs of computing resources. That allows optimizing the information exchange processes between individual units of swarm intelligent systems.

Keywords: Transaction flow · Poisson flow
Exponential distribution · Pearson's criterion · Expectation
Dispersion · Waiting function · Statistical estimation
Intelligent agents

1 Introduction

One of main features of multi-agent swarm systems [1,3] is a continuous data change between units, which may be reduced to two operations: generation transactions to external corresponding units and servicing transaction, arriving from external units. Transactions may be realized as quests to data change procedure [3], process of failures/recoveries [17], receiving commands from human operator in dialogue regimes of control [10], etc. All quests are generated and executed in physical time, and interval between neighboring transactions, for external observer, is a random value. One of diversity of flows is the Poisson one, which has such important feature, as absence of an aftereffect [6,12,15]. Due to this property, simulation of multi-agent swarm system may be substantially simplified. So when working out of such a systems, the question of criterion, which shows degree of approximation of real transaction flow properties to propertied of Poisson flow, arises constantly. On the one hand the criterion should

© Springer International Publishing AG, part of Springer Nature 2018
Y. Tan et al. (Eds.): ICSI 2018, LNCS 10942, pp. 43–52, 2018.
https://doi.org/10.1007/978-3-319-93818-9_5

adequately estimate degree of approximation, and on the other hand computational complexity of estimation should not exceed complexity of solved task of investigation of information system as a whole. The problem of adequate estimation of properties of transaction flow is solved insufficiently, that explains importance and relevance of investigations in this domain.

2   Pearson's Criterion

Let us consider a transaction flow, in which time intervals between neighboring transactions are represented as the simple statistical series

$$\tau = \{t_1, \ldots, t_n, \ldots, t_N\}, \tag{1}$$

where t_n — is the n-th result of measurement of time interval.

In Poisson flow interval between neighboring transactions is described with exponential distribution law [4, 13]:

$$f(t) = \frac{1}{T} \exp -\frac{t}{T}, \tag{2}$$

where T — is the expectation of the exponential law, which can be estimated as

$$T = \frac{1}{N} \sum_{n=1}^{N} t_n. \tag{3}$$

Let us note that estimation (2) is the necessary stage of any statistical processing of series (1).

Conventional method of statistical smoothing of series is the method based on calculation of Pearson's criterion [5, 14, 16, 20]. For the use of such criterion series (1) should be transformed to the histogram as follows

$$g(t) = \begin{pmatrix} \hat{t}_{j-1} \le t \le \hat{t}_j \ \ldots \ \hat{t}_{j-1} \le t \le \hat{t}_j \ \ldots \ \hat{t}_{j-1} \le t \le \hat{t}_j \\ n_1 \qquad\qquad\quad n_j \qquad\qquad\quad n_J \end{pmatrix}, \tag{4}$$

where n_j — is the quantity of results falling to the interval $\hat{t}_{j-1} \le t \le \hat{t}_j$;

$$\sum_{j=1}^{N} n_j = N. \tag{5}$$

Exponential law and histogram are shown on the Fig. 1, where for every rate not only its value is shown, but also spread of the values.

Pearson's criterion for the exponential law (2) is as follows

$$\chi^2 = N \sum_{j=1}^{J} \frac{\left[\frac{n_j}{N} - \exp\left(-\frac{\hat{t}_{j-1}}{T}\right) + \exp\left(-\frac{\hat{t}_j}{T}\right) \right]^2}{-\exp\left(-\frac{\hat{t}_{j-1}}{T}\right) - \exp\left(-\frac{\hat{t}_j}{T}\right)}. \tag{6}$$

Pearson's criterion is rather cumbersome. For its estimation it is necessary to

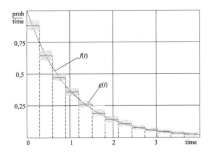

Fig. 1. Exponential law and histogram estimation [19] of experimental data

(1) evaluate T as it is shown in (3);

(2) order series (1) to ascending $\tau \to \tilde{\tau}$, where $\tilde{\tau} = (\tilde{t}_1, \ldots, \tilde{t}_n, \ldots, \tilde{t}_N)$; $\tilde{t}_n \in \tau$; $\tilde{t}_1 \leq \cdots \leq \tilde{t}_n \leq \cdots \leq \tilde{t}_N$;

(3) calculate $\hat{t}_j$ as follows $\hat{t}_j = \tilde{t}_{j-1} + \frac{\tilde{t}_N - \tilde{t}_{11}}{J-1}$;

(4) evaluate   cardinalities n_j $=$ $|\hat{\tau}_j|$,   where
$$\begin{cases} \{\hat{t}|\hat{t}_{j-t} \leq t \leq \hat{t}_{j-t}, \text{ when } 1 \leq j \leq J; \} \\ \{\hat{t}|\hat{t}_{J-t} \leq t \leq \hat{t}_{j-t}, \text{ when } j = J; \} \end{cases}$$

(5) calculate χ^2 with use (6);

(6) evaluate, due to $\chi^2 = u$ and $r \in \{1, 2, \ldots\}$, degree of congruence of exponential law and histogram (4) as follows

$$\varphi_r(u) = \begin{cases} 0, \text{ when } u < 0, \\ \frac{1}{2^{\frac{r}{2}} \cdot \Gamma\left(\frac{r}{2}\right)} u^{\frac{r-2}{2}} e^{-\frac{u}{2}}, \text{ otherwise,} \end{cases} \tag{7}$$

where $\Gamma\left(\frac{r}{2}\right) = \int\limits_0^\infty \xi^{\frac{r}{2}-1} \cdot e^{-\xi} d\xi$ — is the Γ-function.

Computational complexity Pearson's method may be estimated as $\Theta_{\chi^2} = \sum\limits_{i=1}^6 \theta_i$, where θ_i — is the computational complexity of execution of first point of method, which includes $N - 1$ summations and one division; θ_2 in the worst case includes $\frac{(N-1)(N-2)}{2}$ comparisons; θ_3 includes $J - 1$ summations; θ_4 includes J operations cardinality evaluations; θ_5 includes $J + 1$ calculations of exponent, $3J$ summations, J operations of squaring, J divisions and one multiplication; θ_6 includes evaluation of probability, as it follows from (7).

3   Regression Criterion

Regression criterion is based on estimation of standard-mean-square error as follows [7]:

$$\varepsilon_r = \int\limits_0^\infty [g(t) - f(t)]^2 \, dt. \tag{8}$$

where $g(t)$ — is the distribution under estimation.

Let $g(t) = \delta(t - T)$, where $\delta(t - T)$ — is Dirac δ-function. Then $\varepsilon_r = \int_0^\infty [\delta(t - T) - f(t)]^2 \, dt = \varepsilon_{r1} + \varepsilon_{r2} + \varepsilon_{r3}$ where $\varepsilon_{r1} = \int_0^\infty \delta^2(t - T) \, dt =$

$\lim_{a \to 0} \int_{T-a}^{T+a} \left(\frac{1}{2a}\right)^2 dt = \infty$; $\varepsilon_{r2} = -2 \int_0^\infty \delta(t - T_g) \frac{1}{T_f} \exp\left(-\frac{t}{T}\right) dt = -\frac{2}{eT}$; $\varepsilon_{r3} =$

$\int_0^\infty \frac{1}{T^2} \exp\left(-\frac{2t}{T}\right) dt = \frac{1}{2T}$.

Thus criterion ε_r changes from 0 (flow without aftereffect) till ∞ (flow with deterministic link between transactions). Statistical evaluation of (8) is as follows:

$$\varepsilon_r = \sum_{j=1}^{J} \left[\frac{n_j}{N} - \exp\left(-\frac{\hat{t}_{j-1}}{T}\right) + \exp\left(-\frac{\hat{t}_j}{T}\right)\right]^2. \tag{9}$$

For estimation of flow by the criterion (9) it is necessary to

(1) execute pp. 1 — 4 of algorithm of calculation χ^2;
(2) calculate ε_r with use (9).

Computational complexity of regression may be estimated as follows

$$\Theta_r = \sum_{i=1}^{5} \theta_{ri}, \tag{10}$$

where $\theta_{r1} = \theta_{\chi^2 1}$; $\theta_{r2} = \theta_{\chi^2 2}$; $\theta_{r3} = \theta_{\chi^2 3}$; $\theta_{r4} = \theta_{\chi^2 4}$; θ_5 – is computational complexity of calculation of (9), which includes $2J$ calculations of the exponents, $2J$ summations, J divisions and J squaring.

So, computational complexity of calculation of regression criterion is lower then Pearson one.

4   Correlation Criterion

Correlation criterion is as follows [18]:

$$\varepsilon_c = \int_0^\infty g(t) \frac{1}{T} \exp\left(-\frac{t}{T}\right) dt. \tag{11}$$

This criterion changes from $\frac{1}{2T}$ (flow without aftereffect) till $\frac{1}{eT}$, where $e = 2,718$ (deterministic flow). With use the function $\tilde{\varepsilon}_c = \frac{e(1 - 2T\varepsilon_{\tilde{n}})}{e - 2}$ criterion may be done the non-dimensional one, and it fits the interval $0 \leq \tilde{\varepsilon}_c \leq 1$.

Statistical evaluation of (11) is as follows:

$$\varepsilon_{\tilde{n}} = \sum_{j=1}^{J} \frac{n_j}{N} \left[\exp\left(-\frac{\hat{t}_{j-1}}{T}\right) + \exp\left(-\frac{\hat{t}_j}{T}\right)\right]^2. \tag{12}$$

For estimation of flow by the criterion (12) it is necessary to

(1) execute pp. 1 — 4 of algorithm of calculation χ^2;
(2) calculate $\varepsilon_{\tilde{n}}$ with use (12).

Computational complexity of regression may be estimated as follows

$$\Theta_{\tilde{n}} = \sum_{i=1}^{5} \theta_{\tilde{n}i}, \tag{13}$$

where $\theta_{\tilde{n}1} = \theta_{\chi^2 1}$; $\theta_{\tilde{n}2} = \theta_{\chi^2 2}$; $\theta_{\tilde{n}3} = \theta_{\chi^2 3}$; $\theta_{\tilde{n}4} = \theta_{\chi^2 4}$; θ_5 – is computational complexity of calculation of (12), which includes $2J$ calculations of the exponents, J summations, and J multiplications.

So, computational complexity of calculation of regression criterion is lower then Pearson one.

5   Parametric Criterion

Parametric criterion is based on the next property of exponential law [4,6,13]:

$$T^2 = D, \tag{14}$$

where D — is the dispersion, which should be evaluated as follows

$$D = \frac{1}{N-1} \sum_{n=1}^{N} t_n^2 - \frac{N}{N-1} T^2. \tag{15}$$

Parametric criterion, based on property (14) is $\epsilon = \left(\frac{T^2 - D}{T^2} \right)$. From (3) and (15) it follows that $\epsilon = \left[\frac{2N-1}{N-1} - \frac{(N-1) \sum_{n=1}^{N} t_n^2}{\left(\sum_{n=1}^{N} t_n \right)} \right]^2$.

For estimation of criterion it is necessary to

(1) calculate the square of sum of series (1) — computational complexity θ_1 includes $N-1$ summations and one operation of squaring;
(2) calculate sum of squares of units of series (1) — computational complexity θ_2 N operations of squaring, $N-1$ summations and one multiplication;
(3) calculation of criterion — computational complexity θ_3 includes division, summation and squaring.

Common computational complexity is as follows

$$\Theta_{\frac{T^2}{D}} = \sum_{i=1}^{3} \theta_i. \tag{16}$$

So complexity is less, then method based on Pearson's criterion. Decreasing complexity is achieved through excluding such operations as the series ordering, forming the histogram calculation of exponents and evaluation of probability (7).

6   Criterion, Based on Waiting Function

In [9,11] "competition" in parallel stochastic systems were investigated and waiting function was introduces. In the case, when compete an external observer and transaction from the flow, "competition" starts at the moment of previous transaction, observer "wins" and begin to watch, when the next transaction occur, waiting function is as follows

$$f_{w \to g}(t) = \frac{\eta(t) \int_0^\infty w(\tau) g(t + \tau) d\tau}{\int_0^\infty W(t) dG(t)}, \tag{17}$$

where τ — is the subsidiary argument; $\eta(t)$ — is the Heaviside function; $w(t)$ — density of time of "running the distance" by the observer; $g(t)$ — density of time between transactions; $W(t) = \int_0^t w(\tau) d\tau$; $G(t) = \int_0^t g(\tau) d\tau$.

In the Poisson flow, when $g(t) = f(t)$

$$f_{w \to g}(t) = \frac{\eta(t) \int_0^\infty w(\tau) \frac{1}{T} \exp\left[-\frac{t+\tau}{T}\right] d\tau}{1 - \int_{t=0}^\infty \left[1 - \exp\left(-\frac{t}{T}\right)\right] dW(t)} = \frac{1}{T} \exp\left(-\frac{t}{T}\right). \tag{18}$$

Formula (18) expresses absence of hack called aftereffect in the systems with Poisson flows, i.e. for external observer time remaining till the next transaction is distributed in accordance with exponential law, independently from the starting of observation.

In the case, when $g(t) = \delta(t - T)$, expression (17) is as $f_{w \to g}(t) = \frac{\eta(t) w(T-t)}{W(t)}$.

Suppose that $w(t)$ have range of definition $T_{w\,min} \leq \arg w(t) \leq T_{w\,max}$ and expectation $T_{w\,min} \leq T_w \leq T_{w\,max}$. In dependence of location $w(t)$ and T onto time axis, it is possible next cases:

(a) $T < T_{w\,min}$. In this case (18) is senseless.

(b) $T_{w\,min} \leq T \leq T_{w\,max}$. In this case $f_{w \to g}(t)$ is defined as (2), range of definition is $0 \leq \arg \lfloor f_{w \to g}(t) \rfloor \leq T - T_{w\,min}$, and $\int_0^\infty t f_{w \to g}(t) dt \leq T$.

(c) $T > T_{w\,max}$. In this case $f_{w \to g}(t) = w(T - t)$, $T - T_{w\,max} \leq$
$\leq \arg \lfloor f_{w \to g}(t) \rfloor \leq T - T_{w\,min}$, and $\int_0^\infty t f_{w \to g}(t) dt \leq T$.

In such a way, expectation of waiting function $f_{w \to g}(t)$ for the Poisson flow is equal to T. For deterministic flow of transaction expectation of $f_{w \to g}(t)$ changes and depends of function $g(t)$. This obstacle permits to formulate simple criterion, based on expectation of waiting function. Let observer start observation of transactions at the moment $t = T$, where T — is calculated as (3), i.e. $w(t) = \delta(t - T)$.

Density of time of waiting of the next transaction is as follows:

$$f_{\delta \to g}(t) = \frac{\eta(t)g(t+T)}{\int\limits_{T}^{\infty} g(t)dt}. \tag{19}$$

Expectation of (19), and criterion correspondingly are as follows:

$$T_{\delta \to g}(t) = \int\limits_{0}^{\infty} t \frac{g(t+T)}{\int\limits_{T}^{\infty} g(t)dt} dt. \tag{20}$$

$$\epsilon_w = \left(\frac{T - T_{\delta \to g}}{T}\right)^2. \tag{21}$$

Let us define expectation of density $g(t)$ as follows (Fig. 2)

$$\int\limits_{0}^{\infty} tg(t)dt = \int\limits_{0}^{T} tg(t)dt + \int\limits_{0}^{\infty} tg(t+T)dt + T \int\limits_{0}^{\infty} g(t+T)dt = p_{1g}T_{1g} + p_{2g}T_{\delta \to g} + p_{2g}T, \tag{22}$$

where $p_{1g} = \int\limits_{0}^{T} g(t)dt$; $p_{2g} = \int\limits_{T}^{\infty} g(t)dt$.

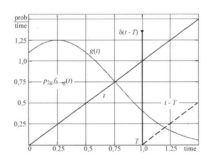

Fig. 2. To calculation of waiting function expectation

If $g(t) = f(t)$, then from equation $p_{1f}T_{1f} + p_{2f}T_{\delta \to f} + p_{2f}T = T$, where $p_{1f} = \frac{e-1}{e}$; $p_{2f} = \frac{1}{e}$; $T_{1f} = T\frac{e-2}{e-1}$, it follows that $T_{\delta \to f} = T$ and confirms (18).

In the case of processing data series (1) T is calculated as (3). Expectation may be calculated as mean value part of series (1)

$$\bar{\tau} = \{\bar{t}_1, \ldots, \bar{t}_n, \ldots, \bar{t}_{\bar{N}}\}; \tag{23}$$

$$T_{\delta \to g} = \frac{1}{\bar{N}} \sum\limits_{n=1}^{\bar{N}} \bar{t}_n; \tag{24}$$

where $\tilde{t}_n \in \tau$; $\bar{N} = |\bar{\tau}|$; $\bar{\tau} = \{\bar{t}|t_n \geq T\}$.

For estimation criterion it is necessary to

(1) calculate the expectation (3) — computational complexity of θ_1 includes $N - 1$ summations and one division;
(2) clip from series (1) part (23) — computational complexity of θ_2 includes N comparisons with T;
(3) calculate the expectation (24) — if $\bar{N} \simeq \frac{N}{2}$, then computational complexity of θ_3 includes $\frac{N}{2} - 1$ summations and one division.
(4) calculate criterion (21) — computational complexity θ_4 includes one subtraction, one division and one squaring.

Thus, from all criteria considered above least computational complexity,

$$\Theta_w = \sum_{i=1}^{4} \theta_i, \tag{25}$$

have criterion based on calculation of expectation of waiting function. Time decreasing is achieved through excluding from calculation such operation, as mass squaring of elements of series.

7   Example

For verification of proposed method direct computer experiment was executed with use the Monte-Carlo method [2]. Transactions are generated by state 1 of semi-Markov process $M = \{A, \boldsymbol{h}(t)\}$, shown on the Fig. 3, in which

$$A = \{1, 2, 3\}; \quad \boldsymbol{h}(t) = \begin{bmatrix} \frac{1}{3} \cdot \psi(t) & \frac{1}{3} \cdot \psi(t) & \frac{1}{3} \cdot \psi(t) \\ \frac{1}{3} \cdot \psi(t) & \frac{1}{3} \cdot \psi(t) & \frac{1}{3} \cdot \psi(t) \\ \frac{1}{3} \cdot \psi(t) & \frac{1}{3} \cdot \psi(t) & \frac{1}{3} \cdot \psi(t) \end{bmatrix};$$

$$f(t) = \begin{cases} \frac{5}{3}, & \text{when } 0,7 \leq t \leq 1,3; \\ 0, & \text{otherwise.} \end{cases}$$

Computer experiment was carried out in accordance with the next classical method.

(1) Reset the counter of number of realizations, $l = 0$.
(2) Assignment the status of current to the first state, $a_l = 1$.
(3) Reset the timer $t_l = 1$.
(4) Receiving a random value $1 \leq \pi \leq 1$ with uniform distribution.
(5) If $0 \leq \pi \leq 0,333$, then $a_l = 1$; if $0,333 \leq \pi \leq 0,666$, then $a_l = 2$; if $0,666 \leq \pi \leq 1$, then $a_l = 3$.
(6) Receiving a random value $1 \leq \pi \leq 1$.
(7) Calculation of time increment on the formula $\Delta_t = 0,6\pi + 0,7s$.
(8) Calculation of current time $t_l := t_l + \Delta_t$.
(9) If $a_l \neq 1$, then 4.
(10) Unloading t_l to array of results.

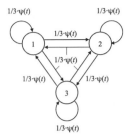

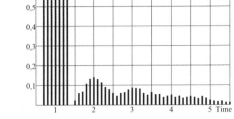

Fig. 3. Semi-Markov generator of transactions

Fig. 4. A histogram of the time between transactions

(11) $l := l + 1$. If $l < L$, then 3.

(12) End of experiment.

During experiment $L = 10^4$. As a result series (1) was formed, where $N = 10^4$. Histogram is shown on the Fig. 4.

Mean time between transactions is $T_{1,1} = 2,996$ [time] with error 0,13%, standard deviation is $\sqrt{D_{1,1}} = 2,493$ [time] with error 0,75%.

Estimation by Pearson's criterion gives coincidence of histogram with exponential law equal to 0,81. Estimation by parametric criterion gives $\epsilon_{\frac{T^2}{D}} = 0,095$. Estimation by waiting function criterion gives $\epsilon_w = 0,083$. In such a way all three criteria show, that flow of transactions is quite alike Poisson flow [8].

8   Conclusions

Paper shows, that criterion based on the expectation of waiting function permits as well as or parametric criteria evaluate properties of transaction flows, but have lower computational complexity. Further investigations in this domain would be directed to establishment of functional dependence between criteria, and estimation of error, of modeling multi-component information systems with non-Poisson flows of transactions.

Acknowledgments. The research was carried out within the state assignment of the Ministry of Education and Science of Russian Federation (No 2.3121.2017/PCH).

References

1. Babishin, V., Taghipour, S.: Optimal maintenance policy for multicomponent systems with periodic and opportunistic inspections and preventive replacements. Appl. Math. Model. **40**(23), 10480–10505 (2016)

2. Berg, B.A.: Markov Chain Monte Carlo Simulations and Their Statistical Analysis: With Web-Based Fortran Code. World Scientific Press, Singapore (2004)

3. Bian, L., Gebraeel, N.: Stochastic modeling and real-time prognostics for multi-component systems with degradation rate interactions. IIE Trans. **46**(5), 470–482 (2014)
4. Bielecki, T.R., Jakubowski, J., Nieweglowski, M.: Conditional Markov chains: properties, construction and structured dependence. Stochast. Process. Appl. **127**(4), 1125–1170 (2017)
5. Boos, D.D., Stefanski, L.A.: Essential Statistical Inference. Springer, New York (2013)
6. Ching, W.K., Huang, X., Ng, M.K., Siu, T.K.: Markov Chains: Models, Algorithms and Applications. International Series in Operations Research & Management Science, vol. 189. Springer, New York (2013). https://doi.org/10.1007/978-1-4614-6312-2
7. Draper, N.R., Smith, H.: Applied Regression Analysis. John Wiley & Sons, New York (2014)
8. Grigelionis, B.: On the convergence of sums of random step processes to a poisson process. Theory Probab. Appl. **8**(2), 177–182 (1963)
9. Ivutin, A., Larkin, E.: Simulation of concurrent games. Bull. South Ural State Univ. Ser. Math. Model. Program. Comput. Softw. **8**(2), 43–54 (2015)
10. Larkin, E., Ivutin, A., Kotov, V., Privalov, A.: Interactive generator of commands. In: Tan, Y., Shi, Y., Li, L. (eds.) ICSI 2016, Part II. LNCS, vol. 9713, pp. 601–608. Springer, Cham (2016). https://doi.org/10.1007/978-3-319-41009-8_65
11. Larkin, E.V., Kotov, V.V., Ivutin, A.N., Privalov, A.N.: Simulation of relay-races. Bull. South Ural State Univ. Ser. Math. Model. Program. Comput. Softw. **9**(4), 117–128 (2016)
12. Limnios, N., Swishchuk, A.: Discrete-time semi-Markov random evolutions and their applications. Adv. Appl. Probab. **45**(01), 214–240 (2013)
13. Lu, H., Pang, G., Mandjes, M.: A functional central limit theorem for Markov additive arrival processes and its applications to queueing systems. Queueing Syst. **84**(3–4), 381–406 (2016)
14. Luedicke, J., Bernacchia, A., et al.: Self-consistent density estimation. Stata J. **14**(2), 237–258 (2014)
15. Markov, A.A.: Extension of the law of large numbers to dependent quantities. Izv. Fiz. Matem. Obsch. Kazan Univ. (2nd Ser.) **15**, 135–156 (1906)
16. O'Brien, T.A., Kashinath, K., Cavanaugh, N.R., Collins, W.D., O'Brien, J.P.: A fast and objective multidimensional kernel density estimation method: fastkde. Comput. Stat. Data Anal. **101**, 148–160 (2016)
17. Song, S., Coit, D.W., Feng, Q., Peng, H.: Reliability analysis for multi-component systems subject to multiple dependent competing failure processes. IEEE Trans. Reliab. **63**(1), 331–345 (2014)
18. Stuart, A.: Rank correlation methods. Br. J. Stat. Psychol. **9**(1), 68–68 (1956). https://doi.org/10.1111/j.2044-8317.1956.tb00172.x. by M. G. Kendall, 2nd edn
19. Ventsel, E., Ovcharov, L.: Theory of probability and its engineering applications. Higher School, Moscow (2000)
20. Wang, B., Wertelecki, W.: Density estimation for data with rounding errors. Comput. Stat. Data Anal. **65**, 4–12 (2013)

Event-Triggered Communication Mechanism for Distributed Flocking Control of Nonholonomic Multi-agent System

Weiwei Xun[1], Wei Yi[1,2($\boxtimes$)], Xi Liu[3], Xiaodong Yi[1,2], and Yanzhen Wang[1,2]

[1] State Key Laboratory of High Performance Computing (HPCL),
School of Computer, National University of Defense Technology,
Changsha, China
yi_wei_cs@163.com
[2] Artificial Intelligence Research Center,
National Innovation Institute of Defense Technology,
Changsha, China
[3] PLA Army Engineering University, Nanjing, China

Abstract. As the scale of multi-agent systems (MAS) increases, communication becomes a bottleneck. In this paper, we propose an event-triggered mechanism to reduce the inter-agent communication cost for the distributed control of MAS. Communication of an agent with others only occurs when event triggering condition (ETC) is met. In the absence of communication, other agents adopt an estimation process to acquire the required information about the agent. Each agent has an above estimation process for itself and another estimation based on Kalman Filter, the latter can represent its actual state considering the measurement value and error from sensors. The error between the two estimators indicates whether the estimator in other agents can maintain a relatively accurate state estimation for this agent, and decides whether the communication is triggered. Simulations demonstrate the effectiveness and advantages of the proposed method for the distributed control of flocking in both Matlab and Gazebo.

Keywords: Event-triggered communication scheme
Distributed control · Multi-agent systems · Flocking

1 Introduction

Multi-agent systems (MAS) can be employed for various tasks, such as security patrol, industrial manufacturing, search and rescue, agricultural production and intelligent detection. Flocking [1] is the collective motion of a large number of self-propelled entities. It is efficient and beneficial to adopt flocking in the

Y. Tan et al. (Eds.): ICSI 2018, LNCS 10942, pp. 53–65, 2018.
https://doi.org/10.1007/978-3-319-93818-9_6

MAS for diversified cooperative tasks. The purpose of flocking control in a MAS setting is to drive a group of autonomous agents to form a flock and collectively accomplish a group task. Due to the uncertainty in the system, for example, the quantity of agents, group motion, exception and so on, distributed control is more applicative than centralized control.

Inter-agent communication plays a crucial role in distributed control for flocking [2]. Agents can exchange information with each other and take other agents' information as a portion of the input, so as to best compute the control output. In most of the existing method for the distributed control of flocking, for instance, the Olfati-Saber algorithm-based method [3] and its extension [4,5], leader-follower method [6,7], consensus strategies [8,9] and others, there is an explicit assumption that communication among agents is performed at every time step. Nevertheless, it neglects the fact that in most cases the motion of an agent would not mutate in a short period of time thus the communication could be unnecessary in such circumstances. Over frequent communication would cause more power consumption and limit the scale of the system. Besides, the communication quality may suffer from finite bandwidth or limited data transmission rates in practical applications.

Event-triggered communication has become a popular research topic in the field of networked systems. The core idea is that the communication is only executed when the certain condition is met. Heemels et al. [10] compared the difference between periodic and event-triggered control systems, and gave an overview of event-triggered and self-triggered control systems where sensing and actuation are performed when needed. Some works concentrate on using event-triggered communication mechanism to the formation control of agents. Dimarogonas et al. [11] considered centralized or distributed self-triggered control for multi-agent systems. Sun et al. [12] adopted a constant threshold for the event-triggered rigid formation control. Ge et al. [13] developed a dynamic event-triggered communication scheme to regulate the inter-agent communication with dynamic threshold parameters and designed event-triggered distributed formation protocol. Distributed control with self-triggered communication mechanism also applies to cooperative path following (Aguiar et al. [14]), target tracking scenario (Zhou et al. [15]) and other technologies in MAS.

In this paper, we attempt to optimize the communication overhead of the distributed control of flocking and propose an event-triggered communication strategy. For each agent, instead of broadcasting its state at each time, we regard the error between two discrepant estimators for itself as an input to decide when is worthwhile to trigger interaction with others. When an agent requires the states of other agents, it adopts a state estimation method to reduce the impact of the lack of communication. The results show our method can reduce communication cost and guarantee the performance of flocking control.

The remainder of the paper is organized as follows. First, a distributed control method for flocking and communication mechanism is briefly introduced. Then we present a detailed description of our approach to solve the flocking problem with event-triggered communication. Next, experimental results with both MATLAB and GAZEBO are presented. Finally, we conclude the paper and point out directions for future work.

2 Preliminaries

2.1 Flocking Problem

Consider a group of N agents, the goal is to form a flock from the initial state followed by an execution of group tasks. For each agent i, its neighbor set is constructed according to the communication topology or a cutting-off distance, denoted by $\mathcal{N}_i$, as shown in Eqs. (1) and (2) respectively,

$$\mathcal{N}_i(t) = \{j | A_{ij} = 1, j \neq i\}, \forall t \tag{1}$$

$$\mathcal{N}_i(t) = \{j | \left\| p_j - p_i \right\| < R, j \neq i\}, \forall t \tag{2}$$

where A is the communication topology matrix, p_i is the position of the i-th agent, and R is the cutting-off distance. The neighbor set of each agent will be time-varying. We use $G = (V, E)$ to represent a dynamic graph, where V is the vertices set for all N agents and E is the incident edges set describing all neighboring relations. Agents can obtain the information of their neighbors and determine their next-step motion according to the governing control law.

We study the distributed control for flocking of nonholonomic agents, for example, fixed-wing UAVs. For each nonholonomic agent $i \in V$, it has the differential drive kinematic described by the following:

$$\begin{cases} \dot{x}_i(t) = v_i(t) \cos(\theta_i) \\ \dot{y}_i(t) = v_i(t) \sin(\theta_i) \\ \dot{\theta}_i(t) = w_i(t) \end{cases} \tag{3}$$

where $p_i = (x_i, y_i)$ is the position, v_i is the linear velocity and w_i is the angular velocity.

Olfati-Saber proposed a flocking algorithm for double integrator agents. Cai et al. [5] introduced a virtual leader-follower mechanism into the Olfati-Saber's algorithm and proposed a distributed control approach for flocking of nonholonomic agents. Set a virtual agent (VA) with double integrator model for each real nonholonomic agent (RA), utilize the Olfati-Saber's algorithm for each virtual agent to obtain control input, and then make the real agent to track the virtual agent, as shown in Fig. 1. Based on this, the definition of a neighbor set is modified by follows:

$$\mathcal{N}_i(t) = \left\{ j \; \middle| \; \begin{array}{l} \left\| p_{v_j} - p_{v_i} \right\| < R, v_j \neq v_i \\ \left\| p_j - p_i \right\| < R, j \neq i \end{array} \right\} \tag{4}$$

[5] also considers group maneuverability and speed restriction for nonholonomic agents. The inter-agent communication and controller update occur in each

timestep. The form of Olfati-Saber's algorithm is as follows, and the output is agent's acceleration:

$$u_i = f_i^g(p) + f_i^d(p,q) + f_i^r(p_i, q_i, p_r, q_r) \tag{5}$$

where $q_i = (v_{xi}, v_{yi})$ is the velocity, f_i^g is utilized to calculate the distance between i and all neighbors; f_i^d is used to harmonize the velocity of agent i with neighbors; f_i^r reflects the navigation of the whole group.

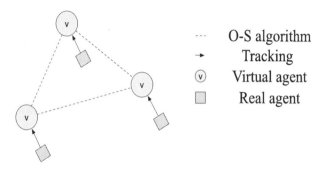

Fig. 1. General view of the flocking algorithm for nonholonomic agent

2.2   Inter-agent Communication

Inter-agent communication is an essential step in distributed control for flocking. The method in [5] adopts a periodic communication mechanism (PCM), all agents broadcast their state at a certain frequency. So, each agent can obtain its state from its sensors and obtain other agents' state through communication. The communication cost consists of broadcasting states of two parts, all real agents and all virtual agents. It is calculated as the following Eq. (6),

$$C = \sum_{k=1}^{T} \sum_{i=1}^{N} m + \sum_{k=1}^{T} \sum_{v_i=1}^{N} m \tag{6}$$

where m is the average communication cost per time, N is the size of the flock, T is the duration of the task. Obviously, the cost is related to the scale of the flock and the duration of the task. The complexity for communication is $o(T * N)$. As the scale of the flock increases, the communication will be costly, even result in occupancy of resources, communication delay and packet dropout in the whole system. Over frequent communication can affect agents' endurance. Besides, the motion of agents will conform to certain law and can not mutate in a short of time so that some unnecessary communication can be reduced. Therefore it is worthwhile to explore when inter-agent communication can be avoided without affecting the overall flocking performance.

3   Proposed Method

For distributed control for multi-agents, we aim at reducing communication cost by trajectory/motion estimation while keeping the accuracy and stability of the flocking process at a controllable level and propose an event-triggered communication mechanism.

3.1   State Estimation

At the k-th timestep, the state vector of an agent is defined by $\mathrm{x} = [x, y, \dot{x}, \dot{y}, \ddot{x}, \ddot{y}]$, which includes position, velocity and acceleration vectors in the x–direction and the y–direction. Each agent can individually obtain its state from its sensor readings. This is called by observation or measurement, which is denoted by z.

$$z_k = H_k \cdot \mathrm{x}_k + v_k \tag{7}$$

where H_k is the observation model which maps the true state space into the observed space, v_k is the measurement noise and is assumed to be zero mean Gaussian.

The state of agents can also be estimated with a computational model for the dynamic system. As the following shows:

$$\mathrm{x}_k = F_k \cdot \mathrm{x}_{k-1} + B_k \cdot u_k + w_k \tag{8}$$

where F_k is a state transform model to generate the new state, x_{k-1} is the history state, B_k is the control-input model which is applied to the control vector, u_k is control vector representing extra control term in controlled systems, w_k is the process noise and is assumed to be drawn from a zero mean multivariate normal distribution.

In our method, assume every agent is moving with a constant acceleration both in the x–direction and the y–direction over a short period of time. So u_k is zero, the F_k and H_k is defined by follows:

$$F_k = \begin{bmatrix} 1 & 0 & t & 0 & \frac{t^2}{2} & 0 \\ 0 & 1 & 0 & t & 0 & \frac{t^2}{2} \\ 0 & 0 & 1 & 0 & t & 0 \\ 0 & 0 & 0 & 1 & 0 & t \\ 0 & 0 & 0 & 0 & 1 & 0 \\ 0 & 0 & 0 & 0 & 0 & 1 \end{bmatrix} \quad H_k = \begin{bmatrix} 1 & 0 & 0 & 0 & 0 & 0 \\ 0 & 1 & 0 & 0 & 0 & 0 \end{bmatrix} \tag{9}$$

where t represents the duration of each timestep. To reflect the influence of noise on the different item in state vector,

$$w_k = G_k w_k = \begin{bmatrix} t & \frac{t^2}{2} & 1 & 0 & 0 & 0 \\ 0 & 0 & 0 & t & \frac{t^2}{2} & 1 \end{bmatrix}^{\mathrm{T}} \cdot w_k \tag{10}$$

Neither x_k nor z_k is the true value. The Kalman filter [16] can make use of both values to obtain a better estimation with two steps of prediction and correction.

For an agent itself, create an estimator based on the Kalman filter with observations and up to date accelerations through control law, which is represented by estimator A for simplicity. It is an accurate value for the agent considering the noise from the direct measurement. Another level of the estimator is just based on the initial state and the state transform model, which is represented by estimator B for simplicity.

3.2 Event-Triggered Communication Mechanism

An event-triggered communication scheme is developed based on the estimators in Sect. 3.1, which aims to reduce unnecessary communication. Agents broadcast states, therefore all agents can individually determine neighbor set and calculate control input. In our method, each agent establishes estimators B for other agents so that it can acquire other agents' states not only by communication but also by estimator B. The availability of estimation depends on the motion of agents and the accuracy of the estimation model. The estimator will be updated after receiving other agents' state.

Under the event-triggered communication scheme, each agent communicates with others when the event triggering conditions are satisfied. It also establishes an estimator B for itself. The estimator will be used to compare with the actual value. If the sensors are errorless, the actual value is the measurement value. Otherwise, it is from the estimator A which combines the measurements and computation model. In our method, we use estimator A instead of the measurement value. We can define an error, as the following shows.

$$\epsilon_i^k = \left\| Est\_A_i^k - Est\_B_i^k \right\|, i = 1, 2, \cdots, N \tag{11}$$

As the Eq. (12) shows, when the difference between the estimation from A and B is over the error tolerance τ_i^{max} at timestep k, an agent realizes that other agents can not have an efficient estimation for it, then it would update estimator B and broadcast its state to the rest of the system followed by the update of the estimator B on other agents.

$$\lambda_{ij}^k = \begin{cases} 1, & \epsilon_i^k \geq \tau_i^{max} \\ 0, & otherwise \end{cases} \tag{12}$$

Where λ_{ij} represents the communication state of agents from id number i to id number j, τ_i^{max} is the maximum error tolerance.

Besides, we introduce an extra minimum error tolerance τ_i^{min}. Let $[\tau_i^{min}, \tau_i^{max})$ be a dynamic and controllable interval in response to the error in advance, making the mechanism more flexible. The variation of error between two timesteps is denoted by $\Delta\epsilon_i^k$ as follows:

$$\Delta\epsilon_i^k = \epsilon_i^k - \epsilon_i^{k-1} \tag{13}$$

If the error keeps growing for $h + 1$ timesteps over the interval $[k, k + h]$, the proposed method predicate that the error will exceed the maximum value after several times and adjust promptly. This is another triggering condition, and the choice of parameter h will influence the algorithm implementation. With the adjustment, the tolerance for triggering is located in the range of $(\tau_i^{min}, \tau_i^{max}]$.

$$
\alpha_{ij}^k = \begin{cases} 1, & \Delta \epsilon_i^l > 0 (l \in [k, k+h]) \\ & \tau_i^{min} \le \epsilon_i^k < \tau_i^{max} \\ 0, & otherwise \end{cases} \tag{14}
$$

α_{ij} is also the communication state. When the communication state $\lambda_{ij} = 1$ or $\alpha_{ij} = 1$, the communication is triggered and agent with ID i shares information with others. The frequency of event detection is the same as the controller update rate, so it can avoid the Zeno behavior that the event is triggered infinite times in limited time.

3.3   A Flock Algorithm with Event-Triggered Communication

In this section, we present a flocking algorithm for nonholonomic agents with the event-triggered communication scheme. The parameter τ_i^{min}, τ_i^{max} and h will influence the final result.

Each agent considers whether other agents have a relatively accurate estimation for it with two estimators. When it detects the error exceeding the allowable range, the communication is triggered. With the ECM, for all T timesteps, the communication time sequence of an agent is changed from $\{1, 2, 3, \cdots, T\}$ to its subset $\{t_1, t_2, t_3, \cdots, n\}$.

When the agent need other agents' state, for PCM, p_j and q_j are from communication at each timestep, while in ECM, p_j and q_j are from the information of $Est\_B_j = [x, y, \dot{x}, \dot{y}, \ddot{x}, \ddot{y}]$. Est_B_i contains two parts, received value at communication moment and estimation value in other moment. As the following shows:

$$
\begin{cases} \hat{p}_j = [1, 1, 0, 0, 0, 0] \cdot Est\_B_j \\ \hat{q}_j = [0, 0, 1, 1, 0, 0] \cdot Est\_B_j \end{cases} \tag{15}
$$

Thus, for the distributed flocking algorithm for nonholonomic agents, the Eqs. (4) and (5) are modified as follows:

$$
\mathcal{N}_i(t) = \left\{ j \;\middle|\; \begin{array}{l} \|\hat{p}_{v_j} - p_{v_i}\| < R, v_j \ne v_i \\ \|\hat{p}_j - p_i\| < R, j \ne i \end{array} \right\} \tag{16}
$$

$$
\begin{cases} f_i^g = \sum_{j \in \mathcal{N}_i} \phi_\alpha (\|\hat{p}_{v_j} - p_{v_i}\|_\sigma) n_{ij} \\ f_i^d = \sum_{j \in \mathcal{N}_i} a_{ij}(p)(\hat{q}_{v_j} - q_{v_i}) \\ f_i^\gamma = -c_1(p_{v_i} - p_r) - c_2(q_{v_i} - q_r) \end{cases} \tag{17}
$$

Considering the motion, at moments when the navigation to the controller changes abruptly, for example, at a sudden turn, the communication will also be triggered for crossing the surging point.

For the Eq. (6), n is less than N, the whole communication cost is reduced. Besides, the estimator can provide the state in abnormal situations where packet loss occurs or communication interrupts, so the system would still work well for a period of time.

4   Experiment

4.1   Simulation with MATLAB

50 nonholonomic agents are set at random initial positions in the safe area with velocities in the range of $[-1, 1]$. The use of virtual agents and parameter settings for Olfati-Saber's algorithm are the same as that in [5]. For the periodic communication mechanism (PCM) tests [5], all virtual agents and all real agents will broadcast state at the frequency of 10 Hz. For the event-triggered communication mechanism (ECM) tests, the state broadcast only occurs in some situations. Both PCM and ECM, the frequency of updating distributed controller is 10 Hz.

We compare the accuracy of the methods by analyzing the errors in distance and velocity, which are defined in [5] as follows:

$$\xi_k^d = \frac{1}{\|\varphi\|} \sum_{(i,j)\in\varphi} \left| \|p_i - p_j\| - D \right| \tag{18}$$

$$\xi_k^v = \frac{1}{N} \sum_{i=1}^{N} \left| \|q_i\| - \|q_{objective}\| \right| \tag{19}$$

where D is the desired distance between agents and φ is the set including all pairs of adjacent agents at current time k.

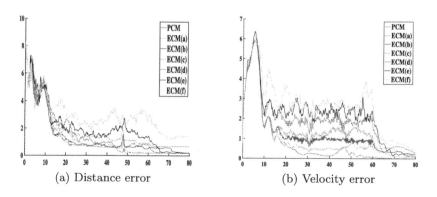

(a) Distance error   (b) Velocity error

Fig. 2. The errors in distance and velocity of the flock at the time $t \in [0, 80]$. ECM with different parameters are simulated, the value of $(\tau^{min}, \tau^{max}, h)$ is as the following: (a): (0.1, 0.2, 5), (b): (0.3, 0.6, 5), (c): (0.5, 1, 5), (d): (1, 2, 5), (e): (1.5, 3, 5), (f): (2, 4, 5). When the $t > 60$, the τ^{min} and h are set by 0.05 and 3 respectively.

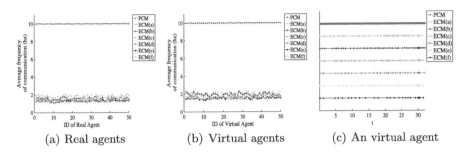

(a) Real agents   (b) Virtual agents   (c) An virtual agent

Fig. 3. Communication comparison of different methods. (a) Average communication frequency of each real agent, (b) Average communication frequency of each virtual agent, (c) Communication time sequences of an agent for $t = [0,32]$.

Figures 2 and 3 show that the results between PCM and ECM with different parameters. Due to the error from the estimator and the asynchronism of communication among agents, each agent's motion may advance or fall behind the method with PCM, which results in the final error of velocity and the difference of shape of the flock. Figure 3 provides a quantitative comparison of the average communication rate with different mechanisms and illustrates that fewer data packets are transmitted through the network by using the ECM. From the results, the following parameters can be a choice to maintain performance with reduced communication: τ^{max} is 0.2, τ^{min} is 0.1, h is 5. For the final horizontal motion, τ^{min} is 0.05 and h is 3. Table 1 provide the detailed data about the communication of an agent.

Table 1. Communication frequency η and communication interval κ with different mechanism for an agent.

	η^{mean}	η^{max}	η^{min}	κ^{max}	κ^{min}
PCM	10 Hz	10 Hz	10 Hz	0.1 s	0.1 s
ECM	1.9125 Hz	6 Hz	0 Hz	1.8 s	0.1 s

Figure 4 depicts the trajectories for all agents with two mechanisms, 50 agents are successfully driven to form a flock and move to an anticipated position safely in both PCM and ECM(a). Figure 5 demonstrates the snapshots of position of the 50 agents under PCM and ECM at $t = 0$ s, $t = 10$ s, $t = 40$ s, and $t = 80$ s, respectively.

From the above, the proposed event-triggered communication mechanism for distributed control of flocking helps in saving a certain amount of communication resources without affecting the overall performance of the distributed control algorithm for flocking.

4.2   Simulation with GAZEBO

To study the effect of the dynamics of robots, we simulate the MAS in Robot Operating System (ROS) and Gazebo simulator with the physical engine.

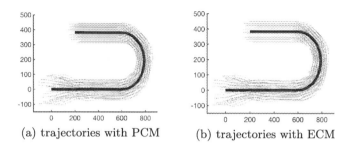

(a) trajectories with PCM   (b) trajectories with ECM

Fig. 4. The overview results by different communication mechanisms.

To evaluate the performance of the proposed algorithm, consider thirty fixed-wing UAVs visualized as quadrotors. The algorithm runs with the following parameters: $\tau^{max} = 0.2$, $\tau^{min} = 0.1$, $h = 3$, other parameters are the same as the paper [5].

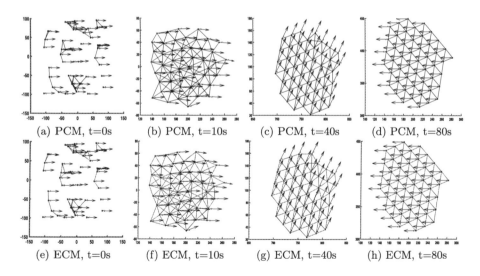

(a) PCM, t=0s   (b) PCM, t=10s   (c) PCM, t=40s   (d) PCM, t=80s

(e) ECM, t=0s   (f) ECM, t=10s   (g) ECM, t=40s   (h) ECM, t=80s

Fig. 5. Snapshots of PCM and ECM(a) at $t = 0$ s, $t = 10$ s, $t = 40$ s, $t = 80$ s.

Each agent is controlled by an independent node and the time steps for different agents are not synchronized, so in fact, the obtaining of the neighboring set and other agents' state at each step may be influenced by transmission delay.

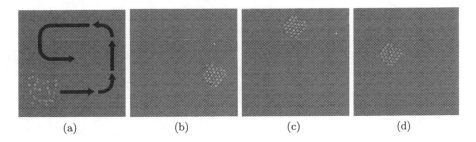

(a)   (b)   (c)   (d)

Fig. 6. Snapshots of the distributed control with event-triggered communication mechanism (ECM) for flocking in Gazebo.

Under the ECM, an estimation method is adopted to provide the state when it is absent. The performance will be impacted by the accuracy of the estimator and the number of communication. Figure 6 and the video (https://youtu.be/1pcL3rBKTtg) show that thirty UAVs are required to form a flock and fly to the center of the scene. The result of Fig. 7 shows our proposed method ECM can reduce communication cost. The number of communication packets sent by virtual agents and real agents is fewer than PCM.

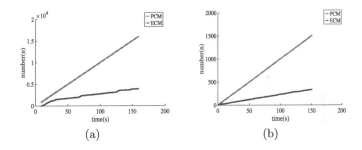

(a)   (b)

Fig. 7. Analysis for communication times. (a) Number of communication packets sent by real agent No. 1. For PCM tests, both the sampling frequency of sensor and the communication frequency of an real agent are 100 Hz. (b) Number of communication packets sent by virtual agent No. 1. For PCM tests, the communication frequency of an virtual agent is 10 Hz.

5   Conclusion

Communication has become a bottleneck as the number of agents increases. Since the motion of the agent cannot mutate in a short time and the state can be estimated, we adopt an event-triggered communication mechanism to the distributed control of flocking based on state estimations. There are two kinds of estimators in our proposed method. One is from Kalman filter based on real-time observation and the computation model; another is only based on the computation model and history state. Only when the difference between the two estimations exceeds a threshold, would the agent update the latter estimator and immediately broadcast its state. To guarantee the performance, each agent maintains a rough estimation for other agents periodically using the second estimator, which is adopted as an input for the distributed controller in the absence of communication. The experiments show that the communication cost can be significantly reduced and the effectiveness of the distributed controller for flocking can be still guaranteed. In our future work, we will consider extending the event-triggered scheme to other flocking algorithms and the formation control algorithm in MAS.

Acknowledgements. This work was supported by NSFC under Grant 91648204 and 61303185 and HPCL Grants under 201502-01.

References

1. Reynolds, C.W.: Flocks, herds and schools: a distributed behavioral model. ACM SIGGRAPH Comput. Graph. **21**(4), 25–34 (1987)
2. Zavlanos, M.M., Jadbabaie, A., Pappas, G.J.: Flocking while preserving network connectivity. In: 2007 46th IEEE Conference on Decision and Control, pp. 2919–2924. IEEE (2007)
3. Olfati-Saber, R.: Flocking for multi-agent dynamic systems: algorithms and theory. IEEE Trans. Autom. Control **51**, 401–420 (2006)
4. Varga, M., Basiri, M., Heitz, G., Floreano, D.: Distributed formation control of fixed wing micro aerial vehicles for area coverage. In: 2015 IEEE/RSJ International Conference on Intelligent Robots and Systems (IROS), pp. 669–674. IEEE (2015)
5. Cai, Z., Chang, X., Wang, Y., Yi, X., Yang, X.J.: Distributed control for flocking and group maneuvering of nonholonomic agents. Comput. Animat. Virtual Worlds **28**(3–4) (2017)
6. Shang, Y., Ye, Y.: Leader-follower fixed-time group consensus control of multiagent systems under directed topology. Complexity **2017** (2017)
7. Yazdani, S., Haeri, M.: Robust adaptive fault-tolerant control for leader-follower flocking of uncertain multi-agent systems with actuator failure. ISA Trans. **71**, 227–234 (2017)
8. Rezaee, H., Abdollahi, F.: Pursuit formation of double-integrator dynamics using consensus control approach. IEEE Trans. Ind. Electron. **62**(7), 4249–4256 (2015)
9. Pan, W., Jiang, D., Pang, Y., Qi, Y., Luo, D.: Distributed formation control of autonomous underwater vehicles based on flocking and consensus algorithms. In: Huang, Y.A., Wu, H., Liu, H., Yin, Z. (eds.) ICIRA 2017, Part I. LNCS (LNAI), vol. 10462, pp. 735–744. Springer, Cham (2017). https://doi.org/10.1007/978-3-319-65289-4_68
10. Heemels, W.P.M.H., Johansson, K.H., Tabuada, P.: An introduction to event-triggered and self-triggered control. In: 2012 IEEE 51st Annual Conference on Decision and Control (CDC), pp. 3270–3285. IEEE (2012)
11. Dimarogonas, D.V., Frazzoli, E., Johansson, K.H.: Distributed event-triggered control for multi-agent systems. IEEE Trans. Autom. Control **57**(5), 1291–1297 (2012)
12. Sun, Z., Liu, Q., Yu, C., Anderson, B.D.: Generalized controllers for rigid formation stabilization with application to event-based controller design. In: 2015 European Control Conference (ECC), pp. 217–222. IEEE (2015)

13. Ge, X., Han, Q.: Distributed formation control of networked multi-agent systems using a dynamic event-triggered communication mechanism. IEEE Trans. Ind. Electron. **64**, 8118–8127 (2017)
14. Jain, R.P., Aguiar, A.P., Sousa, J.: Self-triggered cooperative path following control of fixed wing unmanned aerial vehicles. In: 2017 International Conference on Unmanned Aircraft Systems (ICUAS), pp. 1231–1240. IEEE (2017)
15. Zhou, L., Tokekar, P.: Active target tracking with self-triggered communications. In: 2017 IEEE International Conference on Robotics and Automation (ICRA), pp. 2117–2123. IEEE (2017)
16. Kalman, R.E.: A new approach to linear filtering and prediction problems. J. Basic Eng. Trans. **82**, 35–45 (1960)

Deep Regression Models for Local Interaction in Multi-agent Robot Tasks

Fredy Martínez[✉][iD], Cristian Penagos, and Luis Pacheco

District University Francisco José de Caldas, Bogotá D.C., Colombia
fhmartinezs@udistrital.edu.co,
{cfpenagosb,lapachecor}@correo.udistrital.edu.co
http://www.udistrital.edu.co

Abstract. A direct data-driven path planner for small autonomous robots is a desirable feature of robot swarms that would allow each agent of the system to directly produce control actions from sensor readings. This feature allows to bring the artificial system closer to its biological model, and facilitates the programming of tasks at the swarm system level. To develop this feature it is necessary to generate behavior models for different possible events during navigation. In this paper we propose to develop these models using deep regression. In accordance with the dependence of distance on obstacles in the environment along the sensor array, we propose the use of a recurrent neural network. The models are developed for different types of obstacles, free spaces and other robots. The scheme was successfully tested by simulation and on real robots for simple grouping tasks in unknown environments.

Keywords: Autonomous · Big data · Data-driven · Sensor
Motion planner

1 Introduction

Robotics aims to develop artificial systems (robots) that support human beings in certain tasks. The design of these robots focuses on the problems of sensing, actuation, mobility and control [4]. Each of these elements is dependent on the specific task to be developed by the robot, and the conditions under which it must be developed. Some design criteria used in the development of modern robots are: simplicity, low cost, high performance and reliability [6].

One of the biggest challenges in mobility robots is the autonomous navigation. The problem of finding a navigation path for an autonomous mobile robot (or several autonomous mobile robots in the case of robot swarms) is to make the agent (a real object with physical dimensions) find and follow a path that allows it to move from a point of origin to a point of destination (desired configuration) respecting the constraints imposed by the task or the environment (obstacles, free space, intermediate points to visit, and maximum costs to incur in the task) [13]. This is still an open research problem in robotics [2,7].

© Springer International Publishing AG, part of Springer Nature 2018
Y. Tan et al. (Eds.): ICSI 2018, LNCS 10942, pp. 66–73, 2018.
https://doi.org/10.1007/978-3-319-93818-9_7

For correct navigation in a reactive autonomous scheme, each agent (robot) must sense the pertinent information of the environment [9]. This includes obstacles and restrictions of the environment, communication with nearby agents, and the detection of certain elements in the environment [10]. From this information the robot performs calculations of its estimated position with respect to the destination, traces a movement response, executes it, and verifies the results. This navigation strategy is heavily dependent on the quantity and quality of information processed and communicated.

There are many robot designs for this type of task. Most of these designs include robust and complex hardware with high processing capacity [5, 11]. This hardware is equipped with a high performance CPU, often accompanied by a programmable logic device (CPLD or FPGA) for dedicated processing, and a specialized communication unit. In addition, these robots often have advanced and complex sensors [3]. Due to these characteristics, these robots are expensive and with a high learning curve for an untrained user [8].

Contrary to this trend, this research opts for a minimalist solution. The navigation strategy looks for robots in the swarm to self-organize using as little information as possible [1]. For this purpose, the robots are equipped with a set of distance sensors, and from the data captured by them, and using behavior models previously identified in the laboratory, we program movement policies that determine the final behavior of the swarm [12]. The sensor data is processed in real time by comparing them with the laboratory models, using different metrics of similarity.

The paper is organized as follows. In Sect. 2 presents a description of the problem. Section 3 describes the strategies used to analyze raw data and generate data models for specific environmental characteristics. Section 4 introduces some results obtained with the proposed strategy. Finally, conclusion and discussion are presented in Sect. 5.

2   Problem Statement

One of the most complex parts of robot swarm management is programming the collective system tasks. A first step is to achieve a quick and easy autonomous identification of each individual within the system. In this sense we propose a set of pre-recorded models in the robot that allow it to recognize directly from the raw data of the sensors the type of local interaction that it is detecting (obstacle, free space, edges of the environment or other robots).

Let $W \subset \mathbb{R}^2$ be the closure of a contractible open set in the plane that has a connected open interior with obstacles that represent inaccessible regions. Let $\mathcal{O}$ be a set of obstacles, in which each $O \subset \mathcal{O}$ is closed with a connected piecewise-analytic boundary that is finite in length. Furthermore, the obstacles in $\mathcal{O}$ are pairwise-disjoint and countably finite in number. Let $E \subset W$ be the free space in the environment, which is the open subset of W with the obstacles removed.

Let us assume a set of n agents in this free space. Each of these agents knows the environment E from observations, using sensors. These observations allow them to build an information space I. A information mapping is of the form:

$$q : E \longrightarrow S \tag{1}$$

where S denote an *observation space*, constructed from sensor readings over time, i.e., through an observation history of the form:

$$\tilde{o} : [0,t] \longrightarrow S \tag{2}$$

The interpretation of this information space, i.e., $I \times S \longrightarrow I$, is that which allows the agent to make decisions. The problem can be expressed as the search for a function u for specific environment conditions from a set of sensed data in the environment $y \subset S$ and a target function g.

$$f : y \times g \longrightarrow u \tag{3}$$

Each of these identified functions (models) can then be used for the robot to define motion actions in unknown environments, particularly when detecting other robots in the environment.

3   Methodology

The motivating idea of our research is to simplify the decision making process for each agent of the swarm from the sensor data. However, the function between input data and movement policies corresponds to a complex model.

The problem of model development for specific environmental conditions (obstacle, clear path, and agents) is analyzed as a regression problem. Throughout the tests with the robot in known environments, a sequence of temporary data is produced that must allow to estimate the type of characteristics in the environment for any similar situation. The sequence of data for an obstacle is shown in Fig. 1.

We have chosen to identify the behavior of the dataset through a recurrent neural network, with the intention of knowing the future state of the system from its past evolution. This particular type of data are known as time series, and are characterized by the output that is influenced by the previous events. For this we propose the use of a LSTM (Long Short-Term Memory) network.

The models for each characteristic of the environment are used as reference for the calculation of similarity with respect to the data captured by the robot during navigation. The selected metric corresponds to the two-dimensional representation of the data against time, i.e. by image comparison.

The comparison is made against all channels, i.e. each of the nine channels is compared with each of the nine channels of the model (81 comparisons in each iteration). The distance used as metric for the calculation of similarity was Chi-Square due to its better performance in tests.

Control policies were simplified as a sequence of actions specific to the identified environmental characteristics. For example, an obstacle to the front activates

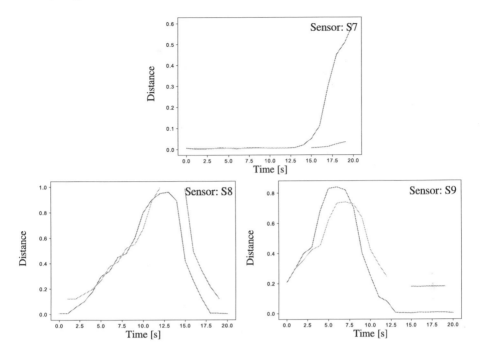

Fig. 1. Obstacle detected by sensors S7, S8 and S9. Normalized reading of infrared sensors (blue), LSTM model (red), and predictions for the training dataset (green). (Color figure online)

the Evation Policy, which in this case consists of stopping, turning a random angle in a random direction, and finally moving forward. Each characteristic of the environment has a control policy, which is adjusted according to how the characteristic is detected by the sensors. The identification of another robot leads to the activation of the Grouping Policy, thanks to which robots follow each other. The initial tests have been carried out with basic grouping tasks (Fig. 2).

4 Results

We have tested our proposed algorithm on a dataset generated by a 45 cm × 61 cm robot (Fig. 3). The robot has nine uniformly distributed infrared sensors around its vertical axis (S1 to S9, with 40° of separation from each other, counterclockwise), each with a range of 0.2 to 0.8 m (Fig. 4). The data matrix delivered by the sensors corresponds to nine standard columns from 0 to 1 with reading intervals between 900 ms.

The performance of the LSTM models are evaluated using cross validation. To do this we separated each dataset in an orderly manner, creating a training set and a test set. For training we use 70% of the data, and we use the rest to test the model. The network has a visible layer with one input, a hidden layer with eight LSTM blocks or neurons, and an output layer that makes a single value prediction. The default sigmoid activation function is used for the LSTM blocks. The network is trained for 100 epochs and a batch size of one is used. The model fit code was written in Python using Keras. We setup a SciPy work environment with Pandas support. Models were evaluated using Keras 2.0.5, TensorFlow 1.2.0 and scikit-learn 0.18.2.

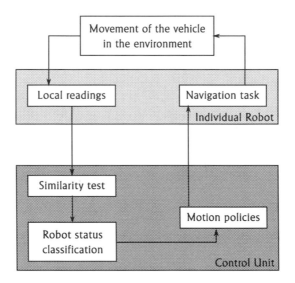

Fig. 2. Flowchart of the proposed motion planner decision making system.

Fig. 3. ARMOS TurtleBot 1 equipped with a set of nine infrared sensors and one DragonBoard 410C development board.

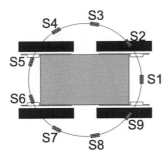

Fig. 4. Top view of the robot and distribution of the distance sensors.

The navigation scheme has been tested in simulation (Fig. 5) and in laboratory with different configurations on a 6 × 6.5 m environment. We have performed more than 100 tests, 98% of them completely successful, that is, the robot managed to navigate the environment and after a certain amount of time he manages to locate the other robots and stays close to them.

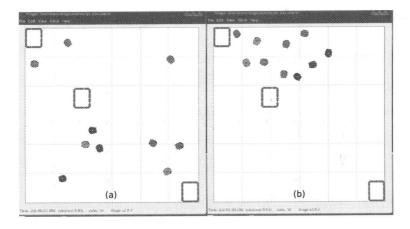

Fig. 5. Simulation of grouping task. (a) Initial random distribution of robots. (b) Position of robots after 2:42 min. Simulation performed in Player-Stage.

Our scheme does not use any other type of communication between robots or with an external control unit. At this point it is necessary to perform a deeper analysis of the algorithm performance, as well as reliable ways to estimate the time required for task development. A statistical analysis can be used to establish the degree of confidence for a given time interval.

5 Conclusions

In this paper we present a behavior model based on LSTM networks for the local interaction of robots within a swarm. The intention is to identify the type of interaction in real time from the raw data of a set of distance sensors, and from this unique information, define the movements of the robots. We build reference images from the two-dimensional representation of the models and compare them with the sensor readings by measuring image similarity. The strategy has been successfully tested by simulation and on real prototypes in simple grouping tasks. We highlight in the strategy the little information required for robot movement, and the speed of decision making by robots. One issue that needs further analysis is related to the estimation of the time required to complete the navigation tasks.

Acknowledgments. This work was supported by the District University Francisco José de Caldas and the Scientific Research and Development Centre (CIDC). The views expressed in this paper are not necessarily endorsed by District University. The authors thank the research group ARMOS for the evaluation carried out on prototypes of ideas and strategies.

References

1. Benitez, J., Parra, L., Montiel, H.: Diseño de plataformas robóticas diferenciales conectadas en topología mesh para tecnología Zigbee en entornos cooperativos. Tekhnê **13**(2), 13–18 (2016)
2. Jacinto, E., Giral, M., Martínez, F.: Modelo de navegación colectiva multi-agente basado en el quorum sensing bacterial. Tecnura **20**(47), 29–38 (2016)
3. Mane, S., Vhanale, S.: Real time obstacle detection for mobile robot navigation using stereo vision. In: International Conference on Computing, Analytics and Security Trends (CAST), pp. 1–6 (2016)
4. Martínez, F., Acero, D.: Robótica Autónoma: Acercamientos a algunos problemas centrales. CIDC, Distrital University Francisco José de Caldas (2015). ISBN 9789588897561
5. Nasrinahar, A., Huang, J.: Effective route planning of a mobile robot for static and dynamic obstacles with fuzzy logic. In: 6th IEEE International Conference on Control System, Computing and Engineering (ICCSE 2016), pp. 1–6 (2016)
6. Nattharith, P., Serdar, M.: An indoor mobile robot development: a low-cost platform for robotics research. In: International Electrical Engineering Congress (iEECON 2014), pp. 1–4 (2014)
7. Oral, T., Polat, F.: MOD* lite: an incremental path planning algorithm taking care of multiple objectives. IEEE Trans. Cybern. **46**(1), 245–257 (2016)
8. Ortiz, O., Pastor, J., Alcover, P., Herrero, R.: Innovative mobile robot method: improving the learning of programming languages in engineering degrees. IEEE Trans. Educ. **60**(2), 143–148 (2016)
9. Rendón, A.: Evaluación de estrategia de navegación autónoma basada en comportamiento reactivo para plataformas robóticas móviles. Tekhnê **12**(2), 75–82 (2015)
10. Schmitt, S., Will, H., Aschenbrenner, B., Hillebrandt, T., Kyas, M.: A reference system for indoor localization testbeds. In: International Conference on Indoor Positioning and Indoor Navigation (IPIN 2012), pp. 1–8 (2012)
11. Seon-Je, Y., Tae-Kyung, K., Tae-Yong, K., Jong-Koo, P.: Geomagnetic localization of mobile robot. In: International Conference on Mechatronics (ICM 2017), pp. 1–6 (2017)

12. Sztipanovits, J., Koutsoukos, X., Karsai, G., Kottenstette, N., Antsaklis, P., Gupta, V., Goodwine, B., Baras, J., Wang, S.: Toward a science of cyber-physical system integration. Proc. IEEE **100**(1), 29–44 (2012)
13. Teatro, T., Eklund, M., Milman, R.: Nonlinear model predictive control for omnidirectional robot motion planning and tracking with avoidance of moving obstacles. Can. J. Electr. Comput. Eng. **37**(3), 151–156 (2014)

Multi-drone Framework for Cooperative Deployment of Dynamic Wireless Sensor Networks

Jon-Vegard Sørli$^{(\boxtimes)}$ (ID) and Olaf Hallan Graven (ID)

University College of Southeast Norway, Kongsberg, Norway
Jon-Vegard.Sorli@usn.no

Abstract. A system implementing a proposed framework for using multiple-cooperating-drones in the deployment of a dynamic sensor network is completed and preliminary tests performed. The main components of the system are implemented using a genetic strategy to create the main elements of the framework. These elements are sensor network topology, a multi objective genetic algorithm for path planning, and a cooperative coevolving genetic strategy for solving the optimal cooperation problem between drones. The framework allows for mission re-planning with changes to drone fleet status and environmental changes as a part of making a fully autonomous system of drones.

Keywords: UAV · Drone · Swarm · Sensor network · Algorithms
Framework

1 Introduction

New technology brings many new possibilities. On such possibility is the use of UAVs, Unmanned Aerial Vehicles (drones) to aid first responders during a scene of an emergency situation such as a natural accident, terrorist attack or an accident.

The aim of this paper is to present a solution to the problem of using multiple drones in the task of gathering vital information about an ongoing emergency situation by deploying a wireless sensor network (WSN) in the situation area. The system of drones must cooperate in deploying wireless sensor nodes in a dynamic environment, hence be able to plan and re-plan the task in an evolving mission situation, and one prone to failure of equipment such as the drones.

1.1 Problem Statement

This paper propose a solution to the problem of planning and re-planning (during mission execution) the deployment of a dynamic wireless sensor network, real

© Springer International Publishing AG, part of Springer Nature 2018
Y. Tan et al. (Eds.): ICSI 2018, LNCS 10942, pp. 74–85, 2018.
https://doi.org/10.1007/978-3-319-93818-9_8

time or close to real time. This is a complex problem containing the following elements:

1. Creating a wireless sensor network topology, updating or expanding an existing WSN based on new information.
2. Planning optimal drone paths.
3. Optimally allocating deployment tasks between a fleet of drones (similar to a multi depot vehicle routing problem [11]).
4. Re-plan based on changes to: the mission area, status of drone fleet (number of drones available, drone failure), deployed/un-deployed sensors, failed sensors.
5. Short execution time to meet real-time constraints.

These elements are strongly connected and solved by different algorithms working together in the framework presented in a continuously running loop, reacting to dynamic changes, i.e. by re-planning. The main focus of this paper is to present the framework and assess its ability to solve the problem stated. The algorithms (components) working in the framework will be presented in short details, but are not the focus of the paper as their refinement is not essential to verify that the framework works or not. They can in essence be interchanged with other algorithms that are able to solve the same kind of problems, such as path planning, as long as they provide the correct data on the interfaces. The hypothesis is that the problem stated can be solved real-time, or close to real time using the proposed framework utilizing the specific implementations for solving the sub-problems.

2   Related Work

Most research related to WSN and drones tend to focus on either:

1. Planning a WSN focusing on optimizing different objectives similar to the WSN planning implementation in this paper. [14] presents a multi-objective genetic algorithm for sensor deployment based on the famous NSGA-II [3] non-dominated genetic algorithm. The algorithm optimizes sensor coverage while maintaining connectivity, minimizing sensors needed and taking obstacles into account. [17] proposes a genetic algorithm for optimal sensor placement on a 2D grid with obstacles to minimize the usage of sensors. It uses a sensing model where detection probability of a sensor decreases exponentially with the distance between target and sensor. [5] proposes a multi-objective genetic algorithm to improve the lifetime and sensing coverage of a WSN during sensor node redeployment. Transmission rate success and total moving costs are used as constraints.
2. Planning paths for drones [13], but not how the WSN is actually going to be deployed, such as using a system of cooperating drones which is the motivation for this work.

There are disaster projects using other strategies such as the U.S. Naval Research Laboratory's CT-analyst [7], a crisis management system performing urban aerodynamic computations to evaluate contaminant transport in cities. The system is used by e.g. [1] as a way of calculating the fitness in a genetic algorithm for sensor placement, using information on time dependent plumes, upwind danger zones and sensor capabilities. Projects combining drones and sensors usually carry sensors on-board drones to do sensing tasks e.g. in [4] UAVs are used to measure air pollution. In [16] UAVs are used to find avalanche victims by detecting their cell phone signals. In [10] multiple UAVs are used as network nodes. UAVs equipped with sensors is not a viable option for a dynamic disaster scenario with unknown time span considering the limited flight time of UAVs, so there is a need for a deployment system. There are some projects aiming to deploy sensors in disaster scenarios. [12] presents an overview of the elements in the AWARE platform, using autonomous UAVs and WSN in disaster management scenarios. The platform seeks to enable cooperation between UAVs and WSN (static and mobile), deploying nodes with an autonomous helicopter. [9] describes the use of the AWARE platform in a mission to deploy a sensor at a location given from a user through a HMI. [15] uses UAVs to deploy sensors in disaster scenarios by dropping them while following predetermined trajectories. The focus is on the localization and navigation system. [6] suggests to deploy WSN nodes using model rockets. In summary, the related work does not provide a solution to the problem statement in this paper, but forms a basis for the work.

3   Swarm Framework for Deployment of Dynamic Sensor Network

The framework is shown in Fig. 1 using a component diagram in UML style format, with provided and required interfaces. This ensures a high level view and separation of tasks between components, ensuring the possibility to solve the task of a component using different algorithms as long as they provide the correct data on their provided interfaces. The components work by reacting to changes on their provided interfaces. The system is started (plan/re-plan) by initiating it though the initiation interface in the Drone fleet component. The latest information on all the provided interfaces is always used during the execution of each component.

3.1   Component Descriptions

Area Model. Responsible for providing a 2D or 3D model of the area and informing the Drone fleet on changes to the area.

Sensor Model. Makes it possible to use different types of sensor and communication devices by informing the sensor network planner on which to use.

Sensor Network Planner. Based on area model, sensor model, communication model input and optionally the sensor payload limitations of one drone run, this component creates the layout of a wireless sensor network. It must have access to a database on sensor and communication models.

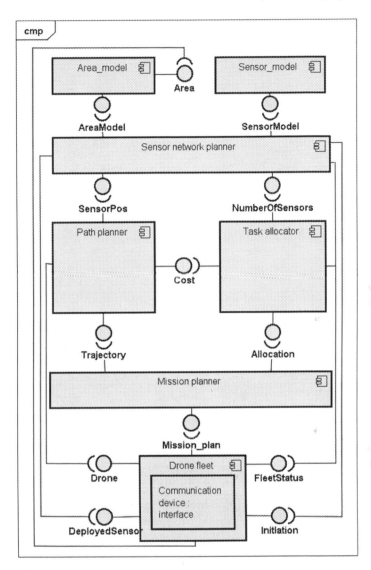

Fig. 1. Framework components diagram

Path Planner. Plans path trajectories between all sensors, drones and the mission base station, and calculates their cost. By accessing a drone specifications database, paths can be optimized on several objectives.

Task Allocator. Based on the number of sensors to be deployed, calculated costs, available payload and remaining energy, allocates the deployment tasks on the available drones.

Mission Planner. Create missions for each drone by combining the task allocation plan with the actual waypoint to waypoint trajectories planned by the Path planner and represented in the cost table.

Drone Fleet. Keeps control of the status of the drone fleet by communication though an interface with the drones. Contains information about the drones used and their positions, which sensors they have deployed and if drones experience failure. This information is used to activate a re-planning phase. It also communicates the mission plan to the drones, and signals how to act at the moment of a re-plan during a mission (this may for example be to wait in the air for a few seconds while the re-plan finishes).

3.2   Interface Descriptions

Interfaces are described using XML examples.

AreaModel. Provides a digital elevation model (DEM) as an array to represent terrain elevation in meters. 2D terrain is represented by using only zeros (no-obstacle) and ones (obstacle).

```
<DEM_size>
        <rows>2</rows>
        <colums>2</colums>
</DEM_size>
< DEM index =0 >
        <E_VALUE index="0">elevationvaluemeters</E_VALUE>
        <E_VALUE index="1">elevationvaluemeters</E_VALUE>
</DEM>
< DEM index =1 >
        <E_VALUE index="0">elevationvaluemeters</E_VALUE>
        <E_VALUE index="1">elevationvaluemeters</E_VALUE>
</DEM>
```

SensorModel. Provide information on which type of sensor and communication device to use.

```
<sensor_model>
        <sensor_type>Sensor model</sensor_type>
        <communication_type>communication model</communication_type>
</sensor_model>
```

SensorPosition. Provides array of planned sensor deployment positions and number of sensors to be deployed. Z position is set to zero for 2D terrain.

```
<Sensor_position >
       <numbers>numberofsensors</numbers>
       <sensor index =0>
       <pos_index ="0">x_position</pos_index>
       <pos_index ="1">y_position</pos_index>
       <pos_index ="2">z_position</pos_index>
       </sensor>
</Sensor_position >
```

NumberOfSensors. Provides the total number of sensors. Indexed from 1 to the total number for identity corresponding to sensor index in SensorPosition.

```
<SensorNumber >
       <numbers>numberofsensors</numbers>
</SensorNumber >
```

Cost. Provides an N by M array of point to point cost of trajectories (containing all intermediate waypoints between points). Costs index = "0" and traj_cost = "1" corresponds to path number 1. Costs index - "0" and traj_cost - "2" corresponds to path number 2. N = M = (1(base position) + Total number of sensors + number of different start positions for drones). Zero costs are included to make indexing easier. Costs are calculated between points in both directions. The order is (Base station) - (sensor positions) - (start positions).

```
<cost>
       <costs index =0>
       <traj_cost ="0">" CostPoint1ToPoint1</traj_cost> <zero cost>
       <traj_cost ="1">" CostPoint1ToPoint2</traj_cost>
       </costs>
</cost>
```

Trajectory. Provides an array of trajectories (series of waypoints) from point to point. Trajectory (traj) with index = "0" corresponds to path number 1.

```
<Trajectory>
       <numbers>numberoftrajectories</numbers>
       <traj index =0>
       <pos_index ="0">x_position_waypoint1</pos_index>
       <pos_index ="1">y_position_waypoint1</pos_index>
       <pos_index ="2">z_position_waypoint1</pos_index>
       <pos_index ="3">x_position_waypoint2</pos_index>
       <pos_index ="4">y_position_waypoint2</pos_index>
       <pos_index ="5">z_position_waypoint2</pos_index>
       </traj>
</Trajectory>
```

Allocation. Provides an allocation list of which drone deploys which sensors.

```
<Allocation >
        <numbers>numberofoperationaldrones</numbers>
        <alloc index =0> <first drone>
        <sensor_index ="0">indexofsensortodeploy</sensor_index>
        <sensor_index ="1">indexofsensortodeploy</sensor_index>
        <sensor_index ="2">indexofsensortodeploy</sensor_index>
        </alloc>
</Allocation >
```

MissionPlan. Provides an array containing mission plans for each drone. The first waypoint for drone one is shown.

```
<Missions>
        <Mission index =0>
        <waypoint_index ="0">x_position_waypoint1</waypoint_index>
        <waypoint_index ="1">y_position_waypoint1</waypoint_index>
        <waypoint_index ="2">z_position_waypoint1</waypoint_index>
        <waypoint_index ="3">waypoint=0 or deployment=1</waypoint_index>
        </Mission>
</Missions>
```

Drone. Provides position of operational drones and model of drone. Provide position of base station for return of drones.

```
<numbers_operational>numberofoperationaldrones</numbers_operational>
<Drone id ="1"> <Drone with id = 1>
        <model>model type</model>
        <pos_x>x_position</pos_x>
        <pos_y>y_position</pos_y>
        <pos_z>z_position</pos_z>
</Drone>
<Base_pos>
        <Base_x>x_position</Base_x>
        <Base_y>y_position</Base_y>
        <Base_z>z_position</Base_z>
</Base_pos>
```

FleetStatus. Provides number of operational drones, available sensor payload and remaining energy.

```
<FleetStatus >
        <numbers>numberofoperationaldrones</numbers>
        <drone id ="1"> <Drone with id = 1>
        <payload>4</payload>
        <energy>Remaining Energy</energy>
```

```
        </drone>
</FleetStatus >
```

DeployedSensor. Provides positions of deployed sensors. Z position is set to zero for 2D terrain.

```
<Sensor_deployed >
        <numbers>numberofdeployedsensors</numbers>
        <sensor index =0>
        <pos_index ="0">x_position</pos_index>
        <pos_index ="1">y_position</pos_index>
        <pos_index ="2">z_position</pos_index>
        </sensor>
</Sensor_deployed >
```

Initiation. Initiate planning and re-planning. Set to one to start. Set to zero for reset before a new start can initiate.

```
<Initiation>
        <start>1</start>
</Initiation>
```

4   Implementation

MATLAB is used for preliminary testing. This section gives a short detailed description of the algorithms used in the main three components (Sensor Network Planner, Path Planner and Task Allocator) during the preliminary testing of the framework. The problem was simplified to a 2D, unmanned ground vehicles (UGV) problem to speed up the preliminary testing phase. The other components need no further description than what is provided in Sect. 3.1 as their tasks are more organizational than algorithmic.

4.1   Sensor Network Planner

During preliminary testing, a simple genetic strategy is used for creating the layout of the WSN. The inputs used are a 2D terrain model, positions of already deployed sensors, payload capacity and a sensing model considering only a sensing radius. For simplicity, no communication model is used. Selection is done using stochastic universal sampling [18]. Fitness is calculated based on the objective of coverage ratio as shown in function (1). Mutation is done by randomly moving sensors around in the environment, one at a time for each individual. Only sensors landing outside of obstacles are allowed, since they cannot be deployed in no go zones. The coverage objective includes coverage of no go zones. Extra sensors are added one at the time until a preset fitness goal has been reached (see Sect. 4.3 Exception Handling for more details).

$$Coverage = \frac{TotalCoverage}{Covered} \qquad (1)$$

4.2 Path Planner

In this work, path planning is performed using a multi objective genetic algorithm inspired by the work in [13]. The genetic operators used are the same, namely the single point crossover [18], single-point mutation, addition and deletion of points. Selection is done using stochastic universal sampling [18]. Path collisions are found using an algorithm inspired by the Bresenham line equation [2]. During the simplified preliminary testing, the fitness function has been limited to optimizing two objectives, the path length in Eq. 2 and a term associated to the collisions in Eq. 3.

$$CostPath = 1 - (\frac{LengthPoint1toPoint2}{LengthTrajectory}) \qquad (2)$$

$$CostCollision = \begin{cases} 0, & \text{Zero collisions} \\ \text{CostCollision}+ \text{Penalty}(=100), & \text{Added each collision} \end{cases} \qquad (3)$$

4.3 Task Allocator

Task allocation which can be viewed as a kind of Vehicle Routing Problem (VRP) is solved using a Cooperative Coevolving Genetic Algorithm, CCGA. The implementation is inspired by [8] using the two subpopulation representations from page 3. Fitness is optimized based on the maximum of a solution, i.e. the cost of the longest path used by one of the UAVs when deploying the sensors, since this maximum cost is the limiting factor. Selection is done using stochastic universal sampling [18]. Two types of mutation are used, one for each type of subpopulation. (1) Random mutation of how many sensors each drone should carry while maintaining the total amount to be deployed. (2) Two point switch mutation (swap), which changes the order of placed sensors while preserving the legal permutations.

Using the data provided on the "NumberOfSensors", "Cost" and "FleetStatus" interfaces, the task of deploying all the sensors is optimally distributed on to the available UAVs and provided on the "Allocation" interface as a list of which drones deploy which sensors, represented by the best solution of the CCGA.

Exception Handling. If there are not enough drones to deploy all the sensors requested by the Sensor Network Planner in one run, there are two alternatives: 1. Allocate as many sensors as possible then initiate a new round based on the deployed sensors after the required extra drones have returned to base station.

2. Based on the information about the payload capacity, the Sensor Network Planner can plan a network that uses fewer sensors on the cost of less coverage. This design option is decided by the designer of the Sensor Network Planner. When using alternative 1, the Sensor network will self initiate a new plan for deploying the remaining sensors when drones become available, i.e. new drones may be added, or returned drones made ready for a new mission.

4.4   Distributed Computing

The bottleneck in this implementation of the framework is the Path planner component. When using multi objective genetic algorithm to plan the paths, each path has an execution time of approximately two-three seconds, and there are many paths to plan. The solution is either using cloud computing or implementing in parallel on hardware such as GPUs. In this implementation the simplest would be to execute code in parallel on workers of the parallel pool in MATLAB.

5   Results and Conclusion

The result of a test run from top to bottom in the framework is shown in Fig. 2. At the bottom left of the figure, we can see four separate departure points for four different drones and their complete paths to deploy a total of fourteen sensors (seen in the middle of each red circle) and in the end return to the base station placed in x = 15. The yellow fields represent the no go, no placement zones. As can be seen, the sensors try to cover the no go zones. The coverage ratio is not set to hundred percent (but close) as this can have significant impacts the total number of sensors needed.

5.1   Conclusion

This paper presents a framework for solving the task of deploying a dynamic sensor network, i.e. planning and re-planning the deployment of sensor network nodes in a dynamic environment, using equipment prone to failure. The framework has been completely implemented as a simulation. The framework is described in a UML diagram, and all its interfaces described using XML format for simplistic usage. The components provide opportunity to use different kinds of algorithms as long as the correct data is provided on the interfaces. The framework has been demonstrated using evolutionary based implementations in all three main components (Sensor Network Planner, Path Planner and Task Allocator), through simulations. This has shown that the proposed framework fulfills the purpose for which it has been designed. Further work will demonstrate the framework using a physical experiment.

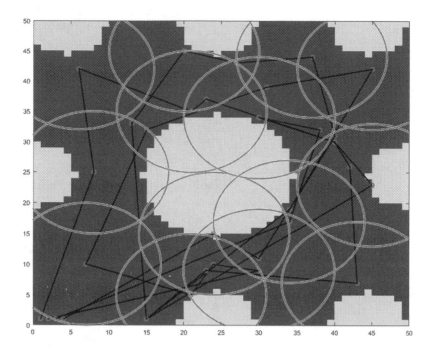

Fig. 2. 2D deployment plan example (Color figure online)

5.2   Further Work

We will now go on to create a physical system to implement and test the framework in a real world experiment using miniature Unmanned Ground Vehicles (UGVs) and a dynamic environment, and later using UAVs by expanding the implementation to 3D environments and refining the algorithms. For the path planner this includes multi objective optimization of shortest collision free paths considering fuel/energy consumption, no fly zones and time. The Sensor Network Planner would include terrain analysis to find the best viable sensor placement points, sensor limitations and wireless communication. Optimization would be multi objective to achieve the best coverage, longest lifetime and optimal conditions for communication.

References

1. Boris, J., Obenschain, K., Patnaik, G.: Using CT-ANALYST TM to optimize sensor placement. In: Proceedings of the Chemical and Biological Sensing V, Orlando, vol. 5416, pp. 14–20 (2004)
2. Bresenham, J.E.: Algorithm for computer control of a digital plotter. IBM Syst. J. **4**(1), 25–30 (1965)
3. Deb, K., Pratap, A., Agarwal, S., Meyarivan, T.: A fast and elitist multiobjective genetic algorithm: NSGA-II. IEEE Trans. Evol. Comput. **6**(2), 182–197 (2002)

4. Evangelatos, O.: AIRWISE - An airborne wireless sensor network for ambient air pollution monitoring. In: Proceedings of the 4th International Conference on Sensor Networks, pp. 231–239 (2015). http://www.scitepress.org/DigitalLibrary/Link.aspx?doi=10.5220/0005203302310239

5. Kuawattanaphan, R., Kumrai, T., Champrasert, P.: Wireless sensor nodes redeployment using a multiobjective optimization evolutionary algorithm. In: IEEE International Conference of IEEE Region 10 (TENCON 2013), pp. 1–6 (2013). http://www.scopus.com/inward/record.url?eid=2-s2.0-84894328390&partnerID=tZOtx3y1

6. Kulau, U., Schildt, S., Wolf, L., Rottmann, S.: Ballistic Deployment of WSN Nodes using Model Rockets (2014)

7. US Naval Research Laboratory: CT-Analyst. http://www.nrl.navy.mil/lcp/ct-analyst

8. Machado, P., Tavares, J., Pereira, F., Costa, E.: Vehicle routing problem: doing it the evolutionary way. Proceedings of the Genetic and Evolutionary Computation Conference, p. 690, January 2002

9. Maza, I., Kondak, K., Bernard, M., Ollero, A.: Multi-UAV cooperation and control for load transportation and deployment. J. Intell. Robot. Syst. Theor. Appl. 57(1–4), 417–449 (2010)

10. Mozaffari, M., Saad, W., Bennis, M., Debbah, M.: Efficient deployment of multiple unmanned aerial vehicles for optimal wireless coverage. IEEE Commun. Lett. 20(8), 1647–1650 (2016)

11. Oliveira, F.B.D.: Cooperative coevolutionary models for the multi-depot vehicle routing problem cooperative coevolutionary models for the multi-depot vehicle routing problem (2015)

12. Ollero, A., Marron, P.J., Bernard, M., Lepley, J., La Civita, M., Van Hoesel, L., De Andrés, E.: AWARE: platform for autonomous self-deploying and operation of wireless sensor-actuator networks cooperating with unmanned AeRial vehiclEs. In: Proceedings of the IEEE International Workshop on Safety, Security and Rescue Robotics, SSRR 2007, September 2007

13. Roberge, V., Tarbouchi, M., Labonte, G.: Comparison of parallel genetic algorithm and particle swarm optimization for real-time UAV path planning. IEEE Trans. Ind. Inform. 9(1), 132–141 (2013). http://ieeexplore.ieee.org/lpdocs/epic03/wrapper.htm?arnumber=6198334

14. Syarif, A., Abouaissa, A., Idoumghar, L., Sari, R.F., Lorenz, P.: Performance analysis of evolutionary multi-objective based approach for deployment of wireless sensor network with the presence of fixed obstacles. In: IEEE Global Communications Conference, GLOBECOM 2014, pp. 1–6 (2014)

15. Tuna, G., Mumcu, T.V., Gulez, K., Gungor, V.C., Erturk, H.: Unmanned aerial vehicle aided wireless sensor network deployment system for post-disaster monitoring. Commun. Comput. Inf. Sci. 304, 298–305 (2012)

16. Wolfe, V., Frobe, W., Shrinivasan, V., Hsieh, T.Y.: Detecting and locating cell phone signals from avalanche victims using unmanned aerial vehicles. In: International Conference on Unmanned Aircraft Systems, ICUAS 2015, pp. 704–713 (2015)

17. Xu, Y., Yao, X.: A GA approach to the optimal placement of sensors in wireless sensor networks with obstacles and preferences. In: 3rd IEEE Consumer Communications and Networking Conference, CCNC 2006, vol. 1, pp. 127–131 (2006)

18. Yu, X., Gen, M.: Introduction to Evolutionary Algorithms. Springer, London (2010). https://doi.org/10.1007/978-1-84996-129-5. http://www.springer.com/gp/book/9781849961288

Swarm Robotics

Distributed Decision Making and Control for Cooperative Transportation Using Mobile Robots

Henrik Ebel[(✉)] and Peter Eberhard

Institute of Engineering and Computational Mechanics,
University of Stuttgart, Pfaffenwaldring 9, 70569 Stuttgart, Germany
{henrik.ebel,peter.eberhard}@itm.uni-stuttgart.de

Abstract. This paper introduces a distributed control scheme tailor-made to the task of letting a swarm of mobile robots push an object through a planar environment. Crucially, there is no centralized control instance or inter-robot hierarchy, and therefore, all decisions are made in a distributed manner. For being able to cooperate, the robots communicate, although the communication sampling time may be several times longer than the control sampling time. Most characteristic for the approach, distributed model predictive controllers are used to achieve a smooth transportation performance with the predicted control errors utilized to plan a suitable object trajectory. Challenging simulation scenarios show the applicability of the approach to the transportation task.

Keywords: Distributed optimization · Communication
Swarm mobile robots · Cooperative object transportation
Distributed model predictive control

1 Introduction

In recent years, the area of robotics has benefited greatly from continuous advancements in reliable wireless communication technology, the ever-increasing efficiency and capability of mobile processors, and the advent of affordable yet reliable sensors and cameras. Hence, the solution of increasingly intricate tasks seems to be within the realm of possibility for robotic systems. In particular, multiple robotic agents may communicate to actively cooperate in the solution of certain assignments, providing potential benefits like improved adaptability to the scale of the task, and improved reliability. Technical failures of individual robots may be compensated for by the remaining robots. This has also sparked interest in control theoretic research, leading to the proposition and analysis of control schemes capable of dealing with systems pursuing a common goal while being independent in their decision making.

Some proposed methods rely on results from algebraic graph theory, describing the communication or information structure within a network of systems, e.g.

© Springer International Publishing AG, part of Springer Nature 2018
Y. Tan et al. (Eds.): ICSI 2018, LNCS 10942, pp. 89–101, 2018.
https://doi.org/10.1007/978-3-319-93818-9_9

a robot swarm, as a graph [1,10]. Other possibilities include methods based on distributed optimization, for instance in the form of distributed model predictive control (DMPC) [14].

In this context, this paper deals with the design and analysis of a control strategy for transporting an object using several independent mobile robots that can communicate with a certain subset of the other robots involved in the task. Specifically, the robots cooperatively push an object in order to move it through a planar environment. This kind of task has previously met continuous interest in robotics research [2,15], having, for instance, potential applications in logistics, if carts of different sizes and shapes, without an own propulsion system, shall be maneuvered through a warehouse. Moreover, it serves as an adequate case study for the practical usefulness of theoretic concepts from distributed control.

One of the novel key ingredients of the control scheme devised in this paper is the incorporation of a distributed model predictive controller that allows for a smooth, cooperative transportation process. Model predictive control (MPC) is an optimization-based approach, allowing the explicit consideration and full, possibly saturating, utilization of state and input constraints [9,11]. In each time step, to establish a feedback in the control loop, an optimal control problem is solved over a finite time horizon, taking into account the most current state measurement or estimate. In turn, distributed model predictive control aims to maintain the key properties of a well-designed model predictive controller, like recursive feasibility, stability and constraint satisfaction, while solving the underlying optimization problem in a distributed manner, with inter-agent communication between subsequent optimizations [6,12,14]. Due to its predictive nature, the incorporation of distributed MPC allows the robots to react to the planned movements of their neighbors. Henceforth, in [3,4], different distributed MPC schemes have performed favorably in simulative and experimental studies in another formation control task, motivating its usage for the present task. Furthermore, in general, the usage of an optimization-based scheme allows an intuitive problem formulation without the introduction of many unphysical control parameters to be tuned. Specifically, those parameters that do exist have a clear meaning, e.g. defining the desired trade-off between control accuracy and control effort.

In this paper's application, apart from the solution of the underlying control problem while moving the object, the robots need to negotiate an agreement on how to organize and reorganize around the object. It is to be expected that a suitable organization is dependent on the object's shape and desired pose. One notable characteristic of this paper's scheme is that all decisions are made in a distributed manner. Therefore, apart from necessary information regarding the object's current pose, each robot calculates its desired trajectory and control input only based on information that has been communicated one or several time steps in the past. Additionally, each robot shall only require information from its immediate neighbors, since long-range communication might be unreliable.

The paper is organized as follows. First, the problem is described in a concise manner, with emphasis on the information actually available to the robots.

Subsequently, the control scheme is described precisely. This is followed by an analysis of the control scheme's performance in simulation scenarios. The findings are then summarized in the concluding section.

2   Problem Formulation

The N robots involved in the object transportation are assumed to be equipped with omnidirectional drives, so that they can move freely in any direction. Therefore, for modeling, mainly their planar positions $q_i \in \mathbb{R}^2$, $i \in \{1, \ldots, N\}$, measured in the inertial frame of reference K_I, are of interest. For control design purposes, it is assumed that the robot dynamics can be appropriately modeled by the second-order dynamics $M \ddot{q}_i + D \dot{q}_i = u_i$, with diagonal mass and damping matrices M and D, and propulsion forces u_i. The robots are assumed to have a circular footprint of radius r. The objects to be transported shall be allowed to take arbitrary polygonal shapes, with dynamics modeled in the form

$$\begin{bmatrix} m_o & 0 & 0 \\ 0 & m_o & 0 \\ 0 & 0 & J_o \end{bmatrix} \ddot{q}_o + \begin{bmatrix} d_p & 0 & 0 \\ 0 & d_p & 0 \\ 0 & 0 & d_r \end{bmatrix} \dot{q}_o = f_c \tag{1}$$

with the object mass m_o, moment of inertia J_o, and non-negative damping parameters d_p, d_r. Hence, $q_o \in \mathbb{R}^3$ consists of the x- and y-positions of the object's center of mass and its rotation around the z-axis. The right-hand side f_c contains the contact forces between the robots and the object, as well as the moment induced by these forces with respect to the center of mass.

The robots know their own positions relative to the object, given in the body-fixed coordinate frame K_R. Furthermore, it is assumed that the robots are provided with a reference path $\gamma_{ref} : \mathcal{I} \subset \mathbb{R}_{\geq 0} \to \mathbb{R}^3$ describing the desired subsequent positions and orientations of the object, given in the inertial frame of reference. This path is not parametrized in time, i.e. there is no predefined velocity along the path. Planning the velocity, and therewith a trajectory, is part of the control scheme. To the end of being able to track this path, the robots are also aware of the object's position and orientation in the inertial frame of reference. For collision avoidance purposes, the robots shall be equipped with distance sensors, e.g. a laser scanner, with finite range and limited accuracy. In addition, they are able to send to and receive information from a certain subset of the other robots involved in the task. These robots will be referred to as neighboring robots. The shape of the object is known to the robots, although, in different applications, it may be deduced from sensor information during a discovery phase executed before the start of the transportation process.

3   Control Scheme

The overall control scheme consists of four main elements. Firstly, depending on the shape of the object, the number of involved robots, and the current tracking error, a suitable positioning of the robots along the edges of the object must be determined. In the following, this will be referred to as the formation synthesis. Then, the robots must communicate to negotiate a mapping that allocates one robot to each position in the formation. Based on its position within the formation and the object's reference path γ_{ref}, each robot individually plans a trajectory so that the object is guided along the path by the formation. Together with some previously communicated information from neighboring robots, this trajectory is fed into the distributed model predictive controller of each robot, calculating appropriate robot velocities. Low-level PI-controllers are used to regulate the propulsion forces according to the provided velocity setpoints. An antiwindup scheme deals with the effects of possible saturations of the constrained propulsion forces.

Crucially, the individual parts of the control loop may be executed at different sampling times. A new formation may only be synthesized if it is not possible to further reduce the tracking error with the current one. Data may be exchanged between the robots at a sampling time $T^{\mathrm{s}}_{\mathrm{comm}}$ that is several times longer than the sampling time $T^{\mathrm{s}}_{\mathrm{ctrl}}$ of the main control loop. The main parts of the scheme are explained in detail in the following subsections.

3.1   Distributed MPC Controllers

Since the robots' propulsion forces are controlled by PI controllers, to reach the velocities commanded by the DMPC controllers, the model used in the controller derivation is the simple single-integrator model $\dot{\boldsymbol{x}}_i = \boldsymbol{u}_i$ with the position $\boldsymbol{x}_i \in \mathbb{R}^2$ of robot i, and the control input $\boldsymbol{u}_i$ being the velocity. In the following, the formula $\boldsymbol{x}_i(k + 1) = \boldsymbol{A}\boldsymbol{x}_i(k) + \boldsymbol{B}\boldsymbol{u}_i(k)$ denotes each robot's single-integrator dynamics discretized with the sampling time $T^{\mathrm{s}}_{\mathrm{ctrl}}$. To the end of being able to formulate the optimization problem solved in each sampling instant, let $\boldsymbol{r}^i_{\mathrm{ref}}(t + k \,|\, t)$, $k \in \{1, \ldots, H\}$, denote the robot's reference trajectory as planned at time step t over the optimization horizon of length H. Analogously, $\boldsymbol{x}_i(\,\cdot\,|\,t)$ denotes the planned state trajectory under the input $\boldsymbol{u}_i(\,\cdot\,|\,t)$. While the above quantities shall be given in the inertial frame of reference K_{I}, $^{\mathrm{R}}\boldsymbol{x}_i(\,\cdot\,|\,t)$ shall signify the planned position of robot i in the current body-fixed coordinate frame of the transported object. Furthermore, the index set $\mathcal{N}_i \subset \{1, \ldots, N\} \setminus \{i\}$ shall reference the set of neighbors of robot i, i.e. those robots whose information shall be used in the cooperative optimization problem. Later, this set will always contain the indices of two robots that will also be neighbors of robot i in a certain geometric sense.

Provided with an aim formation shape around the object, $^{\mathrm{R}}\boldsymbol{\rho}_{i \to j} \in \mathbb{R}^2$ shall denote the vector pointing from the aim position of robot i to that of robot $j \in \mathcal{N}_i$, given in the body-fixed frame. Adopting the above notation, the stage cost for the MPC optimization problem of robot i at step k in the horizon can be defined as

$$L\left(\boldsymbol{x}_i(k\,|\,t),\,\boldsymbol{u}_i(k\,|\,t)\right) = \left\|\boldsymbol{x}_i(k\,|\,t) - \boldsymbol{r}^i_{\text{ref}}(k\,|\,t)\right\|^2_{\boldsymbol{Q}_{\text{t}}}$$
$$+ \sum_{j \in \mathcal{N}_i} \left\|{}^{\text{R}}\boldsymbol{x}_j(k\,|\,t) - {}^{\text{R}}\boldsymbol{x}_i(k\,|\,t) - {}^{\text{R}}\boldsymbol{\rho}_{i \to j}\right\|^2_{\boldsymbol{Q}_{\text{f}}}$$
$$+ \left\|\boldsymbol{u}_i(k\,|\,t)\right\|^2_{\boldsymbol{R}}, \tag{2}$$

with $\|\boldsymbol{v}\|^2_{\boldsymbol{W}} := \boldsymbol{v}^{\text{T}}\boldsymbol{W}\boldsymbol{v}$ for some symmetric positive semi-definite matrix $\boldsymbol{W}$. Hence, the first line of Eq. (2) contains robot i's individual tracking error, while the second line contains the robot's formation error relative to its neighbors. The weighting matrices $\boldsymbol{Q}_{\text{t}}, \boldsymbol{R} \in \mathbb{R}^{2 \times 2}$ are assumed to be positive definite. Maintaining the prescribed relative positions within the formation may be counterproductive while individual robots are still far away from their aim positions relative to the object, e.g. during initial formation acquisition or in the midst of reorganization. Hence, in this paper, $\boldsymbol{Q}_{\text{f}}$ is set to $\boldsymbol{0}$ for large tracking errors. With the stage cost, the MPC optimization problem for robot i can be written as

$$\underset{\boldsymbol{u}_i(\cdot\,|\,t)}{\text{minimize}} \quad \sum_{l_0 = t}^{t+H-1} L\left(\boldsymbol{x}_i(k\,|\,t),\,\boldsymbol{u}_i(k\,|\,t)\right)$$

$$\text{subject to} \quad \boldsymbol{x}_i(k+1\,|\,t) = \boldsymbol{A}\boldsymbol{x}_i(k\,|\,t) + \boldsymbol{B}\boldsymbol{u}_i(k\,|\,t), \ k \in \{t, \dots, t+H-1\}, \tag{3}$$
$$\|\boldsymbol{u}(t+k\,|\,t)\|_\infty \leq v_{\max}, \ k \in \{1, \dots, H-1\},$$
$$\boldsymbol{u}_i(t+H\,|\,t) = \boldsymbol{0},$$
$$\boldsymbol{x}_i(t\,|\,t) = \boldsymbol{x}_i(t).$$

Therein, the control inputs are constrained by the allowed maximum velocity $v_{\max}$, while the velocity at the end of the horizon is constrained to be zero, which simplifies the construction of a feasible candidate solution in the following time step and is also a safety measure so that the robots always plan to be able to stop within the optimization horizon. The minimizing input sequence shall be denoted by $\boldsymbol{u}^\star_i(\cdot\,|\,t)$, with $\boldsymbol{x}^\star_i(\cdot\,|\,t)$ being the corresponding optimal state sequence in the inertial frame, and ${}^{\text{R}}\boldsymbol{x}^\star_i(\cdot\,|\,t)$ in the body-fixed frame. Evidently, the optimization problem (3) cannot be solved in an exact fashion, since it depends on the predicted states of the neighbors ${}^{\text{R}}\boldsymbol{x}_j(\cdot\,|\,t), j \in \mathcal{N}_i$, which in turn are determined by the current optimal input sequences of the neighbors. These are unavailable, since the neighboring robots solve their respective optimization problems concurrently and self-reliantly. Thus, the optimization problem needs to be solved using appropriate approximations of the neighbors' optimal state sequences, based on information communicated in a previous time step. The communication and optimization scheme to obtain this solution is provided in Algorithm 1. In principle, it would be possible to iteratively repeat the communication and optimization cycle in step 3 of the algorithm to improve the solution, giving an iterative distributed MPC scheme. However, this is not done here to keep the number of exchanged data messages low and the sampling time short. The optimization strategy, with the applied control input as a convex combination of the current optimizer and the candidate solution, is closely inspired by the fundamentals from [6, 12, 14]. Although not in the scope of this paper, these references show that, under appropriate assumptions, schemes of this type can be proved to be convergent.

Algorithm 1. Distributed MPC scheme

1: **input:** initial feasible sequences $\hat{u}_i(\cdot \mid 0)$, $^\mathrm{R}\hat{x}_i(\cdot \mid 0)$ $\forall i \in \{1, \dots, N\}$
2: **at all time steps** $t \geq 1$: all robots $i \in \{1, \dots, N\}$ set

$$\hat{u}_i(t + k \mid t) = \begin{cases} u_i(t + k \mid t - 1) & \text{for } k \in \{0, \dots, H - 2\}, \\ 0 & \text{for } k = H - 1, \end{cases}$$

$$^\mathrm{R}\hat{x}_j(t + k \mid t) = \begin{cases} ^\mathrm{R}\bar{x}_j(t + k \mid t - 1) & \text{for } k \in \{0, \dots, H - 1\}, \\ ^\mathrm{R}\bar{x}_j(t + H - 1 \mid t - 1) & \text{for } k = H, \end{cases} \quad \forall j \in \mathcal{N}_i$$

3: **at all time steps** $t \geq 0$:
   in parallel, all robots $i \in \{1, \dots, N\}$
   solve (3) with $x_j(k \mid t) = \hat{x}_j(k \mid t)$ $\forall j \in \mathcal{N}_i$, obtaining $u_i^\star(\cdot \mid t)$
   set $u_i(\cdot \mid t) = (1/(|\mathcal{N}_i| + 1)) \, u_i^\star(\cdot \mid t) + (1 - 1/(|\mathcal{N}_i| + 1)) \, \hat{u}_i(\cdot \mid t)$
   send trajectory $^\mathrm{R}\bar{x}_i(\cdot \mid t)$, predicted using $u_i(\cdot \mid t)$, to all neighbors
4: in parallel, all systems $i \in \{1, \dots, N\}$ apply $u_i(t \mid t)$
5: $t = t + 1$ and go to step 2

As mentioned above, depending on the achievable performance with the robots' communication system, it may be desirable to communicate at a sampling time $T^\mathrm{s}_\mathrm{comm}$ that is longer than $T^\mathrm{s}_\mathrm{ctrl}$. In this case, in those sampling instances in which no recently communicated trajectories $^\mathrm{R}\bar{x}_j(\cdot \mid t)$ are available, the candidate solutions are updated in an open-loop style, by shifting the last communicated prediction further forward in time. Thus, in those cases, in step 2 of the algorithm, $^\mathrm{R}\bar{x}_j(\cdot \mid t - 1)$ is replaced by $^\mathrm{R}\hat{x}_j(\cdot \mid t - 1)$.

3.2   Formation Synthesis

The objective is to derive a formation shape that is suitable to transport a polygonal object by pushing primarily in the normal directions of its edges. This can be interpreted as a one-dimensional deployment problem along the edges of the object, allocating one position to each of the robots. These positions have to account for multiple requirements. On the one hand, the normal directions of the selected points' edges and the corresponding levers with respect to the object's center of mass need to be serviceable to move and rotate the object in the desired directions. Positions close to pointed corners seem undesirable for a robust transportation, while concave corners seem to be rather beneficial. Furthermore, the selected positions should, in the two-dimensional plane, have a Euclidean distance exceeding a minimum value to prevent collisions between the robots. This poses a non-convex constraint on the underlying optimization problem.

In this paper, the formation synthesis problem is approached as follows. Firstly, in a preprocessing step, a dilated version of the object is calculated. In the edges' normal directions, the edges are moved outward by the radius of the calculating robot. The boundary of the resulting dilated object is saved as a piecewise affine function $^R\mathcal{E} : \mathcal{I}_e \subset \mathbb{R}_{\geq 0} \to \mathbb{R}^2$, describing the edges in the body-fixed frame K_R. In this parametrization, pointed corners are left out, so that there is a predefined safety distance between the points on the dilated edge and pointed corners. Alongside $^R\mathcal{E}$, the piecewise constant and piecewise affine functions $^R\mathcal{V} : \mathcal{I}_e \to \mathbb{R}^2$ and $\mathcal{L} : \mathcal{I}_e \to \mathbb{R}$ describing the edges' outer normal vectors and lever arms are calculated. The value of $\mathcal{L}$ is defined to be positive if rotations in the positive z-direction are enabled by the corresponding position, and negative in the converse case. The formation synthesis problem is now a problem of finding a set $\mathcal{P} \subset \mathcal{I}_e$, $|\mathcal{P}| = N$, of N one-dimensional positions that satisfy the aforementioned requirements. In this paper, this is done by successively choosing the positions based on a list of priorities. The first two positions are chosen so that the object's current translational error is a conical combination of the corresponding two inner normal vectors, with lever arms that are as small as possible in their absolute value. The next two are selected based on the value of $^R\mathcal{V}$ being as positive or as negative as possible, enabling rotations in the direction and the counter direction of the current rotational error. The following ones are chosen so that the negative translational error is covered by a conical combination of the inner normals, servicing the remaining two degrees of freedom of the object. Since the robots can only push but not pull, two times the object's degrees of freedom are useful for a smooth motion without reorganization. If more than six robots are present, the additional positions are placed into the longest still unoccupied sections. While choosing the positions, the free Euclidean distance in the plane is checked to be larger than the desired safety distance. Three examples of the results of this algorithm are provided in Fig. 1, in which the dark-gray object shall be moved in the x-direction and rotated around the z-axis. The edges of the dilated object are marked in dark blue, while the light blue circles signify the calculated desired robot positions.

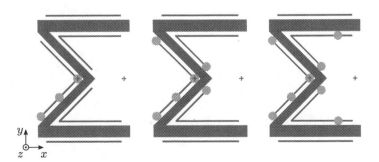

Fig. 1. Desired formations for different numbers of robots (Color figure online)

3.3 Position Allocation Negotiation

Having defined a set of desired positions $\mathcal{P}$, the next step is to devise a reliable distributed algorithm to allocate each robot to one of these positions. For this purpose, at first, each robot calculates the position on $^{\mathrm{R}}\mathcal{E}(\cdot)$ that is closest to its own position $^{\mathrm{R}}\boldsymbol{x}_i$. To this end,

$$\Gamma\left(^{\mathrm{R}}\mathcal{E},\,^{\mathrm{R}}\boldsymbol{x}_i\right) := \left\{ p \in \mathcal{I}_{\mathrm{e}} \mid \left\|^{\mathrm{R}}\boldsymbol{x}_i - {^{\mathrm{R}}\mathcal{E}}(p)\right\|_2 \leq \left\|^{\mathrm{R}}\boldsymbol{x}_i - \boldsymbol{y}\right\|_2 \ \forall \boldsymbol{y} \in {^{\mathrm{R}}\mathcal{E}}(\mathcal{I}_{\mathrm{e}}) \right\} \quad (4)$$

is defined to execute this projection. If $\Gamma\left(^{\mathrm{R}}\mathcal{E},\,^{\mathrm{R}}\boldsymbol{x}_i\right)$ contains more than one element, an arbitrary one is chosen. Let $l_i \in \Gamma\left(^{\mathrm{R}}\mathcal{E},\,^{\mathrm{R}}\boldsymbol{x}_i\right)$ denote the projection of robot i. Considering the projections $\{l_1,\ldots,l_N\}$, $(l_{\pi(1)}, l_{\pi(2)},\ldots, l_{\pi(N)})$ shall denote the sequence of projections sorted in ascending order, i.e. with $l_{\pi(i)} \leq l_{\pi(j)}$ for $i < j$, and a bijective mapping $\pi\colon \{1,\ldots,N\} \to \{1,\ldots,N\}$. The neighbors $\mathcal{N}_i$ of robot i are now defined to be those two robots whose projected value is appearing above and below that of robot i in this sorted list. This shall apply in a toroidal sense, i.e. if robot i is at the beginning or the end of the list, one of the neighbors is then the last or the first robot. In the following, for a more convenient notation, assume that robot i's position is neither first nor last in the sorted list. Now, assuming that $\{j,k\} = \mathcal{N}_i$ with $\pi(j) \leq \pi(k)$, the one-dimensional goal position a_i of robot i is defined as

$$a_i = \max\left\{a \in \mathcal{P} \mid \max\{\bar{a}_j, l_j\} < a < \min\{\bar{a}_k, l_k\}\right\} \quad (5)$$

with $\bar{a}_j$ and $\bar{a}_k$ being the latest goal positions of the two neighbors communicated in a previous time step. These can be communicated together with the data needing to be communicated for the DMPC scheme. If a_i is empty, because there is no applicable member of $\mathcal{P}$ in the interval $(\max\{\bar{a}_j,\ l_j\}, \min\{\bar{a}_k, l_k\})$, it is instead defined as the arithmetic mean of the interval boundaries. The interval boundaries may also be moved further inward for increased safety. Subsequently, $^{\mathrm{R}}\boldsymbol{g}_i = {^{\mathrm{R}}\mathcal{E}}(a_i)$ shall denote the two-dimensional goal position along the edge of the dilated object.

If all robots would pick their goal within the same sampling interval by evaluating Eq. (5), conflicts may arise in the form of robots picking the same goal position. In particular, this may happen when no valid information has yet been communicated, i.e. in the first time step or when a new formation has been calculated. Naturally, this can be solved by letting the robots pick their positions one after another in consecutive time steps, which, in a naive implementation, would necessitate N time steps until all robots have picked a position. Fortunately, non-neighboring robots can pick their positions in parallel, and hence, either two or three time steps are necessary to safely allocate exactly one robot to each goal position.

3.4 Trajectory Generation

To obtain a functioning control scheme, each robot needs a reference trajectory for being able to evaluate the cost function of the DMPC optimization problem (3). For increased robustness, it seems prudent to plan the trajectory based on the control error. The reference path of an individual robot is known via $\boldsymbol{\gamma}_i(w) = \boldsymbol{\gamma}_{\text{ref}}(w) + \boldsymbol{S}^{\text{IR}}_{\gamma_{\text{ref},3}(w)}{}^{\text{R}}\boldsymbol{g}_i$, with $\boldsymbol{S}^{\text{IR}}_{\gamma_{\text{ref},3}(w)}$ denoting the matrix conveying the rotation from the body-fixed frame to the inertial frame, and w being the path parameter of $\boldsymbol{\gamma}_{\text{ref}}$. In the following, it is beneficial to employ two parametrizations of $\boldsymbol{\gamma}_i$ and $\boldsymbol{\gamma}_{\text{ref}}$ to the end of being able to separately limit the translational and the angular velocities along the path. Thus, $\boldsymbol{\gamma}_i(s)$ shall denote a parametrization in the arc length of the two position coordinates of $\boldsymbol{\gamma}_{\text{ref}}$, while $\boldsymbol{\gamma}_i(\nu)$ shall be a parametrization in the arc length of the rotational coordinate of $\boldsymbol{\gamma}_{\text{ref}}$. With this, to plan an error-dependent trajectory over the optimization horizon of the MPC scheme, the principal approach from [4], inspired by [5], can be applied. To this end, we define

$$\beta(\xi, b, \tau) = \max\left\{\frac{1 - \exp(-(b - \xi)/\tau)}{1 - \exp(-b/\tau)},\ 0\right\}, \tag{6}$$

$$\Delta s(k\,|\,t) = v_{\max}\,\beta\left(e_{\text{r}}(k\,|\,t), b_s, \tau_s\right) T^{\text{s}}_{\text{ctrl}}, \tag{7}$$

$$\Delta \nu(k\,|\,t) = \omega_{\max}\,\beta\left(e_{\text{r}}(k\,|\,t), b_\nu, \tau_\nu\right) T^{\text{s}}_{\text{ctrl}}. \tag{8}$$

Apart from the introduced design parameters $v_{\max}, \omega_{\max}, b_s, \tau_s, b_\nu, \tau_\nu > 0$, these expressions contain robot i's predicted control error defined as

$$e^i_{\text{r}}(k\,|\,t) = \left\|\boldsymbol{x}_i(k\,|\,t) - \boldsymbol{r}^i_{\text{ref}}(k\,|\,t)\right\|^2_{Q_{\text{t}}} + \sum_{j \in \mathcal{N}_i}\left\|{}^{\text{R}}\boldsymbol{x}_j(k\,|\,t) - {}^{\text{R}}\boldsymbol{x}_i(k\,|\,t) - {}^{\text{R}}\boldsymbol{\rho}_{i \rightarrow j}\right\|^2_{Q_{\text{f}}}.$$

Setting $s(0\,|\,0) := s(0) := 0$, $\nu(0\,|\,0) := \nu(0) := 0$, we define recursively

$$s(k + 1\,|\,t) = \min\left\{s(k\,|\,t) + \Delta s(k\,|t),\ \tilde{s}(\nu(k\,|\,t) + \Delta\nu(t\,|\,t))\right\}, \quad s(t\,|\,t) := s(t),$$

$$\nu(k + 1\,|\,t) = \min\left\{\nu(k\,|\,t) + \Delta\nu(k\,|t),\ \tilde{\nu}(s(k\,|\,t) + \Delta s(k\,|\,t))\right\}, \quad \nu(t\,|\,t) := \nu(t)$$

with $\tilde{s}(\nu)$ and $\tilde{\nu}(s)$ denoting the conversion from one parametrization to the other. The minimization ensures that the resulting parameter trajectories are consistent in the sense of referencing the same points of the path, while being conservative in the usage of either $\Delta s(k\,|\,t)$ or $\Delta\nu(k\,|\,t)$. The desired reference trajectory is obtained by inserting the predicted parameter trajectories into $\boldsymbol{\gamma}_i$. To establish a feedback between the real state of the transported object and the progression along the path, the object's state is regularly projected onto the path, including a predefined lookahead distance.

4   Simulation Results

In the interest of a meaningful and realistic simulation environment, it is vital that the actual communication between the robots is reproduced in simulation. Meeting this demand, the simulator and the control schemes of every robot each run in their own separate program instances, without any shared memory. Data messages, as necessitated by the introduced control scheme, are then exchanged using the LCM library [8] via UDP multicast. The quadratic programs (3) appearing in the course of Algorithm 1 are solved using qpOASES [7], which is tailor-made for the efficient solution of sequences of multi-parametric quadratic programs as they appear in MPC. The actual simulation is performed in Matlab, with the contact forces between the object and the robots calculated using a penalty-force approach. During situations in which inter-robot collisions or unwanted robot-object collisions may happen, the robots use the VFH+-method [13] to avoid these collisions. In all scenarios, the control sampling time is chosen to be $T^s_{ctrl} = 0.1\,s$, while the communication sampling time T^s_{comm} will vary.

The advantages of employing distributed model predictive control become manifest even in rather simple scenarios. Figure 2 shows two simulation results for a scenario in which a square object shall be transported along a straight line and rotated by 45 degrees. Here and in the following, the robots are depicted as light blue circles and the reference path is dashed in orange. The left plot shows the results with activated DMPC and $T^s_{comm} := 0.2\,s$, while the right plot shows the results for deactivated DMPC, i.e. with $Q_f := 0$ in the MPC stage cost L and in the control error e^i_r. As can be seen, the object's path tracking error is significantly reduced, with considerably smoother robot trajectories, leading to a faster transportation process.

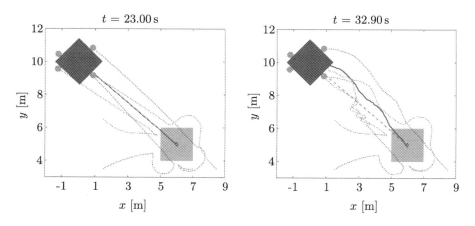

Fig. 2. Object transportation with activated (left) and deactivated DMPC (right), the object's initial pose is marked in transparent gray. (Color figure online)

To study a more complex scenario, four robots shall now transport a different object, starting from the center of a circle, approximated as a linear spline with 32 segments. The object is transported to the circle's border, then along the circumference of the circle, and finally back to its center. During the progression along the circumference, the robots shall rotate the object, so that, ideally, always the same corner of the object points to the circle's center. Figure 3 shows the simulation results for $T^s_{comm} = 0.5\,s$, illustrating that, even with relatively long communication sampling times, a successful transportation is possible. The robots self-reliantly reorganize the formation when leaving and entering the circle, for being able to safely move the object along the prescribed path.

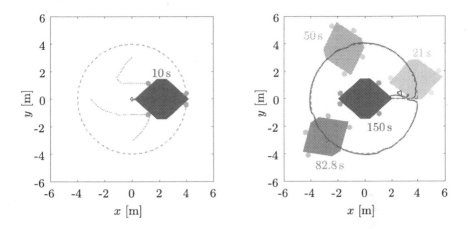

Fig. 3. Object transportation with $T^{\mathrm{s}}_{\mathrm{comm}} = 0.5\,\mathrm{s}$

The results depicted in Fig. 4 indicate that the proposed scheme also seems to be applicable to more complicated object shapes and larger numbers of robots. At the same time, in these results, the robots receive a disturbed pose measurement of the object. The independent normally distributed disturbances on the positions and rotation have zero-mean and standard deviations of $0.05\,\mathrm{m}$ and $0.05\,\mathrm{rad}$, respectively. Even without any filtering of the received measurements, the transportation process is still successful.

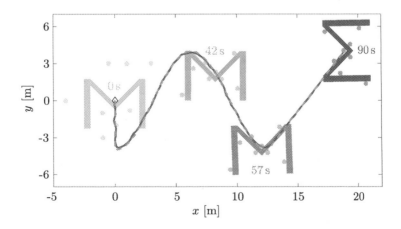

Fig. 4. Object transportation with disturbance and $T^{\mathrm{s}}_{\mathrm{comm}} = 0.2\,\mathrm{s}$

5   Conclusion

This paper introduces a fully distributed control scheme for transporting polygonal objects through planar environments. Each robot communicates with two neighboring robots that are also participating in the transportation task. The communication enables the rather novel usage of a distributed model predictive control scheme for this kind of task, allowing the robots to incorporate their neighbor's predicted trajectories into their control decisions, and providing a prediction of the control error. The latter is useful to plan an error-dependent trajectory, so that the transportation progresses with a velocity that is adequate to the current situation. Furthermore, the robots self-reliantly negotiate their individual positions around the object, so that the object can be safely pushed through the environment. Various simulation results highlight the applicability of the approach, considering the influences of communication sampling times that are longer than the main control sampling time, different object shapes and sizes, and stochastic noise on the pose measurement of the object.

References

1. Bullo, F., Cortés, J., Martínez, S.: Distributed Control of Robotic Networks. Princeton University Press, Princeton (2009)
2. Chen, J., Gauci, M., Li, W., Kolling, A., Groß, R.: Occlusion-based cooperative transport with a swarm of miniature mobile robots. IEEE Trans. Robot. **31**(2), 307–321 (2015)
3. Ebel, H., Sharafian Ardakani, E., Eberhard, P.: Comparison of distributed model predictive control approaches for transporting a load by a formation of mobile robots. In: Proceedings of the 8th Eccomas Thematic Conference on Multibody Dynamics, Prague (2017)
4. Ebel, H., Sharafian Ardakani, E., Eberhard, P.: Distributed model predictive formation control with discretization-free path planning for transporting a load. Robot. Auton. Syst. **96**, 211–223 (2017)
5. Egerstedt, M., Hu, X.: Formation constrained multi-agent control. IEEE Trans. Robot. Autom. **17**(6), 947–951 (2001)
6. Ferramosca, A., Limon, D., Alvarado, I., Camacho, E.: Cooperative distributed MPC for tracking. Automatica **49**(4), 906–914 (2013)
7. Ferreau, H.J., Kirches, C., Potschka, A., Bock, H.G., Diehl, M.: qpOASES: a parametric active-set algorithm for quadratic programming. Math. Program. Comput. **6**(4), 327–363 (2014)
8. Huang, A.S., Olson, E., Moore, D.C.: LCM: lightweight communications and marshalling. In: Proceedings of the 2010 IEEE/RSJ International Conference on Intelligent Robots and Systems, Taipei, pp. 4057–4062 (2010)
9. Maciejowski, J.: Predictive Control with Constraints. Pearson Education, Harlow (2001)
10. Mesbahi, M., Egerstedt, M.: Graph Theoretic Methods in Multiagent Networks. Princeton University Press, Princeton (2010)
11. Rawlings, J.B., Mayne, D.Q.: Model Predictive Control: Theory and Design. Nob Hill Publishing, Madison (2009)

12. Stewart, B.T., Venkat, A.N., Rawlings, J.B., Wright, S.J., Pannocchia, G.: Cooperative distributed model predictive control. Syst. Control Lett. **59**(8), 460–469 (2010)
13. Ulrich, I., Borenstein, J.: VFH+: reliable obstacle avoidance for fast mobile robots. In: Proceedings of the 1998 IEEE International Conference on Robotics and Automation, vol. 2, Leuven, pp. 1572–1577 (1998)
14. Venkat, A.N., Rawlings, J.B., Wright, S.J.: Stability and optimality of distributed model predictive control. In: Proceedings of the 44th IEEE Conference on Decision and Control, Seville, pp. 6680–6685 (2005)
15. Yamada, S., Saito, J.: Adaptive action selection without explicit communication for multirobot box-pushing. IEEE Trans. Syst. Man Cybern. Part C (Appl. Rev.) **31**(3), 398–404 (2001)

Deep-Sarsa Based Multi-UAV Path Planning and Obstacle Avoidance in a Dynamic Environment

Wei Luo[1], Qirong Tang[2(✉)], Changhong Fu[2], and Peter Eberhard[1]

[1] Institute of Engineering and Computational Mechanics, University of Stuttgart,
Pfaffenwaldring 9, 70569 Stuttgart, Germany
[2] Laboratory of Robotics and Multibody System, School of Mechanical Engineering,
Tongji University, No. 4800, Cao An Road,
Shanghai 201804, People's Republic of China
qirong.tang@outlook.com

Abstract. This study presents a Deep-Sarsa based path planning and obstacle avoidance method for unmanned aerial vehicles (UAVs). Deep-Sarsa is an on-policy reinforcement learning approach, which gains information and rewards from the environment and helps UAV to avoid moving obstacles as well as finds a path to a target based on a deep neural network. It has a significant advantage over dynamic environment compared to other algorithms. In this paper, a Deep-Sarsa model is trained in a grid environment and then deployed in an environment in ROS-Gazebo for UAVs. The experimental results show that the trained Deep-Sarsa model can guide the UAVs to the target without any collisions. This is the first time that Deep-Sarsa has been developed to achieve autonomous path planning and obstacle avoidance of UAVs in a dynamic environment.

Keywords: UAV · Deep-Sarsa · Multi-agent · Dynamic environment

1 Introduction

Nowadays unmanned aerial vehicles (UAVs) have been applied in many application fields such as cooperative target search [1], mapping [2], goods transportation [3], observation [4] and rescue [5]. To accomplish these missions, UAVs should have the ability to explore and understand the environment, then take safe paths to the target. Besides that, UAV should be able to react to the obstacles in the scenario and avoid them, especially when the environment is dynamic and the obstacles may move in the environment. All these abilities remain as challenges for UAV research.

For path planning, many studies have been carried out for UAVs. Some algorithms, such as A* algorithms [6,7], artificial potential fields [8], coverage path planning [9], and Q-learning [10,11] perform well in a static environment. They figure out the path to the target and guide UAVs going through a known

© Springer International Publishing AG, part of Springer Nature 2018
Y. Tan et al. (Eds.): ICSI 2018, LNCS 10942, pp. 102–111, 2018.
https://doi.org/10.1007/978-3-319-93818-9_10

environment. However, in most of the cases, the conditions and environment are changing during the mission. For instance, when UAVs shuttle back and forth in the city and transfer goods, they should handle not only static obstacles but also moving ones. Limited by computational capacity and sensor sampling rate, when UAV uses static path planning methods, the previous experience may not be the best choice, since the situation could be changed, and the best action in the last state may even lead to a dangerous scene. Therefore, a dynamic path planning is more practical for real applications.

In this paper, an on-policy algorithm named Deep-Sarsa is selected for path planning and obstacle avoidance for UAVs in a dynamic environment. It combines traditional Sarsa [12] with a neural network, which takes the place of the Q-table for storing states and predicting the best action [13]. Also, the robot operating system (ROS) [14] and the related simulation platform Gazebo [15] are used in our work, since they provide a simulation platform with a physics engine and the implementation in this simulation platform can also be quickly transferred to real UAVs.

The paper is organized as follows. Section 2 describes the principle of Sarsa and the structure of our trained model. In Sect. 3, the training process is introduced, and the experiment in the simulation platform is illustrated. Finally, discussions and conclusions are presented in Sect. 4.

2   Algorithm

Reinforcement learning is one of typical machine learning classes. It is widely used in many robotic applications [16] and obtains rewards from the environment and reinforces the experience. Reinforcement learning algorithms can be divided into two categories: on-policy learning and off-policy learning [17]. Compared with off-policy learning, on-policy learning algorithms gain their experiences during the operation. Therefore, an on-policy algorithm usually has to be more conservative than an off-policy algorithm, since it will not greedily take the maximum reward.

2.1   Sarsa

State-action-reward-state-action (Sarsa) is one of well-known on-policy reinforcement learning algorithms [18]. Exemplary pseudo-code for Sarsa is illustrated in Algorithm 1. Similar to Q-Learning, Sarsa requires a table to store Q-values, which indicate the rewards from the environment on the basis of its rules and depend on the individual state s and action a of robots. During the exploration, a robot agent will interact with the environment and get the updated policy on account of its action. The next state s' and action a' will also have a reward based on the previous stored Q-table. To control the learning process, the learning rate α is set up for control of learning speed and the discount factor γ determines the contribution of future rewards.

Algorithm 1. Pseudo-code for Sarsa

1: initialize $Q(s, a)$ arbitrarily, where s denotes the state of agent and a denotes the action
2: **for** each episode **do**
3:     initialize s
4:     choose a from s using policy derived from Q
5:     **for** each step of episode **do**
6:         take action a, observe reward r, and next state s'
7:         choose the next action a' from s' using policy derived from Q
8:         $Q(s, a) \leftarrow Q(s, a) + \alpha[r + \gamma Q(s', a') - Q(s, a)]$
9:         $s \leftarrow s'; a \leftarrow a'$
10:     until s arrives the terminal state

2.2 Deep Sarsa

The traditional reinforcement learning for path planning usually has a shortcoming since the rules in the certain environment have to be manually constructed. It's a great challenge for the user to find a workable principle to fully describe the connection between the situation of an agent in the environment and the returned reward according to each pair set of state and action. For instance, for the robot path planning, the state usually contains the current position's information of the robot and also other related information about terrains and targets etc. Hence, there may exist plenty of possible states and the dimension of the Q-table could be extremely large. Besides that, if the environment is changed as the terrains or targets move during the operation, the previously stored Q-values may lead to a wrong action and even can cause a collision. Therefore, the traditional Sarsa algorithm can hardly be applied in a dynamic environment.

In literature, Deep Q-Networks [19] have shown a good performance in playing games, and so researchers realized that deep neural networks could be applied in complex situations and they can discover as well as estimate the non linear connections behind the given data. Hence, one promising solution for dynamic situations could be Deep-Sarsa. Instead of constructing a concrete Q-table and rules for each agent in Sarsa, Deep-Sarsa uses a deep neural network to determine which action the UAV needs to take. Owing to the strong generalization ability to cover different situations, Deep-Sarsa can handle complex state combination, such as information from moving terrains, multi-agent. The structure of Deep Sarsa is illustrated in Fig. 1. The neural network requires only initialization at the beginning, then it learns and understands the environment through the given data from training. Therefore, users can naturally and intuitively define the states of relative position and some motion states as inputs. The output of Deep Sarsa is the 'best' action which is determined by the neural network.

3 Experiment and Simulation

To verify the performance of Deep-Sarsa for UAV's path planning and obstacle avoidance, checking different scenarios in the simulation platform is indispensable.

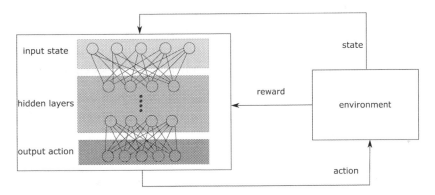

Fig. 1. The structure of Deep-Sarsa

In the experiment, two UAVs in a formation want to pass a small terrain, where two flying obstacles cut their paths and one static obstacle stays in the front of the exit. The simplified environment is illustrated in Fig. 2, where the mission UAVs are marked with red circles and the moving obstacles are in the yellow. Besides, two green triangles form a static obstacle and hamper the path to exit which are marked with two blue circles. The UAVs need to figure out the pattern of obstacles' motion and find the exit they need to reach. The rewards of this experiment are defined quite simple, which it is positively defined when the UAVs arrive at the destination and conversely negatively rated in case of any collision with obstacles.

For this scenario, the Deep-Sarsa model should be trained at first and then applied in a simulation environment. In the training phase, the simplified environment is utilized. The agents in training are treated as mass points, used to test the robustness of the algorithm and also generate the trained model. To check the performance of the trained Deep-Sarsa model, a 3D environment is set up in ROS-Gazebo and provides realistic conditions before performing the experiment on real hardware.

3.1   Training a Model

In the beginning of training, UAVs have no knowledge about the environment. To explore the environment, UAVs take action randomly from five different choices, namely up, down, left, right and still, until they have gained enough experience and 'understand' the situation. To balance exploration and safety a decision parameter ϵ is set up, see Algorithm 2. In each step, once the UAV takes action and gains the state from the environment, the decision parameter ϵ will be multiplied with a const value λ, which is between zero and one, and reduce the possibility of choosing an action too arbitrary.

Using the Algorithms 1 and 2, the flowchart for training a Deep-Sarsa model is illustrated in Fig. 3. In each episode, the current state, the current action and also the next state and action of a UAV will be fed to the Deep-Sarsa model. In this paper, the network used for this scenario is founded through Keras [20]

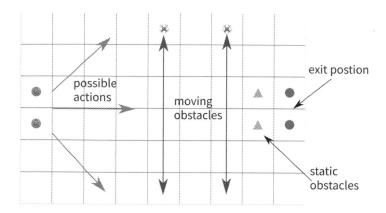

Fig. 2. The simplified training environment (Color figure online)

Algorithm 2. Action selection strategy

1: **for** each step of episode in training **do**
2:     **if** random number $< \epsilon$ **then**
3:         randomly choose an action from up, down, left, right and still
4:     **else**
5:         gain the best action from trained model according to the current state
6:     $\epsilon = \epsilon * \lambda$, where $\lambda = const$

---

and contains three dense layers with totally 549 trainable parameters. The details about the neural network are illustrated in Table 1. In consideration of real experiments for UAVs the input of the Deep-Sarsa model contains 14 components with the information from relative position between UAV and targets, the relative position between UAV and obstacles, obstacles' moving direction and the rewards. And the output of this Deep-Sarsa model is an array of possibilities for five alternative actions for UAV in each step. The UAV can take its next action consulting the predicted action from the Deep-Sarsa model and also its current state.

Based on the training process, 4000 simulation runs are performed to get enough data to train the model. In every episode, if the UAVs successfully arrive in the target zoon, the score will be marked with 1. Otherwise, it will be set to

Table 1. Neural network layout for Deep-Sarsa

Layer index	Output shape	Number of parameters
1	(21, 16)	352
2	(16, 8)	136
3	(8, 4)	36
4	(4, 5)	25

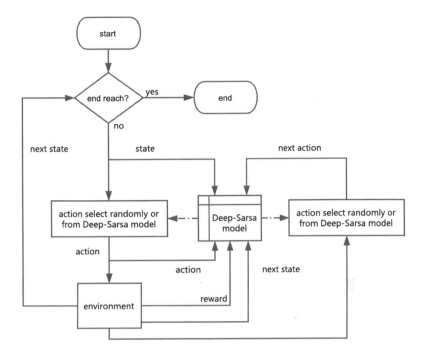

Fig. 3. Flowchart of training a Deep-Sarsa model

−1 if UAVs crash with obstacles. The sum of all scores is illustrated in Fig. 4. In the first 800 runs, UAVs can hardly get to the target and hit the obstacles. Along with the progress of training, the number of success achieving the goal is increased. On the one hand, the occasionality of action is reduced along with the decreasing values of ϵ. On the other side, the trained model is more robust and can help UAVs steering clear of the terrains and finding the path to the target.

3.2 Test of the Trained Model

Since the path planning model for UAVs has been trained in a simplified environment, it's necessary to bring the model in a more demanding test environment before implementation on real UAVs. There are two simplifications in the simplified simulation platform. One is using mass points to indicate the UAVs. In the real experiment, the UAVs act under the fundamental physics laws and the fly performance is restricted to motor power and aerodynamics. The other simplification is considering the training state as discrete since the simplified environment is in the grid. The real readings for sensors of UAVs are obviously more consecutive than the states in the simplified environment, and it needs to be proven that the trained model can also be applied in the real environment. Besides, by training, it ignores the delay of communication and information exchanges, which may also cause severe problems in real hardware experiments.

Considering these problems, the test platform in this work is built based on ROS and Gazebo. In Gazebo, a physics engine is included, which can quickly judge the collision between objects during the simulation. When UAVs have an impact on the terrains, they may lead to a crash or change the moving direction. Additionally, a physical model of a UAV is introduced in the simulation. The fly performance is well simulated, and the controller will not ignore the fly ability of the UAV. The communication between UAVs and trained model is also simulated in the experiment. In the real experiment, the trained model, the UAVs and the server are separated in different network locations according to target requirement. Therefore, the network structure in this work is designed and illustrated in Fig. 5. The bridge between ROS-Gazebo and the trained model is realized through lightweight communications and marshalling (LCM) [21]. It provides a reliable connection and can be deployed not only in the simulation but also for the hardware. During the test, four instances are launched and work parallelly based on the aforementioned structure. Each instance takes charge of one of the operations from the ROS-Gazebo core, broadcasting the state of simulation, Deep-Sarsa model and transmitting the predicted action.

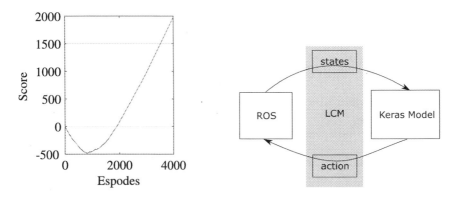

Fig. 4. Training scores of Deep-Sarsa   **Fig. 5.** Communication network structure

In the designed scenario for testing based on ROS-Gazebo, two UAVs are trying to escape from the area, see Fig. 6. The exit is straightforward, but another two UAVs are patrolling in the middle of the terrain and cutting their ways. Based on the trained model in this study, they can take the same strategy, and make a detour to the exit without collisions.

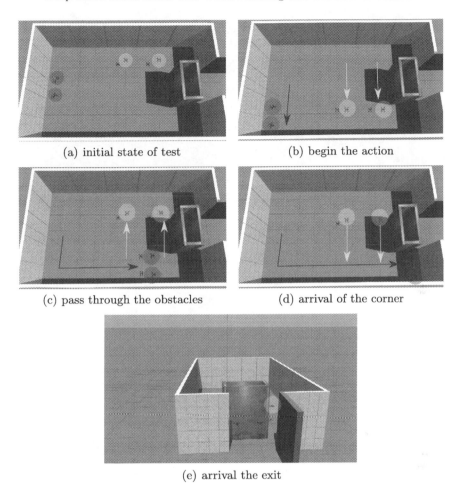

(a) initial state of test

(b) begin the action

(c) pass through the obstacles

(d) arrival of the corner

(e) arrival the exit

Fig. 6. UAV path planning and dynamic obstacle avoidance in ROS-Gazebo test environment

4   Conclusions and Future Works

A method based on Deep-Sarsa for path planning and obstacle avoidance is proposed in this study for UAVs. The proposed approach has been trained in a simplified environment and tested in a ROS-Gazebo simulation platform. The results show the performance of Deep-Sarsa model in the application of path planning and obstacle avoidance, especially in a dynamic environment. The trained Deep-Sarsa model can provide a reliable path for UAVs without collisions, although it requires a pre-training process before applying the model. Meanwhile, since not only the model for UAV but also the communication network between different modules have been taken into consideration, the next step is to implement the model and algorithm with real UAV's hardware.

Acknowledgements. This work is supported by the project of National Natural Science Foundation of China (No. 61603277), the 13th-Five-Year-Plan on Common Technology, key project (No. 41412050101), and the Shanghai Aerospace Science and Technology Innovation Fund (SAST 2016017). Meanwhile, this work is also partially supported by the Youth 1000 program project (No. 1000231901), as well as by the Key Basic Research Project of Shanghai Science and Technology Innovation Plan (No. 15JC1403300). All these supports are highly appreciated.

References

1. Gan, S.K., Sukkarieh, S.: Multi-UAV target search using explicit decentralized gradient-based negotiation. In: IEEE International Conference on Robotics and Automation (ICRA), Shanghai, China, pp. 751–756 (2011)
2. Fu, C., Carrio, A., Campoy, P.: Efficient visual odometry and mapping for unmanned aerial vehicle using ARM-based stereo vision pre-processing system. In: International Conference on Unmanned Aircraft Systems (ICUAS), Colorado, USA, pp. 957–962 (2015)
3. Maza, I., Kondak, K., Bernard, M., Ollero, A.: Multi-UAV cooperation and control for load transportation and deployment. J. Intell. Robot. Syst. **57**(1), 417–449 (2009)
4. Fu, C., Carrio, A., Olivares-Mendez, M.A., Suarez-Fernandez, R., Campoy, P.: Robust real-time vision-based aircraft tracking from unmanned aerial vehicles. In: IEEE International Conference on Robotics and Automation (ICRA) (2014)
5. Hayat, S., Yanmaz, E., Brown, T.X., Bettstetter, C.: Multi-objective UAV path planning for search and rescue. In: IEEE International Conference on Robotics and Automation (ICRA), Singapore, pp. 5569–5574 (2017)
6. Sathyaraj, B.M., Jain, L.C., Finn, A., Drake, S.: Multiple UAVs path planning algorithms: a comparative study. Fuzzy Optim. Decis. Mak. **7**(3), 257–267 (2008)
7. Hrabar, S.: 3D path planning and stereo-based obstacle avoidance for rotorcraft UAVs. In: IEEE/RSJ International Conference on Intelligent Robots and Systems, Nice, France, pp. 807–814 (2008)
8. Bounini, F., Gingras, D., Pollart, H., Gruyer, D.: Modified artificial potential field method for online path planning applications. In: IEEE Intelligent Vehicles Symposium (IV), Los Angeles, USA, pp. 180–185 (2017)
9. Galceran, E., Carreras, M.: A survey on coverage path planning for robotics. Robot. Auton. Syst. **61**(12), 1258–1276 (2013)
10. Zhao, Y., Zheng, Z., Zhang, X., Liu, Y.: Q learning algorithm based UAV path learning and obstacle avoidance approach. In: 36th Chinese Control Conference (CCC), Dalian, China, pp. 3397–3402 (2017)
11. Imanberdiyev, N., Fu, C., Kayacan, E., Chen, I.-M.: Autonomous navigation of UAV by using real-time model-based reinforcement learning. In: 14th International Conference on Control, Automation, Robotics and Vision, Phuket, Thailand, pp. 1–6 (2016)
12. Kubat, M.: Reinforcement learning. In: An Introduction to Machine Learning, pp. 331–339 (2017)
13. Zhao, D., Wang, H., Shao, K., Zhu, Y.: Deep reinforcement learning with experience replay based on SARSA. In: IEEE Symposium Series on Computational Intelligence (SSCI) (2016)

14. Quigley, M., Conley, K., Gerkey, B., Faust, J., Foote, T., Leibs, J., Wheeler, R., Ng, A.Y.: ROS: an open-source robot operating system. In: ICRA Workshop on Open Source Software, Kobe, Japan, pp. 1–6 (2009)
15. Koenig, N., Howard, A.: Design and use paradigms for Gazebo, an open-source multi-robot simulator. In: IEEE/RSJ International Conference on Intelligent Robots and Systems, Sendai, Japan, vol. 3, pp. 2149–2154 (2004)
16. Kober, J., Bagnell, J.A., Peters, J.: Reinforcement learning in robotics: a survey. Int. J. Robot. Res. **32**(11), 1238–1274 (2013)
17. Singh, S., Jaakkola, T., Littman, M.L., Szepesvári, C.: Convergence results for single-step on-policy reinforcement-learning algorithms. Mach. Learn. **38**(3), 287–308 (2000). https://doi.org/10.1007/978-981-10-7515-5_11
18. Sutton, R.S.: Generalization in reinforcement learning: successful examples using sparse coarse coding. In: Touretzky, D.S., Mozer, M.C., Hasselmo, M.E. (eds.) Advances in Neural Information Processing Systems, pp. 1038–1044. MIT Press (1996)
19. Mnih, V., Kavukcuoglu, K., Silver, D., Rusu, A.A., Veness, J., Bellemare, M.G., Graves, A., Riedmiller, M., Fidjeland, A.K., Ostrovski, G., Petersen, S., Beattie, C., Sadik, A., Antonoglou, I., King, H., Kumaran, D., Wierstra, D., Legg, S., Hassabis, D.: Human-level control through deep reinforcement learning. Nature **518**(7540), 529–533 (2015)
20. Ketkar, N.: Introduction to keras. In: Deep Learning with Python, pp. 97–111 (2017)
21. Huang, A.S., Olson, E., Moore, D.C.: LCM: lightweight communications and marshalling. In: IEEE/RSJ International Conference on Intelligent Robots and Systems, Taipei, Taiwan, pp. 4057–4062 (2010)

Cooperative Search Strategies of Multiple UAVs Based on Clustering Using Minimum Spanning Tree

Tao Zhu, Weixiong He$^{(\boxtimes)}$, Haifeng Ling, and Zhanliang Zhang

Army Engineering University of PLA, Nanjing 210014, China
weiwei3381@live.com

Abstract. Rate of revenue (*ROR*) is significant for unmanned aerial vehicle (UAV) to search targets located in probabilistic positions. To improve search efficiency in a situation of multiple static targets, this paper first transfers a continuous area to a discrete space by grid division and proposes some related indexes in the UAV search issue. Then, cooperative strategies of multiple UAVs are studied in the searching process: clustering partition of search area based on minimum spanning tree (MST) theory is put forward as well as path optimization using spiral flying model. Finally, a series of simulation experiments are carried out through the method in this paper and two compared algorithms. Results show that: optimized cooperative strategies can achieve greater total revenue and more stable performance than the other two.

Keywords: UAV · Cooperative search · Clustering · Minimum spanning tree

1 Introduction

Basic missions of present unmanned aerial vehicle (UAV) are still intelligence, surveillance and reconnaissance (ISR) [1]. With increasing complexity of battlefield environment, it is now difficult for a single UAV to search a large area with multiple targets. However, cooperative search task implemented by multiple UAVs sharing information with each other is a well method to overcome sensor limitations and improve search efficiency.

Researches on multi-UAV search for uncertain static targets are now in hotspot, in which approaches can be mostly attributed to search path planning based on information graph. Baum M L proposes distributed protocol for greedy search strategy based on rate of return (*ROR*) map, and multi-UAV cooperative search is studied through optimal theory [2]. Fuzzy C-Mean clustering method is used in Literature [3] to distribute the search area to different UAVs, so that cooperative search case is converted into several single UAV search problems. With distribution of target probabilities given, Literature [4] makes a path planning of cooperative search with minimum cost.

Designing cooperative search strategies is significant for multiple UAVs to reduce return-free consumptions and gain more profits in a specified time. In this paper, multi-UAV search process is analyzed first, and then strategies of area clustering and

© Springer International Publishing AG, part of Springer Nature 2018
Y. Tan et al. (Eds.): ICSI 2018, LNCS 10942, pp. 112–121, 2018.
https://doi.org/10.1007/978-3-319-93818-9_11

path planning are given. Finally, two other algorithms are compared with it to evaluate its search effect.

2 Modeling

2.1 Grid Partition

Suppose that probability density function of all the targets satisfy continuous distribution, and a continuous search area of any shape can be partitioned into grids [5–7], as shown in Fig. 1: in the rectangular coordinate system, the maximum length of a search area along Axis X and Y are respectively l_1 and l_2; the area can be reasonably divided to form a series of cells; each cell is called a search unit.

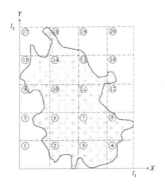

Fig. 1. Grid partition of a search area.

2.2 Related Indicators

Related indicators of UAV search process can be quantitatively described through detection, revenue and *ROR* which are defined as below [2, 3].

Detection function is used to estimate the detection ability of targets in a valuable search unit j with a time consumption of z. And its commonly used exponential form is given as follows:

$$b(j, z) = 1 - e^{-\frac{Wvz}{A}}. \tag{1}$$

where v is UAV search speed, W means scan width, and A stands for unit size.

When multiple UAVs are searching unit j, there is a revenue function defined as follows:

$$e(j, z) = \sum_{i=1}^{n} \omega_i p_i(j) b(j, z). \tag{2}$$

in which ω_i represents weight for target i whose probability in unit j is $p_i(j)$.

The final expectation of multi-UAV cooperative search task is to get a larger profit in a shorter time. Therefore, *ROR* is introduced and a common definition is as follows:

$$\frac{d(e)}{d(z)} = \frac{Wv}{A} \cdot e^{-\frac{Wvz}{A}} \cdot \sum_{i=1}^{n} \omega_i p_i(j). \tag{3}$$

which shows that *ROR* value will decrease if unit j is searched by a UAV when condition of $\sum_{i=1}^{n} \omega_i p_i(j)$ is given.

3   Cooperative Search Strategies

Total revenue of search area is updating because *ROR* values of searching grids are changing. There is an assumption that each UAV can be informed of current *ROR* values of all the search units as well as present and next locations of other UAVs. As a result, UAV cooperative search process is resolved into a problem of putting forward specific strategies for search area distribution and search path planning.

3.1   Clustering of Search Area

To make a maximum *ROR* value in the multi-UAV cooperative search, the search area should be partitioned reasonably so that each part is a connected domain with similar sizes and has units with analogous *ROR* values. A clustering algorithm based on theory of minimum spanning tree (MST) is proposed to segment the search area.

Minimum spanning tree is a subgraph of a connected graph which contains all the original nodes. There is no loop inside and two new tree structures will be generated if one edge is cut off. MST method named Prim Algorithm is adopted in this paper [8], and Fig. 2 shows an example of MST after the grids are connected.

Search area clustering can be transformed into tree division problem after the generation of minimum spanning tree. Stepwise strategy is used that only one edge of one tree is removed at a time. When selecting an edge, we consider its influence on the overall quality of clustering partition.

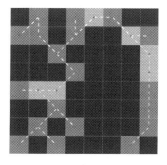

Fig. 2. An example of minimum spanning tree.

SSD, the intracluster square deviation, is a measure of dispersion of attribute values for the objects in a region [9]. Homogeneous regions have small *SSD* values. Thus, the quality measure of partition is the sum of SSD_i, which needs to be minimized. But there are unbalanced situations when only taking *SSD* into account. To solve the disproportion problem, a penalty term is proposed to quality index Q seen as follows:

$$Q = \sum_{i=1}^{k} SSD_i + 100 \cdot \max(\alpha - \frac{\min(G^*)}{\max(G^*)}, 0). \tag{4}$$

where $\min(G^*)$ and $\max(G^*)$ represent the minimum and maximum grid numbers of a connected graph G^* composed of every subtree T_i, and a balance factor α ($0 \leq \alpha \leq 1$) is put forward.

Figure 3 shows the division of a search area with different balance factors. Graph (a) demonstrates that some parts will contain only a few nodes if no balance factor is given, and the other three graphs indicate that it is more balanced when α is increasing. However, similarity of search units in the same partition will decrease if the balance factor enlarges.

The pseudo code of the above clustering algorithm can be seen in Table 1.

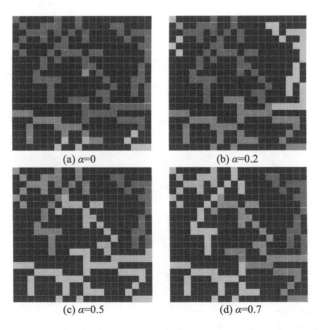

(a) $\alpha=0$ (b) $\alpha=0.2$

(c) $\alpha=0.5$ (d) $\alpha=0.7$

Fig. 3. Division with different values of α.

Table 1. Pseudo code.

Search area partition based on MST clustering.

---

1   Initialize all the grids and generate a connected domain including every search-

ing unit whose *ROR*>0;

2   Let a V={all the searching units of the connected domain}, L={edges generated

by connecting units in V}, k=partition number, V_{new}= ∅ , L_{new}= ∅ ;

3   Select any searching unit v_i from V, let V_{new} ={v_i};

4   **while** V_{new}≠V **do**

5   Find the nearest edge <v_i, v_j> in L, where $v_i \in V_{new}, v_j \notin V_{new}$;

6   Add v_j into V_{new}, and add <v_i, v_j> into L_{new};

7   **end while**.

8   **for** *loop*=1 to k **do**

9   **for** each edge <v_i, v_j> in L_{new} **do**

10   Calculate the quality factor $Q(T_i)$ of subtree T_i including <v_i, v_j>;

11   Calculate del=$Q(T_i)$-($Q(T_{i+1})$+$Q(T_{i+2})$) when removing <v_i, v_j> to divide T_i

into T_{i+1} and T_{i+2};

12   Remove <v_i, v_j> when *del* has a maximum value;

13   **end for**.

14   **end for**.

15   **return** all the subtrees generated by L_{new}.

3.2   Optimizing of Search Path

It is necessary to optimize its path when a UAV is searching a cell, and a spiral flying model is designed with a consideration of its scan width, as shown in Fig. 4. In this way, the UAV can search evenly and gradually fly to the cell periphery so that it is conducive to moving to a next search unit if necessary. When *ROR* value of the cell is high, the UAV only need to continue circling to search more.

   ROR value is decreasing when UAV is searching the unit, so we should plan the search time for every UAV in each cell reasonably. To improve search efficiency, a

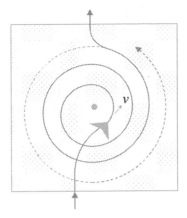

Fig. 4. Spiral flying model.

concept of dynamic break value is introduced in the search process. Suppose that there are number of M search units ranked by ROR values and a quantile is defined as β $(0 < \beta < 1)$, and then ROR value of No.$\lceil \beta M \rceil$ unit is considered as the break value which is also automatically decreasing.

4 Simulation

Some comparison experiments are carried out through the above cooperative search strategies (Algorithm T for short) and two other common methods named Search Algorithm based on Fuzzy C-Mean Cluster (Algorithm C for short) [3] and Greedy Search Algorithm with Distributed Agreement (Algorithm D for short) [2].

4.1 Parameter Conditions

As to $p_i(j)$, the probability of every target in each cell, it is given in advance by intelligence resources [2]. Some major parameters of UAV searching task are listed in Table 2, and one example of initial ROR values with normal distribution is shown in Fig. 5. To ensure a consistent starting state, it is presumed that all UAVs begin flying at the bottom right corner with a minimum velocity value of 10 m/s and the same upward direction. As to UAV flight restrictions, there are axial and lateral acceleration constraints of 2.5 m/s^2 and 0.55 m/s^2 respectively, as well as a speed limit of 35 m/s. What's more, Algorithm T has an additional condition of $\alpha = \beta = 0.3$ and there is a restriction of 50 iterations on Algorithm C.

4.2 Evaluation Index

Within a certain cost of time, a sum of revenue values searched by multiple UAVs in the overall area can reflect the search performance, so total revenue is taken as a measurement of algorithm performance.

Table 2. Major parameters.

Parameter	Value
Size (m)	1066×1066
Area grid	10×10
Target number	8
Search units ($ROR > 0$)	36
UAV quantity	3
Search speed (m/s)	25
Search time (s)	300

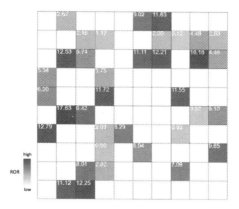

Fig. 5. An example of ROR distribution.

In order to evaluate the stability of algorithm, each algorithm is applied in the same case for many times so that we can get three sets of total revenues. In addition, coefficient of variation (CV) is defined in the following function, where σ is the standard deviation of a group of total revenues with average value μ. It is obvious that algorithm stability is better when CV value is smaller.

$$CV = \sigma/\mu. \tag{5}$$

4.3 Results and Analyses

The UAV search paths using three different algorithms are shown from Figs. 6, 7 and 8 in the order of Algorithm T, C and D, and these trajectories of UAV indicate that there is shortest transfer route in Algorithm T which reveals that its path planning is practical and effective.

Figure 9 shows different changing rules of total revenue with search time through different algorithms. From the beginning to 120 s, there is little difference among three algorithms. Since then, Algorithm T gains faster, and its total earnings are more than others. Further analyses of the other two algorithms are as follows: Algorithm C is

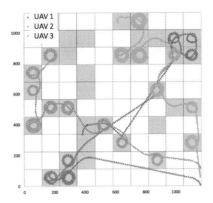

Fig. 6. Search paths using Algorithm T.

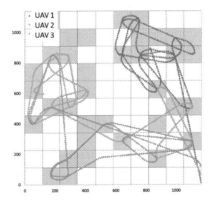

Fig. 7. Search paths using Algorithm C.

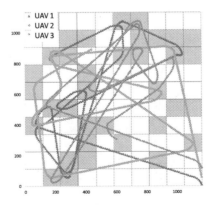

Fig. 8. Search paths using Algorithm D.

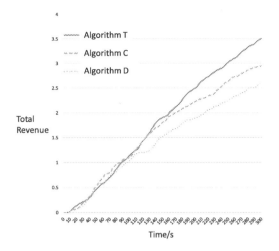

Fig. 9. Changing rules of total revenue.

better than Algorithm D due to some kind of area division, but both are in pursuit of the search unit with highest *ROR*, ignoring the overall revenue; these two algorithms have lower search efficiencies because of longer transfer flight without revenues.

20 experiments of each algorithm are carried out independently, and the results are listed in Table 3. The conclusion shows that the total revenue of Algorithm T is better than the other two, which is about 20.9% higher than Algorithm C and 38.6% higher than Algorithm D. Each algorithm has a small value of *CV*, but the stability of Algorithm T is more obvious. The main reason maybe that Algorithm T which uses MST clustering method is less affected by the initial condition, and there is trade-off analysis of search process.

Table 3. Results of 20 experiments.

Algorithm	μ	σ	*CV*
Algorithm T	**3.496**	0.017	**0.005**
Algorithm C	2.892	0.035	0.012
Algorithm D	2.522	0.050	0.020

5   Conclusion

As to multi-UAV search issue, both area clustering and path planning are of great importance. Cooperative strategies in this paper are both practical and efficient, and the algorithm is effective because of its well stability.

References

1. Department of Defense: Unmanned Systems Roadmap 2007–2032. Createspace Independent Publishing Platform, Washington DC (2015)
2. Baum, M.L., Passino, K.M.: A search theoretic approach to cooperative control for uninhabited air Vehicle. In: AIAA Guidance, Navigation and Control Conference and Exhibit (2002)
3. Yan, M.Q., Liu, B.: Multiple UAVs cooperative search strategy based on fuzzy c-mean cluster. Tactical Missile Technol. **34**(1), 55–63 (2013)
4. Meng, W., He, Z., Su, R., et al.: Decentralized Multi-UAV flight autonomy for moving convoys search and track. IEEE Trans. Control Syst. Technol. **25**(4), 1480–1487 (2017)
5. Stone, L.D.: Theory of Optimal Search, 2nd edn. Academic Press, New York (2004)
6. Liu, Y., Zhu, Q.X., Liu, D.: New method for searching drainage area accidental pollution source based on optimal search theory. Environ. Sci. Technol. **31**(9), 61–65 (2008)
7. Chen, P., Hu, J.G., Yin, Z.W.: Quasi-optimal method for multiple UUVs cooperate to search static target. Fire Control Command Control **38**(4), 53–56 (2013)
8. Jungnickel, D.: Graphs. Networks and Algorithms. Springer, Berlin (1999)
9. Assuncao, R.M., Neves, M.C.G., Camara, et al.: Efficient regionalization techniques for socio-economic geographical units using minimum spanning trees. Int. J. Geogr. Inf. Sci. **20**(8), 797–811 (2006)

Learning Based Target Following Control for Underwater Vehicles

Zhou Hao, Huang Hai[✉], and Zhou Zexing

National Key Laboratory of Science and Technology
for Autonomous Underwater Vehicle, Harbin Engineering University,
145 Nantong Street Harbin, Harbin, China
haihus@163.com

Abstract. Target following of underwater vehicles has attracted increasingly attentions on their potential applications in oceanic resources exploration and engineering development. However, underwater vehicles confront with more complicated and extensive difficulties in target following than those on the land. This study proposes a novel learning based target following control approach through the integration of type-II fuzzy system and support vector machine (SVM). The type-II fuzzy system allows researchers to model and minimize the effects of uncertainties of changing environment in the rule-based systems. In order to improve the vehicle capacity of self-learning, an SVM based learning approach has been developed. Through genetic algorithm generating and mutating fuzzy rules candidate, SVM learning and optimization, one can obtain optimized fuzzy rules. Tank experiments have been performed to verify the proposed controller.

Keywords: Underwater vehicle · Machine learning · Target following

1 Introduction

Recently, underwater vehicles including Autonomous Underwater Vehicles (AUVs) and Remotely Operated Vehicles (ROVs) have attracted growing attentions for the oceanic resources exploration and engineering development [1]. Many research findings and marine engineering development are related with target following with various degree of complexity [2]. However, underwater vehicles confront with more complicated and extensive difficulties in target following than those on the land. For example, the underwater target is insufficient in color features, and vague due to the scattering from particles and water [3]. Thus the underwater vehicles have to search and follow the target at the same time under the disturbance of ocean current in the unknown submarine environment [4].

Considerable researches have been carried out to address the target following issue of underwater vehicle [4]. Taha et al. developed a terminal sliding mode control scheme on the following problem of AUVs in the horizontal plane [5]. Khoshnam et al. studied target following control of an underactuated AUV through neural network adaptive control technique. By utilizing the line-of-sight measurements to track a target, the controller was implemented without knowledge of system dynamics and

Y. Tan et al. (Eds.): ICSI 2018, LNCS 10942, pp. 122–131, 2018.
https://doi.org/10.1007/978-3-319-93818-9_12

environmental disturbances [6]. Xue employed hyperbolic tangent functions in the following controller to generate amplitude-limited control signals to prevent the actuators from the saturation, he particularly relaxed initial conditions when the desired target was far [7]. However, target following process includes target found and locking, motion plan and control for target approaching and following. The underwater vehicle should not only track the target, but also keep the target in the sight [8]. In the complicated submarine environment, the vehicle can't find the target once lost.

With the development of artificial intelligence, autonomous system increasingly applied intelligent and even cognitive architecture with machine learning techniques which can be used for action-decision making problems in unknown and changing environment [9]. Mae et al. proposed a novel semi-online neural-Q-learning (SONQL) controller on target following of underwater vehicle, neural network computing control responses can be updated through Q-learning algorithm [10]. Neural network with Q-learning acts like behavior intelligence can make the controller performance continuously improved. On the other hand, controller with fuzzy rules is also conceived with human intelligence, but not dependent on samples of database [11]. Through the learning based training and generation of fuzzy rules, the underwater vehicle can realize automatic target following control. As a type of effective and reliable machine learning techniques, support vector machine (SVM) have been widely used in classification problems. In compare with neural fuzzy networks, SVM requires less prior knowledge and smaller number of samples [12]. This paper will propose an SVM learning based fuzzy controller for target following of underwater vehicle on the basis of cognitive architecture.

The rest of this paper is organized as follows. Section 2 will introduce cognitive architecture for target following. Section 3 will issue the learning based hybrid rule generation algorithm. Section 4 will make an analysis on target following experiments on open frame ROVs. We will draw conclusions in Sect. 5.

2　Cognitive Architecture for Target Following

In compare with vehicle on the land, underwater vehicle confront with more disturbances and unknown environment in target following missions. The vehicle should not only make full perception to detect and recognize the target in limit watching field, but cruising and floating with stable and accurate control to keep the target in sight. Cognitive architecture originated from human reasoning and intelligence, can realize learning based perception, decision making and automatic control on the basis of knowledge. The cognitive architecture of the underwater vehicle (see Fig. 1) is composed with 5 functions: knowledge base, learning, automatic reasoning and planning, learning based control and perception.

The knowledge base contains the knowledge of target perception and following process such as target models and features training, following plans and strategies control rules and parameters, the base can be online continuously and adaptively updated and expanded with the following missions. The learning module organizes both the success and failure information obtained during the following missions, moreover, this module will help other modules with learning and parameter adaption

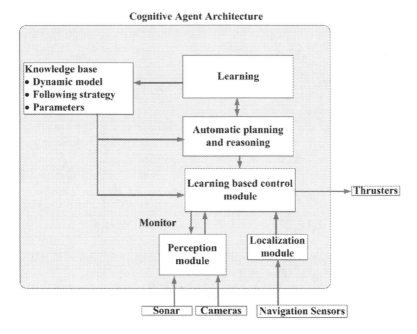

Fig. 1. Cognitive architecture for target following

from the new samples. The automatic reasoning and planning module is designed based on automatic planning and behavior action reasoning methodology; through these methodologies the vehicle reasons about current states, reacts logically to the external feedback and operate with planned behaviors. The learning based control module realizes the planned behaviors with fuzzy controllers and improves the control rules and accuracies with learning strategies which will be detailed discussed in this paper. The perception module will realize target recognition and following through convolutional neural networks so that the vehicle can recognize, lock and continuously track the target through strategy reasoning, learning, learning based control and perception module.

3 Learning Based Hybrid Rule Generation Algorithm

Generally: the fuzzy rules can be set from experience:

$$
\begin{aligned}
R^f &: IF\ x_1^f\ is\ \widetilde{F}_1^f\ and,\dots,and\ x_n^f\ is\ \widetilde{F}_n^f, \\
&THEN\ y_1^f\ is\ w_{U1}^f\ and,\dots,and\ y_p^f\ is\ w_{Up}^f
\end{aligned}
\tag{1}
$$

where $f = 1,\dots,n$ is rule number, $x_i^f, i = 1,\dots,n$ is the rule input, $\widetilde{F}_i^f$ is type-2 fuzzy sets of antecedent part, $w_{Uj}^f, j = 1,\dots,p$ is consequent type-2 interval set. However, in the field experiments and application trials, target following of underwater vehicle will confront with various conditions such as uncertain environmental disturbances, target following speed, relative positions of the target in the vision field, etc. Different states and their combinations need complicated fuzzy rules, which made enumeration and coverage very hard with man power.

The learning based hybrid rule generation algorithm integrates genetic optimization and SVM to generate and optimize reasonable rules through genetic rules mutation and hyper plane classification. Its structure is issued in Fig. 2.

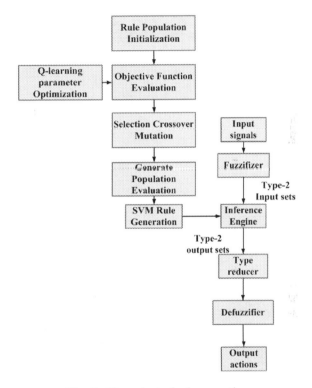

Fig. 2. Flow chart of rule generation

3.1   Genetic Algorithm

As a powerful matheuristic approach, genetic algorithm is to solve difficult combinatorial optimization problems. In the genetic optimization algorithm, rule chromosomes are generated and optimized through iteration, crossover and mutation. In other words, genetic algorithm can help the underwater vehicle to generate and optimize fuzzy rules for target following.

I. Initialization: each binary chromosome individual representation a rule candidate, the total length of the chromosome binary solution vector is 1000 bits. The inputs are

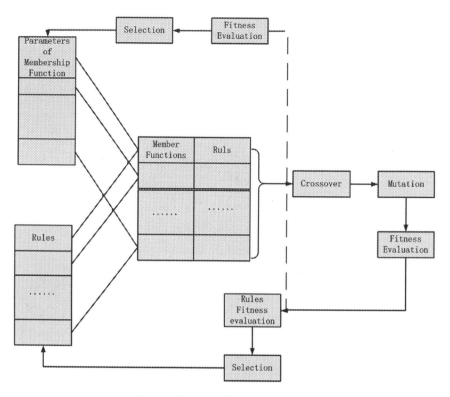

Fig. 3. Diagram of genetic algorithm

the current disturbance, target state in the camera, vehicle speed and headings etc. Each combination of fuzzy rule candidate in a chromosome represents a gene (Fig. 3).

$$FIT = \sum_{i=1}^{m} \left| \frac{k_e(t)(|e_{disi}| + |\dot{e}_{disi}|)}{k_u(t)(\frac{2}{1 + \exp(-k_p e_{disi} - k_d \dot{e}_{disi})} - 1) - a_i} \right| \tag{2}$$

where k_p and k_d are the proportional and derivative gains, k_e and k_u are the parameters of environmental disturbance and vehicle speed, e_{disi} is the distance between the target and the camera core zone, a_i is the corresponding action of fuzzy rule. k_e and k_u can be obtained through Q-learning.

Q-learning is a reinforcement learning algorithm to optimize the action and parameters. It reflects the long term reward by taking the corresponding actions. The parameter of $k_e(t)$ and $k_u(t)$ are obtained through learning and update as follows:

$$\begin{cases} Q(s(t), k_e(t)) = Q(s(t), k_e(t)) + \alpha[r(t+1) + \gamma Q^*(s(t+1)) - Q(s(t), k_e(t))] \\ Q(s(t), k_u(t)) = Q(s(t), k_u(t)) + \alpha[r(t+1) + \gamma Q^*(s(t+1)) - Q(s(t), k_u(t))] \end{cases} \tag{3}$$

where $r(t+1)$ is the reinforcement reward, $Q^*(s(t+1))$ is the optimal estimation in the set of possible actions. the Q value will be updated as:

$$\begin{cases} \Delta Q_{ke} = r(t+1) + \gamma Q^*(s(t+1)) - Q(s(t), k_e(t)) \\ \Delta Q_{ku} = r(t+1) + \gamma Q^*(s(t+1)) - Q(s(t), k_u(t)) \end{cases} \tag{4}$$

The fitness of each individual chromosome will be evaluated through (2). The optimization objective is combined through maximizing the fitness function with the trajectory constraints.

III. Genetic operation: in these operations, new individuals are produced through selection, crossover and mutation. Some of the population are selected and inherited according to roulette-wheel selection. Individuals are chosen at random, crossover is operated so that new individuals are produced.

3.2 Support Vector Machine Optimization Approach

In order to improve the convergence speed and make further rule optimization, support vector machine (SVM) is applied for the system learning. SVM is a reliable and efficient technique to classify and select rules through machine learning. The determine SVM function can be expressed as follows:

$$f(X^l) = w^T \phi(X^l) + b \tag{5}$$

where $X^l = (x_1^l, x_2^l, \ldots, x_{ni}^l)$ is the input signals set. $\phi(X^l)$ is a nonlinear function which maps the input vector X^l into higher dimension feature space, w is ni dimensional weights vector, b is the scalar.

The following optimal problem can be obtained through the two classes separation of a hyper plane:

$$\begin{cases} \min \quad \frac{1}{2} w^T w \\ subject \quad to \quad y_l^i(w^T \phi(X^l) + b_l) \geq 1 \quad \forall l \end{cases} \tag{6}$$

One can formulate the optimal hyper plane through the following optimization problem:

$$\begin{cases} \min \quad \left(\frac{1}{2} w^T w + C \sum_{i=1}^{nr} \xi_i \right) \\ subject \quad to \quad y_i^l(w^T \phi(X^l) + b_i) \geq 1 - \xi_i, \quad \xi_i \geq 0, i = 1, 2, \ldots, nr \end{cases} \tag{7}$$

where $C > 0$ is the regularization parameter which control the trade-off between margin and error for the classification. The primal problem of (7) can be solved by the following Lagrangian function:

$$L = \frac{1}{2}\boldsymbol{w}^T\boldsymbol{w} + C\sum_{i=1}^{nr}\xi_i - \sum_{i=1}^{nr}\alpha_i\xi_i - \sum_{i=1}^{nr}\beta_i[y_i^l(\boldsymbol{w}^T\phi(\boldsymbol{X}^l) + b_i) + \xi_i - 1] \qquad (8)$$

where α_i and $\beta_i(0 \le \beta_i, \alpha_i \le C)$ are Lagrange multipliers. Therefore the following dual quadratic problem can be obtained from (8) and (9):

$$\begin{cases} \max & \left[\sum_{j=1}^{ni}\sum_{i=1}^{ni}\left[\beta_i - \frac{1}{2}\beta_i\beta_jy_i^ly_j^lK\left(x_i^l, x_j^l\right)\right]\right] \\ subject \quad to & \sum_{i=1}^{ni}y_i^l\beta_i = 0, \quad 0 \le \beta_i \le C, i = 1, 2, \ldots, ni \end{cases} \qquad (9)$$

where $K\left(x_i^l, x_j^l\right)$ is a kernel function. $K\left(x_i^l, x_j^l\right)$ is defined as:

$$K\left(x_i^l, x_j^l\right) = \phi\left(x_i^l\right) \cdot \phi\left(x_j^l\right) = \exp\left(-\gamma\left\|x_i^r - x_j^r\right\|^2\right)$$

where γ is the scaling factor. Therefore, the decision function is obtained as:

$$f\left(\boldsymbol{X}^l\right) = \mathrm{sgn}\left[\sum_{i=1}^{ni}\beta_iy_i^lK\left(x_i^l, \boldsymbol{X}^l\right) + b\right] \qquad (10)$$

4   Experimental Results

In order to verify and analyze proposed learning based fuzzy controller, two experiments scenarios are analyzed in a 50 m × 30 m × 10 m tank at the Key Laboratory of Science and Technology on Underwater Vehicle in Harbin Engineering University. Pipe following and organism (sea cucumber) model target following with of open frame ROVs. These two open frame ROVs are both equipped with a depth gauge magnetic, an underwater CCD and a magnetic compass as basic sensors, 6 thrusters including 4 horizontal ones and 2 vertical ones. Moreover the pipe following ROV is equipped with ultrasonic doppler velocity meter (DVL) as position sensors.

In the pipeline following experiment of Figs. 4, 5 and 6, the ROV was cruising with the depth control at 7 m. After image filtering, segmentation, morphological processing and edge detection, the pipeline contour was extracted. The offset distance and angle of pipeline following were obtained through the comparisons between the midline of pipe contour and ROV trace. Figure 5(a) illustrates the pipeline tracking path and reported pipeline position by ROV in the disturbance environment. Figure 5(b) shows the tracking errors and position measurement errors pipeline relative to the actual pipeline position. The inspection results of illustrated precise following and recognizing results in disturbance environment.

The purpose of Figs. 7 and 8 is to manifest the target following experiments of the organism model in the vision based autonomous capture control experiment.

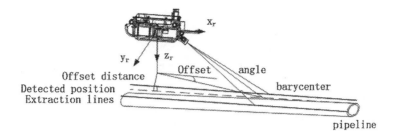

Fig. 4. Pipeline inspection principle

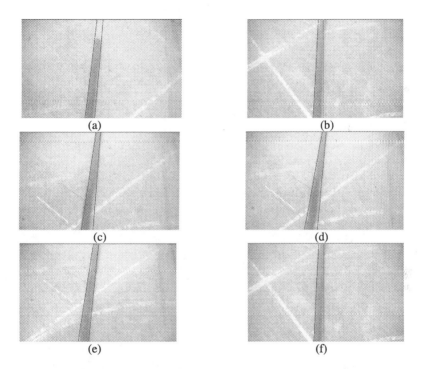

Fig. 5. Pipeline contour extraction and following

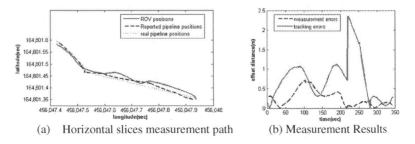

(a)   Horizontal slices measurement path   (b) Measurement Results

Fig. 6. Pipeline following results

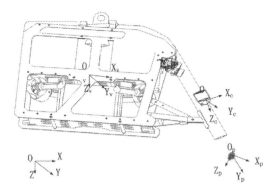

Fig. 7. Target following definition

In the experiment, the ROV recognizes and locks the target in the perception module, trains the ROV learning method and realize target following control with the learning based fuzzy control strategy. The ROV moves towards the recognized target, until the target enter into the absorb range of the absorptive pipe, and realize quick absorption. Since the ROV does not equipped with position or velocity sensor, following and capture can only be realized through the control in the camera coordinate. Thus, the global frame $\sum O$-XYZ, the vehicle frame $\sum O_v$-$X_vY_vZ_v$, the camera frame $\sum O_c$-$X_cY_cZ_c$, and the target frame $\sum O_p$-$X_pY_pZ_p$, have been established in order to realize target following through coordinate transitions.

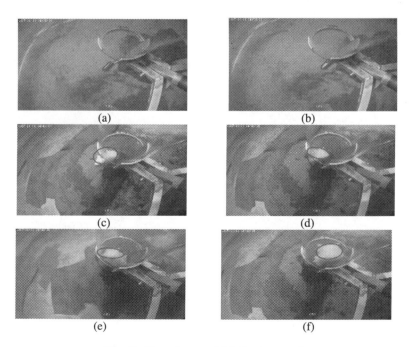

(a)

(b)

(c)

(d)

(e)

(f)

Fig. 8. Organism model following result

5 Conclusions

This study proposes a novel learning based target following control approach through the integration of type-II fuzzy system and support vector maching. In order to overcome uncertain environment disturbance and changing state of the vehicle, the system of type-II fuzzy logic controller is selected. Moreover, in order to generate best fuzzy rules for the target following control, candidate rules have first been initialized and then further generated and mutated through genetic algorithm, finally SVM learning is applied to obtain optimized fuzzy rules. The pipeline following experiments have been performed to verified the proposed controller.

Acknowledgements. This project is supported by National Science Foundation of China (No. 61633009, 51579053, 5129050), it is also supported by the Field Fund of the 13th Five-Year Plan for the Equipment Pre-research Fund (No. 61403120301). All these supports are highly appreciated.

References

1. Benedetto, A., Roberto, C., Riccardo, C., Francesco, F., Jonathan, G., Enrico, M., NiccolÓ, M., Alessandro, R., Andrea, R.: A low cost autonomous underwater vehicle for patrolling and monitoring. J. Eng. Marit. Environ. **231**(3), 740–749 (2017)
2. Mansour, K., Hsiu, M.W., Chih, L.H.: Nonlinear trajectory-tracking control of an autonomous underwater vehicle. Ocean Eng. **145**, 188–198 (2017)
3. Myo, M., Kenta, Y., Akira, Y., Mamoru, M., Shintaro, I.: Visual-servo-based autonomous docking system for underwater vehicle using dual-eyes camera 3D-Pose tracking. In: 2015 IEEE/SICE International Symposium on System Integration (SII), 11–13 December, Meijo University, Nagoya, Japan, pp. 989–994 (2015)
4. Somaiyeh, M.Z., David, M.W., Powers, K.S.: An autonomous reactive architecture for efficient AUV mission time management in realistic dynamic ocean environment. Robot. Auton. Syst. **87**, 81–103 (2017)
5. Taha, E., Mohamed, Z., Kamal, Y.T.: Terminal sliding mode control for the trajectory tracking of underactuated Autonomous Underwater Vehicles. Ocean Eng. **129**, 613–625 (2017)
6. Yanwu, Z., Brian, K., Jordan, M. S., Robert, S. McEwen, et al.: Isotherm tracking by an autonomous underwater vehicle in drift mode. IEEE J. Ocean. Eng. **42**(4), 808–817 (2017)
7. Khoshnam, S., Mehdi, D.: Line-of-sight target tracking control of underactuated autonomous underwater vehicles. Ocean Eng. **133**, 244–252 (2017)
8. Xue, Q.: Spatial target path following control based on Nussbaum gain method for underactuated underwater vehicle. Ocean Eng. **104**, 680–685 (2015)
9. Enric, G., Ricard, C., Narcís, P., David, R., et al.: Coverage path planning with real-time replanning and surface reconstruction for inspection of three-dimensional underwater structures using autonomous underwater vehicles. J. Field Robot. **32**(7), 952–983 (2015)
10. Marc, C., Junku, Y., Joan, B., Pere, R.: A behavior-based scheme using reinforcement learning for autonomous underwater vehicles. IEEE J. Ocean. Eng. **30**(2), 416–427 (2005)
11. Mae, L.S.: Marine Robot Autonomy. Springer, New York (2013)
12. Jong, W.P., Hwan, J.K., Young, C.K., Dong, W.K.: Advanced fuzzy potential field method for mobile robot obstacle avoidance. Comput. Intell. Neurosci. **2016**, 13 (2016). Article ID 6047906

Optimal Shape Design of an Autonomous Underwater Vehicle Based on Gene Expression Programming

Qirong Tang[1]([✉]), Yinghao Li[1], Zhenqiang Deng[1], Di Chen[1],
Ruiqin Guo[1], and Hai Huang[2]

[1] Laboratory of Robotics and Multibody System, School of Mechanical Engineering,
Tongji University, Shanghai 201804, People's Republic of China
qirong.tang@outlook.com
[2] National Key Laboratory of Science and Technology on Underwater Vehicle,
Harbin Engineering University, Harbin 150001, People's Republic of China

Abstract. A novel strategy combining gene expression programming and crowding distance based multi-objective particle swarm algorithm is presented in this paper to optimize an underwater robot's shape. The gene expression programming method is used to establish the surrogate model of resistance and surrounded volume of the robot. After that, the resistance and surrounded volume are set as two optimized factors and Pareto optimal solutions are then obtained by using multi-objective particle swarm optimization. Finally, results are compared with the hydrodynamic calculations. Result shows the efficiency of the method proposed in the paper in the optimal shape design of an underwater robot.

Keywords: Autonomous underwater vehicle · Shape optimization
Gene expression programming
Multi-objective particle swarm optimization

1 Introduction

Being the indispensable carrier to be encountered in the exploration of marine resources, underwater robotics have seen an increasing interest from research institutes to enterprises [1]. At present, the common used underwater robots include remotely operated vehicles (ROVs) and autonomous underwater vehicles (AUVs). Energized by batteries, AUV can adapt to the external environment changes to complete the tasks. Therefore, more and more countries have carried out systematic studies on the AUV in recent years.

Since AUV is usually working in quite a complex environment, and meanwhile, in order to achieve precise positioning, its tasks are often required to have strong resistance to water flow [2]. Therefore, AUV needs to have a configuration of good smoothness of its shape, so as to reduce the friction resistance, reduce energy consumption and as a result to improve its endurance. Numerical

© Springer International Publishing AG, part of Springer Nature 2018
Y. Tan et al. (Eds.): ICSI 2018, LNCS 10942, pp. 132–141, 2018.
https://doi.org/10.1007/978-3-319-93818-9_13

simulation techniques such as computational fluid dynamics (CFD) and finite element analysis, are not only spending plenty of time to solve and optimize the simulation model, but also very expensive which makes it quite impractical to solely rely on the numerical simulation techniques for design and optimization of AUV [3]. To overcome these computational problems, engineers begin to use surrogate models instead of simulation models [4]. The most commonly used surrogate models are response surface model(RSM) [5], Kriging model [6] and radial basis function model(RBF) [7]. All of them have a good effect on the optimization problem of shape of AUVs. However, the prediction accuracy and robustness of RSM are very poor for the highly nonlinear problems. Kriging model is lack of transparency and time-consuming to be constructed. RBF model requires plenty of sample points. What's more, the optimization problem of AUV is often highly nonlinear, and the number of sample points is very limited, so it is necessary and even demanded to use a surrogate model that meets all these requirements.

Based on genetic algorithm and genetic programming, gene expression programming (GEP) is an evolutionary algorithm that is originally put forward for creation of computer programs [8]. It has high transparency and can provide an intuitive and simple explicit function expression. What's more, its prediction accuracy and robustness are not subject to the change of sample scale. As a new adaptive evolutionary algorithm, the impact of GEP is far reaching, e.g., function finding [9], classifier construction [10] and so on. Since the relation between water resistance and section coefficients is highly nonlinear, meanwhile, sample points are limited, GEP is used to establish the surrogate model of resistance and surrounded volume based partially on hydrodynamic calculations.

Multi-objective particle swarm algorithm (MOPSO) is a multi-objective optimization algorithm, which is proposed by Coello and Lechuga in 2002. Because of its ease of implementation, it has been applied on many optimization problems successfully. What's more, it is more effective than GA and other optimization algorithms in many situations. So MOPSO is used to optimize an underwater robot's shape.

This paper is organized as follows. Section 2 describes the gene expression programming model. In Sect. 3, the strategy combining gene expression programming and crowding distance based multi-objective particle swarm algorithm is used to optimize an underwater robot's shape. In Sect. 4, the effectiveness of the proposed method is verified with comparisons. While Sect. 5 concludes the paper.

2   Gene Expression Programming Model

GEP is originally proposed by Ferreira for creation of computer programs [8]. It is a genotype/phenotype genetic algorithm. During reproduction, like genetic algorithm (GA), the individuals in GEP are encoded as linear strings of fixed length. At the fitness evaluation stage, like genetic programming (GP), the chromosomes are translated into expression trees which are nonlinear entities of different sizes and shapes. The detailed introduction of transformation between genotype and phenotype can be found in Ref. [8]. So in GEP, genotype is totally separated from the phenotype which makes it compromise the merits of GA and GP and greatly improves its performance.

Like other evolutionary algorithms, GEP starts from generating the initial population randomly. Then the chromosomes of each individual are translated into expression trees, and the fitness of each expression is calculated. After that the best program is selected to reproduce by genetic manipulation, which includes replication, mutation, inversion, transposition, recombination, then the next generation is created. After that, the fitness of the new generation is evaluated, and the parent is replaced, the next generation is generated by genetic manipulation, and the evaluation is repeated until the end of the evolution is satisfied. The basic theory of GEP is shown as follows.

2.1   Genes and Chromosomes

Different from GA and GP, GEP has an unique chromosomes encoded mode. Its genes are usually composed of a head and a tail, see Fig. 1. Head symbols can be taken from the function set and terminal set, whereas tail symbol can only be selected from terminal set. Usually function set consists of basic arithmetic functions, Boolean operators and nonlinear functions. For example, function set=$\{+, Q, Sin, Not, Nor\}$, where $Q(a)$ represents $\sqrt{a}$. Terminal set includes the inputs of the model such as input variable names or constants. For instance, terminal set=$\{a, b, A, 5\}$. For each problem, the length of the head h is preset by the designer, and the length of the tail t is evaluated in the form of Eq. (1).

$$t = h * (m - 1) + 1, \tag{1}$$

where m is the number of arguments of function which has the most arguments.

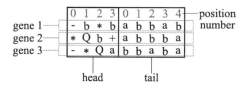

Fig. 1. The gene composition of GEP

In GEP, each chromosome is composed of one or more genes of equal length. The detailed introduction of genes and chromosomes can be found in Ref. [8].

2.2   Fitness Function Design

The chromosomes represent the solution of the problem, and the fitness function is used to evaluate the pros and cons of chromosomes and guide the evolution of the programs. The fitness function is defined in this study in the form of Eq. (2).

$$f_i = 1000 \times \frac{1}{1 + R}, \tag{2}$$

where f_i is the fitness of the program i. $R=\sqrt{\sum_{i=1}^{n}\frac{(y_i-\hat{y}_i)^2}{n}}$, y_i is the actual response value, $\hat{y}_i$ is the predicted value, n is the number of observations.

2.3   Genetic Operation

In GEP, genetic operations are adopted to update the population as they are applied in the GA. The basic genetic operation of GEP is composed of selection, replication, mutation, inversion, transposition, and recombination. Since the mutation operator randomly changes an element of a chromosome into another element, preserving the rule that the tails contain only terminals. What's more, a mutation in the coding sequence of a gene has a much more profound effect: it usually drastically reshapes the expression tree [8], so mutation is one of the most important genetic operators. And its range is suggested from 0.01 to 0.1 by scholars [8]. What's more, insert sequence transposition is the unique operator of GEP.

3   Optimal Shape Design of Autonomous Underwater Vehicle Based on GEP

The optimization of the shape of AUV is an important step in the design process of AUV. Firstly, the initial sample point and its response value are obtained numerically in computer. Then a hybrid optimization method combing GEP and the crowding distance based multi-objective particle swarm optimization algorithm (MOPSO-CD) is used to optimize the shape of AUV. The detailed introduction of MOPSO-CD can be found in [11]. The overall flowchart combing GEP and MOPSO-CD to solve the optimal shape design problem of AUV is shown in Fig. 2.

3.1   Nystrom Linetype

Based on the principle of least resistance, as well taking into account the needs of internal components layout, Nystrom linetype is selected to design AUV, which is shown in Fig. 3. So in the longitudinal direction of AUV, inlet section is a semi-ellipse and outflow section is a parabolic curve. The curve equations of the bow and stern are

$$y = \frac{D_0}{2}\left[1-\left(\frac{X_E}{L_E}\right)^{n_e}\right]^{\frac{1}{n_e}}, \tag{3}$$

$$y = \frac{D_0}{2}\left[1-\left(\frac{X_R}{L_R}\right)^{n_r}\right], \tag{4}$$

respectively, where X_E is the distance between the inlet section and the maximum cross section, X_R is the distance between the outflow section and the maximum cross section, n_e is the index of inlet flow ellipse, n_r is the index of outflow parabola.

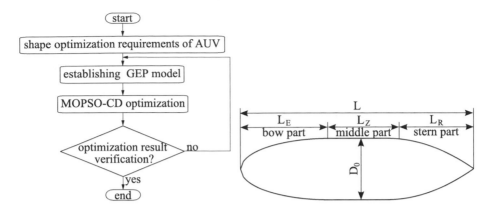

Fig. 2. Flowchart of the whole optimization procedure

Fig. 3. The chart of nystrom revolving hull form

3.2 Establishment of GEP Model

In the process of optimization, the total length of AUV is 2.7 m, the diameter of the middle segment is 0.75 m, the calculated speed is 1.542 m/s. Four design factors are selected, see details in Table 1.

Table 1. The meaning and range of design variables

Design variable	The meaning of variable	The range of variable
x_1	the ratio of the length of bow to the total length	$0.148 - 0.223$
x_2	the ratio of the length of stern to the total length	$0.185 - 0.285$
x_3	shape factor of the bow	$1.5 - 4.0$
x_4	shape factor of the stern	$1.5 - 3.0$

In the process of optimizing the shape of AUV, it is necessary to carry out specific manners of constructing GEP model, so as to obtain the factor sensitivity as simple as possible, i.e., with less sample points. The optimal latin hypercube method is selected to construct GEP model. Design variables in this case are divided into 50 levels in the design space, then the four design variables are combined randomly each time, and each level of the design variables is used only once. Finally 50 datasets are obtained.

Then two mathematical equations based on the GEP method are established in the form of resistance $F = f(x_1, x_2, x_3, x_4)$ and surrounded volume $V = g(x_1, x_2, x_3, x_4)$, where x_1, x_2, x_3 and x_4 are the inputs of the model, i.e. independent variables, resistance and surrounded volume are the model outputs, i.e.

dependent variables. The GEP algorithm in this study comprises thirty chromosomes. Its head size and gene number are eight and three, respectively. An iterative process is employed to select the optimal parameters. The correlation coefficient square (R^2) is calculated to further examine the performance of the model, which is defined in the form of Eq. (5).

$$R^2 = 1 - \frac{\sum_{i=1}^{n}(y_i - \hat{y}_i)^2}{\sum_{i=1}^{n}(y_i - \overline{y})^2}, \tag{5}$$

where $\overline{y}$ is the mean value of actual response. The closer is R^2 to 1, the higher is fitting accuracy of the GEP model.

Based on the Sect. 2, the analytical forms of the proposed GEP models are calculated as following:

$$F = 10^{\arctan\left\{\arccos\{max[(c_0 - x_4) \cdot c_1, \tan(x_1)]\}\right\}} + \cos(x_1 \cdot c_2) \cdot x_3 + \frac{1}{x_2} + max(x_4, c_3)$$
$$+ \arctan\{\ln\{c_4 - \tan[\tan(c_5 + x_4)]\}^2\}, \tag{6}$$

$$V = \sqrt[3]{\exp[\sqrt[3]{\cos(x_3) \cdot (\frac{1}{c_6} - x_1)]}^2} + \sqrt[3]{min|\arctan(A), \arctan\frac{1}{(x_3 - c_7)}|} \tag{7}$$
$$+ \sqrt[3]{\arcsin\{[max(c_{10}, x_1)] \cdot (c_9)^2 - B\}},$$

where,

$$\mathbf{c} = \begin{bmatrix} c_1 & c_2 & c_3 & c_4 & c_5 \\ c_6 & c_7 & c_8 & c_9 & c_{10} \end{bmatrix} = \begin{bmatrix} 1.8852 & 2.0651 & -3.0430 & 5.4558 & 8.4771 \\ -9.5433 & -6.6160 & 8.6543 & -0.1174 & 0.1969 \end{bmatrix},$$

$$A = \frac{1}{(c_8 - x_4 - \frac{x_3 + x_1}{2})}, \quad B = min(\frac{x_2 + x_1}{2}.x_2), \quad c_0 = 1.6126.$$

In order to verify the established GEP model, the response surface models(RSM) of resistance and surrounded volume are constructed. The R^2 and R are selected as the performance indices of the GEP model and RSM, which are listed in Table 2. According to the performance indices values, the GEP model is more accurate than RSM in establishing the surrogate model of resistance, and the GEP model almost has the same accuracy as RSM in establishing the surrogate model of surrounded volume.

Figure 4 illustrates the measured values of resistance in comparison to the predictions of GEP model and RSM in the testing process. Figure 5 illustrates the measured values of surrounded volume in comparison to the predictions of GEP model and RSM in the testing process. These figures indicate that the obtained results for resistance through the GEP model are much closer to the measured values, compared to the results based on RSM, and the obtained results for surrounded volume via the GEP model are almost the same as RSM. So GEP model is more accurate than RSM based in constructing the surrogate model of resistance and surrounded volume.

Table 2. The obtained performance indices values for developed models

Model	Training set		Test set	
	R^2	R	R^2	R
The GEP model of resistance	0.9706	0.1624	0.9561	0.2508
The RSM model of resistance	0.8340	0.3861	0.8359	0.4850
The GEP model of surrounded volume	0.9838	0.0039	0.9851	0.0045
The RSP model of surrounded volume	0.9985	0.0012	0.9979	0.0017

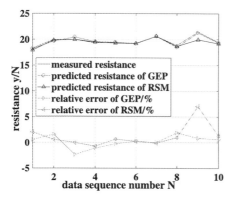

Fig. 4. Resistance prediction curve   **Fig. 5.** Volume prediction curve

3.3   Establishment of Optimization Model

After establishing the GEP model of resistance and surrounded volume of AUV, the shape optimization model of AUV is studied, in which the resistance and the inverse of surrounded volume are set as two optimized factors and x_1, x_2, x_3, x_4 are also selected as design factors. And the optimization model is established as follows

$$\begin{cases} \min(F, \frac{1}{V}), \\ s.t. \quad 0.148 \leq x_1 \leq 0.223, \quad 0.185 \leq x_2 \leq 0.285, \\ \quad\quad 1.5 \leq x_3 \leq 4, \quad\quad\quad\quad 1.5 \leq x_4 \leq 3, \end{cases} \tag{8}$$

3.4   Optimization results

After constructing the optimization model, MOPSO-CD is used to solve it. In the computational procedure, the population size of particle swarm is 200, the evolutionary algebra is 400, the inertia weight $w \in [0.4, 0.9]$, the self cognitive learning factor and social cognitive learning factor $c_1, c_2 \in [0.5, 2.5]$, and the capacity of external archive is 80. The Pareto optimal solution set of resistance and the inverse of surrounded volume is shown in Fig. 6. The scatter diagram expresses the Pareto frontier initially. For the details of MOPSO-CD, please refer to [11].

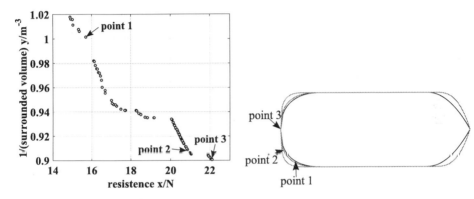

Fig. 6. Pareto optimal solutions of AUV shape design

Fig. 7. Linetype of the selected point

4   Model Verification

In order to verify the effectiveness of the proposed method, three points of the Pareto optimal solution are selected arbitrary, which are shown in Figs. 6 and 7. The multi-objective optimization results for the shape design of AUV are shown in Figs. 8 and 9. According to Figs. 8 and 9, we can find that all the relative errors are smaller than 1.5%, which illustrates that the GEP model can ensure the accuracy of the optimal design. In the case of selecting the design points, it depends on the actual situation and the designers' preferences.

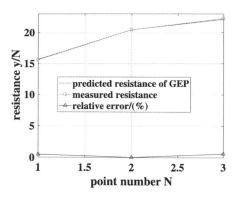
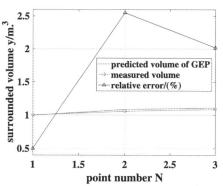

Fig. 8. Pareto optimal solutions of AUV shape design

Fig. 9. Resistance values for developed models

5   Conclusion

This paper puts forward an optimization strategy based on gene expression programming and crowding distance based multi-objective optimization. It is used for optimizing the shape of an autonomous underwater vehicle, where a mathematical model between the design variables and the resistance and surrounded volume of AUV is built. And there is quite a good agreement between the predicted and measured resistance and surrounded volume. What's more, crowding distance based multi-objective optimization method is used to obtain the Pareto optimal solutions of the shape optimization problem.

The proposed methodology has the ability to reduce the cost of CFD simulation, effectively improve the efficiency of optimal shape design of AUV and provide an example for the following AUV design.

Acknowledgements. This work is supported by the project of National Natural Science Foundation of China (No. 61603277; No. 51579053; No. 61633009), the 13th-Five-Year-Plan on Common Technology, key project (No. 41412050101), the Shanghai Aerospace Science and Technology Innovation Fund (SAST 2016017). Meanwhile, this work is also partially supported by the Youth 1000 program project (No. 1000231901), as well as by the Key Basic Research Project of Shanghai Science and Technology Innovation Plan (No. 15JC1403300). All these supports are highly appreciated.

References

1. Sarkar, N., Podder, T.: Coordinated motion planning and control of autonomous underwater vehicle-manipulator systems subject to drag optimization. IEEE J. Oceanic Eng. **26**(2), 228–239 (2001)
2. Zhang, H., Pan, Y.: The resistance performance of a dish-shaped underwater vehicle. J. Shanghai Jiaotong Univ. **40**(6), 978–982 (2006)
3. Jin, R., Chen, W., Simpson, T.: Comparative studies of meta-modelling techniques under multiple modelling criteria. Struct. Multidiscip. Optim. **23**(1), 1–13 (2001)

4. Crombecq, K., Gorissen, D., Deschrijver, D., Dhaene, T.: A novel hybrid sequential design strategy for global surrogate modeling of computer experiments. SIAM J. Sci. Comput. **33**(4), 1948–1974 (2001)
5. Yang, Z., Yu, X., Pang, Y.: Optimization of submersible shape based on multi-objective genetic algorithm. J. Ship Mech. **15**, 874–880 (2011)
6. Song, L., Wang, J., Yang, Z.: Research on shape optimization design of submersible based on Kriging model. J. Ship Mechan. **17**, 8–13 (2013)
7. Shao, X., Yu, M., Guo, Y.: Structure optimization for very large oil cargo tanks based on FEM. Shipbuild. China **49**, 41–51 (2008)
8. Ferreira, C.: Gene expression programming: a new adaptive algorithm for solving problems. Comput. Sci. **2**, 87–129 (2001)
9. Yang, Y., Li, X., Gao, L.: A new approach for predicting and collaborative evaluating the cutting force in face milling based on gene expression programming. J. Netw. Comput. Appl. **36**(6), 1540–1550 (2013)
10. Zhou, C., Xiao, W., Tirpak, T., Nelson, P.: Evolving accurate and compact classification rules with gene expression programming. IEEE Trans. Evol. Comput. **7**(6), 519–531 (2003)
11. Raquel, C., Naval, P.: An effective use of crowding distance in multi-objective particle swarm optimization. In: Proceedings of the 2005 Workshops on Genetic and Evolutionary Computation, June 25–29, Washington DC, pp. 257–264 (2005)

GLANS: GIS Based Large-Scale Autonomous Navigation System

Manhui Sun$^{(\boxtimes)}$, Shaowu Yang, and Henzhu Liu

State Key Laboratory of High-Performance Computing, College of Computer,
National University of Defensive Technology, Deya Street No. 109,
Changsha 410001, China
smh_038@163.com, shaowu.yang@nudt.edu.cn,
hengzhu_liu@263.net

Abstract. The simultaneous localization and mapping (SLAM) systems are widely used for self-localization of a robot, which is the basis of autonomous navigation. However, the state-of-art SLAM systems cannot suffice when navigating in large-scale environments due to memory limit and localization errors. In this paper, we propose a Geographic Information System (GIS) based autonomous navigation system (GLANS). In GLANS, a topological path is suggested by GIS database and a robot can move accordingly while being able to detect the obstacles and adjust the path. Moreover, the mapping results can be shared among multi-robots to re-localize a robot in the same area without GPS assistance. It has been proved functioning well in the simulation environment of a campus scenario.

Keywords: SLAM · GIS database · Navigation at large-scale

1   Introduction

To enable autonomous navigation, SLAM is usually adopted. However, due to the limit of on-board memory and computing power, it is hard for a robot to generate map and autonomously navigate in large-scale environments simultaneously. Traditional SLAM methods have unresolved issues in large-scale environment, such as pose estimation [1] and route searching [2]. The map storage size grows fast while the error accumulates in localization making it impossible to navigate [4].

In this paper, we propose a novel autonomous navigation system GLANS. It consists of a Geographic Information System (GIS) database, a SLAM system and a hybrid path planning module. A topological shortest path is suggested by GIS and a robot can move accordingly while being able to detect the obstacles and adjust the path.

Overall, this paper makes the following contributions:

- We propose a large-scale navigation system GLANS that enables GIS database to provide road path to guide a robot to navigate in a large-scale environment.
- We propose a hybrid navigation method which combines topological navigation with metric navigation. It has been proved functioning well in the simulation environment of a campus scenario.

© Springer International Publishing AG, part of Springer Nature 2018
Y. Tan et al. (Eds.): ICSI 2018, LNCS 10942, pp. 142–150, 2018.
https://doi.org/10.1007/978-3-319-93818-9_14

- We prove the mapping result can be used for re-localization without GPS assistance and the error is tolerable.

2   Related Work

2.1   GIS Based Robotic Application

Geographic information contains a lot of traffic information, satellite maps and other spatial data of a city, which can guide robots in a city. Gutierrez proposed an autonomous spacecraft mission planning framework based on GIS [5]. The framework uses processed GIS information to guide the aircraft, defining the no-fly zones and hot spots to support the mission planning and simulation to improve the flight in real-time. Self-driving car uses GPS and traffic data in Google Map, which is part of GIS. Google and Tesla Motors have been dedicated in this field and have done a lot of work [6–8]. Doersch et al. [14] proposed a localization method of comparing the current image of the camera with the representative landmark image extracted from the Google Street. By recognizing the windows, balconies and other obvious features on the street, the robot can localize itself on the street.

GIS is more powerful than map application for its excellent ability on spatial data calculation and versatility cross systems. However, little work has been done to use spatial data from GIS database on Robot Operating System (ROS) [9] which is the most widely used system on mobile robots.

2.2   Autonomous Navigation at Large-Scale

Autonomous navigation at large-scale area with limited computational resources remains a problem. The memory cost can be really high when it comes to mapping at large scale. Castellanos et al. [3] proposed a method of sub-dividing the map data to save the memory cost at large scale, however it cannot effectively solve the map data problem, and the extended Kalman Filter can bring the error to the whole SLAM state estimation. To enable a robot to navigate in large-scale environment, extra guidance is needed. Konolige [10] proposed a topological navigation method based on odometry and laser-scan results. Adding topological edges between navigable places makes it efficient to plan path in navigation. Lerkerkerer [11] proposed method of long-term mobile robot autonomy in large-scale environments using a novel hybrid metric-topological mapping system. System architecture was proposed that aims at satisfying how robots can take inspiration from humans to perform better in mapping, localization and navigation for large scale.

So far, no extra information other than the scan data is offered to a robot. The robots need more information to understand the surroundings and make better decisions with less computation.

3   System Overview

In this paper, we propose an autonomous navigation system GLANS which consists of GIS database, SLAM system, and navigation module. The system enables a robot to navigate at large-scale by adopting path data in GIS database. The structure of the system is showed as Fig. 1.

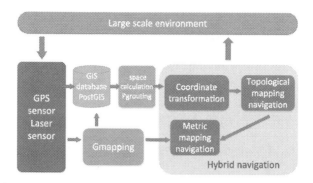

Fig. 1. The structure of GIS-based large-scale autonomous navigation system (GLANS)

For the GIS database, we use PostGIS [12] which is a popular open source database with extended function module pgRouting [13] to calculate shortest path. As we use standard GIS topology data [18], PostGIS can be replaced by other GIS databases as well.

For SLAM part, GMapping [16] is used to generate the local metric map based on 2D laser sensor. It can be replaced by other SLAM systems such as MonoSLAM, ORB-SLAM or even binocular visual SLAM like RTAB-MAP when sensor varies. The system is based on ROS. The source code is publicly available [20].

4   Navigation in Large Scale Environments

4.1   GIS Based Shortest Path Generation

Topological maps are made up out of nodes and edges, like subway map and road map where nodes define places and edges define direct navigability path. Since city road information is usually available in city GIS in standard GIS topology data format, we focus on how a robot can use GIS data. To take advantage of the calculation power GIS database have, a shortest navigable path is suggested by GIS.

When a robot is given a destination from the starting point, it will look up for shortest path between these two spots in GIS database. We use pgRouting [13] to generate the shortest path based on Dijkstra algorithm. Since the path is noted with GPS information, the robot cannot use it directly without transformation. We adopt the normal transformation used in GPS signal processing [21]. First, turn the GPS coordinates into geocentric coordinates under the geocentric fixed coordinate system which is known as Earth-Centered, Earth-Fixed (ECEF) coordinates [14]. Then transform it into local ground East-North-Up (ENU) coordinates where geometric sphere of earth is considered [15]. Finally, transform ENU into rectangular coordinates. The transformation process is shown in Fig. 2. After the transformation, the robot is able to use the shortest path for navigation. A ROS package named rospg is created to realize the process.

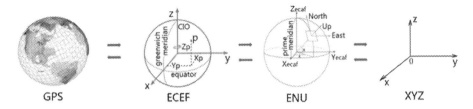

Fig. 2. The transformation of Geographic coordinate system to the Cartesian coordinate system

4.2 Hybrid Navigation in Large-Scale Environment

We propose a hybrid navigation method combining global topological path and local metric map base on [11].

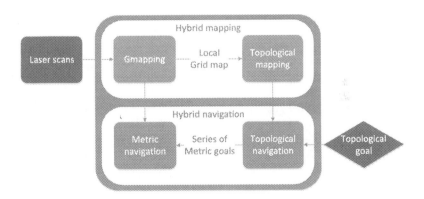

Fig. 3. The main components of hybrid navigation

In global topological planning, the shortest path from GIS database is formed with a bunch of nodes miles from each other. It may out of the sensor rage and make it hard for a robot to follow. We segment the long path into sub-paths where the distance between nodes is adjusted to 10 m. From the starting point, the following point along the path can be served as the next target point of the local metric planning until the robot finally reaches its destination.

In local metric planning, we use GMapping [16] to build the local grid map and to check for navigability. Based on mapping result, the local path planning calculate the lowest cost path and take local obstacles into account, then generate a local path and corresponding velocity instructions based on the global path and the local map. As shown in Fig. 3.

The hybrid navigation algorithm enables a robot to take advantage of the road information in GIS as topological map while adapting itself to local circumstances, so that it can realize autonomous navigation in large-scale environment.

4.3   Re-localization and Path Optimization

After the navigation, we reserve the mapping result of the whole area and try to find if the robot can perform better.

Despite GPS can be quite accurate, it fails between tall buildings or trees. It is better if a robot can independently localize itself on the help of the former mapping result without GPS assistance. We adopt adaptive Monte Carlo localization (AMCL) method [19] which takes in a laser-based map, laser scans, transforms messages, and outputs pose estimates. On startup, AMCL initializes its particle filter according to the parameters provided. Then it base on the result of the map data to adjust the particles to calculate the best location of the robot.

We perform a path optimization to enable the robot to find the best navigable way in when revisiting the same area. During the first navigation, a topological map based on moving trajectory is made with nodes apart every 1 m. All nodes that are navigable directly based on the scanning result are lined up as a path. As Fig. 4 shows, the patrol path around the building is optimized in red path.

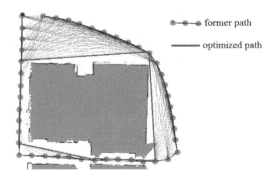

Fig. 4. Path optimization

5   Experimental Evaluation

In the simulation experiment, a campus scene is modeled in Gazebo simulator, which includes office buildings, residential buildings, gas stations, some roadblocks and fences. A Turtlebot was used as a prototype of the mobile robot in the simulation. Specific scenes are shown in Fig. 5.

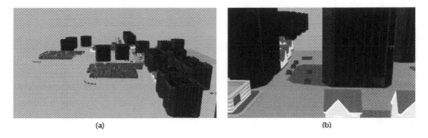

Fig. 5. Simulation environment. (a) is an overview of the environment and (b) is a closer look

We construct the path data of the environment in GIS data standard, calculating the shortest path between two given points in database and display it in QGIS [17], a displaying tool of GIS data, as red line. See Fig. 6.

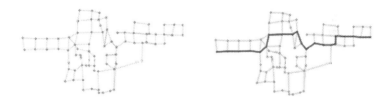

Fig. 6. Shortest path generation.

As shown in Fig. 7, the path given from GIS database is the green line, and the actual moving trajectory is the red line. The green circle nodes are the sub-target points for navigation. It can be seen from the results that the robot successfully use the path data and move accordingly.

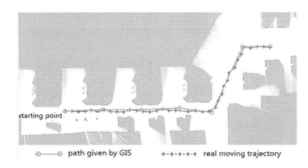

Fig. 7. Comparison of simulation path and navigation path (Color figure online)

Figure 8 shows the results of robot mapping, which covers 80000 square meters of area with laser range of 30 m. The boundaries of the obstacles are clear for obstacle

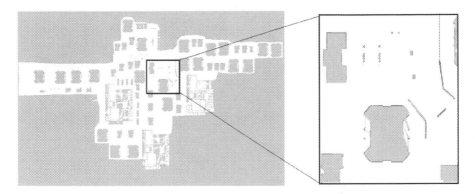

Fig. 8. Mapping results

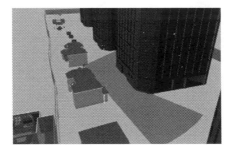

Fig. 9. Obstacle avoidance (Color figure online)

avoidance. In Fig. 9, the robot veers left to bypass the house. The blue shadow is the laser scan zone.

In re-localization experiment, the robot has been moving for 4000 m with the average localization error is 0.1854 m and the variance is 0.01193. Figure 10 shows the trajectory comparison of the truth position and the re-localization method. The localization error has not been accumulated as the moving distance is increasing.

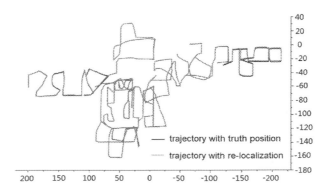

Fig. 10. Trajectory comparison

6 Conclusion and Future Work

In this paper, we propose an autonomous navigation system, GLANS, which enables a robot to navigate in large-scale environment. It consists of GIS database, SLAM and navigation modules. In GLANS, a topological path is suggested by GIS and a robot can move accordingly while being able to detect the obstacles and adjust the path. The re-localization experiments indicate the robot can use the mapping result for localization without GPS assistance.

This work reveals the feasibility of robot using GIS database to gain spatial data and to reserve mapping data. By adding robotic mapping, the original GIS information is enriched. What's more, the conserved mapping result can be used in map sharing for robot swarm.

References

1. Ip, Y.L., et al.: Segment-based map building using enhanced adaptive fuzzy clustering algorithm for mobile robot applications. J. Intell. Robot. Syst. **35**(3), 221–245 (2002)
2. Dissanayake, M.W.M.G., et al.: A solution to the simultaneous localization and map building (SLAM) problem. IEEE Trans. Robot. Autom. **17**(3), 229–241 (2001)
3. Castellanos, J.A., et al.: The SPmap: a probabilistic framework for simultaneous localization and map building. IEEE Trans. Robot. Autom. **15**(5), 948–952 (1999)
4. Shi, C.X., et al.: Topological map building and navigation in large-scale environments. Robot **29**(5), 433–438 (2007)
5. Gutiérrez, P., et al.: Mission planning, simulation and supervision of unmanned aerial vehicle with a GIS-based framework. In: Proceedings of the Third International Conference on Informatics in Control, Automation and Robotics, ICINCO 2006, Setúbal, Portugal, pp. 310–317. DBLP, August 2006
6. He, X.: Vision/odometer autonomous navigation based on rat SLAM for land vehicles. In: Proceedings of 2015 International Conference on Advances in Mechanical Engineering and Industrial Informatics (2015)
7. Liu, D.X.: A research on LADAR-vision fusion and its application in cross country autonomous navigation vehicle. National University of Defense Technology (2009)
8. Lan, Y., Liu, W.W., Dong, W.: Research on rule editing and code generation for the high-level decision system of unmanned vehicles. Comput. Sci. Eng. **37**(8), 1510–1516 (2015)
9. Quigley, M., Conley, K., Gerkey, B., et al.: ROS: an open-source robot operating system. In: ICRA Workshop on Open Source Software (2009)
10. Konolige, K., Marder-Eppstein, E., Marthi, B.: Navigation in hybrid metric-topological maps. In: IEEE International Conference on Robotics and Automation, pp. 3041–3047. IEEE (2011)
11. Lekkerkerker, C.J.: Gaining by forgetting: towards long-term mobile robot autonomy in large scale environments using a novel hybrid metric-topological mapping system (2014)
12. Zheng, J., et al.: A PostGIS-based pedestrian way finding module using OpenStreetMap data **12**, 1–5 (2013)
13. Zhang, L., He, X.: Route Search Base on pgRouting. In: Wu, Y. (ed.) ECCV 2016. AISC, vol. 115, pp. 1003–1007. Springer, Heidelberg (2012). https://doi.org/10.1007/978-3-642-25349-2_133

14. Krzyżek, R., Skorupa, B.: The influence of application a simplified transformation model between reference frames ECEF and ECI onto prediction accuracy of position and velocity of GLONASS satellites. Rep. Geodesy & Geoinformatics **99**(1), 19–27 (2015)
15. Huang, L.: ON NEU (ENU) coordinate system. J. Geodesy Geodyn. (2006). Tianjin
16. Grisetti, G., Stachniss, C., Burgard, W.: Improving grid-based SLAM with Rao-Blackwellized particle filters by adaptive proposals and selective resampling. In: Proceedings of the IEEE International Conference on Robotics and Automation (ICRA) (2005)
17. Macleod, C.D.: An Introduction to Using GIS in Marine Biology: Supplementary Workbook Seven An Introduction to Using QGIS (Quantum GIS). Pictish Beast Publications (2015)
18. Song, X.: Reading of GIS spatial data format. J. Cap. Normal Univ. (2006)
19. Luo, R., Hong, B.: Coevolution based adaptive Monte Carlo localization (CEAMCL). Int. J. Adv. Robot. Syst. **1**(1), 183–190 (2004)
20. https://github.com/xxx. (for anonymous demand)
21. Yuan, D., et al.: The coordinate transformation method and accuracy analysis in GPS measurement. Procedia Environ. Sci. Part A **12**, 232–237 (2012)
22. Tang, M., Mao, X., Guessoum, Z.: Research on an infectious disease transmission by flocking birds. Sci. World J. **2013**(12), 196823 (2013)
23. Tang, M., Zhu, H., Mao, X.: A lightweight social computing. Approach to emergency management policy selection. IEEE Trans. Syst. Man Cybern. Syst. **1**(1–2), 1–13 (2015)

Fuzzy Logic Approaches

Extraction of Knowledge with Population-Based Metaheuristics Fuzzy Rules Applied to Credit Risk

Patricia Jimbo Santana[1], Laura Lanzarini[2] (ID),
and Aurelio F. Bariviera[3]([⊠]) (ID)

[1] Facultad de Ciencias Administrativas, Universidad Central del Ecuador,
Carrera de Contabilidad y Auditoría, Quito, Ecuador
prjimbo@uce.edu.ec
[2] Facultad de Informática, Instituto de Investigación en Informática LIDI,
Universidad Nacional de la Plata, La Plata, Buenos Aires, Argentina
laural@lidi.info.unlp.edu.ar
[3] Universitat Rovira i Virgili, Department of Business,
Avenida de la Universitat, 1 Reus, Tarragona, Spain
aurelio.fernandez@urv.cat

Abstract. One of the goals of financial institutions is to reduce credit risk. Consequently they must properly select customers. There are a variety of methodologies for credit scoring, which analyzes a wide variety of personal and financial variables of the potential client. These variables are heterogeneous making that their analysis is long and tedious. This paper presents an alternative method that, based on the subject information, offers a set of classification rules with three main characteristics: adequate precision, low cardinality and easy interpretation. This is because the antecedent consists of a small number of attributes that can be modeled as fuzzy variables. This feature, together with a reduced set of rules allows obtaining useful patterns to understand the relationships between data, and make the right decisions for the financial institutions. The smaller the number of analyzed variables of the potential customer, the simpler the model will be. In this way, credit officers may give an answer to the loan application in the shorter time, achieving a competitive advantage for the financial institution. The proposed method has been applied to two databases from the UCI repository, and a database from a credit unions cooperative in Ecuador. The results are satisfactory, as highlighted in the conclusions. Some future lines of research are suggested.

Keywords: VarPSO (Variable Particle Swarm Optimization)
FR (Fuzzy Rules) credit risk

1 Introduction

Currently, people apply for a wide variety of loans in financial institutions: commercial loans, consumer loans, mortgages, and microcredits. This leads to financial institutions to analyze a large number of micro-economic variables that allow assess the customer,

© Springer International Publishing AG, part of Springer Nature 2018
Y. Tan et al. (Eds.): ICSI 2018, LNCS 10942, pp. 153–163, 2018.
https://doi.org/10.1007/978-3-319-93818-9_15

and thus give an answer about the access to financial resources. This assessment should advice financial institutions on the amount of the loan and the repayment period. Thanks to technological progress, operations are recorded automatically, giving rise to large repositories of historical information. This records contain not only financial information from customers, but also the result of decisions made, which motivates the interest in learning from past situations, seeking to identify the selection criteria. The aim of this paper is modeling credit risk through classification rules. Proper identification of the most important features will help the credit officer in the decision making process, conducting analysis of the subject of credit in less time. This paper presents a methodology for credit risk which allows obtaining classification rules. The antecedent of the rule is formed by fuzzy variables and nominal variables that contain the knowledge of the credit expert in the database, basically in the membership function that is assigned to each of the fuzzy variables. The use of fuzzy variables will allow credit officer to interpret them more easily and can make decisions properly. To measure the performance of the proposed method, different solutions are analyzed; especially considering the simplicity of the model regarding to:

Cardinality of rules: the lower the number of rules, the better to analyze the generated model,

Average length of the antecedent of the rules and type of variables: the fewer conditions used to form the antecedent of each rule, using fuzzy variables, more easily will be the interpretation of the model.

An association rule is an expression of the form *IF condition1 and condition2 THEN condition3* where condition1 and condition2 may contain fuzzy variables, to allow for a conjunction of propositions of the form (attribute IN fuzzy set X), and whose sole restriction is that the attributes involved in the antecedent of the rule are not part of the consequent. Attributes may be nominal and fuzzy. When the set of association rules shows in the consequent the same attribute, is said that it is a set of classification rules [2, 14].

This article presents a method for obtaining classification rules that combines a neural network with an optimization technique. Emphasis is put on achieving good coverage using a small number of rules, whose antecedent includes fuzzy variables. In this sense it is an extension of previous works [18, 19, 20], aimed at the identification of better classification methods for credit scoring.

The organization is the following: Sect. 2 briefly describes some related work; Sect. 3 develops the proposed method; Sect. 4 presents the results. Finally, Sect. 5 summarizes the findings and describes some future lines of work.

2 Related Work

In the 1960's, the development of the capital markets in United States, showed the need for more scientific models to evaluate the corporate economic and financial 'health'. As a result, Altman [3] developed the first model, known as z score. A survey of techniques applied in the financial area published towards the end of the 1990s [4], does not provide explicit reports of the application of hazard rate models [16] or partial likelihood [17]. However, the survey gives evidence of the use of statistical techniques such as probit and logit, together with techniques of state transition, and other so-called "derivation of actuarial-like probability of default" associated with the bond default. In the following decade, there were developments of application of survival analysis to the measurement of the credit risk [5, 11, 12]. In Latin America, savings and credit cooperatives are considered as a growing industry. It is usual the association between a financial institution with a household appliances store, in order to offer customers quick credit a line. The existence of such financial instrument helps to increase sales. This partnership creates a conflict of interest. On the one hand, the appliance store wants to sell products to all customers; so it is interested in promoting an attractive credit policy. On the other hand, the financial institution wants to maximize revenue from loans, leading to a strict surveillance of the losses on loans. The ideal situation is the existence of transparent policies between appliances shops and financial institutions. There is also the case of financial institutions that grant credits for consumption or production, and also whose goal is the minimization of credit risk. One way of developing such a policy is the construction of objective rules in order to decide to grant or deny a credit application.

Using intelligent computational techniques could produce better results. These techniques, without being exhaustive, include artificial neural networks, theory of fuzzy sets, decision trees, vector support machines, genetic algorithms, among others. In regard to neural networks, there are different architectures, depending on the type of problem to solve. These architectures include popular models, such as back propagation networks, self-organizing maps (SOM) and learning vector quantization (LVQ). Fuzzy sets theory, developed from the seminal work by Zadeh [15] is very useful in cases such as the classification of credit, where the boundaries are not well defined. The data can also be structured in the form of trees, with their respective branches, where the objective is to test the attributes of each branch of the tree. It can also be used support vector machines that, according to the type of discriminant function, enable to build extremely powerful linear and non-linear models. Genetic algorithms as well as particles swarm optimization of particles, are population-based optimization techniques inspired by various biological processes.

If the goal is to obtain association rules, the a priori method [1] or any of its variants can be used. This method is responsible for identifying the sets of attributes that are more common in different nominal, numerical and fuzzy representations. Then it combines them to obtain a set of rules. There are variants of the a priori method that are responsible for reducing computing time. When working with classification rules, the literature identifies different tree-based methods such as the C4.5 [10] or pruned trees as PART [6]. In either case, the fundamental thing is to obtain a set of rules covering the examples, and fulfilling a preset error bound. Tree-based construction methods, which splits the set of samples into subsets, are based on different metrics of the attributes in order to estimate their coverage ability.

3   Methodology

This article presents a hybrid methodology based on the combination of fuzzy rules, optimization by particles swarms of variable population (varPSO), along with LVQ competitive neural networks, which are used to begin the search in promising sectors of the search space. While there are methods for obtaining of rules using the PSO [9], in the first part of this methodology, numeric attributes are fuzzified. In doing so, membership functions are set for each of them. The limits will be defined by credit expert. Nominal attributes are not subject to fuzzification. In this work, we compared the performance of various methods using fuzzy and nominal attributes that combine fixed and variable population. PSO begins with two competitive neural networks, LVQ and SOM. The optimization technique is used to identify the numerical fuzzy and nominal attributes that are more representative. They will form the antecedent of the rules. In other words, the optimization technique is responsible for generating the rules that will be incorporated into the system based on fuzzy rules, with the aim of obtaining good accuracy, interpretability and cardinality.

3.1 Learning Vector Quantization (LVQ)

Learning Vector Quantization (LVQ) is a supervised classification algorithm based on centroids or prototypes [Kohonen, 1990]. This algorithm can be interpreted as a competitive neural network composed of three layers. The first layer is only input. The second is where the competition takes place. The third layer is the output, responsible for the classification. Each neuron in the competitive layer carries a numeric vector of equal dimension than the examples of input and a label which indicates the class which is going to represent. These vectors are the ones that, at the end of the adaptive process contain the information of the centroids or prototypes of the classification. There are different versions of the training algorithm. In the following paragraph, we describe the one used in this article.

At the start of the algorithm, the quantity of K centroids to be used, should be indicated. This allows to define the network's architecture where the number of inputs and outputs are defined by the problem to be solved.

Centroids are initialized by selecting K random examples. Then each of the examples is entered and adapt the position of the centroids. The closest centroid is identified, using a preset distance metric. As it is a supervised process, it is possible to determine if the example and the centroid correspond to the same class. If the centroid and the example belong to the same class, the centroid "approaches" to the example with the objective of strengthening the representation. On contrary, if the classes are different, the centroid "moves away" of the example. These movements are performed using a factor or adaptation speed, which allows to consider the step that is to be performed.

This process is repeated until the change lies below a preset threshold, or until the examples are identified with the same centroids in two consecutive iterations, which-ever comes first.

As a variant on the implementation in this article, it is also considered to the second closest centroid, provided that the class to which they belong is different from the example analyzed, and is located at a distance less than 1.2 times the distance of the first centroid, due to the factor of inertia that was established previously and the applied "detachment". Variations of LVQ can be found in [8].

3.2 Fuzzy Rules (FR)

Fuzzy logic is derived from the theory of fuzzy sets. It takes as a basis the human reasoning, which is approximate, considering that it can be taken as an alternative to classical logic. Fuzzy logic enables to handle human reasoning, interpreting better the inaccurate real world. For example, we can be considered the use of vague data in the analysis of credit management. For example, the variable income "USD. 4000", can be considered as "High income with a membership of 0.3", and as "Median with a membership of 0.6". To provide the membership level of the fuzzy set, we should work with experts, since they know the system. When the antecedent of the rule consists of variables that use the conjunction operator for various conditions, the min or product operator between degrees of membership of the variables can be used.

3.3 Particle Swarm Optimization (PSO)

Particle Swarm Optimization (PSO) is a population metaheuristic proposed by Kennedy and Eberhart [7]. Each individual of the population, called particle, represents a possible solution to the problem, and fits following three factors: its knowledge about the environment (its fitness value), its historical knowledge or previous experiences (memory) and the historical knowledge or past experience of the individuals located in its neighborhood (its social knowledge).

Obtaining classification rules using the PSO, able to operate on numerical, nominal and fuzzy attributes requires a combination of some methods mentioned above, because it is necessary to determine the attributes that will be part of the antecedent. In the case of fuzzy variables, it is necessary to know the membership degree of them.

Taking into account that it is a population-based technique, it is necessary to analyze the required information in each individual of the population. Additionally, we must decide between represent a single rule or the complete set of rules by individual. Finally, we have to choose the scheme of representation of each rule. According to the goals of this work, we follow the Iterative Rule Learning (IRL) [13], in which each individual represents a single rule, and the solution of the problem is built from the best individuals obtained in a sequence of executions. Using this approach implies that population technique is applied iteratively until reaching the required coverage, obtaining a single rule at each iteration: the best individual of the population. It has also decided to use a fixed-length representation, where the antecedent of the rule will only be encoded. Given this approach, we will follow an iterative process involving all individuals of the population with a class by default, which do not requires the encoding of the consequent. PSO uses fuzzified variables, reducing the amount of attributes to choose, which form the antecedent of the rule. Additionally, it uses a criterion of "voting": whenever the fitness function is evaluated, the average degree of membership of the examples that abide by the rule is computed. This information is also used in the movement of the individual.

3.4   Proposed Method for Obtaining Rules: Fuzzy Variables + LVQ + PSO

The sets are determined according to the knowledge of the experts. Fuzzy sets can be represented by triangular or trapezoidal functions, depending on the variable. For example, "age" is represented by a triangular function, since it was defined as young, middle and old. The variable "number of children" is represented by a trapezoidal function. When the variable is equal to 0 or 1, the membership degree to the "low set" is equal to 1. When the variable is equal to 3 the membership is 0.5 to the low set and 0.5 high set. Finally when the variable is equal to or greater than 4, the membership degree is 1 to the high set.

To obtain the rules we use fuzzy variables. Such rules are obtained through an iterative process that analyzes examples that have not been covered by each of the classes starting with those that have higher number of elements. Then an average degree of membership of the examples that satisfy the rule is computed. When a rule has been obtained, the set of examples covered by the generated rule is removed from the input database. This process is performed iteratively, until it reaches to the maximum number of iterations, or until all examples are covered or until the number of examples of each of the resulting classes are considered too few. When the examples are covered by the generated rule, they are removed from the input data set. In order to classify a new example, rules must be applied in the order they were obtained, and the example will be classed with the class corresponding to the consequent of the first rule whose antecedent is verified for the example under examination. Even though, the original data are numerical and nominal, neural networks use numerical attributes. Therefore, the nominal variables are encoded in such a way that each of them has as many binary digits as different values have. Numeric attributes are scaled between 0 and 1. The membership degree of the fuzzy variables defined above, can be treated as nominal or numeric. The similarity measure used is the Euclidean distance. Once the training is completed, each centroid will contain roughly the average of the examples that it represents. For obtaining each of the rules, we need to determine, first of all, the class corresponding to the consequent. In this way it is obtained the rules with high support. The minimum support of each of the classes decreases in the iteration process, as long as the examples of the corresponding class are covered. Consequently, the first generated rules have greater supports. Figure 1 shows the pseudocode of the proposed method.

4   Results

This section benchmarks the performance of the proposed method, with PART and C4.5. This empirical validation is done on two public databases of credit application from the UCI repository, and a database from a savings and credit cooperative from Ecuador. This cooperative is classified as segment 2 by the Superintendency of Popular and Solidary Economy (regulatory authority), given that its assets are between 20,000,000.00 and 80,000,000.00 USD. Regarding the last database, the following variables of the applicants were considered: year and month of credit application,

```
Determine the fuzzy set of each of the variables
Determine the membership function for each of the variables in
each of the defined fuzzy sets.
Train the LVQ network using the training examples
Determine the minimum support for each of the classes
Iteration = 0
While stop criterion is not achieve do
        Choose the class that has the largest uncovered examples
        Construct a population considering LVQ centroids
        Evolve the population using variable population PSO, con-
        sidering the average of the membership degree of the exam-
        ples tan comply with the rule
        Obtain the best population rule
        If the rule complies with the support and confidence then
            Add the rule to the rule set
            Consider as covered the examples that are covered by
            the rule
            Recalculate the minimum support of the considered
            class
        Iteration = Iteration + 1
        End If
End While
```

Fig. 1. Pseudocode of the proposed method

province, loan's purpose, cash savings, total income, total assets, total expenses and total debt. It is also known if the requests for credit was denied or approved.

In the case of the UCI repository databases, triangular fuzzy sets were defined for continuous numerical variables, and trapezoidal fuzzy sets for discrete variables. We used three sets for each continuous numeric variable and two fuzzy sets for discrete numeric variables. To define them, the range of each variable was divided in an equitable manner. Regarding the Ecuadorian database, an expert in the area of credit risk was asked to define fuzzy sets for each of the variables, according to the economy of Ecuador. The following attributes were fuzzified: amount requested, cash savings, total income, total expenses, total assets, and total debts.

We processed the data described above, and compared the performance of several methods that combine two types of PSO, one of fixed population and other variable population, initialized with two different competitive neural networks: LVQ and SOM. These solutions are compared with the C4.5 and PART methods. The way of finding classification rules in the proposed and control methods are different. C4.5 is a pruned tree method, whose branches are mutually exclusive, and allow to classify examples. PART gives a list of rules equivalent to those generated by the proposed method of classification, but in a deterministic way. PART performance is based on the construction of partial trees. Each tree is created in a similar manner to C4.5, but during the process construction errors of each branch are calculated. These errors determine tree pruning.

The proposed method uses random values that makes the movement of the particle not overly deterministic, as is the case with PART. The most important feature of the results obtained, is the combination of an attribute search algorithm (which may be diffuse, numerical or qualitative), with a competitive neural network. As a consequence, we obtain a set of rules with fuzzy variables in the antecedent with a significantly low cardinality (fewer rules). The proposed solution provides greater accuracy, with a reduced set of rules, which makes it easier to understand. The accuracy of the classification obtained in PSO is good. Thus the proposed method meets the objective: that the credit officer can respond fast and accurately, verifying the fewest rules. We believe that this method is an excellent alternative to be used in financial institutions. Results are displayed in Tables 1, 2 and 3

Table 1. Results of fuzzy rules with the Australian database – UCI Repository

Method	Type of prediction	Denied	Accepted	Precision	#rules	Antecedent length
SOM + fuzzy PSO	Denied	0,4472 0.0081	0.1154 0.0211	0.8550	3.0083	1.3076
	Accepted	0,0295 0.0050	0.4079 0.0211	0.0131	0.0009	0.1433
SOM + fuzzy varPSO	Denied	0.4526 0.0101	0.0787 0.0112	0.8957	3.0000	1.3333
	Accepted	0.0255 0.0066	0.4430 0.0120	0.0098	0.0000	0.0896
LVQ + fuzzy PSO	Denied	0.4504 0.0113	0.1066 0.0095	0.8578	3.0000	1.2897
	Accepted	0.0356 0.0060	0.4074 0.0161	0.0109	0.0000	0.2254
LVQ + fuzzy varPSO	Denied	0.4547 0.0123	0.1022 0,0092	0.8689	3.0000	1.4511
	Accepted	0.0288 0.0088	0.4142 0.0178	0.0122	0.0000	0.1493
C4.5	Denied	0.4618 0.0063	0,0847 0.0066	0.8528	18.2200	4.8394
	Accepted	0.0625 0.0120	0.3910 0.0121	0.0124	2.0825	0.2810
PART	Denied	0.3906 0.0288	0.1562 0.0289	0.7469	33.343	2.4926
	Accepted	0.0969 0.0134	0.3564 0.0136	0.0292	1.5793	0.0934

Table 2. Results of fuzzy rules using German database – UCI Repository

Method	Type of prediction	Denied	Accepted	Precision	#rules	Antecedent length
SOM + fuzzy PSO	Denied	0,6031 0.0160	0.0896 0.0201	0.7636	7.7612	2.7926
	Accepted	0,1459 0.0133	0.1605 0.0107	0.0101	0.6540	0.1449
SOM + fuzzy varPSO	Denied	0.5920 0.0131	0.0915 0.0100	0.7697	8.1848	2.8433
	Accepted	0.1385 0.0190	0.1777 0.0111	0.0081	0.5141	0.4493
LVQ + fuzzy PSO	Denied	0.6009 0.0128	0.0961 0.0109	0.7578	8.3595	2.9163
	Accepted	0.1461 0.0078	0.1569 0.0068	0.0091	0.6087	0.2996
LVQ + fuzzy varPSO	Denied	0.5992 0.0132	0.0985 0,0324	0.7592	8.4120	2.6937
	Accepted	0.1418 0.0133	0.1601 0.0124	0.0058	0.5641	0.1921
C4.5	Denied	0.5894 0.0070	0,1106 0.0070	0.7113	86.4600	5.6267
	Accepted	0.1781 0.0069	0.1219 0.0069	0.0079	4.0788	0.1382
PART	Denied	0.5185 0.0091	0.1687 0.0135	0.6940	70.913	3.0138
	Accepted	0.1372 0.0170	0.1754 0.0120	0.0139	2.1575	0.0561

Table 3. Result of fuzzy rules with data from a savings and credit cooperative from Ecuador, belonging to segment 2 of Superintendencia de Economía Popular y Solidaria (assets between 20′000.000,00 and 80′000.000,00 USD)

Method	Type of prediction	Denied	Accepted	Precision	#rules	Antecedent length
SOM + fuzzy PSO	Denied	0,6288 0.0098	0.1067 0.0065	0.8142	3.5925	3.0164
	Accepted	0,0785 0.0078	0.1854 0.0065	0.0062	0.2147	0.2459
SOM + fuzzy varPSO	Denied	0.6238 0.0102	0.0825 0.0128	0.8332	3.9957	2.4328
	Accepted	0.0829 0.0057	0.2094 0.0092	0.0026	0.2968	0.2367
LVQ +fuzzy PSO	Denied	0.6129 0.0143	0.1043 0.0153	0.7448	3.1214	2.1427
	Accepted	0.0778 0.0118	0.1819 0.0043	0.0070	0.2272	0.1971

(*continued*)

Table 3. (*continued*)

Method	Type of prediction	Denied	Accepted	Precision	#rules	Antecedent length
LVQ + fuzzy varPSO	Denied	0.6298 0.0056	0.0780 0,0127	0.8444	4.1498	2.3770
	Accepted	0.0775 0.0094	0.2146 0.0091	0.0089	0.2787	0.1145
C4.5	Denied	0.6320 0.0014	0,1075 0.0013	0.8106	114.2600	9.6752
	Accepted	0.0819 0.0013	0.1786 0.0013	0.0011	6.0543	0.1144
PART	Denied	0.6229 0.0065	0.1036 0.0064	0.8054	42.3567	4.6956
	Accepted	0.0910 0.0065	0.1825 0.0064	0.0023	2.1661	0.0880

5   Conclusions

In this paper, we present a new method of classification rules, whose antecedent is formed by fuzzy variables. We apply this method to the analysis of credit risk, combining competitive neural networks (SOM and LVQ) and population-based optimization techniques (PSO and varPSO). To verify the performance of this method, we used two credit databases. One database is in the UC Irvine Machine Learning Repository. The other database is from a savings and credit cooperative from Ecuador. The results have been satisfactory. The measurements reached by the proposed method has a reduced rule set, which could be used by the credit officer with very good accuracy.

This technique can be considered an optimal model for the credit officer in determining the credit scoring as numerical, nominal and fuzzy attributes from credit applications are being used. A limited number of rules are obtained, whose antecedent is formed by fuzzy variables, facilitating the understanding of the model. Credit officers can assess credit applications in a shorter time frame, with more accuracy, leading to a decrease of credit risk. In future lines of research, we would consider adding to the model the defuzzification of the output variable, indicating the percentage of risk involved in granting the credit. Additionally, we would like to combine in the antecedent of the rule macroeconomic and microeconomic variables, which allow a simpler model while maintaining an adequate accuracy.

References

1. Agrawal, R., Srikant, R., Fast algorithms for mining association rules in large databases. In: Proceedings of the 20th International Conference on Very Large Data Bases, VLDB 1994, pp. 487–499 (1994)
2. Aggarwal, C.C.: Data Mining. Springer, Cham (2015). https://doi.org/10.1007/978-3-319-14142-8

3. Altman, E.I.: Financial ratios, discriminant analysis and the prediction of corporate bankruptcy. J. Finance **23**(4), 589–609 (1968)
4. Altman, E.I., Sounders, A.: Credit risk measurement: developments over the last 20 years. J. Bank. Finance **21**, 1721–1742 (1998)
5. Duffie, D., Singleton, K.J.: Credit Risk: Pricing, Measurement, and Management. Princeton University Press, New Jersey (2003). ISBN 0-691-09046-7
6. Frank, E., Witten, I.H.: Generating accurate rule sets without global optimization. In: Proceedings of the Fifteenth International Conference on Machine Learning, ICML 1998, pp. 144–151 (1998)
7. Kennedy, J., Eberhart, R.: Particle swarm optimization. In: Proceedings of IEEE International Conference on Neural Networks, vol. 4, pp. 1942–1948 (1995)
8. Kohonen, T.: Self-Organizing Maps. Springer Series in Information Sciences, vol. 30. Springer, Heidelberg (2012). https://doi.org/10.1007/978-3-642-56927-2
9. Lanzarini, L., Villa Monte, A., Aquino, G., De Giusti, A.: Obtaining classification rules using lvqPSO. In: Tan, Y., Shi, Y., Buarque, F., Gelbukh, A., Das, S., Engelbrecht, A. (eds.) ICSI 2015. LNCS, vol. 9140, pp. 183–193. Springer, Cham (2015). https://doi.org/10.1007/978-3-319-20466-6_20
10. Quinlan, J.R.: C4.5: programs for machine learning. Morgan Kaufmann Publishers, San Francisco (1993)
11. Roszbach, K.: Bank Lending Policy, Credit Scoring and the Survival of Loans. Sveriges Risksbank Working Paper Series 154. (2003)
12. Saunders, A., Allen, L.: Credit Risk Measurement: New Approaches to Value at Risk and Other Paradigms, 2nd edn. Wiley, New York (2002). ISBN 978-0-471-27476-6
13. Venturini, G.: SIA: a supervised inductive algorithm with genetic search for learning attributes based concepts. In: Brazdil, Pavel B. (ed.) ECML 1993. LNCS, vol. 667, pp. 280–296. Springer, Heidelberg (1993). https://doi.org/10.1007/3-540-56602-3_142
14. Witten, I.H., Eibe, F., Hall, M.A.: Data Mining Practical Machine Learning Tools and Techniques, 3rd edn. Morgan Kaufmann Publishers Inc., San Francisco (2011)
15. Zadeh, L.A.: Fuzzy sets. Inf. Control **8**(3), 338–353 (1965)
16. Nanda, A.K., Shaked, M.: The hazard rate and the reversed hazard rate orders, with applications to order statistics. Ann. Inst. Stat. Math. **53**(4), 853–864 (2001)
17. Insua, J.R.: On the hierarchical models and their relationship with the decision problem with partial information a priori. Trabajos de Estadística e Investigación Operativa **35**(2), 222–230 (1984)
18. Santana, P.J., Monte, A.V., Rucci, E., Lanzarini, L., Bariviera, A.F.: Analysis of methods for generating classification rules applicable to credit risk. J. Comput. Sci. Technol. **17**, 20–28 (2017)
19. Lanzarini, L.C., Villa Monte, A., Bariviera, A.F., Jimbo Santana, P.: Simplifying credit scoring rules using LVQ + PSO. Kybernetes **46**, 8–16 (2017)
20. Lanzarini, L., Villa-Monte, A., Fernández-Bariviera, A., Jimbo-Santana, P.: Obtaining classification rules using LVQ+PSO: an application to credit risk. In: Gil-Aluja, J., Terceño-Gómez, A., Ferrer-Comalat, J.C., Merigó-Lindahl, José M., Linares-Mustarós, S. (eds.) Scientific Methods for the Treatment of Uncertainty in Social Sciences. AISC, vol. 377, pp. 383–391. Springer, Cham (2015). https://doi.org/10.1007/978-3-319-19704-3_31

Fuzzy Logic Applied to the Performance Evaluation. Honduran Coffee Sector Case

Noel Varela Izquierdo[1](✉), Omar Bonerge Pineda Lezama[2],
Rafael Gómez Dorta[3], Amelec Viloria[1], Ivan Deras[2],
and Lissette Hernández-Fernández[1]

[1] Universidad de la Costa (CUC), Calle 58 # 55-66,
Atlántico, Barranquilla, Colombia
{nvarela2, aviloria7, lhernand31}@cuc.edu.co
[2] Universidad Tecnológica Centroamericana (UNITEC), Tegucigalpa, Honduras
{omarpineda, ideras}@unitec.edu
[3] Universidad Tecnológica de Honduras (UTH), San Pedro Sula, Honduras
rafaellucianog@yahoo.es

Abstract. Every day organizations pay more attention to Human Resources Management, because this human factor is preponderant in the results of it. An important policy is the Performance Evaluation (ED), since it allows the control and monitoring of management indicators, both individual and by process. To analyze the results, decision making in many organizations is done in a subjective manner and in consequence it brings serious problems to them. Taking into account this problem, it is decided to design and apply diffuse mathematical procedures and tools to reduce subjectivity and uncertainty in decision-making, creating work algorithms for this policy, which includes multifactorial weights and analysis with measurement indicators that they allow tangible and reliable results. Statistical techniques (ANOVA) are also used to establish relationships between work groups and learn about best practices.

Keywords: Performance evaluation · Fuzzy logic

1 Introduction

The current and dynamic changes in a highly globalized world demand the improvement of organizational efficiency and effectiveness, since customers demand the highest quality in products or services and the rapid response to their requirements (Sueldo et al. [1]).

The Human Capital Models (MCH) (Cuesta [2], Carreón et al. [3]) also focus their objectives on the improvement of organizational results, but from the perspective of human resources, where the evaluation of performance plays an important role in the same. In this aspect, research related to evaluation by competences (Gallego [4]), evaluation by graphic scales (Varela [5]), among others, stand out.

The Performance Evaluation of organizations is vital for the achievement of their objectives and their competitiveness, so it is usual to adopt Models of Management Excellence (MEG) (Kim et al. [6], Sampaio et al. [7], Comas et al. [8]) whose main

© Springer International Publishing AG, part of Springer Nature 2018
Y. Tan et al. (Eds.): ICSI 2018, LNCS 10942, pp. 164–173, 2018.
https://doi.org/10.1007/978-3-319-93818-9_16

objective is the continuous improvement of results through the application of a set of principles of Quality Management (QA) and excellence.

The MEG establish human resource management practices aimed at improving the attitude and behavior of employees at work, as well as the knowledge and skills necessary to implement 'good practices' of management (Ooi et al. [9], Bayo and Merino [10], Escrig and de Menezes [11]). High Commitment Human Resource Management Systems (SAC) are suitable for a context of quality management in general and for the adoption of a model of excellence in particular, (Simmons et al. [12]; Bayo and Merino [10]; Wickramasinghe and Anuradha [13]; Alfalla et al. [14]).

While SACs include performance evaluation and compensation practices based on work performance (Huselid [15]), part of the literature on Quality Management (QA) (e.g., Deming [16]) does not consider them adequate to promote attitudes and behaviors based on collaboration and teamwork, necessary within the framework of a CG initiative. In fact, Soltani et al. [17, 18], Jiménez and Martínez [19], Curbelo-Martínez et al. [20] consider that an unresolved problem in the literature in CG is the analysis of the characteristics that a performance evaluation system should have, which is still considered a topic under discussion.

On the other hand, many organizations or companies perform informal evaluations of work performance based on the employee's daily work. These assessments tend to be insufficient for a correct assessment of performance and therefore to achieve the objectives set by organizations. Therefore, gradually, different methods have been introduced for the evaluation of performance, thus achieving an effective tool for directing policies and measures that improve their performance.

Using ED, organizations obtain information for making decisions on tangible indicators (production goals, quality, sales, etc.) and intangibles (behaviors, attitudes, etc.), so it is very important to develop methods (objectives and high certainty) of performance evaluation for collaborators capable of objectively integrating quantitative and qualitative results and contributing to the fulfillment of strategic and organizational objectives.

For the treatment of subjectivity and uncertainty, (Zadeh [21]) developed the models of Fuzzy Logic, this can be applied to take into account subjective factors in the evaluation of staff performance, reducing uncertainty, which facilitates decision making and It makes it more effective.

The purpose of this paper is to develop an application model of fuzzy mathematics to the evaluation of performance for the treatment of the subjectivity of the same, in which a diffuse performance evaluation model capable of dealing with information and handling will be proposed. The uncertainty provided by the evaluators. We also want to analyze the relationship between groups of works to know their results and best practices applied by them.

2 Materials and Methods

This section shows an analysis of trends, methods and fundamental techniques, which are used for the evaluation of performance, uses of fuzzy mathematics in it and the methodology used for this research.

2.1   Performance Evaluation. Actual Trends

The performance evaluation processes can serve several purposes: administrative and control (Cuesta [2]), for development (Escrig and de Menezes [11]), and human resources planning (Alvarez [22]).

With respect to the treatment of uncertainty, the authors show different points of view. Authors such as (Chiavenato [23]) exposes a wide variety of qualitative methods (critical incidents, forced choice, descriptive phrases, field research, etc.) and quantitative methods (evaluation by results, weighted graphic scales, etc.) according to this author, the use does not depend on the uncertainty but on the real situation and the environment of the organizations.

Other authors (Valdés-Padrón et al. [24] and Gallego [4]) adopt a competency-based assessment approach based on the ability to enhance performance at all levels of the organization, for this, define competencies and modes of action according to the expected results for each process, this approach nevertheless presents a high subjectivity caused by two elements: subjective indicators and very long periods of evaluation.

Sun [25] and Varela [5] highlight the indiscriminate use of qualitative and quantitative techniques, as long as the indicators to be evaluated are objective, with tangible measurement scales and results that show the added value (called "value added"), (Rockwell [26]).

The evaluation of performance is based on the evaluation, by the evaluators, of both objective and subjective indicators. This implies that some indicators are better adapted to a quantitative assessment (objectives) and others to a qualitative assessment (subjective) due to the uncertainty inherently involved, since they are based on the perceptions of the evaluators (Vázquez [27]). However, performance evaluation models propose that evaluators express their evaluations in a single domain of expression (usually numerical), although this implies a lack of expressivity in the evaluators and, therefore, the results may lose representativeness.

The application of fuzzy logic in the measurement of performance has been studied by several researchers, especially in the Asia-Pacific region.

Lau et al. [28] that proposed a methodology to analyze and monitor the performance of suppliers in a company based on the criteria of product quality and delivery time. Ling et al. [29] presents an indicator to assess the level of agility of companies operating in different markets using fuzzy logic focused on the application of linguistic approximation and fuzzy arithmetic to synthesize fuzzy numbers in order to obtain the agility index of manufacturing operations. Silva et al. [30] used diffuse weighted aggregation to formulate problems of optimization of logistic systems, which can be extended to different types of optimization methodologies such as genetic algorithms or ant colony. Arango et al. [31] describe an application of indicators with diffuse logic in the Colombian bakery sector.

In the aspect related to the application of fuzzy mathematics to the evaluation of performance, the literature is scarcer, Özdaban and Özkan [32] develop a research where they apply fuzzy mathematics to a comparative model between the models of individual evaluation and the collective evaluation of the process to which it belongs, where they defend the theory that systems for evaluating individual performance should integrate collective indicators.

2.2 Methodology of Performance Evaluation

For the practical application of the tool the methodology of Performance Evaluation was chosen, Izquierdo et al. [33]. To this methodology some adjustments were made in correspondence with the application of fuzzy mathematics.

The application of the diffuse performance evaluation model allows obtaining the numerical performance indicators for each employee in any area of the organization, as well as the graphs and analysis of historical behaviors, both individual and by areas or processes of the organization. With the defined model, graphical scales are designed for performance evaluation, where each area, process or job, as appropriate, identify the general indicators, the specific indicators, the grades (qualitative evaluation) and the specific weight of each indicator.

2.3 Fuzzy Logic Methodology

Fuzzy logic is multivariate allowing in a practical way to address problems as they occur in the real world. It originates in the theory of fuzzy sets proposed by Zadeh [21], which represents a generalization of the classical theory of sets and applies to categories that can take any value of truth within a set of values that fluctuate between the truth absolute and total falsehood. The foundation of fuzzy sets is the fact that the building blocks of human reasoning are not numbers but linguistic labels; thus, fuzzy logic emulates these characteristics and makes use of approximate data to find precise solutions.

The fuzzy inference system according to (Zadeh [21], Özdaban and Özkan [32]) are expert systems with approximate reasoning that map a vector of inputs to a single (scalar) output. They are based on fuzzy logic to carry out this mapping and consist of several stages:

(a) Fusification

The purpose of fusion is to convert real values into fuzzy values. In the merge, degrees of belonging to each one of the input variables are assigned in relation to the fuzzy sets defined using the belongings functions associated with fuzzy sets.

(b) Diffuse rules

The basis of the fuzzy rule is characterized by the construction of a set of linguistic rules based on the knowledge of the experts. Expert knowledge is usually in the form of if-then rules, which can be easily implemented using diffuse conditional statements.

(c) Diffuse Inference

The inference relates the fuzzy input and output sets to represent the rules that will define the system. In inference, information from the knowledge base is used to generate rules through the use of conditions.

The definition of the fuzzy rules for the mathematical model is a very important aspect for the processing and analysis of the results, authors like (Özdaban and Özkan [32]) refer that the linguistic diffuse sets (degrees), can vary depending on the variables to measure and the meaning of them. For this work were defined as rules the establishment of 4 degrees and their respective diffuse triangular numbers [33].

(d) Defusification

Defusification performs the process of adapting the diffuse values generated in the inference to real values, which are subsequently used in the control process. In defusion, simple mathematical methods are used, such as the maximum method, the centroid method and the height method. (Zadeh [21]).

- Maximum method: The one for which the characteristic function of the fuzzy set is maximum is chosen as the output value. It is not an optimal method, since the value can be reached by several outputs.
- Centroid method: Uses the center of gravity of the characteristic output function as output. With this method you get a single output. (This is the method, applied to this work.)
- Height method: First calculate the centers of gravity for each rule of the diffuse set of output and then the weighted average.

3 Coffee Sector Case Study. Results of the Application

The validation of the Diffuse Performance Evaluation (SEDD) procedure was developed in a company of the Honduran coffee sector, specialized in the benefit of dry coffee and for this a four-step procedure was followed.

1. Select department object of evaluation.
2. Design graphic scale.
3. Apply evaluation using software designed for this method (SEDD).
4. Perform analysis and compare results between the different establishments.

Step 1: The study is carried out in a company in the Honduran coffee sector. This company has several productive departments among which stands out coffee receipt, drying, trillage-classified and the department of packaging and dispatch, of all of them and proposed by the work team decided to select the drying department for the impact it generates in Plant efficiency.

The drying department has 3 work stations located in different geographical areas, which allows the purchase of wet coffee in different areas with significant logistical savings. In each of these stations, three operators work, which are the ones that guarantee the work with the drying machines. The objective is then focused on establishing the evaluation scheme for these workers to know the weak points in their work, compare the different stations with a view to determine where they have good practices and on this basis proceed to improve the performance of the staff.

Step 2: For the design of the graphic scale, a technical analysis of the drying process was carried out, which allowed to elaborate the graphic scale shown in Table 1. In this it can be verified that the performance is evaluated through five indicators very important:

(1) Effectiveness in drying: It refers to the percentage of dryings that meet the moisture criterion. The percentage of humidity for a drying should be between 12 and 13%. This is one of the main skills that the dryer must develop, its ability to provide coffee to the drying process.

Table 1. Graphic scale for dryer operator

Weight	Grades indicators	Bad	Regular	Good	Excellent
50%	**A-Productive Results**				
30%	1 Effectiveness in drying (%)	<85	85–90	90–95	90–95
20%	2 Performance (qq/h)	<8	8–8.5	8.5–9	>9
40%	**B-Quality**				
40%	1 Process Capacity	<1	1.2– 1.33	1.2– 1.33	>1.33
10%	**C-Discipline**				
5%	1 Compliance Procedure (% According to process audit)	<85	90–95	90–95	95–100
5%	2 Safety Compliance (Signs)	<2	1	1	0

(2) Performance. Measures the stability of the drying process that the hot air is responsible for drying the coffee at a reasonable time that does not affect the quality of the coffee and contributes to the rational use of energy and therefore environmental care.

(3) Process capacity. Measure the ability of the process to meet your specifications.

(4) Compliance with procedures: measures the compliance by the operator of the standard work procedure.

(5) Compliance with the safety requirements of the process: it is a measure of the operator's compliance with the safety and hygiene requirements of the work that have been established for the process.

From here the evaluation matrix is built, aided by the SEDD software, (this element constitutes the core of the SEDD), allowing in a flexible way to enter the general, specific indicators, importance weights and degrees for the selected area.

Step 3: Once updated the information of each of the operators of the three establishments of the drying department, we proceeded to the application of the evaluation in the fourth quarter of 2017 (the evaluation is done monthly). Each of the operators of the three establishments was evaluated during each month of the quarter analyzed. Then, in Fig. 1 and as an example, the result of the evaluation for one of the operators in the three months evaluated is presented.

The software allows to take the historical behavior of each employee and show it graphically. The study worker has maintained a sustained performance above the established goal, which is 90% but also allows comparisons with the average of workers in the area and know the strengths and weaknesses of their evaluation.

Step 4: At this time you should proceed to obtain the summary of the results obtained by department. In this aspect, it is sought to determine if there is a relation between the results of each establishment and its qualitative evaluation to identify and establish the best practices and work techniques.

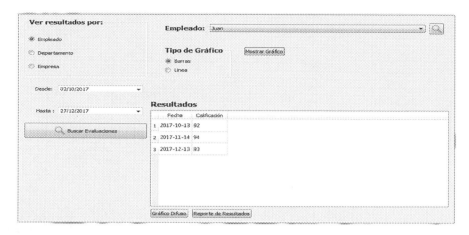

Fig. 1. Results of the evaluation to one of the employees using SEDD (it is shown in the original Spanish language)

A summary of the results achieved by the three departments in the evaluation of the quarter's performance is presented in Table 2.

Table 2. Summary of the performance evaluation for the drying department.

Drying department	Trimester		
	October	November	December
Drying 1	91.5	94	90.6
Drying 2	81	83.3	86.5
Drying 3	82.5	84.5	76.7

The analysis leads to the hypothesis that establishment No.1 presents superior results to establishments 2 and 3. To confirm this hypothesis, an ANOVA was performed, with the help of the STATGRAPHICS Centurion software, the result of the test (p value = 0.009); confirms the hypothesis that there are significant differences in performance between the three drying facilities.

The graph of means in Fig. 2 confirms that the establishment of drying 1 obtains superior results in its performance, so it would be a good reference when forming an improvement strategy, deciding to investigate the procedures and practices that are used to generalize them to the rest of the establishments.

To group the information in such a way as to allow an integral analysis and adopt the decisions on solid bases, Table 3 was elaborated.

Based on the comprehensive analysis of the information presented, it can be stated that the drying establishment 1 presents the best performance, with a satisfactory evaluation in each of the indicators considered, so it is important that for each dryer of the other establishments a training in this establishment, aimed at improving skills

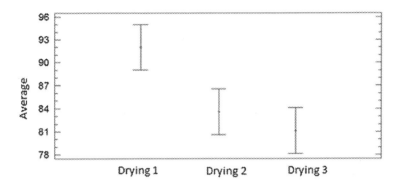

Fig. 2. Graph of average results of ANOVA.

Table 3. Summary of the qualitative evaluation by department.

Establishments	Indicators				
	Productive results		Quality	Discipline	
	Effectiveness in drying	Performance	Processing capacity	Procedures	Security
Drying 1	Good	Good	Good	Excellent	Excellent
Drying 2	Good	Regular	Regular	Good	Good
Drying 3	Good	Regular	Regular	Good	Good

aimed at achieving superior performance, especially with regard to performance optimization procedures and the improvement of process capacity.

4 Conclusions

The application of the SEDD in the company allows to eliminate the subjectivity in the evaluation of the performance, guaranteeing to count on a historical and objective database that allows the realization of integral analysis.

The comparative evaluation made to the drying department of the company made it possible to determine that there are differences in the performance of the different establishments; therefore, an improvement strategy must be defined that allows the established procedures to be effectively developed in each one of them.

The establishments 2 and 3 should use as a reference to the establishment 1 and organize in it, training for its operators that allow you to consolidate their training in relation to the issue of optimization of performance and improvement of the capacity of the process.

References

1. Sueldo, C.S., Urrutia, S., Paravié, D., Rohvein, C., Corres, G.: Una propuesta metodológica para la determinación de capacidades estratégicas en pymes industriales. INGE CUC **10**(2) (2014)
2. Cuesta, A.: Tecnología de Gestión de Recursos Humanos. La Habana, Editorial Félix Varela, Tercera Edición (2010). ISBN 9789590713415
3. Carreón, F.Á., Figueroa, E.G., Montoya, D.A.: El capital humano vs rentabilidad. INCEPTUM Revista de Investigación en Ciencias de la Administración **4**(7), 55–74 (2014)
4. Gallego, M.: Gestión humana basada en competencias contribución efectiva al logro de los objetivos organizacionales. Revista universidad EAFIT **36**(119), 63–71 (2012)
5. Varela, N.: Diseño de un sistema de evaluación del desempeño al personal de ventas de Simplex Group. Revista Innovare, vol. 2, no. 2 (2015). ISSN 2310-290X
6. Kim, D.Y., Kumar, V., Murphy, S.A.: European foundation for quality management business excellence model: an integrative review and research agenda. Int. J. Qual. Reliab. Manag. **27**(6), 684–701 (2010)
7. Domingues, P., Sampaio, P., Arezes, P.M.: New organisational issues and macroergonomics: integrating management systems. Int. J. Hum. Factors Ergon. **1**(4), 351–375 (2012)
8. Comas, A.S., Rodado, D.N., Eras, J.C.: Marcos aplicados a la Gestión de Calidad–Una Revisión Sistemática de la Literatura. Espacios **37**(09) (2016)
9. Ooi, K.B., Bakar, N.A., Arumugam, V., Vellapan, L., Loke, L.K.: Does TQM influence employees' job satisfaction? An empirical case analysis. Int. J. Qual. Reliab. Manag. **24**(1), 62–77 (2007)
10. Bayo, A., Merino, J.: Quality management and high performance work practices: do they coexist? Int. J. Prod. Econ. **73**(3), 251–259 (2001)
11. Escrig, A.B., de Menezes, L.M.: What characterizes leading companies within business excellence models? An analysis of "EFQM Recognized for Excellence" recipients in Spain. Int. J. Prod. Econ. **169**, 362–375 (2015)
12. Simmons, D.E., Shadur, M.A., Preston, A.P.: Integrating TQM and HRM. Empl. Relat. **17**(3), 75–86 (1995)
13. Wickramasinghe, V., Anuradha, G.: High-involvement work practices, quality results, and the role of HR function: an exploratory study of manufacturing firms in Sri Lanka. TQM J. **23**(5), 516–530 (2011)
14. Alfalla, R., Marín, J.A., Medina, C.: Is worker commitment necessary for achieving competitive advantage and customer satisfaction when companies use HRM and TQM practices? Univers. Bus. Rev. **36**, 64–89 (2012)
15. Huselid, M.A.: The impact of human resource management practices on turnover, productivity, and corporate financial performance. Acad. Manag. J. **38**, 635–672 (1995)
16. Deming, E.: Out of the Crisis. Quality, Productivity and Competitive Position. Cambridge University Press, New York (1986)
17. Soltani, E., van der Meer, R., Gennard, J., Williams, M.: Case study: have TQM organisations adjusted their performance management (appraisal) systems? A study of UK based TQM-driven organizations. TQM Mag. **16**(6), 403–417 (2004)
18. Soltani, E., van der Meer, R., Williams, M., Lai, P.: The compatibility of performance appraisal systems with TQM, principles – evidence from current practice. Int. J. Oper. Prod. Manag. **26**(1), 92–112 (2006)
19. Jiménez, D., Martínez, M.: The performance effect of HRM and TQM. Int. J. Oper. Prod. Manag. **29**(12), 1266–1289 (2009)

20. Curbelo-Martínez, D., Pérez-de-Armas, M., Varela-Izquierdo, N.: Diseño y aplicación de un instrumento para la evaluación del contexto de aprendizaje en organizaciones de avanzada del territorio de cienfuegos/. Ingeniería Industrial **32**(2), 123–131 (2011)
21. Zadeh, L.A.: Fuzzy sets. Inf. Control **8**, 338–353 (1965)
22. Álvarez, F.T.: Confiabilidad en procesos de evaluación de 360 grados. Revista Interamericana de Psicología Ocupacional **23**(1), 1–13 (2016)
23. Chiavenato, I.. El capital humano de las organizaciones. 8va Edición (2009)
24. Valdés-Padrón, M., Garza-Ríos, R., Pérez-Vergara, I., Gé-Varona, M., Chávez-Vivó, A.R.: Una propuesta para la evaluación del desempeño de los trabajadores apoyada en el uso de técnicas cuantitativas. Ingeniería Industrial **36**(1), 48–57 (2015)
25. Sun, C.-C.: A performance evaluation model by integrating fuzzy AHP and fuzzy TOPSIS methods. Expert Syst. Appl. **37**(12), 7745–7754 (2010)
26. Rockwell, E.: Contradicciones de la evaluación del desempeño docente: lo que muestra la evidencia cuantitativa. Educación, Formación e Investigación **1**(1) (2015)
27. Vázquez, I.E.: La evaluación del Desempeño en las grandes empresas españolas. Universia Business Review **15**(3), 42–53 (2007)
28. Lau, H., Pang, W., Wong, C.: Methodology for monitoring supply chain performance: a fuzzy logic approach. Logist. Inf. Manag. **15**(4), 271–280 (2002)
29. Ling, C., Chiu, H., Tseng, Y.: Agility evaluation using fuzzy logic. Int. J. Prod. Econ. **101**, 353–368 (2006)
30. Silva, C., Sousa, J., Runkler, T.: Optimization of logistic systems using fuzzy weighted aggregation. Fuzzy Sets Syst. **158**, 1947–1960 (2007)
31. Arango, M.D., Zapata, J., Adarme, A.: Gestión de cadena de abastecimiento con indicadores bajo incertidumbre caso aplicado al sector panificador. Revista ciencia e ingeniería Neogranadina. **20**(1), 97–116 (2010)
32. Özdaban, I., Özkan, C.: A case study on evaluating personnel and jobs jointly with fuzzy distances. Int. J. Ind. Eng. **18**(4), 169–179 (2011)
33. Izquierdo, N., Viloria, A., Gaitán-Angulo, M., Bonerge, O., Lezama, P., Gutiérrez, A.: Methodology of application of diffuse mathematics to performance evaluation. Int. J. Control Theory Appl. (2016). ISSN 0974-5572

Fault Diagnosis on Electrical Distribution Systems Based on Fuzzy Logic

Ramón Perez[1]([✉]), Esteban Inga[1], Alexander Aguila[1],
Carmen Vásquez[2], Liliana Lima[3], Amelec Viloria[4],
and Maury-Ardila Henry[4]

[1] Electronic Department, Universidad Politécnica Salesiana, Quito, Ecuador
{rperezp, einga, aaguila}@ups.edu.ec
[2] Electrical Department, Universidad Nacional Experimental Politécnica
"Antonio José de Sucre", Barquisimeto, Venezuela
cvasquez@unexpo.edu.ve
[3] Basic Sciences Department, Mathematical Section, Universidad Nacional
Experimental Politécnica "Antonio José de Sucre", Barquisimeto, Venezuela
llima@unexpo.edu.ve
[4] Universidad de la Costa, Barranquilla, Colombia
{aviloria7, hamaury}@cuc.edu.co

Abstract. The occurrence of faults in distribution systems has a negative impact on society, and their effects can be reduced by fast and accurate diagnostic systems that allow to identify, locate, and correct the failures. Since the 1990s, fuzzy logic and other artificial intelligence techniques have been implemented to identify faults in distribution systems. The main objective of this paper is to perform fault diagnoses based on fuzzy logic. For conducting the study, the IEEE 34-Node Radial Test Feeder is used. The data was obtained from ATPDraw-based fault simulation on different nodes of the circuit considering three different fault resistance values of 0, 5, and 10 ohms. The fuzzy rules to identify the type of fault are defined using the magnitudes of the phase and neutral currents. All measurements are taken at the substation, and the results show that the proposed technique can perfectly identify and locate the type of failure.

Keywords: Distribution systems · Fault location · Fault type · Fuzzy logic

1 Introduction

Distribution systems are not immune to power outages caused by faults which are difficult to diagnose due to the network topology. When there is a service disruption caused by faults in the distribution system, the fault must be diagnosed, identified and located to repair and restore the service. For this reason, the design and development of fault diagnosis schemes for electrical distribution systems are the main steps in performing smart grid self-healing actions. Smart grids can minimize the negative impact of faults, reducing the time required for restoring of power supply.

© Springer International Publishing AG, part of Springer Nature 2018
Y. Tan et al. (Eds.): ICSI 2018, LNCS 10942, pp. 174–185, 2018.
https://doi.org/10.1007/978-3-319-93818-9_17

The methods based on knowledge, also known as "smart", have been used for diagnosing faults in electrical distribution systems. In [1], a combination of ANN and SVM is presented for locating faults in radial electrical distribution systems, using available measurements at the substation, the circuit breaker, and the relay states. The results of this combined approach demonstrate the feasibility of applying this method in the diagnosis of faults in the systems. Similarly, [2, 3] present an overview of intelligent techniques for locating faults.

In this research, the use of fuzzy logic is proposed to perform fault diagnosis in electrical distribution systems. For this purpose, the first step is to identify the fault type and location. The database is obtained by means of fault simulation with different resistance values on different nodes of a distribution circuit with the use of ATPDraw software and employing the Fuzzy Inference System (FIS).

2   Proposed Methodology

Fault diagnosis in electrical distribution systems is associated with the identification of the type and location of the fault [4]. This research is based on fuzzy logic to perform the analysis and the methodology to be followed consists in the fuzzification of the entries through membership functions. Fuzzy rules will be generated from the knowledge of the behavior of the system that will allow to design the FIS. A FIS defines a non-linear mapping input data vector into a scalar output using fuzzy rules. The assignment process involves membership functions with fuzzy input and output operators, logic rules If – then, aggregation of sets, and output defuzzification. Figure 1 shows the operation scheme of a FIS.

Fig. 1. Operation scheme of a FIS

A. **Fuzzification of the Inputs**
   The first step is to take the inputs and determine the degree to which each fuzzy set designed by membership functions belongs.
B. **Application of Fuzzy Operators**
   If the fuzzy rules have more than one part, i.e., the antecedent and/or consequent with several conditions, fuzzy logical operators are used to evaluate the strength of the rules made by the FIS.
C. **Application of Expert System**
   The Mamdani and Takagi - Sugeno expert systems are used in the FIS. Since each of them feature advantages and disadvantages, a comparative evaluation of these methods is carried out in [5]. Mamdani type expert system was developed in [6], and is the most common of the two mentioned types. This system is explained in detail in [7], describing it as a method of implication and is defined as the

conformation of the output membership function based on the biasing force of the fuzzy rules. Even more, the Takagi-Sugeno system is generally used if knowledge can be extracted from raw data, while the Mamdani system is preferred when human experts develop knowledge. So, the Mamdani system is used in this research.

D. **Defuzzification of All Outputs**

The aggregate output fuzzy set serves as an input to the defuzzificator that generates a clean output. Then, the defuzzificator combines information on the fuzzy inputs for a single variable sharp output (not fuzzy), which is done with defuzzification by the conventional centroid method.

3   Study Case

3.1   Test System and Database Obtaining

To carry out fault diagnosis in electrical distribution systems based on fuzzy logic, the 34-nodes test circuit, developed and published by the IEEE distribution systems analysis subcommittee, is considered with the aim of validating studies in the field of engineering. This feeder is 24.9 kV, the data from this system is in [8], and Fig. 2 shows the scheme.

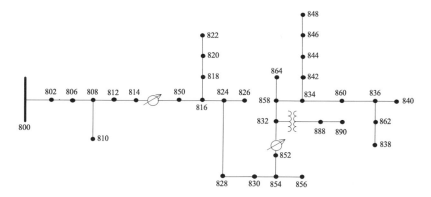

Fig. 2. IEEE 34-nodes feeder [8]

This system is simulated for the various copies of the circuit considering the 11 types of faults that are to be simulated in each node, with three (3) different fault resistance values, which are 0, 5, and 10 ohms, respectively, representing typical values in distribution systems [9]. This combination of different fault types considered with resistances results in a total of 882 to obtain the database needed to perform the fault diagnosis. The database is composed of the magnitudes of the phase and neutral "currents" for identifying the fault type, the impedance magnitudes, and the phase angles of voltages for the fault location. Table 1 shows the different types of faults simulated with the fault number assigned.

Table 1. Types of faults to simulate

Fault type	Nomenclature	Number of fault
Single phase to ground	a-g	1
	b-g	2
	c-g	3
Biphasic	a-b	4
	b-c	5
	c-a	6
Ground biphasic	a-b-g	7
	b-c-g	8
	c-a-g	9
Three phase	a-b-c	10
Grounded three phase	a-b-c-g	11

a: Phase A; b: Phase B; c: Phase C; g: Ground

3.2 Fault Type Identification

From the characteristics that define the different parallel faults that can occur in electrical distribution systems, the fuzzy rules that identify the type of fault are generated. These rules are created just with the database of the phase and neutral current magnitudes measured at the substation. Table 2 shows these rules.

Table 2. Fuzzy rules to identify the type of fault

Rule	$|I_A|$	$|I_B|$	$|I_C|$	$|I_N|$	Fault type
R1	H	N	N	H	a-g
R2	N	H	N	H	b-g
R3	N	N	H	H	c-g
R4	H	H	N	L	a-b
R5	N	H	H	L	b-c
R6	H	N	H	L	c-a
R7	H	H	N	H	a-b-g
R8	N	H	H	H	b-c-g
R9	H	N	H	H	c-a-g
R10	H	H	H	L	a-b-c
R11	H	H	H	N	a-b-c-g

H: High; N: Normal; L: Low

Input fuzzy sets, corresponding to the antecedent of the rule, are represented by a trapezoidal-shaped membership function, which adapts the magnitudes of the phase and neutral currents for different types of faults. Figure 3 shows the membership function. The values of points A, B, C, and D, associated with the trapezoidal membership function representing the input fuzzy sets to identify the type of fault according to the linguistic variable that it describes, are shown in Table 3.

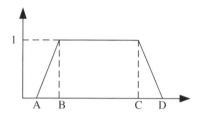

Fig. 3. Trapezoidal-shaped membership function

Table 3. Input fuzzy sets to identify the type of fault

Fuzzy set	Linguistic variables	A	B	C	D
$|I_A|$	Normal	0	4	26	30
	High	32	36	760	850
$|I_B|$	Normal	0	4	26	30
	High	32	36	760	850
$|I_C|$	Normal	0	4	26	30
	High	32	36	760	850
$|I_N|$	Low	0	1	1.5	1.6
	Normal	2	4	8	10
	High	7	8	760	850

The consequent of the rules (type of fault) should also be a fuzzy set. Based on the binary code proposed in [10] and used in [11–14], it is possible to perform the fuzzification of the type of fault that occurs. Thus, defined as a binary code b_3 for phase A, b_2 for phase B, b_1 for phase C, and b_0 for the ground, it is possible to define the Equivalent Number for the Type of Fault (ENTF) by the Eq. (1)

$$ENTF = \sum_{n=0}^{3} 2^n b_n \tag{1}$$

For example, for a single-phase fault in phase A, b_3 is 1, b_2 is 0, b_1 is 0, and b_0 is 1, resulting an ENTF equal to 9. Table 4 shows the ENTF for each fault type.

Table 4. Equivalent number for the type of fault

Fault type	b_3	b_2	b_1	b_0	ENTF
a-g	1	0	0	1	9
b-g	0	1	0	1	5
c-g	0	0	1	1	3
a-b	1	1	0	0	12
b-c	0	1	1	0	6
c-a	1	0	1	0	10
a-b-g	1	1	0	1	13
b-c-g	0	1	1	1	7
c-a-g	1	0	1	1	11
a-b-c	1	1	1	0	14
a-b-c-g	1	1	1	1	15

This output fuzzy set, corresponding to the consequent of the rule, is represented by a triangular membership function as shown in Fig. 4.

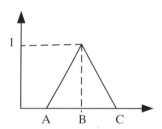

Fig. 4. Triangular membership function

The values of points A, B, and C, associated with the triangular membership function representing the output fuzzy set regarding the type of fault occurring are shown in Table 5.

3.3   Fault Location

To complete the fault diagnosis, the fault is identified and then located. For this purpose, the distribution circuit is divided into zones, grouping nodes with similar profiles impedance and phase angle of voltage, all measured at the substation. These profiles were considered to propose the fuzzy rules to locate the zone of occurrence of the fault. Figure 5 shows the division of circuit zones. Table 6 shows the nodes for each zone in the distribution circuit.

Table 5. Output fuzzy set to identify the fault type

Fault type	A	B	C
a-g	8.5	9	9.5
b-g	4.5	5	5.5
c-g	2.5	3	3.5
a-b	11.5	12	12.5
b-c	5.5	6	6.5
c-a	9.5	10	10.5
a-b-g	12.5	13	13.5
b-c-g	6.5	7	7.5
c-a-g	10.5	11	11.5
a-b-c	13.5	14	14.5
a-b-c-g	14.5	15	15.5

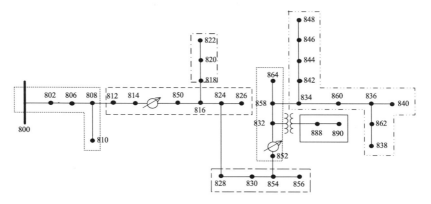

Fig. 5. Distribution circuit division

The FIS is defined for each fault type with a total of 11 FIS, with a fuzzy rule for each containing zone. The fuzzy sets each FIS input variables corresponding to the impedances and voltage phase angles measured at the substation. Table 7 shows the fuzzy rules to locate the fault zone.

In Table 7, the superscripted accompanying the linguistic variable refers to the number of fault, explained in Table 1. The connective for each rule is the operator "AND". Input fuzzy sets are modelled by trapezoidal membership function, with the magnitudes impedance and angles of the voltage per phase. The consequent of the rules (fault zone) also becomes diffuse, like the identification of the type of fault. Thus, in Eq. (2) ENFZ represents the Equivalent Number of the Fault Zone.

$$ENFZ = 2n + 1 \tag{2}$$

Table 6. Nodes for each zone

Zone	Nodes	Label
Z1	800, 802, 806, 810	··················
Z2	812, 814, 816, 824, 826, 850	– – – – – ·
Z3	818, 820, 822	– · – · – · ·
Z4	828, 830, 854, 856	– · — · —
Z5	832,852,858,864	··················
Z6	834, 836, 838, 840, 842, 844, 846, 848, 860, 862	— · · — · ·
Z7	888, 890	—————

Table 7. Fuzzy rules to locate the fault zone

Rule	$|Z_A|$	$|Z_B|$	$|Z_C|$	θ_A	θ_B	θ_C	Fault Zone
R1	VL^1	VL^2	$VL^{3,10,11}$	VH^1	VH^2	$VL^{3,10,11}$	Z1
	$VL^{6,9}$	$VL^{4,7}$	$VL^{5,8}$	$VH^{4,7}$	$TH^{5,8}$	$VL^{6,9}$	
R2	L^1	L^2	$L^{3,10,11}$	H^1	H^2	$L^{3,10,11}$	Z2
	$L^{6,9}$	$L^{4,7}$	$L^{5,8}$	$H^{4,7}$	$VH^{5,8}$	$L^{6,9}$	
R3	M^1	-	-	HM^1	-	-	Z3
R4	LM^1	LM^2	$LM^{3,10,11}$	M^1	HM^2	$LM^{3,10,11}$	Z4
	$LM^{6,9}$	$LM^{4,7}$	$LM^{5,8}$	$M^{4,7}$	$H^{5,8}$	$M^{6,9}$	
R5	HM^1	M^2	$M^{3,10,11}$	LM^1	LM^2	$HM^{3,10,11}$	Z5
	$HM^{6,9}$	$M^{4,7}$	$M^{5,8}$	$LM^{4,7}$	$M^{5,8}$	$HM^{6,9}$	
R6	H^1	H^2	$H^{3,10,11}$	L^1	L^2	$H^{3,10,11}$	Z6
	$H^{6,9}$	$H^{4,7}$	$H^{5,8}$	$L^{4,7}$	$L^{5,8}$	$H^{6,9}$	
R7	VH^1	VH^2	$VH^{3,10,11}$	VL^1	VL^2	$VH^{3,10,11}$	Z7
	$VH^{6,9}$	$VII^{4,7}$	$VII^{5,8}$	$VL^{4,7}$	$VL^{5,8}$	$VH^{6,9}$	

VL: Very Low; L: Low; M: Medium; LM: Lightly Medium;
HM: Highly Medium; H: High; VH: Very High; TH: Too High

This output fuzzy set, corresponding to the consequent of the rule, is represented by a triangular membership function shown in Fig. 4. Table 8 shows the ENFZ and the points A, B, and C of the triangular membership function for each type of fault, with possible values of n for the seven (7) zones of fault.

Table 8. Output fuzzy set to locate the fault zone

Fault zone	ENZF	A	B	C
Z1	1	0	1	2
Z2	3	2	3	4
Z3	5	4	5	6
Z4	7	6	7	8
Z5	9	8	9	10
Z6	11	10	11	12
Z7	13	12	13	14

Table 9. FIS output for faults that include ground

		Fault type							$Rf\ (\Omega)$
		a-g	b-g	c-g	a-b-g	b-c-g	c-a-g	a-b-c-g	
Node	808	9	5	3	13	7	11	15	5
Zone	Z1	1	1	1	1	1	1	1	
Node	812	9	5	3	13	7	11	15	0
Zone	Z2	3	3	3	3	3	3	3	
Node	818	9	-	-	-	-	-	-	10
Zone	Z3	4,1	-	-	-	-	-	–	
Node	854	9	5	3	13	7	11	15	5
Zone	Z4	7	7	7	7	7	7	7	
Node	832	9	5	3	13	7	11	15	0
Zone	Z5	9	9	9	9	9	9	9	
Node	848	9	5	3	13	7	11	15	10
Zone	Z6	11	1	1	11	11	11	11	
Node	888	9	5	3	13	7	11	15	5
Zone	Z7	13	1	1	13	13	13	13	

4   Analysis of Results

Tables 9 and 10 show the results of the outputs from the FIS corresponding to the identification of the fault type and zone for simulations on multiple nodes of the system under study. Tables 9 and 10 show that there is a perfect identification of the fault type for all nodes considered with their respective associated fault resistance Rf. The output value of FIS designed for the type of fault corresponds exactly to the fault occurring in the distribution network. In the specific case of node 818, it only has a single-phase fault result in the phase A. Figure 6 shows the simulated fault and the correctly identified type for each.

Tables 9 and 10 also show the zone where the fault occurs, which is determined by the identification. Comparing this result with Table 8 and Fig. 5, it can be observed that the fault is correctly located. The output value of FIS, designed to locate the fault zone, corresponds exactly to the type of fault that occurs in the distribution network.

By the configuration of the radial distribution networks including different wire sizes, different line lengths, and having a single measurement, some faults are located incorrectly, as shown in Table 11 where the results indicate that, although the fault is correctly identified, the location is incorrect, so the FIS yields an output value that is not associated with any zone, that is, the location of the fault corresponds to more than one zone.

Figure 7 shows bar graphs about the simulated fault type that were correctly located. It is noted that the biggest mistake in the location was in type 1 fault.

The use of hybrid methods requiring more parameters are avoided [14] in this work that represents a contribution for the use of fuzzy logic in the diagnosis of faults in electrical distribution systems, which is not reported in the scientific literature.

Table 10. FIS output for faults that exclude ground

		Fault type				Rf (Ω)
		a-b	b-c	c-a	a-b-c	
Node	808	12	6	10	14	5
Zone	Z1	1	1	1	1	
Node	812	12	6	10	14	0
Zone	Z2	3	3	3	3	
Node	818	-	-	-	-	10
Zone	Z3	-	-	-	-	
Node	854	12	6	10	14	5
Zone	Z4	7	7	7	7	
Node	832	12	6	10	14	0
Zone	Z5	9	9	9	9	
Node	848	12	6	10	14	10
Zone	Z6	11	11	11	11	
Node	888	12	6	10	14	5
Zone	Z7	13	13	13	13	

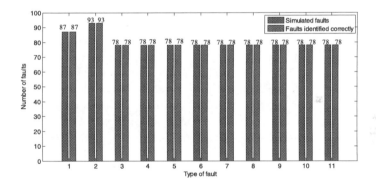

Fig. 6. Fault simulated and correctly identified for each type

Table 11. Errors in fault location

		Fault type			Rf (Ω)
		a-b	b-c	c-a	
Node	828	12	6	10	0
Zone	Z4	5	5	3.46	0
Node	834	12	6	10	0
Zone	Z6	10	10	10	0

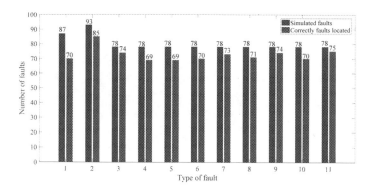

Fig. 7. Simulated faults and correctly located faults

5 Conclusions

In this research, IEEE 34-Nodes fuzzy logic has been applied to perform fault diagnosis. Fuzzy rules for the FIS are established to identify the type of fault that occurs, and the fault location was completed by dividing the circuit zones. The antecedent is represented by trapezoidal membership functions, while the consequent was represented by triangular membership functions. The results show that the identification of 11 types of faults is perfect, just using the magnitudes of phase and neutral currents measured at the substation.

The magnitude of the impedance and the angle of the phase voltage measured by the substation is used for locating the fault zone. At this stage, the location provided satisfactory results since fault zones were located correctly and only some faults were not correctly located. So, the fuzzy logic proved to be adequate for faults diagnosis in electrical distribution systems.

References

1. Thukaram, D., Khincha, H., Vijaynarasimha, H.: Artificial neural network and support vector machine approach for locating faults in radial distribution systems. IEEE Trans. Power Delivery **20**, 710–721 (2005)
2. Mirzaei, M., Kadir, M., Moazami, E., Hizam, H.: Review of fault location methods for distribution power system. Aust. J. Basic Appl. Sci. **3**, 2670–2676 (2009)
3. Prakash, M., Pradhan, S., Roy, S.: Soft computing techniques for fault detection in power distribution systems : a review. In: 2014 International Conference on Green Computing Communication and Electrical Engineering (ICGCCEE), pp. 1–6 (2014)
4. Mustafa, M.: A novel fuzzy cause-and-effect-networks based methodology for a distribution system's. In: 2013 3rd International Conference on Electric Power and Energy Conversion Systems (EPECS), pp. 1–6 (2013)
5. Ying, H., Ying, H., Ding, Y., Ding, Y., Li, S., Li, S., Shao, S., Shao, S.: Typical Takagi-Sugeno and Mamdani fuzzy systems as universal approximators. In: IEEE International Conference on Fuzzy Systems, pp. 824–828 (1998)

6. Mamdani, E., Assilian, S.: An experiment in linguistic synthesis with a fuzzy logic controller. Int. J. Man Mach. Stud. **7**, 1–13 (1975)
7. Schnitman, L., Yoneyama, T.: An efficient implementation of a learning method for Mamdani fuzzy models. In: Proceedings of the Sixth Brazilian Symposium on Neural Networks, vol. 1, pp. 38–43 (2000)
8. Distribution System Analysis Subcommittee: IEEE 34 Node Test Feeder (2000)
9. Pérez, R., Vásquez, C.: Fault location in distribution systems with distributed generation using support vector machines and smart meters. In: IEEE Ecuador Technical Chapters Meeting (ETCM), pp. 1–6 (2016)
10. Das, B.: Fuzzy logic-based fault-type identification in unbalanced radial power distribution system. IEEE Trans. Power Delivery **21**, 278–285 (2006)
11. Mahanty, R., Gupta, P.: A fuzzy logic based fault classification approach using current samples only. Electr. Power Syst. Res. **77**, 501–507 (2007)
12. Babayomi, O., Oluseyi, P., Keku, G., Ofodile, N.: Neuro-fuzzy based fault detection identification and location in a distribution network. In: Proceedings of 2017 IEEE PES-IAS PowerAfrica Conference: Harnessing Energy, Information and Communications Technology (ICT) for Affordable Electrification of Africa, PowerAfrica, pp. 164–168 (2017)
13. Ri, H.: A hybrid wavelet singular entropy and fuzzy system based fault detection and classification on distribution line with distributed generation. In: 2nd IEEE International Conference on Recent Trends in Electronics Information and Communication Technology (RTEICT), pp. 1473–1477 (2017)
14. Izquierdo, N.V., Viloria, A., Gaitán-Angulo, M., Bonerg, O., Lezama, P., Erase, J.J.C., Gutiérrez, A.S.: Methodology of application of diffuse mathematics to performance evaluation. Int. J. Control Theory Appl. (2016). ISSN 0974-5572

Planning and Routing Problems

Using FAHP-VIKOR for Operation Selection in the Flexible Job-Shop Scheduling Problem: A Case Study in Textile Industry

Miguel Ortíz-Barrios[1]($\boxtimes$), Dionicio Neira-Rodado[1],
Genett Jiménez-Delgado[2], and Hugo Hernández-Palma[3]

[1] Department of Industrial Management, Agroindustry and Operations,
Universidad de la Costa CUC, Barranquilla, Colombia
{mortizl, dneiral}@cuc.edu.co
[2] Department of Industrial Engineering,
Corporación Universitaria Reformada CUR, Barranquilla, Colombia
g.jimenez@unireformada.edu.co
[3] Department of Business Management, Universidad del Atlántico,
Puerto Colombia, Colombia
hugohernandezp@mail.uniatlantico.edu.co

Abstract. Scheduling of Flexible Job Shop Systems is a combinatorial problem which has been addressed by several heuristics and meta-heuristics. Nevertheless, the operation selection rules of both methods are limited to an ordered variant wherein priority-dispatching rules are not simultaneously deemed in the reported literature. Therefore, this paper presents the application of dispatching algorithm with operation selection based on Fuzzy Analytic Hierarchy Process (FAHP) and VIKOR methods while considering setup times and transfer batches. Dispatching, FAHP, and VIKOR algorithms are first defined. Second, a multi-criteria decision-making model is designed for operation prioritization. Then, FAHP is applied to calculate the criteria weights and overcome the uncertainty of human judgments. Afterwards, VIKOR is used to select the operation with the highest priority. A case study in the textile industry is shown to validate this approach. The results evidenced, compared to the company solution, a reduction of 61.05% in average delay.

Keywords: Flexible job shop problem · Scheduling · Dispatching algorithm
Fuzzy Analytic Hierarchy Process (FAHP) · VIKOR

1 Introduction

One of the most critical strategies implemented by companies is related to the production process layout. Nevertheless, a good process layout does not ensure customer satisfaction. In this regard, it is also necessary to adequately manage this process to be productive, ensure on-time delivery and be flexible with last-minute orders. However, flexible production scheduling is highly complex [2, 5]. One of the production arrangements is known as *flexible job shop* which is defined as an extension of the classical job shop system which lets an operation to be processed by any machine from

© Springer International Publishing AG, part of Springer Nature 2018
Y. Tan et al. (Eds.): ICSI 2018, LNCS 10942, pp. 189–201, 2018.
https://doi.org/10.1007/978-3-319-93818-9_18

a specified set. This system has gained importance because companies need to produce more customized goods, which requires smaller batches, and machines capable to perform different operations [1, 2], considering that the number of competitors and demand for more customized goods continue to increase [2–4, 29]. Considering the aforementioned aspects, this arrangement can be frequently found in the apparel industry [1, 2, 6]. Nonetheless, the difficulty of addressing flexible job shop problem (FJSP) is a well-known and complex (NP) hard combinational optimization problem [7, 8]. Common objectives are the minimization of the *makespan*, average tardiness or average flow time [9], and throughput [10]. The problem can be mathematically addressed by applying lexicographic optimization or assigning weights with a Pareto front. Considering the complexity of FJSP, different solution techniques such as various meta-heuristics approaches, (e.g. Nature based heuristics, genetic algorithms, simulated annealing) and heuristic approaches have been developed. Normally, scheduling approaches focus on optimizing only one performance measure. Nevertheless, the problem is even sharper when prioritizing operations with multiple criteria to be simultaneously considered. In this regard, the multi-criteria decision making (MCDM) techniques have become a new tool to tackle problems where variables and attributes need to be considered simultaneously [11]. However, when establishing the criteria weights, uncertainty may occur, due to uncompleted preference relationships emanating from human subjective judgments collected during the implementation of several multi-criteria decision-making techniques. Therefore, this paper explores the viability of integrating a heuristic approach with a fuzzy MCDM technique to find an adequate sequence in an FJSP whilst properly satisfying different requirements e.g., due date, throughput, and others. The novelty of this study lies on the fact that the reported literature does not evidence applications simultaneously considering different parameters of interest when scheduling flexible job-shop systems under uncertainty. The remainder of this paper is organized as follows: in Sect. 2, a good overview of the literature regarding Flexible Job-Shop Scheduling techniques is presented; Sect. 3 illustrates the proposed methodology; Sect. 4 describes and analyzes the results of a case study from the textile industry. Finally, Sect. 5 presents the conclusions and future work derived from this study.

2   Flexible Job Shop Problem (FJSP) and Operation Scheduling

FJSP is a prominent topic of study for researchers due to its theoretical, computational, and empirical significance since it was introduced [2]. It is relevant the search for an efficient method to solve FJSP, since the optimization of FJSP help companies to increase its production efficiency; reduce cost and improve product quality [9]. In a flexible job shop problem, each operation can be performed by one out of several machines [12–14]. It is important to point out that the problem of scheduling jobs in FJSPs could be decomposed into two sub-problems: the routing, where each operation is assigned to a relevant machine selected from a set of capable machines, and the scheduling, (sequencing) where the starting times of these operations are calculated for all the machines to obtain a feasible schedule (the technological constraints not violated) and to minimize the predefined objective functions [12, 13, 15]. The problem is considered as very hard and costly to solve [17] due to its complexity. The *makespan* minimization is the commonest optimization objective for FJSPs. Nevertheless, this is often combined with other minimization objectives (e.g., workload, critical machine workload, maximum tardiness, maximum lateness, average completion time, the number of tardy jobs and maximum cost) [15, 16]. To address FJSP, different heuristic procedures such as dispatching rules, local search, meta-heuristics procedures and optimization algorithms (krill herd, monarch butterfly optimization (MBO), earthworm optimization algorithm (EWA), elephant herding optimization (EHO) and moth search (MS) algorithm) have been applied [2]. The most used meta-heuristics to tackle these multi-objective problems are Particle Swarm Optimization (PSO), Simulated Annealing (SA) and HGA (Hybrid genetic algorithms) [13, 18, 19, 25, 27]. There is also a group of multi-objective FJSPs that have been addressed by applying mathematical models consisting of multi-criteria mixed-integer linear or nonlinear mathematical programming [15, 20, 21]. Other authors have addressed the multi-objective FJSP with the use of dispatching rules. In this sense, Ortiz *et al.* [2] developed a dispatching rule-based algorithm to minimize average tardiness for FJSP considering transfer batches, but considering the throughput as the second rule of operation selection, since this measure had not been considered in the mathematical model proposed by Calleja and Pastor [10]. Nonetheless, in these works, operation selection is subject to an ordered variant where the priority dispatching rules are applied in a predefined order. Aiming to determine the importance of each criterion in the dispatching rule Analytic Hierarchy Process (AHP) can be incorporated. AHP is widely used in industry since it establishes dominance priorities of several elements with respect to common criteria [22–25]. It also copes with the rational and irrational when decision makers address multi-objective and multi-criteria decisions with a predefined number of alternatives (e.g. eligible operations). Moreover, in order to overcome the lack of certainty derived from human judgments and to provide a more realistic selection, fuzzy logic can be applied to the implementation of AHP [26, 27]. This will pave the road towards the selection of the operation with the highest priority. For this purpose, it is necessary to rank the eligible operations. In this regard, several methods have been proposed (e.g. TOPSIS, PROMETHEE, VIKOR). Particularly, VIKOR is used in this study since it ranks a set of alternatives in the presence of conflicting criteria [28]. Considering the findings of the literature review, the studies concentrating on FJSP algorithms with operation selection based on the use of FAHP and VIKOR are largely limited. In light of these, we implemented a hybrid approach in this work, which is an adaptation of Calleja and Pastor's [10] in order to provide an effective tool to be used in realistic scenarios of the industry. A case study in textile sector has been developed as an example of this approach.

3   Methods

3.1   Fuzzy Analytic Hierarchy Process (FAHP)

Criteria weights are obtained by applying FAHP. A description of this method can be found below:

- Collect the pairwise judgments for the predefined criteria by applying a survey. The comparisons are expressed in accordance with the fundamental scale of fuzzy triangular numbers as here stated: [1, 1, 1] as "Equal importance", [1, 2, 3] "Weak or slight importance", [2, 3, 4] "Moderate importance", [3, 4, 5] "Moderate plus importance", [4, 5, 6] "Strong importance", [5, 6, 7] "Strong plus importance", [6, 7, 8] "Very strong importance", [7, 8, 9] "Very, very strong importance" and [8, 9, 10] "Extreme importance" The reciprocal of above numbers were assigned to the remaining judgments.

- Organize the judgments into a fuzzy comparison matrix $\tilde{A}^k(a_{ij})$ for criteria (Eq. 1). The values on the diagonal are always [1, 1, 1] due to an element is equal to itself.

$$\tilde{A}^K = \begin{bmatrix} \tilde{d}_{11}^k & \tilde{d}_{12}^k & \cdots & \tilde{d}_{1n}^k \\ \tilde{d}_{21}^k & \tilde{d}_{22}^k & \cdots & \tilde{d}_{2n}^k \\ \cdots & \cdots & \cdots & \cdots \\ \tilde{d}_{n1}^k & \tilde{d}_{n2}^k & \cdots & \tilde{d}_{nn}^k \end{bmatrix}. \tag{1}$$

Here $\tilde{d}_{ij}^k$ represents how much the criterion ith dominates the criterion jth according to the kth expert's preference. When the judgments are made by a group of experts, $\tilde{d}_{ij}^k$ is obtained by applying Eq. 2. After this, the fuzzy judgment matrix is updated as described in Eq. 3.

$$\tilde{d}_{ij} = \frac{\sum_{k=1}^{K} \tilde{d}_{ij}^k}{K}. \tag{2}$$

$$\tilde{A} = \begin{bmatrix} \tilde{d}_{11} & \cdots & \tilde{d}_{1n} \\ \vdots & \ddots & \vdots \\ \tilde{d}_{n1} & \cdots & \tilde{d}_{nn} \end{bmatrix}. \tag{3}$$

- Establish the geometric mean of fuzzy judgment numbers of each criterion via applying Eq. 4. Here, $\tilde{r}_i$ represents triangular numbers.

$$\tilde{r}_i = \left(\prod_{j=1}^{n} \tilde{d}_{ij} \right)^{1/n}, \ i = 1, 2, \ldots, n. \tag{4}$$

- Calculate the fuzzy weights of each criterion $(\tilde{w}_i)$ by using Eq. 5.

$$\tilde{w}_i = \tilde{r}_i \otimes (\tilde{r}_1 \oplus \tilde{r}_2 \oplus \ldots \oplus \tilde{r}_n)^{-1} = (lw_i, mw_i, uw_i). \tag{5}$$

- Defuzzify ($\tilde{w}_i$) via applying Centre of Area method (refer to Eq. 6). M_i represents a non-fuzzy number. After this, normalize M_i (refer to Eq. 7).

$$M_i = \frac{lw_i + mw_i + uw_i}{3}. \tag{6}$$

$$N_i = \frac{M_i}{\sum_{i=1}^{n} M_i}. \tag{7}$$

3.2 VIKOR Method

VIKOR is a method that is used to rank eligible operations under non-commensurable and decision criteria. The procedure of VIKOR is detailed as follows:

- A set of m eligible operations denoted as E_1, E_2, ..., E_m is stated for the operation selection problem. Here, each operation E_i is defined by a number of prioritizing criteria (n). The value of each criterion C_j is represented by f_{ij} and is introduced in matrix A (refer to Eq. 8)

$$A = \begin{array}{c} E_1 \\ E_2 \\ E_3 \\ \vdots \\ E_m \end{array} \begin{bmatrix} C_1 & C_2 & \cdots & C_n \\ f_{11} & f_{12} & \cdots & f_{1n} \\ f_{21} & f_{22} & \cdots & f_{2n} \\ f_{31} & f_{32} & \cdots & f_{3n} \\ \vdots & \vdots & \cdots & \vdots \\ f_{m1} & f_{m2} & \cdots & f_{mn} \end{bmatrix}. \tag{8}$$

- Define the best (f_j^*) and the worst (f_j^-) values in each criterion via applying Eqs. 9 and 10.

$$f_j^* = \begin{cases} \max_i f_{ij}, & \text{for benefit criteria} \\ \min_i f_{ij}, & \text{for cost criteria} \end{cases}, \quad i = 1, 2, \ldots, m. \tag{9}$$

$$f_j^- = \begin{cases} \min_i f_{ij}, & \text{for benefit criteria} \\ \max_i f_{ij}, & \text{for cost criteria} \end{cases}, \quad i = 1, 2, \ldots, m. \tag{10}$$

- Determine the S_i and R_i values by performing Eqs. 11 and 12. Here, w_j represents the weight of the criterion C_j. This measure is an output provided by the FAHP method.

$$S_i = \sum_{j=1}^{n} \frac{w_j \left(f_j^* - f_{ij} \right)}{f_j^* - f_j^-}. \tag{11}$$

$$R_i = \max_j \left(\frac{w_j \left(f_j^* - f_{ij} \right)}{f_j^* - f_j^-} \right). \tag{12}$$

- Calculate the Q_i values by applying Eqs. 13, 14 and 15. Here, v denotes the weight of the strategy for the maximum group utility.

$$Q_i = v \frac{S_i - S^*}{S^- - S^*} + (1 - v) \frac{R_i - R^*}{R^- - R^*}. \tag{13}$$

$$S^* = \min_i S_i, S^-. \tag{14}$$

$$R^* = \min_i R_i, R^-. \tag{15}$$

- Rank the eligible operations based on S_i, Q_i and R_i values.
- Establish a compromise solution $(P^{(1)})$ by selecting the best-ranked operation in accordance with Q_i ranking list and satisfying the conditions below:
  - *Acceptable advantage* (refer to Eqs. 16 and 17):

$$Q\left(P^{(2)}\right) - Q\left(P^{(1)}\right) \geq DQ. \tag{16}$$

$$DQ = \frac{1}{m - 1}. \tag{17}$$

Here $Q\left(P^{(2)}\right)$ is the eligible operation with the second highest priority in the Q_i ranking list. The number of alternatives, in this case *jobs*, is represented by m.
  - *Acceptable stability in decision making*: The operation $(P^{(1)})$ must be also the best-ranked in S_i and R_i lists.
    If one of the aforementioned conditions is not satisfied, select one of these solutions:

  - $(P^{(1)})y(P^{(2)})$ if there is not an acceptable stability in decision making.
  - $(P^{(1)})$, $(P^{(2)})$, ..., (P^m) if there is not an acceptable advantage. Here, $(P^{(m)})$ is subject to the following formula:

$$Q\left(P^{(m)}\right) - Q\left(P^{(1)}\right) < DQ.$$

3.3   Integration of FAHP, VIKOR and Dispatching Methods

The Flexible Job-shop Problem is stated as follows: Let $J_i = \{J_1, J_2, ..., J_n\}$ be a set of n orders which can be produced by m machines where $M_k = \{M_1, M_2, ..., M_m\}$. Each order J_i has a predefined sequence of n_i operations P_{ij} ($j = 1, 2, ..., n_i$). The operation P_{ij} is performed on a machine selected from a specific set of available machines. Here, R_{ki} is defined as the availability time of operation (i, j). Moreover, f_{pk} represents the earlier time to start a new operation on the machine k (*Note: if no queue, an infinite value is assigned*). In this regard, the objective is to minimize average tardiness of orders and by considering *order quantity, product throughput, monthly product demand, order delay* and *customer type* criteria simultaneously. In addition, some assumptions are considered:

- The machines perform one operation at a time.
- Setup times and transfer batches are deemed.
- Eligible operations are prioritized in accordance with the rank obtained by FAHP-VIKOR
- The release time of all the orders is 0.

The proposed procedure can be described as below (refer to Fig. 1)

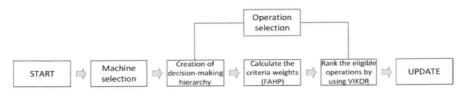

Fig. 1. Proposed methodology for FJSS with high-throughput orders

Start: The first operations of the orders must be introduced in the *eligible operations* (E_i) subset with their r_{1i} values correspondingly. After this, determine f_{pk} for each machine. Finally, identify the machine with f_{pmin}. (See Eq. 21)

Machine selection: If $f_{pmin} = \infty$, all operations have been already programmed. Otherwise, select a machine with f_{pmin}. However, if there is a set of machines with f_{pmin}, select the operation with the highest closeness coefficient by applying FAHP-VIKOR. Closeness coefficient is related with the fact of how close is an alternative (a job in this case) from the ideal solution (job giving the best values for each criterion). The calculation of the coefficient will be described in Sect. 3.3.

Operation Selection: If there is one operation in E_i, this must be scheduled. Otherwise, select the operation with the highest closeness coefficient by using FAHP-VIKOR. For this, it is first necessary to create the decision-making hierarchy selecting the operation with the highest priority. Then, FAHP is applied to calculate the criteria weights while considering the vagueness stemming from human judgments (refer to Subsect. 3.1). The weights are then incorporated into VIKOR method which finally ranks the operations in accordance with the company preferences (refer to Subsect. 3.2).

Update: Program the selected operation (j, i) by setting its start and final time (refer to Eqs. 18 and 19)

$$t_{start}(j, i) = rp_{j,j,k}. \tag{18}$$

$$t_{final}(j, i) = t_{start}(j, i) + Dp_{j,i,k}. \tag{19}$$

Here, D denotes the order size and $p_{j,i,k}$ represents the unit processing time of operation j of the order i in the machine k. Then, introduce the selected operation in the subset of programmed operations. If this is not the last operation of order i, move its next operation from N_i (Unavailable operations) to E_i. On the other hand, taking into account that k' is the machine associated with the next operation of order i, Q represents the transfer batch size and t_q is defined as the time to move a transfer lot size Q, the release date $(r_{j+1,i})$ can be then determined as detailed in Table 1:

Table 1. Formulas for release date considering transfer batches.

Relation between k and k'	Relation between $p_{(j, i, k)}$ and $p_{(j+1, i, k)}$	$r_{(j + 1, i, k)}$
$k = k'$	All relations between $p_{j.i.k}$ and $p_{j+1.i.k}$	$t_{final(j,i)}$
$k \neq k'$	$p_{(j+1.i.k')} \geq p_{(j.i.k)}$	$tstart(j,i) + (tq + Qp(j,i,k))/60$
	$p_{(j+1.i.k')} < p_{(j.i.k)}$	$tfinal(j,i) - Dp_{(j.i.k)} + (tq + Qp(j,i,k))/60$

Now, it is necessary to update f_k. In this respect, if the machine k' has not already used, $f_k = 0$. But, if any operation in machine k has been programmed, then, $f_k = t_{final}$ (j, i) i.e., the machine j will have an availability time f_k that is equal to the final time of the last scheduled operation in the machine k. Then, determine $rp_{j,i,k}$ (refer to Eq. 20)

$$rp_{j,i,k} = max\left(r_{j,i}, f_k\right).$$ (20)

Finally, determine f_{pmin} (refer to Eq. 21):

$$fp_{min} = min\left(rp_{j+1,i}\right).$$ (21)

4   A Case Study in Textile Industry

The proposed approach was implemented in a textile production system. Particularly, this company offers three product lines to the market: Towels, Bedspreads, and Muleras. The manufacturing system configuration is comprised of 5 activities and each product line has an operational sequence. Some operations can be performed by any machine from a predefined set but with different production ratios. However, some products (e.g. hotel towels) can be processed by certain resources due to the high-quality standards required by these customers. The processing times (min) for each operation are detailed in Table 2. Here, the cells with cross mark denote that the activity is not part of the predefined processing route of the product. The throughput and monthly demand are shown in Table 3. The orders for each product reference are also tabled (refer to Table 3). The due date for each order is indicated in *brackets* (day – month).

Table 2. Current processing times for each operation

Reference	Weaving			Dyeing				Cutting		Side seam		Cleaning	
Resource	A1	A2	A3	T1	T2	T3	T4	C1	C2	S1	S2	L1	L2
SBS	3,74	4,5	4,4	1,56	1,61	1,9	1,6	1,49	1,49	3	3	2,43	2,43
SFBS	X	X	3,75	1,67	1,73	2,08	1,72	1,49	1,49	3	3	2,43	2,43
SSB	3,74	4,5	4,4	1,56	1,61	1,9	1,6	1,49	1,49	2	2	1,43	1,43
DB	5,23	X	4,84	2,1	2,19	2,77	2,18	1,49	1,49	2,33	2,33	1,54	1,54
DFBS	X	X	7,57	1,84	1,92	2,35	1,89	1,49	1,49	2,33	2,33	1,54	1,54
SDB	5,23	X	4,84	2,1	2,19	2,77	2,18	1,49	1,49	2,33	2,33	1,54	1,54
SSBS	X	X	4,6	1,55	1,61	1,89	1,59	1,49	1,49	1,5	1,5	1,43	1,43
SSFB	X	X	3,7	1,67	1,73	2,07	1,71	0,51	0,51	1,5	1,5	1,43	1,43
SDBS	X	X	6,4	1,67	1,73	2,07	1,71	0,51	0,51	1,5	1,5	1,43	1,43
SDFBS	X	X	5,34	1,67	1,73	2,07	1,71	0,51	0,51	1,5	1,5	1,43	1,43
P	1,74	X	1,86	X	X	X	X	0,12	0,12	1,87	1,87	2,4	2,4
YP	X	1,76	1,86	X	X	X	X	0,12	0,12	1,87	1,87	2,4	2,4
M	5,28	X	5,98	X	X	X	X	0,04	0,04	1,87	1,87	5,37	5,37

To prioritize eligible operations, a FAHP-VIKOR method was applied. For this purpose, five criteria (refer to Fig. 2) were selected by the production managers in accordance with the company goals: *order quantity, product throughput, monthly product demand, order delay* and *customer type*. In this regard, *order quantity* (OQ) represents the amount of product required by customers in each order. *Product throughput* (PT) denotes the ratio earnings/time in the bottleneck so that high-profitable products can be identified. *Monthly product demand* (MPD) is a measure considering the product acceptability in the market. *Order delay* (OD) is deemed as the time period between the due date and the real delivery time of an order. Finally, *customer type* (CT) represents the client profile in accordance with their payment history.

Regarding the inclusion of FAHP-VIKOR method in operation selection, the pairwise comparisons were made by the operation managers through a survey and then analyzed via using Superdecisions® software (refer to Table 4). The relative weights of prioritizing criteria are detailed in Fig. 2. These measures are used as insights for VIKOR method. To implement this technique, a metric was defined for each criterion: *order quantity* (order size), *product throughput* (throughput), *monthly product demand* (average monthly demand), *order delay* (order lateness) and *customer type* (client category). The critical measure of VIKOR method is the closeness coefficient (CC). In this regard, the eligible operation whose coefficient is closer to 1, will have the highest priority. On the other hand, Table 4 presents the first seven programmed operations via applying the integrated approach. The first operation that must be scheduled is O_{13SSB} which denotes *weaving*, Order 3 and SSB. This operation achieved the highest closeness coefficient (0.8915). This table also specifies the selected resources for each operation. Particularly, in this case, 27 orders were taken into account (refer to Table 2) with $Q = 42$ units. The results evidenced that average tardiness could be reduced (5.23 days) in comparison with the proposed company solution, Pareto-based grouping discrete

Table 3. Orders, throughput and monthly demand per product reference

Product reference	Throughput (USD/min)	Monthly demand (Kg/month)	Orders		
			Order 1	Order 2	Order 3
SBS	1,13	3782,46	173 (16 – 05)	190 (9 – 05)	149 (2 – 05)
SFBS	1,13	2287,51	136 (16 – 05)	118 (9 – 05)	
SSB	1,51	1276,38	112 (16 – 05)	174 (9 – 05)	226 (2 – 05)
DB	1,10	541,11	178 (16 – 05)	124 (9 – 05)	
DFBS	0,71	862,59	121 (16 – 05)	112 (9 – 05)	
SDB	1,47	198,41	136 (16 – 05)	172 (2 – 05)	
SSBS	1,16	2166,56	12 (16 – 05)	125 (2 – 05)	256 (25 – 06)
SSFB	1,16	323,60	126 (16 – 05)	182 (5 – 05)	
SDBS	0,87	2166,56	124 (16 – 05)		
SDFBS	0,70	327,84	121 (16 – 05)		
P	1,19	2665,23	3276 (20–04)	2651 (13 – 04)	
YP	1,44	2664,23	1101 (17 – 06)	951 (14 – 05)	
M	0,50	2811,65	3551 (18 – 06)	3551 (2 – 05)	

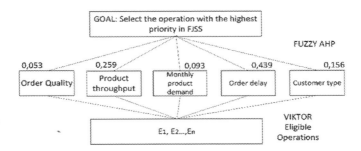

Fig. 2. Multi-criteria decision-making model for operation selection in FJSP

Table 4. Direct-relation matrix for fuzzy AHP

	OQ	PT	MPD	OD	CT
OQ	[1. 1, 1]	[1/6, 1/5, 1/4]	[1/4, 1/3, 1/2]	[1/6, 1/5, 1/4]	[1/4, 1/3, 1/2]
PT	[4, 5, 6]	[1. 1, 1]	[2, 3, 4]	[1/4, 1/3, 1/2]	[2, 3, 4]
MPD	[2, 3, 4]	[1/4, 1/3, 1/2]	[1. 1, 1]	[1/6, 1/5, 1/4]	[1/4, 1/3, 1/2]
OD	[4, 5, 6]	[2, 3, 4]	[4, 5, 6]	[1. 1, 1]	[2, 3, 4]
CT	[2, 3, 4]	[1/4, 1/3, 1/2]	[2, 3, 4]	[1/4, 1/3, 1/2]	[1. 1, 1]

harmony search algorithm (PGHDS) [30] and the integrated HHS/LNS method [31] by 61.05% (8.39 days), 2.6% (5.36 days) and 1.8% (5.32 days) respectively (Table 5).

On the other hand, a Mann-Whitney test (given a non-parametric stochastic distribution of the variables) was conducted to determine whether the median delay for high-throughput orders (>1 USD/min) in FAHP-DEMATEL-VIKOR method

Table 5. First six scheduled operations under the proposed approach

Product reference	Operation	CC	Order Number	Candidate resources	Selected resource	t_q (h)	t – start (h)	t – end (h)
SSBS	Weaving	0,8915	3	A3	A3	0	0	19,62
P	Weaving	0,7211	1	A1	A1	0	0	95,0
SSB	Weaving	0,3478	3	A2	A2	0	0	16,95
SBS	Weaving	0,3285	3	A2	A2	0	16,95	28,12
SSB	Dyeing	0,3478	3	T1	T1	0	9,30	15,17
P	Weaving	0,6523	2	A3	A3	10	19,62	101,8

($M = 1day$) was significantly lower than the median delay obtained with the company solution ($M = 2days$). In this case, considering a W = 347.0 and p-value = 0.0035 (adjusted for ties), it can be concluded that the proposed approach provides a reduced delay for high-throughput orders (refer to Fig. 3).

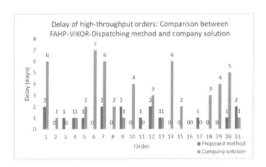

Fig. 3. Effects of FAHP-VIKOR-dispatching method on the delay of high-throughput orders

5   Conclusions and Future Work

Scheduling Flexible Job-Shop Systems combined with multi-criteria prioritizing criteria is both relevant and arduous when increasing the competitiveness and firm performance of different industrial sectors. Nonetheless, approaches considering different indicators (i.e. throughput, monthly sales) simultaneously in operation selection are largely limited. The importance of including these indicators lies in the fact that decision making in a company cannot see a problem isolated from the rest of the organization. Contrariwise, decision must be made considering how the decision affects other metrics. To fulfill this gap, this paper proposed an integration of Dispatching Algorithm and FAHP-VIKOR methods. In this work, setup times, transfer batches, order variables and other assumptions were deemed to schedule operations in a company from the textile industry. This aspect is even more important when ensuring customer satisfaction and avoiding possible sanctions because of delayed orders. Moreover, a closer look can be taken at the system throughput aiming to increase the revenues. The main output is a methodology that underpins FJSP under multi-criteria environments based on the combined FAHP-VIKOR. Particularly, this approach contributed to reducing tardiness of high-throughput orders. The proposed method is scalable and adaptable in any FJSP. Future works aim to create models introducing the preemption and break down assumptions.

References

1. Neufeld, J.S., Gupta, J.N.D., Buscher, U.: A comprehensive review of flowshop group scheduling literature (2016)
2. Ortiz, M., Neira, D., Jiménez, G., Hernández, H.: Solving flexible job-shop scheduling problem with transfer batches, setup times and multiple resources in apparel industry. In: Tan, Y., Shi, Y., Li, L. (eds.) ICSI 2016. LNCS, vol. 9713, pp. 47–58. Springer, Cham (2016). https://doi.org/10.1007/978-3-319-41009-8_6
3. Neira Rodado, D., Escobar, J.W., García-Cáceres, R.G., Niebles Atencio, F.A.: A mathematical model for the product mixing and lot-sizing problem by considering stochastic demand. Int. J. Ind. Eng. Comput. **8**(2), 237–250 (2016)
4. Landinez-Lamadrid, D.C., Ramirez-Ríos, D.G., Neira Rodado, D., Parra Negrete, K., Combita Niño, J.: Shapley Value: its Algorithms and Application to Supply Chains El valor de Shapley: sus Algoritmos y Aplicación en Cadenas de Suministro, Enero-Junio, vol. 13, no. 2, pp. 61–69 (2017)
5. Atencio, F.N., Prasca, A.B., Rodado, D.N., Casseres, D.M., Santiago, M.R.: A comparative approach of ant colony system and mathematical programming for task scheduling in a mineral analysis laboratory, vol. 9712 (2016)
6. Ortiz Barrios, M., Neira Rodado, D., Jiménez, G., López Meza, P.: Integration of dispatching algorithm and AHP-TOPSIS method for flexible job-shop scheduling problem: a case study from the apparel industry. Int. J. Control Theory Appl. (2016)
7. Conway, R.W., Maxwell, W.L.: Theory of Scheduling. Dover, New York (2003)
8. Melanie, M.: An Introduction to Genetic Algorithms Library of Congress Cataloging − in − Publication Data (1998)
9. Kumar, R., Jain, A.: Assessment of makespan performance for flexible process plans in job shop scheduling, pp. 1948–1953 (2015)
10. Calleja, G., Pastor, R.: A dispatching algorithm for flexible job-shop scheduling with transfer batches: an industrial application. Prod. Plan. Control **25**(2), 93–109 (2014)
11. Dargi, A., Anjomshoae, A., Galankashi, M.R., Memari, A., Tap, M.B.M.: Supplier selection: a fuzzy-ANP approach. Procedia Comput. Sci. **31**, 691–700 (2014)
12. Demir, Y., Kürşat İşleyen, S.: Evaluation of mathematical models for flexible job-shop scheduling problems. Appl. Math. Model. **37**(3), 977–988 (2013)
13. Zhang, G., Gao, L., Shi, Y.: An effective genetic algorithm for the flexible job-shop scheduling problem. Expert Syst. Appl. **38**(4), 3563–3573 (2011)
14. Brucker, P., Schlie, R.: Job-shop scheduling with multi-purpose machines. Computing **45**(4), 369–375 (1990)
15. Genova, K., Kirilov, L., Guliashki, V.: A survey of solving approaches for multiple objective flexible job shop scheduling problems
16. Brandimarte, P.: Routing and scheduling in a flexible job shop by tabu search. Ann. Oper. Res. **41**(3), 157–183 (1993)
17. Wu, Z.: Multi-agent workload control and flexible job shop scheduling. University of South Florida (2005)

18. Tanev, I.T., Uozumi, T., Morotome, Y.: Hybrid evolutionary algorithm-based real-world flexible job shop scheduling problem: application service provider approach. Appl. Soft Comput. **5**(1), 87–100 (2004)
19. Pezzella, F., Morganti, G., Ciaschetti, G.: A genetic algorithm for the flexible job-shop scheduling problem. Comput. Oper. Res. **35**(10), 3202–3212 (2008)
20. Low, C., Yip, Y., Wu, T.-H.: Modelling and heuristics of FMS scheduling with multiple objectives. Comput. Oper. Res. **33**(3), 674–694 (2006)
21. Fattahi, P., Saidi Mehrabad, M., Jolai, F.: Mathematical modeling and heuristic approaches to flexible job shop scheduling problems. J. Intell. Manuf. **18**(3), 331–342 (2007)
22. Saaty, T.L.: Decision making with dependence and feedback: the analytic network process, pp. 83–135. RWS Publications (2001)
23. Ortíz, M.A., Cómbita, J.P., Hoz, Á.L.A.D.L., Felice, F.D., Petrillo, A.: An integrated approach of AHP-DEMATEL methods applied for the selection of allied hospitals in outpatient service. Int. J. Med. Eng. Inform. **8**(2), 87–107 (2016)
24. İç, Y.T., Yurdakul, M.: Development of a decision support system for machining center selection. Expert Syst. Appl. **36**(2), 3505–3513 (2009)
25. Lee, S.H.: Using fuzzy AHP to develop intellectual capital evaluation model for assessing their performance contribution in a university. Expert Syst. Appl. **37**(7), 4941–4947 (2010)
26. Zavadskas, E.K., Govindan, K., Antucheviciene, J., Turskis, Z.: Hybrid multiple criteria decision-making methods: a review of applications for sustainability issues. Economic Research-Ekonomska Istraživanja **29**(1), 857–887 (2016)
27. Ertuğrul, Ð., Karakasoğlu, N.: Performance evaluation of Turkish cement firms with fuzzy analytic hierarchy process and TOPSIS methods. Expert Syst. Appl. **36**(1), 702–715 (2009)
28. Opricovic, S., Tzeng, G.H.: Compromise solution by MCDM methods: a comparative analysis of VIKOR and TOPSIS. Eur. J. Oper. Res. **156**(2), 445–455 (2004)
29. Barrios, M.A.O.: Teoría de restricciones y modelación PL como herramientas de decisión estratégica para el incremento de la productividad en la línea de toallas de una compañía del sector textil y de confecciones. Prospectiva **11**(1), 21–30 (2013)
30. Gao, K.Z., Suganthan, P.N., Pan, Q.K., Chua, T.J., Cai, T.X., Chong, C.S.: Pareto-based grouping discrete harmony search algorithm for multi-objective flexible job shop scheduling. Inf. Sci. **289**, 76–90 (2014)
31. Yuan, Y., Xu, H.: An integrated search heuristic for large-scale flexible job shop scheduling problems. Comput. Oper. Res. **40**(12), 2864–2877 (2013)

A Solution Framework Based on Packet Scheduling and Dispatching Rule for Job-Based Scheduling Problems

Rongrong Zhou, Hui Lu$^{(\boxtimes)}$, and Jinhua Shi

School of Electronic and Information Engineering, Beihang University,
Beijing 100191, People's Republic of China
mluhui@vip.163.com

Abstract. Job-based scheduling problems have inherent similarities and relations. However, the current researches on these scheduling problems are isolated and lack references. We propose a unified solution framework containing two innovative strategies: the packet scheduling strategy and the greedy dispatching rule. It can increase the diversity of solutions and help in solving the problems with large solution space effectively. In addition, we propose an improved particle swarm optimization (PSO) algorithm with a variable neighborhood local search mechanism and a perturbation strategy. We apply the solution framework combined with the improved PSO to the benchmark instances of different job-based scheduling problems. Our method provides a self-adaptive technique for various job-based scheduling problems, which can promote mutual learning between different areas and provide guidance for practical applications.

Keywords: Job-based scheduling · Unified solution framework
Packet scheduling · Dispatching rule · Improved PSO

1 Introduction

Scheduling problems have been widely investigated in many fields, such as manufacturing industry, service industry, cloud computing, Internet of things and so on [1–6]. Job-based scheduling problems represent one important branch of scheduling, including flexible job shop scheduling problem (FJSP), test task scheduling problem (TTSP), parallel machine scheduling problem (PMSP) and so on. These scheduling problems consist of a series of sequential or parallel execution tasks. The goal of scheduling is to assign all tasks to independent resources reasonably. In the research process of job-based scheduling problems, scheduling algorithms have been greatly improved. However, the design process of algorithms is unsupervised in most cases. In addition, job-based scheduling problems have many similarities in the problem characteristics, like scheduling objectives, solution methods and development process. However, the researches of job-based scheduling problem in different fields are isolated from each other

© Springer International Publishing AG, part of Springer Nature 2018
Y. Tan et al. (Eds.): ICSI 2018, LNCS 10942, pp. 202–211, 2018.
https://doi.org/10.1007/978-3-319-93818-9_19

and lack mutual references and general analysis. This is not conducive to the theoretical research of the scheduling problems.

In this paper, we make full use of the inherent relations of different job-based scheduling problems, and propose a unified solution framework based on the problem characteristics. In the aspect of task scheduling, we propose a packet scheduling strategy. All tasks are randomly divided into several groups with the same number of tasks, and an intelligent optimization algorithm is used to optimize within a group. Meanwhile, in the aspect of resource allocation, a dispatching rule called probability-based scheme choice rule (PBSCR) is proposed. The shorter the completion time of a task with a resource, the greater the probability of the resource to be selected. The two strategies interact with each other, which can reduce the difficulty of solving high dimensional problems.

2   The Proposed Solution Framework

The solution framework is based on decomposing a job-based scheduling problem into task sequence and resource allocation. A schematic figure of the solution framework is shown in Fig. 1 and Opt. is the abbreviation of optimization.

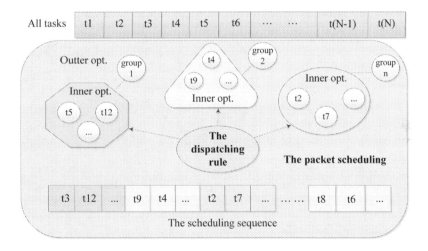

Fig. 1. The schematic figure of the solution framework

2.1   The Packet Scheduling Strategy

The packet scheduling strategy adopts the idea of grouping optimization. The whole solution space is divided into several groups to be optimized separately. The optimal results of groups are connected to obtain the optimal solution. The specific steps are as Algorithm 1.

Algorithm 1. The packet scheduling strategy

---

1 **Initialization**: Select an intelligent optimization algorithm, and it will be used for the outer layer optimization of the packet mode. Initialize the population of the outer layer optimization as $P_1(0) = I_1, I_2, \cdots, I_{N_1}$, N_1 is the number of individuals. Each individual represents a packet mode. The iteration number $iter_1$ is set to 0;

2 **Optimize grouping mode**: **while** *not find "good enough" solution or not reach the pre-determined maximum number of iterations* **do**

3   **Grouping**: Based on the packet mode, randomly divide all N tasks into n groups. Each group has the same number of tasks. The groups are denoted by $G_1, G_2, \cdots, G_n$. Set the group number gn equal to 1. The start time of resources is set to 0;

4   **while** *gn not reach the maximum number of groups* **do**

5   **Initialization**: Initialize the population $P_2(0) = I_1, I_2, \cdots, I_{N_2}$, where N_2 is the number of individuals. Each individual corresponds to a sequence of tasks within the group after decoding. The iteration number $iter_2$ is set to 0;

6   **while** *iter_2 not reach the pre-determined maximum number of iterations* **do**

7   **Inner scheduling optimization within a group**: Use **PBSCR** dispatching rule to select the reasonable resource for each task in each sequence. Thus, the fitness value of each individual in P_2 is determined. Obtain the updated population $P_2(iter_2)$.

8   The optimal fitness value of group gn is denoted by f_{gn}.

9   **Update**: Update resource status as the initial condition for the next task grouping.

10   The optimal solutions of groups are connected in turn. The fitness value of the whole problem under the current packet mode is f_n.

2.2 The Dispatching Rule

Selecting the optimal resource allocation scheme for a given task sequence still has an enormously large solution space. To solve this problem quickly and efficiently, we propose a dispatching rule called PBSCR. It is designed to find the proper resource allocation scheme for the current scheduling task with the smallest completion time.

Assume that there are tn tasks in the task sequence, and the ith task has m_i resource allocation options. The detailed description of PBSCR is shown as Algorithm 2. PBSCR is an improved greedy algorithm with accepting a worse solution probability. It increases the diversity of solutions and improves the ability of local search.

2.3 Optimization Objective Within a Group

For different scheduling problems, the scheduling scheme in the earlier groups may have different effects on the latter groups. Therefore, the factors of the

---

Algorithm 2. The dispatching rule

---

1 **Initialization**: Set task ID i to 1, and the start times of resources are set to zero;
2 **while** i *not reach the task number tn* **do**
3   Traverse the resource options of task i to compute the completion time. The completion time of the 1st scheme to the m_i^{th} scheme is denoted by $t_{i1}, t_{i2}, \cdots, t_{im_1}$;
4   Calculate the selective probability of each scheme, $p_i(j) = \exp(-t_j)/\sum_{q=1}^{m_i} \exp(-t_q)$, where j is the scheme number;
5   Calculate the cumulative probability of scheme j, $cp_i(j) = \sum_{q=1}^{j} p_i(q)$;
6   Produce a uniformly distributed random number r in interval $[0,1]$;
7   If $r < cp_i(1)$, the first scheme is selected. Otherwise, select scheme k satisfying $cp(k-1) < r \leq cp(k)$ as the resource allocation scheme for task i;
8   Update the start time or available time of the resource occupied by scheme k;

---

optimization objective that need to be considered may be different. The task of a latter group can be inserted into the idle time of the earlier groups in FJSP and PMSP. Therefore, the idle time is not considered in the objective function. As for TTSP, the idle time of the earlier group cannot be used. In this circumstance, the optimization goal of the group is no longer the minimization of makespan, but the minimization of the completion time of each instrument. Therefore, we modify the optimization objective as:

$$f_{gn} = makespan + \sum_{m=1}^{M} (idle_m/fin_m)/M \qquad (1)$$

Here, M is the number of instruments. $idle_m$ and fin_m represent the sum of idle time and the finish time of all the tasks on instrument m. The integral part of f_{gn} is the makespan and the fractional part of f_{gn} is the normalized mean idle time.

3   The Improved Particle Swarm Optimization

3.1   Variable Neighborhood Local Search Mechanism

The particle swarm optimization (PSO) algorithm is originally introduced by Kennedy and Eberhart [7]. In this paper, a variable neighborhood local search mechanism is proposed to optimize the individual optimal solution. It can effectively improve the success rate and the optimization precision of the traditional PSO algorithm. Specifically, there is a point $X(x_1, x_2, \cdots, x_d)$ in D dimensional space. δ is a positive number, and $(x_i - \delta, x_i + \delta)$ is called a δ neighborhood on dimension i. The gather of δ neighborhood on all the dimensions is called the dimension based δ neighborhood of point X. Based on this concept, the local search mechanism is designed as follows.

(1) Before the individual optimal solution of each particle is updated, the optimal solution of the particle is set as the initial solution, and the initial solution is set as the current solution.
(2) Generate the dimension based δ neighborhood of the current solution. m derivative solutions are generated randomly in the neighborhood, and the fitness values of these derivative solutions are evaluated.
(3) If a derivative solution is better than the current solution, the derived solution is set to the current solution, and return to (2); otherwise go to (4).
(4) If all derivative solutions are worse than the current solution, expand the neighborhood radius (the value of δ), and return to (2); If the local search space of the current solution has been extended for ω times and no better solution has been found, the optimal solution of the particle is unchanged.

3.2   Perturbation Strategy

To increase the diversity of the solutions when the particles gather to the individual optimal solution and the global optimal solution, we add a perturbation strategy to the PSO after the fitness value of a particle is updated. The detailed steps are as follows.

(1) Set the particle that has just been updated as the current particle. The position of the current particle is denoted as X_s. Set the perturbation rate as p.
(2) Generate a random number $rand$ between 0 and 1. If $rand < p$, go to (3); otherwise terminate the perturbation process.
(3) The population size is denoted as N. Generate two random numbers between 1 and N, and denoted them as m and n.
(4) Generate a new particle and the position is $X_{new} = X_s + r \times (X_m - X_n)$, where r is a random number following a uniform distribution. X_m and X_n are the positions of the mth particle and the nth particle in the population.
(5) Check if the value on any dimension of the new particle is within the specified range. If the value on a dimension is out of range, the value is replaced by a random number within the range.
(6) The fitness value of the new particle is calculated. If the fitness value is better than the current one, the new particle is used instead of the current particle to participate in the latter steps of PSO.

4   Experiment and Analysis

The optimization algorithm in the proposed solution framework is self-adaptive, and it could be any search algorithm. We illustrate this adaptability and choose a good search algorithm for the solution framework in Sect. 4.1. In addition, we conduct the experiment on TTSP, FJSP and PMSP in Sect. 4.2. The runtime environment is an Intel(R) Core (TM) i5-4590T 2.00 GHz CPU, with 4 GB of memory and a Microsoft Windows 7 SP1 32 bit operating system.

4.1   The Experiments with Different Algorithms

The solution framework provides a self-adaptive technique to solve job-based scheduling problems. To verify the generality and effectiveness of the framework with different search algorithms, we combine GA, PSO, VPSO (PSO with variable neighborhood local search mechanism) and IPSO (PSO with variable neighborhood local search mechanism and perturbation strategy) with the solution framework respectively, and compare their performance on the benchmark instances of TTSP. They are instance 20×8 and 40×12 employed from [8,9]. The parameter settings are illustrated in Table 1. P_c and P_m are the crossover probability and the mutation probability of genetic algorithm. δ, m, ω and p are the radius of the neighborhood, the number of derivative solutions, the cycle number of local search and the perturbation rate. n_p represents the number of population or particle and n_{iter} means the number of iteration. There are 10 tasks in each group. Finally, the performance indicators are in Table 2. BV represents the best optimal fitness and SR represents the probability to find the optimal solution. MBF represents the average of all the optimal fitness values found in 10 times, and Time represents the CPU time.

Table 1. The parameter settings of each method.

Algorithm	Parameter setting
PSGA	Outer layer GA: $n_p = 30$; $n_{iter} = 10$; $P_c = 0.9$; $P_m = 0.1$;
	Inner layer GA: $n_p = 20$; $n_{iter} = 15$; $P_c = 0.9$; $P_m = 0.1$;
PSPSO	Outer layer PSO: $n_p = 30$; $n_{iter} = 10$;
	Inner layer PSO: $n_p = 20$; $n_{iter} = 15$;
PSVPSO	Outer layer VPSO: $n_p = 20$; $n_{iter} = 10$; $\delta = 0.1$; $m = 10$; $\omega = 2$; $p = 0$;
	Inner layer PSO: $n_p = 10$; $n_{iter} = 10$; no local search and perturbation;
PSIPSO	Outer layer IPSO: $n_p = 20$; $n_{iter} = 10$; $\delta = 0.1$; $m = 10$; $\omega = 2$; $p = 0.3$;
	Inner layer PSO: $n_p = 10$; $n_{iter} = 10$; no local search and perturbation;

The results show that the solution framework can be combined with any algorithms like GA and PSO. As for instance 20×8, the best optimal values found by the four algorithms are the same. However, the value of SR obtained by PSGA, PSPSO, PSVPSO and PSIPSO increases from 0.1 to 1, which indicates that the performance stability of the four algorithms is in an increasing order. In addition, the value of MBF decreases, indicating that the average scheduling performance of the four algorithms is also in an increasing order. Therefore, the VPSO improves the search performance of PSO, and IPSO improves the search performance of VPSO even further, and they are better than GA within similar CPU time. As for instance 40×12, the change rule of the performance indicators is basically the same as instance 20×8. PSGA did not find the best known solution, and the value of MBF is the worst. Although PSVPSO also did not find the best known solution, the value of SR is 1, which indicates that the algorithm performance is very stable. PSIPSO also obtains the best value of BV and MBF. Although the difficulty of instance 40 × 12 increases substantially, PSIPSO is still the best method and obtains good performance. To sum up, this group of experiments confirm that the proposed solution framework can be combined with any search algorithm, and the improved PSO is effective and has good performance.

Table 2. The performance indicators of the three methods.

Algorithm	Instance 20 × 8				Instance 40 × 12			
	BV	SR	MBF	Time	BV	SR	MBF	Time
PSGA	28	0.4	29	189.5	39	0.2	40	510
PSPSO	28	0.7	28.3	228	38	0.1	39.1	468
PSVPSO	28	0.9	28.1	219	39	1	39	397
PSIPSO	*28*	*1*	*28*	214	*38*	*0.1*	*38.9*	398

4.2   The Experiments on Different Scheduling Problems

To verify the proposed framework and PSIPSO, we apply our method to TTSP, FJSP, and PMSP, and compare the results with existing methods. We combine them with random key encoding [10], using integration method to solve these problems. The mathematical model of TTSP and other methods including GASCR, PGA and GASA are mentioned in paper [11]. For GA, $n_p = 500$ and $n_{iter} = 600$. For PSO, $n_p = 300$ and $n_{iter} = 500$. The experimental results are shown in Table 3. The results obtained by GA and PSO are worse, compared with the results obtained by PSGA and PSPSO in Table 2. This indicates that the search ability of single GA and PSO is not very good when the solution space is enormous. The framework can improve the algorithm performance significantly, especially for large-scale problems. In other methods, PGA and GASA are even worse. Although GASCR is the best known algorithm, the three indicators obtained by it are all worse than those of PSIPSO. To sum up, the proposed framework is helpful to improve the performance of search algorithms, and PSIPSO is better than existing methods.

Meanwhile, the mathematical model of FJSP and the test set with 10 examples in [12] were used. The parameter settings of the PSIPSO are the same as the one in Table 1. Table 4 shows the experimental results (minimizing makespan) of the proposed PSIPSO and other algorithms ($n \times m$ means that this problem contains n jobs and m machines). GA, Heuristic, TABC, HGTS and MA2 represent the reported algorithms from the references [13–17]. S_{bst} is the best known makespan. In Table 4, no method can obtain all the best known solutions (S_{bst}) for these problems. The results of the proposed PSIPSO are better or equal to the S_{bst} in most cases, except Mk05, Mk06, Mk10. However, the experiments still illustrate that PSIPSO is an effective method and can complete the scheduling task with high quality in most cases.

Table 3. The experimental results of TTSP.

Algorithm	Instance 20 × 8			Instance 40 × 12		
	BV	SR	MBF	BV	SR	MBF
GA	31	1	31	45	0.2	46.1
PSO	31	0.2	31.8	45	0.2	47.8
PGA	31	0.2	33.8	42	0.1	44.8
GASA	32	0.2	33.9	47	0.1	49.2
GASCR	28	0.5	29	40	0.4	40.6
PSIPSO	*28*	*1*	*28*	*38*	*0.4*	*38*

Table 4. The optimal makespan of FJSP obtained by different methods.

Example	$n \times m$	S_{bst}	GA	Heuristic	TABC	HGTS	MA2	PSIPSO
Mk01	10 × 6	40	40	42	40	40	40	*35*
Mk02	10 × 6	26	26	28	26	26	26	*24*
Mk03	15 × 8	204	204	204	204	204	204	*172*
Mk04	15 × 8	60	60	75	60	60	60	*57*
Mk05	15 × 4	172	173	179	173	*172*	*172*	186
Mk06	10 × 15	57	63	69	60	*57*	59	70
Mk07	20 × 5	139	139	149	139	139	139	*129*
Mk08	20 × 10	523	523	555	523	523	523	*416*
Mk09	20 × 10	307	311	342	*307*	*307*	*307*	*307*
Mk10	20 × 15	197	212	242	202	*198*	202	232

In addition, the mathematical model of PMSP and the test instances are derived by [18]. All these instances are available from http://www.soa.iti.es. The optimal solution for each instance is obtained by ILOG-IBM CPLEX 10, which is also available from the same web page. Due to the small number of tasks, all tasks can be viewed as one group. The number of particles and the number of iterations of the outer IPSO are both set to 1. The number of particles and the number of iterations of the inner IPSO are set to 200 and 50, respectively. We run the proposed method 5 times for each instance, and calculate the relative percentage deviation (RPD) from the reference solution as follows.

$$(C_{max} - C^*_{max}) \times 100/C^*_{max} \tag{2}$$

Here, C^*_{max} is the optimal solution. C_{max} is the makespan obtained by the given method. The experimental results (average RPD) of the proposed PSIPSO and the other algorithms proposed by [18] are shown in Table 5.

The smaller the RPD, the closer the optimal solution is to the best known one. The experimental results show that the values of RPD obtained by PSIPSO are much smaller than those of Meta and MetaC. Therefore, PSIPSO is much better

Table 5. The average relative percentage deviation of each instance of PMSP.

$n \times m$	Meta	MetaC	GAK	GA1	GA2	PSIPSO
6×2	5.29	5.39	1.28	*0.00*	*0.00*	*0.00*
6×3	5.92	6.33	0.19	0.15	*0.08*	0.18
6×4	10.33	11.24	*0.00*	0.40	0.27	0.06
6×5	16.08	15.96	0.36	0.23	0.21	*0.06*
8×2	3.98	4.80	1.58	0.07	0.03	*0.00*
8×3	4.55	5.60	1.23	0.20	0.24	*0.16*
8×4	8.67	9.55	2.65	0.66	*0.39*	*0.39*
8×5	11.28	13.38	8.78	0.49	0.20	*0.01*
10×2	2.72	3.34	2.61	0.19	*0.17*	0.46
10×3	3.86	4.82	2.71	0.26	*0.20*	*0.20*

than Meta and MetaC. For most instances, the performance of PSIPSO is better than GAK, GA1 and GA2. Therefore, PSIPSO has a very good performance on PMSP. The experiments on TTSP, FJSP and PMSP demonstrate the good performance of the proposed method on different job-based scheduling problems.

5   Conclusion

Job-based scheduling problems contain task scheduling and resource allocation. Based on this characteristic, we propose an adaptive solution framework to deal with these problems. The framework can choose various search algorithms adaptively. To provide an effective intelligent algorithm for the solution framework, we improve the traditional PSO by adding the variable neighborhood local search mechanism and the perturbation strategy. The application results on TTSP, FJSP and PMSP illustrate that the method has good performance on different job-based scheduling problems. The solution framework can provide reference for the research and application of similar problems in different fields, and improve existing scheduling algorithms. Future work includes applying the method to more benchmark instances of different problems and further promoting the integration and mutual reference in different fields.

Acknowledgement. This research is supported by the National Natural Science Foundation of China under Grant No. 61671041.

References

1. Li, K., Zhang, X., Leung, Y.T., Yang, S.L.: Parallel machine scheduling problems in green manufacturing industry. J. Manuf. Syst. **38**, 98–106 (2016)

2. Liu, W., Liang, Z., Ye, Z., Liu, L.: The optimal decision of customer order decoupling point for order insertion scheduling in logistics service supply chain. Int. J. Prod. Econ. **175**, 50–60 (2016)
3. Abdullahi, M., Ngadi, M.A., Abdulhamid, S.M.: Symbiotic organism search optimization based task scheduling in cloud computing environment. Futur. Gener. Comput. Syst. **56**, 640–650 (2016)
4. Sharma, R., Kumar, N., Gowda, N.B., Srinivas, T.: Probabilistic prediction based scheduling for delay sensitive traffic in Internet of Things. Procedia Comput. Sci. **52**(1), 90–97 (2015)
5. Kong, W., Lei, Y., Ma, J.: Virtual machine resource scheduling algorithm for cloud computing based on auction mechanism. Optik Int. J. Light Electron Opt. **127**(12), 5099–5104 (2016)
6. Freitag, M., Hildebrandt, T.: Automatic design of scheduling rules for complex manufacturing systems by multi-objective simulation-based optimization. CIRP Ann. Manuf. Technol. **65**(1), 433–436 (2016)
7. Kennedy, J., Eberhart, R.: Particle swarm optimization. In: Proceedings of the IEEE International Conference on Neural Networks, vol. 4, pp. 1942–1948, November 1995
8. Lu, H., Niu, R., Liu, J., Zhu, Z.: A chaotic non-dominated sorting genetic algorithm for the multi-objective automatic test task scheduling problem. Appl. Soft Comput. **13**(5), 2790–2802 (2013)
9. Lu, H., Zhu, Z., Wang, X., Yin, L.: A variable neighborhood MOEA/D for multi-objective test task scheduling problem. Math. Prob, Eng. **2014**(3), 1–14 (2014)
10. Bean, J.C.: Genetics and random keys for sequencing and optimization. In: Production Scheduling (1993)
11. Shi, J., Lu, H., Mao, K.: Solving the test task scheduling problem with a genetic algorithm based on the scheme choice rule. In: Tan, Y., Shi, Y., Li, L. (eds.) ICSI 2016. LNCS, vol. 9713, pp. 19–27. Springer, Cham (2016). https://doi.org/10.1007/978-3-319-41009-8_3
12. Brandimarte, P.: Routing and scheduling in a flexible job shop by tabu search. Ann. Oper. Res. **41**(3), 157–183 (1993)
13. Wang, J.F., Du, B.Q., Ding, H.M.: A genetic algorithm for the flexible job-shop scheduling problem. In: Shen, G., Huang, X. (eds.) CSIE 2011. CCIS, vol. 152, pp. 332–339. Springer, Heidelberg (2011). https://doi.org/10.1007/978-3-642-21402-8_54
14. Ziaee, M.: A heuristic algorithm for solving flexible job shop scheduling problem. Int. J. Adv. Manuf. Technol. **71**(1–4), 519–528 (2014)
15. Gao, K.Z., Suganthan, P.N., Chua, T.J., Chong, C.S., Cai, T.X., Pan, Q.K.: A two-stage artificial bee colony algorithm scheduling flexible job-shop scheduling problem with new job insertion. Expert Syst. Appl. **42**(21), 7652–7663 (2015)
16. Palacios, J.J., González, M.A., Vela, C.R., Gonzlez-Rodríguez, I., Puente, J.: Genetic tabu search for the fuzzy flexible job shop problem. Comput. Oper. Res. **54**(1), 74–89 (2015)
17. Yuan, Y., Xu, H.: Multiobjective flexible job shop scheduling using memetic algorithms. IEEE Trans. Autom. Sci. Eng. **12**(1), 336–353 (2014)
18. Vallada, E.: A genetic algorithm for the unrelated parallel machine scheduling problem with sequence dependent setup times. Eur. J. Oper. Res. **211**(3), 612–622 (2011)

A Two-Stage Heuristic Approach for a Type of Rotation Assignment Problem

Ziran Zheng[1(⊠)] and Xiaoju Gong[2]

[1] School of Management Science and Engineering,
Shandong Normal University, Jinan, China
zzr_nature@163.com
[2] Shandong Provincial Hospital Affiliated to Shandong University, Jinan, China

Abstract. A two-stage heuristic algorithm is proposed for solving a trainee rotation assignment problem in a local school of nursing and its training hospital. At the first stage, the model is reduced to a simplified assignment problem and solved using a random search procedure. At the second stage, a problem-specific operator is designed and employed with a hill climber to further improve solutions. We benchmark our algorithm with instances generated based on the real-life rules. Results show that the proposed algorithm yields high-quality solutions in less computation time for large scale instances when compared with integer linear programming formulation using the commercial solver Cplex.

Keywords: Trainee rotation assignment · Personnel scheduling
Heuristic

1 Introduction and Related Work

In this proposal, a class of rotation assignment problem in a local school of nursing is addressed. Figure 1 presents an example of such a problem instance and its solution. The whole time range has seven time periods and we want to assign two rotations to three trainees. At each time period, the internship hospital has one available position for each rotation and in each row every rotation must be performed by one trainee. For each trainee, rotations of the same type must be assigned consecutively along time periods, which is called consecutive constraint in this work. Let n, r and m be the number of whole periods, rotations and trainees respectively. The l and u be the minimum and maximum number of periods that each one can take. In this solution the consecutive constraints are all satisfied. This solution is clearly feasible and three soft constraints are violated.

The work is supported by the Project of Shandongp Province Higher Educational Science and Technology Program (Grant No. J14LN10) and National Natural Science Foundation of China (Grant No. 61472231).

Periods	Trainee 1	Trainee 2	Trainee 3
1	R_1	R_2	
2	R_1	R_2	
3		R_1	R_2
4		R_1	R_2
5	R_2	R_1	
6	R_2		R_1
7	R_2		R_1

Fig. 1. A feasible solution for a rotation assignment problem instance. Here $n = 7, r = 2, m = 3, l = 2$ and $u = 3$. The cells with bold border represent the undesired periods of trainees. We use different colors together with R_1 and R_2 to denote different rotations. Let $p_{i,j}$ denote penalty values of undesired periods in period i for trainee j. Suppose the values are: $p_{2,1} = 2$, $p_{5,1} = 1$, $p_{6,2} = 3$ and $p_{3,3} = 3$, and the cost value of this solution is 6.

The problem can be mathematically formulated as an integer linear programming model. The model is described as follows.

R_k: set of rotations and let $R_k, k = 1, ..., r$ denote a type of rotation;
T_j: set of trainees and let $T_j, j = 1, ..., m$ denote a single trainee;

$$\text{Minimize} \quad \sum_{i=1}^{n}\sum_{j=1}^{m}\sum_{k=1}^{r} p_{ij}x_{ijk} \tag{1}$$

Subject to:

$$\sum_{k=1}^{r} x_{ijk} \leq 1, \forall i = 1, ..., n \text{ and } \forall j = 1, ..., m, \tag{2}$$

$$\sum_{j=1}^{m} x_{ijk} = 1, \forall i = 1, ..., n \text{ and } \forall k = 1, ..., r, \tag{3}$$

$$\sum_{i=1}^{n} x_{ijk} \geq l, \forall k = 1, ..., r \text{ and } \forall j = 1, ..., m, \tag{4}$$

$$\sum_{i=1}^{n} x_{ijk} \leq u, \forall k = 1, ..., r \text{ and } \forall j = 1, ..., m, \tag{5}$$

$$y_{1jk} = x_{1jk}, \forall j = 1, ..., m \text{ and } \forall k = 1, ..., r \tag{6}$$

$$y_{ijk} \geq x_{ijk} - x_{(i-1)jk}, \forall i = 2, ..., n, \forall j = 1, ..., m \text{ and } \forall k = 1, ..., r, \tag{7}$$

$$\sum_{i=1}^{n} y_{ijk} = 1, \forall j = 1, ..., m \text{ and } \forall k = 1, ..., r, \tag{8}$$

$$y_{ijk}, x_{ijk} \in \{0, 1\}, \forall i = 1, ..., n, \forall j = 1, ..., m \text{ and } \forall k = 1, ..., r. \tag{9}$$

Periods	Trainee 1	Trainee 2	Trainee 3
1	R_1	R_2	
2	R_1	R_2	
3		R_1	R_2
4		R_1	R_2
5	R_2	R_1	
6	R_2		R_1
7	R_2		R_1

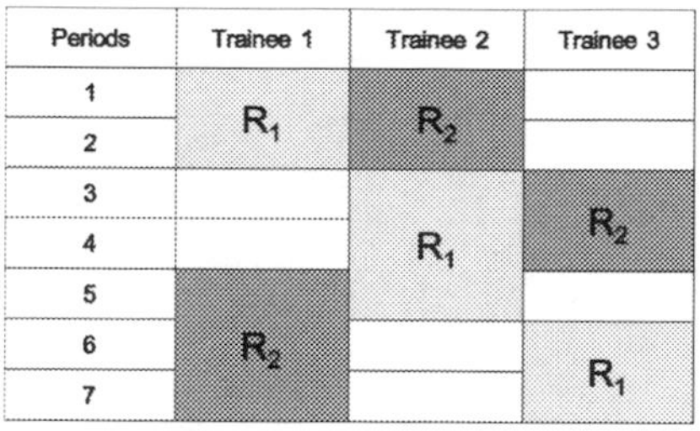 Periods	Trainee 1	Trainee 2	Trainee 3
1	R_1	R_2	
2			
3		R_1	R_2
4			
5	R_2		
6			R_1
7			

(a) Solution in normal form   (b) Solution in block form

Fig. 2. Two equivalent solutions in two forms

There are two sets of binary decision variables. The first set defines rotation type in each period:

$$x_{ijk} = \begin{cases} 1, & \text{in period } i \text{ trainee } j \text{ perform rotation } k \\ 0, & \text{otherwise} \end{cases}$$

Another set defines the start of a rotation:

$$y_{ijk} = \begin{cases} 1, & \text{trainee } j \text{ perform rotation } k \text{ starts at period } i \\ 0, & \text{otherwise} \end{cases}$$

The models are very problem-dependent and there is no generalized and suitable model definition for all situations among literature [1–9]. Regarding the solution approach for solving staff scheduling problem, although a large number of methods are proposed [3], little attention is given to develop approaches for solving the model in this paper. As noted in [1], for this problem, developing robust heuristic solution procedure that provide good solutions in small computation times is an interesting direction and our work addresses this. In this paper, a two-stage heuristic algorithm is proposed for solving this problem. To the best of our knowledge, there is no work about heuristic algorithm for solving such rotation assignment problem before.

2   Solution Approach

2.1   Overview of the Algorithm

Our algorithm uses two stages in order to produce feasible, high-quality solutions. The idea is that because rotations must be performed in consecutive periods, these periods can be seen as a block of this type of rotation. Throughout this paper, such groups of rotations of same type are called *rotation blocks*. Figure 2 presents a solution the same as in Fig. 1 together with its corresponding view based on rotation blocks.

In the first stage, we optimize the solution based on rotation blocks. Since the solution space is much larger than solutions only through this stage alone, in the next a problem-specific operator is employed in order to further explore solution space to search better solutions. These two stages are executed repeatedly until the running time limit is reached, and the algorithm will return the best solution found during the process. The overall algorithm is presented by the pseudo-code in Fig. 3 and details of these two stages are described in following sections.

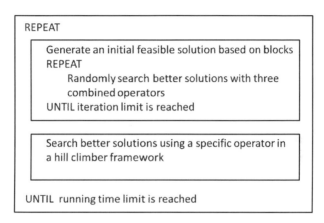

Fig. 3. Overview of the proposed algorithm

2.2   First Stage

Periods Partition. In the first stage, in order to generate a feasible solution based on rotation blocks, rows (periods) of a solution are firstly grouped into blocks to reduce the whole periods into a new set. Note that each rotation block has to be performed by every trainee exactly once and in each period the blocks of the same type will not overlap due to the constraints (3). Given these reasons, in the whole time period, the number of blocks of each rotation must be equal to the number of trainees. So the whole periods are partitioned into m (number of trainees) groups. Let $i', i' = 1, ..., m$ be the new index of periods in blocks. To keep the solution feasible, in each block of period, rotations of all types must be performed by distinct trainees. To produce a solution in blocks, this partition should be fixed first. In this paper, it is assumed that instances to be solved are always feasible since in real-life scenario, this can be guaranteed by the rule maker of the training program in school.

Assume we have an instance with period set $I = \{1, 2, ..., n\}$. We partition this set into a new form $\tilde{I} = \{a_1, a_2, ..., a_m\}$, where $a_{i'}, i' = 1, ..., m$ are subsets of I such that $\cup_{i'=1}^{m} a_{i'} = I$, $a_{i'} \cap a_{j'} = \emptyset, \forall i \neq j$, and $|a_{i'}| \in [l, u], \forall a_{i'} \in \tilde{I}$. While partitioning, the order and position of periods should keep unchanged. For example, when $I = \{1, 2, 3, 4, 5, 6, 7\}$, two possible partitions are $\tilde{I} = \{\{1, 2\}, \{3, 4\}, \{5, 6, 7\}\}$ and $\tilde{I} = \{\{1, 2\}, \{3, 4, 5\}, \{6, 7\}\}$, where $l = 2, u = 3$

and $m = 3$. Although the partition will influence quality of the final solution, we cannot employ any fitness function to evaluate it at this stage and it is generated randomly.

Problem Reduction. After the partition configuration is fixed, the original problem is transformed into a simplified version, where the number of periods are reduced from n to m and the cells of solution are also grouped together. Figure 4 presents an example of a feasible solution based on block forms and its corresponding original solution. It is clear that a feasible solution to reduced problem is also feasible to the original problem.

Periods	Trainee 1	Trainee 2	Trainee 3
1	R_1	R_2	
2		R_1	R_2
3	R_2		R_1

(a) A feasible solution of the reduced model

Periods	Trainee 1	Trainee 2	Trainee 3
1	R_1	R_2	
2	R_1	R_2	
3		R_1	R_2
4		R_1	R_2
5	R_2		R_1
6	R_2		R_1
7	R_2		R_1

(b) The corresponding solution of the original model

Fig. 4. In (a), the periods are partitioned to the form $\tilde{I} = \{\{1, 2\}, \{3, 4\}, \{5, 6, 7\}\}$, and the new preference costs are: $\tilde{p}_{3,1} = p_{5,1} + p_{7,1}$, $\tilde{p}_{1,2} = p_{1,2}$, $\tilde{p}_{2,2} = p_{4,2}$, $\tilde{p}_{2,3} = p_{3,3}$, $\tilde{p}_{3,3} = p_{6,3}$ and other penalties are 0.

To deal with this new model, we use a random iterative search algorithm instead of the exact method. The reason is that the method in the next stage only searches the local optima in a deterministic way and we want to obtain different solutions from the first stage to diversify the search.

Overview of First Stage. In Algorithm 1, the first stage of the proposed algorithm is presented in detail. A feasible solution can be firstly produced using a simple procedure. After an initial solution is generated, better solutions are searched iteratively using three operators described as follows.

- *Row_swap*: two rows of a solution are randomly selected and swapped;
- *Column_swap*: two columns of a solution are randomly selected and swapped;
- *Partial_row_swap*: for two rows, if there exists a subset of columns (trainees) where they perform two equal subsets of rotations, then the rotations in such columns between these two rows are swapped. For instance, in Fig. 5, trainees T_1, T_2 and T_3 performs R_1 and R_2 both in periods P_2 and P_3, and thus their rotations can be swapped between these two periods.

Algorithm 1. Overview of the first stage

---

    input : A feasible instance
    output: A feasible solution
1   Produce a feasible solution X;
2   asdfasdfas test; //asdfasdfasd
3   **while** *iteration limit is not reached* **do**
4      $X' = X$;
5   Generate b in $[0, 1]$ randomly;
6   **if** $b > 0.5$ **then**
7 | *Row_swap* to X';
8   **else**
9 | *Column_swap* to X';
10   **end**
11   **foreach** *violated preferences P_{ij}* **do**
12 | *Partial_row_swap* to X';
13   **end**
14   **if** X' *is better than* X **then**
15 | $X = X'$;
16   **end**
17 **end**
18 **return** X;

During one iteration of the search, the *row_swap* and *column_swap* are selected randomly with equal probability and perform to the current solution. Then all violated rotations are checked and use *part_swap_operator* to see if this violation can be eliminated. Note that the number of violated rotation is $O(m)$ and the possible swaps for each one is $O(m^2)$. All of these operators will not influence the hard constraints of a solution. Figure 5 is also an example of using the *part_swap_operator* to eliminate a violated assignment. When stopped, the best solution obtained enters the next stage. As for the stop criterion of this stage, we generate a number in $[10, 220]$ randomly and use this value to be the iteration limit of the first stage. Note that this interval is fixed for all instances. It is obvious that the best solution of reduced problem could not be reached in this manner. If we fix it, however, same solutions could be obtained among different runs of first stage. Given that the second stage is not stochastic, this phenomenon could lead to stagnation in local optima. To avoid this, we use this stochastic mechanism to diversify the search for the second stage.

2.3 Second Stage

Since the neighbourhood in first stage is only based on rotations blocks, solution space of the original model is apparently larger than solutions of the reduced problem. In this stage, a neighbourhood defined by a *move_and_repair* procedure is incorporated to further explore solution space.

Periods`	Trainee 1	Trainee 2	Trainee 3	Trainee 4	Trainee 5
1					
2	R_1	R_2		R_3	
3		R_1	R_2		R_3
4					

(a)Solution before the operation

Periods`	Trainee 1	Trainee 2	Trainee 3	Trainee 4	Trainee 5
1					
2		R_1	R_2	R_3	
3	R_1	R_2			R_3
4					

(b)Solution after the operation

Fig. 5. In (a), the cost is 2 and in (b) the cost is reduced to 1 after *Part_swap_operator* is performed to T_1,T_2 and T_3 between P_2 and P_3. Here we assume that the undesired periods are also in bold border and the penalties are all set to 1.

Operator: Move_and_Repair. The *move_and_repair* procedure consists of two steps. At the first step, an operator which aims to move rotations between blocks of rotations is defined. We call it *one_step_move* and it is always performed to blocks of the same type. Intuitively, this operator mimics the act of adjustment by a human solution to change the structure of a solution when trying to find better ones. Figure 6 illustrates an example of this operator. In order to express the concept clearly, the blocks in the figure are of the same rotation type while blocks of other rotations are omitted. In the following description, a single cell is also referred to as a unit.

As shown in the figure, a top unit of block 3 can be moved to the bottom of block 1 while the feasibility is still maintained if rotation blocks of other types are ignored temporarily. During this process, lengths of blocks between the two blocks will not change but the position will shift vertically. Implementation steps we use to carry out this operator are shown in (b) and (c), where a unit of assignment is moved to the bottom of the adjacent upper block iteratively until the top block is reached. It is worth noting that in our approach, we only consider the direction of move from bottom up.

An issue of this operator is that if blocks of other rotations are taken into account, this shift can influence assignments of other blocks. For example, the positions taken up by blocks of other types of rotations will be replaced during this process. Consequently, at that period, the rotation being replaced is broken, and thus the solution becomes infeasible. In Fig. 7(a) and (b) provide an example of this case between two blocks R_i and R_j, where the same move as in Fig. 6(b) is performed to R_i. When such situation occurs, the second step of *move_and_repair* is employed which aims to repair this broken point.

To fix this, we perform a similar move to pairs of blocks of R_j which contains the broken period. As shown in Fig. 7(c), we find *Block* 2 and *Block* 3 of rotation R_j (deep color) are also an available pair, so we can perform another *one_step_move* to them, which can still cause another broken rotation. We continue using this procedure iteratively until no such broken rotation exists so that the solution becomes feasible again.

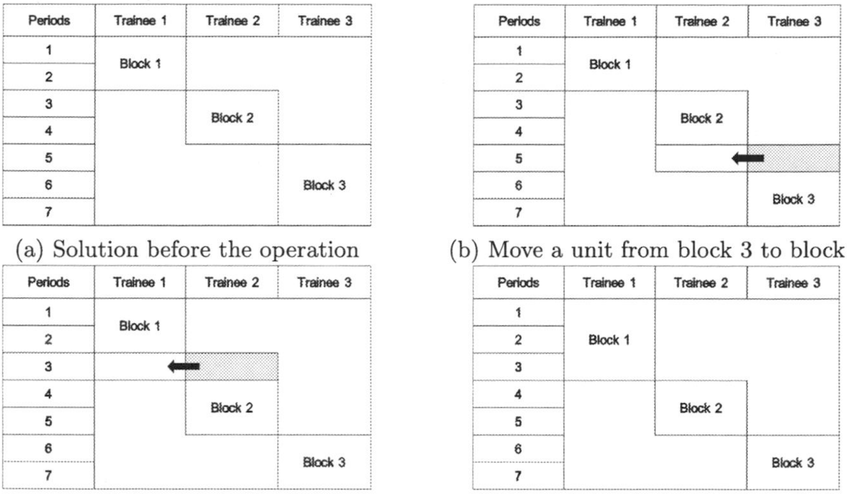

Periods	Trainee 1	Trainee 2	Trainee 3
1	Block 1		
2			
3		Block 2	
4			
5			
6			Block 3
7			

(a) Solution before the operation

Periods	Trainee 1	Trainee 2	Trainee 3
1	Block 1		
2			
3		Block 2	
4			
5		←	
6			Block 3
7			

(b) Move a unit from block 3 to block 2

Periods	Trainee 1	Trainee 2	Trainee 3
1	Block 1		
2			
3	←		
4		Block 2	
5			
6			Block 3
7			

(c) Move a unit from block 2 to block 1

Periods	Trainee 1	Trainee 2	Trainee 3
1	Block 1		
2	Block 1		
3			
4		Block 2	
5			
6			Block 3
7			

(d) Solution after the operation

Fig. 6. *One_step_move* operator description. Here the three rotation blocks are of the same type.

Algorithms of Second Stage. Algorithm 2 presents overview of the second stage of our algorithm. Note that the input solution is the one generated from the first stage. We use *move_and_repair* for a hill climber. We check for all rotations, and for each one we loop through all available pairs to try the operator. If a better solution is found, we start over the whole procedure from this better solution. If either the *move_and_repair* does not success, or the solution does not become better, the changed solution will be recovered and we continue to try the next pair.

3   Computational Results

3.1   Problem Instances

To test our algorithm, we solved randomly generated instances based on rules of training program and the history data of five years from school of nursing in Shandong University. Training program in the school has two types according to the number of trainees. Each type also has two subtypes according to number of rotations. Table 1 presents the specific values of these parameters for each type.

3.2   Experimental Protocol

We compare our algorithm with Cplex using the integer linear programming formulation(ILP) provided in Sect. 1. Since for larger instances(especially type II), Cplex will spend very much time in finding initial feasible integer solutions,

---

Algorithm 2. Overview of second stage

---

input : A solution X generated by the first stage
output: An optimized solution
1 **foreach** R_i *of* X **do**
2   **foreach** *feasible pairs of block* $B_i(p,q)$ *of* X **do**
3         $X' = X$;
4   **if** *move_and_repair to* $B_i(p,q)$ *of* X' *return True* **then**
5   **if** X' *is better than* X **then**
6                 $X = X'$;
7   goto step 1;
8   **end**
9   **end**
10   **end**
11 **end**
12 **return** X';

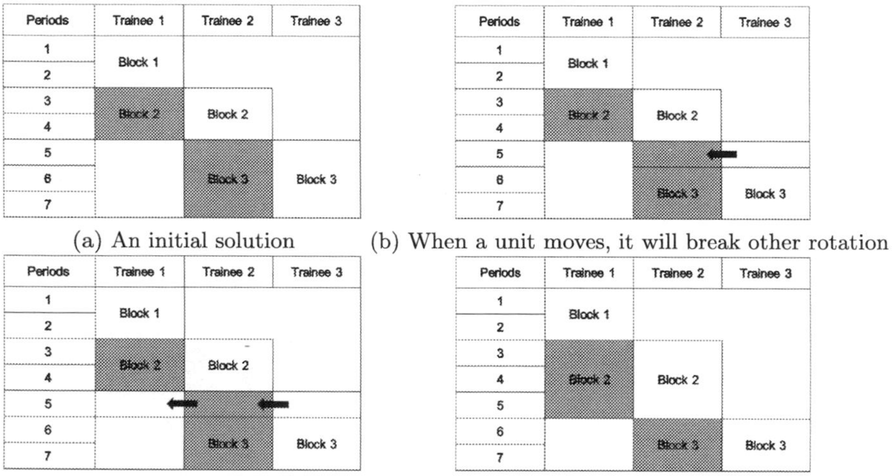

(a) An initial solution   (b) When a unit moves, it will break other rotation

(c) Repair the borken rotation   (d) Solution after *move_and_repair*

Fig. 7. A case of broken rotation caused by the *one_step_move* operator and the repair process. Here we use deep color to denote R_j and white color to denote R_i. We find that the rotation in deep color is broken when the white color rotation moves. In (c), we use a identical move to repair the broken rotation.

we also provide initial feasible integer solution using Algorithm 2 for Cplex warm start for all instances. Instance files and source code can be downloaded from https://github.com/zzrnature/rotation for reproduction. We use Cplex 12.6.3 to solve all instances and the proposed algorithm is implemented in C++ using Visual Studio 2010. Since our algorithm is random in nature, we run 20 times for each instance. There are no other parameters to be tuned in our algorithm.

Table 1. Parameter values based on real-life rules for experiments

Type I		Type II	
Trainees	Rotations	Trainees	Rotations
8	5, 6	12	9, 10
Total periods (undesired periods)		Total periods (undesired periods)	
26(5), 29(6), 32(7), 35(7), 38(7)		40(8), 44(9), 48(9), 52(10), 57(11)	

Table 2. Results and comparison with ILP formulation using Cplex

Instances				ILP formulation		Proposed algorithm			
No.	Trainees	Rotations	Periods	Best	Lower bound	Min	Max	Avg	Std
1	8	5	26	7	7	11	11	11	0.00
2				13	13	**13**	13	13	0.00
3				7	7	12	13	12.4	0.49
4	8	5	29	5	5	9	12	11	0.89
5				7	7	15	17	15.8	0.60
6				14	14	17	20	19.1	0.94
7	8	5	32	16	12	21	23	22.7	0.64
8				24	5.8	**22**	25	23.6	0.66
9				11	6.7	22	27	25.4	1.36
10	8	5	35	23	6.15	26	28	26.5	0.67
11				25	6	**22**	24	23.6	0.66
12				16	7	21	23	22.2	0.60
13	8	5	38	31	4.4	**24**	26	25.4	0.80
14				18	3	19	20	19.90	0.30
15				27	4.1	**23**	34	23.10	0.30
16	8	6	26	26	18	**26**	26	26	0.00
17				25	15	26	29	27.6	0.92
18				26	8.7	**22**	23	22.9	0.30
19	8	6	29	24	13.1	**24**	27	23.4	0.80
20				23	15	27	29	28.4	0.66
21				27	18	**26**	27	26.4	0.49
22	8	6	32	37	25	38	40	39.2	0.75
23				40	20	41	44	42.9	0.94
24				37	22	**36**	40	38.2	1.16
25	8	6	35	43	11	**35**	37	35.8	0.60
26				44	22.6	**44**	45	44.3	0.46
27				38	19.5	**33**	36	35.2	0.87

(*continued*)

Table 2. (*continued*)

Instances				ILP formulation		Proposed algorithm			
No	Trainees	Rotations	Periods	Best	Lower bound	Min	Max	Avg	Std
28	8	6	38	54	22.7	**49**	49	49	0.00
29				45	18	**38**	39	38.9	0.30
30				41	14.6	**40**	42	41.1	0.83
31	12	9	40	62	23	**62**	64	62.8	0.75
32				86	19	**63**	65	63.6	0.8
33				103	17	**53**	57	55	1.48
34	12	9	44	73	16.3	**72**	76	74.2	1.07
35				83	31	**73**	75	73.8	0.60
36				65	24	69	72	69.7	0.90
37	12	9	48	65	13	**65**	70	67.5	1.50
38				74	15	**71**	76	74.4	1.50
39				83	14	**75**	79	76.8	1.25
40	12	9	52	100	15	**78**	85	82.2	2.09
41				172	12.7	**82**	89	86.7	2.53
42				113	14	**78**	81	79.9	1.14
43	12	9	57	170	22	**103**	110	107.1	1.92
44				201	26	**106**	111	108.6	1.28
45				161	15	**92**	100	98.1	2.3
46	12	10	40	111	45	**91**	95	93.6	1.02
47				112	57	**89**	94	91.5	1.28
48				107	39	**86**	89	87.6	1.11
49	12	10	44	131	57	**98**	103	100.9	1.58
50				122	58	**103**	109	106.2	2.09
51				119	51	**119**	99	97.3	2.10
52	12	10	48	127	53	**127**	103	101	1.41
53				186	53	**107**	115	111.9	2.30
54				172	39	**172**	98	96.9	1.30
55	12	10	52	180	51	**115**	120	118.3	1.68
56				209	53	**122**	127	125	1.26
57				192	51	**112**	119	116.4	2.10
58	12	10	57	235	71	**156**	159	157.8	0.87
59				216	67.2	**148**	152	150.6	1.28
60				200	67	**131**	134	132.4	0.92

3.3   Results and Comparison with ILP Formulation

Table 2 presents the results of our algorithm and the comparison with ILP formulation. The first column (No.) includes the instance number; the next three columns presents the main parameters of each instance; next two column, best solution and lower bound values are provided; in the last four columns, we offer the minimum (min), maximum (max), average (avg) and standard deviation (std) values for each instance. We use bold to mark better solutions with our algorithm than Cplex. One can see that for the first 6 instances (No. 1–No. 6), Cplex can find optimal solutions within the time limit and our algorithm only solved one to optimal. For the next 18 instances (No. 7–No.24), our method finds equal or better solutions for 50% of them. For the rest instances (No. 25–60), our algorithm yields better solutions all but only one instance (No. 36) whose gap is only 1. It is clearly to see that, as the input scales become larger, our algorithm finds much better solutions. Overall, our two-stage heuristic obtain no worse solutions for 75% of all instances with significant less computation times and shows great advantage for larger instances. Regarding the stability, standard deviations are more than 2.00 for only 7 instances out of 60, thus we conclude that our algorithm is very stable.

4   Conclusions and Future Research

In this paper, A two-stage heuristic approach is proposed to tackle a rotation assignment problem. Compared with Cplex in integer linear programming formulation, our heuristic approach can obtain high-quality solutions with much less computation time, especially for large instances. Further direction primarily includes improvement of the algorithm.

References

1. Beliën, J., Demeulemeester, E.: Scheduling trainees at a hospital department using a branch-and-price approach. Eur. J. Oper. Res. **175**(1), 258–278 (2006)
2. Beliën, J., Demeulemeester, E.: On the trade-off between staff-decomposed and activity-decomposed column generation for a staff scheduling problem. Annal. Oper. Res. **155**(1), 143–166 (2007)
3. Bergh, J.V.D., Beliën, J., Bruecker, P.D., Demeulemeester, E., Boeck, L.D.: Personnel scheduling: a literature review. Eur. J. Oper. Res. **226**(3), 367–385 (2013)
4. Bettinelli, A., Cacchiani, V., Roberti, R., Toth, P.: An overview of curriculum-based course timetabling. TOP **23**(2), 313–349 (2015)
5. Burke, E.K., Mareček, J., Parkes, A.J., Rudová, H.: Penalising patterns in timetables: novel integer programming formulations. In: Kalcsics, J., Nickel, S. (eds.) Operations Research Proceedings 2007, vol. 2007. Springer, Heidelberg (2008). https://doi.org/10.1007/978-3-540-77903-2_63
6. Burke, E.K., Marecek, J., Parkes, A.J., Rudová, H.: Decomposition, reformulation, and diving in university course timetabling. Comput. Oper. Res. **37**(3), 582–597 (2010)

7. Guo, J., Morrison, D.R., Jacobson, S.H., Jokela, J.A.: Complexity results for the basic residency scheduling problem. J. Sched. **17**(3), 211–223 (2014)
8. Smalley, H.K., Keskinocak, P.: Automated medical resident rotation and shift scheduling to ensure quality resident education and patient care. Health Care Manag. Sci. **19**, 1–23 (2014)
9. Wang, C., Sun, L., Jin, M., Fu, C., Liu, L., Chan, C., Kao, C.: A genetic algorithm for resident physician scheduling problem. In: Proceedings of Genetic and Evolutionary Computation Conference, GECCO 2007, London, England, UK, 7–11 July 2007, pp. 2203–2210 (2007)

An Improved Blind Optimization Algorithm for Hardware/Software Partitioning and Scheduling

Xin Zhao[1,2], Tao Zhang[1,2(✉)], Xinqi An[1,2], and Long Fan[1,2]

[1] School of Electrical and Information Engineering,
Tianjin University, Tianjin 300072, China
zhangtao@tju.edu.cn
[2] Texas Instruments DSP Joint Lab, Tianjin University, Tianjin 300072, China

Abstract. Hardware/software partitioning is an important part in the development of complex embedded system. Blind optimization algorithms are suitable to solve the problem when it is combined with task scheduling. To get hardware/software partitioning algorithms with higher performance, this paper improves Shuffled Frog Leaping Algorithm-Earliest Time First (SFLA-ETF) which is a blind optimization algorithm. Under the supervision of the aggregation factor, the improved algorithm named Supervised SFLA-ETF (SSFLA-ETF) used two steps to better balance exploration and exploitation. Experimental results show that compared with SFLA-ETF and other swarm intelligence algorithms, SSFLA-ETF has stronger optimization ability.

Keywords: Hardware/software partitioning · Blind optimization algorithms
SSFLA-ETF · High performance

1 Introduction

Compared with single-core processor system, multi-core processor system usually shows better performance. Therefore, complex multi-core embedded systems have become the mainstream of development for meeting higher requirements. Many complex embedded systems are composed of software units and hardware units. Because hardware units and software units have different performance when execute different tasks, it is crucial to balance the proportion of different units in design scheme.

Hardware/Software partitioning is to achieve the most effective system design scheme by assigning tasks with different complexity to software units or hardware units. It is a NP-hard problem. The problem have higher computational complexity because of its large-scale tasks and multiple optimization objectives. In general, solving the problem with exact algorithms such as Dynamic Programming (DP) [1], Integer Linear Programming (ILP) [2], Branch and Bound (B&B) [3] is very time-consuming and difficult to perform. Compared with exact algorithms, heuristic algorithms are efficient in solving complex optimization problems. Therefore, many creative heuristic algorithms are applied to hardware/software partitioning, such as the greedy algorithm [4], tabu search [5], evolutionary algorithms [6] and Swarm intelligence algorithms [7–10].

© Springer International Publishing AG, part of Springer Nature 2018
Y. Tan et al. (Eds.): ICSI 2018, LNCS 10942, pp. 225–234, 2018.
https://doi.org/10.1007/978-3-319-93818-9_21

In work [11], heuristic algorithms are further categorized into blind optimization algorithms and non-blind optimization algorithms. It demonstrates that blind optimization algorithms are more suitable for solving complex optimization problems.

Hardware/Software partitioning mainly completes the work of tasks assignment, and task scheduling usually should be performed after that. Work [11] demonstrates that some better solutions may be missed if task scheduling is not considered during the process of hardware/software partitioning. Therefore, work [11] combines hardware/software partitioning with task scheduling. Because problem becomes more complex, swarm intelligence algorithms which is belong to blind optimization algorithm is selected to address. Work [11] combines Shuffled Frog Leaping Algorithm (SFLA) and a task scheduling algorithm named Earliest Tim First (EFT) [12] to generate a new algorithm SFLA-ETF. Experimental results show that SFLA-ETF can solve the hardware/software partitioning problem effectively when task scheduling is considered.

Although SFLA-ETF is an effective algorithm, the performance of the algorithm needs to be further improved to better meet the requirements in the aspects such as the quality of the solutions, the running time of algorithm and so on. Therefore, on the basis of work [11], we continue to focus on the hardware/software partitioning problem combined with task scheduling and try to improve the performance of algorithm further. This paper proposes an improved SFLA-ETF algorithm whose update process is supervised by the aggregation factor. The new algorithm is named SSFLA-ETF (Supervised SFLA-ETF).

The rest of the paper is organized as follows. In Sect. 2, the mathematical model is described and the original algorithm SFLA-ETF is introduced. In Sect. 3, the improved algorithm SSFLA-ETF is proposed. In Sect. 4, the experimental results is given. In Sect. 5, we conclude this paper.

2 Related Knowledge

2.1 The Mathematical Model

In this paper, we used the simplified model same with work [11]. Assume that one task consists of n subtask nodes, it can be described by $G = <V, E>$, where $V = \{V_0, V_1, \cdots V_i \cdots V_n\}$ denotes the n subtask nodes and V_i is the ith subtask node. $V_i = \{V^i_{type}, (T^i_{sw}, T^i_{hw}), (A^i_{hw})\}$, where V^i_{type} denotes the processing unit which subtask V_i is assigned to, $V^i_{type} = sw$ represents V_i is assigned to software and $V^i_{type} = hw$ represents V_i is assigned to hardware. T^i_{sw} and T^i_{hw} represent the software execution time and hardware execution time respectively. A^i_{hw} represents the area requirement of hardware. The area requirement of software is ignored. $E = \{e_1, e_2 \cdots e_j \cdots e_m\}$ denotes the dependency relationship among subtask nodes. Where $e_j = \{(V_{aj}, V_{bj}, c_{aj,bj}) | V_{ai}, V_{bj} \in V\}$ denotes there is a dependency between nodes V_{aj} and V_{bj}. Task V_{bj} can be executed when task V_{aj} is completed. $c_{aj,bj}$ is the communication time between V_{aj} and V_{bj}.

When hardware/software partitioning is combined with task scheduling, the scheduling length $T_{sch}(V)$ is used as an optimization objective and the total area requirement A_{sum} is used as the constraint condition. The problem can be described as formula (1):

$$min : T_{sch}(V) = max\{TE(V_i)|i = 1, 2, \cdots n\}$$

$$subject\ to : \sum_{i=1}^{n} A_{hw}^i(V_{type} = hw) \leq AreaLimit \tag{1}$$

Where *AreaLimit* is the area constraint and $TE(V_i)$ is the completion time of V_i after task scheduling.

2.2   SFLA-ETF

SFLA-ETF is generated by combining SFLA with EFT. The key of SFLA-ETF algorithm is that the evaluation of a solution is based on the scheduling length. In other words, when a new solution is generated, it should be scheduled. The flow chart of SFLA-ETF is shown in Fig. 1.

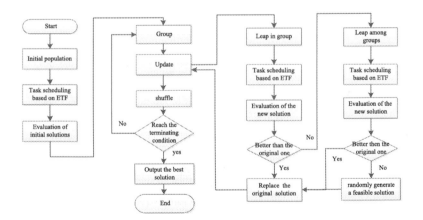

Fig. 1. The flow chart of SFLA-ETF

3   SSFLA-ETF Algorithm

3.1   Analysis of SFLA-ETF

To improve the performance of swarm intelligence algorithm, the most important thing is to balance the exploration and exploitation.

(1) For the exploration, it is important to keep the diversity of the population. In order to further analyze the relationship between the population diversity and the optimization ability of the algorithm, aggregation factor *Dis* is used as an indicator of population diversity. The calculation formula of *Dis* is shown as follows:

$$f_d(x_1, x_2) = \sum_{i=1}^{n} |x_1(i) - x_2(i)|$$

$$f_a(x) = \begin{cases} 1, & x < Dis\_min \\ 0, & x \geq Dis\_min \end{cases} \tag{2}$$

$$Dis = \sum_{i=1}^{N-1} \sum_{j=i}^{N} f_a(f_d(S_i, S_j))$$

Where x_1 and x_2 are two n-dimensional vectors and n is the number of subtask nodes. $x_1(i)$ represents the value of the ith dimension of x_1. *Dis_min* is a threshold. N is the number of solutions in the population. S_i and S_j are the ith and jth solution in the population. It can be seen from the formula that the larger the *Dis* is, the closer the distance among the individuals are. When SFLA-ETF is used to solve the problem of 500 subtask nodes and *Dis_min* is set to $n/50$. The relationship between the optimal solution's fitness value and the population's *Dis* is shown in Fig. 2

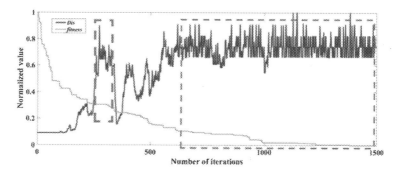

Fig. 2. Relationship between fitness and *Dis*

As illustrated in Fig. 2, when the value of *Dis* is large, the descending speed of the fitness curve is slow. Especially at the later stage of the iterations, *Dis* keeps a high value and the descending speed of the fitness curve obviously keeps slow.

(2) For the exploitation, the setting of the search step size is an important work. Large search step size can speed up the descending of the fitness curve, but it may cause the algorithm to fall into a local optimal. Small search step size has better global optimization ability, but it may slow down the decline speed of the fitness curve. Therefore, if the search step size can be adjusted adaptively in the algorithm process, the ability of the exploitation will be increased effectively. In SFLA-ETF,

poor solutions will move to optimal solutions to update themselves. Finding a suitable method to adaptively adjust the step size of the movement is benefit to SFLA-ETF.

3.2 SSFLA-ETF

Based on the above analysis, a Supervised SFLA-ETF algorithm is proposed. In this algorithm, aggregation factor Dis is calculated in each iteration and used as a supervision. Based on this supervision, the original algorithm is improved by introducing the following two strategies.

(1) Regenerating the population. When the Dis is higher than a threshold D_LIM, the best solution in the population is reserved and other solutions are regenerated based on formula (3).

$$S_{new} = S_{ori} + Rand * Csize \tag{3}$$

Where S_{ori} is the original solution, S_{new} is the new solution, $Rand$ is a random value between 0 and 1, $Csize$ is the update step size. The positions of the solutions before and after regeneration is shown in Fig. 3. Where the red circle represents the best solution and other circles represent other solutions. It can be seen from Fig. 3 that the aggregation degree of the population has become smaller. In addition, the reservation of the best solution of the original population is necessary. Because the previous achievement is beneficial for improving the search speed of the new population.

(2) Adjusting the search step size adaptively. The moving step size of the solutions are also adjusted based on the aggregation factor Dis. The calculation formula of the step size is as follows:

$$Step_{new} = Step_{max} - (Step_{max} - Step_{min}) * Dis/D\_LIM \tag{4}$$

Where $Step_{new}$ is the new step size, $Step_{max}$ and $Step_{min}$ is the maximum and minimum step size. It can be seen from formula (4) that when the degree of aggregation increases, the step size will become smaller. That is because the more concentrated the distribution of the solutions is, the greater the probability of the emergence of the optimal solutions is. When the area is not easy to appear optimal solutions, a large step

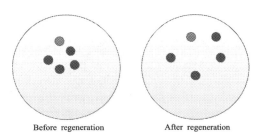

Before regeneration   After regeneration

Fig. 3. Positions of solutions before and after the update (Color figure online)

Table 1. Pseudo code of SSFLA-ETF

Algorithm SSFLA-ETF
___
Begin

1 Population_size=N, Group_num=M, Max_repeat_num=MR; /* Initialize basic parameters*/

2 Init_frogs(); /*Initialize frog population*/

3 **For** repeat_num=1 to MR **do**

  3.1 Dis=Cac_Dis();/* Calculate Dis based on formula (2)*/

    While $Dis>D\_LIM$ **do**

      Regenerate_frogs(); /* Regenerate population based on formula (3)*/

      Dis=Cac_Dis();

    End while

  3.2 ETF(all_solutions); /*Task scheduling based on ETF*/

  3.3 Cac_Fit(all_solutions);/*Calculate the fitness of all solutions*/

  3.4 Group();/*Group solutions*/

  3.5 $Step_{new}$ =Cac_step();/*Calculate step size based on formula (4)*/

  3.6 **For** i=1 to M **do**

      $S_{i,temp}$ =$S_{i,worst}$ + $Rand*Step_{new}*(S_{i,best}-S_{i,worst})$;

      ETF($S_{i,temp}$);

      $Fit_{i,temp}$ = Cac_Fit($S_{i,temp}$)

      If Is_valid(S_{temp})&& $Fit_{i,temp}$ < $Fit_{i,worst}$ **then**

        $S_{i,worst}$ = $S_{i,temp}$;

      Else

        $S_{i,temp}$ =$S_{i,worst}$ + $Rand*Step_{new}*(S_{BEST}-S_{i,worst})$;

        ETF($S_{i,temp}$);

        $Fit_{i,temp}$ = Cac_Fit($S_{i,temp}$)

        If Is_valid($S_{i,temp}$)&& $Fit_{i,temp}$ < $Fit_{i,worst}$ **then**

          $S_{i,worst}$ = $S_{i,temp}$;

        Else do

          $S_{i,temp}$ =random_frog(); /*Randomly generate a solution*/

          While !is_valid($S_{i,temp}$)

          $S_{i,worst}$ = $S_{i,temp}$

        End while

      End if

    End if

  End for

  End for

4 **Output** solution;

End.

---

size will increase the speed of optimization. On the contrary, when the optimal solutions are easy to appear, searching with a small step size is helpful to find the optimal solutions. The pseudo code is shown in Table 1, where $S_{i,worst}$, $S_{i,best}$, S_{BEST} are the worst solution in group i, the best solution in group i and the best solution in the population respectively. *Rand* is a random value between 0 and 1.

4   Empirical Results

In this section, some experiments are designed to test the performance of SSFLA-ETF. These algorithms are implemented in C++ and tested on a computer Intel core i5-6400 @ 2.70 GHz with 8 GB RAM. The instances are generated randomly in accordance with [11]. The TGFF tool is used to generate the instances of hardware/software partitioning problem.

For better comparing two algorithms, we set one algorithm as the Anchor Basis (AB), and the other algorithm as the tuned algorithm. The improvement ratio ρ. tuned algorithm to the AB is calculated as (5).

$$\rho = \left(1 - \frac{T_{sch}^{TUN}}{T_{sch}^{AB}} \right) \times 100\% \tag{5}$$

Where T_{sch}^{TUN} represents the scheduling length of tuned algorithm and T_{sch}^{AB} represents the scheduling length of AB.

4.1   Comparison of SFLA-ETF and SSFLA-ETF

SFLA-ETF and SSFLA-ETF are run based on task sets with different scale. For each task set, algorithms will run 10 times to get the average value. The number of iterations of each algorithm is 1500.

Table 2. The comparison of results between SFLA-ETF and SSFLA-ETF

Node number	SFLA-ETF		SSFLA-ETF		ρ/%
	Scheduling length	Running time	Scheduling length	Running time	
50	22879.80	0.7328	22606.47	0.7497	1.19
100	44045.82	3.5028	42074.07	3.5471	4.48
200	89807.21	21.2344	86285.27	21.5387	3.92
300	142684.58	65.2533	137898.00	67.3858	3.35
500	243006.48	281.2161	235557.18	289.7792	3.07
700	353802.55	763.2726	346247.29	775.7454	2.14
1000	505451.57	2180.2415	499932.57	2206.7198	1.10

Table 2 shows the comparison of results over scheduling length and running time between SFLA-ETF and SSFLA-ETF, where SFLA-ETF is the AB and SSFLA-ETF is

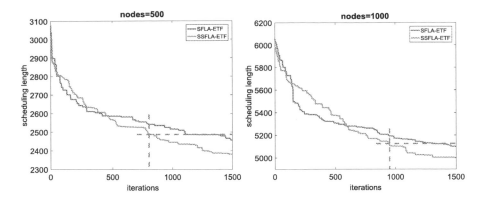

Fig. 4. The fitness curves of SFLA-ETF and SSFLA-ETF

the turned algorithm. As shown in Table 2, under the same number of iterations, SSFLA-ETF can get better solutions. The running time of SSFLA-ETF is a little longer than SFLA-ETF. The main reason is that the calculation of *Dis* increase the running time.

Figure 4 illustrates the fitness curves of SFLA-ETF and SSFLA-ETF based on the task sets with 500 nodes and 1000 nodes. In the early stage, the descending speed of SFLA-ETF is faster than SSFLA-ETF, which is because regenerating the population will temporarily reduce the overall quality. But SSFLA-ETF can keep a stable descending speed and gradually exceed SFLA-ETF. Especially in the later stage, the descending speed of SFLA-ETF becomes slow while SSFLA-ETF is still fast. This illustrates SSFLA-ETF has a stronger optimization ability. In addition, it can be seen that the solution obtained by 1000 iterations of SSFLA-ETF can achieve the same quality as the solution obtained by 1500 iterations of SFLA-ETF. Therefore, although the running time of SSFLA-ETF is longer than SFLA-ETF under the same number of iterations, to get solutions with the same quality, SSFLA-ETF needs shorter running time.

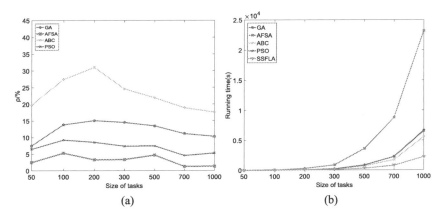

Fig. 5. Comparison of SSFLA-ETF and other swarm intelligence algorithms

4.2   Comparison of SSFLA-ETF and Other Swarm Intelligence Algorithms

To further evaluate the performance of SSFLA-ETF, it is compared with GA, AFSA, ABC and PSO. Figure 5 (a) presents the improvement ratio of SSFLA-ETF to other algorithms and Fig. 5 (b) presents the running time of different algorithms. It can be seen that SSFLA-ETF can get the highest quality solutions with the shortest running time among the five algorithms. It indicates that the proposed algorithms in this paper have outstanding performance when it is used to solve the hardware/software partitioning problem.

5   Conclusion

In this paper, we propose an improved blind algorithm SSFLA-ETF which is used to solve the hardware/software partitioning problem combined with task scheduling. On the basic of SLFA-ETF, the improved algorithm first use aggregation factor as a supervision, then regenerate the population and adjust the search step size based on the supervision results. Experimental results show that the proposed algorithm has better performance than SFLA-ETF and other swarm intelligence algorithms. In the process of research, we find that the parameters such as *Csize* and *D_LIM* may affect the algorithm performance. The parameters setting of the algorithm need to be studied further.

References

1. Shi, W., Wu, J., Lam, S.: Algorithmic aspects for bi-objective multiple-choice hardware/software partitioning. Comput. Electr. Eng. **50**(3), 127–142 (2016)
2. Kuang, S.-R., Chen, C.-Y., Liao, R.-Z.: Partitioning and pipelined scheduling of embedded system using integer linear programming. In: 11th International Conference on Parallel and Distributed Systems, pp. 37–41. IEEE Computer Society, Fukuoka (2005)
3. Jigang, W., Chang, B., Srikanthan, T.: A hybrid branch-and-bound strategy for hardware/software partitioning. In: 8th IEEE/ACIS International Conference on Computer and Information Science, pp. 641–644. IEEE, Shanghai (2009)
4. Lin, G.: An iterative greedy algorithm for hardware/software partitioning. In: 9th International Conference on Natural Computation, pp. 777–781. IEEE, Shenyang (2013)
5. Jemai, M., Dimassi, S., Ouni, B., et al.: A meta-heuristic based on tabu search for hardware/software partitioning. Turk. J. Electr. Eng. Comput. Sci. **25**(2), 901–912 (2017)
6. Tong, Q., Zou, X., Tong, H., et al.: Hardware/software partitioning in embedded system based on novel united evolutionary algorithm scheme. In: International Conference on Computer and Electrical Engineering, pp. 141–144. IEEE, Phuket (2008)
7. Zhang, T., Zhao, X., Yi-Ke, Y., et al.: Reserch on hardware/software partitioning method of improved shuffled frog leaping algorithm. J. Signal Process. **2015**(9), 1055–1061 (2015)
8. Dawei, W., Sikun, L., Yong, D.: Collaborative hardware/software partition of coarse-grained reconfigurable system using evolutionary ant colony optimization. In: Asia and South Pacific Design Automation Conference, pp. 679–684. IEEE, Seoul (2008)

9. Tong, Q., Zou, X., Zhang, Q., et al.: The hardware/software partitioning in embedded system by improved particle swarm optimization algorithm. In: 5th IEEE International Symposium on Embedded Computing, pp. 43–46. IEEE, Beijing (2008)

10. Luo, L., He, H., Dou, Q., et al.: Hardware/software partitioning for heterogeneous multicore SoC using genetic algorithm. In: 2nd International Conference on Intelligent System Design and Engineering Application, pp. 1267–1270. IEEE, Sanya (2012)

11. Zhang, T., Zhao, X., An, X., Quan, H., Lei, Z.: Using blind optimization algorithm for hardware/software partitioning. IEEE Access 5, 1353–1362 (2017)

12. Duan, Z., Zhang, Z.L., Hou, Y.T.: Fundamental trade-offs in aggregate packet scheduling. IEEE Trans. Parallel Distrib. Syst. 16(12), 1166–1177 (2005)

Interactive Multi-model Target Maneuver Tracking Method Based on the Adaptive Probability Correction

Jiadong Ren[1,2,3], Xiaotong Zhang[2,3(✉)], Jiandang Sun[2,3],
and Qingshuang Zeng[1]

[1] School of Astronautics, Harbin Institute of Technology, Harbin 150001, China
[2] Shanghai Institute of Spaceflight Control Technology,
Shanghai 201109, China
xjtu_llzxt@126.com
[3] Shanghai Key Laboratory of Space Intelligent Control Technology,
Shanghai 201109, China

Abstract. Non-cooperative target tracking is a key technology for complex space missions such as on-orbit service. To improve the tracking performance during the unknown maneuvering phase of the target, two methods including the IMM (interactive multi-model) algorithm based on extended CW equation and the variable IMM algorithm based on CW and extended CW equation are presented. The analysis and simulation results show that the higher the maneuvering index of the target is, the more obvious the advantages of the classical augmented IMM method are. However, the variable dimension IMM method has consistent performance for all the maneuver index interval of the target, and it is relatively suitable for engineering applications due to the lower complexity of algorithm.

Keywords: Augmentation · Relative navigation · Target maneuver
Interactive multi-model

1 Introduction

The geostationary orbit (GEO) satellite is widely used in the fields of meteorology, surveying and mapping. Under the influence of the gravitational perturbation of sun, moon and earth, the GEO satellite may drift in the direction of the longitude and latitude. A stationary orbit satellite needs to maneuver at regular intervals to maintain the position. The maneuver characteristics of the target will degenerate the performance of the traditional relative navigation method.

In the motion estimation of non-cooperative maneuvering target, it is difficult for any single model to achieve high accuracy estimation and rapid tracking in maneuvering process simultaneously due to the difference between maneuvering and non-maneuvering state. The single model navigation method often improves the maneuvering target tracking performance by adjusting filter parameters, detecting target maneuvering and designing adaptive filtering algorithm, as in literature [1–3]. In literature [8–11], a variety of adaptive filtering methods are designed by combining the

© Springer International Publishing AG, part of Springer Nature 2018
Y. Tan et al. (Eds.): ICSI 2018, LNCS 10942, pp. 235–245, 2018.
https://doi.org/10.1007/978-3-319-93818-9_22

interacting multiple model algorithm with a variety of filtering methods. But there are some problems such as limited navigation error and long delay.

In order to satisfy both the high accuracy filtering estimation in target non-maneuvering situation and the quick tracking requirement in target maneuvering situation, the relative navigation model based on two different bandwidth augmented CW equations is combined, and the model probability updating method is improved to achieve the complementarity of the advantages of these two models. Then considering the requirement of reducing the amount of computation in engineering application, the navigation method of variable dimension interacting multi-model method is designed, which has good comprehensive performance for relative navigation of maneuvering targets after adjustment.

2 Interactive Multi-model Design Based on Augmented CW Equation

2.1 Augmented CW Equation

According to the engineering practice, the acceleration can be modeled as a constant. The state variable is taken as $X = [\ x\ \ y\ \ z\ \ \dot{x}\ \ \dot{y}\ \ \dot{z}\ \ ax\ \ ay\ \ az\ ]^T$, and the state equation is as follows:

$$\dot{X}_1 = A_1 X_1 + B_1 w_1 \tag{1}$$

Where,

$$A_1 = \begin{bmatrix} & & 0_{3\times3} & I_{3\times3} & 0_{3\times3} & & \\ 0 & 0 & 0 & 0 & 0 & 2\omega & \\ 0 & -\omega^2 & 0 & 0 & 0 & 0 & I_{3\times3} \\ 0 & 0 & 3\omega^2 & -2\omega & 0 & 0 & \\ & & & 0_{3\times9} & & & \end{bmatrix}, B_1 = \begin{bmatrix} 0_{6\times3} \\ I_{3\times3} \end{bmatrix}, \quad w_1 \text{ represents}$$

the noise of the thrusts. Discretizes the Eq. 1, the following equation is obtained:

$$X_1(t_k) = \Phi_1(\delta_k) X_1(t_{k-1}) + G_1(\delta_k) w_1(t_{k-1}) \tag{2}$$

The observation equation is as follow, where ρ is the distance between two satellites, ψ and θ is the azimuth and the pitch angle measured by radar, $v(t)$ is measurement noise.

$$Z = \begin{bmatrix} \rho \\ \psi \\ \theta \end{bmatrix} = \begin{bmatrix} \sqrt{x^2 + y^2 + z^2} \\ \arctan\frac{y}{\sqrt{x^2+z^2}} \\ \arctan\frac{-z}{x} \end{bmatrix} + v(t) \tag{3}$$

The relative navigation method formed by the above state equation and observation equation is defined as augmented CW equation relative navigation method.

2.2   Multi-model Interaction Design

In order to satisfy the high accuracy of filtering estimation in target non-maneuvering situation and the fast tracking requirement in target maneuvering situation, an interactive multi-model method based on augmented CW equation is proposed. Only the variance matrix of the process noise is different between two models, $Q_k^1 = 0.01Q_k^2$.

The interactive multi-model algorithm mainly consists of four steps:

(1) Input interaction

$$\begin{cases} \widehat{X}_{k-1/k-1}^{0i} = \widehat{X}_{k-1/k-1}^{1}\mu_{k-1/k-1}^{1|i} + \widehat{X}_{k-1/k-1}^{2}\mu_{k-1/k-1}^{2|i} \\ P_{k-1/k-1}^{0i} = \mu_{k-1/k-1}^{1|i}\left(P_{k-1/k-1}^{1} + \alpha_1\alpha_1^T\right) + \mu_{k-1/k-1}^{2|i}\left(P_{k-1/k-1}^{2} + \alpha_2\alpha_2^T\right) \end{cases} \quad (4)$$

Where,

$$\alpha_j = \left[\widehat{X}_{k-1/k-1}^{j} - \widehat{X}_{k-1/k-1}^{0i}\right] \quad (5)$$

$$\mu_{k-1/k-1}^{j|i} = P\{\mu_{k-1}^{j}|\mu_k^i, Z^{k-1}\} = \frac{1}{c^i}\pi_{ji}\mu_{k-1}^{j} \quad (6)$$

$$c^i = \sum_{j=1}^{N}\pi_{ji}\mu_{k-1}^{j} \quad (7)$$

$$\pi_{ji} = \Pr\{M_j(k+1)|M_i(k+1)\} \quad (8)$$

Usually, $\pi = \begin{bmatrix} 0.9 & 0.1 \\ 0.1 & 0.9 \end{bmatrix}$.

(2) The extended Kalman filter of each model:

$$\begin{cases} X_{k/k-1}^{i} = \Phi_i\widehat{X}_{k-1/k-1}^{0i} \\ P_{k/k-1}^{i} = \Phi_i P_{k-1/k-1}^{0i}\Phi_i^T + Q_i \end{cases} \quad (9)$$

Where

$$K_k^i = P_{k/k-1}^{i}H^T(S_k^i)^{-1} \quad (10)$$

$$\widehat{X}_{k/k}^{i} = \widehat{X}_{k/k-1}^{i} + K_k^i v_k^i \quad (11)$$

$$P_{k/k}^{i} = \left(I - K^i H\right)P_{k/k-1}^{i} \quad (12)$$

$$v_k^i = Z_k - H^i\widehat{X}_{k/k-1}^{i} \quad (13)$$

$$S_k^i = H^i P_{k/k-1}^{i}\left(H^i\right)^T + R^i \quad (14)$$

(3) Model probability updating:

$$\mu_k^i = P\{m_k^i|Z^k\} = \frac{1}{c}\Lambda_k^i\sum_{j=1}^{N}\pi_{ji}\mu_{k-1}^j \tag{15}$$

$$c = P\{Z_k|Z^{k-1}\} = \sum_{j=1}^{N}\Lambda_k^i c^i \tag{16}$$

$$\Lambda_k^i = \frac{1}{(2\pi)^{m/2}\sqrt{|S_k^i|}}\exp\left\{-0.5\left(v_k^i\right)^T\left(S_k^i\right)^{-1}\left(v_k^i\right)\right\} \tag{17}$$

$\left|S_k^i\right|$ represents the norm of S_k^i, and m represents the dimension of the innovation.
(4) Output interaction:

$$\widehat{X}_{k/k} = \widehat{X}_{k/k-1}^1\mu_k^1 + \widehat{X}_{k/k-1}^2\mu_k^2 \tag{18}$$

$$P_{k/k-1} = \mu_k^i\left[P_{k/k}^i + \left[\widehat{X}_{k/k}^i - \widehat{X}_{k/k}\right]\left[\widehat{X}_{k/k}^i - \widehat{X}_{k/k}\right]^T\right] + \mu_k^i\left[P_{k/k}^i + \left[\widehat{X}_{k/k}^i - \widehat{X}_{k/k}\right]\left[\widehat{X}_{k/k}^i - \widehat{X}_{k/k}\right]^T\right] \tag{19}$$

3   The Improved Model Probability Updating Method

When the filtering process is in steady state, the values of the likelihood functions of the models are approximately equal:

$$\Lambda_k^1 \approx \Lambda_k^2 \approx \cdots \approx \Lambda_k^r \Rightarrow \mu_k^1 \approx \mu_k^2 \approx \cdots \approx \mu_k^r \approx \frac{1}{r} \tag{20}$$

This results the probability of each model is approximately equal, which can't achieve the complementary advantages among the multiple models. The acceleration estimation of model 2 is to be used as an intervening factor to update the model probability. In theory, the distribution of model 2 acceleration estimation error meets:

$$P\left(\begin{bmatrix}\hat{\ddot{x}}_k & \hat{\ddot{y}}_k & \hat{\ddot{z}}_k\end{bmatrix}\right) \sim N(\begin{bmatrix}\ddot{x}_k & \ddot{y}_k & \ddot{z}_k\end{bmatrix}, P\_a_k) \tag{21}$$

Where $P\_a_{k/k-1} = P_{k/k-1}^2(7:9;\ 7:9)$ represents the variance of the acceleration state in the state estimation variance matrix of model 2; $[\ddot{x}_k \quad \ddot{y}_k \quad \ddot{z}_k]$ represents the true state of the target maneuvering acceleration. The normalized likelihood function of acceleration based on zero mean expectation is conducted, which can be expressed as:

$$\Lambda\_a_k^2 = \exp\left\{-0.5(\begin{bmatrix}\hat{\ddot{x}}_k^2 & \hat{\ddot{y}}_k^2 & \hat{\ddot{z}}_k^2\end{bmatrix})^T(P\_a_k)^{-1}(\begin{bmatrix}\hat{\ddot{x}}_k^2 & \hat{\ddot{y}}_k^2 & \hat{\ddot{z}}_k^2\end{bmatrix})\right\} \tag{22}$$

The characteristics of $\Lambda\_a_k^2$ are as follows: (1) If the target is not maneuvering, it is consistent with the likelihood function of zero-mean white noise with an amplitude of about 1; (2) If the target is maneuvering, the value of $\Lambda\_a_k^2$ is small due to the non-zero expected value of acceleration estimation; (3) The value of $\Lambda\_a_k^2$ decays rapidly with the increase of the target maneuvering index.

The correction coefficient of model 1 is defined as $\kappa_k^1 = 1$, and the correction coefficient κ_k^2 of model 2 is shown below:

$$\kappa_k^2 = \gamma_3 \left(\gamma_2^{\gamma_1 \left(1 - \Lambda\_a_k^2 \right)} \right) \tag{23}$$

Where the value of $\gamma\,(\gamma > 1)$ is related with the parameter configuration (such as process noise β) of model 2. After setting, κ_k^2 meets:

$$\kappa_k^2 = \begin{cases} <0.1 & \left\| \begin{bmatrix} \ddot{x}_k & \ddot{y}_k & \ddot{z}_k \end{bmatrix} \right\| < \lambda_{min} \\ \approx 2 & \left\| \begin{bmatrix} \ddot{x}_k & \ddot{y}_k & \ddot{z}_k \end{bmatrix} \right\| \approx \lambda_{ave} \\ > 10 & \left\| \begin{bmatrix} \ddot{x}_k & \ddot{y}_k & \ddot{z}_k \end{bmatrix} \right\| > \lambda_{max} \end{cases} \tag{24}$$

Where λ is defined as the maneuver index, which is the satellite's maneuvering acceleration. According to the current configuration of high-orbit satellites, the maneuver index interval of the target is determined as shown in Table 1.

$$\lambda_i = \sigma_{wi} \quad i = x, y, z$$

Table 1. Index interval of target maneuvering

Sequence number	Maneuver index	Maneuver acceleration	Configuration
1	λ_{min}	0.00005 m/s^2	100 mN(thrust), 2000 kg (platform);
2	λ_{ave}	0.002 m/s^2	10 N(thrust), 5000 kg (platform);
3	λ_{max}	0.01 m/s^2	20 N(thrust), 2000 kg (platform);

Now, the model probability updating method can be expressed as:

$$\mu_k^i = P\{m_k^i | Z^k\} = \frac{1}{c} \kappa_k^i \Lambda_k^i \sum_{j=1}^{N} \pi_{ji} \mu_{k-1}^j \tag{25}$$

$$c = P\{Z_k | Z^{k-1}\} = \sum_{j=1}^{N} \Lambda_k^i c^i \tag{26}$$

$$\Lambda_k^i = \frac{1}{(2\pi)^{m/2}\sqrt{|S_k^i|}} \exp\left\{-0.5\left(v_k^i\right)^T \left(S_k^i\right)^{-1}\left(v_k^i\right)\right\}$$

(27)

After correction, when the target is not maneuvered, the probability of Model 2 is greatly reduced. When the target is maneuvering, the probability of Model 2 is greater than Model 1.

The above method is called the improved augmented CW equation interaction multi-model method.

4   Variable Dimension Interacting Multi-model Method

In engineering application, the augmented algorithm has a higher system dimension and a larger amount of computation. Therefore, the method of variable dimension integration is considered: Model 1 adopts classical relative navigation method (CW equation), it has better steady-state filtering performance. Model 2 adopts relative navigation design based on augmented CW equation.

Model 1: The state variable is $X = [x \ \ y \ \ z \ \ \dot{x} \ \ \dot{y} \ \ \dot{z}]$, the classical relative navigation system is based on CW equation.

Model 2: The state variable is $X = [x \ \ y \ \ z \ \ \dot{x} \ \ \dot{y} \ \ \dot{z} \ \ ax \ \ ay \ \ az]^T$, the relative navigation method of augmented CW equation in Sect. 1.1 is adopted.

In the current model configuration, model 1 is 6-dimensional and model 2 is 9-dimensional. The transformation matrix T_{69} is used to transform the dimension, so that the state models with different dimensions are combined and filtered by the interacting multi-model method. Since the estimated state of acceleration and the noise state are not included in the 6-dimensional state, Therefore, it isn't equivalent in the input interaction:

$$\begin{aligned}\widehat{X}_{k-1/k-1}^{02} &= \left[T_{69}\widehat{X}_{k-1/k-1}^1 \mu_{k-1/k-1}^{1|2} + \widehat{X}_{k-1/k-1}^2 \mu_{k-1/k-1}^{2|2}\right] \Rightarrow \widehat{X}_{k-1/k-1}^{02}(7:9) \\ &= \widehat{X}_{k-1/k-1}^2(7:9)\mu_{k-1/k-1}^{2|2}\end{aligned}$$

(28)

When the target is not maneuvering, the above equation still meets the expected unbiased tracking characteristic:

$$E\left(\widehat{X}_{k-1/k-1}^{02}(7:9)\right) = \mu_{k-1/k-1}^{2|2} E\left(\widehat{X}_{k-1/k-1}^2(7:9)\right) = E\left(X_{k-1/k-1}(7:9)\right) = 0 \quad (29)$$

However, in the case of target maneuvering tracking, the above equation does not hold due to the existence of the model probability $\mu_{k-1/k-1}^{2|2}$:

$$E\left(\widehat{X}_{k-1/k-1}^{02}(7:9)\right) = \mu_{k-1/k-1}^{2|2} E\left(\widehat{X}_{k-1/k-1}^2(7:9)\right) \neq E\left(X_{k-1/k-1}(7:9)\right) \quad (30)$$

In order to solve this problem, the following two requirements need to be met in the improved application of variable dimensional interaction: (1) The expectation of model 2 acceleration estimation is unbiased; (2) Modify the model interaction probability to satisfy $\mu^{2|2}_{k-1/k-1} \approx 1$ when the target is maneuvering;

A new interaction method is adopted to achieve variable dimensional multi-model interaction. This method adopted in this paper interacts with model 1 only in the input interaction stage. The interactive multi-model algorithm mainly includes four steps:

(1) Input interaction: input interactive states and variance of each model are:

$$
\begin{cases}
\widehat{X}^{0i}_{k-1/k-1} = T^i_{VD} \left[T_{69} \widehat{X}^1_{k-1/k-1} \mu^{1|i}_{k-1/k-1} + \widehat{X}^2_{k-1/k-1} \mu^{2|i}_{k-1/k-1} \right] \\
P^{0i}_{k-1/k-1} = T^i_{VD} \left[T_{69} \mu^{1|i}_{k-1/k-1} \left(P^1_{k-1/k-1} + \alpha_1 \alpha^T_1 \right) T^T_{69} + \mu^{2|i}_{k-1/k-1} \left(P^2_{k-1/k-1} + \alpha_2 \alpha^T_2 \right) \right] \left(T^i_{VD} \right)^T
\end{cases}
$$

$$(31)$$

Where α_j, $\mu^{j|i}_{k-1/k-1}$, π_{ji} are valued respectively by Eqs. 5, 6 and 7. $T_{69} = \begin{bmatrix} E_{6\times6} & 0_{6\times3} \end{bmatrix}^T$ is a dimensional transformation matrix; T^i_{VD} represents i-th model's Variant Dimension matrix $T^1_{VD} = T^T_{69}$, $T^2_{VD} = E_{9\times9}$.

(2) Extended Kalman filter for each model: steps are shown from Eqs. 9, 10, 11, 12, 13 and 14.

(3) Model probability updating: the same improvement method as augmented method is adopted, the correction coefficient of Model 1 is defined as $\kappa^1_k = 1$. Thus, the method of updating the model probability can be expressed as Eqs. 28, 29 and 30.

(4) Interactive output

$$
\widehat{X}_{k/k} = \widehat{X}^1_{k/k-1} \mu^1_k + T^T_{69} \widehat{X}^2_{k/k-1} \mu^2_k
\tag{32}
$$

$$
P_{k/k-1} = \mu^i_k \left[P^i_{k/k} + \left[\widehat{X}^i_{k/k} - \widehat{X}_{k/k} \right] \left[\widehat{X}^i_{k/k} - \widehat{X}_{k/k} \right]^T \right] + T^T_{69} \mu^i_k \left[P^i_{k/k} + \left[\widehat{X}^i_{k/k} - T_{69} \widehat{X}_{k/k} \right] \left[\widehat{X}^i_{k/k} - T_{69} \widehat{X}_{k/k} \right]^T \right] T_{69}
$$

$$(33)$$

The above method is called a Variable dimension interacting multi-model method, which is referred to as a variable dimensional IMM method for short.

5   Simulation Verification

The two satellites are in geostationary orbit. The initial conditions are as follows: 20 km apart, 2 km in relative motion plane, 1 km out-of-plane size, simulation time 6000 s; 0 s–4000 s, the target satellite is in free floating state, 4000 s–5000 s, the target satellite maneuvers continuously in the normal direction of the orbital plane (axis Y direction); 5000 s–6000 s, target maneuvering stops.

Radar measurement noise takes

$$E\left[V, V^T\right] = diag\left[(0.0005\rho)^2 m^2, (0.01/57.3)^2 rad^2, (0.01/57.3)^2 rad^2\right].$$

The relevant parameters of different methods are set as follows:
Classic augmented IMM model:

Model 1: $\beta = \frac{\sigma_w^2}{T^2/2}$; Model 2: $\beta = 100 \times \frac{\sigma_w^2}{T^2/2}$; $\sigma_w^2 = 10E - 7$.

The improved augmented IMM model: $\kappa_k^2 = 0.05\left(20^{5\left(1-\Lambda-a_k^2\right)}\right)$.

Variable Dimensional IMM Model: $\kappa_k^2 = 0.05\left(20^{5\left(1-\Lambda-a_k^2\right)}\right)$

In order to evaluate the adaptability of the algorithm, the minimum, average and maximum maneuver indexes are simulated with the same configuration parameters to analyze the synthesis performance of three kinds of algorithms. Comprehensive performance evaluation is divided into three stages with the same weighting factors.

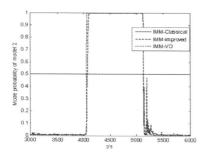
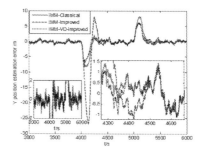

Fig. 1. Model interaction probability of each method (maximum maneuver index)

Fig. 2. Position estimation error of Y-axis of each method (maximum maneuver index)

Stage 1: 3000 s–4000 s, the stage after maneuver initiation;
Stage 2: 4000 s–5000 s, the stage during maneuver;
Stage 3: 5000 s–6000 s, the stage after maneuver termination;

Maximum maneuver index, maneuver acceleration 0.01 m/s^2, the simulation diagram as shown in Figs. 1 and 2; Average maneuver index, maneuver acceleration 0.002 m/s^2, the simulation diagram as shown in Figs. 3 and 4; Minimum maneuver index, maneuver acceleration 5E-5 m/s^2, the simulation diagram as shown in Figs. 5 and 6;

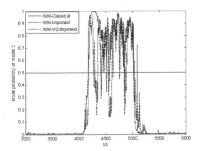

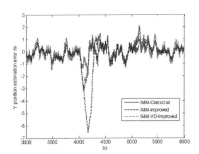

Fig. 3. Model interaction probability of each method (average maneuver index)

Fig. 4. Position estimation error of Y-axis of each method (average maneuver index)

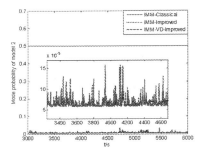

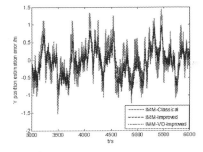

Fig. 5. Minimum maneuver index interaction probability of each method model

Fig. 6. Position estimation error of Y-axis of each method (minimum maneuver index)

Table 2. Relative position error comparison of three methods

Maneuver index	Relative position:m	Classical augmented IMM	Improved augmented IMM	Improved variable dimensional IMM
0.01 m/s^2	synthetical error(1σ)	2.1895	4.6766	1.7049
	steady state error(1σ)	0.4650	0.3394	0.3277
	tracking error(1σ)	2.5172	7.5530	2.0721
	recovery error(1σ)	2.3606	1.8081	1.7121
2E-3 m/s^2	synthetical error(1σ)	0.5739	1.3316	0.6423
	steady state error(1σ)	0.4927	0.3744	0.3636

(*continued*)

Table 2. (*continued*)

Maneuver index	Relative position:m	Classical augmented IMM	Improved augmented IMM	Improved variable dimensional IMM
5E-5 m/s²	tracking error(1σ)	0.6181	2.2005	0.9901
	recovery error(1σ)	0.6021	0.5760	0.3522
	synthetical error(1σ)	0.5039	0.3649	0.3840
	steady state error(1σ)	0.4927	0.3744	0.3636
	tracking error(1σ)	0.5332	0.3581	0.4201
	recovery error(1σ)	0.4839	0.3617	0.3652

The numerical performance statistics of each stage are shown in Table 2. Simulation results show that:

1. The classical augmented IMM method has good filtering and tracking performance under all conditions, and the transitional process time is about 200 s. The final output of the algorithm is actually the combination of equal weight of two models.
2. The improved augmented IMM method changes the coefficient of model interaction. The model interaction coefficients of the three stage models are 1, 0.5 and 1, respectively, and the performance of the algorithm is slightly better than that of the augmented IMM algorithm.
3. In general, the variable dimensional improved IMM method possesses the compromise performance of the above two methods. The proposed algorithm has better steady-state performance than the classical augmented IMM method and therefore has the best estimation accuracy because of the tracking process is superior to the improved IMM method.

6 Conclusions

Aiming at solving the existing dilemma that the high performance of the stable state and the fast tracking response of the unknown maneuvering phase cannot be satisfied at the same time, three IMM relative navigation methods based on augmented CW equation are proposed. The simulation and numerical analysis results show that these three methods all have the good comprehensive performance differing only with the index of the maneuvering. The higher the maneuvering index is, the more obvious the advantages of the classical augmented IMM method are compared with the augmented IMM method. The variable dimensional IMM method has the advantages of comprehensive performance, and it has consistent filtering estimation performance in different maneuver index interval. Meanwhile, the algorithm complexity is relatively low, thus it is suitable for engineering applications.

References

1. Liu, T., Xie, Y.: A relative navigation algorithm for a chaser tracking a non-cooperative maneuvering target in space, **31**(5), 1338–1344 (2010) (In Chinese). https://doi.org/10.3873/j.issn.1000-1328.2010.05.014
2. Qian, G.H., Li, Y., Luo, R.J.: One maneuvering frequency and the variance adaptive filtering algorithm for maneuvering target tracking. J. Radars **2**(6), 258–264 (2013). (In Chinese)
3. Jiyuan, L., Jun, Z., Yingying, L.: Applying auto-adaptation filter to tracking of maneuvering target in special relative navigation. J. Northwest. Polytech. Univ. **4**, 013 (2011). (In Chinese)
4. Kim, H.S., Park, J.G., Lee, D.: Adaptive fuzzy IMM algorithm for uncertain target tracking. Int. J. Control Autom. Syst. **7**(6), 1001–1008 (2009)
5. Liu, W., Li, Y., Wang, M.: An adaptive UPF algorithm for tracking maneuvering target in compound K noise environment. Acta Electronica Sinica **40**(6), 1240–1245 (2012). https://doi.org/10.3969/j.issn.0372-2112.2012.06.029. (in Chinese)
6. Naidu, V., Gopalaratnam, G., Shanthakumar, N.: Three Model IMM-EKF for Tracking Targets Executing Evasive Maneuvers. In: AIAA Aerospace Sciences Meeting & Exhibit (2007)
7. Yang, C., Blasch, E.: Characteristic errors of the IMM algorithm under three maneuver models for an accelerating target. In: International Conference on Information Fusion. IEEE, 2008
8. Jiangw, L.V.Z.J., Lan, Y.: IMM-CKF algorithm based on variable dimension interaction. Comput. Appl. Softw. **30**(5), 4–6 (2013)
9. Sun, Q., Kong, X., Lu, C., Deng, J.: Two new IMM algorithms for nonlinear maneuvering target tracking. Electron. Opt. Control **08**, 14–19+31 (2008). (in Chinese)
10. Xiong, K., Wci, C.: Spacecraft relative navigation based on multiple model adaptive estimator. J. Syst. Sci. Math. Sci. **34**(07), 828–837 (2014). (in Chinese)
11. Shaofeng, M., Xinxi, F., Yulei, L., Zhang, W., Xiaomei, Z.: A variable dimension adaptive IMM tracking algorithm. Electron. Opt. Control **22**(02), 36–40+45 (2015). (in Chinese)

Recommendation in Social Media

Investigating Deciding Factors of Product Recommendation in Social Media

Jou Yu Chen[1], Ping Yu Hsu[1], Ming Shien Cheng[2(✉)],
Hong Tsuen Lei[1], Shih Hsiang Huang[1], Yen-Huei Ko[1],
and Chen Wan Huang[1]

[1] Department of Business Administration, National Central University, No. 300,
Jhongda Road, Jhongli 32001, Taoyuan, Taiwan (R.O.C.)
984401019@cc.ncu.edu.tw
[2] Department of Industrial Engineering and Management, Ming Chi University
of Technology, No. 84, Gongzhuan Road, Taishan Disrict,
New Taipei City 24301, Taiwan (R.O.C.)
mscheng@mail.mcut.edu.tw

Abstract. With the growing popularity of social media, the number of people using social media to communicate and interact with others has increased steadily. As a result, social commerce has become a new phenomenon. In the past, most of the product recommendations in microblogging only dealt with personal preferences and interests, and ignored other possible factors such as Crowd Interest, Popularity of Products, Reputation of Creators, Types of Preference and Recent. Nowadays, these variables used by Facebook to recommend posts to their users. Therefore, this research adapted those five aspects and analyzed their effectiveness to recommend products on social media. This study used the Plurk API to develop and implement recommended robots that recommend products at specific times of the day so that they can get product information and meet recommended tasks in the social circle. The empirical results showed that the Interest, Popularity and Type have significant impacts on recommendation effectiveness.

Keywords: Social media · Recommendation · NewsFeed

1 Introduction

Microblogging user messages are relatively short compared to other social media platforms due to its text limit, thus failing to specifically described information in detail. However, due to the featured simpler message sending, users can have more interactions and discussions with friends on a micro blog that is more active than other social media sites. Messages sent through a micro blog can instantaneously reflect user's emotions, thoughts and opinions [2]. In other words, we can find out users' emotions or their degree of preference for a product through user message content. Additionally, with the rise of today's e-commerce websites and social media, product recommendations have also become important channels through which products sold. Meanwhile, e-commerce, besides blending into social media sites to interact with users,

© Springer International Publishing AG, part of Springer Nature 2018
Y. Tan et al. (Eds.): ICSI 2018, LNCS 10942, pp. 249–257, 2018.
https://doi.org/10.1007/978-3-319-93818-9_23

also recommends products to consumers through different ways of advertising, including sharing by celebrities or a recommendation algorithm, including resource semantics similarity, user preference, behavior and user relationship networks.

According to the previously mentioned background motivation, this study adopted the dynamic algorithm "News Feed" on social media site Facebook as a theoretical basis, which was modified to replace the five factors affecting the algorithms manifested in dynamic articles, namely: Interest, Post, Creator, Type, and Recent. With social media users' preference for creators (or individuals), Degree of Product Popularity, Creator Reputation, Product Category Preference, and Product Launch Time as factors for determining consumer preferences, the above factors are used to establish models and predict changes in product click rates.

This paper organized as follow: (1) Introduction: research background, motivation and purpose. (2) Related work: a review of recommendations through microblogs and dynamic algorithm applications on social media. (3) Research methodology: content of research process in this study. (4) Statistical analysis: description the experimental results and the discussion of the test results. (5) Conclusion and future research: contribution of the study, and possible future research direction discussed.

2   Related Work

2.1   Recommendations Through Microblogs

Many researchers today determine users' preferences and interests through messages published on micro blogs. For example, Banerjee et al. in 2009 [2] discovered users' preferences based on articles they recommended, and established a recommendation system to meet users' possible preferences. Bai in 2013 [1] set up a product recommendation system on Plurk and discovered that, compared to experts; a recommendation system or a popular product recommendation produce excellent personalized recommendation results. Among many social media platforms, micro blog Plurk selected as the product research platform in this study. Through articles published on Plurk, replies could instantaneously received. Moreover, article sequencing is done chronologically, which is more objective compared to Facebook that needs to compute the degree of intimacy between friends.

2.2   Dynamic Algorithm Applications on Social Media

In order for users to browse quickly through their friends' messages as well as important and useful posts, Facebook also uses an algorithm backstage for computing and analysis. Before 2014, EdgeRank, also known as Blade Ranking, was the algorithm used [5]. Similar to PageRank algorithm used by Google, both algorithms are used to determine the importance of a particular webpage. EdgeRank based on the computed product of affinity of each edge, weights, and time decay score. The higher the value, the more frequent the posts of friends with whom the user interacts with will appear. Kincaid in 2010 [4] pointed out that the original problem of EdgeRank was the appearing lies in the user who chats with close friends instead of interacting with them on the dynamic timeline. In addition, interactions between the user and the user's friends and webpage viewing are the keys leading to changes on Facebook, which subsequently lead to FB algorithm change. In order to meet users' preferences, the algorithm changed to News Feed algorithm. News Feed dynamic algorithm is the main algorithm used by Facebook to compute the dynamic timeline layout [6, 7]. In particular, News Feed consists of posts on the dynamic timeline. The equation below is as follows:

$$News\ Feed\ Visibility = I * P * C * T * R. \qquad (1)$$

Description of Variable Names

I (Interest) =   The user's interest in the content creation user
P (Post) =   The rate of others users' interaction with the post
C (Creator) =   The rate of other users' interaction with the content creation user's previous posts
T (Type) =   The category of posts of interest to the user (dynamics, images, links, etc.)
R (Recent) =   The recent of the post

News Feed visibility is the product of interest, post, creator, type, and recent. The higher the numerical value result, the more frequent the appearance of posts of the user's friends with whom the user interacts. The algorithm separately computes the user, friends, and public figures to derive at results that are more accurate. News Feed algorithm underwent restructuring in this study. With the algorithm for computing the importance of messages on popular social media platform Facebook as the cause, it inferred that the equation placed on other social media platforms. Such as Plurk, changing the equation into primary analysis suitable for carrying out product recommendations, and the degree of impact of the factors on products could determine by the click rate.

3   Research Methodology

This study uses the Plurk API to develop and implement recommended robots that recommend products at specific times of the day so that they can get product information and meet recommended tasks in the social circle. With the robot, in addition to obtaining the number of hits for the product by a plurker, it is also possible to communicate with a large number of instantaneous plurkers and understand which products are preferred.

This study carried out modification in reference to News Feed algorithm of Facebook. The product website page click rate *item (a,b)* of the recommended creator is the variable for observed product recommendation effectiveness. The higher the product recommendation click rate, the better the product recommendation effectiveness.

1. Interest (I): represents users' preference for the creator. The Eq. 2 is as follows:

$$I(a) = \sum_{v \in U} \frac{\left| \sum_{b \in B(a)} like\,(v, b) \right|}{B(a)}. \tag{2}$$

B(a): The all products of creator a; $like(v, b) = \begin{cases} 1 = v\ likes\ b \\ 0\quad 0/w \end{cases}$;

U: The all Plurkers; v: a Plurker; b: a book; a: a creator

2. Popularity (P): It represents the degree of popularity of a product recommended. This study measured popularity based on the search level on Google Trends. The Eq. 3 is as follows:

$$P^k(b) = \frac{\sum_{d \in M} g_b^k(d)}{|M|}. \tag{3}$$

M: The date set of data collection; $g_b^k(d)$: the query volume of product b based on product k in Google Trend; d: days; k: based book

3. Creator Reputation (C): It represents the number of creator searches that represents the product on Google Trends. The Eq. 4 is as follows:

$$C^u(a) = \frac{\sum_{d \in M} g_a^u(d)}{|M|}. \tag{4}$$

M: The date set of data collection; $g_a^u(d)$: the query volume of creator u based on creator u in Google Trend; d: days; u: a creator; a: based creator

4. Type (T): It calculates the degree of popularity of products in the same category. The Eq. 5 is as follows:

$$T(b) = \frac{\sum_{v \in U, e \in \Psi(b)} like(v, e)}{|\Psi(b)|}. \tag{5}$$

$\Psi(b)$: The same category books with b; $like(v, e) = \begin{cases} 1 = v\ likes\ e \\ 0\quad 0/w \end{cases}$; *U: all*

Plurkers

5. Recent (R): It represents the time between product launch and the time of survey. The Eq. 6 is as follows:

$$R(b) = \frac{\max_{n \in B} Pd(n) - Pd(b) + 1}{\max_{n \in B} Pd(n)}. \tag{6}$$

Pd(): The published month of book; B: all books;

Inference: *Item (a,b) should be positive correlation with I(a), $P^k(b)$, $C^u(a)$, T(b), R(b). b represents book; a represents creator; Item represent clicks.*

4   Data Collection and Statistical Analysis

4.1   Data Collection

On current social media, users have increasingly diversified, searching for sites according to their own browsing preferences. On www.books.com.tw, a variety of books and products are available, which meet consumers' need to pursue diversified products and categories. In particular, the books under the Chinese category available on the site can divided into 20 types: literary fiction, business finance, art design, humanities history, social science, natural science, psychological inspiration, health care, diet, lifestyle, tourism, religion, parenting, children's books/teenage literature, light novels, language learning, examination books, computer information, and professional/text books/government publications. In 2013, www.books.com.tw ranked one of Taiwan's top 100 websites for five consecutive years; in 2014, it received the Technological Innovation Business Award sponsored by the Institute for Information Industry; it also collaborated with 7-Eleven and President Transnet Corp. to enhance goods claim convenience and timeliness, making www.books.com.tw the number one choice for Taiwanese consumers to purchase books online.

Therefore, this study adopted the Chinese books of www.books.com.tw as recommended books. First, the monthly book sales starting December 2016 were tallied. From the 20 categories of books on the website, the top 10 more popular categories summarized, and books were randomly selected. The books selected were mainly the books by authors who published more than one book. In two months, 122 books selected.

In this study, the robot that setup book recommendations used as the account for sharing articles. The robot randomly embedded books into discussion strings that might be of interest to users or instantly recommended books on www.books.com.tw. When chatting with plurkers using the emotional thesaurus of Chuo Shu-Ling et al. [3]. The plurkers added by the robot used as targets for recommending books. At the beginning of the research, the recommended system had 1,270 friends and 326 followers. From 2017/1/1 to 2017/2/28 three to four articles were shared daily. The information posted in the articles included: book links recommended on www.books.com.tw, author names, book introduction, images, and prices. In addition, pluckers "like" count, forwards, replies, and click count were collected.

The user ID of those who replied "like" under the articles, the quantity of "likes", the quantity of forward, and the click count sent back to the report.

The operational variable defined as following:

1. Interest: This variable explains the degree of preference for the author targeting plurkers who clicked like between January and February 2016.
2. Popularity: This variable explains the degree of popularity for the books from January to February 2017. The names of the 122 books collected within two months placed on Google Trends (https://trends.google.com.tw/trends/) to carry out search. Since the searched values were relative values, a base point needed. Hence, from the 122 books, one base book selected. The base book selected was "The Courage to be Not Liked 2", and the time was set within the data range.

3. Creator: This variable explains the popularity of the author from January to February 2017. The 53 authors collected within two months placed on Google Trends (https://trends.google.com.tw/trends/) to carry out search. First, one among 53 authors chosen as the base author. In this study, Takashi Saito selected as the base author and compared with the other authors. The time was set within the range of data search.
4. Type: This variable is the degree of book category preference of users who clicked like in January and February 2017. There are 20 categories of Chinese books. The top ten categories among the monthly best-selling books in December 2016 chosen, including language learning, parenting, business finance, literary fiction, social sciences, travel, health care, religion, and children's books/teenage literature. The quantities of the 122 books different types of plurkers like tallied. Then, the computing done by way of averaging the total numbers of books in respective categories.
5. Recent: This variable measures the time of book publication. As Robert Brown mentioned, the time series situation shows stability or regularity. Therefore, the time series could reasonably and homeopathically delayed. In statistical principles, it also mentioned that financial forecast uses time as an added weight. Recent data has a major influence, and vice versa. The farther the variable setting time, the smaller the numerical value. Therefore, the farthest date of data publication was found and set as one, which incrementally increased every month. The closer the data to the recent times, the larger it is. After normalization, this variable could calculate.

4.2   Data Analysis Results

The five variables and number of clicks were substituted into the linear regression in statistical software SPSS for analysis. The results are as shown in Tables 1 and 2. The research results show that R square is 0.347, and the regression model explains 34.7% of variance. Among the 5 variables, three have reached significance, including: interest, popularity, and type. It is an indication that interest, popularity, and type have reached a significant correlation with the click rate. The three significant variables used to establish a regression model, which was used for predicting click rates. According to Table 2, we build a regression equation as following:

Table 1. Summary of regression model

R	R^2	Adjusted R	Estimated σ	F value	P value
0.589	0.347	0.319	1.9663	12.319	0.000

$$Item(a,b) = 5.586 * I(a) + 2.373\ P^k * (b) + 3.144 * T(b) - 1.537$$

In order to test whether or not the recommended product regression equation can predict rates, the 122 entries of book data from 2017/1/1 to 2017/2/28 were divided into: 70% training data and 30% verification data. The three significant variables analyzed in the above section used to establish a regression model and collect

Table 2. B Value and significant test

Model	Non-standardized coefficients		Standardized coefficients	T value	Significant
	B	Standardized ε	Beta		
Constant	−1.537	1.415		−1.086	
interest	5.586	0.893	0.482	6.256	0.000
popularity	2.373	0.913	0.199	2.598	0.011
creator	−0.537	1.074	−0.038	−0.500	0.618
type	3.144	1.480	0.165	2.125	0.036
recent	**0.802**	**0.936**	**0.066**	**0.857**	0.393

additional test data. The time was set as 017/4/15-2017/4/30. Two to three articles shared daily, and information pasted in the articles, including www.books.com.tw recommended book links, author names, book introductions, images, and prices. The number of plurkers that clicked like, forwarded, and replied examined the following day, and the click rates viewed to determine the book recommendation effectiveness. The test data selected from the 122 entries of book information in the training and test data, which shared again.

The error between the predicted click rate and the actual rate expressed by the equation below:

$$E^2 = \left(Y_o - Y_p\right)^2$$

E^2: The error of Click; Y_o: Actual Click; Y_p: Predicted Click
After running testing data, the result is showed as in Table 3.

Table 3. Average and standard deviation of clicks

	Recommend book	N	Average	σ
Original click Y_o	Training and verification data	122	3.754	2.382
	Testing data	36	4.778	1.437
Predicted click Y_p	Training and verification data	122	2.965	1.383
	Testing data	36	6.461	0.826
E^2	Training and verification data	122	4.338	10.346
	Testing data	36	4.502	5.038

According to the research results and from Table 4, Lavene test for equality of variances, it shows that the value did not reach significant differences. Thus, the "t" value of "equality of variances" should selected. "T" test result in Table 5 shows that "t" error value is similar without differences, which conforms to the regression prediction model. In view of this, the prediction model obtained with the regression model is stable.

Table 4. Lavene test for equality of variances

	F	Significant
E^2	0.505	0.478

Table 5. T test of predicted book click

		T	df	p	95% Confidence interval	
					Lower bound	Upper bound
E^2	Same variance	−0.092	156	0.927	−3.693	3.364

5   Conclusion and Future Research

The purpose of this study is to gain an insight into the many determining factors of microblogging (Plurk) product recommendations; and what factors can enhance the click rates of product recommendation articles. Currently, it has confirmed that recommended products on social media adopt "user preference" as the target. In this study, the other five factors adopted to determine product recommendations. The experimental results show that there are indeed three factors, namely, the user's preference for the author, the degree of book popularity, and the book type preference affects the user's link to articles, leading to higher click rates.

In the experiment with books as recommended products, it was found in this study that the quantity of book articles users click "like" and their preference for an author indeed affect click rates, which indirectly explain users' preferences affect click rates. Although in the study the author popularity does not significantly affect click rates, whether or not the users themselves like the author is still very important. "Book popularity affects click rates" also explains when books receive mass attention in the Internet world, users will click and view books because either they have heard of them before, or they do it out of curiosity. On www.books.com.tw, books divided into many types. Specific types of books such as literature novels or psychological inspiration preferred by the masses. For this reason, every time popular book types recommended, click rates increase as well. The regression model R^2 in this study reached 0.347, indicating good predictive results. Viewing the training and test data errors that show no significant differences, the regression model possesses certain stability.

Microblogging Plurk data adopted in this study to carry out reach. However, whether or not similar or differed results papered for Facebook, Google+, Weibo, Twitter, and other popular social media site platforms, it recommended that different platform use this method in the future in order to compare whether differed social media platforms resulted in differences. In this study, books used as experimental product recommendation products. However, different products also have varied impact factors, or factor significance may give rise to different results. For "degree of product popularity" and "creator reputation" product recommendation factors, Google Trends website used to calculate relative values, possibly leading to errors and different degrees of impacts in different time settings. It recommended that other computing methods used in the future.

References

1. Bai, S.-W.: Study of product recommendation on micro-blog considering time factor (2013)
2. Banerjee, N., Chakraborty, D., Dasgupta, K., Mittal, S., Joshi, A., Nagar, S., Madan, S.: User interests in social media sites: an exploration with micro-blogs. In: Proceedings of the 18th ACM Conference on Information and Knowledge Management, pp. 1823–1826. ACM, November 2009
3. Chiu, C.M., Hsu, M.H., Wang, E.T.: Understanding knowledge sharing in virtual communities: an integration of social capital and social cognitive theories. Decis. Support Syst. **42**(3), 1872–1888 (2006)
4. Kincaid, J.: EdgeRank: The secret sauce that makes Facebook's news feed tick. Techcrunch (2010)
5. http://www.inboundjournals.com/edgerank-is-dead-facebooks-news-feed-algorithm-factors/ EdgeRank into the past - to explore Facebook dynamic message algorithm
6. https://sproutsocial.com/insights/facebook-news-feed-algorithm-guide/ Edgerank: A Guide to the Facebook News Feed Algorithm
7. https://www.singlegrain.com/social-media-news/facebooks-news-feed-algorithm/ Facebook's News Feed

Using the Encoder Embedded Framework of Dimensionality Reduction Based on Multiple Drugs Properties for Drug Recommendation

Jun Ma, Ruisheng Zhang$^{(\boxtimes)}$, Rongjing Hu, and Yong Mu

School of Information Science and Engineering, Lanzhou University,
Lanzhou 730000, China
{junma, zhangrs, hurj}@lzu.edu.cn

Abstract. After obtaining a large amount of drug information, how to extract the most important features from various high-dimensional attribute datasets for drug recommendation has become an important task in the initial stage of drug repositioning. Dimensionality reduction is a necessary and important task for getting the best features in next step. In this paper, three important attribute data about the drugs (i.e., chemical structures, target proteins and side effects) are selected, and two deep frameworks named as F_1 and F_2 are used to accomplish the task of dimensionality reduction. The processed data are used for recommending new indications by collaborative filtering algorithm. In order to compare the results, two important values of Mean Absolute Error (MAE) and Coverage are selected to evaluate the performance of the two frameworks. Through the comparison with the results of Principal Components Analysis (PCA), it shows that the two deep frameworks proposed in this paper perform better than PCA and can be used for dimensionality reduction task in the future in drug repositioning.

Keywords: Machine learning · Autocoder · Encoder
Dimensionality reduction · PCA · Drug recommendation

1 Introduction

It is known that there are about 5000 human diseases but about 250 diseases have certain drugs that can be treated, because the development of safe and effective medicines is intricate, expensive and time consuming [1]. In general, a single new molecular entity costs more than \$2 billion and can take 14 years to develop [2] in drug discovery. Therefore, one alternative strategy is drug repositioning used in drug discovery, that is the therapeutic use of a drug or drug candidate for a disease other than that for which it was originally developed [3]. A successful example is Sildenafil was approved for erectile dysfunction and then later for pulmonary arterial hypertension [4].

For candidate drugs, their attribute information collected from various databases has high dimensionality. In general, the 2D structure of a compound come from DRAGON [5] is 726 dims and the 3D structure of a compound is 1000 dims. A binary ChemAxon [6] compounds descriptors is 2048 dims. How to reduce these high-dimensional data

© Springer International Publishing AG, part of Springer Nature 2018
Y. Tan et al. (Eds.): ICSI 2018, LNCS 10942, pp. 258–266, 2018.
https://doi.org/10.1007/978-3-319-93818-9_24

effectively and keep its important information is a very significant problem, because the results can improve the accuracy of drug repositioning.

2 Related Work

The dimensionality reduction from all drug properties information is the decisive step in the drug recommendation process [7–10]. Besides this key factor, Tan et al. [11] also mentioned that a reduction of the attribute space leads to a better understandable model and simplifies the usage of different visualization techniques. Dimensionality reduction is the transformation of high-dimensional data into a meaningful representation of reduced dimensionality. Maaten et al. [12] summarized a review and systematic comparison of these techniques. The most common techniques have Principal Components Analysis (PCA) [13, 14], Local Linear Embedding (LLE) [15], Autoencoder [16, 17] etc. PCA is a well-known data preprocessing method to capture linear dependencies among attributes of a data set. The central idea of PCA is to reduce the dimensionality of a data set consisting of a large number of interrelated variables, while retaining as much as possible of their variances [18]. PCA has found widespread application in molecular modeling and drug design, and it is common practice to visualize compound distributions using the first two or three principal components [19]. In the field of dimensionality reduction, there is a nonlinear technique which is the neural network (NN). Currently, the adapting advanced neural network frameworks for pharmaceutical research is borrowed from the field of deep learning [20]. Zhang et al. [21] used Restricted Boltzmann Machine to realize the dimensionality reduction task.

3 Material and Methods

3.1 Datasets

In this paper, four datasets are come from the paper [22]. In [22], the chemical structure information of drugs is from PubChem [23], which includes 122,022 associations between 1007 drugs and 881 PubChem chemical substructures. The protein data is from DrugBank [24], which includes 3152 associations between 1007 drugs and 775 target proteins. The data of drugs and side effects is come from SIDER [25], which includes 61,102 associations between 888 drugs and 1385 side-effect terms. The data of drugs and diseases is from National Drug File [26], which includes 3250 treatment relationships between 799 drugs and 719 diseases. In this paper, all same drugs in the four datasets will be selected out. There are 536 same drugs in the four datasets. D_c denotes the dataset of the drugs' chemical substructures, D_p denotes the dataset of the drugs' proteins, D_s denotes the dataset of the drugs' side effects, D_d denotes the dataset of drugs and diseases. In the fourth dataset, there are 593 drugs and 719 diseases, if one drug could be treated one disease, the score is 1 otherwise the score is 0. D_d is the rating matrix used in this paper.

3.2   The Proposed Method

In this paper, two frameworks are proposed for multi-properties of drugs datasets. The two frameworks are named as F_1 and F_2. D_{En1}, D_{En2} denote two different results after reducing dimensionality by two frameworks F_1 and F_2. In Fig. 1, it shows the structures of the two frameworks. The two frameworks are composed by the Encoder unit (Fig. 1). In the two frameworks, the Encoder of AE is used as the unit embedding the models.

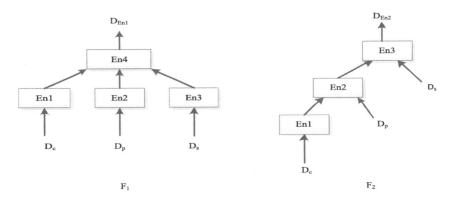

Fig. 1. Two different frameworks, F_1 and F_2. (In F_1, it has two layers and there are four different Encoders. In F_2, it has three layers and there are three different Encoders.)

In this paper the part of an Autoencoder model, Encoder model, is exploited for reducing the dimensionality of the multiple drugs properties information. The Encoder of an Autoencoder model is selected as a unit to build the reducing dimensionality frameworks. The basic Autoencoder model is a neural network that is trained to attempt to copy its input to its output. In general, an Autoencoder model is composed by an Encoder and a Decoder. G. E. Hinton and R. R. Salakhutdinov used deep Autoencoder networks to learn low-dimensional codes that work much better than PCA as a tool to reduce the dimensionality of data.

The Autoencoder model is full connections between each layer, and there is no connection in each layer. The basic model is three layers, the layer L_1 is the input layer, the layer L_2 is the hidden layer and the layer L_3 is the output layer. The Encoder section is composed of the layer L_1 and the layer L_2, the decoder section is composed of the layer L_2 and the layer L_3. Actually, according different datasets and tasks, the layer L_2 could be increased. The parameters of this model are optimized by the average reconstruction error, when the average reconstruction error is minimized, the parameters of the model are best. In this paper, the squared error is used as loss function, as follows formula (1).

$$L(x, z) = ||x - z||^2 \tag{1}$$

The general training procedure is that the first layer L_2 is trained as the encoders to minimize the reconstruction error of the input data L_1, the hidden units' outputs in L_2 are used as input for another layer L_3. The Encoder units that make up frameworks F_1 and F_2 are come from a three layers Autoencoder. The three layers Autoencoder model is used to train all parameters in each dataset for getting the optimal value of weights. After finishing the training task, the Encoder model is used to build our deep frameworks.

In F_1 framework, the formula (2) describes the process of dimensionality reduction.

$$D_{En1} = En4\big(W_4\big(En1(W_1D_c) + En2\big(W_2D_p\big) + En3(W_3D_s)\big)\big) \tag{2}$$

where $En1$, $En2$ and $En3$ are lied in the first layer, W_1, W_2 and W_3 are different weights and come from different Autoencoders. We train each Autoencoder for each dataset to get the weights, and these weights are used in the first layer. In the second layer we use the output of the first layer as the input, finally the result is obtained by $En4$.

First for each dataset the Autoencoder is used to get the weight W_i, then the Encoder using W_i becomes a unit in the framework in each layer, at last the output of the frameworks are the reducing dimensionality result of three drugs' properties information. In the Fig. 1, the first framework has two layers, four different Encoders are used in it, the three datasets D_c, D_p, D_s are reduced to 20 dimensions by three different Encoders in the first layer, the three results is combined as new input of the second layer, the output of the second layer is final result of the first model. D_{En1} denotes the final result.

In the Fig. 1, the second framework has three layers, while three different Encoders are used in it. In the second framework, the drugs' properties dataset is incorporated layer by layer. In the first layer, D_c is the original dataset. In the second layer, the two parts merge into the input, one part is the output of the first layer, the other is D_p. The second layer's output and D_s are merged into the input of the third layer. After the third layer, the final output D_{En2} is the result of reducing dimensionality. The Formula (3) describes the process.

$$D_{En2} = En3'(W_3'\big(En2'\big(W_2'\big(En1'\big(W_1'D_c\big) + D_p\big)\big) + D_s\big)) \tag{3}$$

where $En1'$, $En2'$ and $En3'$ are lied in different layers, W_1', W_2' and W_3' are different weights. The first Autoencoder is trained to get W_1', the result of $En1'$ ($W_1'D_c$) and D_p are the input of the second layer. The same operation is in the third layer. D_{En2} is the output of the second framework.

In next step, D_{En1} and D_{En2} are used to compute the similarity of drugs, respectively. Based on the two different similarities, the collaborative filtering algorithm is applied to realize drug recommendation and compare the values of MAE and Coverage. The collaborative filtering algorithm is in the Formula (4).

In drug discovery, PCA is one of the most common dimensionality reduction algorithms. In this paper, PCA is used as baseline algorithm to process all datasets. Through repeated testing, when all datasets are reduced to 20 dimensions, the recommended effect is most accurate. Therefore, when the two frameworks are applied to reduce datasets dimension, the dimensionality is set to 20. The detail of the workflow is shown in Fig. 1. From the Fig. 1, it describes the whole calculation process.

In order to evaluate the performance of reducing dimensionality, the collaborative filtering technique to recommend the indications for each drug is used in the workflow. In the workflow, d_i denotes a drug. For a drug d_i, the formula (4) is used to compute the recommendation result (Fig. 2).

$$R_i = \frac{\sum_{j=1}^{k} sim_j \times score_{disease}}{\sum_{j=1}^{k} sim_j} \tag{4}$$

where sim_i is Person similarity of d_i, k is the number of all drugs in D_d, $score_{disease}$ is 0 or 1 which come from the rating matrix D_d. R_i is the recommendation result of d_i.

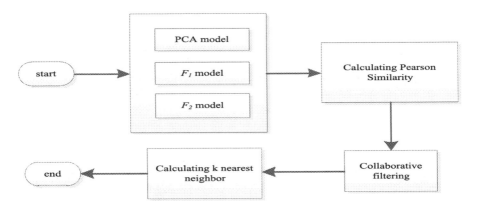

Fig. 2. The workflow for comparing the results of three dimensionality reduction models

4   Results and Analysis

There are two indicators to evaluate the two frameworks results, one is Mean Absolute Error (MAE), and the other is Coverage. Assumed that d_i has the recommended values for the n diseases, the set of the recommended values of d_i is denoted as $p = \{p_1, p_2, ..., p_n\}$, the set of the true values of d_i and the n diseases is denoted as $r = \{r_1, r_2, ... r_n\}$, s represents the number of recommended values in p. The two computational formulas are shown in the formula (5) and (6). In general, if the smaller MAE value, the better recommendation quality is. The larger the value of the Coverage, the better the method is.

$$MAE = \frac{\sum_{i=1}^{n} |p_i - r_i|}{n} \tag{5}$$

$$Coverage = \frac{s}{n} \tag{6}$$

In Fig. 3, the X-axis is k-near values which denote k nearest neighbors in the recommended results. When k is 10, it represents 10 drugs that are similar in chemical structure, target protein, and side effects with the drugs in the test set. The Y-axis is MAE values. From the Fig. 3, we can conclude that in the recommendation results, the values of MAE and Coverage of F_1_framework and F_2_framework have better performance than PCA. In Fig. 3(a), when the k value changes from 10 to 100, the performance of the F_1_framework and F_2_framework curves is always better than PCA curve in the three curves. When the k value is between 30 and 70, the PCA curve has the worst performance. When k is 70, the MAE of PCA is close to 0.15 which is the most value in the three curves. After that, the MAE value descends with the increased k value. In the three curves the performance of F_1_framework has some fluctuations, from the beginning the MAE ascends. When the k value is between 40 and 70, the MEA is close to the PCA curve, when the k value is greater than 70, the MAE value descends. The F_2_framework curve has best performance in the three curves, with the increase of the k value the MEA is always the smallest. In the three curves, when k is 20, the values of three curves are the minimum in the interval and there are 0.0488, 0.0327 and 0.0298 respectively. From the Fig. 3(b), F_2_framework has the best performance in the three

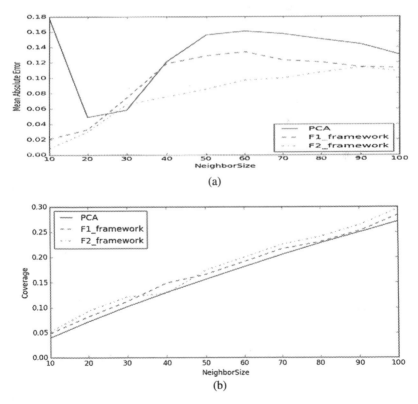

Fig. 3. The MAE values and Coverage values based on the two deep frameworks and PCA. (a) shows the MAE values of the three recommendation results. (b) shows the Coverage values of the three recommendation results

curves. Therefore, in the two frameworks, the result of $F_2\_framework$ is better than $F_1\_framework$. It demonstrates that in the learning process the method of inputting drugs' properties layer by layer can learn more latent information.

There are several hyper parameters must be adjusted in Autoencoder model, the range of hyper parameters by performing a grid search on the framework is investigated, and the stochastic gradient descent algorithm for training the frameworks is used. In the experiments, learning rate is 0.005, maximum number of epochs is 10000 and L2reg is 0.0001. In the whole calculation process, 10-fold cross validation method is used to test the models.

In order to verify the validity of our frameworks, the top 20 drugs for each disease are recommended. In the Table 1, 10 records are selected from the result of the top 20.

In Table 1, we search in DrugBank.com to find each drug's description, categories, indication or related articles. In the paper [27], it introduces *abacavir* can be used for the treatment of HIV-1 infection. In DrugBank.com the description of *propranolol* is that a widely used non-cardio selective beta-adrenergic antagonist. *Propranolol* is used in the treatment or prevention of many disorders and one of its categories is Cardio-vascular System. In the paper [28], it investigates the curative effect of *Cefoperazone-sulbactam* of different doses in the treatment of simple gonorrhea. In DrugBank.com the description of *sotalol* is that an adrenergic beta-antagonist that is used in the treatment of life-threatening arrhythmias and the categories are Cardiovascular Agents and Cardiovascular System. In the DrugBank.com, the description of *trifluoperazine* is that it is used as an antipsychotic and an antiemetic, the indication of *aztreonam* is that for the treatment of the following infections caused by susceptible gram-negative microorganisms: urinary tract infections, lower respiratory tract infections, septicemia, skin and skin-structure infections, intra-abdominal infections, and gynecologic infections. For the recommended results, the frameworks proposed in this paper will help drug researchers narrow the scope to some disease and the process is likely to further accelerate the speed of development of drugs for new indications.

Table 1. Some recommended drugs and scores in the result

Disease	Drug	Score
AIDS-related opportunistic infections	abacavir	0.0167
Atrial fibrillation	propranolol	0.0274
Gonorrhea	cefoperazone	0.0398
Heart failure	sotalol	0.0839
Nausea	trifluoperazine	0.0188
Pneumonia, Bacterial	aztreonam	0.0445

5 Conclusion

In this paper, we exploit two the Encoder embedded frameworks to realize the reduction dimensionality of multiple drug's properties data, then we use a collaborative filtering algorithm to recommend drugs for each disease, at last the results are compared with PCA. From the result of the experiment the two frameworks have good performance. According the recommendation result, several recommended drugs have been proved in the DrugBank.com. Therefore, the Encoder embedded frameworks are efficient way to characterize features of high dimensional multiple drugs data and could be fitted for the reducing dimension of multiple drugs' properties in drug reposition.

In the future, based on the second framework, there are two aspects of the work to be done. One is that we will combine diseases' characteristics in the framework to predict drugs for specific diseases. The other is that we will try to integrate other deep learning algorithms into our deep framework to resolve the problems in drug repositioning.

Acknowledgments. This work was supported by the Fundamental Research Funds for the Central Universities (No. lzujbky-2017-195).

References

1. Paul, S.M., Lewis-Hall, F.: Drugs in search of diseases. Sci. Transl. Med. **5**(186), 228–235 (2013)
2. Paul, S.M., Mytelka, D.S., Dunwiddie, C.T., Persinger, C.C., Munos, B.H., Lindborg, S.R., Schacht, A.L.: How to improve R&D productivity: the pharmaceutical industry's grand challenge. Dressnature Rev. Drug Discov. **9**(3), 203–214 (2010)
3. Ashburn, T.T., Thor, K.B.: Drug repositioning.: identifying and developing new uses for existing drugs. Nat. Rev. Drug Discov. **3**(8), 673–683 (2004)
4. Ghofrani, H.A., Osterloh, I.H., Grimminger, F.: Sildenafil: from angina to erectile dysfunction to pulmonary hypertension and beyond. Nat. Rev. Drug Discov. **5**(8), 689–702 (2006)
5. Dragon. http://www.talete.mi.it
6. ChemAXon. https://chemaxon.com/
7. Janecek, A., Gansterer, W.N., Demel, M., Ecker, G.: On the relationship between feature selection and classification accuracy. J. Mach. Learn. Res. **4**, 90–105 (2008)
8. Schneider, G., So, S.S.: Adaptive Systems in Drug Design. Landes Bioscience, Austin (2002)
9. Reutlinger, M., Schneider, G.: Nonlinear dimensionality reduction and mapping of compound libraries for drug discovery. J. Mol. Graph. Model. **34**(2), 108 (2012)
10. Hinton, G.: Where do features come from? Cogn. Sci. **38**(6), 1078 (2014)
11. Tan, P.N., Steinbach, M., Kumar, V.: Introduction to Data Mining, 1st edn., vol. 18(4), pp. 86–103 (2005)
12. Maaten, L.J.P.V., Postma, E.O., Herik, H.J.V.D.: Dimensionality reduction: a comparative review. J. Mach. Learn. Res. **10**(1), 1–22 (2007)
13. Karl Pearson, F.R.S.: LIII. On lines and planes of closest fit to systems of points in space. Philos. Mag. **2**(11), 559–572 (1957)
14. Hotelling, H.: Analysis of a complex of statistical variables into principal components. Br. J. Educ. Psychol. **24**(6), 417–520 (1932)
15. Roweis, S.T., Saul, L.K.: Nonlinear dimensionality reduction by locally linear embedding. Science **290**(5500), 2323–2326 (2000)
16. Demers, D., Cottrell, G.W.: Non-linear dimensionality reduction. In: Advances in Neural Information Processing Systems, pp. 580–587 (1992)

17. Hinton, G.E., Salakhutdinov, R.R.: Reducing the dimensionality of data with neural networks. Science **313**(5786), 504–507 (2006)
18. Jolliffe, I.T.: Principal Component Analysis. Springer (2005)
19. Linusson, A., Elofsson, M., Andersson, I.E., Dahlgren, M.K.: Statistical molecular design of balanced compound libraries for QSAR modeling. Curr. Med. Chem. **17**(19), 2001–2016 (2010)
20. Bengio, Y.: Learning deep architectures for AI. Found. Trends® Mach. Learn. **2**(1), 1–127 (2009)
21. Zhang, R., Li, J., Lu, J., Hu, R., Yuan, Y., Zhao, Z.: Using deep learning for compound selectivity prediction. Curr. Comput. Aid. Drug. **12**, 1 (2016)
22. Wang, F., et al.: Exploring the associations between drug side-effects and therapeutic indications. J. Biomed. Inform. **51**, 1568–1577 (2014)
23. Wang, Y., Xiao, J., Suzek, T.O., Zhang, J., Wang, J., Bryant, S.H.: PubChem: a public information system for analyzing bioactivities of small molecules. Nucleic Acids Res. **37**, W623–W633 (2009)
24. Wishart, D.S., Knox, C., Guo, A.C., Cheng, D., Shrivastava, S., Tzur, D., Gautam, B., Hassanali, M.: DrugBank: a knowledgebase for drugs, drug actions and drug targets. Nucleic Acids Res. **36**, D901–D906 (2008)
25. Kuhn, M., Campillos, M., Letunic, I., Jensen, L.J., Bork, P.: A side effect resource to capture phenotypic effects of drugs. Mol. Syst. Biol. **6**(343), 2016 (2010)
26. Comparative Toxicogenomics Database. http://ctdbase.org/
27. Gandhi, M., Gandhi, R.T.: Single-pill regimens for HIV-1 infection. N. Engl. J. Med. **371**(19), 1845–1846 (2014)
28. Yang, J.: Clinical efficacy of cefoperazone sulbactam combined with uncomplicated gonorrhea in the treatment of uncomplicated gonorrhea. J. Math. Med. **29**(8), 1220–02 (2016)

A Personalized Friend Recommendation Method Combining Network Structure Features and Interaction Information

Chen Yang, Tingting Liu[✉], Lei Liu, Xiaohong Chen[✉], and Zhiyong Hao

College of Management, Shenzhen University, Shenzhen, China
liutingting2017@email.szu.edu.cn,
lrene.hong@foxmail.com

Abstract. With the popularity of social network platforms in the crowd, more and more platforms begin to develop friend recommendation services to fit the users' demands. Current research on friend recommendation strategies are mainly based on the nodes structural characteristics and path information of the friendship network. The recommendation strategies that consider node information are more efficient for large-scale networks, such as the Adamic-Adar Index. However, it solely utilizes the degree information of common neighbors and ignores the structural characteristics of the target nodes themselves. In this paper we attempted to improve the friend recommendation performance by incorporating the structural characteristics of the target nodes and the interactions between these nodes into the Adamic-Adar Index. In order to verify the effectiveness of our proposed algorithms, we conducted several groups of comparative experiments. The experimental results show that our proposed algorithm can effectively improve the recommendation performance comparing with the benchmark.

Keywords: Social network structure · Friend recommendation service
Link prediction · Adamic-Adar Index

1 Introduction

According to the surveys investigated by the organizations "Hootsuite" and "We Are Social", in 2017, the total scale of the social network in the world is about 3.028 billion while the population of the whole world is only 7.5 billion. People use SNS (Social Network Service) not only to reach out to friends they made before, but also to develop new social network relationships by making new friends [1].

However, because of the large scale of the social network and the overload information, it's hard for users to make new friends they want. Therefore, all the platforms are dedicated to designing friend recommendation strategies. But the most important and hardest is whether the strategies can recommend accurate friends.

Social recommendation is the most commonly used recommendation method and it mainly contains two kinds of algorithms. One of them is based on the social network nearest neighbor model. Take Jaccard's coefficient [2] as an example. This algorithm

© Springer International Publishing AG, part of Springer Nature 2018
Y. Tan et al. (Eds.): ICSI 2018, LNCS 10942, pp. 267–274, 2018.
https://doi.org/10.1007/978-3-319-93818-9_25

tries to recommend friends to friends since the more common friends two users have, the more likely they are to become friends. The other one is based on the graph model. For example, D. Liben-Nowell et al. proved that the more friends the common friends have, the less chance his or her friends to be friends [3]. Moreover, Armentano et al. [4] proposed an algorithm based on network topology structure and the algorithm uses network topology for different factors to find a good source of information.

The recommendation algorithms based on social network are simple and easy to operate. But in fact, they cannot always reflect users' friend relationships correctly in most cases, and the algorithms are too simple to ignore important information. From the real life we know that the importance of the users' each friend is different and some users may have quite a lot of friends who are made with the needs of specific occasions. When the specific occasions displace, the relationships are over (but they still maintain relationships on networks). It is easy to find that the relationships in specific situations like those are not strong. With that point, some scholars found that the records near the target users are more beneficial than other interactive records and the addition of the interactive information makes the algorithms perform better than those based only neighborhood [5].

The points above indicate that social networks are not always static but are constantly updated and self-developed. Therefore, all the interactions among users on social networks like sending messages can represent the intensity of relationships. In a word, the more frequent the interactions are, the stronger the relationships are [6].

We find that the number of users' friends will have positive impacts on users' loyalty and dependence, and the loyalty as well as the dependence affect users' trust toward the platforms directly [7]. Moreover, according to the Matthew effect, users with more friends may make more new friends in future [8]. Therefore, in this paper, we propose new kind of algorithms considering interaction and the willingness to make new friends.

This paper is organized as follow: In Sect. 2, we give a brief description of the link prediction and friend recommendation. In Sect. 3, we introduce the Adamic-Adar Index and propose our algorithms. Finally, we show the results of the experiments in Sect. 4 and make a conclusion in Sect. 5.

2   Related Work

Online recommendation is a system which can evaluate and recommend new "resources" to users automatically [9]. In 2003, Amazon proposed collaborative filtering (CF) algorithm which is the most widely used recommendation algorithm at present. This kind of algorithm can be divided into two types: collaborative filtering based on model [10] and collaborative filtering based on memory [11]. In addition, common recommendation algorithms include content-based recommendation algorithm (CB) [12] and hybrid recommendation strategy.

Similarity can be used to measure the relationships among nodes such as demographic similarity in demographic recommendation and content similarity in CB algorithm. This kind of recommendation belongs to the link prediction and is the simplest one of them [14]. In fact, link prediction recommendation mainly includes machine learning, probability model and social network structure. Among them, machine learning and probability model apply a large number of nodes' external attributes. However, it is hard for systems to get the information, so the link prediction recommendation which only based on the social network structure is becoming more and more popular and gets more and more concerns from scholars.

The improved algorithms proposed in this paper are based on the topology graphs of the network structure. Each user is a node in the graphs and the two-way connections between two nodes represent their friend relationships. According to the existing connections we calculated the similarities and the possibility of connecting among users who are not connected. It is generally believed that users with high similarities are more likely to be a pair of new friends and can definitely be recommended to each other [15]. Literature [6] proposed a definition method based on network topology graph and they compared the results of different prediction methods in large-scale scientists' network experiments. It was found that the Adamic-Adar Index performed best on the basis of the number of common neighbors [16]. In the view of the sparsity and hugeness, paper [17] proposed an algorithm based on local random walking which has higher accuracy and lower complexity. All above are friend recommendation algorithms based on network structure. This type of algorithms can be divided into two categories: global indices and local indices. Algorithms used global indices such as Katz Index, Leicht-Holme-Newman Index and Matrix Forest Index generally need to consider global network topology graphs [18]. This kind of algorithms can obtain a higher degree of recommendation accuracy but the overall calculation is more complex and expensive. Opposite to that are algorithms used local indices such as the Jaccard's coefficient. At the expense of some accuracy, we can get faster calculation speed.

Similarity-based approaches pay attention to the existing social network. Scholars usually consider the users' behaviors as well as internal regularities. In contrast, if we consider the similarities among nodes based on the structure of social networks, the scope of application will be actually larger. Sometimes, the users we recommended are the users who have been familiar by the target users before, though they are not friends now. This is a great advantage of the algorithms.

However, most of the previous recommendation algorithms based on social network structure consider the importance of the users to be the same, and neglect users' personalized characteristics such as the attitude and willingness to make new friends. Social networks can help users develop and maintain interpersonal relationships (Erving Goffman, 2008), so as to meet the need of the sense of belonging which is a main psychological need of users [19]. Related research showed that all people can get gratification from social networks [18]. Literature [7] found that the number of online friends have significant positive effects on the use of social networks. In other words, the number of online friends can reflect the users' willingness to use social networks. Those with fewer friends are more likely to drop out of the platforms, because it is easy for them to interact with their friends on other platforms [8]. In addition, the stronger the relationships among nodes in the network structure are, the more likely it is to maintain high network loyalty toward the network structure. On the contrary, those with fewer friends may tent to quit the network structure [8]. It's not hard to associate that if the users learn about their importance for the platforms, or they feel that they are in the core of their relationship networks, they may gain the sense of responsibility for other nodes on the platforms. The sense of responsibility makes them dependent heavily on the platforms and keep the activity. Realizing those, users will be more willing to expand the peripheral nodes. All of above highlight two points: (1) the higher the users' loyalty and dependence toward the platforms, the higher the trust of the new friends recommended by the platforms; (2) the higher the trust of the new friends, the more likely the new friends to be accepted.

The views in the last paragraph and the Matthew effect lead to the instability of the algorithms on users' differences. Under the background of such problems, this paper proposes new social network structure optimization algorithms which enhance the wide applicability of local indices methods based on similarity.

3   The Proposed Approaches

In all the equations: $\Gamma(x)$ are the neighbors of nodes x and y. z is a common neighbor of the nodes x and y. Mes(xz) represents the account of the messages x send to z.

A. *Adamic-Adar Index (AA for short)*

Adamic-Adar Index is an algorithm to develop link prediction with the measure of "proximity" among different network nodes [3]. The main idea of it is the greater the number of friends is, the lower the importance of each friend is. The formula of Adamic-Adar Index is as follows:

$$\text{AdamicAdar\_Index}_{(xy)} = \sum_{z \in \Gamma(x) \cap \Gamma(y)} \frac{1}{log|\Gamma(z)|} \tag{1}$$

B. *AA Considering the Number of Users' Friends*

Besides the point that mentioned before, users with so many friends may have greater willingness to make new friends than those with a few friends. That is to say, the possibility between two unconnected nodes maybe is positively related to their willingness to make new friends, and we can quantify the willingness with the number of their friends. We try to conclude an index and its formula is as follow:

$$\text{WIL\_AA}_{(xy)} = \sum_{z \in \Gamma(x) \cap \Gamma(y)} \frac{log|\Gamma(x)| * log|\Gamma(y)|}{log|\Gamma(z)|} \tag{2}$$

C. *AA Considering Interaction Frequency*

The literature [9] has shown that taking into account the interaction information between two nodes is more effective than simply considering the nearest neighbors' recommendation model. However, the paper had not found a suitable index to calculate the similarity between two unconnected nodes. This paper attempts to propose the following index:

$$MES\_AA_{(xy)} = \sum\nolimits_{z\in\Gamma(x)\cap\Gamma(y)} \frac{Mes_{xz} + Mes_{yz}}{log|\Gamma(z)|} \tag{3}$$

D. *AA Considering Interaction Frequency and the Number of Users' Friends*

Based on the Adamic-Adar Index, we consider not only the willingness of users to make new friends but also the importance of common friends. So, we try to improve the Adamic-Adar index and conclude the new formula as follow:

$$MES\_WIL\_AA_{(xy)} = \sum\nolimits_{z\in\Gamma(x)\cap\Gamma(y)} \frac{log|\Gamma(x)| * (Mes_{xz} + Mes_{yz}) * log|(\Gamma(y)|}{log|\Gamma(z)|} \tag{4}$$

4 Experiment Results

The friend network data used in the experiments are collected by a large social network platform in Shenzhen. There are two experiments. The first one is to test our assumption that whether it will be more effective if an index considers the users' willingness to make new friends. The other one is similar to the first one, but the methods we cut the data set are different.

Before proceeding with the first experiment, we randomly divided the dataset into the test set and training set at a 4:1 ratio. We then randomly selected 20 times negative links to add to the test set. The method we used to partition data set is to select a certain percentage of users who have more than 200 friends and then put them into the test set. The final training set includes 170,000 pairs of links, and the test set includes 45,000 pairs of links. Adamic-Adar Index (AA for short) is the benchmark and precision, Recall and F-measure were the evaluation indicators.

Tables 1, 2 and 3 show the precision, recall and F-measure of the four algorithms. We bold the maximums of each column and underlined the minimums of each column.

Table 1. Results of test algorithms in Precision.

	P@1	P@2	P@3	P@5	P@10
MES_WIL_AA	**0.981439**	**0.853828**	0.749420	**0.612065**	0.406729
MES_AA	**0.981439**	0.852668	**0.750193**	**0.612065**	**0.406961**
WIL_AA	0.974478	0.850348	0.747973	0.608817	0.404640
AA	0.972158	0.846868	0.748647	0.607889	0.403712

From Tables 1, 2 and 3, we learn that the performance of the AA is always the worst, no matter how many friends recommended to the users. And MES_WIL_AA performs best on the recall but if there are so many recommended candidates, the performance may not as good as before. On the other hand, MES_AA performs best on precision and seems to be more suitable to recommend more candidates.

Table 2. Results of test algorithms in Recall.

	R@1	R@2	R@3	R@5	R@10
MES_WIL_AA	**0.450457**	**0.645199**	**0.746234**	**0.863025**	0.961834
MES_AA	0.450273	0.644815	0.746199	0.862898	**0.961939**
WIL_AA	0.445618	0.639467	0.743378	0.860364	0.959581
AA	0.445047	0.637933	0.742625	0.859924	0.959137

Table 3. Results of test algorithms in F-measure.

	F@1	F@2	F@3	F@5	F@10
MES_WIL_AA	**0.617498**	**0.734996**	0.747824	**0.716197**	0.571703
MES_AA	0.617325	0.734316	**0.748191**	0.716153	**0.571951**
WIL_AA	0.611571	0.729983	0.745668	0.713056	0.569241
AA	0.610576	0.727700	0.745624	0.712268	0.568244

In the second experiment, we tried another 3 methods to cut the data sets. Take one of them as an example. We first put one part of the users whose friends are more than 300 (so as the 250 and 150) into the test set and put the other part of them into the training set. After that, we put all of the users whose friends are less than 300 into the training set. In order to control the proportion of the test sets and training sets in an appropriate range, we adjust the datasets properly. The follow-up experiment processes are the same as the first experiment.

Tables 4 and 5 list the precision and F-measure of four algorithms. The bolding data represent the maximums in the same row.

From Tables 4 and 5, we find that not all the best performances are P@1 and F@10. Moreover, the precision and F-measure will increase if more candidates are recommended to the target users who have more friends. It means that for users with

Table 4. Results of test algorithms in Precision.

		P@1	P@2	P@3	P@5	P@10
300	MES_WIL_AA	0.963068	0.961648	0.962121	0.962500	**0.971023**
	MES_AA	0.957386	0.960227	0.959280	0.960227	**0.970739**
	WIL_AA	0.894886	0.924716	0.934659	0.947159	**0.955114**
	AA	0.914773	0.936080	0.945076	0.951136	**0.958523**
250	MES_WIL_AA	**0.974719**	0.893258	0.817416	0.703371	0.536517
	MES_AA	**0.971910**	0.893258	0.816479	0.702247	0.538202
	WIL_AA	**0.960674**	0.879213	0.810861	0.700562	0.533146
	AA	**0.966292**	0.883427	0.814607	0.703933	0.535112
150	MES_WIL_AA	**0.977226**	0.855072	0.772257	0.650104	0.468530
	MES_AA	**0.975155**	0.855072	0.772257	0.653830	0.469979
	WIL_AA	**0.971014**	0.846791	0.765355	0.649689	0.465217
	AA	**0.973085**	0.847826	0.763975	0.648033	0.464596

Table 5. Results of test algorithms in F-measure.

		F@1	F@2	F@3	F@5	F@10
300	MES_WIL_AA	0.071023	0.136706	0.198302	0.309409	**0.537669**
	MES_AA	0.069989	0.136243	0.198250	0.310787	**0.537240**
	WIL_AA	0.066253	0.132024	0.193093	0.304760	**0.529569**
	AA	0.067554	0.133280	0.194410	0.304860	**0.530552**
250	MES_WIL_AA	0.500884	0.649271	0.697651	**0.712859**	0.658046
	MES_AA	0.499893	0.648227	0.700958	**0.719309**	0.664810
	WIL_AA	0.577182	0.684239	0.717964	**0.715822**	0.617597
	AA	0.498115	0.643793	0.696317	**0.713511**	0.656556
150	MES_WIL_AA	0.579285	0.688540	**0.722530**	0.716297	0.621120
	MES_AA	0.580924	0.690216	**0.723533**	0.720697	0.623956
	WIL_AA	0.577182	0.684239	**0.717964**	0.715822	0.617597
	AA	0.578329	0.685047	**0.717118**	0.714620	0.616932

more friends, we can increase the number of recommended friends appropriately to enhance the recommendation performance. However, for users with fewer friends, it is not suitable to recommend too many new friends. This is also the further evidence that users with different numbers of friends are not equally receptive to new friends. That is to say, their willingness to make new friends are different.

5 Summary

According to the number of neighbor nodes as well as the interaction frequency among the nodes, we explored the improvement of Adamic-Adar Index. In this paper, we tested 3 new algorithms. All the new algorithms devote to calculate the similarity of the social network structure based on the neighborhoods. The experimental results showed that considering the number of neighbor nodes and the interaction frequency among the common nodes could improve the recommendation effect to a certain extent. If the numbers of recommended candidates are in reasonable interval, it will be the best choice to consider the above two points together. Finally, we were surprised to find that for those users who have more neighbor nodes, increasing the recommended candidates as appropriate can improve the recommendation performances. In the future, we try to find suitable weights between the number of neighbor nodes and the frequency of interactions, so that we can maximize the effect of recommendation.

Acknowledgements. This work is supported by National Natural Science Foundation of China (Project No. 71701134), The Humanity and Social Science Youth Foundation of Ministry of Education of China (Project No. 16YJC630153), and Natural Science Foundation of Guangdong Province of China (Project No. 2017A030310427).

References

1. Magnier-Watanabe, R., Yoshida, M., Watanabe, T.: Social network productivity in the use of SNS. J. Knowl. Manag. **14**(6), 910–927 (2010)
2. Jaccard, P.: The distribution of the flora in the alpine zone. New Phytol. **11**(2), 37–50 (1912)
3. Liben-Nowell, D., Kleinberg, J.: The link-prediction problem for social networks. John Wiley & Sons, Inc., New York (2007)
4. Armentano, M.G., Godoy, D., Amandi, A.: Towards a followee recommender system for information seeking users in twitter. In: International Workshop on Semantic Adaptive Social Web, pp. 27–38 (2013)
5. Agarwal, V., Bharadwaj, K.K.: A collaborative filtering framework for friends recommendation in social networks based on interaction intensity and adaptive user similarity. Soc. Netw. Anal. Min. **3**(3), 359–379 (2013)
6. Lo, S., Lin, C.: WMR–a graph-based algorithm for friend recommendation. In: IEEE/WIC/ACM International Conference on Web Intelligence, pp. 121–128. IEEE (2007)
7. Weijia, Z.H.A.O.: The effect of social network sites use on self-esteem in college students: mediating of the number of online friends and moderating of gender. Psychol. Technol. Appl. **5**(7), 403–412 (2017)
8. Shu, W.: Community Network and Fans' Consumer Behavior. Fudan University (2014)
9. Yang, J., Xiao, H., Li, X.: Educational inequality and income inequality: an empirical study on China. Manag. World **4**(3), 413–434 (2009)
10. Li, Q., Yao, M., Yang, J., et al.: Genetic algorithm and graph theory based matrix factorization method for online friend recommendation. Sci. World J. **2014**(1), 162148 (2014)
11. Shi, Y., Larson, M., Hanjalic, A.: Exploiting user similarity based on rated-item pools for improved user-based collaborative filtering. In: ACM Conference on Recommender Systems, Recsys 2009, New York, NY, USA, pp. 125–132. DBLP, October 2009
12. Balabanović, M., Shoham, Y.: Fab: content-based, collaborative recommendation. Commun. ACM **40**(3), 66–72 (1997)
13. Liben-Nowell, D., Kleinberg, J.: The link prediction problem for social networks. J. Assoc. Inf. Sci. Technol. **58**(7), 1019–1031 (2007)
14. Ahn, M.W., Jung, W.S.: Accuracy test for link prediction in terms of similarity index: the case of WS and BA models. Phys. Stat. Mech. Appl. **429**(1), 177–183 (2015)
15. Adamic, L.A., Adar, E.: Friends and neighbors on the Web. Soc. Netw. **25**(3), 211–230 (2003)
16. Yao, Q., Huawei, M.A., Yan, H., et al.: Analysis of social network users' online behavior from the perspective of psychology. Adv. Psychol. Sci. **22**(10), 1647 (2014)
17. Lü, L., Zhou, T.: Link prediction in complex networks: a survey. Phys. Stat. Mech. Appl. **390**(6), 1150–1170 (2011)
18. Liu, W., Lu, L.: Link prediction based on local random walk. EPL (Europhys. Lett.) **89**(5), 58007–58012 (2010)

A Hybrid Movie Recommendation Method Based on Social Similarity and Item Attributes

Chen Yang, Xiaohong Chen$^{(\boxtimes)}$, Lei Liu$^{(\boxtimes)}$, Tingting Liu, and Shuang Geng

College of Management, Shenzhen University, Shenzhen, China
lrene.hong@foxmail.com, liulei_0912@163.com

Abstract. With the increasing demand for personalized recommendation, traditional collaborative filtering cannot satisfy users' needs. Social behaviors such as tags, comments and likes are becoming more and more popular among the recommender system users, and are attracting the attentions of the researchers in this domain. The behavior characteristics can be integrated with traditional interest community and some content features. In this paper, we put forward a hybrid recommendation approach that combines social behaviors, the genres of movies and existing collaborative filtering algorithms to perform movie recommendation. The experiments with MovieLens dataset show the advantage of our proposed method comparing to the benchmark method in terms of recommendation accuracy.

Keywords: Movie recommendation · Matrix factorization · Feature selection

1 Introduction

As an effective tool to solve the problem of information overload, the recommendation systems have a great impact in the world. With the sharply increasing demand for personalized recommendation for different products, many experts have been putting forward a lot of kinds of models to achieve accurate recommendation for different products. Collaborative Filtering (CF) [1] is the most classic outcome. CF strategy can recommend the information that the users' interests with the same preference or the common experience of a group. It can use machine algorithms to filter information that is difficult to analyze content automatically. However, CF still has many problems such as data sparseness, cold start and etc.

As for Content-Based Recommendation [2], it is another method to recommend the information to users. It makes use of the features of the content that the user has chosen before to make a similar recommendation. But not all the features of the content can be easily extracted, such as the features of music and movies. However, some social content annotations [3, 4] are helpful to understand users' preference, such as tags and classification. So, it also becomes a popular subject.

At present, more and more social applications spread widely, such as micro blog, social games, e-commerce and instant messaging. Users like watching photos, live videos, movies and listening music and so on. All of those contain huge information of

© Springer International Publishing AG, part of Springer Nature 2018
Y. Tan et al. (Eds.): ICSI 2018, LNCS 10942, pp. 275–285, 2018.
https://doi.org/10.1007/978-3-319-93818-9_26

users. Therefore, studying the Content-Based Recommendation on users' browsing history can help us find out what users maybe interest in.

Considering the problems above, this paper is aimed at putting forward a hybrid technology recommendation model for movie platforms. It combines the traditional Collaborative Filtering algorithm and Content-Based Recommendation model. This model not only can effectively solve the problem of the new users' recommendation, but also can solve the problem of the sparse data of the user evaluations.

2 Backgrounds and Notations

2.1 Backgrounds

With the development of social networking, such as Netflix and other platforms are increasingly active. There are many researches show that the movie attributes are becoming more and more important. Now, the user's tags on the film, the user's evaluation of the movie and the introduction of the movie are always used to study the movie attributes and to discover the movies that the user may be interested in. However, it is very difficult to obtain the complete content features of the film through the film attributes. And even in practical applications, it is also very difficult to get all users' evaluate of the view history.

Therefore, many scholars have proposed a hybrid recommendation system which is based on Collaborative Filtering algorithm and Content- Based recommendation system to recommend movies accurately. Lei Li and Gai Li et al. improved the CF algorithm based on Singular Value Decomposition (SVD) [5]. The improved Collaborative Filtering recommendation system introduces a regularized Collaborative Filtering algorithm based on iterative least square method on the basis of the traditional Matrix Factorization model.

Xiaolin Zheng et al. had proposed a movie recommendation system via movie tags [6]. And they designed a social movie networks through the folksonomy, and then combined the social characteristics to predict the users' interest by using a preference model. This algorithm is aimed at studying the relationship between social network and movie, which is better for understanding the users' interests.

2.2 Matrix Factorization

Different from SVD, Matrix Factorization (MF) [7] also can gives a way to learn users and object location with less complexity. So in this paper, we uses MF instead of SVD. It sorts and extracts the "user-item rating" matrices and then factorizes the matrixes. So a user's implicit vector matrix and an object hidden vector matrix can be obtained. For example, in Fig. 1 there is a rating matrix R about the information of users and movies with M * N.

M: The number of items
N: The number of users
w_{NM}: The rating of User N for the Item M.

	Item1	Item2	Item3	......	Item M
User1		w_{12}		......	w_{1M}
User2	w_{21}			......	......
User3		w_{32}	w_{33}	......	......
......				......	......
User N		w_{N2}		......	w_{NM}

Fig. 1. A rating matrix R about user's and movie's information with M * N

From the matrix above, we can see that the matrix is sparse for the reason that the number of the users and items are larger than the number of rating. And it's not helpful to recommend films for users. Now we assume that all the movies have several genres. And there are G genres in movies. According to the factorizing of the matrix R, we can obtain two new matrices Q and P as follow (Fig. 2):

	genre1	genre2	genre3	......	genre G
User1	w_{11}^{ug}	w_{12}^{ug}	w_{13}^{ug}	......	w_{1G}^{ug}
User2	w_{21}^{ug}	w_{22}^{ug}	w_{23}^{ug}	......	w_{2G}^{ug}
User3	w_{31}^{ug}	w_{32}^{ug}	w_{33}^{ug}	......	......
......	......	......	......	......	......
User N	w_{N1}^{ug}	w_{N2}^{ug}	w_{N3}^{ug}	......	w_{NG}^{ug}

	Item1	Item2	Item3	......	Item M
genre1	w_{11}^{gi}	w_{12}^{gi}	w_{13}^{gi}	......	w_{1M}^{gi}
genre2	w_{21}^{gi}	w_{22}^{gi}	w_{23}^{gi}	......	w_{2M}^{gi}
genre3	w_{31}^{gi}	w_{32}^{gi}	w_{33}^{gi}	......	......
......	......	......	......	......	......
genre G	w_{G1}^{gi}	w_{G2}^{gi}	w_{G3}^{gi}	......	w_{GM}^{gi}

Fig. 2. Two new matrices Q and P

With these matrices, we can calculate the rating of the user i on item j using the formula and complete the matrix R. So that the system can mitigate the effects of cold start problem.

$$w_{ij} = \sum_{g=1}^{G} w_{ig}^{ug} w_{gj}^{gi} \tag{1}$$

To get matrices Q and P, it still needs to make QP^T and R have smaller distance with iteration method. We use Gradient Descent to set a loss function as follow:

$$\arg\ min_{Q,P} = L(R, QP^T) + \gamma\left(\|Q\|_F^2 + \|P\|_F^2\right) \tag{2}$$

L(A, B): The loss function measuring the distance between matrices A and B
$\left(\|Q\|_F^2 + \|P\|_F^2\right)$: A regular term used to constrain parameters and avoid over fitting
$\|\cdot\|_F$: F-Norm

2.3   Bayesian Personalized Ranking Model

The core of the Bayesian Personalized Ranking (BPR) [8] model is to establish a partial sequence pair for each user to represent users' preferences. And it trains a recommendation model by using these partial orders instead of using a content-feedback item which is in the implicit feedback matrix D.

The establishment of partial sequence pairs that represent user preferences is as follow:

$$P = \left\{(u,i,j)|i \in I_u^+ \wedge j \in I\backslash I_u^+\right\} \tag{3}$$

(u, i, j): User u likes the content i more than content j
I_u^+: User u with a set of implicit feedback content
$I\backslash I_u^+$: User u without a set of implicit feedback content

From the Bayesian Probability, there is:

$$p(\Theta| >_u) \propto p(>_u|\Theta)p(\Theta) \tag{4}$$

$$p(>_u|\Theta) = \prod_{(u,i,j\in P)} p(i >_u j|\Theta) \tag{5}$$

Definition:

$$p(i >_u j|\Theta) = \sigma\left(x_{uij}(\Theta)\right) \tag{6}$$

$x_{uij}(\Theta)$: Shows any real function of the model parameter Θ and shows the preference relationship between user u and content i and j
$\sigma()$: Logistic function with "s" shape

The final optimization objective is:

$$maxO_\Theta = lnp(\Theta| >_u) = \sum\nolimits_{(u,i,j \in P)} ln\,\sigma\big(x_{uij}(\Theta)\big) - \lambda_\Theta \|\Theta\|^2 \tag{7}$$

2.4   BPR-MF Model

In BPR model, we choose Matrix Factorization (MF) model as training model, which is called BPR - MF algorithm [9]. The MF model is based on latent semantic analysis (Latent Class Model), which assumes that the attributes and user preferences can be represented in lower dimensional space with lower dimension. The traditional MF model is used to estimate the user score by using the content feature vector and the inner product of the users' preference vector while the MF based on BPR is used to estimate the target preference.

Therefore, the definition is:

$$x_{ui} = <w_u, h_i> \; = \sum\nolimits_{f=1}^{k} w_{uf}, h_{if} \tag{8}$$

$$x_{uij} = x_{ui} - x_{uj} \tag{9}$$

(8) can be written in matrix form as $x = W \cdot H^t$, and x is the object preference matrix. So we can get a parameter $\Theta = (W, H)$

The final expression of BPR-MF can be as follow:

$$min\,O_{W,H} = - \sum\nolimits_{u,i,j \in P} ln\,\sigma\big(x_{uij}\big) + \lambda \Big(\|W\|_F^2 + \|H\|_F^2 \Big) \tag{10}$$

2.5   Term Frequency-Inverse Document Frequency and Text Similarity

Term Frequency-Inverse Document Frequency (TF-IDF)[1] is a statistical method used to evaluate the importance of words to one of the files or a corpus. A word will become more importance when it appears more frequently in the document. However, if it appears in a corpus, it seems be not so important. So term frequency can help us finding keywords in the files and the inverse document frequency can measures the importance of a term in a file.

As for term frequency (*tf*), there is:

$$tf_{i,j} = \frac{n_{i,j}}{\sum_{k=1}^{K} n_{k,j}} \tag{11}$$

$n_{i,j}$:   The number of times term i appears in the file j

---

[1] https://en.wikipedia.org/wiki/Tf%E2%80%93idf

As for inverse document frequency (*idf*), there is:

$$idf(t, \text{D}) = log\frac{N}{|\{d \in D : t \in d\}|} \tag{12}$$

$$idf(t, \text{D}) = log\frac{N}{1 + |\{d \in D : t \in d\}|} \tag{13}$$

N: the number of the documents in the corpus
$|\{d \in D : t \in d\}|$: The number of terms t exists in document D when $idf(t, \text{D}) \neq 0$
$1 + |\{d \in D : t \in d\}|$: The number of terms t exists in document D when $idf(t, D) = 0$.

To calculate the similarity between two texts, it still needs some algorithms to calculate the values of similarity. Such as Cosine Similarity, Pearson Similarity and so on. Take Cosine Similarity as an example, the process of calculation is as follows:

(1) Find out all the keywords in the texts with TF-IDF.
(2) Take a number of keywords in each text, merge into a set and calculate the term frequency in its text.
(3) Generate the respective term frequency vectors of the two texts.
(4) Calculate the cosine similarity of two vectors, and the more similar the value is, the more similar they are.
(5) The formula of Cosine Similarity is as follow:

$$\cos\theta = \frac{\sum_{i=1}^{n}(A_i * B_i)}{\sqrt{\sum_{i=1}^{n}(A_i)^2} * \sqrt{\sum_{i=1}^{n}(B_i)^2}} \tag{14}$$

3   Proposed Approach

In this paper, we put forward a hybrid recommendation with combining Collaborative Filtering and Content-based Recommendation. As for CF, we used BPR-MF to solve the problem of matrix sparsity. And as for Content-based Recommendation, we used TF-IDF algorithm to calculate the similarity of tags and genres and then get the final predictive rating. The hybrid recommendation system was implemented in two phases work.

The first stage is that use BPR-MF model to train the training dataset and obtain a refined candidate set according to the rating. After training the dataset, we predicted the rating of movies that did not exist in the training dataset for every user. Then we sorted the rating of the items and got the candidate set. Every candidate set of each user in training dataset has several top items.

The second stage is comparing the similarities between the candidate movies and the movies that users had rated in training dataset. We then recommend the movies that users may be interested in according to the similarities. The method to calculate the similarity between two movies is combining the similarities of tags [10, 11] and genres of the movies. After testing and removing with the greedy algorithm, we can get:

$$sim_{ij} = \alpha * g_{simij} + (1 - \alpha) * t_{simij} \tag{15}$$

sim_{ij}: The similarity between item i and item j
t_{simij}: The similarity of tags between item i and item j
g_{simij}: The similarity of genres between item i and item j
α: The weight of the similarity of tags.

In order to solve the problem of tag matrix sparseness, the prediction scores of the first stage were regarded as a factor of users' interest and were combined with the similarities of the films to get the final predictive rating. The details are as followed:

$$pre\_rate_{ui} = \beta * pre_{ui} + (1 - \beta) * sim_{ij} \tag{16}$$

pre_rate_{ui}: The user's predictive rating on the item i
pre_{ui}: The user's predictive rating on the item i in the first stage with BPR-MF
sim_{ij}: The similarity between item i and item j that user had seen
β: The weight of pre_{ui} in the first stage.

Combining (15) and (16), we can get:

$$pre\_rate_{ui} = \beta * pre_{ui} + (1 - \beta) * \alpha * g_{simij} + (1 - \beta) * (1 - \alpha) * t_{simij} \tag{17}$$

A history item and rating dataset were established for every user. So that the candidate set can compare with the history set. The compared items in the history set had rated high and it could be make sure that it's the user's interest. As for α and β, we found the optimal solution by using greedy algorithm. The result will be shown in part four.

4   Experiment

4.1   Data

The movie dataset contains 671 users, 9125 movies, 100005 movie ratings and 1297 tags that users marked for the movies. The dataset is collected from MovieLens[2] and released in March, 2014. It is known that MovieLens has long history. Therefore, it is significant to study this dataset.

The tag of different movies is used to calculate the similarity in order to judge whether two movies are similar or not. The tags are marked by the users' own subjective consciousness. Different films with similar tags mean that the films have a certain extent

---

[2] http://www.movielens.org

similarity. The similarities of tags are calculated by the TF-IDF model of Gensim[3]. For the reason that users can mark tags for a movie without a limited number of times, all the tags of the same users for the same movies were arranged into a long tag.

The similarities of genres of different movies are also calculated by the TF-IDF model of Gensim to distinguish the similarities of the movie genres. All the movies in the dataset were compared to other movies and gained a list of similarities of genres. Then all the lists were generated a matrix. The upper or the lower trigonometric parts of the matrix can be seen as non-repetition of the genre data. It is helpful and convenient to compare the similarity between two movies.

4.2   Evaluation Methods

To evaluate whether a recommendation system is helpful, there is a lot of ways to do. Some scholars may calculate the error between the real rating and predictive rating including using algorithm of Mean Absolute Error. And some may calculate the hit rate of the predicted results, such as presicion@N and recall@N. In this paper, we use Root Mean Square Error and Mean Absolute Error.

Root Mean Square Error (RMSE) and Mean Absolute Error (MAE) are both evaluation indicators of recommendation system. They can intuitively show the accuracy of the recommendation system. They are also suitable for the system of scoring prediction and evaluating the accuracy of off-line data. However, they are not suitable for evaluating sorting performance for the reason that they just calculate the error between the predicted value and the actual value.

Root Mean Square Error (RMSE) is the square root of Mean Square Error (MSE). It can evaluate the degree of change in the data. It calculates the square of the error and it can magnify error. The smaller the value it is, the better the prediction model is. However, when an error in a dataset is too large, it will affect the value of the RMSE and make a harmful impact on evaluating the system.

The formula of RMSE is as follow:

$$\text{RMSE} = \sqrt{\frac{\sum (i,j \in \Omega_{test})(a_{i,j} - b_{i,j})^2}{|\Omega_{test}|}} \tag{18}$$

Ω_{test}: The test dataset
$|\Omega_{test}|$: The number of test dataset
$a_{i,j} - b_{i,j}$: The error between the predict value and actual value

Mean Absolute Error calculates the mean of all the absolute error in the dataset. MAE can better reflect the actual situation of the predicted value error. Unlike RMSE, MAE can ignore the error which is too large or too small. It can measure the error in a balanced way.

---

[3] https://radimrehurek.com/gensim/

The formula of MAE is as follow:

$$\text{MAE} = \frac{\sum (i,j \in \Omega_{test}) |a_{i,j} - b_{i,j}|}{|\Omega_{test}|} \tag{19}$$

4.3   Results and Discussion

From Fig. 3 and Table 1, we can summarize the results of the experiment. The values of MAE indicate that the hybrid recommendation system is better than only Collaborative Filtering algorithm. Although the final data of RMSE and MAE was not significantly lower than the data of BPR-MF, it still presents a better trend. And it is proved that on the base of BPR-MF, calculating the similarity of tags and genres can recommend movies more accurately. Besides, the little changes in the data reflect a connection between the tag and the genre.

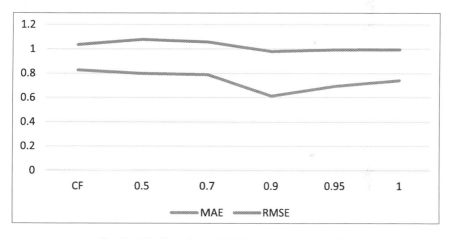

Fig. 3. The line chart of MAE and RMSE varieties

Figure 3 shows that the precision of the hybrid recommendation system increases with the increase of the value of α, β until α, β was 0.9. For the reason that when we doing research with using the greedy algorithm, $\alpha = \beta$ was the optimal solution. So we set $\alpha = \beta$. And the result shows that 0.9 is the optimal solution. The reason is that the tags that users marked have little information while the rating data and movies data have ten times larger than tag data. The recommendation system can get less information on the content of the tags, so using the similarities of the tags as one of the main components of movie similarities will be hard and could not be helpful. So the chart shows that the similarities of tags have low importance in calculating the precision.

What's more, the lines of MAE and RMSE in the Fig. 3 all present the same trend. But the effect of MAE seems better than the effect of RMSE. It reflects that the error of the predicted value of the actual situation is small while the precision of the

Table 1. The proportion of the similarities of tags and genres

	CF	$\alpha, \beta = 0.5$	$\alpha, \beta = 0.7$	$\alpha, \beta = 0.9$	$\alpha, \beta = 0.95$	$\alpha, \beta = 1$
MAE	0.827	0.798532	0.789271	0.612981	0.693728	0.74122
RMSE	1.036	1.078570	1.058479	0.979840	0.994671	0.99599

recommendation system is not high. It means that the recommendation system still has problems and is not stable and helpful.

To sum up, the hybrid recommendation system still shows a better trend than traditional CF and only BPR-MF. If we further analyze and improve it, the hybrid recommendation system still has the chance to surpass the only collaborative filtering and achieve to be a precise recommendation.

5   Conclusion and Future Work

In the study, we propose a hybrid recommendation combining Collaborative Filtering and Content-based Recommendation. While studying the relation between the similarity of items and predictive score of users, we found that the content of movies can greater influence users' behaviors such as giving a tag or a like. So we use BPR-MF and calculate the similarities of movies to predict the rating of users based on Combinatorial Innovation.

To recommend movies accurately, it often needs the information about users' behavior history, interests, social networks and the directors, actors, genres, contents of movies and so on. However, even if we have the information above, it's still very hard to provide an accurate recommendation service. Consequently, we try to establish a hybrid recommendation system to study users' interest content and combine mathematic algorithm to gain the implicit information. According to the users' behavior including ratings and tags, we analyzed users' preference. Movie genre helps us to distinguish which movie may users interested in.

In the future, we will take users' satisfactions and the synopsis and directors of movies as factors into account and put them into our model. We will further excavate the contents of films and connect the users' satisfactions to recommend films. For example, a famous director must have fans. So if a user is the director's fan, the user may be more inclined to watch the movie. Besides, synopsis of movie can be connected with directors and users. So we can establish a model to set up a network of users and directors in order to confirm if director can influence users' preference. In this way, can the hybrid movie recommendation be more personalized and robust.

Acknowledgements. This work is supported by National Natural Science Foundation of China (Project No. 71701134), The Humanity and Social Science Youth Foundation of Ministry of Education of China (Project No. 16YJC630153), and Natural Science Foundation of Guangdong Province of China (Project No. 2017A030310427).

References

1. Breese, J.S., Heckerman, D., Kadie, C.: Empirical analysis of predictive algorithms for collaborative filtering, vol. 461, San Francisco, CA (1998)
2. Tatemura, J., Santini, S., Jain, R.: Social and content-based information filtering for a web graphics recommender system. In: Proceedings of the IEEE ICIAP 1999 (1999)
3. Chelmis, C., Prasanna, V.K.: Social link prediction in online social tagging systems. ACM Trans. Inf. Syst. 2013. 31(204)
4. Hoi, S.C.H., et al.: Social Media Modeling and Computing. Springer-Verlag New York Inc. (2011)
5. Li, G., Li, L.: Collaborative filtering algorithm based on matrix decomposition. Comput. Eng. Appl. **47**(30), 4–7 (2011)
6. Wei, S., Xiao, L., Zheng, X., et al.: A hybrid movie recommendation approach via social tags. In: IEEE, International Conference on E-Business Engineering. IEEE Computer Society, pp. 280–285 (2014)
7. Lee, D.: Learning the parts of objects with nonnegative matrix factorization. Nature **401**(6755), 788 (1999)
8. Rendle, S., Freudenthaler, C., Gantner, Z., et al.: BPR: Bayesian personalized ranking from implicit feedback. In: Conference on Uncertainty in Artificial Intelligence, pp. 452–461. AUAI Press (2009)
9. Hu, G.-N., Dai, Xin-Yu.: Integrating reviews into personalized ranking for cold start recommendation. In: Kim, J., Shim, K., Cao, L., Lee, J.-G., Lin, X., Moon, Y.-S. (eds.) PAKDD 2017. LNCS (LNAI), vol. 10235, pp. 708–720. Springer, Cham (2017). https://doi.org/10.1007/978-3-319-57529-2_55
10. Ji, K., Shen, H.: Addressing cold-start: scalable recommendation with tags and keywords. Knowl. Based Syst. **83**, 42–50 (2015)
11. Cantador, I., Szomszor, M., Alani, H., Fernández, M., Castells, P.: Enriching ontological user profiles with tagging history for multi-domain recommendations. In: CISWeb (2008)

Multi-feature Collaborative Filtering Recommendation for Sparse Dataset

Zengda Guan$^{(\boxtimes)}$

Business School, Shandong Jianzhu University, Jinan, Shandong, China
guanzengda@sdjzu.edu.cn

Abstract. Collaborative filtering algorithms become losing its effectiveness on case that the dataset is sparse. When user ratings are scared, it's difficult to find real similar users, which causes performance reduction of the algorithm. We here present a 3-dimension collaborative filtering framework which can use features of users and items for similarity computation to deal with the data sparsity problem. It uses feature and rating combinations instead of only ratings in collaborative filtering process and performs a more complete similarity computation. Specifically, we provide a weighted feature form and a Bayesian form in its implementation. The results demonstrate that our methods can obviously improve the performance of collaborative filtering when datasets are sparse.

Keywords: Collaborative filtering · Sparse dataset
Multi-feature similarity

1 Introduction

Recommender systems can help people find the interesting and valuable information from books, articles, webpages, movies, music and so on. Collaborative filtering (CF) filters for information or patterns using techniques involving collaboration among multiple agents, viewpoints, data sources, etc [1].

CF is easy to implement and perform well in very many situations [2]. However, it's seriously dependent on human ratings, performs decreasingly when data are sparse, and cannot recommend for new-coming users and items. The similarity measure in CF relies on those users/items with many common ratings and therefore it will become untrustworthy when data don't have enough common ratings, which causes performance degradation even failure. In reality, people usually have lots of data such as users' demographic data and behavior data, which can potentially be helpful for recommendations. This inspires us to consider integrating these non-rating data into CF framework to alleviate the difficulty of CF in sparse-data situation while conventional CF cannot use these data directly.

Our idea is simple and natural, and it comes from this intuition. If recommendations need to satisfy only one constraint, a wide range of recommendations are fit, while if they need to satisfy many constraints, only some real ones could

© Springer International Publishing AG, part of Springer Nature 2018
Y. Tan et al. (Eds.): ICSI 2018, LNCS 10942, pp. 286–294, 2018.
https://doi.org/10.1007/978-3-319-93818-9_27

be fit. More strict conditions can bring more accurate and intense recommendations, somehow because they are taken into consideration in human choice and hence show more value. Here, we take the data features of users and items as conditional constraints of collaborate computation, which produces a strong representation for users' interests in items. It could be thought that users with more common relevant features have stronger common interests. This view is also consistent when it's applied to conventional CF. For conventional CF, if two users/items have more common ratings of user-items, their ratings to target items/users will be more similar. Simply, the rating-based similarity can be generalized to multi-feature-based similarity.

In details, we implement the idea in a 3-dimension CF framework. We firstly construct feature vectors for every user-item and the vectors are consisted of relevant features including ratings and other features instead of only ratings, then compute the similarity between user-item vectors to obtain neighbors of the target user-item, and finally compute the ratings of the target users on the items. We use a prediction function to reweight the features in the vectors for a good performance. Moreover, we also employ a Bayesian view to construct a similarity comparison form between user-items. The results of the experiments demonstrate our methods perform much better than conventional CF.

The remainder of the article is organized as follows. In Sect. 2, we introduce the related work about CF, especially CF for sparse data. In Sect. 3, we present our methods in details. In Sect. 4, we give the experiments and the result analyses. In the last section, we conclude our work.

2   Related Work

There have been a large number of studies on CF [3]. CF algorithms have performed well in a broad domain as recommendation technology [2]. GroupLens was a pioneering in collaborative filtering [4,5]. The GroupLens team initially implemented a neighborhood-based CF system for rating Usenet articles. They used a 1–5 integer rating scale and computed distance using Pearson correlations. Delgado [6] took an agent-based approach to CF, developing several algorithms that combined ratings data with other sources of information such as the geographic location of the user, and weighted majority voting was used to combine recommendations from different sources.

The data sparsity problem is fundamental [7] and is a major bottleneck in CF [8]. Specifically, when new users or items have come into the CF system, it's difficult to find their similar neighbors because it lacks enough information, sometimes called cold start problem [3]. Many research dealt with this problem by generating reasonable values for the missing rating. Herlocker et al. [9] studied small intersection sets for user-item matrix by reducing the weight of users with few common items. Chee et al. [10] constructed cliques of users who were approximately similar and extended users' rating history with the clique's averages. Breese et al. [11] assumed a neutral or somewhat negative preference for the unobserved ratings and then computed the users' similarity on the resulting ratings data. Su et al. [12] proposed using an imputation technique to fill in the missing data. Other methods were also proposed to alleviate the data sparsity problem. Principle Component Analysis (PCA) [13], and Latent Semantic Indexing (LSI) [14] were proposed to address the sparsity problem by removing unrepresentative or insignificant users or items through reducing the dimensionality of the user-item matrix. Najafabadi et al. [15] tackled data sparsity problem using clustering and association rules mining on massive data.

Besides, hybrid CF approaches were also proposed to incorporate both CF technology and content-based features content, such as users' profiles, item descriptions and users' rating history, to cope with the sparsity difficulties. Content-boosted CF algorithm [16] used external content information to produce predictions on non-rating data, and then provided personalized suggestions through CF. Greinemr et al. [17] developed TANELR as the content-predictor on data subsets, and then used CF to improve prediction performance. These methods used content features to predict the ratings, which might produce extra bias because of not so accurate predicted ratings.

3   Multi-features CF

3.1   CF and Features

It is known that the fundamental assumption of conventional CF is that if users X and Y rate n items similarly, and hence they will rate on other items similarly. CF uses the ratings of these similar users to evaluate the target ratings. The basic formula is as follows:

$$r_{tt'} = \sum_{i=1}^{i \neq t} sim\,(u_i, u_t)\, r_{it'} \tag{1}$$

where u_t denotes the target user, u_i denotes any other user, $r_{tt'}$ and $r_{it'}$ denote the rating of user u_t and user u_i on the target item t', respectively. For the similarity computation $sim\,(u_i, u_t)$, conventional CF usually depends only on ratings. The similarity computation can also be explained in a conditional probabilistic prospect. In details, it is as follows:

$$
\begin{aligned}
sim\,(u_i, u_t) &= Pr(r_{it'} = r_{tt'} | r_{i1}, ..., r_{in}, r_{t1}, ..., r_{tn}) \\
&\approx Pr(g(r_{i1}, ..., r_{in}) = g(r_{t1}, ..., r_{tn})) \\
&\approx simf((r_{i1}, ..., r_{in}), (r_{t1}, ..., r_{tn}))
\end{aligned} \tag{2}
$$

where n is the number of items, $r_{i1}, ..., r_{in}$ represents all the ratings of user u_i except the rating $r_{it'}$, $g(r_{i1}, ..., r_{in})$ represents a prediction function for $r_{it'}$, and $simf((r_{i1}, ..., r_{in}), (r_{t1}, ..., r_{tn}))$ represents the similarity between two users based on their ratings. $Pr(r_{it'} = r_{tt'} | r_{i1}, ..., r_{in}, r_{t1}, ..., r_{tn})$ represents the probability with which u_i has the rating of $r_{tt'}$. It then can be empirically computed by the probability with which both $g()$ function values are equal. Finally, it is computed by the similarity function $simf()$, since it is assumed that $g()$ is continuous and smooth and hence $g(r_{i1}, ..., r_{in})$ and $g(r_{t1}, ..., r_{tn})$ are similar when $(r_{i1}, ..., r_{in})$

and $(r_{t1}, ..., r_{tn})$ are similar. From a wider perspective, $Pr(r_{it'} = r_{tt'}|...)$ can be computed integrating other significant features which are helpful for predicting $r_{tt'}$. Or in other word, the function $g()$ can be trained by all kinds of features involved in recommendation, not limiting to only ratings. Thus, $simf()$ can also be computed by other features besides rating.

In reality, users' ratings are usually accompanied with some features which are correlated to the rating. That also inspires us to consider replacing ratings similarity with a combination of features and ratings. On one hand, the feature combination can work when the rating are missing, on the other hand, it can improve the representation for users' interests.

We further explain the theory that the interest similarity between users increases as the number of their common related features increases. Let us give an example. When many users rate the same film. some rate the film high for its actor, some rate high for its director, and some rate high for its plot. All rate similar values for different reasons, so they may rate differently on other films. On the contrary, if people rate many films similarly for the same reasons, they will rate another film similarly more probably. This would be much more useful in sparse data situation where we can use feature information as the reason for choice instead of only ratings.

3.2 Vector-Based Similarity

A simple way is to compute the similarity of two vectors directly which consist of features and ratings. We choose the cosine similarity, which can support our assumption well, i.e., more similar features bring stronger relationship between users. In details, we can choose some plausible or relevant features, insert ratings and them into the vectors of user-item, and compute the similarity between the vectors. Its significance lies that it can compute the similarity between users using the features, even without the rating, in which situation we treat the rating value as 0. The formula is presented as follows:

$$sim(u_i, u_t) = simcos(mat(f_{i·1}, ..., f_{i·m}, r_{i·}), mat(f_{t·1}, ..., f_{t·m}, r_{t·})) \qquad (3)$$

where $f_{i·k}$ and $r_{i·}$ denote a column vector which includes the kth features and the ratings for the user u_i on all items, respectively. $f_{t·k}$ and $r_{t·}$ are used in a similar way. Matrix $mat(f_{i·1}, ..., f_{i·m}, r_{i·})$ contains m features and the rating of the user u_i, and matrix $mat(f_{t·1}, ..., f_{t·m}, r_{t·})$ is used similarly.

We then discuss the risk produced by (3). We denote the risk of conventional CF by c_{risk}, and the risk of vector-based similarity CF by v_{risk}. If all features have nothing to do with the rating and users' interests, v_{risk} will be much bigger than c_{risk}. If all features are equivalent to the rating, v_{risk} will be equal to c_{risk}. If these features can help enhance the similarity of interests of users compared with only-rating, v_{risk} will be smaller than c_{risk}. If all features are equivalent to the real rating and the rating values are all missing, v_{risk} will be reasonably small and c_{risk} will be unable to compute. Moreover, if we think these features are constraints of interest similarity computation, we obtain smaller neighbor sets of target users than conventional CF, which will be easier to compute.

In summary, compared with conventional CF, it can use the features of users and items to reduce the variance of similar users and interests. While compared with content-based recommenders, it can use CF technology to help predict the user's interests better.

3.3   Reweighting the Features

In fact, the weight of each element in feature-rating vectors can be different, and it is expected to be set reasonable values for better recommendation performance. If we take the rating values as predicted results of a function involving the features, we can use the parametric functional coefficients as the weight values. Here, linear functions should be a prior choice for their simplicity and directness for weight settings. For a classification problem, we can choose logistic regression to determine the weights of features and ratings, taking the probability of predicted ratings and the coefficients of the feature variables as their own weights. For a regression problem, the option can be a linear function in which the coefficients of the features are used as their weights directly.

3.4   A Bayesian View

Then, we provide a Bayesian view to illustrate a new CF. Compared with non-Bayesian way, it assumes that the features belonging to different ratings have little significant relationship, thus they make little contribution to similarity computation between users. This seems to be reasonable because the features are so many and complicated that they can overwhelms the true similarity in computations. Moreover, it can reduce the feature dimensions to compute in this Bayesian way, which alleviates the "high dimension curse" in similarity estimations. The similarity between two users is represented as follows:

$$
\begin{aligned}
sim(u_i, u_t) &\approx simf((f_{i\cdot}, r_{i\cdot}), (f_{t\cdot}, r_{t\cdot})) \\
&= Pr(f_{i\cdot}, r_{i\cdot}, f_{t\cdot}, r_{t\cdot}) \\
&= Pr(r_{i\cdot}, r_{t\cdot})Pr(f_{i\cdot}, f_{t\cdot}|r_{i\cdot}, r_{t\cdot}) \\
&\approx Pr(r_{i\cdot} = r_{it'}, r_{t\cdot} = r_{it'})Pr(f_{i\cdot}, f_{t\cdot}|r_{i\cdot}, r_{t\cdot})
\end{aligned}
\tag{4}
$$

where $r_{it'}$ denotes the rating for the user i on the target item t'. The first equation above is obtained due to (2) by integrating the features $f_{i\cdot}$ and $f_{t\cdot}$. $Pr(r_{i\cdot} = r_{it'}, r_{t\cdot} = r_{it'}) = 1.0$ when $r_{i\cdot} = r_{it'}$ and $r_{t\cdot} = r_{it'}$, while $Pr(r_{i\cdot} = r_{it'}, r_{t\cdot} = r_{it'}) = 0.0$ when $r_{i\cdot} \neq r_{it'}$ or $r_{t\cdot} \neq r_{it'}$. It says that we compute the similarity between users only using the features with the same rating $r_{it'}$.

In details, for classification problems, the method computes the similarity between the target user and other users on each class, i.e., each rating label. Firstly, for each class, it selects the users whose rating on the target item belongs to the class. Then, it assigns 0 to the feature vectors of all selected users' items on which the rating has a different class label from the rating on the target item, and computes the similarity between these users and the target user. Finally, it uses the similarity and the rating of non-target users on the target item to compute the rating value of the target user on the target item. The similarity computation formula is further represented in a cosine similarity form:

$$sim(u_i, u_t) = simcos(mat(f_{i\cdot 1}, ..., f_{i\cdot m}), \bar{mat}(f_{t\cdot 1}, ..., f_{t\cdot m}))$$
$$s.t. \quad r_{i\cdot} = r_{t\cdot} = r_{it'} \tag{5}$$

The formula can be computed easily.

4   Experiment

We performed two experiments to evaluate our methods. One experiment is for predicting repeat buyers, and the other experiment is for predicting movie ratings.

4.1   Predicting Repeat Buyers

The data of this experiment was from Tmall IJCAI-15 Competition Dataset (https://tianchi.shuju.aliyun.com/) which contained anonymous users' shopping logs in the past 6 months before and on the "Double 11" day, and the label information indicating whether they were repeat buyers. We preprocessed the source dataset simply, and obtained a dataset including 10000 users and 4993 items, which has sparse ratings with a sparse rate 0.158%. The dataset has user features including age and gene, item features including categories and brands, and user-item features including time-stamps, user behaviors(such like click, add-to-chart, purchase and add-to-favorite). The rating values are enumerated type 0, 1, where 1 means repeat buyer, and 0 means non-repeat buyer.

We test how conventional CF (CF), logistic regression (LR), logistic regression CF (LRCF), vector CF (VCF), weighted vector CF (WVCF) and Bayesian CF (BCF) perform on the dataset. LRCF uses logistic regression to predict the missing ratings and then perform conventional CF. VCF denotes the vector based CF whose every element has a default weight 1.0. WVCF is another kind of VCF that we compute and set weight of every element of the vectors by logistic regression. BCF is the Bayesian multi-feature CF described in the previous sector. For this task, we use precision rate and recall rate as the test index, and perform a 10 repetitions to obtain the results.

Table 1. Precision and recall rate comparison between CF, LR, LRCF, VCF, WVCF and BCF

Condition	CF	LR	LRCF	VCF	WVCF	BCF
Precision	0.0	0.9380	0.9841	0.9779	0.9879	0.9946
Recall	0.0	0.0	0.9875	0.9032	0.9912	0.9938

The final results are described in Table 1. CF doesn't work on this dataset because somehow the dataset are complicated and sparse so that it's failed to calculate the similarity between users. All multi-feature CF perform well and obtain better results than LR. Specifically, WVCF and BCF are the best methods on both precision and recall test on this dataset. WVCF behaves better than VCF because it sets a fit weight to each feature. BCF obtained the best performance in all the methods, and it's also robust, suggested by the fact that the feature weights of BCF are all not man-made and equals to 1.0.

4.2   Predicting Movie Ratings

In this experiment, we used a Yahoo! dataset [18] to test the methods. Our dataset has 1910 users and 2978 items, with a sparse rate less than 0.013%. The dataset includes movie user ratings of movies, user features including birthyear and gender, and item features including MPAA rating, release date, list of genres, list of directors, list of actors, average critic rating, the number of critic ratings, list of anonymized review owners, global non-personalized popularity and so on. To be noted, this dataset has a difference with the dataset of last experiment that it does not have features related to user and item simultaneously. We select some features from the dataset for training a model. We compare CF only using ratings (i.e. conventional CF, called CF), CF only using features(FCF), CF using features and ratings(FRCF) and Bayesian CF(BCF), in order to testify whether multi-feature CF is better than CF. The results are showed in Table 2, and MAE and RMSE are used for error measurement.

Table 2. Predicted results comparison between CF, FCF, FRCF, and BCF

Condition	CF	FCF	FRCF	BCF
MAE	1.3079	1.1636	1.1256	0.9731
RMSE	1.8596	1.7426	1.6961	1.3088

From Table 2, it can be seen that all multi-feature CF methods excel CF. BCF achieves the best performance on this dataset. At the same time, FRCF with fit weight values behaves better than CF and FCF.

We also take an experiment to study the impact of weights of features to the performance of FRCF, which is shown in Fig. 1. We first set a basic weight to each feature of FRCF according to the parametric coefficients in the regression models, and then use a series of values to multiply the basic weight. The results shows that the performance can be affected much by the feature weights.

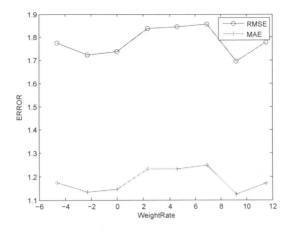

Fig. 1. The impact of weights of features to the performance of FRCF

5   Conclusions

In this paper, we present an effective approach to use data features and ratings together for CF. We set the weights of the features in CF by prediction models like logistic regression, and we also propose a Bayesian way to compute the similarity between users. Then, we perform two experiments to verify that our methods can behave better than conventional CF and other methods in the case of sparse data. In the future, we'll explore CF with complex features which can exist in many situations.

Acknowledgements. The author gratefully acknowledges the generous support from the Doctoral Fund of Shandong Jianzhu University (XNBS1527).

References

1. Terveen, L., Hill, W.: Beyond recommender systems: helping people help each other. In: HCI in the New Millennium, p. 6. Addison-Wesley (2001)
2. Linden, G., York, J.: Amazon.com recommendations: item-to-item collaborative filtering. IEEE Internet Comput. **7**(1), 76–80 (2003)
3. Su, X., Khoshgoftaar, T.: A survey of collaborative filtering techniques. Adv. Artif. Intell. **2009**, 19 (2009)
4. Resnick, P., Iacovou, N., Suchak, M., Bergstrom, P., Riedl, J.: GroupLens: an open architecture for collaborative filtering of netnews. In: Proceedings of the ACM Conference on Computer Supported Cooperative Work (1994)
5. Konstan, T., Miller, B., Maltz, D., Herlacker, J., Gordon, L., Riedl, J.: GroupLens: applying collaborative filtering to usenet news. Commun. ACM **40**(3), 77–87 (1997)
6. Delgado, J.: Agent-based information filtering and recommender systems on the Internet. Ph.D. thesis, Nagoya Institute of Technology (2000)

7. Xue, G., Lin, C., Yang, Q., Xi, W., Zeng, H., Yu, Y., Chen, Z.: Scalable collaborative filtering using cluster-based smoothing. In: Proceedings of the 28th Annual International ACM SIGIR Conference on Research and Development in Information Retrieval, pp. 114–121. ACM (2005)

8. Li, B., Yang, Q., Xue, X.: Can movies and books collaborate? cross-domain collaborative filtering for sparsity reduction. In: IJCAI-09, vol. 9, pp. 2052–2057 (2009)

9. Herlocker, J.L., Konstan, J.A., Borchers, A., Riedl, J.: An algorithmic framework for performing collaborative filtering. In: Proceedings of the Conference on Research and Development in Information Retrieval (SIGIR 1999), pp. 230–237 (1999)

10. Chee, S.H.S., Han, J., Wang, K.: RecTree: an efficient collaborative filtering method. In: Kambayashi, Y., Winiwarter, W., Arikawa, M. (eds.) DaWaK 2001. LNCS, vol. 2114, pp. 141–151. Springer, Heidelberg (2001). https://doi.org/10.1007/3-540-44801-2_15

11. Breese, J., Heckerman, D., Kadie, C.: Empirical analysis of predictive algorithms for collaborative filtering. In: Proceedings of the 14th Conference on Uncertainty in Artificial Intelligence (UAI 1998) (1998)

12. Su, X., Khoshgoftaar, T.M., Greiner, R.: A mixture imputation-boosted collaborative filter. In: Proceedings of the 21th International Florida Artificial Intelligence Research Society Conference (FLAIRS 2008), Coconut Grove, Fla, USA, pp. 312–317, May 2008

13. Goldberg, K., Roeder, T., Gupta, D., Perkins, C.: Eigentaste: a constant time collaborative filtering algorithm. Inf. Retr. 4(2), 133–151 (2001)

14. Fisher, D., Hildrum, K., Hong, J., Newman, M., Thomas, M., and Vuduc, R.: SWAMI: a framework for collaborative filtering algorithm development and evaluation. In: Proceedings of the 23rd Annual International Conference on Researech and Development in Information Retrieval (SIGIR) (2000)

15. Najafabadi, M.K., Mahrin, M.N.R., Chuprat, S., Sarkan, H.M.: Improving the accuracy of collaborative filtering recommendations using clustering and association rules mining on implicit data. Comput. in Hum. Behav. 67, 113–128 (2017)

16. Melville, P., Mooney, R.J., Nagarajan, R.: Content boosted collaborative filtering for improved recommendations. In: Proceedings of the 18th National Conference on Artificial Intelligence (AAAI 2002), Edmonton, Canada, pp. 187–192 (2002)

17. Greinemr, R., Su, X., Shen, B., Zhou, W.: Structural extension to logistic regression: discriminative parameter learning of belief net classifiers. Mach. Learn. 59(3), 297–322 (2005)

18. Yahoo! Webscope movie data set. http://research.yahoo.com

A Collaborative Filtering Algorithm Based on Attribution Theory

Mao DeLei[1(✉)], Tang Yan[1], and Liu Bing[1,2]

[1] Southwest University, Chongqing 400715, China
mdelei@163.com
[2] Dazhou Vocational and Technical College, Dazhou 635001, Sichuan, China

Abstract. The Collaborative filtering algorithm predicts the user's preference for the project to complete a recommendation by analyzing the user preference data, and usually takes the user's rating as the user preference data. However, there is a bias between user's preference and user's score of the real scene, so the user's rating as user preference can lead to lower recommendation accuracy. For this problem, this paper proposes a user preference extraction method based on attribution theory, calculates user preferences by analyzing user rating behavior. Then, combining preference similarity and rate similarity, making up the bias between user rating and user preference in collaborative filtering algorithm. Experimental verification on universal Dataset Movies lens-1m results shows that the algorithm is preferable to the existing collaborative filtering algorithm.

Keywords: Attribution theory · User preference · Collaborative filtering
Recommender system

1 Introduction

The personalized recommendation system is a type of business intelligence platform based on massive data mining, which provides personalized information service and decision support to users through the recommendation algorithm [1]. The collaborative filtering algorithm was first proposed in the 1992 Year by the Goldberg [2]. It is a part of the most widely used personalized recommendation algorithms at present. The collaborative filtering algorithm finds users with similar interests through analyzing user preference data, and recommends interesting items to users based on the association with similar users. The most influential source of user preference data is the user - project rating, thus highlighting two issues: 1. Incomplete rating data leads to sparse user preference data; 2. user ratings and user preferences may have a bias. The above problems lead to the lack of recommendation accuracy of collaborative filtering algorithm, and there are still some defects in the cold-start [3].

For all aspects of collaborative filtering algorithm, researchers propose various methods to improve the collaborative filtering algorithm. Son [4] presented a method for fusing fuzzy similarity-based on user features and user similarity-based on historical rating. Joshi [5] proposed an asynchronous stochastic gradient collaborative filtering algorithm based on matrix decomposition, and the rating matrix is distributed on

© Springer International Publishing AG, part of Springer Nature 2018
Y. Tan et al. (Eds.): ICSI 2018, LNCS 10942, pp. 295–304, 2018.
https://doi.org/10.1007/978-3-319-93818-9_28

different machines, the parameters are updated by stochastic gradient optimization in the network. In addition, a regularization method based on similarity is introduced. Kim [6] proposed a Bayesian binomial mixed-model for collaborative filtering, modeling the missing data through three factors related to users, projects, and rating values. Hofmann [7] referred to the LSI in information retrieval (Latent Semantic Indexing) technology, used subspace instead of the original data set to improve the feasibility of locating neighbors. The above research work has improved the cold-start problem and the algorithm accuracy by diverse methods. However, there are no analysis and improvement of the bias between user ratings and user preferences. Therefore, this paper analyzes and improves the bias in order to increase the accuracy of the algorithm.

Bias between user ratings and user preferences means that same ratings reflect different degrees of user preference. This bias does exist, because according to the attribution theory, people's behavior will be influenced by consistency, distinctiveness, social expectations, positive and negative preferences and other factors. It is caused by the above factors that even the same user rating may reflect different user preferences. For example: (1) A and B, two users have different rating habits, A user is accustomed to low ratings, B user is accustomed to high ratings; (2) A user more objective, even user do not like the item that is still given an objective rating, B user will only give a low rating on items he do not like; (3) A user will give high scores because of their behavior, B users will not; Analysis of the above situations, A and B, two users will reflect different preferences on the same rating.

Owing to the bias between user ratings and user preferences, a collaborative filtering algorithm based on attribution theory is proposed (AT-CF). Firstly, the user's rating behavior is analyzed by attribution theory, and the user preference is extracted. Attribution theory analysis user rating behavior that involves three of information, namely: Consensus, Distinctiveness, positive and negative preference, with these three information to quantify user preferences. Then, combining preference similarity and rating similarity, we can compensate for the bias between user's rating and user preference in collaborative filtering algorithm. Improve collaborative filtering algorithm (AT-CF) compare with traditional CF, HU-FCF [4], SGO Based regularization [5] BM/CPT-v [6]. The test results demonstrate that the ATP-CF has a better recommended effect, and an average absolute error (MAE) with a smaller value.

2 Related Theories

2.1 Collaborative Filtering Algorithm

Collaborative filtering algorithm was proposed in 1992 Year by Goldberg [2] to develop the recommendation system Tapestry. So far, it is still the most widely personalized recommendation technology. The algorithm analysis user preference data, mining the similarity between users for predicting the user's preference to complete a recommendation. When the similarity between users is computed, these methods are generally used, such as modified cosine similarity, Jaccard, Pearson correlation coefficient and so on. A brief idea of collaborative filtering algorithm the following Fig. 1:

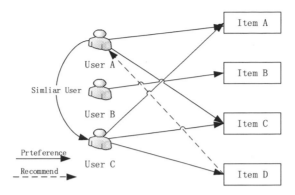

Fig. 1. Method of collaborative filtering algorithm

As a result of the high application value and research value of the collaborative filtering algorithm, the research on collaborative filtering has traditionally been hot. In the recommended systems for well-known web sites such as Amazon.com, Taobao.com, YouTube, Collaborative filtering algorithm is the major components. In academic research, ACM recommender system (recsys), ACM SIGIR, AI Communications, IEEE Intelligent Systems related to the recommendation system, there are often articles published on research and improvement of collaborative filtering algorithms.

In contemporary research of collaborative filtering algorithm, a lot of new methods and new ideas are proposed, and the algorithm is improved better. However, it ignores the possible bias between user rating and user preference. Therefore, this paper analyzes the bias to improve the accuracy of the algorithm.

2.2   Attribution Theory

As the subject of cognitive activity, people will be corresponding behavior in the specific environment structure, and the attribution theory is the method to analyze this behavior process [10]. Jones and K.E. Davis proposed an attribution method called corresponding inference, which presents the concept of societal expectation. The corollary says to be difficult to infer people's true attitude when their behavior meets society expectation. Therefore, positive and negative user preferences can be inferred by societal expectations.

Kelly's three-dimensional attribution theory suggests that attribution of behavior to people always involves three factors: (1) actors; (2) objective stimuli; (3) The relationship or environment. Attribution to the above three factors depends on the following three behavioral messages: (1) Consensus: Refers to whether other people have the same reaction to the same stimuli as the actors. (2) Distinctiveness: Whether the performer responds to similar stimuli in the same way. (3) Consistency: Refers to whether the actors in an environment and at any time have same response to the unified stimulus, and the behavior of the actors is stable and durable.

Kelly thinks that these three aspects of information constitute a covariant three-dimensional framework. So depending on the above three kinds of behavioral information, we can attribute the action of people to actors, objective stimuli or environment.

It is because attribution theory may infer the exact attitude of people's behavior, so the bias between user rating and user preference can be compensated by analysis the user rating behavior. Attributed user rating behavior to the actors, i.e. the user's preference affected the rating behavior. Therefore, we can quantify user preferences through Consensus, Distinctiveness, and societal expectations (positive and negative preferences) mentioned above.

3 Collaborative Filtering Algorithm Based on Attribution Theory

To solve the bias between user rating and user preference, this paper proposes a collaborative filtering algorithm based on attribution theory (AT-CF). AT-CF algorithm analyzes three types of user rating behavior information: consistency, distinctiveness, positive and negative preference. Calculating these three behavioral information, and combination of three kinds of behavioral information to quantify user preferences, so as to better reflect the user's real preferences. The method of weighted fusion of rating similarities and preference similarities can compensate for bias between user rating and user preferences. Calculating the nearest neighbor set of the user, predict the rating of the target user on the unrated item.

3.1 Attribution Theory Extract User Preference

In order to extract user preference, the attribution theory is utilized to analyze the user rating behavior, which involves three kinds of behavioral information: Consensus, Distinctiveness and positive and negative preference.

Consensus

Consensus [10] refers to the deviation between user and other users in rating item. The greater the deviation, the lower the Consensus, and when the Consensus is low, it may reflect the user's preference for the item. Consensus is measured by mean square root error, the greater the mean square root error, the smaller the Consensus. Calculate Consensus by formula (1):

$$Consensus(u, i) = \sqrt{\frac{\sum_{v \in V_{ui}} (r_u - r_v)^2}{n}} \tag{1}$$

Parameter description in the formula (1): v_{ui} represent user collection with other user rate the same item, r_u, r_v Represents a user rating, n is the number of v_{ui}.

Distinctiveness

Distinctiveness [10] refers to the rating deviation of similarity item. The smaller the deviation of the user's rating in similar items, the lower distinctiveness, and it can reflect the user's preference towards the project. Similarly, the mean square root error is used to compute the distinctiveness, as showed in the formula (2):

$$Distinctiveness(u, i) = \sqrt{\frac{\sum_{C_i \in I_{sim(i)}} (r_{ui} - r_{uC_i})^2}{n}}$$

(2)

Parameter description in the formula: $I_{sim(i)}$ represents a collection of similar items, $r_{ui} r_{uC_i}$ represents a user rating for similar item, n represents the number of similar items.

For the experimental data in this paper, the categories of movies processed as a dimension vector of a category feature, represented by a matrix Category. A row of a matrix represents an item, the column represents a category label for the item. Calculate the category similarity of the item by using of formula (3). N item with the highest similarity to the project is then taken as a collection of similar items, the in formula 2.

$$Category = \begin{pmatrix} 100000001000000100 \\ 000000001000000001 \\ 000100000000001000 \\ \vdots \\ 010000000000000000 \end{pmatrix}$$

(3)

$$Similarity(I_a, I_b) = \frac{1}{5} \left(\overrightarrow{I_a} \cdot \overrightarrow{I_b} \right)$$

Positive or Negative Preferences

The societal expectation of an item is to distinguish the positive and negative preferences. The difference between user's rating and social expectation indicates the user's preference to item. The social expectation score value of the item is calculated by a weighted average, as showed in the formula (4): Positive and negative preferences such as Formula (5):

$$ERate(i) = \frac{\sum_{j=1}^{5} n_j \times j}{n}$$

(4)

$$Preference(u, i) = r_{ui} - ERate(i)$$

(5)

User Preference Extraction

To sum up, three informations about user rating behavior is extracted by attribution theory: positive and negative preference, Consensus, Distinctiveness. By using the formula (6), compute the attribution theory user preference (ATP):

$$ATP = \begin{cases} Preference + Consensus + Distinctiveness & Preference > 0 \\ Preference - Consensus - Distinctiveness & Preference < 0 \end{cases}$$

(6)

3.2   Similarity Fusion

Although the bias between user ratings and user preferences is a problem, they are still in line with a positive correlation. Therefore, the preference similarity cannot replace the rating similarity, through fusion preference similarity and rating similarity, to compensate for the bias between user ratings and user preferences.

Rating Similarity Usage Pearson Similarity [11] to calculate, Pearson similarity is a central to the user's rating interval when processing the rating data, which may avoid the differences caused by different rating habits. Such as formulas (7):

$$Sim_{Rcore}(u,v) = \frac{\sum_{i \in I_{uv}} (r_{ui} - \overline{r_u})(r_{vi} - \overline{r_v})}{\sqrt{\sum_{i \in I_{uv}} (r_{ui} - \overline{r_u})^2} \sqrt{\sum_{i \in I_{uv}} (r_{vi} - \overline{r_v})^2}} \tag{7}$$

The calculated data of the preference similarity are derived from the user preference extracted by the attribution theory, using the Adjusted Cosine [11] calculates preference similarity. The Adjusted Cosine can take into account the two directions of user preference, namely: positive and negative preference, and the degree of user preference. Such as formulas (8):

$$Sim_{ATP}(u,v) = \frac{\sum_{i \in I_{uv}} (r_{ui} - \overline{r_u})(r_{vi} - \overline{r_v})}{\sqrt{\sum_{i \in I_u} (r_{ui} - \overline{r_u})^2} \sqrt{\sum_{i \in I_v} (r_{vi} - \overline{r_v})^2}} \tag{8}$$

Formula (7) and (8) parameter Description: I_{uv} is the collection that users collectively rating, I_u, I_v is the collection that users rating for item, r_{ui}, r_{vi} are users rating for item, $\overline{r_u}$, $\overline{r_v}$ are users average rating for item.

When fusion rating similarity and preference similarity, α and β parameters controls the weight of two similarity fusion, and the similarity fusion takes the formula (9):

$$Sim(u,v) = \alpha * Sim_{ATP}(u,v) + \beta * Sim_{Raing}(u,v) - (1 - \alpha - \beta)Sim_{ATP}(u,v)$$
$$\cdot Sim_{Rating}(u,v) \tag{9}$$

3.3   AT-CF Algorithm

The collaborative filtering algorithm based on attribution theory (AT-CF) is implemented by Pseudo code, as shown in Table 1:

Table 1. AT-CF is implemented by Pseudo code

Require: R, r_{ui}, $r_{ui} \in R$
  1: R Rating matrix
  2: r_{ui} Predicted score
  3: U User
  4: I Item
Ensure: AT-CF
  5: for $u \in U$, $i \in I$ do
  6: calculate $Consensus(u, i)$,$Distinctiveness(u, i)$, $Preference(u, i)$
      by Attribution Theory.
      Calculate **ATP** by formula (6).
  7: End for
  8: for $u, v \in U \wedge u \neq v$ do
  9:    Calculate ATP Similarity: $Sim_{ATP}(u, v)$
        Calculate rating Similarity: $Sim_{Rating}(u, v)$
  10: end for
  11: Calculate Similarity Fusion $Sim(u, v)$ by formula (9).
  12: Select the nearest user collection:$N(u)$
  13: for $v \in N(u)$ do
  14:    $RatingSum$+= $Sim(u, v) \times r_{vi}$
         $SimSum$+= $Sim(u, v)$
  15: end for
  16: $r_{ui} = \frac{RatingSum}{SimSum}$

---

4 Experiment

4.1 Dataset

Movie lens-1m [12] provided by the Group Lens project team, 6040 User rate 3952 item. It is widely used in recommendation system evaluation, and the sparsity is higher 95.8%. The dataset is split into training sets and test sets, each accounting for 80% and 20%. Since dataset are extremely sparse and divided into training and test sets, there is no over fitting problem. In the experiment, using Training sets to predict the rating of un-rating item, and then comparing actual rating with the predict rating in test sets.

4.2 Evaluation Criteria

MAE (mean absolute error) is the average of the absolute error, which can reflect the actual situation of predictive error. The smaller the value of MAE, the higher accuracy of the algorithm. As follows formula (10):

$$MAE = \frac{1}{N} \sum |r_{pi} - r_i| \tag{10}$$

Formula parameter Description: r_{pi} represents a predictive rating for item, MAE represents the true rating of item.

4.3   Experiment Result

Comparing AT-CF with Traditional CF

In order to verify the AT-CF algorithm proposed in this paper, AT-CF is compared with the traditional collaborative filtering algorithm that with Adjust cosine similarity and Pearson similarity. In the experiment, the nearest neighbor number of users is 5, 10, 15, 20, 25, 30, 35, 40, 45, 50, which compares the recommended effect of ATP-CF and traditional collaborative filtering algorithm under different nearest neighbor values. The comparison result is displayed in Fig. 2.

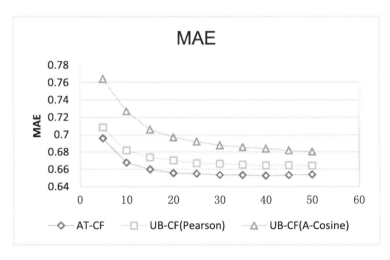

Fig. 2. MAE value of AT-CF and the traditional CF

Comparing with the collaborative filtering algorithm which uses the Adjust cosine similarity, the accuracy of algorithm increase 3%. Comparing with Pearson's similarity-based collaborative filtering algorithm, the accuracy of algorithm increase 1.5%.

Comparing AT-CF with Exiting CF

In order to test the optimization degree of AT-CF algorithm, the paper compares the algorithm with extra research work. The object of comparison: Son HU-FCF [4] (2014), bikash Joshi SGO Based regularization [5] BM/CPT-v (2016), Kim [6] (2014). The consequence is the following Fig. 3.

Influence of α and β

The parameters α and β in the formula (9) are controlled, and α and β represent the respective weights when the similarity of the score and the preference similarity are merged. Figure 4 display the results of the experiments where the nearest neighbor number is 5 when α = [0.1 1] and β = [0.1 1]. When the nearest neighbor number is not 5, the trend of algorithm is still following the Fig. 4.

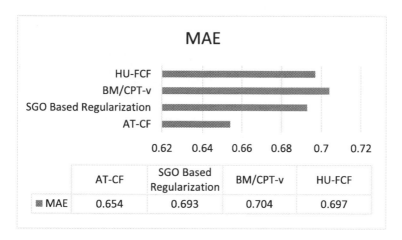

	AT-CF	SGO Based Regularization	BM/CPT-v	HU-FCF
▨ MAE	0.654	0.693	0.704	0.697

Fig. 3. MAE value of AT-CF and the exiting CF

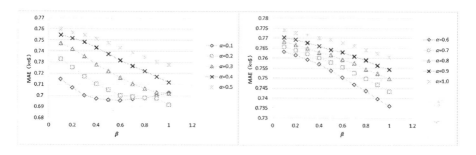

Fig. 4. Influence of α and β

As can be seen in Fig. 4, for each combination of parameters, as the β increases, the MAE value decreases and the test result gets better. When α = 0.1 and β = 0.6, the MAE value is the smallest, and the test result is the best. Therefore, the experiment part is carried out under the condition of this parameter.

Experiments show that the accuracy of AT-CF algorithm is increased by 4%–5% of MAE, when the similarity fusion parameters α = 0.1 and β = 0.6. Therefore, the AT-CF algorithm utilizes the attribution theory to analyze consistency, distinctiveness, positive and negative preferences, and can indeed quantify user preferences better. The weighted method between rating similarity and preference similarity can compensate for user's bias and user's preference.

5 Conclusion

This paper proposes a collaborative filtering algorithm based on attribution theory. We use three types of behavior information to analyze the user rating behavior: positive and negative preferences, consistency and distinctiveness. To some extent, the method of combining the rating similarity of preference similarity can compensate for the bias between user's rating and user's preference. Experimental results on the Movies Lens dataset show that the AT-CF algorithm has a better recommendation and the recommendation accuracy is increased by 4%–5%.

Because Kelly's attribution theory overemphasizes logic and makes it idealistic, Kelly supplements several principles such as the principle of reinforcement and the principle of compensation, and further work needs to consider such factors as the principle of enhancement. And, in many cases cannot get the relevant behavioral information. In this regard, further work must take into account the additional information and environmental aspects of the actors involved references.

References

1. Jie, L., Dianshuang, W., Mao, M., Wang, W., Zhang, G.: Recommender system application developments: a survey. Inf. Syst. **74**(4), 12–32 (2015)
2. Goldberg, D., Nichols, D., Oki, B.M., et al.: Using collaborative filtering to weave an information tapestry. Commun. ACM **35**(12), 61–70 (1992)
3. Son, L.H.: Dealing with the new user cold-start problem in recommender systems: a comparative review. Inf. Syst. **58**(5), 87–104 (2016)
4. Son, L.H.: HU-FCF: A hybrid user-based fuzzy collaborative filtering method in recommender system. Expert Syst. Appl. **41**(5), 6861–6870 (2014)
5. Joshi, B., Iutzeler, F., Amini, M.R.: Asynchronous distributed matrix factorization with similar user and item based regularization. In: ACM Conference on Recommender Systems, pp. 75–78 (2016)
6. Kim, Y.D., Choi, S.: Bayesian binomial mixture model for collaborative prediction with non-random missing data. In: ACM Conference on Recommender Systems, pp. 201–208 (2014)
7. Hofmann, T.: Latent semantic models for collaborative filtering. ACM Trans. Inf. Syst. (TOIS) **22**(1), 89–115 (2004)
8. Zou, C., Zhang, D., Wan, J., Hassan, M.M., Llloret, J.: Using concept lattice for personalized recommendation system design. IEEE Syst. J. **11**(1), 305–314 (2017)
9. Patra, B.K., Launonen, R., Ollikainen, V., Nandi, S.: A new similarity measure using bhattacharyya coefficient for collaborative filtering in sparse data. Knowl.-Based Syst. **82**(7), 163–177 (2015)
10. Kelley, H.H.: Attribution theory in social psychology. Nebr. Symp. Motiv. **15**(6), 192–238 (1967)
11. Sarwar, B., Karypis, G., Konstan, J., Riedl, J.: Item-based collaborative filtering recommendation algorithms. In: International Conference on World Wide Web, vol. 4(1), pp. 285–295 (2001)
12. Harper, F.M., Konstan, J.A.: The movie lens datasets: history and context. ACM **5**(4), 19 (2015)

Investigating the Effectiveness of Helpful Reviews and Reviewers in Hotel Industry

Yen Tzu Chao[1], Ping Yu Hsu[1], Ming Shien Cheng[2(✉)],
Hong Tsuen Lei[1], Shih Hsiang Huang[1], Yen-Huei Ko[1],
Grandys Frieska Prassida[1], and Chen Wan Huang[1]

[1] Department of Business Administration, National Central University, No. 300,
Jhongda Rd., Jhongli City, Taoyuan County 32001, Taiwan (R.O.C.)
984401019@cc.ncu.edu.tw
[2] Department of Industrial Engineering and Management,
Ming Chi University of Technology, No. 84, Gongzhuan Rd., Taishan Dist.,
New Taipei City 24301, Taiwan (R.O.C.)
mscheng@mail.mcut.edu.tw

Abstract. With the growth of e-commerce, online consumer reviews have become important attributes that influence purchasing decisions. Especially, hotel industry has strongly influenced by online reviews due that most tourists cannot experience all hotels personally and the service levels among hotels are very different. However, the flood of online consumer reviews has caused information overload, making it difficult for consumers to choose reliable reviews. Therefore, helpful remarks of hotel review should potentially have strong influence on users. Previous research focused on how to predict the helpful scores of reviews, but it has not explored the influence of reviews marked with helpfulness. The aim of this study is to investigate whether the helpful reviews and reviewers who contribute many reviews really have effects on the marks hotel received. With analysis of reviews contributed in Tripadvisor.com for three hundred hotels scattered in ten cities of U.S., this study found both reviewer contribution, and helpful review has a positive effect on marks of hotels. Moreover, the research also discovered that the helpfulness of reviews is negatively relates to the ratings. Also, the research found that the standard deviation of review mark is positively relates to hotel ranks.

Keywords: Online ratings · Helpful reviews · On-line hotel reviews
Tripadvisor

1 Introduction

The tourism and hotel industry provide intangible services, falling under short-term experiential consumption. Consumers are quite dependent on Internet word-of-mouth when making a purchasing decision. The survey results show that among consumers', most searched hotel community websites and review websites, Trip Advisor and AAA websites rank the highest. In the past, factors affecting helpful reviews showed contradictions. Some scholars studied important factors affecting helpful reviews, such as review characteristics, product type, review length, and so on, all of which intended to find factors affecting consumers' determination of helpful reviews. Travel review websites often use "helpful reviews" as indicators that aid in evaluating review quality. Other studies found that "rating" directly affected sales, rating and sales showed non-linear growth. A high rating does not affect high sales. When the rating is between 4.2 and 4.5, it means positive reviews affect sales and consumers' purchase rate increases.

Therefore, the purpose of this study is to explore whether reviews labeled "helpful" affect hotel owners, thereby exploring whether the influence of message senders affect hotel owners. The hotel reviews targeting the top ten popular scenic spots in North America on global travel review website Trip Advisor will adopted as research participants.

This paper organized as follow: (1) Introduction: research background, motivation and purpose. (2) Related work: a review of attributes of helpful reviews and message senders. (3) Research methodology: content of research process in this study. (4) Statistical analysis: experimental results and the discussion of the test results; (5) Conclusion and future research: contribution of the study and possible future research direction is discussed.

2 Related Work

2.1 Attributes of Helpful Reviews

According to a survey report of TheSkift.com, Internet reviews are one of the top three important factors for hotel reservations. About 89% global travelers and 64% global hotel owners find Internet reviews to have an influence on hotel reservations. Helpful voting is the most commonly used indicator for consumers to measure whether a review is helpful. Therefore, many scholars are searching which reviews are helpful. As showed in Table 1, numerous previous studies carried out research targeting factors voted as helpful reviews. Hence, five factors would compiled in this study: message sender characteristic, review rating, and review characteristic such as emotional characteristic, readability, and quality.

In view of past scholars' research that explore helpful review attributes, it was found that message sender characteristics, review ratings, the emotional characteristics of review contents, readability, and quality factors are all relevant factors affecting helpful reviews. This study explored whether helpful reviews and message senders produce actual impacts on consumers, which have a complementary relationship with the factors found above. In this paper, Trip Advisor travel reviews were adopted as examples. According to information provided in reviews, including the "like" clicks the review receives, review rating, the "like" clicks the message sender receives, and the message sender's total review contribution quantity divided into review attributes and message sender attributes.

Table 1. Summary of helpful review attributes in past research

Research	A	S	R	Q	F	Product	Source
Kim et al. (2006) [5]	✓	✓		✓		MP3/Digital Camera	Amazon
Ghose and Ipeirotis (2007) [4]	✓	✓	✓	✓	✓	Video Player/Digital Camera/Video CD	Amazon
Liu et al. (2007) [6]		✓	✓	✓		Digital Camera	Amazon
Otterbacher (2009) [10]	✓		✓	✓	✓	Electronic Product/Video CD/Software	Amazon
O'Mahony and Smyth (2010) [9]	✓	✓		✓		Hotels	TripAdvisor
Mudambi and Schuff (2010) [8]				✓	✓	MP3/Video CD/Video Game Console/ Smart Phone/Digital Camera/Laser Printer	Amazon
Cao et al. (2011) [1]				✓	✓	News	CNET
Pan and Zhang (2011) [11]	✓			✓	✓	Video CD/Video Game Console/Electronic Product/Software/Health Care Products	Amazon

2.2 Review Attributes and the Attributes of Message Senders Adopted in This Study

Review attributes divided into review ratings and the review "like" clicks a review receives. Review rating is the most direct expression of a review's product attitude. On the other hand, "like" clicks indicate consumers find information provided in a review to be helpful.

1. Review Rating: When the consumer browses reviews on a review website, compared to review contents, review ratings had better enable consumers to obtain information within a short period time. Review ratings are usually review indicators, ranking from ratings of 1–5 that represent a comprehensive assessment of a product or service [11]. Since consumers' time and attention are limited, it is more difficult to read all determinable items in a large quantity of reviews. With simplified numerical values, information could easily understand, thus reducing information-processing complexity. This study deems "rating" to facilitate consumers' quick reading of product information contained in the Internet reviews with an information overload.

2. Review "Like" Clicks: Review websites assist consumers in speeding up purchase decision-making. After the consumer finished viewing others' reviews and found the information in a review to be helpful to consumers, the "voting" function used to inform consumers the review is a helpful one. When a review voted by consumers to be helpful, it means: (1) the review has been read; (2) the review is valuable to consumers and may affect purchase decision-making; (3) the review can

provide more information compared to reviews with no vote. Hence, this study deems that the "like" clicking behavior of consumers after reading a review indicates the review was helpful to consumers.

At present, many eWOM researches involve user contribution behaviors, such as their sharing motivation or self-awareness [3, 12] found in their study that the message sender's characteristics change with varied degrees of contribution, indicating relevance between the message sender's contribution degree and the message sender's characteristics. According to [2], users' information shared on social networking platforms or review websites affect consumers' decision prior to making a purchase. This paper deems that when the message sender shares personal experience, knowledge, or feelings for a particular field, the higher the information contribution, the higher the involvement in the field and more knowledge and experiences accumulated.

3   Research Methodology

The research process is showing in the following Fig. 1. Firstly, we describe the data selection, then depict the selection of reviews and preprocessing, finally describe the definition of variable.

Fig. 1.   Research process

1. Data Source Selection: Trip Advisor is an American travel website, the largest travel website in the world with over 3.15 members and more than 46.5 billion entries of hotels, restaurants, and travel scenic spots, as well as other related travel store comments and reviews. The survey by [7] shows that among the hotel review websites most frequently searched by consumers, Trip Advisor website has the highest ranking.
2. Number of Reviews Selected: Targeting hotel reviews on Trip Advisor, this study adopted the top travel scenic spots in North American regions as the data sources. Therefore, in this paper, the top 30 hotel reviews will select, and the total reviews for each hotel totaled about 800 to 1500 entries. About 1/10 of the total reviews was selected for each hotel, accounting for approximately 80 entries. Hence, the reviews for each region were about just over 2400 entries of review information.
3. Data Preprocessing: Repeated reviews, and review ratings with null values will delete. Reviews or message senders without receiving any likes will directly set zero. Table 2 shows the data after compiling the ten data sets.

Table 2. The top 10 most popular North American hotel reviews after arranging

Rank	City	Deleted entries	Data volume	Messages volume
1	New York City	6	2,383	2,364
2	Houston	5	2,381	2,372
3	Los Angeles	6	2,394	2,372
4	San Antonio	19	2,382	2,363
5	San Diego	22	2,779	2,761
6	Orlando	14	2,386	2,368
7	San Francisco	10	2,391	2,373
8	New Orleans	11	2,390	2,378
9	Miami Beach	5	2,396	2,354
10	Las Vegas	10	2,393	2,381

4. The Definition of Variable: Fig. 2 shows the column explored in this study includes hotel ranking, review rating, review helpfulness, etc.

Fig. 2. Review field of TripAdvisor correspond to the variable

(1). Hotel Ranking: According to the hotel popularity ranking algorithm provided by Trip Advisor official website, unlike other websites that rank hotels by price or hotel rating, Trip Advisor adopts message senders' rating as the hotel quality indicator. The quantity of reviewed hotels indicates travelers' comments and hotel information volume; the review newness indicates the newer a review the more it represents the hotel's actual recent situation, which is helpful for consumers. In view of the above-mentioned message sender rating, quantity of reviewed hotels, and review newness, the three items are popularity-ranking indicators that determine overall traveler satisfaction.

(2). Review Rating: This study deems that ratings can enable consumers to quick read product information from an overload of Internet review information. Rating and helpful reviews is related, as shown in Fig. 2. Review ratings designed beside reviews. While reading reviews, consumers can also quickly browse message senders' attitude towards a hotel. Review ratings represented by $s(r)$.

(3). Rating Differences: In this study, rating differences regarded to be influential to hotel owners. The rating difference of a particular review is the difference among all reviews after the review had published. In other words, the higher the rating difference, the greater the rating difference, the greater the rating difference between the particular review and a subsequent review. As far as hotel owners are concerned, that particular article is crucial; as it is the review that has a major impact on hotel owners. The rating difference formula defined as following.

$$\frac{\sum_{r_2 \in R, r_1 \ll r_2} s(r_2)}{|\{r_2|r_2 \in R, r_1 \ll r_2|} - s(r_1) \tag{1}$$

R: Review database; $r_1 \ll r_2$: the posting time of r_2 is after r_1

(4). Reviews with Helpfulness: This study deems that the "click like" indicator design for review websites to be intended to lead consumers into believing a particular review possesses helpfulness. After consumers' finish reading the review, they click "like" to show they find the review to be helpful. Review helpfulness and rating differences underwent relevant testing to test if the helpful reviews affected hotels.

(5.) Average Contribution of Message Senders: This study considers the total number of reviews of message senders as their degree of contribution. The average degree of contribution of the message sender represents the number of "like" clicks on each article of the message sender. The number of "like clicks" of the message sender divided by the message sender's total number of reviews to obtain the message sender's average contribution.

4   Statistical Analysis and Result

In this study, SPSS 20 statistical software employed to carry out correlation analysis. Based on the review ratings, the reviews were divided three parts: positive, neutral, and negative. Positive divided into four parts; neutral divided into three parts; negative is divided into two parts. Since the 1–5 rating limited by the system design, rating differences cannot reflect the impact on hotel owners, and thus excluded from the test. The review attributes were first tested. If a review possessed helpfulness, the message sender's attributes then examined, such as the correlation between the message sender's average contribution and rating difference. Whether or not the review and message sender attributes produced impacts on hotel owners examined.

1. According to Table 3(a), among the positive reviews, New York City, San Antonio, San Diego, San Francisco, New Orleans had significantly correlated relationships. Since the top 30 hotels in rank will selected from each region, the positive reviews were approximately five times more than the neutral reviews. On the other hand, the negative review entries were fewer than the neutral reviews, and thus excluded from the test. The results show that the positive review ratings showed a significantly positive correlation with rating difference in five regions. The neutral review ratings in the same region showed the same effect.

Table 3. Review helpfulness and rating differences correlated analysis

(a) Positive Review

ID	Dataset	Pearson correlation coefficient	Significant (two tail)
1	New York City	.183**	0
2	Houston	0.031	0.833
3	Los Angeles	0.255	0.174
4	San Antonio	.180*	0.033
5	San Diego	.204*	0.03
6	Orlando	0.012	0.951
7	San Francisco	.367*	0.036
8	New Orleans	.256**	0.003
9	Miami Beach	0.048	0.588
10	Las Vegas	0.113	0.511

(b) Neutral Review

ID	Dataset	Pearson correlation coefficient	Significant (two tail)
1	New York City	0.179	0.465
2	Houston	-0.467	0.204
4	San Antonio	0.183	0.286
6	Orlando	-0.046	0.992
7	San Francisco	.485**	0.003
8	New Orleans	0.185	0.287
9	Miami Beach	-0.157	0.243
10	Las Vegas	0	1

2. Correlated Testing of the Average Contribution of the Message Sender and the Rating Difference: According to Table 4(a–c), the positive reviews in three regions produced a significantly positive correlation. The neutral reviews in one region produced a significantly positive correlation; and two regions produced a significantly negative correlation. For the negative reviews, three regions produced a significantly negative correlation. That is, among positive reviews, the review has an influence as far as hotel owners are concerned. In negative reviews, other reviews following the said review also tend to lead to a negative hotel review.

Table 4. Average contribution of the message sender and the rating difference correlated analysis

(a) Positive Review

ID	Dataset	Pearson correlation coefficient	Significant (two tail)
1	New York City	.144*	0.022
2	Houston	-0.045	0.452
3	Los Angeles	0.01	0.846
4	San Antonio	0.05	0.73
5	San Diego	-0.044	0.366
6	Orlando	0.115	0.334
7	San Francisco	0.011	0.823
8	New Orleans	.240**	0.005
9	Miami Beach	0.006	0.919
10	Las Vegas	.100*	0.042

(b) Neutral Review

ID	Dataset	Pearson correlation coefficient	Significant (two tail)
1	New York City	0.283	0.062
2	Houston	-0.085	0.464
3	Los Angeles	0.196	0.081
4	San Antonio	0.134	0.572
5	San Diego	0.033	0.677
6	Orlando	.677*	0.045
7	San Francisco	0.032	0.772
8	New Orleans	-.294*	0.004
9	Miami Beach	-0.005	0.96
10	Las Vegas	.191*	0.039

(c) Negative Review

ID	Dataset	Pearson correlation coefficient	Significant (two tail)
1	New York City	-0.138	0.625
2	Houston	0.1	0.667
3	Los Angeles	-.734*	0.038
4	San Antonio	0.163	0.633
5	San Diego	0.109	0.722
6	Orlando	-.894*	0.016
7	San Francisco	0.289	0.097
8	New Orleans	-.319*	0.047
9	Miami Beach	-0.225	0.147
10	Las Vegas	-0.18	0.249

3. Correlated Testing of Helpfulness and Review Ratings: Table 5 shows that New York City, San Antonio, New Orleans, and Miami Beach regions showed a significantly negative correlation.

Table 5. Review helpfulness and review ratings correlated analysis

ID	Dataset	Pearson correlation coefficient	Significant (two tail)
1	New York City	−.212**	0
2	Houston	0.245	0.132
3	Los Angeles	0.04	0.688
4	San Antonio	−.182**	0
5	San Diego	0.002	0.969
6	Orlando	−0.09	0.324
7	San Francisco	−0.017	0.67
8	New Orleans	−.210**	0
9	Miami Beach	−.278**	0
10	Las Vegas	0.127	0.133

Table 6. Hotel ranking and hotel rating standard deviation correlated analysis

ID	Dataset	Pearson correlation coefficient	Significant (two tail)
1	New York City	.590**	0.001
2	Houston	.498**	0.005
3	Los Angeles	.509**	0.004
4	San Antonio	.604**	0
5	San Diego	.603**	0
6	Orlando	.596**	0.001
7	San Francisco	.494**	0.006
8	New Orleans	.490**	0.006
9	Miami Beach	0.079	0.68
10	Las Vegas	.499**	0.005

4. Correlated Testing of hotel ranking and Hotel Rating Standard Deviation: According to Table 6, nine regions are positive correlation.

Finally, this study further analyzed the correlation between rating and other variables. Reviews with helpfulness and review rating show a negative correlation, with four regions having a significant correlation, namely, New York City, San Antonio, New Orleans, and Miami Beach. As for the correlation between hotel rating and hotel ranking, it was found that hotel rating standard deviation and hotel ranking had a positive correlation, with nine significant regions. It means the farther back the hotel ranking, the greater the rating standard deviation and the more inconsistent the message senders' opinions. Table 7 shows the table of research test results.

Table 7. Research test results list

Testing result of variable correlation	No. of significant area
Review helpfulness and rating differences is positive correlated	6
Average contribution of the message sender and the rating difference is correlated (5 Positive, 4 Negative)	9
Review helpfulness and review ratings is negative correlated	4
Hotel ranking and hotel rating standard deviation is positive correlated	9
Hotel ranking and hotel positive and negative change frequency is positive correlated	8

5 Conclusion and Future Research

The study finding shows review "helpfulness" in positive and neutral reviews have an influence on hotel owners, while the message sender's "average contribution", whether in positive, neutral, or negative reviews, produce a significant relationship. It means higher message sender's average contribution leads to a positive and high hotel rating following a positive review; in a negative review scenario, consumers also give the hotel a negative review. Moreover, "helpfulness review" and "rating review" have a negative correlation, indicating the lower the review rating, the higher the review helpfulness. Furthermore, hotel rating standard deviation and hotel positive and negative change frequency can used to evaluate hotel ranking. The higher the hotel rating standard deviation and hotel positive and negative change frequency, the more inconsistent the hotel rating and the more unstable the hotel quality.

In the future hotels with lower rankings or hotels with lower total rankings may targeted to carry out relevant research. Extended discussions on reviews for other types of products, such as books, brands, electronic appliances, and cosmetics, may be included. This study recommends that in addition to considering review ratings, emotional characteristics as evaluation factors may also be included. Finally, this study suggests that the message sender's past experiences be included as a consideration.

References

1. Cao, Q., Duan, W., Gan, Q.: Exploring determinants of voting for the "helpfulness" of online user reviews: a text mining approach. Decis. Support Syst. **50**(2), 511–521 (2011)
2. Cheung, M.Y., Luo, C., Sia, C.L., Chen, H.: Credibility of electronic word-of- mouth: Informational and normative determinants of on-line consumer recommendations. Int. J. Electron. Commer. **13**(4), 9–38 (2009)
3. De Bruyn, A., Lilien, G.L.: A multi-stage model of word-of-mouth influence through viral marketing. Int. J. Res. Mark. **25**(3), 151–163 (2008)
4. Ghose, A., Ipeirotis, P.G.: Estimating the helpfulness and economic impact of product reviews: mining text and reviewer characteristics. IEEE Trans. Knowl. Data Eng. **23**(10), 1498–1512 (2011)
5. Kim, S.-M., Pantel, P., Chklovski, T., Pennacchiotti, M.: Automatically assessing review helpfulness. Paper presented at the Proceedings of the 2006 Conference on empirical methods in natural language processing (2006)
6. Liu, J., Cao, Y., Lin, C.-Y., Huang, Y., Zhou, M.: Low-quality product review detection in opinion summarization. Paper presented at the EMNLP-CoNLL (2007)
7. McCarthy, L., Stock, D., Verma, R,.: How travelers use online and social media channels to make hotel-choice decisions (2010)
8. Mudambi, S.M., Schuff, D.: What makes a helpful review? a study of customer reviews on Amazon.com (2010)
9. O'Mahony, M.P., Smyth, B.: A classification-based review recommender. Knowl.-Based Syst. **23**(4), 323–329 (2010)
10. Otterbacher, J.: 'Helpfulness' in online communities: a measure of message quality. Paper presented at the Proceedings of the SIGCHI conference on human factors in computing systems (2009)
11. Pan, Y., Zhang, J.Q.: Born unequal: a study of the helpfulness of user-generated product reviews. J. Retail. **87**(4), 598–612 (2011)
12. Rafaeli, S., Raban, D.R.: Information sharing online: a research challenge. Int. J. Knowl. Learn. **1**(1–2), 62–79 (2005)

Mapping the Landscapes, Hotspots and Trends of the Social Network Analysis Research from 1975 to 2017

Li Zeng[(✉)], Zili Li[(✉)], Zhao Zhao[(✉)], and Meixin Mao[(✉)]

College of Advanced Interdisciplinary Studies, National University of Defense Technology, Changsha 410073, China
`crack521@163.com, zilili@163.com, z_costa@163.com,`
`452368828@qq.com`

Abstract. A Bibliometric analysis was applied in this paper to quantitatively evaluate the social network analysis research from 1975 to 2017 based on 7311 bibliographic records collected from the Science Citation Index (SCI) database. Firstly, a comprehensive analysis was conducted to reveal the current landscapes such as scientific outputs, international collaboration, subject categories, and research performances by individuals, we then use innovative methods such as Burst Detection, Referenced Publication Years Spectroscopy and Keyword Semantic Clustering to provide a dynamic view of the evolution of social network analysis research hotpots and trends from various perspectives. Results shows that social network analysis research has developed rapidly in the past four decades and is in the growth period with a maturity of 50.00%, the total of 7311 articles cover 120 countries (regions) and the top five most productive countries are USA, England, China, Canada and Germany. Among the 1181 major journal related to social network analysis, University of Illinois, University of Sydney and Carnegie Mellon University ranked as the top three. In addition burst keywords such as Knowledge Management, Centrality, Modularity, Community, Link Prediction, Learning Analytics and Big Data demonstrate the trends of this field. The result provides a dynamic view of the evolution of Social Network Analysis research landscapes, hotspots and trends from various perspectives which may serve as a potential guide for future research.

Keywords: Social network analysis · Bibliometric · Research hotspots

1 Introduction

One of the most predominant perspectives in social science is that individuals are embedded tightly in social relations and interactions [1]. Social network analysis (SNA) theory provide a pathway to investigating such structures through the use of networks and graph theory [2]. Over last few decades, SNA had been widely resear-ched in many fields, such as Computer Science [3], Management [4], Education [5], Behavioral Ecology [6], Health [7], Psychology [8], Political [9] and so on. In fact, SNA is an old and yet hot field of research, which has gained huge popularity in these days. SNA has been researched with respect to theory and application. For example,

© Springer International Publishing AG, part of Springer Nature 2018
Y. Tan et al. (Eds.): ICSI 2018, LNCS 10942, pp. 314–325, 2018.
https://doi.org/10.1007/978-3-319-93818-9_30

Butts (2008) [10] review the fundamental concepts of social network analysis, as well as a range of methods currently used in the field. Borgatti (2009) [1] reviewed the kinds of things that social scientists have tried to explain using social network analysis and provide a nutshell description of the basic assumptions, goals, and explanatory mechanisms prevalent in the field. Besides these researches, a Bibliometric analysis of SNA could offer an innovative way of bringing to light global research landscapes, hotspots and trends in SNA and could may serve as a potential guide for future research, thus a scientometric review of the landscape and trend of published SNA research is performed by investigating annual scientific outputs, distribution of countries, institutions, journals, research performances by individuals and subject categories. Moreover, innovative methods such as Burst Detection, Referenced Publication Years Spectroscopy and Keyword Semantic Clustering with the aim to offer a dynamic view of the evolution of social network analysis research hotpots and trends from various perspectives.

2   Data and Methods

Samples are collected from Web of Science (WOS) of CLARIVATE ANALYTICS on December 31, 2017 and the time span is limited to 1975 and 2017. The query string looked like this: Topic: ("Social Network* Analy*") Indexes: SCI-EXPANDED, SSCI, A&HCI, CPCI-S, CPCI-SSH, BKCI-S, BKCI-SSH, ESCI, CCR-EXPANDED, and IC, Timespan = 1975–2017. After data reduction, 7311 bibliographic records were retrieved and downloaded. Then we used a Bibliometric approach to evaluate current research landscapes, hotspots and trends on SNA.

3   Result and Discussion

3.1   Characteristics of Article Outputs

In total, the average increase number about SNA research is 16.9 papers per year. From annual curve of research paper numbers (Fig. 1), we found that a substantial interest in SNA research did not emerge until 2006, although a few articles related to SNA were published previously. The peak of the annual number curve appears in 2016 which means that this fields is still very popular in recent times. According to the TRIZ theory [11], the evolution of a technology system goes through four stages: infancy, growth, maturity, and decline, and each stage presents different characteristics. In this paper, we use the logistic model [12] to fit the cumulative number curve which can evaluate the maturity of SNA, and the final fitting formula look like this: ($y = 12795.099/$ $(1 + e^{640.07 - 0.31749x})$ $r^2 = 0.9904$), where x denotes year and y denotes the article number. According to this formula, we divide the development of SNA into four stages: infant period (before 2006), growth period (2007–2023), mature period (2023–2028) and decline period (after 2028). According to the above stage division, the research of Social Network Analysis in 2017 was in the growth period with a maturity of 50.00%.

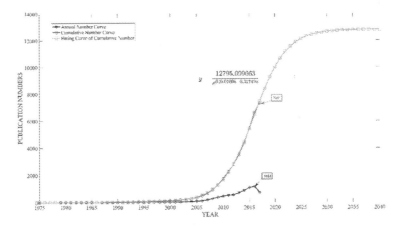

Fig. 1. Quantity change curve of literature

3.2   Characteristics of Document Type

The distribution of the document type was displayed in Fig. 2. Overall, the papers about Social Network Analysis Research involving a total of seventeen document types, and the details are as follows: Article (4183 papers, 57.22%), Proceedings Paper (2453 papers, 33.55%), Book Chapter (174 papers, 2.38%), Article & Proceedings Paper (154 papers, 2.11%), Review (146 papers, 2.00%), Others (201 papers, 0.92%). The distribution of document type suggested the high priority of Article and Proceedings Paper in the Social Network Analysis research.

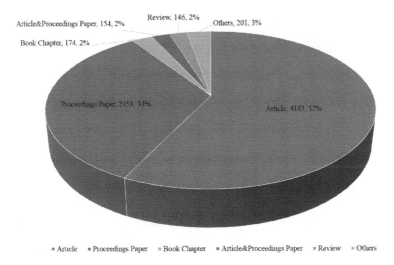

Fig. 2. Distribution of document type

3.3   Subject Categories Distribution and Co-occurring Network

The distribution of the subject categories identified by the Institute for Scientific Information (ISI) was analyzed and the result was displayed in Fig. 3. The total of 7311 articles covered 50 ISI identified subject categories in the SCI databases. The ten most common categories were Computer Science (2946 articles, 27.83%), Engineering (1105 articles, 10.44%), Business & Economics (804 articles, 7.59%), Information Science & Library Science (501 articles, 4.73%), Education & Educational Research (434 articles, 4.10%), Environmental Sciences & Ecology (389 articles, 3.67%), Psychology (377 articles, 3.56%), Science & Technology - Other Topics (305 articles, 2.88%), Sociology (297 articles, 2.81%) and Telecommunications (239 articles, 2.26%).

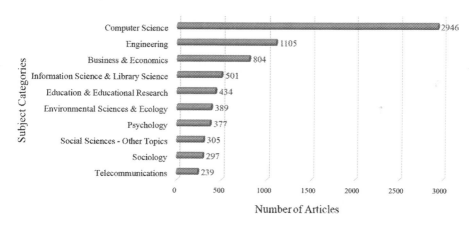

Fig. 3. Distribution of subject categories

In order to reveal temporal patterns of Subject Categories of SNA, we use the Theme River algorithm [13] to mining the literature of SNA between 1975 and 2017 (Fig. 4). Overall, SNA research involves more and more disciplines. Computer Science, Business & Economics, Engineering and Information Science & Library Science are the mainstream in this research field. As the time goes by, the proportion of these disciplines is also gradually increasing.

3.4   Geographic Distribution Map of Countries (Regions) and International Collaboration

Data on geographic information were generated from author affiliations. Figure 5 shows the geographic distribution of countries (regions) in the field of "SNA". From the figure, we can conclude that the authors of this field are mainly located in North America, Europe, Southeast Asia and Oceania. The total of 7311 articles covered 120 countries (regions) and the top five countries (regions) were USA with 1996 papers and 30756 citations, England with 556 with 8521 citations, China with 869 papers and 3341 citations, Canada with 358 papers and 4485 citations, Germany with 358 papers and 3422 citations.

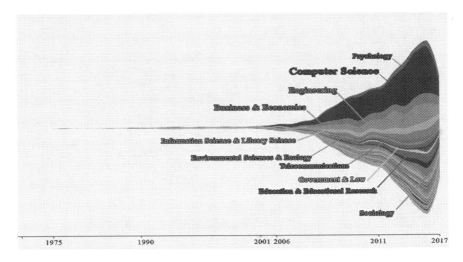

Fig. 4. Subject categories theme river between 1975 and 2017

In order to deeply explore the cooperation between countries (regions), we use VOSViewer [14] to visualize the Countries (Regions) collaboration network based on Co-authorship and use CiteSpace [15] to calculate the Network centrality and find the citation bursts of Countries (Regions). Network centrality measures the relative importance of nodes within networks and could be used as an indicator of a subject category's position within the network [16], while citation burst is a metric which can be used to find the research front [17]. We can find that the USA took part in more co-occurring relationship, with England, Canada and China as close neighbors (Fig. 6). In addition, five countries (regions) have citation bursts: USA (34.3242), ENGLAND (2.709), GERMANY (6.6941), HUNGARY (2.7465), and SLOVENIA (2.3191), suggesting that they have abrupt increases of citations, and the details are listed in the Table 1.

3.5   Institutions Distribution and Co-occurring Network

Overall, a total of 1181 research institutes in the world were engaged in Social Network Analysis Research during 1975 and 2017. And the top ten of them are: univ illinois (70 papers, 1390 citations), Univ Sydney (63 papers, 711 citations), Carnegie Mellon Univ (55 papers, 1905 citations), Arizona State Univ (54 papers, 626 citations), Univ Maryland (52 papers, 685 citations), Penn State Univ (51 papers, 240 citations), Univ Oxford (50 papers, 663 citations), Wroclaw Univ Technol (50 papers, 1513 citations), Wuhan Univ (46 papers, 856 citations) and Yeungnam Univ (45 papers, 228 citations). Obviously, most of the top 10 institutes come from the United States, indicating that USA occupies an important position in the field of SNA (Fig. 7).

Figure 8 shows the visualization of the distribution of institutions. In order to show the core institutions of this field, we filter out the institutions with small number of publications and get an institute co-occurring network with 494 nodes and 603 links. Obviously, Harvard Univ and Univ Minnesota are the earliest institutions involved in

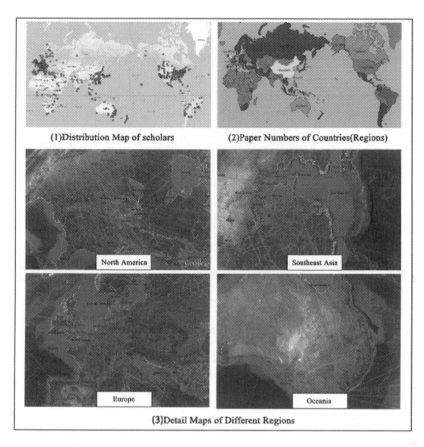

(1)Distribution Map of scholars

(2)Paper Numbers of Countries(Regions)

North America

Southeast Asia

Europe

Oceania

(3)Detail Maps of Different Regions

Fig. 5. Geographic distribution map of countries (regions)

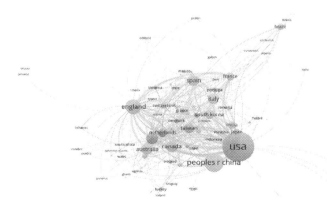

Fig. 6. Cooperation network of countries (regions) on SNA research papers

Table 1. Top five countries (regions) with strongest citation bursts.

Countries (regions)	Strength	Begin	End	1975 - 2017
USA	34.3242	1975	2004	▆▆▆▆▆▆▆▆▆▆▆▆▆▆▆▆▆▆▆▆▆▆▆▆▆▆▆▆▆▆▂▂▂▂▂▂▂▂
ENGLAND	2.709	1998	2001	▂▂▂▂▂▂▂▂▂▂▂▂▂▂▂▂▂▂▂▂▂▂▂▆▆▆▆▂▂▂▂▂▂▂▂▂▂
GERMANY	6.6941	2002	2006	▂▂▂▂▂▂▂▂▂▂▂▂▂▂▂▂▂▂▂▂▂▂▂▂▂▆▆▆▆▆▂▂▂▂▂▂
HUNGARY	2.7465	2005	2009	▂▂▂▂▂▂▂▂▂▂▂▂▂▂▂▂▂▂▂▂▂▂▂▂▂▂▂▆▆▆▆▆▂▂▂▂
SLOVENIA	2.3191	2006	2010	▂▂▂▂▂▂▂▂▂▂▂▂▂▂▂▂▂▂▂▂▂▂▂▂▂▂▂▂▆▆▆▆▆▂▂▂

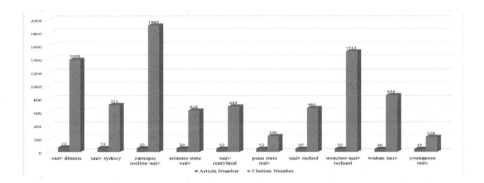

Fig. 7. Distribution of Institutes

the study since 1975, while University Illinois is the most productive university with 72 papers since 2001 and is also the node with the highest betweenness centrality in the institution co-occurring network, fully demonstrating its import role in SNA research. Carnegie Mellon Univ is the institute with the highest citations which started the research from 1999 with 55 papers. MIT is the node with the highest burst which has started SNA research from 2005 with 28 papers. Apart from that, there are still other institutions actively participating in SNA research such as Arizona State Univ (61 papers, 626 citations), Univ Maryland (52 papers, 658 citations), Chinese Acad Sci (51 papers, 240 citations), Penn State Univ (50 papers, 1513 citations), Univ Arizona (50 papers, 663 citations), Univ Oxford (46 papers, 856 citations), Wuhan Univ (42 papers, 107 citations) and so on.

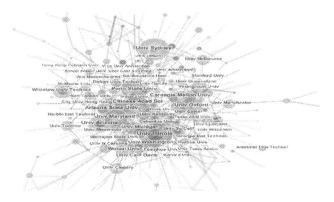

Fig. 8. Institutes co-occurring network with 494 Nodes and 603 Links

3.6   Research Hotspots and Emerging Trends of Social Network Analysis

References co-citation network can effectively detect the intellectual structure, land-scapes, dynamics, emerging trends and paradigm shifts in a certain domain [18]. Figure 9 shows the cited references network of Social Network Analysis. In order to show the backbone of the whole network, G-index [19] was used to prune the network. At last, a network of cited references with 722 unique nodes and 1494 links was generated. Clusters are identified and labeled using author keywords of the articles in these clusters. The largest cluster is #0 Knowledge Management, located on the center of the visualization. It contains 61 articles with an average year of publication of 1999. Cluster #1 community detection, near the right of the image, it contains 59 articles with an average year of publication of 2002. Cluster #2 learning analytics, is the third largest cluster with 46 articles and an average publication year of 1999. Cluster #3 scientific network, is located in the west of the image, it contains 31 articles with an average year of publication of 2003. Cluster #4 ICANN, is not only the fifth largest cluster of 28 articles but also the youngest one. Its average publication year is 2004 (Table 2).

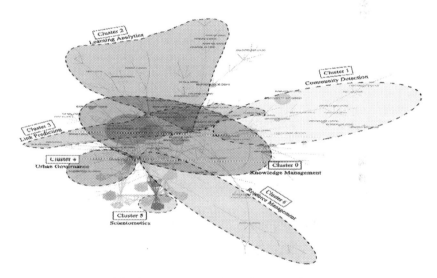

Fig. 9. Network of cited references of SNA

In order to find the landmark papers of SNA, a quantitative method named reference publication year spectroscopy (RPYS) introduced by Bornmann [20] was used to determine the historical roots of Social Network Analysis and evaluate their impact on current research. RPYS is based on the analysis of the frequency with which references are cited in the publications of a specific research field in terms of the publication years of these cited references [21]. Figure 10 shows the RPYS of SNA, the blue curve represents the change in the cited number of publication over time, and the red curve is the deviation from median cited number of publication. In order to find important publications in this fields, the peaks in the blue curves are we highlighted. The year corresponding to these

Table 2. The largest five clusters in the 722 core articles network.

ID.	Size	Silhouette	Mean (year)	Top Terms
0	61	0.896	1999	knowledge management, knowledge sharing, knowledge creation
1	59	0.984	2002	community detection, clustering, graph mining, label propagation
2	46	0.906	1999	learning analytics, collaborative learning, organizational learning
3	31	0.987	2003	scientific network, co-authorship, team formation, g-index
4	28	0.943	2004	Governance, construction management, sustainability

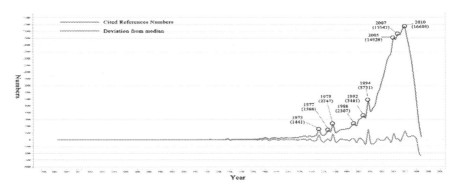

Fig. 10. Reference publication year spectroscopy of SNA

peaks are the periods when important breakthroughs occurred. According to these results, the landmark papers of SNA are listed as follows. Granovetter (1973) proposed the concept of weak ties and emphasize that weak ties have a strong impact on diffusion of influence and information, mobility opportunity, and community organization [22]. Linton C. Freeman (1977) introduced a set of measures of centrality based on betweenness [23]. Freeman (1979) also reviewed the intuitive background for measures of structural centrality in social networks and evaluated existing measures in terms of their consistency with intuitions and their interpretability [16]. Coleman (1988) introduced the concept and forms of social capital and examined the social structural conditions under which it arises [24]. Burt (1992) developed the concept of Structural holes and attempted to explain the origin of differences in social capital [25]. Wasserman and Faust (1994) talked about the methods and applications of social network analysis [26]. Hanneman and Riddle (2005) gave a detailed introduction to social network methods [27]. Robins et al. (2007) introduced an exponential random graph (p*) models for social networks [28]. Fortunato (2010) made a detailed overview of the series of methods for community detection in graphs [29].

In scientometrics, keywords are often used to describe the hotspots of technology development, in order to find the research hotspots about SNA in detail, we use word2vec [30] based technology to calculate the semantic vectors of keywords, and use word frequency indicates the heat of these keywords, based on which a keyword landscape map of this field is generated. Figure 11 shows the result of the algorithm, in which similar words form a cluster, and the height of the mountain indicates the heat of the keyword. The keywords with high frequent are social network, network, complex network, social media, big data and so on. In addition, ten keywords are found to have citation bursts: knowledge management (17.1968), communication (14.6057), social structure (13.6032), data mining (8.0411), organization (7.4167), centrality (7.3949), modularity (7.084), visualization (7.0731), link prediction (7.0017) and politics (6.9908), suggesting that they have abrupt increases of citations detected. Figure 12 shows the temporal graph of these burst keywords detected by CiteSpace which can be seen as the research front of social network analysis research.

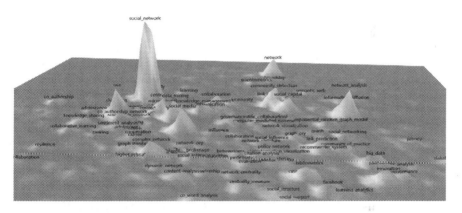

Fig. 11. Keyword landscape map of SNA

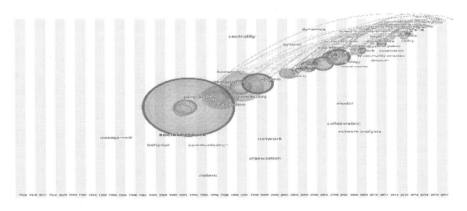

Fig. 12. Temporal graph of research fronts in SNA

4   Conclusion

This paper demonstrates a comprehensive assessment of publication data in the Social Network Analysis domain. A Bibliometric method to quantitatively assessing current research hotspots and trends on Social Network Analysis, using the related literature in the Science Citation Index (SCI) database from 1975 to 2017. References about Social Network Analysis were concentrated on the analysis of scientific outputs, geographic distribution, institutions, journals and subject categories. Moreover, innovative methods such as co-citation analysis, Burst Detection, Reference Publication Year Spectroscopy and keyword semantic clustering were applied which can vividly reveal the landscape and trends from various perspectives.

References

1. Borgatti, S.P., Brass, D.J., Labianca, G.J., Mehra, A.: Network analysis in the social sciences. Science **323**(5916), 892–895 (2009)
2. Otte, E., Rousseau, R.: Social network analysis: a powerful strategy, also for the information sciences. J. Inf. Sci. **28**(6), 441–453 (2002)
3. Kossinets, G., Watts, D.J.: Empirical analysis of an evolving social network. Science **311** (5757), 88–90 (2006)
4. Zheng, X., Le, Y., Chan, A.P.C., Hu, Y., Li, Y.: Review of the application of social network analysis (sna) in construction project management research. Int. J. Project Manage. **34**(7), 1214–1225 (2016)
5. Cela, K.L., Sicilia, M.Á., Sánchez, S.: Social network analysis in e-learning environments: a preliminary systematic review. Educ. Psychol. Rev. **27**(1), 219–246 (2015)
6. Hasenjager, M.J., Dugatkin, L.A.: Social network analysis in behavioral ecology. Adv. Study Behav. **47**, 39–114 (2015)
7. Martínez-López, B., Perez, A.M., Sánchez-Vizcaíno, J.M.: Social network analysis. review of general concepts and use in preventive veterinary medicine. Transbound. Emerg. Dis. **56** (4), 109–120 (2009)
8. Butts, C.T.: Social network analysis: a methodological introduction. Asian J. Soc. Psychol. **11**(1), 13–41 (2010)
9. Ingold, K.: Network structures within policy processes: coalitions, power, and brokerage in swiss climate policy. Policy Stud. J. **39**(3), 435–459 (2011)
10. Butts, C.T.: Social network analysis: a methodological introduction. Asian J. Soc. Psychol. **11**(1), 13–41 (2008)
11. Al'tshuller, G.S. (Genrikh Saulovich), Shulyak, L.A., Rodman, S.: The innovation algorithm: triz, systematic innovation and technical creativity. Aseanheartjournal Org (1999)
12. Rogosa, D., Brandt, D., Zimowski, M.: A growth curve approach to the measurement of change. Psychol. Bull. **92**(3), 726–748 (1982)
13. Havre, S.L., Hetzler, E.G., Nowell, L.T.: ThemeRiver: Visualizing Theme Changes over Time. INFOVIS (2000)
14. Eck, N.J., Waltman, L.: Software survey: VOSviewer, a computer program for bibliometric mapping. Scientometrics (2009)
15. Chen, C.: Citespace ii: detecting and visualizing emerging trends and transient patterns in scientific literature. J. Assoc. Inf. Sci. Technol. **57**(3), 359–377 (2009)
16. Freeman, L.C.: Centrality in social networks conceptual clarification. Soc. Netw. **1**(3), 215–239 (1979)

17. Kleinberg, J.M.: Bursty and Hierarchical Structure in Streams. Data Min. Knowl. Disc. **7**, 373–397 (2002)
18. Chen, C.: Mapping Scientific Frontiers: The Quest for Knowledge Visualization by Chaomei Chen. Springer, New York (2003). 256 pps, $79.95 (ISBN: 0-85233-494-0). Information Retrieval, 8, 505–507
19. Egghe, L.: Theory and practise of the g-index. Scientometrics **69**, 131–152 (2006)
20. Bornmann, L., Barth, A., Leydesdorff, L., Marx, W.: Detecting the historical roots of research fields by reference publication year spectroscopy (RPYS). JASIST **65**, 751–764 (2014)
21. Bornmann, L., Haunschild, R., Leydesdorff, L.: Reference publication year spectroscopy (rpys) of eugene garfield's publications. Scientometrics **114**(2), 1–10 (2018)
22. Granovetter, M.S.: The strength of weak ties. Am. J. Sociol. **78**, 1360–1380 (1973)
23. Freeman, L.C.: A set of measures of centrality based on betweenness. Sociometry **40**(1), 35–41 (1977)
24. Coleman, J.S.: Social Capital in the Creation of Human Capital. Am. J. Sociol. **94**, S95–S120 (1988)
25. Burt, R.S.: Structural Holes: The Social Structure of Competition. Harvard University Press, Cambridge (1992)
26. Wasserman, S., Faust, K.: Social Network Analysis: Methods and Applications, p. 506. Cambridge University Press, Cambridge (1994)
27. Hanneman, R.A., Riddle, M.: Introduction to social network methods. Department of Sociology University of California Riverside (2005)
28. Robins, G., Pattison, P., Kalish, Y., Lusher, D.: An introduction to exponential random graph (p *) models for social networks. Circuits Syst. & Sig. Process. **29**(2), 173–191 (2007)
29. Fortunato, S.: Community detection in graphs. Phys. Rep. **486**(3), 75–174 (2009)
30. Mikolov, T., Sutskever, I., Chen, K., Corrado, G., Dean, J.: Distributed representations of words and phrases and their compositionality, 26, pp. 3111–3119 (2013)

Predication

A Deep Prediction Architecture for Traffic Flow with Precipitation Information

Jingyuan Wang[1], Xiaofei Xu[1], Feishuang Wang[1], Chao Chen[2], and Ke Ren[1(✉)]

[1] School of Computer and Information Science, Southwest University,
Chongqing, China
wjykim@email.swu.edu.cn, 513178837@qq.com
[2] Online and Continuing Education College, Southwest University,
Chongqing, China

Abstract. Traffic flow prediction is an important building block to enabling intelligent transportation systems in a smart city. An accurate prediction model can help the governors make reliable traffic control strategies. In this paper, we propose a deep traffic flow prediction architecture P-DBL, which takes advantage of a deep bi-directional long short-term memory (DBL) model and precipitation information. The proposed model is able to capture the deep features of traffic flow and take full advantage of time-aware traffic flow data and additional precipitation data. We evaluate the prediction architecture on the dataset from Caltrans Performance Measurement System (PeMS) and the precipitation dataset from California Data Exchange Center (CDEC). The experiment results demonstrate that the proposed model for traffic flow prediction obtains high accuracy compared with other models.

Keywords: Traffic flow prediction · Bi-directional LSTM
Deep hierarchy · Precipitation information

1 Introduction

Traffic flow prediction has been long regarded as a critical problem for intelligent transportation systems (ITS) [1]. The aim of traffic flow prediction is to predict the number of vehicles within a given time interval on the basis of the historical traffic information. Traffic flow prediction has an important significance in real-time route guidance and reliable traffic control strategies [2]. Accurate real-time traffic flow prediction can offer information and guidance to road users to optimize their travel decisions and to reduce costs. And according to prediction, the authorities can use advanced traffic management strategies to mitigate congestion. Many traffic flow prediction models have been proposed in the past decades. They can be broadly divided into parametric and nonparametric models.

The traditional methods for traffic flow prediction are parametric approaches. In earlier studies, linear time series models have been widely applied. Time series

© Springer International Publishing AG, part of Springer Nature 2018
Y. Tan et al. (Eds.): ICSI 2018, LNCS 10942, pp. 329–338, 2018.
https://doi.org/10.1007/978-3-319-93818-9_31

methods, such as the autoregressive integrated moving average (ARIMA) [3], were employed to forecast short-term traffic flow. Moreover, some improved ARIMA models like space-time ARIMA [4] and seasonal ARIMA (SARIMA) [5] were also proposed to predict traffic flow. The parametric approach has simple and explicit architecture, which is easy for implementation. However, due to the stochasticity and nonlinearity of the traffic flow, parametric approaches cannot describe traffic flow precisely.

More and more researchers are dipping their toes in the waters of the nonparametric approach, for nonparametric approaches can capture the complicated nonlinearity of the traffic flow and take the uncertainty into consideration. Jin et al. [6] employed support vector regression (SVR) to predict traffic flow. Leshem et al. [7] developed a random forest regression (RF) method. And neural network (NN) models were reported in [8].

The rapid development of intelligent transportation system and data collecting technology makes it possible to get access to huge amount of traffic data as well as environmental data. However, both the typical parametric and nonparametric models tend to make assumptions to ignore additional influencing factors like precipitation. Recent advances in deep learning have enabled researchers to model the complex nonlinear relationships and have shown promising results in computer vision and natural language processing fields [9]. This success has inspired several attempts to use deep learning techniques on traffic prediction problems. Huang et al. [1] incorporated multitask learning (MTL) into deep belief networks (DBN) for traffic flow prediction. Lv et al. [10] proposed a stacked auto-encoder (SAE) model. Tian et al. [11] used long short-term memory (LSTM) recurrent neural network to forecast traffic flow. Yao et al. [12] tried to model both spatial and temporal relations. The shallow structure of current deep learning models makes them unable to mine deep features of traffic flow. And ignoring additional influencing factors leads to the fact that they are hard to improve the prediction accuracy.

In this paper, we propose a deep architecture for traffic flow prediction considering precipitation impact. It is worthwhile to highlight the main contributions of our work: (1) We propose a deep bi-directional long short-term memory (DBL) by introducing long short-term memory (LSTM) recurrent neural network, residual connections, deeply hierarchical networks and bi-directional traffic flow. A regression layer is used above the DBL for supervised prediction. (2) We take precipitation factor into consideration when predicting traffic flow. The features of traffic flow under various precipitation conditions can be learned after training using traffic data and precipitation data. In this way, we promote the DBL model to the P-DBL model. (3) We adopt dropout training method to avoid overfitting problem.

The rest of this paper is organized as follows. Section 2 formalizes the problem of traffic flow prediction and introduces long short-term memory (LSTM) model. Section 3 proposes the P-DBL architecture for traffic flow prediction. Section 4 discusses the experiment design and performance of the proposed architecture, and comparison with several selected models. Finally, Sect. 5 is the conclusion.

2   Related Work

2.1   Traffic Flow Prediction

Traffic flow prediction is a typical temporal and spatial process. The traffic flow prediction problem can be stated as follows. The traffic flow of the i_{th} observation point (road, segment or station) at the t_{th} time interval is denoted as $f_{i,t}$. At time t', the prediction task is to forecast the traffic flow $f_{i,t'+1}$ at time $t' + 1$, which is based on the traffic flow sequence $F = \{f_{i,t} | i \in O, t = 1, 2, ..., t'\}$ in the past. O is the full set of observation points. The prediction time interval is the interval between time t and $t + 1$, which is denoted as Δt. According to the length of the prediction time interval, the traffic flow prediction can be divided into three types: long-term, mid-term and short-term traffic flow prediction. Traffic flow prediction has a significant meaning in real-time route guidance and reliable traffic control strategies.

2.2   Long Short-Term Memory Network

Long Short-Term Memory (LSTM) [13] is an effective approach to handle sequential data, which takes advantage of the three multiplicative units in the memory block to determine the optimal time lags dynamically.

$$h_t = H(W_{xh}x_t + W_{hh}h_{t-1} + b_h) \tag{1}$$

$$y_t = W_{hy}h_t + b_y \tag{2}$$

$$i_t = \sigma(W_{xi}x_t + W_{hi}h_{t-1} + W_{ci}c_{t-1} + b_i) \tag{3}$$

$$f_t = \sigma(W_{xf}x_t + W_{hf}h_{t-1} + W_{cf}c_{t-1} + b_f) \tag{4}$$

$$c_t = f_t c_{t-1} + i_t g(W_{xc}x_t + W_{hc}h_{t-1} + b_c) \tag{5}$$

$$o_t = \sigma(W_{xo}x_t + W_{ho}h_{t-1} + W_{co}c_t + b_o) \tag{6}$$

$$h_t = o_t h(c_t) \tag{7}$$

$$\sigma(x) = \frac{1}{1 + e^{-x}} \tag{8}$$

$$g(x) = \frac{4}{1 + e^{-x}} - 2 \tag{9}$$

$$h(x) = \frac{2}{1 + e^{-x}} - 1 \tag{10}$$

2.3   Precipitation Impact

It is widely accepted that weather plays a significant role in the performance of the surface transportation system [14]. Certainly, extreme weather events, such as thick fog, can bring traffic to a halt. However, beyond these extreme conditions, more common weather events, such as precipitation, have also been shown to impact traffic conditions. Many researchers have focused on studying the precipitation impact on traffic characteristics such as road capacity and vehicle speed. Both road capacity and vehicle speed will greatly impact the traffic flow. Therefore, it is quite necessary to consider precipitation impact when predicting traffic flow.

Due to the lack of data, many previous scholars have to make assumptions to ignore weather factors like precipitation. However, with the rapid development of intelligent transportation system and data collecting technology, tons of weather data can be collected for traffic flow research. The speed-flow-occupancy relationship under adverse weather conditions was examined by using dummy variables within a multiple regression model, and the results of capacity loss are marginal in light rain but about 15% in heavy rain are indicated [15]. Thus, using precipitation data can make the model be more in line with the reality and gain better performance.

3   Traffic Flow Prediction Architecture: P-DBL

3.1   Deep Bi-Directional Long Short-Term Memory (DBL) Model

The structure of deep bi-directional long short-term memory model is shown in Fig. 1. The input n-length historical traffic flow sequence is denoted as $x^0 = \{x_0^0, x_1^0, x_2^0, ..., x_{n-1}^0\}$, where $x_i^0 (i = 0, 1, 2, ..., n-1)$ is the traffic flow at the t_{th} time interval. $x^i (i = 1, 2, ..., m)$ is the output of the i_{th} layer. BiLSTM is the bi-directional long short-term memory network, where $\overrightarrow{LSTM}$ encodes the input sequence from the start to the end and $\overleftarrow{LSTM}$ encodes the input sequence from the end to the start. Due to the strong ability to handle the sequential data, biLSTM has been successfully applied in natural language processing and image processing. By using biLSTM, the traffic flow information of both directions can be taken into consideration.

In this paper, we use 7 biLSTM layers. The deep hierarchy structure always results in the gradient vanishing problem. To achieve the idea of modeling differences between an intermediate layers output and the targets, we introduce residual connections among the DBL layers in a stack (the red line shown in Fig. 1. Residual connections performed well in the past [16,17]. With residual connections in the DBL model, the equations are as follows.

$$c_t^i, h_t^i = biLSTM^i(c_{t-1}^i, h_{t-1}^i, x_t^{i-1}; \theta^i)$$ (11)

$$x_t^i = x_t^{i-1} + h_t^i$$ (12)

$$c_t^{i+1}, h_t^{i+1} = biLSTM^{i+1}(c_{t-1}^{i+1}, h_{t-1}^{i+1}, x_t^i; \theta^{i+1})$$ (13)

where c_t^i and h_t^i are the memory states and hidden states of $biLSTM^i$ at the t_{th} time interval for the i_{th} layer, respectively; x_t^i is the input at the t_{th} time interval for the i_{th} layer; θ^i is the set of parameters of $biLSTM^i$ for the i_{th} layer.

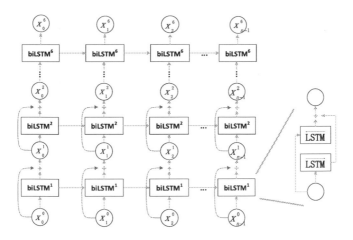

Fig. 1. The structure of deep bi-directional long short-term memory model (Color figure online)

3.2   The Prediction Architecture: P-DBL

As shown in Fig. 2, the prediction architecture mainly consists of four parts: the embedding layer, the DBL, the mean pooling layer and the softmax regression layer. $\{x(0), x(1), ..., x(n-1)\}$ is the input which represents corresponded traffic flow data and precipitation data, and each $x(i)(i = 0, 1, ..., n-1)$ is a piece of corresponded traffic flow data and precipitation data at a time interval encoded by one-hot representation. The corresponded traffic flow data and precipitation data is mapped into a space of same dimension, which is a 128-dimensional vector space. After the DBL encodes the time-aware traffic flow information and precipitation data, a sequence $\{h(0), h(1), ..., h(n-1)\}$ is produced. Then, the mean pooling layer extracts mean values of the sequence over time intervals. Besides, the mean pooling layer makes the features encoded into a vector h. The vector h is fed into the softmax regression layer at the top of the prediction architecture.

To avoid overfitting problem [18] and improve the generalization capability of the model, we adopt the dropout method [19,20] in the embedding layer. The key idea of the dropout method is to randomly drop units (along with their connections) from the neural network during training, which can prevent units from co-adapting too much. During training, dropout samples from numerous different thinned networks. When testing, it becomes easy to approximate the effect of averaging the predictions of all these thinned networks and it can be achieved by a single unthinned network with smaller weights.

4   Experiments and Results

4.1   Experimental Settings

There are mainly two types of traffic flow data in the real world. The first type is the loop detector data, which is collected by sensors on each road, such

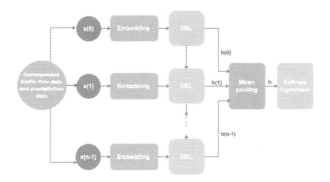

Fig. 2. The structure of the prediction architecture: P-DBL

as inductive loops. The second type is the entrance-exit station data, which is collected at the entrance and exit of a road segment. The prediction task for the first type of data is to forecast the traffic flow on each road or segment, while the prediction task for another type is to forecast the traffic flow in each station, particularly the exit station.

In this paper, we evaluate our model and other comparison models on the dataset from Caltrans Performance Measurement System (PeMS)[1]. The precipitation data is from California Data Exchange Center (CDEC)[2]. PeMS is the most widely used dataset in traffic flow prediction. PeMS constantly collects loop detector data in real time for more than 8100 freeway locations throughout the State of California. Thus, the PeMS dataset is a typical dataset of the loop detector data and the prediction task for PeMS is to forecast the traffic flow on each road or segment. The California Data Exchange Center installs, maintains, and operates an extensive hydrologic data collection network including automatic snow reporting gages for the Cooperative Snow Surveys Program and precipitation and river stage sensors for flood forecasting. We obtain corresponding hourly precipitation data from CDEC. We use the data of five months (from January to May) in 2017 as the training set and the later one month (June) as the testing set.

We used one-hot encoding to transform discrete features (e.g., holidays and weather conditions) and used Max-Min normalization to scale the continuous features (e.g., the average of demand value in last three time intervals).

The models used in comparison experiments are explained as follows.

- **ARIMA:** autoregressive integrated moving average;
- **SVR:** support vector regression [6];
- **DBN:** deep belief network [1];
- **SAE:** stacked auto-encoder [10];
- **LSTM:** long short-term memory recurrent neural network [11];

---

[1] Caltrans Performance Measurement System (PeMS), http://pems.dot.ca.gov.
[2] California Data Exchange Center (CDEC), http://cdec.water.ca.gov.

- **DBL:** we remove the precipitation data from the proposed architecture;
- **P-DBL:** the proposed prediction architecture.

4.2 Experimental Results

To evaluate the effectiveness of the traffic flow prediction models, we use two performance indexes, which are the Mean Absolute Percentage Error (MAPE) and the Root Mean Square Error (RMSE). According to them, we can evaluate the relative error and the absolute error. They are defined as follows.

$$MAPE(f, \hat{f}) = \frac{1}{n} \sum_{i=1}^{n} \frac{|f_i - \hat{f}_i|}{f_i} \tag{14}$$

$$RMSE(f, \hat{f}) = \left[\frac{1}{n} \sum_{i=1}^{n} (|f_i - \hat{f}_i|)^2 \right]^{\frac{1}{2}} \tag{15}$$

where f is the observation (real) value of traffic flow, and $\hat{f}$ is the prediction value of traffic flow.

The Prediction Accuracy Comparison. To evaluate the prediction accuracy of the P-DBL model, we use P-DBL to predict 30-min interval traffic flow of a whole day (June 1, 2017) using the data collected from No.312139 observation road on D03-5 freeway in California. As shown in Fig. 3, the red line represents the real traffic flow, and the blue line shows the prediction of traffic flow. From Fig. 3, we can notice that the performance of the P-DBL model is quite good during most of the day. Besides, there are mainly three fluctuating periods, which are around 7:00, 12:00 and 19:00 respectively. Those fluctuating periods are all peak traffic periods during which the performance of the P-DBL model is not as stable as other periods. The MAPE of P-DBL is 3.23% and the RMSE of P-DBL is 110.43, which manifests that P-DBL obtains a high prediction accuracy.

Table 1. The results of traffic flow prediction with 30-min time intervalThe results of traffic flow prediction with 30-min time interval

Models	MAPE(%)	RMSE
ARIMA	8.63	171.26
SVR	5.97	143.42
DBN	7.44	165.43
SAE	6.81	151.09
LSTM	4.26	135.32
DBL	**3.87**	**124.31**
P-DBL	**3.23**	**110.43**

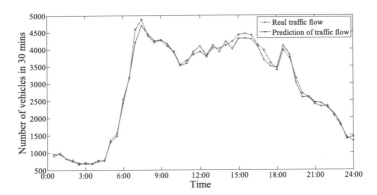

Fig. 3. The comparison between real traffic flow and prediction of traffic flow (Color figure online)

The performance of seven models is tested and the results of them are listed in Table 1. As shown in Table 1, both MAPE and RMSE of P-DBL are lowest among the prediction models. We can notice that deep bi-directional architecture improves the performance of LSTM. And the precipitation information enhances the prediction ability of DBL.

The Effect of Precipitation Information. To verify the effectiveness of the precipitation information, we use DBL and P-DBL to predict 30-min interval traffic flow of a whole day. We evaluate the proposed method with the baseline model on 876 observation roads and achieve the similar results. Next, we will illustrate the details for one randomly selected road and omit the details of others owing to the space limit. The comparison between DBL and P-DBL is shown in Fig. 4. It is immediately visible from the graph that P-DBL outperforms DBL significantly. In our experiment, we notice that a precipitation event occurs from 10:30 to 14:30, and P-DBL predicts more precisely than DBL does in this period.

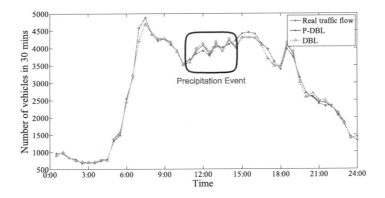

Fig. 4. The comparison between P-DBL and DBL

We find that the MAPE and the RMSE of P-DBL are both lower than those of DBL, which means that the precipitation information is an effective tool to improve the prediction accuracy.

5   Conclusion

To address the traffic flow prediction problem, we propose a deep bi-directional long short-term memory (DBL) model which is able to capture the deep features of traffic flow and take full advantage of time-aware traffic flow data. Moreover, we introduce the DBL model, precipitation information, regression layer and dropout training method into a traffic flow prediction architecture P-DBL. To verify the performance of the P-DBL model, the dataset from PeMS is used in the proposed model and other six comparison models (ARIMA, SVM, DBN, SAE, LSTM, DBL) and the dataset from CDEC is used for precipitation information. In the exprimental results, P-DBL obtains high accuracy.

In the follow-up work, we will take both spatial features and temporal features into consideration. We attempt to use convolutional neural network (CNN) to capture the spatial features and use long short-term memory model (LSTM) to capture the temporal features.

Acknowledgement. This work is supported by "Fundamental Research Funds for the Central Universities" (XDJK2017C027) and "CERNET Innovation Project" (NGII20170516).

References

1. Huang, W., Song, G., Hong, H., Xie, K.: Deep architecture for traffic flow prediction: deep belief networks with multitask learning. IEEE Trans. Intell. Transp. Syst. **15**(5), 2191–2201 (2014)
2. Abadi, A., Rajabioun, T., Ioannou, P.A.: Traffic flow prediction for road transportation networks with limited traffic data. IEEE Trans. Intell. Transp. Syst. **16**(2), 653–662 (2015)
3. Ahmed, M.S., Cook, A.R.: Analysis of freeway traffic time-series data by using Box-Jenkins techniques (1979)
4. Kamarianakis, Y., Vouton, V.: Forecasting traffic flow conditions in an urban network: comparison of multivariate and univariate approaches. Transp. Res. Rec. **1857**(1), 74–84 (2003)
5. Williams, B.M., Hoel, L.A.: Modeling and forecasting vehicular traffic flow as a seasonal arima process: theoretical basis and empirical results. J. Transp. Eng. **129**(6), 664–672 (2003)
6. Jin, X., Zhang, Y., Yao, D.: Simultaneously prediction of network traffic flow based on PCA-SVR. In: Liu, D., Fei, S., Hou, Z., Zhang, H., Sun, C. (eds.) ISNN 2007. LNCS, vol. 4492, pp. 1022–1031. Springer, Heidelberg (2007). https://doi.org/10.1007/978-3-540-72393-6_121
7. Leshem, G.: Traffic flow prediction using adaboost algorithm with random forests as a weak learner. Enformatika **193** (2011)

8. Chan, K.Y., Dillon, T.S., Singh, J., Chang, E.: Neural-network-based models for short-term traffic flow forecasting using a hybrid exponential smoothing and Levenberg-Marquardt algorithm. IEEE Trans. Intell. Transp. Syst. **13**(2), 644–654 (2012)

9. LeCun, Y., Bengio, Y., Hinton, G.: Deep learning. Nature **521**(7553), 436 (2015)

10. Lv, Y., Duan, Y., Kang, W., Li, Z., Wang, F.Y.: Traffic flow prediction with big data: a deep learning approach. IEEE Trans. Intell. Transp. Syst. **16**(2), 865–873 (2015)

11. Tian, Y., Pan, L.: Predicting short-term traffic flow by long short-term memory recurrent neural network. In: IEEE International Conference on Smart City/SocialCom/SustainCom, pp. 153–158 (2015)

12. Yao, H., Wu, F., Ke, J., Tang, X., Jia, Y., Lu, S., Gong, P., Ye, J.: Deep multi-view spatial-temporal network for taxi demand prediction. arXiv preprint arXiv:1802.08714 (2018)

13. Hochreiter, S., Schmidhuber, J.: Long short-term memory. Neural Comput. **9**(8), 1735 (1997)

14. Wang, Y.Q., Jing, L.: Study of rainfall impacts on freeway traffic flow characteristics. Transp. Res. Procedia **25**, 1533–1543 (2017)

15. Ibrahim, A.T., Hall, F.L.: Effect of adverse weather conditions on speed-flow-occupancy relationships (1994)

16. Wu, Y., Schuster, M., Chen, Z., Le, Q.V., Norouzi, M., Macherey, W., Krikun, M., Cao, Y., Gao, Q., Macherey, K.: Google's neural machine translation system: bridging the gap between human and machine translation (2016)

17. He, K., Zhang, X., Ren, S., Sun, J.: Deep residual learning for image recognition. In: Computer Vision and Pattern Recognition, pp. 770–778 (2016)

18. Hawkins, D.M.: The problem of overfitting. Cheminform **35**(19), 1 (2004)

19. Hinton, G.E., Srivastava, N., Krizhevsky, A., Sutskever, I., Salakhutdinov, R.R.: Improving neural networks by preventing co-adaptation of feature detectors. Comput. Sci. **3**(4), 212–223 (2012)

20. Srivastava, N., Hinton, G., Krizhevsky, A., Sutskever, I., Salakhutdinov, R.: Dropout: a simple way to prevent neural networks from overfitting. J. Mach. Learn. Res. **15**(1), 1929–1958 (2014)

Tag Prediction in Social Annotation Systems Based on CNN and BiLSTM

Baiwei Li[1]([✉])(ID), Qingchuan Wang[2], Xiaoru Wang[1], and Wei Li[3]

[1] Beijing University of Posts and Telecommunications, Beijing 100876, China
{libaiwei,wxr}@bupt.edu.cn
[2] Beijing Information Science and Technology University, Beijing 100192, China
qingchuan97@163.com
[3] Beijing University of Technology, Beijing 100124, China
18811353239@163.com

Abstract. Social annotation systems enable users to annotate large-scale texts with tags which provide a convenient way to discover, share and organize rich information. However, manually annotating massive texts is in general costly in manpower. Therefore, automatic annotation by tag prediction is of great help to improve the efficiency of semantic identification of social contents. In this paper, we propose a tag prediction model based on convolutional neural networks (CNN) and bi-directional long short term memory (BiLSTM) network, through which, tags of texts can be predicted efficiently and accurately. By Experiments on real-world datasets from a social Q&A community, the results show that the proposed CNN-BiLSTM model achieves state-of-the-art accuracy for tag prediction.

Keywords: Tag prediction · Convolutional neural network
Prediction · Bi-directional LSTM · Deep learning

1 Introduction

Social annotation systems have been playing an important role in social media platforms, where users are required to annotate large-scale texts with tags for complex tasks, e.g., understanding tagged texts and quickly searching for relevant information. As a large amount of unannotated texts stream into social media platforms, annotation by individual users is in general costly in manpower and inefficient to meet the requirement of real-time data processing. Therefore, automatic tag prediction is of crucial importance for semantically understanding social contents.

Conceptually, tag prediction falls into text classification tasks, which are increasingly fundamental and important in machine learning. Lewis et al. [16] research 804414 news of Reuters and found that the average of each news at the same time belong to 2.6 different categories. In the ACM Computing classification system [17], there are 11 primary and secondary categories, and the

Y. Tan et al. (Eds.): ICSI 2018, LNCS 10942, pp. 339–348, 2018.
https://doi.org/10.1007/978-3-319-93818-9_32

author can select a number of different categories for each article. Snoek [18] analyses 43907 audio clips from Africa, China and the United States, as well as 101 tags associated with these audio clips, and found that each audio segment has an average of 4.4 Different labels. This kind of problem is called multi-label classification. Vens et al. [13] use decision trees for multi-label classification that is efficient to obtain good results with large-scale data, which ignores the relevance among properties and is hard to avoid overfitting. Some methods usually employ the state-of-the-art methods such as support naive Bayes (NB), K Nearest Neighbor (KNN) and vector machines (SVMs) classifiers. The accuracy of tag prediction is also far from our expectation. Recently many kinds of prediction methods are based on neural networks which is a good progress being made there. A neural network algorithm named BP-MLL [1] is proposed based on Back-propagation. Multi-label prediction with BP-MLL obtains a good result.

In this paper, we propose a CNN-BiLSTM prediction model that shows an improved performance with datasets from the social Q&A community. The main contributions are as follows.

- We combine the CNN and Bi-LSTM model to train the title and the description of texts, which are represented by both word vectors and character vectors in order to extract more information from texts.
- In concatenation for output generated by the two models, we simulate the gradient descent to adjust the weight of each model by using the cross entropy loss function. Finally, the model output the prediction probability of each tag through the fully connected layer and the sigmoid layer.
- Conventionally, tag prediction methods usually involve simple representation to express texts. Instead, we use vectors generated by Google word2vec [2] as input of CNN-BiLSTM which obtains comprehensive sentiment representation for the texts. As a result, our model shows better performance through experiments on real-word datasets.
- Specially, optimization in model training is tailored in order to improve prediction accuracy. We use dynamic learning rate to optimize the network structure and adjust network parameters such as the size of the convolution kernel, the number of each convolution kernel, the dropout parameter, the coefficient of l2 regularization, the batch size, the optimizer type and so on. Experiment shows better performance with these optimization methods.

2   Related Work

Recently, tag prediction problems attract wide attention. Tag prediction methods are mainly divided into two parts, Problem Transformation (PT) based methods [10] and Algorithm Adaptation (AA) based methods [20].

The key to PT based methods is to transfer multi-label problem into a group of single-label classification problems. Early research on text classification mainly focus on training each label with an independent classifier. McCallum [3] propose a mixture model trained by EM to generate the class set of the documents. It ignores the relationship among labels. As a result, the accuracy cannot satisfy the present requirement. Hullermeier [5] proposes a classification method based on pairwise comparision which means constructing many classifiers to compare relationships between two labels. It can be applied to fewer label types.

AA based methods are also widely used in recent years which aims at transforming the existing single-label classification methods to deal with multi-tag prediction problems. Zhang [1] uses artificial neural network to solve tag prediction problems by defining global optimization parameters. It provides an efficient way to annotate texts.

Building on these ideas from previous works, we propose CNN-BiLSTM model to predict tags of texts. The main distinction of our work is that we design a deep and complex neural network structure to improve the experiment performance. In the model concatenation part, we simulate the gradient reduction method to linearly fuse the multiple models, and adjust the weight of each model by using the F1 score of the validation set. Results show the improvement on the accuracy and recall rate by using many optimization methods experimented with real-world datasets.

3   Model

In this section, we propose CNN-BiLSTM prediction model to solve the multi-tag prediction problems. As shown in Fig. 1, we design a combined neural network structure with CNN and BiLSTM. The model consists of four main parts which are data preprocessing, feature extraction, model concatenation and sigmoid output. We design the neural network structure applied to tag prediction.

3.1   Model Structure

We design a deep and complex convolutional neural network structure. The CNN consists of four main layers which are an input layer, two hidden layers and an

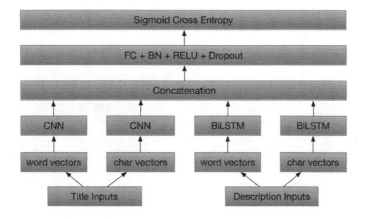

Fig. 1. CNN-BiLSTM model

output layer. In the hidden layer, we use different filter width to get the feature representations with more information. Our CNN is a word-level Convolutional Neural Network. The word is a kind of unit in the natural language processing. The words consist of the matrixes and then high-level features are extracted with the model. We use word2vec to transform the texts into character or word embedding and train the model to update the embedding. We define x_i as the embedding of the word w_i which is a dense vector. W is a matrix that transforms the neuron point into the neuron point of the next hidden layer. After we obtain the representation x_i of the word w_i, we apply the activation function tanh to the neural network structure as shown in the following equations.

$$Y_i = f(WX_i + b) \tag{1}$$

$$f(x) = \frac{1 - e^x}{1 + e^x} \tag{2}$$

Y_i is a text semantic representation vector in which each dimension represents the latent information of the text. Figure 2 shows the overall structure of our CNN encoder.

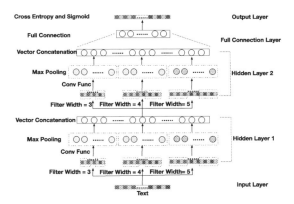

Fig. 2. ML-CNN model structure

The basic idea of Bi-directional Long Short-Term Memory (BiLSTM) is to propose that both forward and backward training sequence are LSTM, and both of them are connected to an output layer. The structure provides the complete context information of past and future for each point in the input layer. The following figure shows the BiLSTM that runs along time (Fig. 3).

In the forward pass, all input data slice $1 \leq t \leq T$ trough the LSTM and determine the predicted outputs. s_t of hidden layer is related to s_{t-1}.

$$o_t = g(Vs_t + V's'_t) \tag{3}$$

$$s_t = f(Ux_t + W's_{t-1}) \tag{4}$$

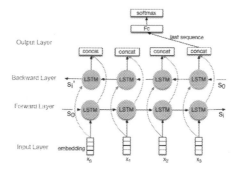

Fig. 3. Bidirectional LSTM model structure

In the backward pass, the part of the objective function derivative is calculated for the slice $1 \leq t \leq T$ in the forward pass. s_t of hidden layer is related to s_{t+1}.

$$s_t = f(Ux_t + W' s'_{t+1}) \tag{5}$$

3.2 Combining the Models

After each of the character and word embeddings of texts is extracted by CNN and BiLSTM, we can improve the difference of the models by combining the models and then the performance is improved obviously. We simulate the gradient descent to adjust the weight of the models.

The effect and the target of the optimization are concerned with the loss function definition. In order to output continuous and derivative values, we combine cross entropy with sigmoid active function which is used by each output tag to solve multi-tag prediction problems. The loss function is defined as Eq. 6.

$$J(W, b, x^L, y) = -\sum y_k \ln x_k^L \tag{6}$$

The gradient of each layer in the network is calculated as Eq. 7.

$$\delta^l = \frac{\partial J(W, b, x^l, y)}{\partial z^l} \tag{7}$$

The gradient shows the difference between prediction value and real value. The loss function without the derivative of the activation function speeds the convergence of back propagation progress.

4 Experiment

In order to prove that our model can be applied to solve multi-tag prediction problems, in this section, we experiment with Zhihu datasets which is a topic forum, so as to further support our motivation.

4.1 Datasets

The experiment datasets is from 2017 Zhihu Kan Shan Cup Machine Learning Challenge Competition. The tagged data contains 3,000,000 questions with titles and description. Each of the questions has one or more tags for a total of 1999 tags. For protecting the user privacy, all the original text has been encoded with special methods. The question title and description are concatenated and transformed into word identification sequences which are served as features of data. Google word2vec is used to get the 256 dimension word vectors and data show highest cosine distance values in vector space of the nearest words. Each text is transformed into 256*N dimension matrix with the method. N is the biggest length of the texts. For the reason that the texts have different lengths, we set N as the standard length and fill in the short text with zero to reach the standard length. One-Hot encoding method is used to get the labels of data.

4.2 Experiment Result and Analysis

In our experiment, we set a lot of model parameters which are made up of two parts hyperparameters and training parameters. Table 1 shows the hyperparameters parameter setting and Table 2 shows the training parameter setting.

Table 1. Hyperparameters parameter setting

Hyperparameters	
$Dimension\,of\,character\,or\,word\,embedding$	256
$Size\,of\,convolution\,kernel\,(filter\,width)$	$3, 4, 5$
$Number\,of\,filters\,per\,filter\,width$	1024
$Dropout\,keep\,probability$	0.5
$L2\,regularization\,lambda$	0.0005
$Learning\,rate$	0.0008
$Decay\,rate$	0.75

In addition to the parameter setting, we propose a method to evaluate the experiment performance. If a prediction label is one of the real labels, it is regarded as the right prediction. After we calculate the precision rate and recall rate, we use F1-Score in the following equation as the final evaluating indicator.

$$Precision = \sum_{pos=1}^{p} \frac{Right\,Num}{Sample\,Num * \log(1.0 + p)} \tag{8}$$

$$Recall = \frac{Right\,Num}{Labeled\,Num} \tag{9}$$

$$F1 - Score = 2 * \frac{Precision * Recall}{Precision + Recall} \tag{10}$$

Table 2. Training parameter setting

Training parameters	
Batch size	64
Number of training epochs	10
Number of steps to evaluate model on dev	50
Number of steps to save models	200
Number of checkpoints to store	5
Number of training steps	15000

We train our model for 15000 epochs and record the precision and recall for every ten epochs. F1-Score is calculated with the precision and recall. We choose batch size as 32, 48, 64 and 80 from the training dataset. For each kind of batch size, we train three models which are CNN, LSTM and our CNN-BiLSTM. The accuracy of our model is significantly more efficient than the others. Figure 4 shows the real-time changes of the precision, the recall and the F1-Score.

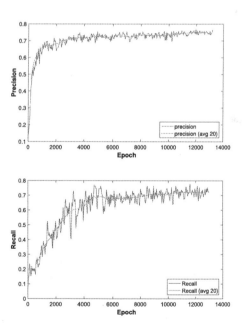

Fig. 4. Precicion and recall of BiLSTM

Traditional research on tag prediction mainly focus on training each tag with an independent classifier. Our model combine CNN and BiLSTM to train data which learns latent features and predicts tags more accurately. Figure 5 shows that our fusion model has a better performance compared with the single CNN or BiLSTM. The result shows that the models perform better if the batch size is above 64. However, the complexity of algorithm increases with $O(n^3)$ and the program runs at a low speed with the batch size increasing. In that case, the batch size is set to 64 which is not too large considering efficiency and precision.

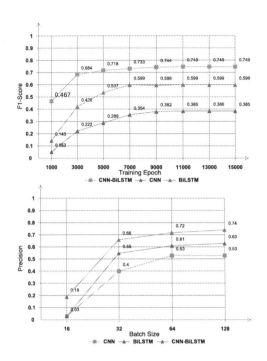

Fig. 5. F1-Score and precision comparison of different models

5   Conclusion

In this paper, we propose CNN-BiLSTM model applied to tag prediction by combining CNN and BiLSTM. The CNN is designed with different sizes of kernels which extract more information from text titles and the BiLSTM is a powerful sequence model which can capture the long-term contextual information of text descriptions, what's more it performs better in the nonlinear ability. We combine the models with simulated gradient declination to adjust the weight of the models. Experiment shows an improved performance with real-world Zhihu datasets. Further research is needed to see whether a more complex neural network gets better performance or not. With the increase in the ability of computer calculation, there will be a great progress in this area.

Acknowledgements. This work was supported by the National Natural Science Foundation of China (NSFC) grant funded by the China government, Ministry of Science and Technology(No.61672108).

References

1. Zhang, M.-L., Zhou, Z.-H.: Multilabel neural networks with applications to functional genomics and text categorization. IEEE Trans. Knowl. Data Eng. **18**(10), 1338–1351 (2006)
2. Goldberg, Y., Levy, O.: word2vec explained: deriving Mikolov et al'.s negative-sampling word-embedding method. arXiv preprint arXiv:1402.3722 (2014)
3. McCallum, A.: Multi-label text classification with a mixture model trained by EM. In: AAAI workshop on Text Learning (1999)
4. Zhang, M.-L., Zhou, Z.-H.: A k-nearest neighbor based algorithm for multi-label classification. In: 2005 IEEE International Conference on Granular Computing, vol. 2. IEEE (2005)
5. Hllermeier, E., et al.: Label ranking by learning pairwise preferences. Artif. Intell. **172**(16–17), 1897–1916 (2008)
6. Sriram, B., et al.: Short text classification in twitter to improve information filtering. In: Proceedings of the 33rd International ACM SIGIR Conference on Research and Development in Information Retrieval. ACM (2010)
7. Melville, P., Gryc, W., Lawrence, R.D.: Sentiment analysis of blogs by combining lexical knowledge with text classification. In: Proceedings of the 15th ACM SIGKDD International Conference on Knowledge Discovery and Data Mining. ACM (2009)
8. Ghamrawi, N., McCallum, A.: Collective multi-label classification. In: Proceedings of the 14th ACM International Conference on Information and Knowledge Management. ACM (2005)
9. Huang, W., Qiao, Y., Tang, X.: Robust scene text detection with convolution neural network induced MSER trees. In: Fleet, D., Pajdla, T., Schiele, B., Tuytelaars, T. (eds.) ECCV 2014. LNCS, vol. 8692, pp. 497–511. Springer, Cham (2014). https://doi.org/10.1007/978-3-319-10593-2_33
10. Read, J.: A pruned problem transformation method for multi-label classification. In: Proceedings of the 2008 New Zealand Computer Science Research Student Conference (2008)
11. Zhou, D., Schölkopf, B.: Learning from labeled and unlabeled data using random walks. In: Rasmussen, C.E., Bülthoff, H.H., Schölkopf, B., Giese, M.A. (eds.) DAGM 2004. LNCS, vol. 3175, pp. 237–244. Springer, Heidelberg (2004). https://doi.org/10.1007/978-3-540-28649-3_29
12. PadmaPriya, G., Duraiswamy, K.: An approach for text summarization using deep learning algorithm. J. Comput. Sci. **10**(1), 1–9 (2014)
13. Vens, C., et al.: Decision trees for hierarchical multi-label classification. Mach. Learn. **73**(2), 185–214 (2008)
14. Chen, L., Qu, H., Zhao, J.: Generalized correntropy induced loss function for deep learning. In: 2016 International Joint Conference on Neural Networks (IJCNN). IEEE (2016)
15. Ding, S., et al.: Deep feature learning with relative distance comparison for person re-identification. Pattern Recogn. **48**(10), 2993–3003 (2015)
16. Lewis, D.D., et al.: RCV1: a new benchmark collection for text categorization research. J. Mach. Learn. Res. **5**, 361–397 (2004)
17. Sebastiani, F.: Machine learning in automated text categorization. ACM Comput. Surv. (CSUR) **34**(1), 1–47 (2002)
18. Van De Sande, K., Gevers, T., Snoek, C.: Evaluating color descriptors for object and scene recognition. IEEE Trans. Pattern Anal. Mach. Intell. **32**(9), 1582–1596 (2010)

19. Yousfi, S., Berrani, S.-A., Garcia, C.: Deep learning and recurrent connectionist-based approaches for Arabic text recognition in videos. In: 2015 13th International Conference on Document Analysis and Recognition (ICDAR). IEEE (2015)
20. Widrow, B., McCool, J.: A comparison of adaptive algorithms based on the methods of steepest descent and random search. IEEE Trans. Antennas Propag. **24**(5), 615–637 (1976)

Classification

A Classification Method for Micro-Blog Popularity Prediction: Considering the Semantic Information

Lei Liu[1(✉)], Chen Yang[1], Tingting Liu[1(✉)], Xiaohong Chen[1],
and Sung-Shun Weng[2]

[1] College of Management, Shenzhen University, Shenzhen, China
liulei_0912@163.com, liutingting2017@email.szu.edu.cn
[2] Department of Information and Finance Management, National Taipei
University of Technology, Taipei, Taiwan

Abstract. Predicting the scale and quantity of reposting in micro-blog network have significances to the future network marketing, hot topic detection and public opinion monitor. This study proposed a novel two-stage method to predict the popularity of a micro-blog prior to its release. By focusing on the text content of the specific micro-blog as well as its source of publication (user's attributes), a special classification method—Labeled Latent Dirichlet allocation (LLDA) was trained to predict the volume range of future reposts for a new message. To the authors' knowledge, this paper is the first research to utilize this multi-label text classifier to investigate the influence of one micro-blog's topic on its reposting scale. The experiment was conducted on a large scale dataset, and the results show that it's possible to estimate ranges of popularity with an overall accuracy of 72.56%.

Keywords: Popularity prediction · Classification · Semantic information
Short contents · LLDA · Micro-blog

1 Introduction

With the rapid development of computer technology and network information technology, human has entered into an era which fuses the real world and virtual network together. The online social network is becoming an important channel for people to communicate, contact and disseminate information with each other. As a new online social media platform, micro-blog attracts a large number of users because it is characterized with low threshold, easy to use and rapid information transfer. It has evolved a vast network of social relations and information dissemination. Therefore, major media, enterprises and institutions have headed toward micro-blog, trying to use this platform to carry out network marketing or publicity and communication.

Micro-blog is a kind of information sharing and dissemination platform, which is built based on user relationships. On that people can write their own ideas and opinions in text, or they can also upload such as pictures, videos, stickers or other multimedia contents on it. The main features in micro-blog include posting/tweet, reposting/retweet,

© Springer International Publishing AG, part of Springer Nature 2018
Y. Tan et al. (Eds.): ICSI 2018, LNCS 10942, pp. 351–360, 2018.
https://doi.org/10.1007/978-3-319-93818-9_33

commenting, liking and the function of @. Among these features, user's reposting behavior is the ultimate cause that micro-blog information spreads continuously and the amount of information rapidly explodes in the Internet. This unique way of information dissemination broadens the research field of complex network information communication and arouses the widespread concern of the academic circles. Scholars try to use statistics, infectious disease dynamics, data mining and machine learning to systematically study the factors that affect reposting prediction and information dissemination, and then mine and extract information of social and commercial value.

Micro-blog reposting prediction is an important research topic related to social network. This problem can be divided into two sub problems: the local prediction and the global prediction. The local prediction refers to the problem whether a particular user will repost a specific micro-blog message or not. This problem is related to the target user's properties, the history micro-blog information he or she has posted, and even the time the user read that micro-blog or the users on the micro-blog reposting chain. And the global prediction refers to predicting the popular time and popularity of a specific micro-blog message on the social network. Due to the spirited competition for attention and the time-sensitive aspect, accurately predicting the popularity to which a specific micro-blog will spread on the social network is extremely valuable to content publishers, advertisers and micro-blog recommendation system. It is also important for activists and politicians who are using this micro-blog platform increasingly more to influence public opinion [1]. Hence, this paper is aimed at studying the global prediction problem. That is to predict the popularity (reposting scale) of a specific micro-blog message on the social network.

Some micro-blogs can attract a lot of traffic and become virally popular, while some micro-blogs can only receive little attention so that cannot be effectively transmitted. It should be said that various reasons make the micro-blog to be propagated, and it is interesting to investigate why some micro-blogs can be spread quickly and widely in the social network [2].

However, estimating online popularity of micro-blog messages is a challenging task. First, emergencies or a large number of internet mercenaries that affect the population will make this prediction difficult. Furthermore, users' different properties can add other layers of complexity to this problem. That is to say, even the same contents which are posted by diverse users will receive vastly different interaction rates. Most significantly, intuition suggests that the content of a message must play a crucial role in its popularity [1]. Content that resonates with heavy users such as a major world-wide event (e.g. ice bucket challenge) can be expected to gather wide attention while specific content relevant only to a few may not spread widely. And due to the previous feature that no more than 140 words of one micro-blog message, most users are still used to posting short contents in their micro-blog, which also increases the difficulty in prediction.

In this paper, we investigated the influence of one micro-blog text's topic on its transmission range by using a special classification method—Labeled Latent Dirichlet allocation (LLDA). As a mutation of the classical topic model—Latent Dirichlet allocation (LDA), LLDA improves expressiveness on analyzing the semantic information of a document by adding an additional layer of class label information. According to our summary, this paper is the first research to utilize this multi-label text classifier to study the influence of one micro-blog's topic on its reposting scale. Our goal is to discover if any predictors relevant only to the micro-blog's text exist and if it is possible to make a reasonable forecast of the spread of a micro-blog based on its text. The experiment was conducted on a large scale dataset, and the results show that our method is competitive compared to three common classification models.

2 Related Works

Compared to repost prediction problem (the local prediction), there is less research on the micro-blog popularity prediction (the global prediction). It might be because there are too many factors as mentioned above that affect a specific micro-blog's reposting size and quantity in some cases [3].

At present, there are two ideas for the research of micro-blog popularity prediction. One way is to study this problem as a regression or a probability problem. Xiong et al. [4] used PCA (Principle Components Analysis) to extract the most important features of user and tweet, and then built a PCA-based linear predicating model to predict the popularity of a newly submitted tweet. But the authors thought that semantic analysis (especially Chinese semantic analysis) was a challenging research topic, so they did not analyze the semantic information of the tweet. And the content features they used in their model mainly referred to the special symbols (e.g. #URL, #Image, #Emotion) contained in that specific tweet. Yang et al. [2] proposed a factor graph model to predict the spread of messages. They defined message's content features by using TF-IDF (Term Frequency-Inverse Document Frequency) values of keywords, not considering the semantic information too. Li et al. [5] used SVM algorithm with five features to solve the local prediction problem. And then they proposed an iterative algorithm to predict the exact values of retweet scale on the basis of SVM. Similar to previous work's [2] basic idea, they treated the micro-blog reposting path as a retweet tree. In one tree the root node was the user who released the original tweet. The intermediate nodes and the leaf nodes represented the users who did and did not retweet that message respectively. Therefore, predicting retweet scale is to calculate the number of nodes in the retweet tree except the root and leaf nodes. They gave a method to evaluate the predict accuracy by themselves and their experiment with Sina Weibo data showed a good result.

The other idea is to formulate the prediction task into a classification problem. This method usually splits the numbers of reposts into several levels. Then predict the target micro-blog's reposting level, rather than having to predict the exact number of reposts. Bandari et al. [1] predicted the popularity of news articles prior to their release by verifying the influence of four characteristics (the source of the article, the category, subjectivity in the language and the named entities mentioned) on news retweeting scale. The authors examined both regression and classification algorithms. First, they applied regression to produce exact values of retweet counts, and next they defined popularity classes (Range of tweets: 1–20; 21–100; 101–2400) and predicted which class a given article will belong to. They discovered that one of the most important predictors of popularity was the source of the article. Hong et al. [6] used Logistic Regression as the classifier to investigate the problem of predicting the popularity of tweets. The authors considered a wide spectrum of features, including the content and topical information of messages, graph structural properties of users, temporal dynamics of retweet chains and meta-information of users. For content features, they used TF-IDF values as a baseline and utilize LDA to obtain the topic distributions for each tweet. The results showed that their method can successfully predict tweet which will receive thousands of retweets with good performance. The features studied in this paper are very instructive to micro-blog's reposting problem. However, this paper is too short so that many details are not clear. Li et al. [7] extracted a feature system for predicting the government micro-blog retweeting scale from the three aspects of users' feature, content feature and release time feature. They considered the topic information of the micro-blog, but only defined two popularity classes when splitting the numbers of reposts (less than 500 and more than 500).

3   Proposed Approach

About propagation effect of micro-blog, most of the current studies considered the popularity prediction as a classification problem. In this paper, we divided the prediction process into two stages. First, we categorized users by their historical counts of been reposted. Then we trained a multi-class classifier to predict the volume range of future reposts for a new message. The proposed approach is shown in Fig. 1.

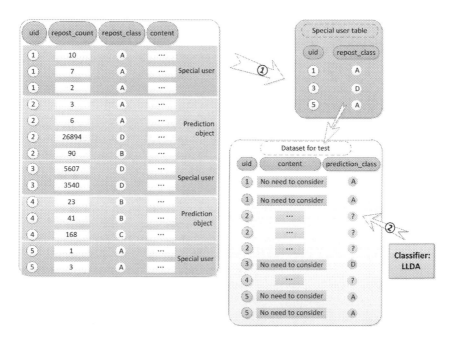

Fig. 1. The proposed approach

3.1   Extracting Attributes of User

Instead of directly predicting the exact number of reposts, we divided the micro-blog messages into four different repost volume "classes": A (1-20); B (21-100); C (101-1000); D (1001-). Most users have only one popularity class, or they have a high proportion in one class. That is, to a large extent the micro-blog messages posted by the same user may receive similarity attention or repost counts over a period of time. Therefore, we can categorize users by their historical counts of been reposted.

In this part, we extracted the users who only had one popularity class to generate "special user table". When predicted the popularity class of one micro-blog in the testing data, if that particular micro-blog was released by one special user, then we had no need to consider the content of that micro-blog message and could directly determine the popularity class by the user's historical counts of been reposted.

3.2   Analyzing Text Content of Micro-Blogs

Short text classification is different from traditional document in its high sparse features, strong context dependency and noise [8]. Given the character of micro-blog's short text, LDA [9] is more suitable for analyzing user's interest because it can find implicit semantic information of the document. It is an unsupervised Bayesian model which has three-layer structure of document-topic-word. As one of the most popular topic models, LDA makes the generative assumption that each document contains multiple topics in varying proportions.

In contrast to the standard probabilistic topic model, a supervised model can take full advantages of the additional information in a document. For example, in the document classification task, there may be some documents whose categories are known. These can be input to the model and play an important role in modeling. As a mutation of LDA, LLDA [10] can be used to do multi-classification on labeled documents, which establishes one-to-one mapping from topic to label and learns the relationship between words and labels. It adds an additional layer of class label information and improves the problem of compulsive allocation compared with the traditional LDA model.

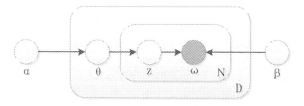

Fig. 2. Graphical model of LDA: N is the number of words in each document; ω is represented the word; z is the topic sampled from topic vector θ; α and β are the parameters of the Dirichlet Distribution.

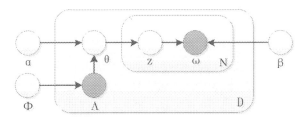

Fig. 3. Graphical model of LLDA: Λ is represented the label; Φ is the label prior for topic k

Figures 2 and 3 show the graphical model representation of LDA and LLDA, respectively. We can see that unlike LDA, LLDA incorporates supervision by simply constraining the topic model to use only those topics that correspond to a document's (observed) label set. The generative process for LLDA is shown in Table 1.

Table 1. Generative process for LLDA

1   For each topic $k \in \{1, \dots, K\}$:

2   Generate $\beta_k = (\beta_{k.1}, \dots, \beta_{k,V})^T \sim \text{Dir}(\cdot \,|\eta)$

3   For each document d :

4   For each topic $k \in \{1, \dots, K\}$

5   Generate $\Lambda_k^{(d)} \in \{0,1\} \sim \text{Bernoulli}(\cdot \,|\Phi_k)$

6   Generate $\alpha^{(d)} = L^{(d)} \times \alpha$

7   Generate $\theta^{(d)} = \left(\theta_{l_1}, \dots, \theta_{l_{M_d}}\right)^T \sim \text{Dir}(\cdot \,|\alpha^{(d)})$

8   For each i in $\{1, \dots, N_d\}$:

9   Generate $z_i \in \left\{\lambda_1^{(d)}, \dots, \lambda_{M_d}^{(d)}\right\} \sim \text{Mult}(\cdot \,|\theta^{(d)})$

10   Generate $\omega_i \in \{1, \dots, V\} \sim \text{Mulit}(\cdot \,|\beta_{z_i})$

λ is the vector of document's labels. L is a document-specific label projection matrix. Please see the original work [10] for more details.

In this paper, we used the popularity classes as the labels of each micro-blog and then trained LLDA to do the multi-class classification. Our goal is to discover if any predictors relevant only to the short social network content exist and if it is possible to make a reasonable forecast of the spread of a micro-blog based on its topics. We conducted our experiments on a large scale dataset.

4 Dataset Descriptions

Sina Weibo is a Chinese micro-blog website. It is one of the most popular sites in China, with a market penetration similar to Twitter. By 2017 the number of monthly active users in Sina Weibo has reached 392 million, accounting for 50.7% of the

Chinese netizen [11]. And "Weibo" is a Chinese word for "micro-blog". User behaviors such as reposting, commenting and liking are important factors that can be used to estimate the quality of a certain weibo and implement the recommendation and feed controlling strategy. In this work, we used "reposts" as a measure of popularity and addressed the problem by utilizing machine learning techniques to predict in which range of popularity new messages will be reposted in the future.

We got the datasets from a Sina Weibo Interaction-prediction Competition. The dataset samples on users and takes out the original weibos of each target user in half a year (from 20140701 to 20141231). All the user id and weibo id are encrypted. The data structure is shown in Table 2.

Table 2. Data structure

Attribute	Description
uid	user id. Sampled and encrypted
mid	weibo id. Sampled and encrypted
time	post time. Format YYYYMMDDHHmm
repost_count	amount of repost within one week after posting
comment_count	amount of comment within one week after posting
like_count	amount of like within one week after posting
content	weibo content

Figure 4 shows the log distribution of total weibos over all data, demonstrating a long tail shape which is in agreement with other findings on distribution of Twitter information cascades [12]. The graph also indicates that weibos with zero reposts lie outside of the general linear trend of the graph because they did not propagate on the weibo social network.

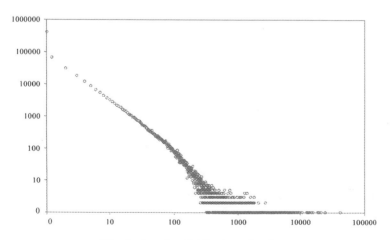

Fig. 4. Log-log distribution of weibos

5 Experiment

We focus this work on the content of a weibo as well as its source of publication. Therefore, we mainly analyze the text contents of weibos and extract the attributes of the users according to their historical counts of been reposted. As discussed in Sect. 4, there is evident in how the zero-repost weibos do not follow the linear trend of the rest of data points in Fig. 4. Consequently, we did not include a zero-repost class in our classification scheme and performed the classification by only considering those weibos that were reposted.

In the first part, we extracted the users who only had one popularity class to generate "special user table". Finally, we got 4462 special users, accounting to 37.14% of all the 12015 users in the training data.

In the second part, we should process the text content first. Given the openness and arbitrariness of the social media, the choice of words in weibo is not really normative. Therefore, we should wash the data before handling it, including word segmentation, deleting web links and special symbols, stemming English terms and remove the stop words. The weibo text less than three terms after washing will be excluded. Finally we got 220,161 weibo messages totally.

For the multi-class classification problem, we report accuracy for each class. Five-fold cross validation was used to test the accuracy of our method. In the comparison experiment, we selected three common classification models: Naïve Bayes, J48 and Logistic regression. The feature that input in the model was word frequency matrix.

We achieved a stable accuracy of 65.78% by using LLDA, which was better than these three common classification models (see Table 3). And we also got an overall accuracy of 72.56% by using this two-stage method for weibo popularity prediction. Table 4 shows the prediction accuracy of each class. The results are better in Class A and Class D but poor in Class B and Class C, which is similar to this work [6].

Table 3. Prediction accuracy of four models

Model	LLDA	Naïve Bayes	J48	Logistic regression
Prediction accuracy	65.78%	51.74%	60.27%	61.03%

Table 4. Prediction accuracy of each class

Class name	Accuracy
A	68.88%
B	49.06%
C	32.43%
D	65.83%

6 Discussion and Conclusion

In this work we predicted the popularity of a weibo by focusing on its text content as well as its source of publication (user's attributes). First, we categorized users by their historical counts of been reposted. Then, we applied LLDA to predict the popularity class of that specific weibo if it was not posted by the special users. Our results show that this method can be effective in providing a range of popularity for weibo.

The result in Table 3 indicates that LLDA performs better than these classification algorithms in predicting weibos' popularity, even if it is not a specialized classification model. This is in agreement with the intuition that people understand the meaning of entire text rather than just looking at the words one by one. That is to say, after receiving the semantic information of the micro-blog, users usually compare that micro-blog with their interests and needs, then decide to repost or not. And our experiments show that it's possible to estimate ranges of popularity with an overall accuracy of 72.56% only considering short text contents and people's historical reposting levels. It means that it's really helpful to think that most users have only one popularity class over a period of time.

Based on this, the article has three main contributions. First, implicit semantic information has been considered. Most studies just analyzed the content at the level of words and ignored the semantic information when studying micro-blog reposting prediction problem. Our goal is to discover if any predictors relevant only to the micro-blog's text exist and if it is possible to make a reasonable forecast of the spread of a micro-blog based on its text. Now this article demonstrates that considering the topic or the implicit semantic information of the text content is really helpful in predicting the micro-blog popularity. Second, according to our summary, this paper is the first research to utilize LLDA this multi-label text classifier to study the influence of one micro-blog's topic on its reposting scale. And the overall accuracy demonstrates that this two-stage method can effectively predict the popularity of a micro-blog prior to its release. Third, the model can be interpretable. Unlike those specialized classification algorithms, the results produced by LLDA are semantically meaningful and declarative. Also, LLDA can generate top-n relevant words of each label class, so it's easy to figure out which words are most relevant in each category. That is to say, if we used some words selectively in weibo, we may get better reposting results.

In Table 4, we can see that the prediction accuracy of class A and class D are better than the other two middle classes. It indicates that weibos only receiving a small audience and attracting a great number of reposts might be very different from the weibos in the medium levels (especially class C). And it is also important to keep in mind that while it is intriguing to pay attention to the most popular weibos—those that become viral on the social network—huge weibos actually spread in medium numbers. However, it's difficult to predict the medium level as the results show. Therefore, more features will be considered to make the prediction results more precisely.

This research mainly investigated the influence of semantic information in a micro-blog on its popularity. Therefore, future works could extend this research by studying other features, such as emotional factors, special symbols in micro-blogs.

Acknowledgements. This work is supported in part by National Natural Science Foundation of China (Project No. 71701134), The Humanity and Social Science Youth Foundation of Ministry of Education of China (Project No. 16YJC630153), National Taipei University of Technology-Shenzhen University Joint Research Program (Project No. 2018003), and Natural Science Foundation of Guangdong Province of China (Project No. 2017A030310427).

References

1. Bandari, R., Asur, S., Huberman, B.A.: The pulse of news in social media: forecasting popularity. In: 6th International AAAI Conference on Weblogs and Social Media, pp. 26–33. AAAI Press, Dublin (2012)
2. Yang, Z., Guo, J., Cai, K., Tang, J., Li, J., Zhang, L., Zhong, S.: Understanding retweeting behaviors in social networks. In: 19th ACM International Conference on Information and Knowledge Management, pp. 1633–1636. ACM Press, Toronto (2010)
3. Romero, D.M., Meeder, B., Kleinberg, J.: Differences in the mechanics of information diffusion across topics: idioms, political hashtags, and complex contagion on Twitter. In: 20th International Conference on World Wide Web, pp. 695–704. ACM Press, Hyderabad, India (2011)
4. Xiong, X., Zhou, G., Huang, Y., Ma, J.: Predicting popularity of tweets on Sina Weibo. J. Inf. Eng. Univ. **13**(4), 496–502 (2012)
5. Li, Y., Yu, H., Liu, L.: Predict algorithm of micro-blog retweet scale based on SVM. Appl. Res. Comput. **30**(9), 2594–2597 (2013)
6. Hong, L., Dan, O., Davison, B.D.: Predicting popular messages in Twitter. In: 20th International Conference on World Wide Web, pp. 57–58. ACM Press, Hyderabad, India (2011)
7. Li, Q., Jiang, J., Li, Y., Liu, Y.: The retweeting scale classification prediction of government micro-blogs in China. J. Intell. **37**(1), 95–99 (2018)
8. Tan, C.: Short text classification based on LDA and SVM. Int. J. Appl. Math. Stat. **51**(22), 205–214 (2013)
9. Blei, D.M., Ng, A.Y., Jordan, M.I.: Latent Dirichlet allocation. J. Mach. Learn. Res. **3** (2003), 993–1022 (2003)
10. Ramage, D., Hall, D., Nallapati, R., Manning, C.D.: Labeled LDA: a supervised topic model for credit attribution in multi-labeled corpora. In: The 2009 Conference on Empirical Methods in Natural Language Processing, pp. 248–256. ACL Press, Singapore (2009)
11. Sina Science and Technology Homepage. http://tech.sina.com.cn/i/2018–02-13/doc-ifyrmfmc2280063.shtml. Accessed 2018/4/6
12. Zhou, Z., Bandari, R., Kong, J., Qian, H., Roychowdhury, V.: Information resonance on Twitter: watching Iran. In: 1st Workshop on Social Media Analytics, pp. 123–131. ACM Press, Washington (2010)

VPSO-Based CCR-ELM for Imbalanced Classification

Yi-nan Guo, Pei Zhang, Ning Cui, JingJing Chen, and Jian Cheng[(⊠)]

School of Information and Control Engineering, China University of Mining
and Technology, Xuzhou 221008, Jiangsu, China
chengjian@cumt.edu.cn

Abstract. In class-specific cost regulation extreme learning machine
(CCR-ELM) for the class imbalance problems, the key parameters, including the
number of hidden nodes, the input weights, the hidden biases and the tradeoff
factors are normally chosen randomly or preset by human. This made the algorithm responding slowly and generalization worse. Unsuitable quantity of hidden
nodes might form some useless neuron nodes and make the network complex. So
an improved CCR-ELM based on particle swarm optimization with variable
length is present. Each particle consists of above key parameters and its length
varies with the number of hidden nodes. The experimental results for nine
imbalance dataset show that particle swarm optimization with variable length can
find better parameters of CCR-ELM and corresponding CCR-ELM had better
classification accuracy. In addition, the classification performance of the proposed classification algorithm is relatively stable under different imbalance ratios.

Keywords: Variable length · Particle swarm optimization
Class-specific cost regulation extreme learning machine · The class imbalance

1 Introduction

In many real-world classification problems, the amount of data in a class is far less than
the other classes. We call them imbalance datasets. Two kinds of imbalance classification methods had been studied by researchers. One is data-based imbalance classification strategies. They weakened the deviation of data size in different class by
over-sampling for minority samples or under-sampling for majority class. Synthetic
minority over-sampling technique (SMOTE) [1] and SMOTE-based improved sampling algorithms [2, 3] were the popular data-based strategies. Algorithm-based
strategies enhanced the classification performances by improving the traditional classification algorithms according to the data features. For instance, the classification cost
was introduced into the weight updating strategy of AdaBoost to highlight the effect of
minority class [4]. Kernel was employed to adjust the classification boundary of
support vector machine for the imbalanced learning [5]. A weighted extreme learning
machine [6] was presented to strengthen the role of minority class by assigning an extra
weight to each sample. Xiao [7] proposed a class-specific cost regulation extreme
learning machine (CCR-ELM), together with its kernel-based extension, to solve
binary or multiclass classification problems with imbalance distribution.

© Springer International Publishing AG, part of Springer Nature 2018
Y. Tan et al. (Eds.): ICSI 2018, LNCS 10942, pp. 361–369, 2018.
https://doi.org/10.1007/978-3-319-93818-9_34

In recent years, extreme learning machine had become an attention-attracting method due to its faster speed and better generalization. It provided a unified learning platform by employing generalized single hidden layer feed-forward networks (SLFNs) and least-square-based learning algorithm [8]. To solve different kinds of regression or classification problems, some improved ELM algorithms were proposed. Online sequential extreme learning machines employed additive hidden nodes with radial basis function in SLFNs show better generalization to deal with online data flow [9]. Incremental extreme learning machine [10] randomly added hidden nodes and manually adjusted the output weights linking the hidden layer and the output layer. Semi-supervised ELM and unsupervised ELM fit for tackling the classification problems that collecting large amount of labeled data was hard and time-consuming [11]. However, above ELM-based learning algorithms might result in ill-condition problems due to the randomly selected input weights and hidden biases. Non-optimal or redundant input weights and hidden biases also made ELM responding slowly and led to worse generalization [12]. Thus, some population-based intelligence optimization algorithms, such as genetic algorithm (GA) [13], particle swarm optimization(PSO) [14, 15] and krill herd algorithm [16], were introduced to find the optimal parameters of the activation function in ELM-based learning algorithms so as to improve the classification accuracy.

In order to improve the classification accuracy of the imbalance learning problems, the network's structure of CCR-ELM decided by the number of hidden nodes, the input weights, the hidden biases and two tradeoff factors is optimized by particle swarm optimization with variable length, so as to avoid the useless neuron nodes and simplify the complex of the network. Especially, the length of the particles vary from the number of hidden nodes.

2   Class-Specific Cost Regulation Extreme Learning Machine

In extreme learning machine, the input weights and hidden biases of SLFNs were randomly chosen. Corresponding output were analytically determined by generalized inverse operation of output matrix in the hidden layer. Suppose there are N distinct samples (X_i, t_i) with $X_i = [x_{i1}, x_{i2}, \ldots, x_{in}]^T \in R^n$ and $t_i = [t_{i1}, t_{i2}, \ldots, t_{im}]^T \in R^m$. Let a_i and β_i be the input and output weights, respectively. b_i is the biases. A SLFN with L hidden nodes is modeled as follows [7].

$$\sum_{i=1}^{L} \beta_i g(a_i, b_i, X_j) = o_j, j = 1, \ldots, N \tag{1}$$

Here, $g(\bullet)$ is the activation function. The error between the estimated outputs o_j and the actual outputs t_i shall be zero once the SLFNs can exactly approximate the feature of data. Let $\beta = [\beta_1^T, \ldots, \beta_L^T]^T$ and $T = [T_1^T, \ldots, T_N^T]^T$. The model with the actual outputs can be simplified as $H\beta = T$.

$$
H = \begin{bmatrix} g(a_1,b_1,X_1) & \cdots & g(a_L,b_L,X_1) \\ \vdots & \ddots & \vdots \\ g(a_1,b_1,X_N) & \cdots & g(a_L,b_L,X_N) \end{bmatrix}_{N \times L} \tag{2}
$$

H is so-called output matrix of hidden layer. During the training process, the parameters in each hidden node, including a_i and b_i, are not adjusted after randomly generated. Let $H^\dagger$ be the Moore–Penrose generalized inverse of H. The optimal output weights are gotten by minimizing the cost function $\|o - t\|$. For the class imbalance problems, two parameters, include C^+ for minority positive samples and C^- for majority negative samples, are employed to make both classes rebalanced by the optimal classification plane. Suppose the number of the minority positive samples and majority negative samples are l_1 and l_2. The CCR-ELM is modelled as follows [7].

$$
\min \left(\frac{1}{2}\|\beta\|^2 + \frac{1}{2}C^+ \sum_{\substack{i=1|t_{i}=+1}}^{l_1} \xi_i^2 + + \frac{1}{2}C^- \sum_{\substack{i=1|t_{i}=-1}}^{l_2} \xi_i^2 \right) \tag{3}
$$

$$
s.t. \ h(x_i)\beta = t_i - \xi_i, i = 1, \ldots N.
$$

Corresponding output weights are estimated as follows.

$$
\hat{\beta} = H^\dagger T = \begin{cases} \left(\dfrac{I}{C^+} + \dfrac{I}{C^-} + H^T H \right)^{-1} H^T T, L < N \\ H^T \left(\dfrac{I}{C^+} + \dfrac{I}{C^-} + H^T H \right)^{-1} T, L \geq N \end{cases} \tag{4}
$$

In CCR-ELM, there are five key parameters, including the number of hidden nodes L, the input weights a_{ij}, the hidden biases b_i, C^+ and C^-. The former three parameters decide the structure of SLFNs and all of them have the direct impact on the classification accuracy.

3   CCR-ELM Based on Variable Length Particle Swarm Optimization

Five key parameters in CCR-ELM consist of a particle. Because the number of the input weights and hidden biases depend on the number of hidden nodes, the length of corresponding particles also vary with L. However, the length of each particle in traditional PSO algorithm is fixed and similar. Therefore, an improve particle swarm optimization with variable length (VPSO) is employed to find the optimal parameters in CCR-ELM. We call it VPSO-based CCR-ELM.

Assume that a particle is denoted by $x_i = (x_{i1}, x_{i2}, x_{i3}, \ldots, x_{iD})$. The local best and global best are expressed by $p_i = (p_{i1}, p_{i2}, p_{i3}, \ldots, p_{iM})$ and $p_g = (p_{g1}, p_{g2}, p_{g3}, \ldots, p_{gN})$. Their dimensions denoted by D, M and N respectively may be different. During the evolution process of VPSO, once D is different from M and N, the chord-length parameterization method is employed to calculate the equivalent local best and global best denoted by $\overline{p_{id}^t}$ and $\overline{p_{gd}^t}$ [17]. The chord-length is mathematically defined as the distance of two particles along any dimension, denoted as follows.

$$cl(x_{ij}, x_{ik}) = \left\| x_{ij} - x_{ik} \right\|_2 \tag{5}$$

The equivalent length of x_i, p_i and p_g are defined as $\|x_i\| = \sum_{j=1}^{D-1} cl(x_{ij}, x_{i(j+1)})$, $\|p_i\| = \sum_{j=1}^{M-1} cl(p_{ij}, p_{i(j+1)})$ and $\|p_g\| = \sum_{j=1}^{N-1} cl(p_{gj}, p_{g(j+1)})$, respectively. According to the geometric proportion of the chord-length, as x_i^t flies toward the local best p_i^t, x_{id}^t must be close to $\overline{p_{id}^t}$ and $\overline{p_{id}^t}$ satisfies Eq. 6.

$$\begin{cases} \overline{p_{id}^t} = p_{id}^t & d = 1, D \\ \frac{cl(\overline{p_{id}^t}, p_{i1}^t)}{\|p_i^t\|} = \frac{cl(x_{id}^t, x_{i1}^t)}{\|x_i^t\|} & d \in (1, D) \end{cases} \tag{6}$$

Similarly, as x_i^t flies toward the global best p_g^t, $\overline{p_{gd}^t}$ satisfies Eq. 7.

$$\begin{cases} \overline{p_{gd}^t} = p_{gd}^t & d = 1, D \\ \frac{cl(\overline{p_{gd}^t}, p_{g1}^t)}{\|p_g^t\|} = \frac{cl(x_{id}^t, x_{i1}^t)}{\|x_i^t\|} & d \in (1, D) \end{cases} \tag{7}$$

The velocity $v_{id}^{(t+1)}$ and position $x_{id}^{(t+1)}$ of ith particle are updated as follows.

$$v_{id}^{(t+1)} = \omega v_{id}^t + c_1 r_1 \left(\overline{p_{id}^t} - x_{id}^t \right) + c_2 r_2 \left(\overline{p_{gd}^t} - x_{gd}^t \right) \tag{8}$$

$$x_{id}^{(t+1)} = x_{id}^t + v_{id}^{(t+1)}. \tag{9}$$

In order to evaluate the classification accuracy of each particle, the fitness function is defined as the root mean square error on the training set.

$$F = \sqrt{\frac{\sum_{j=1}^{N} \left\| \sum_{i=1}^{L} \hat{\beta}_i g(a_i, b_i, X_j) - t_j \right\|_2}{N}} \tag{10}$$

The detailed algorithm steps of VPSO-based CCR-ELM are shown as follows.

Algorithm 1: VPSO-based CCR-ELM

Step 1:The imbalanced dataset $X = \{(x_i,t_i), i = 1,2,...N\}$ is divided into the training set X_{train} and testing set X_{test}.

Step 2:The initial population P is randomly generated based on the defined lower and upper bounds of variables.

Step 3:Finding the optimal parameters of CCR-ELM by VPSO and output these optimal parameters.

Step 4:Classify the imbalanced dataset by CCR-ELM with the optimal parameters.

---

4 Experimental Results and Discussion

In order to fully analyze the performances of the proposed classification method, nine binary-class imbalanced datasets chosen from UCI Machine Learning Repository [18] are employed in the experiments. Detailed information about these datasets are listed in Table 1. The imbalanced ratio varies from 0.1 to 0.4.

Table 1. The detailed information about binary-class datasets from UCI

Dataset	The number of attributes	The number of training data	The number of testing data	Imbalance ratio
Wine1	13	100	78	0.3333
Wine 2	12	2898	2000	0.2461
Adult	14	28842	20000	0.2500
WPBC	34	100	98	0.2533
WDBC	32	300	317	0.4000
Dota2	116	50000	52944	0.1000
Iris	4	75	75	0.3333
Car	6	1000	728	0.2997
Poker hand	11	25010	100000	0.2382

To evaluate the imbalance classification methods, not only the overall accuracy of all samples defined in Eq. 11, but also the classification accuracy obtained within each class are concerned. However, because the overall accuracy is sensitive to the class distribution and cannot fully reflect the imbalance classification performances, G-mean is present [19]. Suppose TP, TN, FP, FN stand for the number of data with true positive, true negative, false positive and false negative, respectively.

$$overall\,accuracy = \frac{TP + TN}{TP + FP + TN + FN} \tag{11}$$

$$G - mean = \sqrt{\frac{TP}{TP + FN} \times \frac{TN}{TN + FP}} \tag{12}$$

In CCR-ELM, the sigmoid function expressed by $g(a, b, x) = 1/(1 + exp(-(ax + b)))$ is employed as the activation function. The bound of input weight and biases are $a_i, b_i \in [-1, 1] \cdot C^+, C^- \in \{2^{-24}, 2^{-23}, \ldots, 2^{25}\}$ and $L \in \{10, 20, \ldots, 1000\}$. Taking Car dataset as an example, the effect of L on the classification performance is shown in Fig. 1. With the increasing of L, the classification accuracy becomes better. And G-mean is relatively stable as $L \geq 500$. However, larger L means the networks contains more hidden nodes, which increases the computational complexity. The classification performance under different C^+ and C^- as $L = 400$ is shown in Fig. 2. Obviously, G-mean is sensitive to both C^+ and C^-. And the classification accuracy retains worse as C^+ and C^- are less than 2^{-10}.

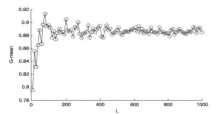
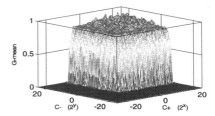

Fig. 1. The G-mean under different L

Fig. 2. The G-mean under different C^+ and C^-

To improve the generalization of CCR-ELM, GA, PSO and VPSO were introduced to optimize the key parameters of CCR-ELM. During the experiments, the terminal iteration is 1500 and the population size is 20 for all methods. For GA-based CCR-ELM, the crossover probability is 0.9, the mutation probability is 0.01, and the generation gap is 0.9. For PSO-based CCR-ELM, $c_1 = 1.5, c_2 = 1.7$ and the inertia weight $w = 1$. The parameter of VPSO is the same as PSO. The half of the solutions will be re-initialized every 200 generations [8]. By comparing above all CCR-ELM, the statistical results under 30 running times are listed in Tables 2 and 3.

The overall accuracy indicate that all of methods have the similar classification accuracy except for Iris dataset. By further comparing G-mean shown in Table 3, we see that traditional CCR-ELM has the worse classification accuracy. After optimizing the parameters of CCR-ELM, the classifiers have better accuracy for most datasets. Hence, to optimize the key parameters of CCR-ELM is necessary. The overall accuracy and G-mean of GA-, PSO- and VPSO-based CCR-ELM show that VPSO-based CCR-ELM has best performances, especially for the large-scale datasets, such as Adult, Dota2 and Poker hand datasets.

In order to analyze the impact of the imbalanced ratios on the classification performance, the experiments under the imbalanced ratios changing from 0.1 to 0.4 are

Table 2. Compare the overall accuracy of CCR-ELM and GA-, PSO-, VPSO-based CCR-ELM

Dataset	CCR-ELM	GA-based CCR-ELM	PSO-based CCR-ELM	VPSO-based CCR-ELM
	(C^+,C^-, L) Max/average	(C^+,C^-, L) Max/average	(C^+,C^-, L) Max/average	(C^+,C^-, L) Max/average
Wine	$(2^7,2^6,70)$ 96.87/95.41	$(6.59^7,3.44^6,70)$ 92.55/91.17	$(3.76^6,9.78^6,50)$ 97.75/97.23	$(1.82^5,1.72^5,70)$ 98.75/97.10
Wine 2	$(2^3,2^{-10},10)$ 97.30/96.55	$(5.37^3,1.12^3,250)$ 98.91/97.96	$(1.74^3,1.81^4,170)$ 99.06/98.95	$(5.75^6,3.70^6,60)$ 99.24/99.03
Adult	$(2^7,2^{-1},600)$ 76.53/75.71	$(1.43^7,5.11^6,310)$ 81.72/79.77	$(6.34^7,5.12^6,130)$ 80.48/78.98	$(2.81^4,1.68^4,30)$ 86.14/84.85
WPBC	$(2^{-12},2^4,20)$ 82.47/80.82	$(3.38^6,2.89^7,90)$ 85.30/83.99	$(3.32^7,1.77^7,90)$ 72.16/70.61	$(6.77^3,5.32^3,150)$ 92.88/91.43
WDBC	$(2^7,2^{-21},60)$ 90.82/90.13	$(4.46^7,7.43^6,80)$ 90.12/89.01	$(5.38^6,1.22^7,220)$ 91.50/90.37	$(8.39^2,1.54^3,40)$ 92.41/91.55
Dota2	$(2^{13},2^6,90)$ 85.69/85.14	$(2.32^5,6.65^6,340)$ 84.42/81.11	$(4.42^5,1.33^6,60)$ 83.10/81.32	$(2.81^4,1.68^4,90)$ 85.42/85.04
Iris	$(2^0,2^1,30)$ 41.33/37.86	$(1.22^6,8.09^6,120)$ 60.33/59.63	$(4.99^5,2.54^7,280)$ 35.52/34.66	$(2.53^7,4.92^6,30)$ 100/99.54
Car	$(2^{-8},2^6,60)$ 84.14/82.81	$(4.96^7,3.78^7,60)$ 84.64/83.77	$(3.09^7,2.30^7,420)$ 84.74/83.73	$(9.62^4,1.20^6,60)$ 85.69/81.94
Poker hand	$(2^{11},2^{-17},70)$ 78.42/74.98	$(5.41^4,3.86^4,130)$ 85.33/83.46	$(2.42^6,2.33^7,120)$ 86.53/83.23	$(8.42^7,5.50^6,130)$ 89.87/88.98

Table 3. Compare the G-mean among CCR-ELM and GA-, PSO-, VPSO-based CCR-ELM

Dataset	CCR-ELM	GA-based CCR-ELM	PSO-based CCR-ELM	VPSO-based CCR-ELM
	(C^+,C^-,L) Max/average	(C^+,C^-,L) Max/average	(C^+,C^-,L) Max/average	(C^+,C^-,L) Max/average
Wine	$(2^{-4},2^{-3},20)$ 0.9616/0.9540	$(6.77^6,1.46^6,160)$ 0.9263/0.9143	$(1.97^7,2.38^7,120)$ 0.9832/0.9788	$(6.13^4,3.60^4,60)$ 0.9858/0.9794
Wine 2	$(2^{-2},2^{-23},20)$ 0.9612/0.9526	$(3.42^5,9.47^7,120)$ 0.9804/0.9724	$(2.73^7,1.51^7,10)$ 0.9819/0.9800	$(9.49^5,7.71^4,130)$ 0.9891/0.9877
Adult	$(2^{18},2^{-12},370)$ 0.6616/0.6540	$(6.31^4,6.78^5,30)$ 0.8407/0.8367	$(4.20^6,1.55^6,40)$ 0.8223/0.8108	$(6.93^4,6.23^6,70)$ 0.8858/0.8647
WPBC	$(2^7,2^{-1},30)$ 0.6896/0.6062	$(3.43^6,3.97^6,140)$ 0.8426/0.8352	$(6.69^6,3.15^7,100)$ 0.7009/0.6364	$(9.90^6,1.21^6,60)$ 0.8905/0.8766
WDBC	$(2^4,2^{-13},10)$ 0.8616/0.8540	$(5.23^6,6.21^6,60)$ 0.9057/0.8982	$(1.54^6,8.07^6,30)$ 0.9123/0.9037	$(1.40^7,2.32^7,160)$ 0.9185/0.9127
Dota2	$(2^4,2^{21},30)$ 0.0036/0.020	$(4.76^5,3.53^6,90)$ 0.8508/0.8437	$(3.67^5,7.43^4,50)$ 0.8406/0.8312	$(6.45^5,2.41^6,30)$ 0.8779/0.8696
Iris	$(2^{-8},2^{-16},60)$ 0.2464/0.1963	$(4.23^4,2.61^6,120)$ 0.6421/0.6372	$(2.94^7,2.25^7,150)$ 0.2132/0.1414	$(1.97^7,1.32^7,10)$ 1/0.9926
Car	$(2^{-1},2^5,530)$ 0.7802/0.7419	$(8.44^7,8.00^7,80)$ 0.8522/0.8436	$(2.25^7,2.80^7,100)$ 0.8640/0.8486	$(5.11^4,2.21^4,90)$ 0.8927/0.8738
Poker hand	$(2^4,2^{17},80)$ 0.4266/0.3676	$(6.67^5,3.98^4,210)$ 0.8212/0.8011	$(1.10^6,7.84^6,130)$ 0.7963/0.7748	$(5.53^5,2.65^4,220)$ 0.8958/0.8821

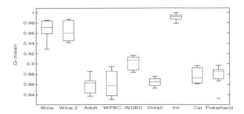

Fig. 3. The boxplot of the G-mean

done for above nine datasets. The G-mean under different imbalanced ratios shown in Fig. 3 indicate that no matter the imbalance ratios change or not, VPSO-based CCR-ELM has the relatively stable classification performance.

5   Conclusions

To improve the generalization and classification accuracy, VPSO-based CCR-ELM is proposed to deal with the class imbalance problems. VPSO is employed to find the optimal parameters of CCR-ELM, including the number of hidden nodes, the input weights, the hidden biases and the tradeoff factors. All above parameters compose of a particle of VPSO and its length varies with the number of hidden nodes. The experimental results for nine imbalance dataset show that VPSO can find better parameters of CCR-ELM and corresponding CCR-ELM had better classification accuracy than other optimization algorithms, such as GA and PSO. In addition, the classification performance of the proposed classification method is relatively stable under different imbalance ratios. The applications of the proposed algorithm in practical class imbalance problems are our future works.

Acknowledgements. This work is supported by National Natural Science Foundation of China under Grant 61573361, National Key Research and Development Program under Grant 2016YFC0801406, and Six talent peaks project in Jiangsu Province under Grant No.2017-DZXX-046.

References

1. Chawla, N.V., Bowyer, K.W., Hall, L.O., et al.: SMOTE: synthetic minority over-sampling technique. J. Artif. Intell. Res. **16**(1), 321–357 (2002)
2. Ramentol, E., Caballero, Y., Bello, R., et al.: SMOTE-RS B: A hybrid preprocessing approach based on oversampling and undersampling for high imbalanced datasets using SMOTE and rough sets theory. Knowl. Inf. Syst. **33**(2), 245–265 (2012)
3. Gao, M., Hong, X., Chen, S., et al.: A combined SMOTE and PSO based RBF classifier for two-class imbalanced problems. Neurocomputing **74**(17), 3456–3466 (2011)
4. Sun, Y., Kamel, M.S., Wong, A.K.C., et al.: Cost-sensitive boosting for classification of imbalanced data. Pattern Recogn. **40**(12), 3358–3378 (2007)

5. Wu, G., Chang, E.Y.: KBA: kernel boundary alignment considering imbalanced data distribution. IEEE Trans. Knowl. Data Eng. **17**(6), 786–795 (2005)
6. Zong, W., Huang, G.B., Chen, Y.: Weighted extreme learning machine for imbalance learning. Neurocomputing **101**, 229–242 (2013)
7. Xiao, W., Zhang, J., Li, Y., et al.: Class-specific cost regulation extreme learning machine for imbalanced classification. Neurocomputing **261**, 70–82 (2017)
8. Rong, H.J., Huang, G.B., Sundararajan, N., et al.: Online sequential fuzzy extreme learning machine for function approximation and classification problems. IEEE Trans. Syst. Man Cybern. Part B **39**(4), 1067–1072 (2009)
9. Mirza, B., Lin, Z., Liu, N.: Ensemble of subset online sequential extreme learning machine for class imbalance and concept drift. Neurocomputing **149**, 316–329 (2015)
10. Huang, G.B., Chen, L., Siew, C.K.: Universal approximation using incremental constructive feedforward networks with random hidden nodes. IEEE Trans. Neural Netw. **17**(4), 879–892 (2006)
11. Huang, G., Song, S., Gupta, J.N., et al.: Semi-supervised and unsupervised extreme learning machines. IEEE Trans. Cybern. **44**(12), 2405–2417 (2014)
12. Huang, D.S., Ip, H.H., Law, K.C., et al.: Zeroing polynomials using modified constrained neural network approach. IEEE Trans. Neural Netw. **16**(3), 721–732 (2005)
13. Ertam, F., Avcı, E.: A new approach for internet traffic classification: GA-WK-ELM. Measurement **95**, 135–142 (2016)
14. Guo, Y.N., Zhang, P., Cheng, J., et al.: Interval multi-objective quantum-inspired cultural algorithms. Neural Comput. Appl. 1–14 (2016)
15. Han, F., Yao, H.F., Ling, Q.H.: An improved evolutionary extreme learning machine based on particle swarm optimization. Neurocomputing **116**, 87–93 (2013)
16. Guo, Y.-n., Zhang, P., Cheng, J., Zhang, Y., Yang, L., Shen, X., Fang, W.: An improved weighted ELM with Krill Herd algorithm for imbalanced learning. In: Tan, Y., Takagi, H., Shi, Y., Niu, B. (eds.) ICSI 2017. LNCS, vol. 10386, pp. 371–378. Springer, Cham (2017). https://doi.org/10.1007/978-3-319-61833-3_39
17. Hu, C.Y., Hu, B.J., Xiong, Y.H.: Mobile agent routing using variable-dimension PSO algorithm based on chord-length parameterization. National Doctoral Academic Forum on Information and Communications Technology, IET, 7–7 (2013)
18. Frank, A., Asuncion, A.: UCI Machine Learning Repository. University of California, Irvine, School of Information and Computer Sciences (2010). http://archive.ics.uci.edu/mlS
19. Yu, H., Sun, C., Yang, X., et al.: ODOC-ELM: Optimal decision outputs compensation-based extreme learning machine for classifying imbalanced data. Knowl.-Based Syst. **92**, 55–70 (2016)

An Ensemble Classifier Based on Three-Way Decisions for Social Touch Gesture Recognition

Gangqiang Zhang[1($\boxtimes$)], Qun Liu[1], Yubin Shi[1], and Hongying Meng[2]

[1] Chongqing Key Laboratory of Computational Intelligence,
Chongqing University of Posts and Telecommunications,
Chongqing 400065, People's Republic of China
tszgq2015@163.com
[2] Department of Electronic and Computer Engineering,
Brunel University London, Uxbridge, UK

Abstract. Touch is an important form of social interaction. In Human Robot Interaction (HRI), touch can provide additional information to other modalities, such as audio, visual. In this paper, an ensemble classifier based on three-way decisions is proposed to recognize touch gestures. Firstly, features are extracted from six perspectives and four classifiers are constructed on different scales with different preprocessing methods. Then an ensemble classifier is used to combine the four classifiers to classify touch gestures. Our method is tested on the public Corpus of Social Touch (CoST) dataset. The experiment results not only verify the validity of our method but also show a better performance of our ensemble classifier.

Keywords: Touch gesture recognition · Data preprocessing
Ensemble classifier · Three-way decisions

1 Introduction

Touch behavior is one of the important non-verbal forms of social interaction, which can describe the intensity emotions communicated by other modalities [1]. Touch is able to affect the emotions, attitude and social behavior in the communication between humans [2]. As a novel subject, it has drawn growing attention. Humans can understand the meaning of social touch such as emotions. Robot and other interfaces also need to understand social touch. In the social human-robot interaction, touch gesture can be used together with audio-visual cues to improve affect recognition performance [3]. So far, many researches have been carried out to design suitable devices for capturing and classifying social touch to reach the social intelligent interaction. Envisioned applications for these interfaces are like: robot therapy, remote communication and interactive stuffed animal [4–6].

© Springer International Publishing AG, part of Springer Nature 2018
Y. Tan et al. (Eds.): ICSI 2018, LNCS 10942, pp. 370–379, 2018.
https://doi.org/10.1007/978-3-319-93818-9_35

To spark the further study of social touch, the Social Touch Gesture Challenge was organized in 2015 [7], which focused on the recognition of touch gesture with social meaning performed by hand on a pressure-sensitive surface. Two datasets were given, CoST [5] and Human-Animal Affective Robot Touch (HAART) [8]. The challenge was summarized in the 2015 ACM International Conference on Multi-model Interaction (ICMI). In the challenge, Hughes et al. [9] used deep neural networks with hidden Markov models (DNN-HMMS), geometric moments and gesture level features to identify the two datasets, they got 56% accuracy of CoST, 71% accuracy of HAART. Balli Altuglu et al. [10] used image features, Hurst exponent, Hjorth parameters and autoregressive model coefficients as features, they got accuracy from 26% to 95% of CoST and around 60% to 70% of HAART. Gaus et al. [11] used the random forests classifier, and got the accuracy 59% and 67% separately. Ta et al. [12] proposed 273 features and used random forests classifier, got the accuracy for CoST 61.34%, and HAART 70.91%. The above 4 papers received top 4 in this challenge.

Three-way decisions is a kind of decision making model that conforms to human cognition, and it believes that people can make decisions immediately in the process of actual decision making if they have full confidence in accidence in acceptance or rejection. For those which they cannot make immediate decisions, people tend to postpone the judgment [13]. The essential ideas of three-way decisions are commonly used in everyday life and widely applied in many fields and disciplines, including medical decision-making, social judgment theory, hypothesis testing in statistics, peering review process, and management sciences [14].

The contributions of this paper is to explore an ensemble classifier based on three-way decisions for the recognition of social touch gestures. We use Corpus of Social Touch (CoST) introduced by Jung et al. [5] as our experimental dataset. In order to achieve a higher recognition accuracy, two kinds of preprocessing methods are proposed. The first one depends on the analysis of the procedure of data collection and the other one is inspired by banalization of gray-scale image. Firstly, four base classifiers are trained on different scale dataset by different preprocessing methods. Then based on three-way decisions, a new ensemble classifier is proposed to recognize touch gestures. Compared with the existing results, our method has obtained better performance.

The remainder of the paper is organized as following. In Sect. 2, the methods of preprocessing and features extraction are described. The ensemble classifier based on three-way decisions will be illustrated in Sect. 3. Section 4 contains the results analysis of experiments by comparing our method with other previous works. Finally, the conclusion is given in Sect. 5.

2 Data Preprocessing

2.1 Preprocessing Methods

As we all know removing the noise from the dataset is beneficial on receiving high quality data. In this section, two different preprocessing methods are proposed in our work, which is named "cutout" and "removing background".

Cutout. After performing a gesture, the participants need to press a key to see next gesture's instruction, which is shown on the computer monitor. So many invalid frames may be contained during segmentation between key strokes and the next gesture. We used the threshold of the maximum pressure sequence of each frame of the gesture as the reference, then truncated the signal bellowing the threshold on the earlier part and later part of each frame. In order to find the suitable sequence thresholds for "cutout", we tried the different ratio for the mean, median and maximum of the pressures sequence.

Removing Background. Some gestures are always performed too fast or too gently, so the signals captured by the sensor may be very weak and difficult to classify accurately. In order to enhance the valid part of frames as much as possible, we used the binarization method of gray-scale image for preprocessing. Each pressure value of the channel will be preserved if it is greater than the threshold, otherwise will be set to 0. Similarly, to find the suitable threshold for "removing background", we tried Otsu [15] value, the mean value and 50% maximum for all 64 sensors as the thresholds respectively. Using the random forest classifier to do many experiments, it was found the Otsu value could perform the best as the threshold.

2.2   Feature Extraction

We extract features from six different perspectives, some referenced the work of other researchers, some are obtained by ourselves through analyzing the characteristics of datasets. The total number of features is 331. They are illustrated as follows:

Basic Features. This part of the features are defined in [5], including duration, mean pressure, maximum pressure, mean pressure per column, mean pressure per row, pressure variability and displacement. There are total 24 features.

Histogram-Based Features. The whole pressure range (0–1023) is discretized by bins and each pressure for frames of the gestures is put into the bins depending on its value. The number of each bins is used as the features. Wingerden et al. [16] evaluated the amount of bins from 2 to 32, and find 8 bins performed best. There are total 8 features.

Sequence Features. We compute statistical metrics of the mean, maximum and sum for the pressure matrix of each frames separately as the features, including maximum, mean, median, mode, range, midrange, variance, standard deviation, coefficient of variation and peak count. Hence, there are total 39 features.

Gradient-Based Features. In order to extract the difference between the channels, we calculate the absolute difference between each single channel and its neighbor channel, including horizontal, vertical and diagonal for each frame. Firstly, the mean and maximum of these 210 gradient values for each frame are calculated to consist of two sequences, then the statistical metrics like the above are computed on these two sequences as the features. So there are 26 features totally.

Contact Area Features. It is necessary to extract the contact area for different gestures because of their characteristics. We take Otsu value, mean and 50% maximum of each frame as the threshold to consist of three sequences. Then statistical metrics like the above are computed on these three sequences as the features. In addition, we also take the contact area of the frame with the maximum summed pressure to be the features. There are a total of 42 features.

Channel-Based Features. Since there are 64 pressure sensors used on simulated skin to capture the variation of gestures, it is important to extract features based on every channels so as to get more precise and complete information. Hence, we captured the mean value of pressure, the variation of mean pressure and the percentage which is the number of pressure points greater than the Otsu threshold of each frame and the total number of frames for a channel. The number of these features are 192.

3   An Ensemble Classifier Based on Three-Way Decisions

After using our preprocessing method, 4 different datasets can be gotten, they are the original dataset, the dataset preprocessed by "cutout", the dataset preprocessed by "removing background" and the dataset preprocessed by both "cutout" and "removing background". We analysis and extract features from these datasets, then use random forest classifier to classify them by 10-fold cross validation separately. The experimental results illustrate that different preprocessing methods are suitable for different gestures' classification. Obviously, every gesture has its own characteristic. In order to combine the advantages of the above 4 preprocessing methods together, an ensemble classifier based on three-way decisions will be proposed in this section.

3.1   Three-Way Decisions

m-Category Classification Transformation. In order to take advantage of better base classifiers and reduce the influence of worse base classifiers, three-way decisions will be introduced. In [14], U is supposed as a finite nonempty set and C is a finite set of criteria. Three-way decisions divide U into three pair-wise disjoint regions, namely POS, NEG, and BND, which is called the positive, negative, and boundary regions, respectively. The positive and negative regions can be used to induce rules of acceptance and rejection; whenever it is impossible to make an acceptance or a rejection decision, the third non-commitment decision is made. And the three regions are defined by:

$$POS_{(\alpha,\beta)}(X) = \{x \in U \mid Pr(X \mid [x]) \geq \alpha\} \tag{1}$$

$$BND_{(\alpha,\beta)}(X) = \{x \in U \mid \beta < Pr(X \mid [x]) < \alpha\} \tag{2}$$

$$NEG_{(\alpha,\beta)}(X) = \{x \in U \mid Pr(X \mid [x]) \leq \beta\} \tag{3}$$

where $Pr(X \mid [x])$ is the conditional probability of the classification.

However, the three-way decisions can be just used to solve the two-category classification problems. In this paper there are m(m = 14) gestures to be classified. So it is necessary to transform m-category classification problem to m two-category classification problems at first. For example, referring the method of literature [17], obj_1, obj_2, obj_3 are supposed to belong to one of 3 categories C_1, C_2, C_3. The transformation procedure of a 3 two-category classification is shown in Table 1.

Table 1. The transformation procedure with three-way decisions.

Test data	$C_1(C_1, \neg C_1)$	$C_2(C_2, \neg C_2)$	$C_3(C_3, \neg C_3)$	Decision results
obj_1	BND	NEG	POS	$C_1(BND), C_2(NEG), C_3(POS)$
obj_2	BND	NEG	BND	$C_1(BND), C_2(NEG), C_3(BND)$
obj_3	POS	NEG	NEG	$C_1(POS), C_2(NEG), C_3(NEG)$

Calculating the Threshold. Reasonable thresholds α and β play key roles in solving the decision problems. Yao [13] introduced the Bayes decision procedure into rough set model, proposed the decision theoretic rough set that gave the theoretical basis of threshold calculation. Jia et al. [18] proposed an adaptive learning parameters algorithm based on the decision theoretic rough set. Their algorithm summarizes the 6 decision risks in three-way decisions, and build the target model of the minimum total risk to get the optimal thresholds.

In our model, we need transform m-category classification to m two-category classification. The target model in [18] is not suitable for our problem because it is just used for two category classification. Therefore, the statistical method for calculate the threshold of three-way decisions is put forward. We use Random Forest (RF) in Weka to calculate the prediction probability on train dataset by leave-one-out cross validation, and also analyzed the experiment results of the 14 gestures, the conclusions are the same. Namely, we take the first quartile (Q1) of True Positive (TP) as the threshold α and the third quartile (Q3) of False Negative (FN) as the threshold β.

3.2　The Model of the Ensemble Classifier

In this section, based on three-way decisions, the model of a new ensemble classifier are described in detail that is combined with 4 base classifiers built on different preprocessing methods. Each base classifier uses the same feature set and RF algorithm as their classifiers. It is divided into two steps: (1) Decision of single base classifier: Transform the m-category classification to m two-category classification problems firstly. Then calculate three-way decisions' thresholds for every two-category classification according to the methods discussed in Sect. 3.1. Next make decisions for m two-category classification depending on the rules of three-way decisions; Finally select a reasonable result according to the procedure described in Table 1. (2) Final prediction decision: Through the step 1, each prediction result has been divided depending on 3 regions *POS*, *NEG*, and *BND*. Next, compute the weight for the decisions in 3 region *POS* by the Eq. (4), select a class in the region *POS* with the maximum weight as the final prediction result. If no results in the region *POS*, discuss the results in the region *BND* by the same way. Otherwise as well as the region *NEG*. These two steps are illustrated in Fig. 1.

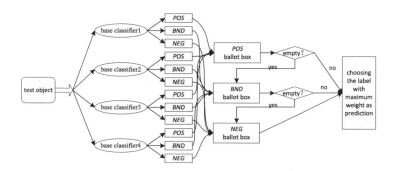

Fig. 1. The procedure of the ensemble classifier based on three-way decisions.

Using the RF algorithm, 4 base classifiers are trained based on four datasets preprocessed by different methods. In the training phase, the training set is preprocessed and extracted features to get the corresponding 4 datasets. Then 10-fold cross validationis used to get the F-measure of each classifier as each gestureas the conf in Eq. (4). Next three-way decisions threshold is calculated for each two-category classification through the method described in Sect. 3.1. During the test phase, the last prediction result is obtained. The algorithm is shown as the Algorithm 1 in detail.

Let $G = \{g_1, g_2, ..., g_{14}\}$ denotes the 14 different gestures, $C = \{c_1, c_2, c_3, c_4\}$ denotes the 4 base classifiers. The weight adopted in our algorithm is defined below:

$$w_{ij} = conf_{ij} \times P_{ij} \tag{4}$$

Where w_{ij} is the weight of base classifier C_i voting to the gesture g_i, $conf_{ij}$ denotes the accuracy rate which classifier C_i can make the right decision for the gesture g_i. In our algorithm, we take F-measure of classifier C_i for the gesture g_i as $conf_{ij}$. P_{ij} denotes the prediction probability that the gesture g_i is predicted correctly by classifier C_i.

3.3   The Analysis of Experimental Results for Ensemble Classifier

Figure 2 show the comparison results between ensemble algorithm and each single base classifier on the metrics, such as recall, precision, and F-measure respectively. From the mean value of these 3 metrics, our ensemble algorithm receives all the best results. For the single gesture, the classification accuracy of gesture "hit", "massage", "pinch", "poke", "stroke" have been promoted on the recall; the classification accuracy of gesture "pat", "rub", "scratch", "squeeze", and "tap" have been improved on the precision; on the F-measure, the gesture of "pat", "poke", "squeeze", "stroke", and "tickle" have been promoted.

But there are still some gestures whose recognition rate are lower than the base classifiers. Because these gestures' data are confused due to the procedure of data collection and preprocess caused by their characteristics. However, most of gestures' recognition rate have been improved.

Algorithm 1. A new ensemble classifier.

    Input: train set , test object , number of labels.
    Output: output prediction result.

1 **Training process:** Extract features, get the 4 data sets $\{s_1, s_2, s_3, s_4\}$; Train the 4 base classifiers $\{c_1, c_2, c_3, c_4\}$; Get $conf_{ij}$; Calculate the three-way decisions threshold $(\alpha, \beta)_{ij}$ of each classifier;

2 **Test process:** Preprocess and extract features to get $\{obj_1, obj_2, obj_3, obj_4\}$; Create ballot boxes *POS, BND, NEG*, Vote contains (label, weight);

3 **for** $i = 1$ *to* 4 **do**

4   **for** $j = 1$ *to* M **do**

5         $w_{ij} = conf_{ij} \times P_{ij}$ // calculate vote weight

6   **if** $\Pr(X \mid [x]) \geq \alpha$ **then**

7 | $POS.add\,(j, w)$ // decision region is POS

8   **end**

9   **if** $\beta < \Pr(X \mid [x]) < \alpha$ **then**

10 | $BND.add\,(j, w)$ // decision region is BND

11   **end**

12   **if** $\Pr(X \mid [x]) \leq \beta$ **then**

13 | $NEG.add\,(j, w)$ // decision region is NEG

14   **end**

15   **end**

16 **end**

17 **if** *POS ballot box is not empty* **then**

18 | choose the label with maximum summation weight.

19 **else**

20   **if** *BND ballot box is not empty* **then**

21 | choose the label with maximum summation weight.

22   **else**

23 | choose the label with maximum summation weight.

24   **end**

25 **end**

26 **return** *the gestures label.*

4   Experiments

4.1   The CoST Dataset

The CoST dataset was introduced in [5]. During the gathering process, the simulated arm is covered with 8*8 grid pressure sensor, and the pressure values of the 64 channels are ranged from 0 to 1023. Before performing gestures, gesture sample video was shown on the computer screen. Then participants pressed the start button and performed, and the end button is pressed if they finished. There are 31 participants' gestures collected in CoST dataset and every gesture was performed 6 times in 3 variations. The dataset provided by the social touch Gesture challenge 2015 only contains two variations, namely normal and gentle. In this challenge, the organizer divided the dataset into training set (3524 gestures) and test set (1769 gestures) randomly.

(a)   (b)   (c)

Fig. 2. The comparison results between ensemble algorithm and each single base classifier on the metrics, including Recall, Precision and F-measure.

4.2   Comparison of Experimental Results

In the Social Touch Gesture Challenge 2015, the highest recognition accuracy results are obtained by literature [9–12]. In the literature [11,12], they classified with two different algorithms respectively. In this section, we just compare the higher accuracy one in their works. The classification results are shown in Fig. 3 on the metrics of recall, precision, and F-measure between other researches and ours.

From the Fig. 3, it can be seen that literature [12] gets the highest mean value on the above 3 metrics, but our results are close to it. Just comparing the single metrics, for the recall metric, the gestures "grab", "hit", "massage", "poke", "press" and "rub" have been gotten the best recognition accuracy by our algorithm; the gestures "pinch", "rub", "scratch", and "squeeze" are the highest than others on the precision metrics, as well as the recognition of gestures "grab", "pinch", "poke", "rub", "slap", and "tickle" on the F-measure metric. Generally, the better accurate recognition rate has been obtained compared with the other researches.

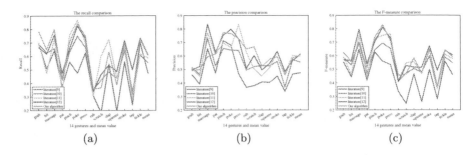

Fig. 3. The comparison results between our algorithm and other literatures.

5   Conclusion

A new touch gesture classification method is proposed in this paper. Firstly, two kinds of data preprocessing methods were proposed to extract features from six perspectives. These two preprocessing methods was called "cutout" and "background removing", which is effective to eliminate the interference of noise data for some gestures. Then an ensemble algorithm is proposed to recognize touch gestures on CoST corpora based on three-way decisions. From the analysis of experiment results, the accuracy of touch gesture classifying is improved by our ensemble algorithm. Although we proposed a statistical method to compute the thresholds of three-way decisions and achieved the better results, it still has some drawbacks. In the future, we will design the reasonable target model of the minimum total risk for the m category classification, then we can compute the better thresholds and to obtain the better classification results.

Acknowledgments. The work is supported by the Key Research and Development Program of Chongqing (cstc2017zdcy-zdyfx0091) and the Key Research and Development Program on AI of Chongqing (cstc2017rgzn-zdyfx0022) and the National Nature Science Foundation of China (61572091).

References

1. Hertenstein, M.J., Verkamp, J.M., Kerestes, A.M., Holmes, R.M.: The communicative functions of touch in humans, nonhuman primates, and rats: a review and synthesis of the empirical research. Genet. Soc. Gen. Psychol. Monogr. **132**(1), 5–94 (2006)
2. Gallace, A., Spence, C.: The science of interpersonal touch: an overview. Neurosci. Biobehav. Rev. **34**(2), 246–259 (2010)
3. Zeng, Z., Pantic, M., Roisman, G.I., Huang, T.S.: A survey of affect recognition methods: audio, visual, and spontaneous expressions. IEEE Trans. Pattern Anal. Mach. Intell. **31**(1), 39–58 (2009)
4. Jung, M.M., Poel, M., Poppe, R., Heylen, D.K.: Automatic recognition of touch gestures in the corpus of social touch. J. Multimodal User Interfaces **11**(1), 81–96 (2017)

5. Jung, M.M., Poppe, R., Poel, M., Heylen, D.K.: Touching the void-introducing cost: corpus of social touch. In: Proceedings of the 16th International Conference on Multimodal Interaction, pp. 120–127. ACM (2014)
6. Silvera-Tawil, D., Rye, D., Velonaki, M.: Interpretation of social touch on an artificial arm covered with an eit-based sensitive skin. Int. J. Soc. Robot. **6**(4), 489–505 (2014)
7. Jung, M.M., Cang, X.L., Poel, M., MacLean, K.E.: Touch challenge'15: Recognizing social touch gestures. In: Proceedings of the 2015 ACM on International Conference on Multimodal Interaction, pp. 387–390. ACM (2015)
8. Yohanan, S., MacLean, K.E.: The role of affective touch in human-robot interaction: human intent and expectations in touching the haptic creature. Int. J. Soc. Robot. **4**(2), 163–180 (2012)
9. Hughes, D., Farrow, N., Profita, H., Correll, N.: Detecting and identifying tactile gestures using deep autoencoders, geometric moments and gesture level features. In: Proceedings of the 2015 ACM on International Conference on Multimodal Interaction, pp. 415–422. ACM (2015)
10. Balli Altuglu, T., Altun, K.: Recognizing touch gestures for social human-robot interaction. In: Proceedings of the 2015 ACM on International Conference on Multimodal Interaction, pp. 407–413. ACM (2015)
11. Gaus, Y.F.A., Olugbade, T., Jan, A., Qin, R., Liu, J., Zhang, F., Meng, H., Bianchi-Berthouze, N.: Social touch gesture recognition using random forest and boosting on distinct feature sets. In: Proceedings of the 2015 ACM on International Conference on Multimodal Interaction, pp. 399–406. ACM (2015)
12. Ta, V.C., Johal, W., Portaz, M., Castelli, E., Vaufreydaz, D.: The grenoble system for the social touch challenge at ICMI 2015. In: Proceedings of the 2015 ACM on International Conference on Multimodal Interaction, pp. 391–398. ACM (2015)
13. Yao, Y.: Three-way decisions with probabilistic rough sets. Inf. Sci. **180**(3), 341–353 (2010)
14. Yao, Y.: An outline of a theory of three-way decisions. In: Yao, J.T., Yang, Y., Słowiński, R., Greco, S., Li, H., Mitra, S., Polkowski, L. (eds.) RSCTC 2012. LNCS (LNAI), vol. 7413, pp. 1–17. Springer, Heidelberg (2012). https://doi.org/10.1007/978-3-642-32115-3_1
15. Otsu, N.: A threshold selection method from gray-level histograms. IEEE Trans. Syst. Man Cybern. **9**(1), 62–66 (1979)
16. Wingerden, S., Uebbing, T.J., Jung, M.M., Poel, M.: A neural network based approach to social touch classification. In: Proceedings of the 2014 Workshop on Emotion Representation and Modelling in Human-Computer-Interaction-Systems, pp. 7–12. ACM (2014)
17. Yao, Y., Zhao, Y.: Attribute reduction in decision-theoretic rough set models. Inf. Sci. **178**(17), 3356–3373 (2008)
18. Jia, X.Y., Li, W.W., Shang, L., Chen, J.J.: An adaptive learning parameters algorithm in three-way decision-theoretic rough set model. Dianzi Xuebao (Acta Electronica Sinica) **39**(11), 2520–2525 (2011) (in Chinese)

Engineering Character Recognition Algorithm and Application Based on BP Neural Network

Chen Rong[1(✉)] and Yu Luqian[2]

[1] Audit S&T Research Institution, Nanjing Audit University, Nanjing, China
Chenr2001_125@163.com
[2] School of Government Audit, Nanjing Audit University, Nanjing, China
Ylq180256@163.com

Abstract. Character recognition algorithm can directly affect the accuracy and speed of character recognition. This algorithm uses BP neural network to train samples, preserve neural network weights, and recognize photographed images. The software algorithm integrates image-processing and neural network modules. Image-processing modules include pre-treatment processes, such as, binaryzation, denoising, dilation, erosion, rotation and character segmentation and extraction of images collected by cameras. Neural network modules include network training, identification, display, saving, loading, and other modules, such as image preprocessing and recognition. A prototype of online engineering character recognition system has been developed. Test results indicate that the duration of a single picture is approximately 100 ms, and the detection time displayed by the interface includes the zooming time of display interface that is approximately 200 ms.

Keywords: Engineering character recognition · BP neural network
Online automatic recognition

1 Rationale of BP Neural Network

Character recognition can increase the speed of character information entry, reduce the work intensity of people, recognize the printing error of engineering characters online, and promote the detection efficiency of engineering automation. Along with the development of computer vision and image processing technology, character recognition algorithm has been extensively applied in various sectors considering the years of continuous improvement and perfection. Although many achievements have been attained from studies on character recognition algorithm, further research is still needed on the error recognition of engineering printing characters on industrial production lines, error recognition of printing characters in large-scale building engineering projects, and online character recognition application of other engineering characters. Literature (1) applies the CNN method for the text classification of natural scenes and conducts post-processing according to character characteristics after classification, acquiring an accurate positioning effect. Literature (2) determines the positioning and recognition of numbers in natural scenes in connection with hidden Markov model (HMM) and deep learning methods. Literature (3) proposes a type of algorithm of

© Springer International Publishing AG, part of Springer Nature 2018
Y. Tan et al. (Eds.): ICSI 2018, LNCS 10942, pp. 380–388, 2018.
https://doi.org/10.1007/978-3-319-93818-9_36

marshaling characters in connection with convolutional neural network and random forest statistical algorithm. The present thesis applies BP neural network algorithm for automatic online recognition application of medicine bottle characters.

In 1985, Rumelhart et al. proposed BP neural network algorithm (error back propagation, EBP) that aims to minimize the objective function of training errors according to the weight and threshold value of iterative adjustment network toward the declining direction of the negative gradient. This algorithm systematically solves the learning problem of the hidden unit layer connection in the multilayer neural network and provides complete derivation.

The model of neural network that uses BP neural network algorithm is generally referred to as BP neural network. Figure 1 shows the topographical structure of multilayer neural network model, which comprises input layer, hidden layer (interlayer), and output layer. The hidden layer can be one or more layers, with each layer having many single nerve cells.

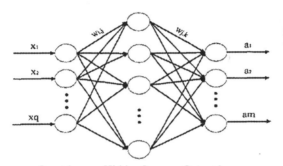

Input layer   Hidden Layer   Output layer

Fig. 1. The structure of BP neural network

The learning process of BP neural network comprises two parts: forward-propagation and counter-propagation. Input information is transmitted to the output layer from the input layer via the hidden unit layer. The state of neural cells in each layer can only affect that in the next layer. If expected output cannot be acquired in the output layer, then counter-propagation will begin. The error signals are returned along the original connection channel of neural cells. In the returning process, the connection weights of neural cells in each layer are corrected one by one. This process is iterated continuously, eventually enabling signal errors to be within the allowable scope [5].

BP neural network algorithm uses continuously differentiable sigmoid function as the excitation function of neural cells, e.g. S-type function

$$f(x) = \frac{1}{1 + e^{-x}}.$$

(1)

It has P training samples, namely P input-output pairs:

$$(X_k, T_k), (k = 1, 2, \cdots, P) \tag{2}$$

Therein,

X_k is the kth sample input vector:

$X_k = (x_{k1}, x_{k2}, \cdots, x_{kM})$, M is an input vector dimension number;

T_k is the kth sample output vector (expected output):

$T_k = (t_{k1}, t_{k2}, \cdots, t_{kN})$, N is output vector dimension number; the actual output vector of network is:

$$O_k = (O_{k1}, O_{k2}, \cdots, O_{kN}). \tag{3}$$

ω_{ji} is the weight for the ith neural cell in the preceding layer to be put into the jth neural cell in the following layer.

With regard to the kth sample, the status definition of the jth neural cell is:

$$Net_{kj} = \sum_i \omega_{ji} o_{ki}. \tag{4}$$

Then, the output of the jth neural cell is:

$$O_{kj} = f_j(Net_{kj}). \tag{5}$$

2   Online Engineering Character Detecting System

2.1   System Structure

This thesis selects a tubular medicine bottle as an experiment target, for the online detection and recognition of the printed characters of the medicine bottle (Fig. 2).

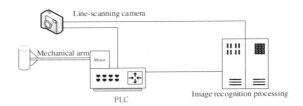

Fig. 2. The structure of character recognition system

Online engineering character detecting system (OECDS) comprises five subsystems, including visual sensing, image processing, control mechanism, movement mechanism, and mechanical arm. Visual sensing uses a line-scanning camera to photograph the medicine bottle. A PLC drives a servo motor to rotate the medicine bottle at a constant speed, and controls the scanning camera for continuous scanning. Scanned images are communicated via the CameraLink image transmission interface and processing server. Image character recognition is conducted as well.

1. Visual sensing subsystem. This subsystem generally uses two types of camera: area-array and line-scanning camera. This thesis uses the latter to conduct real-time collection of pictures running continuously on detected articles, and transmit these collected images to a computer for image processing via the CameraLink image collection card, an automatic assembly-line movement. The defect detection of continuously-moving character images includes positioning, detection, and product NG judgment of moving characters. The location mark of character defect is determined through NG judgment.
2. Image processing subsystem. This subsystem includes four modules: image pre-processing, image training, character recognition, and system management.
3. Movement control subsystem. This subsystem uses the PLC control system. PLC can be used to control the circular movement or linear movement of the detected object. PLC controls the movement of servo motor (driving the single-axis or multi-axis location control module of stepping or servo motor) and the photographing of the line-scanning camera.
4. Servo motor subsystem. This subsystem can control speed and location, and convert voltage signal into torque and rotating speed to drive the control object. The rotor-rotating speed of servo motor is controlled by the input signal of PLC control subsystem, which can convert the received electric signal into angular displacement or speed on the motor reel for output, and manage the movement of mechanical arm (Fig. 3).
5. Mechanical gripper subsystem. This subsystem controls the constant-speed rotation of the medicine bottle managed by the servo motor.

2.2 Software Composition

Image processing subsystem is a core function of online detection, and it comprises image pre-processing, image training, character detection, and system control.

1. Image pre-processing. This module filters noise, reinforces useful information, and restores degraded information. OECDS pre-processing uses character binaryzation, character segmentation, character refining, and character standardization.
2. Image training. The entire character after binaryzation is trained as characteristics by using the BP neural network (see Sect. 3 for the algorithm).
3. Classified recognition. BP neural network algorithm is used for automatic classification.
4. System control. This module includes log service, configuration management, and movement control module.

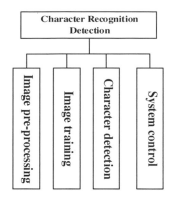

Fig. 3. Composition of character recognition software

3   Character Recognition BP Neural Network Algorithm

Considering that BP neural network algorithm requires using a nonlinear continuously derivable excitation function, character recognition in this thesis uses the S-type function as excitation function:

$$f\left(Net_{kj}\right) = \frac{1}{1 + e^{-Net_{kj}}}. \tag{6}$$

In the equation: $Net_{kj} = \sum_{i} \omega_{ji} o_{ki} + \theta_{j}$

The basic steps of character recognition BP neural network algorithm are as follows:

1. Conduct sample training using the entire image pre-processing binaryzation character as input;
2. Set the initial weight value: $\omega_{ji}(0)$, $\theta_{j}(0)$ is a small random non-zero value.
3. Give input/output sample set:
   Input vector: $X_k, k = 1, 2, \cdots, P$;
   Expected output: $d_k, k = 1, 2, \cdots, P$;
   Conduct the following 4–5 iterations to each input sample;
4. The actual output of BP neural network and the state of hidden-layer cell:

$$O_{kj} = f_j\left(\sum_{i} \omega_{ji} O_{ki} + \theta_{j}\right). \tag{7}$$

5. Calculate the training error of neural network:
   Output layer:

$$\delta_{kj} = O_{kj}\left(1 - O_{kj}\right)\left(t_{kj} - O_{kj}\right). \tag{8}$$

Hidden layer:

$$\delta_{kj} = O_{kj}(1 - O_{kj}) \sum_m \delta_{km}\omega_{mj}. \tag{9}$$

6. Correct the weight and threshold value of neural network:

$$\omega_{ji}(t+1) = \omega_{ji}(t) + \eta\delta_j O_{ki} + \alpha\left[\omega_{ji}(t) - \omega_{ji}(t-1)\right]. \tag{10}$$

$$\theta_j(t+1) = \theta_j(t) + \eta\delta_j + \alpha\left[\theta_j(t) - \theta_j(t-1)\right]. \tag{11}$$

7. After k goes through 1 to P each time, determine whether the index meets the precision requirement:

$$E_{all} \le \varepsilon\varepsilon : \text{precision}. \tag{12}$$

Repeat the above process until the condition of convergence is met;
8. After pre-processing, character image is inputted to the detection module;
9. Through BP neural network, the detection module conducts character detection classification.

4   Experiment and Results

4.1   Software Interface

Character recognition software is classified into recognition and training model, with the former open to users. The keyboard triggers the analog photographing process, the pictures are read to conduct the pre-processing segmentation and recognition, the recognition result is obtained, and the operating time and pictures are displayed on the interface. Under the recognition model, the display interface is as follows:

Fig. 4. Image process software

The training model runs at the background. According to different product demands, we can select whether to open the training model to users. Under the training model, we must process, segment, and classify the collected samples. Afterward, a neural network is trained to meet the error requirement following the sample and save the weight value (Fig. 4).

4.2 Experiment Results

The experiment results are shown in Tables 1, 2, 3, 4 and 5.

Table 1. Net head

1	128	128	1	100	36	36	800	0.6	1	0.1	0.0001

Table 2. Train target

0.9	0.1	0.1	0.1	0.1	0.1	0.1	0.1	...	0.1	0.1	0.1	0.1	0.1	0.1
0.1	0.9	0.1	0.1	0.1	0.1	0.1	0.1	...	0.1	0.1	0.1	0.1	0.1	0.1
0.1	0.1	0.9	0.1	0.1	0.1	0.1	0.1	...	0.1	0.1	0.1	0.1	0.1	0.1
0.1	0.1	0.1	0.9	0.1	0.1	0.1	0.1	...	0.1	0.1	0.1	0.1	0.1	0.1
0.1	0.1	0.1	0.1	0.9	0.1	0.1	0.1	...	0.1	0.1	0.1	0.1	0.1	0.1
0.1	0.1	0.1	0.1	0.1	0.9	0.1	0.1	...	0.1	0.1	0.1	0.1	0.1	0.1
0.1	0.1	0.1	0.1	0.1	0.1	0.9	0.1	...	0.1	0.1	0.1	0.1	0.1	0.1
0.1	0.1	0.1	0.1	0.1	0.1	0.1	0.9	...	0.1	0.1	0.1	0.1	0.1	0.1
0.1	0.1	0.1	0.1	0.1	0.1	0.1	0.1	...	0.1	0.1	0.1	0.1	0.1	0.1
0.1	0.1	0.1	0.1	0.1	0.1	0.1	0.1	...	0.1	0.1	0.1	0.1	0.1	0.1
0.1	0.1	0.1	0.1	0.1	0.1	0.1	0.1	...	0.1	0.1	0.1	0.1	0.1	0.1
0.1	0.1	0.1	0.1	0.1	0.1	0.1	0.1	...	0.1	0.1	0.1	0.1	0.1	0.1
...	...	...	...	...	...	...	...		...	...	...	...	...	...
0.1	0.1	0.1	0.1	0.1	0.1	0.1	0.1	0.1	0.1	0.1	0.1	0.1	0.9	0.1
0.1	0.1	0.1	0.1	0.1	0.1	0.1	0.1	0.1	0.1	0.1	0.1	0.1	0.1	0.9

Table 3. Input layer weights

0.04482	0.018941	-0.03322	0.114248	-0.04919	0.058867	-0.122 ...	0.112807	-0.07782	-0.01647	-0.04652	-0.00303
0.046883	-0.06622	0.08178	0.01832	0.009225	0.037254	-0.06 ...	0.03986	-0.00535	-0.04033	-0.05272	-0.0588
0.025074	0.068683	0.061649	-0.02171	0.007403	0.092799	-0.032 ...	0.011342	0.072047	-0.02117	-0.04797	0.048465
-0.085	-0.08971	-0.10024	-0.00268	0.023738	-0.0011	-0.024 ...	-0.12376	-0.05088	0.015898	-0.05649	-0.0534
0.083669	0.005645	0.047134	-0.03617	-0.10391	-0.03188	0.1539 ...	-0.05449	0.060636	0.026568	0.020439	0.007519
0.014966	0.047205	0.033414	-0.0152	0.004809	-0.01517	-0.004 ...	-0.02538	0.005232	0.150934	0.087487	0.034265
0.100995	0.096927	0.017801	0.052181	0.028157	0.023089	-0.022 ...	-0.00901	-0.02482	0.050087	0.017329	-0.03357
0.015223	-0.00811	-0.00866	0.03762	-0.03754	0.012838	-0.113 ...	-0.03165	-0.07391	0.125057	-0.00587	-0.02016
0.034682	-0.00363	-0.03941	-0.0405	-0.09856	-0.12945	0.0674 ...	-0.10906	-0.00878	-0.02339	-0.08241	-0.05214
-0.05036	0.017601	0.022058	0.023512	0.017207	0.067196	-0.048 ...	-0.02964	-0.00914	0.010033	0.012736	0.102559
-0.00165	0.033087	0.013027	-0.06663	-0.05578	-0.0501	-0.153 ...	-0.00419	0.021419	0.000079	-0.0317	0.033602
-0.00349	-0.0096	0.04572	0.099569	-0.00711	0.096498	-0.099 ...	0.024837	-0.0481	-0.03848	-0.04995	-0.00581
...	...	...	...	...	...	...	...	...	...	...	...
-0.00669	0.054433	0.038397	0.008726	0.062906	0.094989	0.0971	0.004235	-0.00405	-0.06876	-0.06949	-0.0195	0.056215
0.048448	-0.05845	-0.05726	-0.04878	-0.06406	-0.12691	0.1444	-0.0889	-0.03723	0.071837	0.069538	0.082519	-0.01908

Table 4. Hidden layer weights

0.312371	0.175745	0.012099	0.090633	-0.06633	0.047157	0.086836	0.010455	...	-0.01934	-0.0301	0.261716	0.157223	-0.03053	0.094059	-0.15978	0.03666
0.017574	-0.02851	0.03737	0.085091	-0.04745	0.083651	0.060009	0.04796	...	-0.09034	0.011583	0.067667	-0.00828	-0.05931	-0.06338	0.013371	0.000363
-0.21791	-0.14269	0.02469	0.343326	-0.00723	0.047453	-0.04688	-0.10684	...	-0.05498	0.114225	-0.32006	-0.02602	-0.02927	-0.01001	0.197551	-0.07368
0.165647	0.061303	-0.01129	-0.0769	-0.05651	-0.00831	0.032009	0.100122	...	0.064693	-0.06251	0.059905	0.046721	0.005883	-0.1344	-0.05524	-0.05858
0.087701	0.13089	0.003941	-0.20672	-0.05446	-0.06888	-0.0295	-0.02627	...	0.116917	-0.09317	0.203241	0.004841	0.034114	-0.02971	-0.05924	0.021828
0.046135	0.040816	-0.04252	0.030687	-0.03968	0.064785	-0.0012	0.015507	...	0.0572	-0.02601	0.040691	-0.04112	0.016515	-0.06573	-0.00736	0.025677
0.051359	0.03425	0.021413	0.115507	0.123252	-0.04831	0.058428	-0.09408	...	-0.03503	0.071624	-0.01082	0.091775	0.069784	0.015936	0.202604	0.034027
0.106398	0.162474	0.009989	-0.14935	-0.10731	0.031967	0.049044	-0.11726	...	-0.09054	-0.05765	0.164393	-0.0541	0.025427	0.024164	-0.08853	-0.03363
0.078673	0.024812	-0.00511	-0.03278	0.045496	-0.02059	0.043593	0.113643	...	0.022677	-0.03696	0.020491	0.072881	-0.03178	-0.05842	-0.01542	-0.02457
0.197157	-0.0271	-0.13098	-0.168	0.026806	-0.1658	0.034027	0.018466	...	-0.05402	0.023531	0.028859	0.031615	-0.03773	0.044561	-0.22721	-0.13424
-0.00644	-0.01633	0.018292	0.059566	-0.05399	-0.00378	-0.01418	-0.01437	...	0.05509	-0.05621	0.094038	-0.05653	0.093969	0.062623	-0.04581	0.003666
0.094666	-0.00975	-0.01737	-0.12155	0.027696	0.002713	0.045063	0.104182	...	0.014004	-0.05225	0.025854	0.069346	0.019504	-0.0513	-0.00656	0.002389
-0.00696	-0.0622	0.006741	0.096773	0.039032	-0.07357	0.05102	-0.02174	...	0.099416	0.014911	-0.05112	0.01621	0.033489	0.093011	0.035593	0.075254
0.063374	0.031612	0.011614	-0.02373	-0.14775	0.090905	0.057906	0.064946	...	-0.20641	0.073615	-0.05761	0.087962	-0.13048	-0.07094	-0.21247	-0.12433
...	...	...	...	...	...	...	...		...	...	...	...	...	...	...	...
0.16521	0.087841	-0.02284	0.039274	0.031811	-0.0613	0.026243	0.001157	0.080773	0.013065	-0.03689	0.102895	0.09724	0.032674	-0.01171	-0.08239	0.070045
-0.15184	0.022947	0.032455	0.014807	-0.01518	0.032108	-0.06198	-0.12595	-0.16838	-0.0658	0.024772	0.021404	-0.09928	0.071714	0.120191	-0.02362	0.011616

Table 5. Output layer weight

0.361318	-0.01995	1.005055	-0.3257	-0.50129	-0.16013	0.244724	⋯	-0.33772	-0.12297	-0.01633	0.021104
0.708475	-0.15219	-0.02479	-0.01518	0.112014	-0.08964	-0.10917	⋯	-0.0367	0.260772	-0.41509	-0.13953
-0.78055	0.248247	-0.26424	0.024057	0.173195	0.023287	0.206635	⋯	0.084353	-0.32405	-0.18533	0.056915
-0.06695	-0.0288	-0.01312	0.05943	-0.10569	-0.02112	-0.00971	⋯	0.014012	-0.04472	-0.03211	-0.03402
0.009079	-0.06906	-0.10794	-0.09503	-0.10534	-0.01584	-0.02416	⋯	-0.04335	-0.01115	-0.03067	-0.09778
0.294774	-0.13409	-0.3089	0.34414	-0.4083	0.16552	0.287894	⋯	-0.18162	0.143428	-0.66542	-0.11611
-0.03404	0.045935	-0.05199	0.011851	-0.04486	-0.11431	-0.0271	⋯	0.026085	-0.04371	-0.07926	-0.11802
0.236712	-0.03381	-0.3048	-0.03798	0.060512	0.023103	-0.96987	⋯	-0.03847	-0.09736	0.310735	-0.06189
-0.05094	-0.10898	-0.06126	0.028283	-0.02484	0.022065	-0.06798	⋯	-0.05251	-0.0388	-0.0684	-0.1183
-0.04006	-0.08612	-0.06338	-0.05765	-0.0321	-0.0476	-0.10375	⋯	-0.12734	0.025907	0.037517	-0.14822
⋯	⋯	⋯	⋯	⋯	⋯	⋯	⋯	⋯	⋯	⋯	⋯
0.045526	-0.0553	-0.07578	-0.03323	-0.0356	-0.03765	-0.02202		-0.02587	-0.01163	0.019321	-0.00847
-0.08827	-0.05885	-0.02236	0.007832	-0.07369	-0.06154	0.038818		0.0203	-0.10053	0.004824	-0.05913

The results indicate that this algorithm exhibits high precision and convergence rate.

5 Conclusion

This thesis proposes an online engineering character detection system based on BP neural network. This algorithm can concurrently detect rhythm and performance index. As indicated by the experiment results, the proposed BP neural network algorithm exhibits superior accuracy and efficiency over many existing detection methods. The proposed method is feasible and highly efficient. Character recognition is classified as pattern recognition, and its algorithm can be summed up as a character recognition algorithm based on template matching [6], character recognition algorithm based on machine learning [7] and character recognition algorithm based on feature matching [8]. BP neural network is a character recognition algorithm based on fuzzy matching. Although the algorithm does not calculate the latest algorithm in character recognition [9, 10], it is true that the timeliness and efficiency of engineering font detection is the innovation of this paper compared with other character recognition algorithms. Although the complex and detailed algorithm experiments and steps are not provided, the purpose of this paper is to illustrate the feasibility of BP neural network for on-line detection of Engineering fonts through simple experiments.

References

1. Kobchaisawat, T., Chalidabhongse, T.H.: Thai text localization in natural scene images using convolutional neural network. In: 2014 Asia-Pacific Signal and Information Processing Association Annual Summit and Conference (APSIPA), pp. 1–7. IEEE (2014)
2. Guo, Q., Lei, J., Tu, D., Li, G.: Reading numbers in natural scene images with convolutional neural networks. In: 2014 International Conference on Security, Pattern Analysis, and Cybernetics (SPAC), pp. 48–53. IEEE (2014)
3. Xu, H., Su, F.: A robust hierarchical detection method for scene text based on convolutional neural networks. In: IEEE International Conference on Multimedia & Expo, pp. 1–6 (2015)

4. Wang, G.: Detecting text in natural scene images with conditional clustering and convolution neural network. J. Electron. Imaging **24**(5), 053019 (2015)
5. Yang, J.: Practical Course on Artificial Neural Networks. Publishing House of Zhejiang University, Hangzhou (2001)
6. Sarfraz, M., Ahmed, M.J., Ghazi, S.A.: Saudi Arabian license plate recognition system. In: 2003 Proceedings International Conference on Geometric Modeling and Graphics, pp. 36–41. IEEE (2003)
7. Kunyan, Z., Yiya, Z., Songchi, M., Guijuan, W.: A BP neural network license plate character recognition system based on global threshold two valued method. Comput. Eng. Sci. (02), 88–90+134 (2010)
8. Leutenegger, S., Chli, M., Siegwart, R.Y.: BRISK: Binary robust invariant scalable keypoints. In: 2011 IEEE International Conference on Computer Vision (ICCV), pp. 2548–2555. IEEE (2011)
9. Nijhuis, J.A.G., Ter Brugge, M.H., Helmholt, K.A., Pluim, J.P.W., Spaanenburg, L., Venema, R.S., Westenberg, M.A.: Car license plate recognition with neural networks and fuzzy logic. In: 1995 Proceedings of IEEE International Conference on Neural Networks, vol. 5, pp. 2232–2236. IEEE (1995)
10. Dalal, N., Triggs, B.: Histograms of oriented gradients for human detection. In: 2005 IEEE Computer Society Conference on Computer Vision and Pattern Recognition, CVPR 2005, vol. 1, pp. 886–893. IEEE (2005)

Hand Gesture Recognition Based on Multi Feature Fusion

Hongling Yang[1]($\boxtimes$), Shibin Xuan[2], and Yuanbin Mo[3]

[1] Guangxi Computer Software Laboratory, Guangxi University for Nationalities,
Nanning 530006, Guangxi, China
1826955085@qq.com
[2] Multimedia Technology Laboratory, Guangxi University for Nationalities,
Nanning 530006, Guangxi, China
[3] Embedded Technology Laboratory, Guangxi University for Nationalities,
Nanning 530006, Guangxi, China

Abstract. In view of the influence of complex and changeable gestures on recognition, a gesture recognition method based on multi feature phase fusion is proposed. Firstly, the skeleton feature and contour feature of the gesture area are extracted. Then the feature fusion method is used to obtain the fusion features of the gestures. Finally, support vector machine, decision tree, random forest and convolution neural network are used to recognize the skeleton feature, contour feature and fusion feature of gesture area respectively. The results show that under different data sets, gesture recognition based on multi feature fusion improves the recognition accuracy by 2% compared with single feature recognition algorithm, reaching 98.57%.

Keywords: Gestures recognition · Multi feature fusion · Neural network

1 Introduction

In recent years, with the rapid development of machine learning in computer vision and human-computer interaction technology, all kinds of novel and free interactive ways are also appearing. From the traditional mouse and keyboard to the popular touch screen and voice interaction, human-machine interaction equipment is also from complex to simple, and the way of interaction is more and more humanized, and it also meets people's needs. The purpose of efficient human-machine interaction is to enable computer to understand human body language and gesture as an important body language. It is a common way of natural human-machine interaction. It is also a simple and free means of human-machine interaction. It has a very broad application prospect.

Present hand gesture recognition can be divided into gesture recognition based on data glove and gesture recognition based on vision. Gesture recognition based on data glove has become the main direction of gesture recognition because of its high value and convenience. However, in the process of gesture recognition based on vision, it is often necessary first to extract the features from the gesture and then to recognize based the extracted gesture features.

© Springer International Publishing AG, part of Springer Nature 2018
Y. Tan et al. (Eds.): ICSI 2018, LNCS 10942, pp. 389–398, 2018.
https://doi.org/10.1007/978-3-319-93818-9_37

Gesture feature extraction is the basis of gesture recognition and the accuracy and identifiably of the extraction often affects the subsequent gesture recognition results. At present, gesture features commonly used in gesture recognition include shape and contour features, histogram features and skeleton characteristics, and the number of fingertips, contour circumference and area ratio are extracted. Currently, the common gestures features in gesture recognition are those. For example, the recognition method based on neural network has strong ability of classification, recognition and classification [1, 2]. But if the number of neural network layers is generally shallow, it is easy to overmatch. The recognition method based on geometric features can extract gesture structure, edge and contour features for gesture recognition [3–5]. It has good stability, but it can't improve the recognition rate at the same time of raising the sample size. The recognition method based on the hidden Markov model has the ability to describe the temporal and spatial changes of gestures, but the recognition speed of the method is not satisfactory [6]. At the same time, with the rapid development of deep learning, the method based on convolution neural network also brings new ideas to the task of gesture recognition [7, 8].

Therefore, a gesture recognition method based on multi feature fusion is proposed in this paper. Support vector machine, decision tree, random forest and convolution neural network are used to identify the skeleton features, contour features and fusion features of gesture area respectively. Experiments show that this method has good recognition effect. Compared with gesture recognition based on multi feature fusion, the recognition algorithm based on single feature is increased by 2%, and it can reach 98.57% under different data sets.

2   Research Framework

The ability to use computers instead of humans to learn and improve their processing problems is machine learning. Its purpose is to estimate and predict the output of the system based on training samples. With the rapid development of computer technology, the field of machine learning has gradually expanded, such as statistics, artificial intelligence and psychology. The commonly used machine learning methods include supervised learning, unsupervised learning, and intensive learning. In view of the complexity of gestures, a gesture recognition method based on multi-feature fusion is proposed. Skeleton features, contour features and fusion features of gesture regions are identified respectively by classification methods such as support vector machine, decision tree, random forest and convolution neural network. The specific algorithm flowchart as shown in Fig. 1.

The original image is collected by gesture input, the original image by filtering and denoising pretreatment skeleton and edge feature extraction, feature fusion and feature fusion to obtain through the graph with the edge of the skeleton, the support vector machine, decision tree, random forest and convolution neural network for single feature and feature fusion gesture recognition model, feature selection and classification model by comparing the optimal.

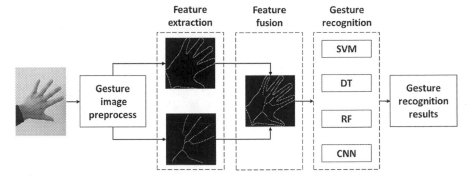

Fig. 1. Flow chart of gesture recognition algorithm. The algorithm mainly consists of three parts: gesture feature extraction, feature fusion and gesture recognition.

3   Feature Extraction

Due to the complexity of the change of gestures, people often pay more attention to the meaning represented by the gesture when performing gesture recognition. However, the original gesture image contains a lot of unnecessary detail information, thereby increasing the difficulty of recognition. Therefore, in order to increase the accuracy of gesture recognition rate, reduce the computational complexity, we usually extracting features to reduce the data in the image information in the gesture recognition. In order to explore the impact of multi-fusion features on gesture recognition, the fusion of these two features based on single skeleton or contour feature extraction can not only reduce the interference from unnecessary detail information in gesture recognition, Able to better describe the meaning of gestures.

3.1   Feature Extraction of Gesture Skeleton

Skeleton, as a form of object, can keep geometry, shape and topology information of objects. It is an excellent shape description feature and can effectively describe the information that an object wants to express. Therefore, the skeleton is widely used in many fields, such as computer graphics and graphics, computer geometry and so on. Gesture skeleton as a way to represent the nature of gesture information, can describe the physical meaning of the gesture well. The gesture skeleton information can be used as a type of gesture recognition feature description. This paper uses fast parallel thinning algorithm, by iteration to remove the image boundary points and key points of retaining skeleton. At the same time maintaining the gesture framework connectivity improves the speed and efficiency of the refinement of gesture skeleton extraction, the results as shown in Fig. 2(b) shows.

3.2   Feature Extraction of Gesture Edge

The edge, as an important feature of the image, exists in a place where the gray, texture, or color changes of the image are dramatically changed. The edge of gesture can reflect the meaning of gesture to some extent. Therefore, the edge information of gesture can also be an important feature of gesture recognition. Common edge operators are Roberts's operator, Sobel operator, Laplace operator, canny operator and so on. Compared to other operators, the canny operator using two different thresholds respectively. So this paper uses Canny edge detection operator has higher SNR and detection accuracy for edge feature extraction, the results as shown in Fig. 2(c) shown.

3.3   Gesture Feature Fusion

Although a single gesture skeleton or edge feature can explain the meaning of gesture well, the key information contained is defective. Therefore, a fusion method based on multi features is applied to fuse the skeleton features and the edge features, and get the fusion feature with stronger expression of gesture information to gesture recognition. The concrete fusion method is as follows:

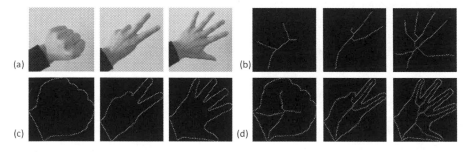

Fig. 2. Flow chart of gesture recognition algorithm. The algorithm mainly consists of three parts: gesture feature extraction, feature fusion and gesture recognition.

(1)   Two types of feature images are amplified or reduced to the same size. At the same time, an equal size blank image If is created to store the fusion features.

$$I_f + I_s = I_e. \tag{1}$$

(2)   On the skeleton feature image and edge feature, the sequence is traversed along the sequence of the X axis and the Y axis of the image from the point of origin. When a pixel is searched for a gray value of 255 in an image, the point of the same position in the image If is set to 255, otherwise 0. The fusion results are shown as shown in Fig. 2(d).

$$I_{f(x,y)} = 255 = \begin{cases} 255 & \text{if } (I_{s(x,y)} = 255 \, or \, I_{e(x,y)} = 255) \\ 0 & else \end{cases} \tag{2}$$

4 Gesture Recognition

Template matching method, support vector machine based on neural network based method are the common ways of gesture recognition method. This paper compared to single feature and feature fusion as the pros and cons of gesture recognition through different machine learning methods, so as to obtain the optimal features and identification methods.

4.1 Gesture Recognition Based on Support Vector Machine

Support vector machine was a learning algorithm first proposed by Vapnik et al. in 1995 to solve many unique advantages in small sample, nonlinear and high-dimensional pattern recognition. It is a learning theory of VC dimension theory and structural risk minimization principle on the basis of statistics, according to the limited sample information to search for the best compromise between model complexity and learning ability, in order to obtain the best generalization ability.

Because of the complexity of gesture itself, this paper transforms the fused feature image into one dimension eigenvector which is needed for training when support vector machine is used as input, and trains and gets the classification model for gesture recognition.

4.2 Gesture Recognition Based on Decision Tree

Decision tree learning is an inductive learning algorithm based on an example. It focuses on the classification rules that deduce the form of decision tree representation from a set of unordered and irregular cases. It is usually used to form a classifier and a prediction model to classify or predict the unknown data. After Quinlan JR put forward the ID3 algorithm in 1986, and with the improvement of C4.5 and CART generating decision tree algorithm, the decision tree method has been further applied and developed in machine learning and knowledge discovery. And it has a very important theoretical and practical value in the field of artificial intelligence and human-computer interaction.

In view of the complexity of the gestures, we transform the fused feature images into one dimension data structure as the input of the decision tree training. Then the ID3 learning algorithm is used to generate the decision tree and reduce the branch. Finally, the input feature fusion image is predicted by the decision tree generated by the training.

According to the decision tree generation algorithm for gesture recognition, the unique tree structure can not only reduce the recognition time, but also directly reflect the characteristics of the data. There is a certain degree of credibility. But for image data, high latitude data training has a problem of classification accuracy.

4.3   Gesture Recognition Based on Random Forest

In machine learning, a random forest is a classifier that contains multiple decision trees. It is the type of output mode by individual output categories depending on the tree.

The input of the random forest learning algorithm is similar to the decision tree, and is also the input of the training by converting the fused feature images into one dimensional data structure. Each tree is built according to the following algorithms:

(1) The number of training samples is represented by N, and M indicates that the image is transformed into one dimension data structure as a feature of training.
(2) From the N training samples, the samples were sampled and sampled N times to form a set of training sets.
(3) For the sampled samples, the M feature (m<<M) is selected randomly, and the best segmentation method is calculated, and a decision tree is generated by training.
(4) To select 20 data sets for training, each tree will grow intact without pruning.

According to the random forest algorithm to identify the gestures, compared to the decision tree, the results according to the mode of multi tree and output. As a result, the accuracy of the decision tree is improved to a certain extent. But the prediction of a number of trees will also lead to a rise in time.

4.4   Gesture Recognition Based on Convolution Neural Network

With the rapid development of deep learning, convolutional neural network has been widely applied in various fields, such as speech recognition [9], handwritten font recognition [10], license plate recognition [11], face recognition and so on [12].

Its efficient recognition precision and speed have a positive effect on gesture recognition. Therefore, this paper uses the method of deep learning to carry on the gesture recognition, and constructs the structure of the deep convolution neural network. The hand gesture classification model is obtained by a supervised learning method to identify the gestures.

The convolution neural network (CNN) has three basic features: local connection, weight sharing and down sampling. Reduce training parameters through local connection and weight sharing, at the same time reduce the training parameters by down sampling to improve the robustness of the model. Therefore, according to the characteristics of the convolution neural network, it usually contains two special network neuron layers: the convolution layer and the lower sampling layer. Because the classification task of this article is relatively simple. Therefore, the network structure based on AlexNet is streamlined, and the specific network structure is shown in Fig. 3. The initial values of convolution kernel and all bias parameters are randomly generated. After input samples, we update the parameters through the forward propagation and back propagation algorithm to train the network.

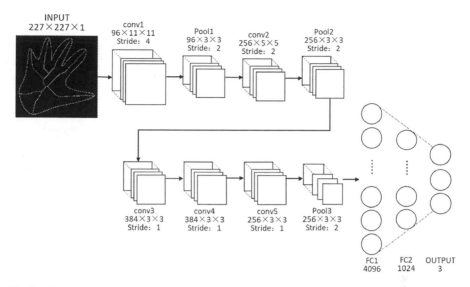

Fig. 3. Convolution neural network structure of gesture recognition. A total of 6 layers, Input Layer as the input layer, specifically for the gesture features of the 64*64 fusion image. Layer1–Layer3 is a convolution layer. Layer4–Layer5 is a fully connected layer. Layer6 Output is the output layer, and there are 3 output layer neurons, representing hand gesture categories: stone, scissors, and cloth.

5   Experimental Results and Analysis

5.1   Experimental Results

The method proposed in this article is verified on two databases. The first database is a gesture image database that is collected in the indoor scene. In the collected gesture database, 100 images of different environments and different types of gesture images under different rotation angles are used for testing the performance of an algorithm through a common camera; second Moeslunds Gesture Recognition database using Thomas Database, also selected 100 images of all kinds of gestures used to test the algorithm performance. At the same time, we use different recognition algorithms in two databases to verify the two methods of skeleton, edge and fusion feature from the recognition accuracy and recognition speed. The experimental results are shown in Figs. 4 and 5.

From the experiment, we can see that in the accuracy of gesture recognition, the recognition method based on convolution neural network (CNN) and support vector machine (SVM) has little difference. Based on random forest (RF) method relative to both difference is not large, but based on decision tree (DT) method is slightly inferior. But in the process of recognition, the average consumption time based on the DT method is the shortest and the SVM is the longest.

In feature selection, no matter which recognition algorithm is used, the accuracy rate based on the fusion feature is higher than the single skeleton feature or edge

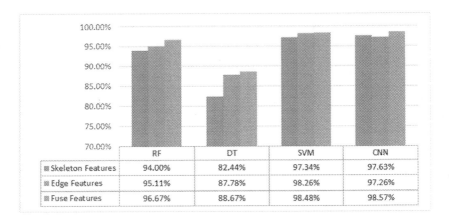

Fig. 4. The influence of different features and different recognition methods on the recognition rate of gestures.

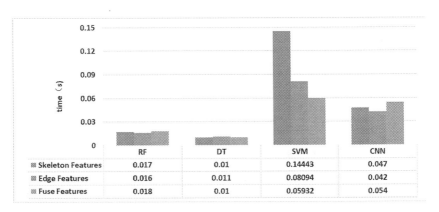

Fig. 5. The influence of different features and different recognition methods on the speed of gesture recognition.

feature. Therefore, we consider the use of a convolution neural network based on multi feature fusion to make gestures.

5.2   Comparison and Analysis of Experiments

In order to further verify the performance of the algorithm, the recognition rate of the experimental results obtained in this paper is compared with that of other domestic scholars. The following table shows the comparison of the recognition rate and time consumption of the gesture samples under different methods (Table 1).

Through contrast, we can find that the recognition rate of the algorithm is relatively high: the skeleton and edge fusion feature of gesture image, as the input of convolution neural network, can describe the physical meaning represented by gesture, and achieve

Table 1. Comparison of the performance of this method and other methods.

Methods	Average time	Average recognition rate
This paper	0.0054 s	98.57%
Literature [7]	0.0050 s	95.00%
Literature [8]	0.0080 s	96.80%
Literature [13]	0.0030 s	87.25%
Literature [14]	0.1200 s	84.00%

better recognition effect. And the network structure is relatively simple, reducing the consumption time of recognition to a certain extent, so as to realize fast and accurate gesture recognition.

6 Summary

In this paper, a new gesture recognition method based on multi feature fusion is proposed in view of the complexity of gestures. It recognizes the input of the algorithm by the fusion of the edge of the gesture and the skeleton features. At the same time, support vector machine, decision tree, random forest and convolution neural network are used to compare the accuracy and recognition speed of single feature and fusion feature in gesture recognition. Experiments show that the accuracy of gesture recognition based on the fusion of Dortmund has high recognition speed, and also in the acceptable range. Next, we will continue to consider the characteristics of gesture change, and improve the accuracy of gesture recognition without affecting the recognition speed. At the same time, we need to achieve dynamic gesture recognition.

Acknowledgments. This research work is supported by Innovation Project of Guangxi University for Nationalities Graduate Education (gxun-chxzs2017112); National Natural Science Fund (21466008, 21566007); Guangxi Natural Science Foundation (2015GXNSFAA13911).

References

1. Stergiopoulou, E., Papamarkos, N.: Hand gesture recognition using a neural network shape fitting technique. Eng. Appl. Artif. Intell. **22**, 1141–1158 (2009)
2. Li, J., Ruan, Q.Q.: Research on gesture recognition based on neural network. Journal of Beijing Jiaotong University (2006)
3. Liu, Y., Yin, Y., Zhang, S.: Hand gesture recognition based on HU moments in interaction of virtual reality. In: International Conference on Intelligent Human-Machine Systems and Cybernetics. IEEE (2012)
4. Dong, L., Ruan, J., Ma, Q., et al.: Application of gesture recognition and machine, micro. invariant moments and support vector machine (2012)
5. Sui Yunheng, Guo Yuan Fusion of Hu moments and BoF-SURF support vector machines for hand gesture recognition [J]. computer application research, (2014)
6. Morton, P.R., Fix, E.L., Calhoun, G.L.: Hand gesture recognition using neural networks (1996)

7. Wang, L., Liu, H., Wang, B., Li, P.: Computer engineering and application combined with skin model and convolution neural network gesture recognition method (2016)
8. Xiaowen, F., Hua, Z.: Research on gesture recognition based on convolution neural network. Microcomput. Appl. (2016)
9. Sukittanon, S., Surendran, A.C., Platt, J.C., et al.: Convolutional networks for speech detection. In: INTERSPEECH 2004 - ICSLP, International Conference on Spoken Language Processing, Jeju Island, Korea. DBLP, October 2004
10. Chen, Y.N., Han, C.C., Wang, C.T., et al.: The application of a convolution neural network on face and license plate detection. Pattern Recognit. (2006)
11. Lauer, F., Suen, C.Y., Bloch, G., et al.: A trainable feature extractor for handwritten digit recognition. Pattern Recognit. (2007)
12. Sun, Y., Wang, X., Tang, X.: Deep convolutional network cascade for facial point detection. In: Computer Vision and Pattern Recognition(CVPR) (2013)
13. Stergiopoulou, E., Papamarkos, N.: Hand gesture recognition using a neural network shape fitting technique. Eng. Appl. Artif. Intell. (2009)
14. Cai, J., Cai, J., Liao, X., et al.: The application of hand gesture recognition based on convolution neural network. Comput. Syst. Appl. (2015)

Application of SVDD Single Categorical Data Description in Motor Fault Identification Based on Health Redundant Data

Jianjian Yang[1], Xiaolin Wang[1(✉)], Zhiwei Tang[1], Zirui Wang[1],
Song Han[1], Yinan Guo[2], and Miao Wu[1]

[1] China University of Mining and Technology (Beijing), Beijing 100083, China
396082938@qq.com
[2] China University of Mining and Technology, Xuzhou 221116, China

Abstract. The system's self-protection mechanism immediately stops the motor when motor system in the event of a malfunction, so it is difficult to collect the fault data when monitoring the motor status. Under the premise of only collecting motor's health data, using SVDD algorithm to train health data and building non-health data sets based on practical experience in this paper. Based on BP neural network, a random self-adapting particle swarm optimization algorithm (RSAPSO) is used to substitute the original gradient descent method in BP network, training speed and accuracy of BP network training is improved. Three commonly used test functions were used to test the performance of the improved PSO, and the improved particle swarm optimization is compared with the standard particle swarm optimization, particle swarm optimization with compression factor and adaptive particle swarm optimization. In this paper, three asynchronous motor Y225S-4 output shaft vibration acceleration signal in healthy state as a case to test the effectiveness of the algorithm, results show that in the case of only health data, the new algorithm based on single classification has better performance and can effectively monitor the working state of the motor.

Keywords: Fault identification · Health redundant data
Support vector data description · Particle swarm optimization

1 Introduction

Three asynchronous motor has the advantages of simple structure, strong stability, light weight, low cost, so it has been widely used in industry. As the key equipment in continuous production system, once the motor breaks down, it will often affect the normal operation of the whole production system, resulting in huge economic loss. So, fault diagnosis is of great significance [1].

A large number of data tests show that the motor vibration signal and its working conditions are closely linked. After processing, vibration sensor output signal is compared with the known fault characteristic frequency to find out the nature of the fault and fault location. Fault identification in motor is difficult to collect fault data, firstly, its production line is unmanned management, secondly, system exists self-protection

© Springer International Publishing AG, part of Springer Nature 2018
Y. Tan et al. (Eds.): ICSI 2018, LNCS 10942, pp. 399–410, 2018.
https://doi.org/10.1007/978-3-319-93818-9_38

mechanism. The motor will stop working immediately when a fault occurs. Therefore, the lack of faulty vibration data is a major challenge in motor fault identification. Using support vector data description (SVDD) can effectively solve this problem. Training health data with SVDD can classifies components health and non-health data.

It needs to be diagnosed and analyzed for the degree of failure after obtaining the device's health and non-health data. Currently used fault diagnosis methods include expert system diagnostics [3, 4], neural network diagnostics [5, 7], fault tree diagnostics [8, 9] and signal processing based diagnostic methods [10]. BP neural network has good nonlinear mapping ability, self-learning and self-adaptive ability, generalization ability and capacity, it represents a huge advantage when dealing with unconventional issues. However, the BP algorithm has the disadvantage of slow convergence rate and easy local optimization. Therefore, many researchers propose to train the network to replace the original BP algorithm with the algorithm with global optimization performance, Li Huimin [11] applied particle swarm optimization (PSO) to neural networks to overcome the shortcomings of the BP network to assess the degree of rock burst risk. It has higher accuracy than standard BP network diagnostics. In order to further improve the global and local search ability of the PSO algorithm, the researchers proposed a variety of improved particle swarm optimization, such as CLPSO algorithm [12], APSO algorithm [13] and CFPSO algorithm [14].

In view of the lack of fault data and the need of dividing the fault degree in the research of motor fault diagnosis. Based on the standard BP network diagnostics, SVDD is introduced to train health data and construct non-health data sets based on field experience, adopting an improved PSO algorithm for motor fault identification to replace the original gradient descent algorithm in BP network, compared with the results obtained by the mainstream PSO such as standard PSO and CFPSO, the proposed method has higher accuracy and faster convergence rate.

2 Algorithm Description

Standard PSO algorithm [14] adjusts the weight value formula has a greater limitation, small adjustment range of weights, and therefore often appear local optimum and search accuracy is not high. In order to improve the search accuracy of the algorithm and reduce the probability of falling into the local optimum. This article uses a RSAPSO algorithm. In the algorithm, random adaption is introduced to let the particles randomly reset the position with a certain probability, so that it jumps out of the original position to search again, reducing the probability of particle swarm into local minima.

The standard PSO formula is as shown in formulas (1)–(4)

$$v_{id}(t+1) = v_{id}(t) + c_1 r_1 \left(P_{id}(t) - x_{id}(t) \right) + c_2 r_2 \left(P_{gd}(t) - x_{id}(t) \right) \tag{1}$$

$$x_{id}(t+1) = x_{id}(t) + v_{id}(t+1) \tag{2}$$

$$v_{id} = \begin{cases} v_{max} & if \quad v_i^d > v_{max} \\ -v_{max} & if \quad v_i^d < -v_{max} \\ v_{id} & if \quad |v_{id}| < v_{max} \end{cases} \tag{3}$$

$$w = w_{max} - \frac{(w_{max} - w_{min}) \times t}{T_{max}} \tag{4}$$

Where v_{id} is the velocity of the current particle i; x_{id} is the position of the current particle i; c_1, c_2 are the learning factors; r_1, r_2 is the random number between [0, 1]; P_{id} is The individual's optimal position found by particle i; P_{gd} is the global optimal position found by particle i; v_{max} is the maximum velocity; w_{max} is the maximum inertia weight, w_{min} is the minimum inertia weight, t is the number of iterations, T_{max} is the maximum number of iterations.

This method is easy to fall into a local optimum, and the search accuracy is not high. Therefore, this article uses a RSAPSO algorithm to adjust the weight update formula, as shown in Eq. (5).

$$w = w_{max} - \frac{(w_{max} - w_{min}) \times (f_{max} - fitness(i))}{f_{max} - f_{min}} \tag{5}$$

Where $fitness(i)$ is the fitness value of the i-th particle; f_{max} is the maximum fitness value of the particle; f_{min} is the minimum fitness value in the particle.

The RSAPSO algorithm used in this paper is tested by three commonly used test functions, Rosenbrock, Griewanks and Rastrigin optimization test functions and is compared with several classical particle swarm optimization algorithms such as standard PSO algorithm, CLPSO algorithm and CFPSO algorithm Comparison, comparison of fitness values shown in Figs. 1, 2 and 3.

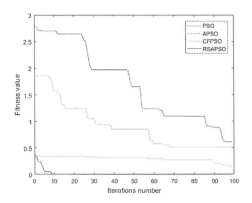

Fig. 1. Comparison of fitness values under Griewank function

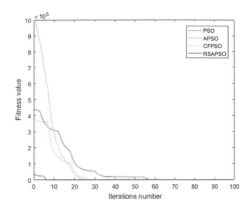

Fig. 2. Comparison of fitness values under Rosenbrock function

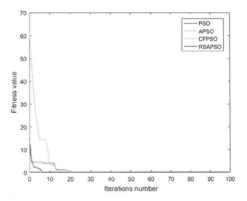

Fig. 3. Comparison of fitness values under Rastrigin function

As can be seen from Figs. 1, 2 and 3, the convergence speed of RSAPSO algorithm used in this paper is relatively superior.

The algorithm in this paper runs for five times. When the maximum number of iterations is reached, the minimum fitness values of the three algorithms are shown in Table 1.

Table 1. Minimum fitness under 4 test functions

Test functions	PSO	CFPSO	APSO	RSAPSO
Griewank	0.9492	0.0351	0.9357	1.5639e−11
Rosenbrock	1.8803e−07	0.0841	0.0399	1.1094e−14
Rastrigin	7.1054e−15	3.2676e−05	3.0811e−05	0

As can be seen from Table 1, the minimum fitness of the RSAPSO algorithm is far less than the other three algorithms after the algorithm is run five times and statistically. From this we can see that RSAPSO algorithm has the highest stability and convergence accuracy.

3 Sample Data Classification Based on SVDD

Currently, SVDD is used in algorithm evaluation for a variety of device evaluation, identification and diagnosis [15–20]. The SVDD principle is described in the literature [15]. For a given set of datasets for a motor output shaft vibration data signal sample containing n samples $\{x_i | i = 1, 2, \ldots, K, \ldots n\}$, we need to satisfy the following formula:

$$minF(a, r) = r2 + C\frac{1}{n}\sum_{i=1}^{n} \varepsilon_i \qquad (6)$$

F (a, r) is a hyperspherical center centered at a and r is a radius; C is a penalty constant that controls the penalty on the misclassification sample to maintain the balance between the volume of the hypersphere and the number of mispredictions; ε_i is Relaxation factor.

Through the three motor Y225S-4 output shaft vibration characteristics of the signal analysis, take $C = 0.5$.

Determine the recognition rate of SVDD according to the different values of ε_i: When the numerical ε_i is small, most of the samples are hyperspherical envelopes. At this time, the SVDD recognition rate is higher and the data is health data. When the ε_i increases, the number of hyperspherical envelopes and the number of scattered samples outside the hypersphere are relatively balanced. At this moment, the recognition rate of SVDD decreases, the recognition rate is not 100%, and the data is the critical value of the fault. When ε_i continue to increase, most of the samples scatter outside the hyperspherical shape. At this time, the SVDD recognition rate is low or even close to zero, and the data is fault data.

Based on practical experience, the accuracy of the data and the data type should have the relationship as shown in Eq. (7):

$$Z(A) = \begin{cases} 1 & A = 100\% \\ 0 & A \neq 100\% \\ -1 & A = 0\% \end{cases} \qquad (7)$$

Z (A) is the indicator function, A is the recognition accuracy, 1 is the health data, 0 is the critical data, and −1 is the fault data.

Based on the above principles, this paper selects another group of healthy samples that can be identified by SVDD to classify them into healthy data sets, critical data sets and fault data sets.

4   Instance Data Analysis

4.1   Sample Data Extraction

The data used in this paper is the vibration acceleration signal of Y225S-4 output shaft of three asynchronous motors collected by Fushun, a data logger developed by China University of Mining and Technology (Beijing). The original waveform is shown in Fig. 4.

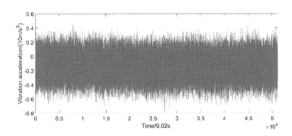

Fig. 4. Original waveform of motor vibration data

Using MATLAB to analyze the vibration acceleration signal, and normalized to get the waveform shown in Figs. 5, 6 and 7.

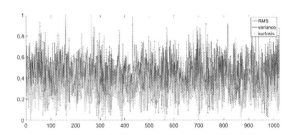

Fig. 5. RMS, Variance, Kurtosis Eigenvalue normalized waveform

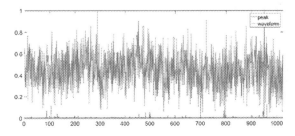

Fig. 6. Peak, Waveform indicators Eigenvalue normalized waveform

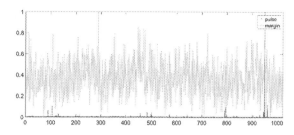

Fig. 7. Pulse, Margin Eigenvalue normalized waveform

In the objective function, select six groups of data as the original sample, select one as a training sample, the remaining five as a test sample.

4.2 Non-health Data Structure

After obtaining the sample data, the SVDD method was used to train the original training samples, and another original test sample was used to test the trained SVDD. The accuracy of the recognition is 100% under the condition of the motor health.

According to the method proposed in this paper, another 5 groups of test data are selected, with 100 samples in each group. The relationship between linear weights and recognition accuracy is shown in Tables 2, 3, 4, 5 and 6.

Table 2. The first group's Relationship between linear weights and recognition accuracy

Accuracy	The linear weight	Accuracy	The linear weight
100%	1.05	45%	1.8
90%	1.1	19%	2.3
77%	1.3	7%	3
62%	1.5	0	3.3

Table 3. The second group's Relationship between linear weights and recognition accuracy

Accuracy	The linear weight	Accuracy	The linear weight
100%	1.04	30%	1.8
91%	1.1	15%	2.3
75%	1.3	6%	3
49%	1.5	0	3.2

Table 4. The third group's relationship between linear weights and recognition accuracy

Accuracy	The linear weight	Accuracy	The linear weight
100%	1.04	44%	1.8
92%	1.1	17%	2.3
85%	1.3	6%	3
66%	1.5	0	3.3

Table 5. The fourth group's relationship between linear weights and recognition accuracy

Accuracy	The linear weight	Accuracy	The linear weight
100%	1.05	35%	1.8
93%	1.1	18%	2.3
85%	1.3	5%	3
59%	1.5	0	3.4

Table 6. The fifth group's Relationship between linear weights and recognition accuracy

Accuracy	The linear weight	Accuracy	The linear weight
100%	1.06	33%	1.8
93%	1.1	14%	2.3
76%	1.3	4%	3
59%	1.5	0	3.1

The formula in Table 7 is constructed from Tables 2, 3, 4, 5 and 6

Table 7. The linear weights range and data construction formula of various types of data

The data type	Linear weight	Data structure formula
Healthy data	1–1.04	$S_{1i} = s_i \times R_{1i}$
The critical data	1.04–3.1	$S_{2i} = s_i \times R_{2i}$
Failure data	More than 3.1	$S_{3i} = s_i \times R3i$

In Table 7, S_{1i} is the ith health data, S_{2i} is the ith failure threshold data, S_{3i} is the ith failure data, s_i is the ith primary health data, R_1 is a random number between 1 and 1.04, and R_2 is A random number between 1.04 and 3.1. R_3 is a random number above 3.1, where $i = 1, 2, \ldots,100$.

The original data samples are used to construct three types of data according to the data construction principle shown in Table 7, and each sample uses 100 training samples and 50 test samples to obtain the SVDD classification map as shown in the following Fig. 8.

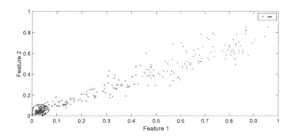

Fig. 8. Target data division based on SVDD

4.3   Target Data Test

Select the motor vibration acceleration signal RMS, kurtosis and kurtosis index as the neural network input vector, the number of nodes in the input layer is 3; In this paper, the working status of the motor is divided into three kinds, that is, the health status, the critical status of the fault and the fault status. Therefore, the data label of the output layer is divided into [1], [0], [−1], respectively, corresponding to the three working state of the motor. Use a hidden layer to achieve the purpose of classification, the number of nodes is seven. After the input vector is normalized, the data is [0, 1], so the input layer activation function uses *logsig*. The output vector data is [−1, 1], so the output layer activation function uses *tansig*.

According to the formula (8):

$$N = (S1 + 1) \times S2 + (S2 + 1) \times S3 \tag{8}$$

It can be determined that the population size $N = 40$ is the most suitable, the maximum number of iterations $M = 1000$, the maximum inertia weight $w_{max} = 0.9$, the minimum inertia weight $w_{min} = 0.4$ and the learning factor $c_1 = c_2 = 2.05$. Since the input vector in this paper is between [0, 1], the maximum velocity $v_{max} = 1$.

The fitness function selected in this paper is the mean square error between the target output and the actual output. The mathematical formula is as follows:

$$F = \frac{1}{n}\sum\nolimits_{i=1}^{n}(P_i - T_i)^2 \quad i = 1, 2, 3 \ldots n \tag{9}$$

Where n is the number of samples, P_i is the ideal output value of the ith sample and T_i is the actual output value of the ith sample.

A total of 300 training samples of health, fault criticality and fault constructed in Section 3.2 were brought into the RSAPSO-BP network for training. The fitness decline curve of BP neural network is shown in Fig. 9.

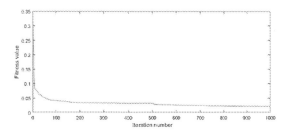

Fig. 9. Fitness decline curve

As can be seen from Fig. 9, the fitness value of RSAPSO-BP neural network declines rapidly and achieves high convergence accuracy.

The trained neural network is tested with 150 sets of test samples in Section 3.2 to obtain the test results as shown in Table 8.

Table 8. Test results

	Healthy state	Critical state	Failure state
Recognition rate	100%	98%	100%
Average recognition rate		99.3%	
Average error		0.0117	

As can be seen from Table 8, RSAPSO-BP neural network has a high recognition rate of the three data, with an overall recognition rate of 99.3% and a small average error.

Table 9 shows the minimum fitness function values obtained from running 10 RSAPSO-BP runs over 10 runs each, and the mean and variance of the minimum fitness functions.

Table 9. Minimum fitness, average value and variance

	1	2	3	4	5
Minimum fitness value	0.0128	0.0134	0.0151	0.0103	0.0119
Average	0.0203	0.0166	0.0213	0.0154	0.0166
Variance	1.31e−05	1.433e−05	1.669e−05	1.596e−05	1.439e−05
	6	7	8	9	10
Minimum fitness value	0.0206	0.0157	0.0195	0.0113	0.0134
Average	0.0263	0.0198	0.0293	0.0143	0.0167
Variance	1.69e−05	1.561e−05	1.784e−05	1.267e−05	1.336e−05

As can be seen from Table 8, the values of fitness, mean and variance after RSAPSO-BP neural network training remain basically stable. The test results show that the RSAPSO-BP network used in this paper has high accuracy.

5   Conclusion

In order to meet the requirements of real-time performance and high-precision of motor fault identification in actual production, this paper proposes a neural network method to identify. In view of the fact that there is only a large number of healthy redundant data and fault data is short, we put forward a single taxonomy that supports vector description. Aiming at the problem that the traditional PSO algorithm is easy to fall into the local minima and the precision is not high, the RSAPSO algorithm is used to optimize the neural network. The random adaptive algorithm is introduced to reduce its Fall into the local optimum probability. The simulation results show that the support vector data used in this paper can effectively use a large number of healthy redundant data to build a non-healthy sample set. Compared with the standard PSO, the improved PSO algorithm, which improves the accuracy of motor fault identification, and provides a new way for motor fault identification in the actual production has the advantages of fast convergence rate, high search accuracy and it is not easy to fall into the local Excellent features.

Acknowledgments. This research is supported by National Program on Key Basic Research Project of China (973 Program) (2014CB046306) and National Natural Science Foundation of China under Grant 61573361.

References

1. Zhong, B.L., Huang, R.: Introduction to Machine Fault Diagnosis. Mechanical Industry Press, Beijing (2006)
2. Zheng, L., Zhe, Z., Xiang, Y.: A summary of on-line condition monitoring and fault diagnostics for 3-phase induction motors. J. Wuhan Yejin Univ. Sci. Technol. **24**(3), 285–289 (2001)
3. Park, Y.M., Kim, G.W., Sohn, J.M.: A logic based expert system (LBES) for fault diagnosis of power system. IEEE Trans. Power Syst. **12**(1), 363–369 (1997). https://doi.org/10.1109/59.574960
4. Vazquez, E., Chacon, O.L., Altuve, H.J.: An on-line expert system for fault section diagnosis in power systems. IEEE Trans. Power Syst. **12**(1), 357–362 (1997). https://doi.org/10.1109/59.574959
5. Wen, L., Li, X., Gao, L., Zhang, Y.: A new convolutional neural network based data-driven fault diagnosis method. IEEE Trans. Ind. Electron. **65**(7), 5990–5998 (2017). https://doi.org/10.1109/tie.2017.2774777
6. Saucedo-Dorantes, J., Delgado-Prieto, M., Osornio-Rios, R., Romero-Troncoso, R.: Multi-fault diagnosis method applied to an electric machine based on high-dimensional feature reduction. IEEE Trans. Ind. Appl. **PP**(99), 1 (2016). https://doi.org/10.1109/tia.2016.2637307
7. Zhang, Y., Ding, X., Liu, Y., Griffin, P.J.: An artificial neural network approach to transformer fault diagnosis. IEEE Trans. Power Delivery **11**(4), 1836–1841 (2002). https://doi.org/10.1109/61.544265
8. Shu, M.H., Cheng, C.H., Chang, J.R.: Using intuitionistic fuzzy sets for fault-tree analysis on printed circuit board assembly. Microelectron. Reliab. **46**(12), 2139–2148 (2006). https://doi.org/10.1016/j.microrel.2006.01.007
9. Volkanovski, A., Čepin, M., Mavko, B.: Application of the fault tree analysis for assessment of power system reliability. Reliab. Eng. Syst. Saf. **94**(6), 1116–1127 (2009). https://doi.org/10.1016/j.ress.2009.01.004
10. Gao, J., Hu, N., Jiang, L., Fu, J.: A new condition monitoring and fault diagnosis method of engine based on spectrometric oil analysis. Wear **110**, 117–124 (2011). https://doi.org/10.1016/j.wear.2007.02.022
11. Huimin, L.I., Zhenlei, L.I., Rongjun, H.E., Yan, Y.: Rock burst risk evaluation based on particle swarm optimization and bp neural network. J. Min. Saf. Eng. **31**(2), 203–207+231 (2014)
12. Han, X.H., Xiong, X., Duan, F.: A new method for image segmentation based on BP neural network and gravitational search algorithm enhanced by cat chaotic mapping. Appl. Intell. **43**(4), 855–873 (2015). https://doi.org/10.1007/s10489-015-0679-5

13. Niu, M., Sun, S., Wu, J., Zhang, Y.: Short-term wind speed hybrid forecasting model based on bias correcting study and its application. Math. Prob. Eng. **2015**, 1–13 (2015). https://doi.org/10.1155/2015/351354
14. Liu, Y.M., Niu, B.: Theory and Practice of New Particle Swarm Optimization, Beijing (2013)
15. Jie, W.U., Shangguan, W.B., Jing, T., Song, Z.S., Huang, Z.L.: Robust analysis for decoupling layout of a powertrain mounting system. J. Vibr. Shock (2009)
16. Banerjee, A., Burlina, P., Meth, R.: Fast hyperspectral anomaly detection via SVDD. In: IEEE International Conference on Image Processing, vol. 4, pp. IV-101–IV-104. IEEE (2007). https://doi.org/10.1109/icip.2007.4379964
17. Luo, H., Jiang Cui, Y.W.: A SVDD approach of fuzzy classification for analog circuit fault diagnosis with FWT as preprocessor. Expert Syst. Appl. **38**(8), 10554–10561 (2011). https://doi.org/10.1016/j.eswa.2011.02.087
18. Yang, Z., Wang, S., Fu, X.: Pattern recognition-based chillers fault detection method using support vector data description (SVDD). Appl. Energy **112**(4), 1041–1048 (2013). https://doi.org/10.1016/j.apenergy.2012.12.043
19. Liu, Y.H., Lin, S.H., Hsueh, Y.L., Lee, M.J.: Automatic target defect identification for TFT-LCD array process inspection using kernel FCM-based fuzzy SVDD ensemble. Expert Syst. Appl. **36**(2), 1978–1998 (2009). https://doi.org/10.1016/j.eswa.2007.12.015
20. Tao, X.M., Chen, W.H., Du, B.X., Xu, Y., Dong, H.G.: A novel model of one-class bearing fault detection using SVDD and genetic algorithm. In: IEEE Conference on Industrial Electronics and Applications, ICIEA 2007, pp. 802–807. IEEE (2007). https://doi.org/10.1109/iciea.2007.4318518

Finding Patterns

Impact of Purchasing Power on User Rating Behavior and Purchasing Decision

Yong Wang[1], Xiaofei Xu[1], Jun He[1], Chao Chen[2], and Ke Ren[1(✉)]

[1] School of Computer and Information Science,
Southwest University, Chongqing, China
wy8654@email.swu.edu.cn, 214433287@qq.com
[2] Online and Continuing Education College,
Southwest University, Chongqing, China

Abstract. Recommender system have broad and powerful applications in e-commerce, news promotion and online education. As we all know, the user's rating behavior is generally determined by subjective preferences and objective conditions. However, all the current studies are focused on subjective preferences, ignoring the role of the objective conditions of the user. The user purchasing power based on price is the key objective factor that affects the rating behavior and even purchasing decision. Users' purchasing decisions are often affected by the purchasing power, and the current researches did not take into account the problem. Thus, in this paper, we consider the influence of user preferences and user purchasing power on rating behavior simultaneously. Then, we designed a reasonable top-N recommendation strategy based on the user's rating and purchasing power. Experiments on Amazon product dataset show that our method has achieved better results in terms of accuracy, recall and coverage. With ever larger datasets, it is important to understand and harness the predictive purchasing power on the users' rating behavior and purchasing decisions.

Keywords: Recommender system · Rating behavior
Purchasing power · Purchasing decision

1 Introduction

At present, recommendation system has been widely used in the field of electronic commerce. It play an important role in providing personalized information to users and helping address the in information overload problem [7,14]. In other words, the recommendation system can help users to find the products they want more quickly and more accurately.

It is a matter of course that we design the recommendation system to recommend the products the users might be interested in. However, we all know that users' purchasing decisions are closely related to their objective economic conditions, in addition to their preferences. Further, the recommendation system

© Springer International Publishing AG, part of Springer Nature 2018
Y. Tan et al. (Eds.): ICSI 2018, LNCS 10942, pp. 413–422, 2018.
https://doi.org/10.1007/978-3-319-93818-9_39

should take full account of the user's purchasing power and personal preferences. On the other hand, users will be affected by the price of products when they give a rating. So we often see such a commodity evaluation: It's a good thing, but it's not worth the price. We can see that the impact of price runs through the whole process of shopping. Of course, we know that different users have different attitudes towards the same price, and the user purchasing power is the root cause of this phenomenon.

Former Amazon scientists Greg Linden[1] believed that a good recommendation system is designed to find goods which users could be interested in, rather than make accurate rating prediction when users bought these goods. Thus, cater to the actual needs, we will also discuss the effect of the top-N recommendation in addition to predicting the consumer score.

In fact, if the user knows what he want to buy, then he doesn't need the help of recommendation system. We believe that the user's purchasing decision is determined during the browsing process. In other words, at the beginning, users only knew what they wanted to buy, but some external features such as the style and color were determined when browsing the item list. Further, the users' browsing record contains their current selection preferences. For example, the user wants to buy a watchband, and Fig. 2 shows a set of selection records and the final purchasing one (Fig. 1).

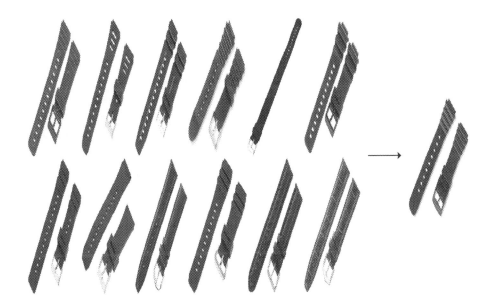

Fig. 1. Records of the selecting watchstrap. (Color figure online)

---

[1] https://cacm.acm.org/blogs/blog-cacm/22925-what-is-a-good-recommendation-algorithm/fulltext.

In this paper, first of all, we will calculate the price level of each item and the purchasing power level of users according to their purchase records. Next, we will jointly consider the user's personal preference and the purchasing power impact to establish a reasonable model for the rating prediction. Finally, we will also design a reasonable list of recommendations based on the user's purchasing power. Experiments show that our method can not only predict the user's rating accurately, but also generate a reasonable list of recommendations.

2   Related Work

Preference matching has been richly studied in area of recommender systems, which two kinds of approaches of interest have been developed: content-based approaches [10,12] where explicit user profiles or item information are used as features, and collaborative filtering approaches where preference predictions mainly rely on users' previous behavior. Collaborative filtering algorithm has been attracting more and more attention because of its good performance [2,5,6,14]. Among them, the core idea of latent factor model is contacting the characteristics of user interest and items by implicit features. Since the start of the Netflix Prize competition, latent factor model has gradually gained a higher degree of concern. As one kind of latent factor model, matrix factorization techniques have been widely applied for recommender system due to their accuracy and scalability [1,4,8,13].

Many factors affect user purchase behavior and can be leveraged to improve recommendation performance. Wang et al. [18] and Zhao et al. [19] considered the impact of time factors on the effectiveness of the recommendation. Chen [3] pointed out that user comment is another factor that affects user purchase behavior. Besides, in social recommender systems, considerable work has considered the social influence. Ma et al. [11] incorporated users' social network for items recommendation using matrix factorization. Tang et al. [15] explored the impact of local and global context information in the model. The idea of price sensitivity in recommender systems has been mentioned as a potential direction in a classic survey [9]. In addition, these two papers [16,17] have also been engaged in this field of research. These work is mainly to consider the relationship between price change and overall profit. However, few researches consider the impact of user purchasing power on ratings and shopping decisions from the user level.

3   Model Specification

3.1   Price Level Model and User Purchasing Power Model

As we all know, there will be a great difference in the price of the different kinds of commodities. In simple terms, commodities of the same category can be compared directly with the price. Therefore, we generally define the price level of a commodity as the ratio of the price of the commodity to the average price in its category. We use p_i to express the price of the commodity i and use p_c to express the average price of its category c. Then, the following formula indicates the commodity price level pl_i:

$$pl_i = \frac{p_i}{p_c} \tag{1}$$

The classification rules of the commodities are carried out according to the Amazon website classification standard. We all know that, even in the same category, the price of commodities could be very different. The price of some goods may greatly affect the average price of the whole category. For example, in general, a common scarf will not exceed three hundred yuan($45), but there will be a thousand yuan($151) or even more. So if the average value is calculated in a general way, the result will not be representative. In order to cope with this situation, we have two steps to deal with:

1. We can use the four division method in statistics to remove the outliers. From the Fig. 2, we divide the Amazon electronic data set into 8 categories according to the classification principles of the website itself, and then 5% minimal outliers and 10% maximal abnormity values are screened out.
2. Each price is weighted according to the popular ranking. Because we think the average price should represent the vast majority of users. The unpopular items should have a smaller weight.

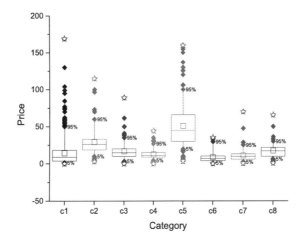

Fig. 2. The removal of outliers. (Color figure online)

We use r_i to indicate the popularity ranking of the commodity i in its category, then the weight of the commodity i is $\frac{1}{\ln(e+r_i-1)}$. So the average price(p_c) of type c is expressed as:

$$p_c = \frac{\sum\limits_{i \in l_c} p_i * \frac{1}{\ln(e+r_i-1)}}{\sum\limits_{i \in l_c} \frac{1}{\ln(e+r_i-1)}} \tag{2}$$

where l_c represents the collection of items under the category c and p_i represents the price of the item i. $I_u = \{i_1, i_2, \cdots, i_n\}$ represents the collection of goods purchased by the user u. We have already calculated the price level of each commodity before, then the I_u's price level sequence $pl_u = \{pl_1, pl_2, \cdots, pl_n\}$. Then, user purchasing power bp_u can be indicated like:

$$bp_u = \frac{\sum\limits_{i \in I_u} pl_i}{n} \tag{3}$$

3.2   Rating Prediction Model

We believe that the more appropriate interpretation of the user's purchasing power should be the user's sensitivity to the price, and the closer the user is, the more comfortable the user will feel. In the rating behavior, the user will balance the individual preferences and prices based on their own purchasing power to make the final evaluation. In user-based collaborative filtering algorithm [2], we use similar users' ratings to express the current user's. The higher the weight value given by the more similar purchasing power, the weight function is used by the Gaussian kernel function which is a weighted function commonly used in machine learning. δ needs to be specified, which depends on the final prediction effect. Here we use a similar way to show the impact of price on the user and user's preference for items could be represented by a matrix factorization model. So, the rating of the user u for the item i is expressed as

$$r_{ui} = p_{ui} + \lambda_{ui} * \sum_{v \in N(u,L)} e^{\frac{|bp_u - bp_v|}{-2\delta^2}} (r_{vi} - p_{vi}) \tag{4}$$

Here, $p_{ui} = \sum\limits_{k=1}^{K} \theta_{uk}\beta_{kj}$ represents the preference of user u to item i and $N(u, L)$ is a collection of L users most similar to u. The parameter λ which can be obtained through training represents the weight between the individual preferences and the price selection.

4   Experiments and Results

4.1   Rating Prediction

First, let's take a look at the general situation of the user's purchasing power and the user's ratings. Since the overall distribution of the two data sets is similar, we use an electronic product dataset as the main explanation. As we can see from Fig. 3, most users are willing to make high marks(4&5). And most of the users' purchasing power is concentrated between 0.7 and 1.2. More accurately, it should be hovering around 1. This shows that most users will consider selecting items near the average price level when they buy items.

Although the score prediction is not our ultimate goal, it will serve as an important basis for the final top-N recommendation. It will tell us whether the

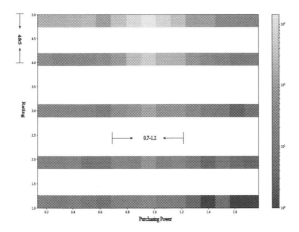

Fig. 3. Ratings and user purchasing power.

user will be interested in this item. In our opinion, users will not only consider personal preferences, but also take into account their own economic conditions.

In order to analyze the effect of the model, we use root mean square error (RMSE) as the standard of comparison. That is, for our test set T we report

$$RMSE(T) = \sqrt{\frac{1}{|T|} \sum_{r_{ui} \in T} (r_{ui} - \hat{r}_{ui})^2} \tag{5}$$

Among them, r_{ui} represents the actual value, and $\hat{r}_{ij}$ represents the predictive value.

The δ parameter determines the span of the weight, and we choose the value of δ with the final prediction effect. That is to say, we choose the value that makes the error minimum. Figure 4 shows the selection process. Due to the small sensitivity of the electronic product dataset to the changes of δ, we put it alone in the subgraph in order to be more obvious. We mark the results of the selection of two datasets in red. In addition, when the δ is increasing, the error will be too large and it will cause calculation overflow.

The final results are shown in Table 1. The experiment shows that considering the price factor in the rating prediction can make the prediction result more accurate.

4.2   Purchasing Power and Purchasing Decision

Next, Let's study the relationship between the price level and the purchasing power. We first calculated the difference between the price level of the items and the purchasing power of the users in each record.

As shown in Fig. 5, the X axis represents the purchasing power of the user, and the Y axis indicates the difference between the price level of the items and the purchasing power. We can find that most of the dots are clustered near the line

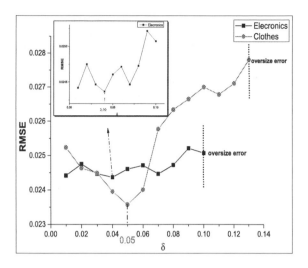

Fig. 4. The choice of parameter δ. (Color figure online)

Table 1. Experimental results (RMSE).

	Electronic	Clothes
PMF	0.0433	0.0584
User-IIF	0.0374	0.0786
ItemCF-IUF	0.0327	0.0429
bp-MF	**0.0293**	**0.0335**

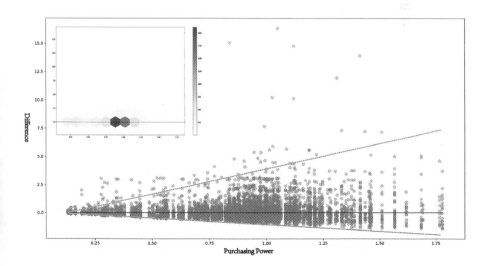

Fig. 5. Purchasing power and purchasing decision. (Color figure online)

of $y = 0$, which means that the price level of users will not be too far from their purchasing power. In order to illustrate this feature more clearly, we represent the process with a density map (subgraph). In addition, we mark the range of most points with two green lines in the scatter plot. As you can see, the higher the purchasing power level, the greater the range of the difference between the price level and the purchasing power. This is an interesting phenomenon: users with high purchasing power are more willing to buy items beyond their purchasing power. In other words, their consumption behavior is more "irrational".

4.3   Top-N Recommendation

It is not just personal preference that ultimately affects their purchase decision. After all, no one knows whether the item is worth buying before it is used. So, we can't ignore the objective factor of personal purchasing power.

We think that, under similar ratings, if the price level of some goods is closer to the user's purchasing power level, the user will be more inclined to buy such items. We also have two options for the generation of the recommended list:

1. We think that the ratings more than 4 could be in the range of praise. So we first screen out the item list of high ratings, and then order them according to the price level and the purchasing power distance, and finally generate the recommended list according to the ranking results.
2. We set a distance threshold and assume that items the price of which less than this threshold can attract the user. Then the items are sorted by the ratings to generate a list of recommendations.

We choose the first as an experimental method. We all know that the model has strict requirements for the parameters, so when we do independent control experiments, we all choose the optimal parameters of the model. The final results(two datasets) are shown in Table 2.

Table 2. Experiment result.

Comparison model	Accuracy		Recall		Coverage	
PMF	21.54%	23.26%	14.04%	12.63%	23.22%	21.18%
User-IIF	24.22%	22.57%	12.84%	11.79%	21.13%	19.67%
ItemCF-IUF	20.62%	19.04%	14.16%	11.54%	23.91%	25.73%
bp-MF-sf	**24.52%**	**23.37%**	**14.33%**	**13.47%**	**22.24%**	**23.92%**

Experiments show that when we create a list of recommendations, considering the user's purchasing power level can effectively improve the effectiveness of the recommendation. The purchasing power factor can affect the consumer's purchasing decision to a great extent.

5   Conclusions

As the most important influence factor in the consumption activity, the user purchasing power can affect the user's rating behavior and the purchase decision. In this paper, we first calculate the user's purchasing power according to the historical purchasing records of the user, and then weigh the impact of user preferences and user purchasing power to make a rating prediction. Finally, in the practical application, the recommendation list is created by considering the user rating and the user purchasing power factor. Experiments show that our ideas can achieve a good effect. It not only enhances the prediction of the rating, but also improves the effect of the recommendation.

Acknowledgements. This work is supported by "Fundamental Research Funds for the Central Universities" (XDJK2017C027) and "CERNET Innovation Project" (NGII20170516).

References

1. Baltrunas, L., Ludwig, B., Ricci, F.: Matrix factorization techniques for context aware recommendation. In: ACM Conference on Recommender Systems, Recsys 2011, Chicago, IL, USA, pp. 301–304, October 2011
2. Breese, J.S., Heckerman, D., Kadie, C.: Empirical analysis of predictive algorithms for collaborative filtering **7**(7), 43–52 (2013)
3. Chen, H.: The impact of comments and recommendation system on online shopper buying behaviour. J. Netw. **7**(2), 345–350 (2012)
4. Forbes, P., Zhu, M.: Content-boosted matrix factorization for recommender systems: experiments with recipe recommendation. In: ACM Conference on Recommender Systems, pp. 261–264 (2011)
5. Jamali, M., Ester, M.: Trustwalker: a random walk model for combining trust-based and item-based recommendation. In: ACM SIGKDD International Conference on Knowledge Discovery and Data Mining, pp. 397–406 (2009)
6. Karypis, G.: Evaluation of item-based top-n recommendation algorithms. In: Tenth International Conference on Information and Knowledge Management, pp. 247–254 (2001)
7. Koren, Y.: Collaborative filtering with temporal dynamics, pp. 447–456 (2009)
8. Koren, Y., Bell, R., Volinsky, C.: Matrix factorization techniques for recommender systems. Computer **42**(8), 30–37 (2009)
9. Liu, F., Tang, B., Yuan, X., Yang, X.: Recommender system in e-commerce. In: International Conference on E-Business and E-Government, pp. 700–703 (2012)
10. Lops, P., De Gemmis, M., Semeraro, G.: Content-based recommender systems: state of the art and trends (2011)
11. Ma, H., Yang, H., Lyu, M.R., King, I.: Sorec: social recommendation using probabilistic matrix factorization. In: ACM Conference on Information and Knowledge Management, pp. 931–940 (2008)
12. Pazzani, M.J., Billsus, D.: Content-based recommendation systems. In: Brusilovsky, P., Kobsa, A., Nejdl, W. (eds.) The Adaptive Web. LNCS, vol. 4321, pp. 325–341. Springer, Heidelberg (2007). https://doi.org/10.1007/978-3-540-72079-9_10

13. Rendle, S.: Factorization machines with libFM. ACM Trans. Intell. Syst. Technol. **3**(3), 1–22 (2012)
14. Salakhutdinov, R., Mnih, A.: Probabilistic matrix factorization. In: International Conference on Neural Information Processing Systems, pp. 1257–1264 (2007)
15. Tang, J., Hu, X., Gao, H., Liu, H.: Exploiting local and global social context for recommendation. In: International Joint Conference on Artificial Intelligence, pp. 2712–2718 (2013)
16. Umberto, P.: Developing a price-sensitive recommender system to improve accuracy and business performance of ecommerce applications. Int. J. Electron. Commer. Stud. **6**(1), 1–18 (2015)
17. Wan, M., Wang, D., Goldman, M., Taddy, M., Rao, J., Liu, J., Lymberopoulos, D., Mcauley, J.: Modeling consumer preferences and price sensitivities from large-scale grocery shopping transaction logs. In: International Conference on World Wide Web, pp. 1103–1112 (2017)
18. Wang, J., Zhang, Y.: Opportunity model for e-commerce recommendation: right product; right time, pp. 303–312 (2013)
19. Zhao, G., Lee, M.L., Hsu, W., Chen, W.: Increasing temporal diversity with purchase intervals, pp. 165–174 (2012)

Investigating the Relationship Between the Emotion of Blogs and the Price of Index Futures

Yen Hao Kao[1], Ping Yu Hsu[1], Ming Shien Cheng[2(✉)],
Hong Tsuen Lei[1], Shih Hsiang Huang[1], Yen-Huei Ko[1],
and Chen Wan Huang[1]

[1] Department of Business Administration, National Central University,
No. 300, Jhongda Road, Jhongli City 32001, Taoyuan County, Taiwan (R.O.C.)
984401019@cc.ncu.edu.tw
[2] Department of Industrial Engineering and Management,
Ming Chi University of Technology, No. 84, Gongzhuan Road, Taishan District,
New Taipei City 24301, Taiwan (R.O.C.)
mscheng@mail.mcut.edu.tw

Abstract. As the financial derivatives tradable market developed quickly in Taiwan, the trading volumes in futures grew quickly in recent years. At the same time, many people posted and shared opinion on social media. Many research in economics and behavioral finance have posited and confirmed that investor's "mood" correlated with the performance of financial market. Several researches had devoted to study the relationship between the volatility of financial market and sentiments expressed in social media. On the other hand, even though emotion can describe the feeling of people more precisely than sentiment, to the best of our knowledge, only one research has tried to discover the relationship between futures performance and emotion fluctuation. The research tracked the evolvement of specific events. Instead of tracking long-term emotional fluctuation, this study strived to predict price change of derivatives with emotion expressed in social media in previous day. The result confirmed that there was a significant correlation between the intensity of emotion "fear" and the market decline. When the major emotions were "good" and "sad", the strength of emotion was significantly correlated with the change of the market price.

Keywords: Emotion analysis · Social media · Taiwan index futures

1 Introduction

"Taiwan Stock Exchange Capitalization Weighted Stock Index (TAIEX)" compiled by the Taiwan Stock Exchange Corporation (TSEC) is Taiwan's most familiar stock index, often regarded as a window for Taiwan's economy trend. The calculation is based on the market value of the stock market in 1966 set as 100 points, including all the listed stocks except the preferred stocks and full-cash delivery stocks. The calculation of weighted stock price index based on the circulation-listed stocks as weight, so the stocks with larger share capital have greater impact on the index than the stocks

© Springer International Publishing AG, part of Springer Nature 2018
Y. Tan et al. (Eds.): ICSI 2018, LNCS 10942, pp. 423–431, 2018.
https://doi.org/10.1007/978-3-319-93818-9_40

with smaller share capital, especially those with high market value such as TSMC, Hon Hai, and China Steel.

On July 21, 1998, the Taiwan Futures Exchange launched the first futures on TAIEX, "TAIEX Futures Contract". Then, it launched the first options, "TAIEX Options" on December 24, 2001, to add variety to Taiwan's financial derivatives. Therefore, investors could hedge their investments using call options or put options, benefiting greatly from the financial market. After several decades of development, currently TAIEX futures and TAIEX options have a great influence on the market. This study would like to find a reference index with high credibility through researching TAIEX futures, hoping to help investors determine the direction of future market and improve their investment efficiency.

In recent years, many scholars have shown that investors are not entirely rational, such as Shleifer (2000) who pointed out that investors often display irrational behavior and investment decisions did not present randomly but presented to the same direction. In addition, investor sentiment would directly affect the behavior of investors (Baumeister 2007). Rystrom (1989) also pointed out that the investor's inner emotions would affect their investment decisions in financial markets. Moreover, sentiment was one of the factors that made investors make irrational deals. It represented the subjective judgment of investors for the future market or the current situation; there was also a research on the use of emotions to predict the 2–3 years short-term returns (Brown and Cliff 2002). Therefore, investors' view of the future on the market is extremely important because when the investor sentiment is too high or too low, investors may ignore or overreact to the market-related information and overestimate or underestimate the future market prices. In recent years, the concept of crowd sourcing has been proposed, and investment has long been considered a very professional technology, especially "Wall Street" that is synonymous with professional financial market. With the development of financial technology, currently the use of the crowd sourcing to analyze the financial market through algorithm has become a trend. For example, social media site Estimation has used technology to establish an open market forecast platform for predicting revenues of the major companies through crowd sourcing models. So, many researches captured sentiment words from the social media sites such as Facebook and Twitter post comments and judged the posts as with positive or negative emotions. However, the Chinese and English languages are very different in terms of characteristics and Chinese language needs more additional treatment, so researches on Chinese sentiment words are fewer than those in English.

Because investors have expectations of the future trend of the market, which may go up or down, so the sentiment indicator is important and influential. This study would like to further use the daily discussions of investors and switch to more detailed emotional indicators than sentiment as a tool to measure the investor sentiment in current market.

This paper organized as follow: (1) Introduction: Research background, motivation and purpose. (2) Related work: Review of scholars' researches on the influence of sentiment on investor behavior. (3) Research methodology: Content of research process in this study. (4) Statistical analysis: Experimental results and the discussion of the test results. (5) Conclusion and future research: Contribution of the study, and possible future research direction is discussed.

2 Related Work

In the past, many behavioral economists have studied the impact of psychological or emotional factors in decision-making, as well as the impact on gains and risks in stock market. Psychological research identified that sentiment factors have a significant impact on people's decision-making besides external information (Dolan 2002). Behavioral economists further argued that investors tended to be driven by their emotions when they made decisions in investment (Nofsinger 2005). Therefore, public sentiment and other factors such as economic factors determine the share prices in stock market.

Since the 1980s, efficient market hypothesis meet challenged. The challenge presented by the New York Stock Market crash on October 19, 1987. However, presently many research showed that the stock market prices have not shown a random trend, and confirmed that investor sentiment has been one of the important factors in the determination of prices, so some researchers believe that it is possible to obtain some indicators of price reaction from online social media sites. Schumaker Schumaker and Chen (2009) applied the machine learning method to financial news articles and found that the sentiment in news articles immediately affected the market prices, with the best effect in the prediction model, so the news article regarded as a factor. In addition, there have been researches using the expert classification system to obtain sentiment from the posts in Yahoo financial discussion area. Liu (2006) described the relationship between sentiment and stock prices. Gibert (2010) used "Live Journal" as the source to extract the feelings of anxiety, worry and fear from the website articles, finding that the rise of anxious mood led to the imminent fall S & P 500 index. There have been other studies using Granger causality. Bollen (2010) examined the correlation between the collective emotional state of a large number of tweets from Twitter and the Dow Jones Industrial Average (DJIA) index over time. The results showed that there was a positive correlation between the emotional state of "calm" and the prices of the index. Similarly, based on tweets from Twitter, Zhang (2011) found that both emotion and sentiment could use to predict the Nasdaq Composite index and S & P 500 index.

Although sentiment has confirmed as one of the factors affecting the stock prices, past researches used bivariate sentiment, but multivariate emotions hardly used. Therefore, this study investigates whether the emotional indicator related to the next day's opening prices.

3 Research Methodology

The research process shows in the following Fig. 1. First, we describe the sample selection and the time range, then depict the operating environment and explain how to calculate the emotional scores and the related variables and finally we developed the data analysis steps.

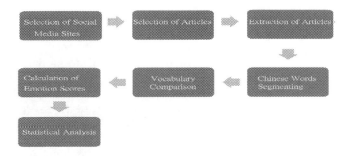

Fig. 1. Research process

3.1 Selection of Social Groups and Articles

For this research, the Professional Technology Temple (PTT) and National Taiwan University (NTU) selected for the collection of comments about stock market. The reason that selected PTT is that it has the largest discussion forum in Bulletin Board System (BBS) in Taiwan. With increasing users, it has gradually become one of the largest network discussion forums. Currently total about 1.5 million users have registered in PTT, which divided into many boards based on themes, and more than 150,000 users in the peak period log on to PTT, to discuss the same or similar matters. More than 20,000 new articles and 500,000 posts published every day (Ptt website 2017).

The Option board has selected for this study. On the option board, the content of discussion is the information related to options, question posts, chats about moods and so on. Among these articles, there are the chats about moods that appear daily and intraday chat and after-hour chat about TAIEX futures during trading days. Because the intraday chats and after-hour chats attract the most attention and responses, the response strings under these two articles will used for this study, to sort out and merge them, and then calculate the intensity of various emotions shown by investors on a certain day. From the board, the chats could collected as early as April 1, 2014, so the chats selected from April 1, 2014 to December 31, 2016. Totally 1,360 articles published on PTT over 660 days were collected.

3.2 Extraction of Articles and Chinese Words Segmenting

In this study, the operating environment version is Python 2.7, the development environment is IPython notebook, and the related articles of the Option board extracted. Chinese word segmenting is the first step of text mining. Unlike English, there is no blank between Chinese characters, so the separation between Chinese words is particularly vague. Therefore, it is necessary to segment Chinese words to obtain each word for meaningful analysis. The Python used to write the Chinese words segmenting for this study, and the dynamic programming in Package Jieba of Python used to find the most likely combination of words. It can also self-built dictionary and create vocabulary.

3.3   Calculation of Emotion Scores

As described above, after extracting what needed from the original response data, we used the Chinese segmentation tool, Jieba, to separate the articles into different words. The next step was to generate words and Chinese emotional vocabulary from these responses, and make a comparison between them to find whether the word is in the vocabulary. For this part, the Chinese emotional vocabulary compiled by the IR laboratory of Dalian University of Technology used for this study. Chinese emotional vocabulary based on Ekman's six basic emotions, and the emotional category "good" has added to the vocabulary, in order to strengthen it for the analysis of Chinese words expressing emotion of comfort, which is widely used for researches on Chinese text mining. Table 1 below shows all the seven categories of emotional words in the vocabulary and their 21 sub-categories.

Table 1. Emotional category table. (Source: IR laboratory of Dalian University of Technology, China http://ir.dlut.edu.cn)

No.	Emotional Category	Emotional Sub-Category	Example
1	Happy(樂)	Joy(快樂)	Delight(喜悅)
2		Reliable(安心)	Practical(踏實)
3	Good(好)	Respect(尊敬)	Respectful(恭敬)
4		Praise(讚揚)	Handsome(英俊)
5		Believe in(相信)	Trust(信任)
6		Favorite(喜愛)	Admiration(傾慕)
7		Wish for(祝願)	Longing(渴望)
8	Angry(怒)	Angry(憤怒)	Anger(氣憤)
9	Sad(哀)	Sad(悲傷)	Depressed(憂傷)
10		Disappointments(失望)	Pity(哀事)
11		Guilty(疚)	Compunction(內疚)
12		Miss(思)	Thinking(思惹)
13	Fear(懼)	Panic(慌)	Flurry(慌張)
14		Fear(恐懼)	Timid(膽怯)
15		Shy(羞)	Blush(害羞)
16	Hate(惡)	Bored(煩悶)	Oppressed(憋悶)
17		Evil(憎惡)	Oppressed(反感)
18		Derogatory(貶責)	Dull(呆板)
19		Jealous(妒忌)	Envious(眼紅)
20		Suspicious(懷疑)	Heart(多心)
21	Surprise(驚)	Surprisingly(驚奇)	Strange(奇怪)

Each emotional word in the Chinese emotional vocabulary has its own emotional category label, such as "joy". There will be strength and polarity marks. So the emotion scores of daily characters and words that have sorted out could calculated using the calculation method as follows: Definition 1.

Definition 1. Let d be the date, $r(d)$ for the index futures intraday, after-hours articles related palindrome after the collection of word segmenting. For the emotion category e, $W(e)$ is the main category of words, where $e = \{1,2,3,4,5,6,7\} \rightarrow \{\text{Good, Happy, Hate, Fear, Sad, Angry, Surprise}\}$, $S(x,e)$ is the score of word x in emotion e.

$$Emotion\ (d)_e = \sum_{\{x \in r(d) \wedge x \in W(e)\}} (S(x,e))$$

4   Statistical Analysis

4.1   Exploration into the Relationship Between Emotional Intensity and Changes of Futures Prices

In this study, the five categories of emotional scores were set as independent variables. The difference between the closing price and the opening price of the next day was set as the dependent variable, to examine the regression relationship. The statistical software SPSS is used to calculate the regression equation shown in Table 2. Each explanatory variable analyzed as follows:

Table 2. Relationship between emotional category and changes of next day futures prices

Model	Non-Standardized Coefficients		Standardized Coefficients	T Value	Significant
	B	Standardized ε	Beta		
Constant	-176.304	689.865		-.256	.798
Good(好)	-2.715	6.425	-.022	-.423	.673
Happy(樂)	3.538	6.252	.031	.566	.572
Hate(惡)	5.541	6.533	.045	.848	.397
Fear(懼)	-14.647	7.386	-.105	-1.983	.048
Sad(哀)	.971	6.607	.008	.147	.883

The study shows that only investor sentiment "fear" negatively correlated with the opening prices of the next day. That is, the greater the "fear" expressed by posts and responses is, the greater the decline.

4.2 The Relationship Between Single Emotion Intensity and Change of TAIEX Futures Price

Because only the kind of emotion "fear" is significant as mentioned in the previous paragraph, whether emotions correlated with the extent if up or down has been known will be explored in this paragraph.

The correlation coefficient is used for this study on the condition that the ups-and-downs of opening prices the next day have been known. The correlations between five emotional indicators and the fluctuation in opening prices will discussed separately. In this paragraph, only the intensity of the main emotions is used for discussion because among the five emotions the gap between the intensity (scores) of main emotions and that of minor emotions is large (Tables 3 and 4).

Table 3. Correlation analysis of emotional categories and price decrease

ID	Emotional Category	Pearson correlation coefficient	Significant(Two-tailed)
1	Good(好)	-.038	.755
2	Happy(樂)	-.04	.702
3	Hate(惡)	-.185	.223
4	Fear(懼)	-.605**	.005
5	Sad(哀)	-.473**	.000

Table 4. Correlation analysis of emotional categories and price increase

ID	Emotional Category	Pearson Correlation Coefficient	Significant (two-tailed)
1	好	.411**	.000
2	樂	.174	.054
3	惡	.152	.189
4	懼	.088	.691
5	哀	-.062	.602

The study shows when the major emotion is "fear" or "sad" and the opening prices the next day decline, the intensity of these two main emotions correlated with the next day's decline in opening price.

The study shows that when the main emotion is "good" and the opening price rises the next day, the intensity of the main emotion "good" correlated with the rise.

5 Conclusion and Future Research

In the past, the relevant researches also showed that negative emotions negatively correlated with the prices, but the difference in this study is that the negative emotions subdivided into three kinds of emotions, "dislike", "fear" and "sadness". Among them, the emotion "fear" and "sadness" has caused the prices to decline, but the emotion "dislike" has no effect. Because of the comprehensive study, the relationship between the emotion indicators and the index futures price described as follows. The intensity of the emotion "fear" negatively correlated with the change of the prices the next day. When the intensity of the emotion is strong, the prices will decline and the reward will reduce. When the intensity of the emotion is weak, the prices will rise and the reward will increase. The emotion indicators that are worth discussing are "good" and "sadness". Although the two variables are not significant in the regression, if they are separately analyzed, it was found that the emotion "good" was significantly correlated the rise of prices the next day, indicating the heated discussion among investors is positively correlated with the prices. In addition, the appearance of emotion "sadness" would also affect the price changes the next day, indicating that although the intensity of the emotion did not affect the prices, it still had a certain degree of relevance. Compared with the emotional dichotomy, this study shows that multivariate emotion indicators can provide investors with more accurate investment references.

This study shows that the negative emotion indicators are negatively correlated with the futures prices and suggests that the trading strategy is that when the negative emotional intensity is strong, the investors should sell futures and when the negative emotional intensity is strong, the investors should buy futures. That is, investors who have a long position and encounter the main emotions "fear" and "sadness" advised to sell it to reduce the loss of security deposit. On the contrary, investors who hold a short position and encounter the main emotions "fear" and "sadness" advised to buy a long position, to offset the short and make a profit.

This study shows that if the emotion is extracted form professional news, it may be possible to respond to Schumaker and Chen (2009) conclusion that news factors could use to obtain high pay. So it may be more feasible to collect news about an industry or some concept stocks in Taiwan. Therefore, this study suggests that using professional news to analyze emotion deserves further research.

In addition, taking into account the characteristics of PTT in Taiwan, some indicators have been against the public opinions. If related data of the advanced countries can analyzed, may be the anti-target characteristics could avoid and more accurate correlation between emotion indicators and market can achieve.

References

Baumeister, R.F., Vohs, K.D., DeWall, C.N., Zhang, L.: How emotion shapes behavior: feedback, anticipation, and reflection, rather than direct causation. Personal. Soc. Psychol. Rev. **11**(2), 167–203 (2007)

Bollen, J., Mao, H., Zeng, X.: Twitter mood predicts the stock market. J. Comput. Sci. **2**(1), 1–8 (2010)

Brown, G.W., Cliff, M.T.: Investor sentiment and near term stock market. J. Empir. Financ. **11**, 1–27 (2002)

Dolan, R.J.: Emotion, cognition, and behavior. Science **298**(5596), 1191–1194 (2002)

Ekman, P., Friesen, W.V.: Measuring facial movement. Environ. Psychol. Nonverbal Behav. **1**, 56–75 (1976)

Gilbert, E., Karahalio, E.: Widespread worry and the stock market. In: International AAAI Conference on Weblogs and Social Media (2010)

Nofsinger, J.R.: Social mood and financial economics. J. Behav. Financ. **6**(3), 144–160 (2005)

Rystrom, D.S., Benson, E.D.: Investor psychology and the day-of-the-week effect. Financ. Anal. J. **45**(5), 75–78 (1989)

Schumaker, R.P., Chen, H.: Textual analysis of stock market prediction using breaking financial news: the AZF in text system. J. ACM Trans. Inf. Syst. **27**, 1–19 (2009)

Shleifer, A.: The Inefficient Markets: An Introduction to Behavioral Finance (2000)

Zhang, X., Fuehres, H., Gloor, P.A.: Predicting stock market indicator through Twitter. "I hope it is not as bad as I fear". Procedia – Soc. Behav. Sci. **26**, 55–62 (2011)

Ptt Website: (2017). https://zh.wikipedia.org/wiki/批踢踢

A Novel Model for Finding Critical Products with Transaction Logs

Ping Yu Hsu[1], Chen Wan Huang[1(✉)], Shih Hsiang Huang[1],
Pei Chi Chen[1], and Ming Shien Cheng[2]

[1] Department of Business Administration, National Central University,
No. 300, Zhongda Road, Zhongli District, Taoyuan City 320, Taiwan (R.O.C.)
105481015@cc.ncu.edu.tw
[2] Department of Industrial Engineering and Management,
Ming Chi University of Technology, No. 84, Gongzhuan Road, Taishan District,
New Taipei City 24301, Taiwan (R.O.C.)
mscheng@mail.mcut.edu.tw

Abstract. For the consumer market, finding valuable customers is the first priority and is assumed to assist companies in obtaining more profit. If we could discover critical products that are related with valuable customers, then it will lead to better marketing strategy to fulfill those essential customers. It will also assist companies in business development. This study selects real retail transaction data via the recency, frequency, and monetary (RFM) analysis and adopts the K-means algorithm to obtain results. Moreover, the Apriori algorithm with minimum support and skewness criteria is used to filter and find critical products. In this research, we found a novel methodology through setting the minimum support and skewness criteria and utilized the Apriori algorithm to identify 31 single critical products and 60 critical combinations (two products). This study assist companies in finding critical products and important customers, which is expected to provide an appropriate customer marketing strategy.

Keywords: RFM · K-means · Association rules · Skewness
Frequent itemsets

1 Introduction

In the new retail era and highly competitive consumer market, finding the right product selling strategy and profitable customer are the key successful factor for companies. Consumers agree to pay different prices according to the distinct product or service level. Especially their buying behavior has been difficult to know well in recent years. How to know your important products, valuable customer and buying behavior should be the industry major tasks.

Direct marketers have been using recency, frequency, and monetary (RFM) analysis to predict customer buying behavior for more than 50 years. It is one of the most powerful techniques available to a database marketer [7]. And the discovery of association rules is one of the major techniques of data mining [8]. The Safeway stores using mining methodology to find which significant items are important because 25%

© Springer International Publishing AG, part of Springer Nature 2018
Y. Tan et al. (Eds.): ICSI 2018, LNCS 10942, pp. 432–439, 2018.
https://doi.org/10.1007/978-3-319-93818-9_41

of high spending customers often buy these items. Although such product sales volume has a lower sales ranking, but those unique products are very critical. Therefor discover the important customer according to the critical commodities, marketers could have an appropriate sales strategy to help and achieve the company business marketing plan. There has been far less research in identifying the correlation between critical products and important customers.

Song [11] proposed a statistic-based approach to value latent users via the time-series segmenting time interval of RFM in a large-scale dataset, and Khajvand [9] presented the results of calculated CLV for different segments to explain the marketing and sales strategies by a company. Grami [10] extracted loyal customers by using the RFM criterion to obtain more reliable answers and create relevant datasets. Bhandari [4] presented efficiency research under the association rules algorithm, and Hu [6] defined the RFM pattern and developed a novel algorithm to discover the complete set of RFM patterns. Those literatures focus on RFM methodology or customer database. Nevertheless, this study is expected to enhance critical commodity research and complete consumer product analysis, important customer mining and provide the related managerial implication.

The purpose of this study is to develop a novel method of data mining algorithm and statistical model to obtain critical products and then explore the valuable customers for a company. The contributions of this research are as follows:

1. The study of our proposed novel framework lead to a better understanding of finding critical products and combination products.
2. The experimental results assist both for academic research and managerial implication such as provide an appropriate customer sales strategy and reduce unnecessary selling costs.

And the experimental results found 31 critical product and 60 critical combination (two products) and managerial implication such as product marketing strategy.

This paper is organized as follows: (1) Introduction: This part explains the research background, motivation and purpose; (2) Related Work: This part contains a review on customer data mining analysis, RFM methodology and the association rules; (3) Research Design: This part describes the content of the research framework design in this study; (4) Experiment Result: This part describes the research data acquisition process. Numerical tables and values are also used to present the experimental results; and (5) Conclusion and Future Research: The contribution of the novel methodology in this study is proposed, and possible future research directions are discussed.

2   Related Work

The related work in this chapter includes customer data mining, RFM methodology and the association rules algorithm.

2.1   Data Mining and Customer Marketing

In some places, data mining can be termed as knowledge discovery in databases as it generates hidden and interesting patterns, and it also comprises of an amalgamation of methodologies from various disciplines such as statistics, neural networks, database technology, machine learning, information retrieval, etc. [4].

Hu [6] noted that the aim of database marketing is to improve the effectiveness of customer service, enhance the quality of sales, and retain valuable customers in the most profitable way. In marketing practice, businesses have begun to analyze customer databases while building their marketing plans. In the market segmentation process, a market is separated into groups of customers with distinct characteristics that might require different marketing mixes. Companies can adopt appropriate marketing strategies based on the characteristics of different segments or select the market segments on which they want to focus on. Therefore, they can perform targeted marketing at the right time and place [3].

2.2   Customer Management and RFM Analysis

If a company can customize the appropriate selling combination by different valuable clients, it is efficient to utilize marketing resources and reduce unnecessary development cost. Companies analyze valuable customers through current transaction data and segment them to define different strategies from their contributions. For successful customer relationship management, a firm starts by identifying the customers' true value and loyalty since customer value can provide basic information to deploy more targeted and personalized marketing [9].

Song [11] indicated that conventional customer relationship management (CRM) is typically based on the RFM model, whose parameters are the recency, frequency and monetary aspects of target customers. Previous studies revealed that recency, frequency and monetary (RFM) analysis and frequent pattern mining can be successfully integrated to discover valuable patterns. Based on customers' historical purchasing behavior, RFM analysis can identify a valuable customer group [6].

The use of RFM to guide communications will always improve profits over any other method. RFM works with the consumer and with business-to-business customer files. It works with any type of industry in which one communicates with customers for marketing purposes. One of the most powerful methods is RFM analysis [2].

2.3   Association Rule and Apriori

An association rule plays an important role in recent data mining techniques. The purchasing of one product along with another related product represents an association rule. Association rules are used to show the relationships between data items. Association rules are frequently used for different purposes such as marketing, advertising and inventory. The mining of association rules in a large database is a challenging task. The Apriori algorithm is widely used to find the frequent item sets from a database [12]. Abirami [1] stated that association rule mining is classified under unsupervised models. Association models detect associations between discrete events, products, or attributes.

The Apriori algorithm is one of the most popular algorithms in data mining for learning the concept of association rules. It is being used by many people specifically for transaction operations, and it can be used in real-time applications by collecting the items bought by customers over time so that frequent item sets can be generated [4]. The Apriori algorithm computes the frequent itemsets in the database through several iterations [3]. The Apriori algorithm operates by finding all rules satisfying the minimum confidence and support specifications [5]. Grami [10] noted that an important topic that is widely used in data mining is association rules. Association rule mining is a method for discovering interesting relations between variables in large databases. These rules are used to discover the relations between data in a dataset. Formally, these rules are used to analyze shopping carts. Using data mining is an alternative to discovering frequent patterns and association rules from datasets.

3   Research Design

The method to carry out this study was using the customer evaluation methodology and data mining algorithm to experiment and explore critical products and valuable customers. Our research materials consisted of real retail transaction logs. The data were collected from the retail transaction database. The source data were extracted, membership information was kept, and the transaction records included membership number, transaction date, time, sales volume and purchase product list.

3.1   Data Analysis

This research included four phases for data analysis as described in the following: (1) RFM phase: Build a daily transaction file, and sort the customer ranking by calculating recency, frequency and monetary records to evaluate the customer value. And according to the RFM calculation to obtain each indicator score and summarize these three indicators to obtain a final RFM score; (2) K-means phase: Use RFM score and K-means algorithm to divide customers into five groups. Obtain the central score of five groups and the customer quantity of each group. Assign customer level from 1 to 5 according to RFM score and K-means result. And integrate purchase product list and customer level information; (3) Apriori algorithm phase: The Apriori algorithm utilizes the candidate itemset according to the preceding table to determine the frequent itemsets. First, all single-item candidate sets are utilized and candidate 1-itemset is generated. The minimum support threshold is set for filtering, and frequent itemsets data are obtained. From the rule, large 1-itemset is selected. The methodology is utilized to discover large 2-itemsets and 3-itemsets, until there is no more frequent itemsets. The research applies the Apriori algorithm to identify the frequent itemset and to cut unqualified minimum support and shrink the search space; (4) Skewness phase: For those items that meet the minimum support threshold, this study also considers the coefficient of skewness. The coefficient of skewness measures the skewness of a distribution, and the formula is shown below:

$$\beta_1 = \frac{\frac{1}{N}\sum_1^N (\chi_i - \mu)^3}{\sigma^3}.$$ (1)

We assume that $\beta_1 < 0$ is skewed to the left; $\beta_1 > 0$ is skewed to the right; and $\beta_1 = 0$ is symmetric. The purpose in this paper is to dig out those that fulfill the minimum support threshold and are skewed to the left, to indicate products assembled in the important customer group. The candidate 1-itemset meets both the minimum support threshold and skewness criteria, that is, the single critical product, which is our first purpose in this research. According to the Apriori algorithm, the subset in one of the large itemsets should be belong to this large itemsets. This frequent item should be the critical product, and further data mining process is unnecessary. The next step is to weed out those data that do not pass the minimum support threshold, keep those that fit the minimum support and are not skewed to the left and congregate to the combination candidate. The minimum support threshold and skewness criteria are utilized to verify the combination candidate again. The combination candidate that fulfills both conditions is searched until there is no more frequent itemsets.

3.2   Research Framework

Here is the research framework of this paper (Fig. 1):

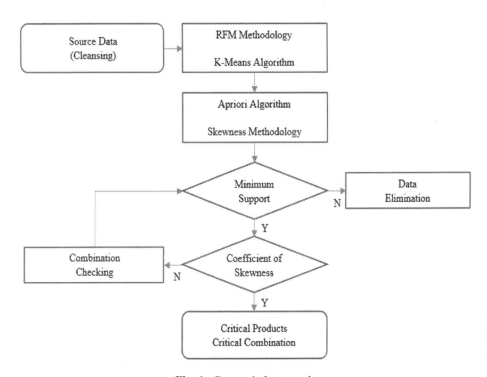

Fig. 1. Research framework.

4 Experiment Result

4.1 Data Collection and Preparation

The research used the open source R language and statistical software package. First, data with no membership number information are filtered and deleted, and 3,819 membership data including 640,623 product transaction records are kept, excerpted as shown in Table 1.

Table 1. Transaction details.

T-Date	Member ID	Product	Amount
0108	M0060	P00233	24
0108	M0060	P00016	10
0109	M0823	P00191	18

4.2 RFM Model Results

For the preparation of RFM methodology analysis, the data are sorted by transaction date and membership sale amount and integrated as 85,271 transaction records, excerpted as shown in Table 2. The summary data of RFM scores are obtained according to recency, frequency and monetary information for each membership.

Table 2. Transaction table.

T-Date	Member ID	Sales
105	M0269	63
107	M0703	17
109	M0823	40

4.3 K-means and Segmentation

Utilize K-means algorithm to divide customers into five groups, and the integrated results are excerpted in Table 3.

Table 3. RFM with customer level.

Member ID	Recency	Frequency	Monetary	R	F	M	Star
M0065	0528	1	106	1	3	1	1
M0075	1030	21	12,705	4	8	6	3
M0080	1105	4	2,562	4	4	6	2
M0262	1127	173	74,724	9	9	9	5
M0283	1116	83	24,826	5	9	5	4

4.4   Association Rules and Novel Skewness Experiment Result

The novel method of minimum support threshold and coefficient of skewness criteria are utilized to discover the critical product and combination products for essential customers. After different threshold data tests, we conclude that minimal support greater than 30 to find useful observations.

According to customer grade experiment, data integration and thru novel coefficient of skewness experiment to conclude the parameters and get valuable insight of critical products and great result.

This study extract 70% data of source transaction database included 10,000 products above, then discover thirty-one single critical products and sixty critical combinations (two products), which are excerpted in Table 4.

Table 4. Experimental result for critical products.

Single critical product	Critical combination (two products)
P01895	P02168 and P03891
P03127	P02126 and P03479
P00060	P01809 and P00458

And experiment the other 30% testing data to find 80% of critical product skewed to important customer.

5   Conclusion and Future Research

In this paper, we utilized RFM and K-means and Apriori data mining algorithms to analyze the important customers according to the membership number and purchasing information and discovered thirty-one single critical products and sixty critical combinations (two products). Companies could utilize a similar evaluation to explore the potential and valuable customers for business development.

This research found the valuable insight. If we only considered the critical product must fulfill both two conditions in the same time. It is possible to eliminate those potential critical combination. Thus, in this paper, we found a novel methodology by setting the minimum support and coefficient of skewness criteria and utilizing the Apriori algorithm to discover the single critical products and critical combinations.

This study is relevant to real industry by analyzing customer behavior, which does not violate the legal rules of personal information. For managerial implications, this research study assist companies in finding critical products, which is expected to provide an appropriate customer marketing strategy to reduce unnecessary selling costs.

In the real word, there could still be some uncontrollable research limitations. There might be different types of important customers and critical product combination in different geographic locations and population conditions. Thus, we refer to the literature and assume some definitions to obtain a valuable result and explanation in this research. We expect future research to find the customer purchasing behavior and recommendations by different customer segmentations. Additionally, other real industry data should be selected to discover different critical products for cross industries.

References

1. Abirami, M., Pattabiraman, V.: Data mining approach for intelligent customer behavior analysis for a retail store. In: Vijayakumar, V., Neelanarayanan, V. (eds.) ISBCC 2016. SIST, vol. 49, pp. 283–291. Springer, Cham (2016). https://doi.org/10.1007/978-3-319-30348-2_23
2. Agrawal, R., Srikant, R.: Fast algorithms for mining association rules. In: Proceedings of the 20th International Conference on Very Large Data Bases, VLDB (1994)
3. Beheshtian-Ardakani, A., Fathianb, M., Gholamian, M.: A novel model for product bundling and direct marketing in e-commerce based on market segmentation. Decis. Sci. Lett. **7**, 39–54 (2018)
4. Bhandari, A., Gupta, A., Das, D.: Improvised apriori algorithm using frequent pattern tree for real time applications in data mining. Procedia Comput. Sci. **46**, 644–651 (2015)
5. Cho, Y.S., Moon, S.C., Ryu, K.H.: Mining association rules using RFM scoring method for personalized u-Commerce recommendation system in emerging data. In: Kim, T.-H., Ramos, C., Abawajy, J., Kang, B.-H., Ślęzak, D., Adeli, H. (eds.) MAS/ASNT 2012. CCIS, vol. 341, pp. 190–198. Springer, Heidelberg (2012). https://doi.org/10.1007/978-3-642-35248-5_27
6. Hu, Y.H., Yeh, T.W.: Discovering valuable frequent patterns based on RFM analysis without customer identification information. Knowl. Based Syst. **61**, 76–88 (2014)
7. Hughes, A.M.: Strategic Database Marketing. McGraw-Hill Pub. Co., New York (2001)
8. Kantardzic, M.: DATA MINING: Concepts, Models, Methods and Algorithms. John Wiley & Sons, Inc., Hoboken (2001)
9. Khajvand, M., Zolfaghar, K., Ashoori, S., Alizadeh, S.: Estimating customer lifetime value based on RFM analysis of customer purchase behavior: case study. Procedia Comput. Sci. **3**, 57–63 (2011)
10. Grami, M., Gheibi, R., Rahimi, F.: A novel association rule mining using genetic algorithm. In: 2016 Eighth International Conference on Information and Knowledge Technology (IKT), Hamedan, Iran (2016)
11. Song, M., Zhao, X., Haihong, E., Ou, Z.: Statistics-based CRM approach via time series segmenting RFM on large scale data. Knowl. Based Syst. **132**, 21–29 (2017)
12. Vasoya, A., Koli, N.: Mining of association rules on large database using distributed and parallel computing. Procedia Comput. Sci. **79**, 221–230 (2016)

Using Discrete-Event-Simulation for Improving Operational Efficiency in Laboratories: A Case Study in Pharmaceutical Industry

Alexander Troncoso-Palacio[1], Dionicio Neira-Rodado[1],
Miguel Ortíz-Barrios[1(✉)], Genett Jiménez-Delgado[2],
and Hugo Hernández-Palma[3]

[1] Department of Industrial Management, Agroindustry and Operations,
Universidad de la Costa CUC, Barranquilla, Colombia
{atroncos1, dneiral, mortiz1}@cuc.edu.co
[2] Department of Industrial Engineering, Corporación Universitaria Reformada
CUR, Barranquilla, Colombia
g.jimenez@unireformada.edu.co
[3] Department of Business Management, Universidad del Atlántico, Puerto
Colombia, Colombia
hugohernandezp@mail.uniatlantico.edu.co

Abstract. Just-in-time delivery has become a key aspect of pharmaceutical industry when loyalizing customers and competing internationally. Additionally, prolonged lead times may lead to increased work-in-process inventory, penalties for non-compliance and cost overrun. The problem is more complex upon considering a wide variety of products as often noted in pharmaceutical companies. It is then relevant to design strategies focusing on improving the delivery performance. Therefore, this paper proposes the use of Discrete-event simulation (DES) to identify inefficiencies and define solutions for the delivery problem. First, input data were gathered and analyzed. Then, a DES model was developed and validated. Finally, potential improvement scenarios were simulated and analyzed regarding productivity rate and proportion of tardy jobs. A case study in a pharmaceutical laboratory is presented to validate the proposed methodology. The results evidenced that, by implementing the best scenario, the productivity may be augmented by 44.83% which would generate zero tardy jobs.

Keywords: Discrete-event simulation (DES) · Pharmaceutical industry
Productivity rate · Proportion of tardy jobs

1 Introduction

Economy globalization has been positive for final users since they have access to more customized and cheaper products. Nevertheless, this implies a great effort to companies when competing internationally. In this regard, companies will have to search for new ways to continuously improve their processes and value chain. This is particularly true

© Springer International Publishing AG, part of Springer Nature 2018
Y. Tan et al. (Eds.): ICSI 2018, LNCS 10942, pp. 440–451, 2018.
https://doi.org/10.1007/978-3-319-93818-9_42

in pharmaceutical companies where it is necessary to tackle the insufficient drug supply problem. Additionally, in Colombia, the expected sales increment is 7% [1] which demands a better productivity rate from this industry. On the other hand, it is also important to take into account the complexity of the pharmaceutical market and the introduction of new international competitors which end up with affecting the internal production and raising the stringency levels in terms of quality and on-time delivery. In this respect, a Computers & Chemical Engineering paper [2] conducted a study on the challenges and opportunities in the pharmaceutical industry where it was established that further research is needed on capacity planning, modeling of decision alternatives and identification of critical parameters limiting system performance.

Much coordination is needed between system resources to ensure that a continuous flow of products can be effectively achieved. This requires complex operational and tactical strategies that should be supported by decision support tools in order to both tackle operational inefficiencies and provide real-time solutions. Moreover, it is necessary to incorporate the uncertainties of the system, e.g. equipment breakdowns and absenteeism so that a reliable model can be finally enhanced.

Such considerations have led to several methodological proposals aiming at determining the main causes of low productivity and off-time delivery. More recently, the use of Discrete-event simulation (DES) has gained considerable attention in the industry [3–5]. Some applications can be seen in construction sector [6, 7], chemical industry [8, 9], food industry [10, 11], semiconductor manufacturing industry [12], semi-process industry [13] and automobile sector [14, 15]. However, its implementation in pharmaceutical industry is largely limited. Additionally, even when DES can provide a means to pretest changes in manufacturing systems before implementation in an effective manner, the evidence base is poorly developed.

In this paper, we model the analysis lab of a pharmaceutical company first motivated by a desire to establish a baseline against which a number of streamlining scenarios may be evaluated. Another novelty lies in the use of DES to increase productivity in a lab with a wide variety of products (52). Furthermore, once we have developed the simulation model, we can analyze the impact of potential improvement scenarios. Particularly, we will focus on determining the adequate way to allocate the laboratory resources so that tardy jobs can be also minimized. We will also endeavor to address the issues identified in [2], mainly with regard to modeling decision alternatives and identifying critical parameters limiting system performance.

The remainder of this paper is organized as follows: In Sect. 2, a literature review on DES applications in pharmaceutical industry is presented. Then, the proposed methodology is explained in Sect. 3. In Sect. 4, results from a case study in a pharmaceutical lab are described and analyzed. Finally, Sect. 5 presents the conclusions.

2 Primary Studies from the Literature

In recent years, the Discrete-Event Simulation (DES) has been used as an important tool for the diagnosis, evaluation, and improvement of operations and as support of the decision-making process [16], since it is able to describe and represent the characteristics of a real system with high fidelity [17]. There are several benefits derived from the application of DES (e.g. increased operational efficiency, time reduction, cost savings and customer satisfaction). However, these benefits have not been extended to all companies and economy sectors [18], especially healthcare and pharmaceutical sectors which present constant challenges due to the market dynamic, whereas high-quality products are demanded at competitive prices and short delivery times.

We reviewed the reported scientific literature where different academic articles showing the use of the DES technique were found [19]. In this regard, DES applications with a focus on improving the operational efficiency in manufacturing environments were first identified. For example, in [20], DES was used for production line balancing aiming at reducing excess inventory, operational costs and delivery times. Also, there are studies where DES has been applied in complex environments related to the pharmaceutical industry, such as healthcare services. Here, DES was implemented for process analysis and performance improvement measured in terms of operational efficiency, service delivery times, appointment lead-time and waiting time in maternal-child hospitals [18], elderly outpatient clinics, emergency departments [21, 22] and hospital pharmacies [23].

When considering case studies relating to laboratory services and the pharmaceutical industry, a few studies were found. In [24] performance of planning policies in a clinical laboratory when addressing different demand scenarios. Also, DES has been found to improve efficiency and effectiveness in the workflows of clinical laboratories [25]. DES applications in pharmaceutical companies also include the supply chain optimization and manufacturer selection [26], the improvement of the decision-making process in the biopharmaceutical industry, investment alternative selection [27] and the reduction of operational inefficiencies associated with the equipment use and response capacity of quality control laboratories supporting drug manufacturing process [28].

In light of the aforementioned facts, it can be concluded that studies directly concentrating on improving operational efficiency in pharmaceutical industry, with the use of discrete-event simulation, are largely limited. Therefore, we implemented this technique in the present work in order to provide a useful decision-making tool that can be used for supporting the improvement of productivity rate in realistic scenarios whilst reducing the gap identified in the literature.

3 Proposed Methodology

For an appropriate implementation of DES in manufacturing systems from the pharmaceutical industry, it is critical to consider the number and range of pathways along the entire product journey in addition to the multi-dimensional dynamic interactions affecting the resource utilization, productivity rate and proportion of tardy jobs. Hence, it is highly important to reach a satisfactory level of equivalence between the real manufacturing system and the simulation model in terms of structure, performance, and variability. Considering the nature of pharmaceutical manufacturing systems, it is therefore relevant to reach a systemic progress instead of searching for local solutions. In this regard, a 4-phase procedure (refer to Fig. 1) has been proposed to (i) effectively identify problems contributing to process inefficiencies, (ii) assist production managers in decision-making, (iii) allocate production resources properly and (iv) consequently diminish the proportion of tardy jobs and increase production rate. This methodology has been created to be implemented in practical scenarios. Moreover, it is even more valuable when considering the scant evidence base relating to the application of DES models as stated in Sects. 1 and 2.

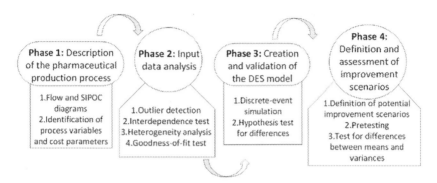

Fig. 1. Methodological approach for the implementation of DES models in pharmaceutical companies: diagnosis and evaluation of potential improvement strategies

- **Phase 1 (Description of the pharmaceutical production process):** The production managers and operational staff are required to provide information on the variables and process sequence so that the real manufacturing system can be fully and effectively characterized. In addition, it is necessary to identify the cost parameters so that we can later provide a financial analysis complementing the performance diagnosis. After this, the data concerning the aforementioned variables and parameters should be adequately gathered from the company information sources so that high-quality information can be incorporated into the simulated model. To this end, flow and SIPOC (Supplier-Input-Process-Output-Customer) diagrams are highly recommended to produce a detailed model of the real system [29]. This characterization will be further deemed for the correct modeling of the pharmaceutical production process.

- **Phase 2 (Input data analysis):** After finishing the Phase 1, it is relevant to first examine the presence of potential outliers for ensuring high-quality data. If some outliers are detected, they should be then investigated to determine whether these data represent an abnormal behavior of the system. If this statement is true, the outliers should be removed from the dataset. The next task is then to conduct an interdependence test (e.g. scatterplot, run test and autocorrelation analysis) to verify the randomness of data distribution ($\alpha = 0.05$). Afterwards, a heterogeneity analysis should be carried out in order to detect potential sub-groups of data. In this respect, statistical methods such as Analysis of Variance (ANOVA), log-rank and Kruskal-Wallis and log-rank can be useful for this purpose. If the data are found to be heterogeneous, each sub-group must be modeled separately; otherwise, the dataset is represented by one probability distribution. Once this is finished, a goodness-of-fit test is used to define whether a stochastic model appropriately fits the data and then calculate the distribution parameters that should be introduced into the simulation model.

- **Phase 3 (Creation and validation of the DES model):** A sophisticated simulation tool is used to support the creation of a virtual representation of the pharmaceutical manufacturing process. Furthermore, it contributes to user engagement by animating the resources and product journey associated with the production system. To verify the model reliability, key performance metrics and simulation run length are initially established. Afterwards, 10 runs are carried out to estimate the sample size (number of computational runs) that is required to represent the variability of the real-world process. Once the computational runs are complete, a hypothesis test is performed to determine whether the simulated model is statistically equivalent to the real manufacturing system [30]. In this regard, if the p-value is greater than the alpha level (0.05), the model is concluded to be realistic and suitable for pretesting. Otherwise, it should be verified and modified to guarantee high reliability and usefulness.

- **Phase 4 (Definition and assessment of improvement scenarios):** Useful interventions are characterized by offering solutions whose implementation can be fully pretested. In this sense, potential improvement strategies should be identified and then assessed in terms of the previously defined performance metrics. The strategies are designed with the aid of production managers and operational staff in order to guarantee that they are aligned with the organizational goals and can be applied without violating existing restrictions (e.g. budget availability and quality constraints). After this, a simulation model (modified version of the initial model) is created to pretest each strategy before implementation. To this end, 10 runs are executed to calculate the sample size (number of simulation runs) that will be used to statistically compare the current pharmaceutical manufacturing process with each scenario considering the predefined performance metrics of interest. If the resulting p-value is lower than the alpha level (0.05), the proposed scenario is beneficial for the company. On the contrary, it is concluded as non-significant and should not be then considered for implementation.

4   An Illustrative Example: Modelling an Analysis Lab from a Pharmaceutical Company

4.1   Description of the Pharmaceutical Production Process

The company under study has found that 35% of customers complained of tardy delivery. In addition, it was detected that during 2015, 30% of the analysis that were requested to the laboratory, was released several days after the due date. Thus, considering the proposed methodology, a SIPOC diagram was developed to describe the entire product journey from the analysis request to the elaboration of quality reports. Our model was based on a 1-year prospective dataset extracted from the Production Management System (PMS) which evidences all the production orders received by the analysis lab between 1 January 2016 and 31 December 2016. PMS is a database that

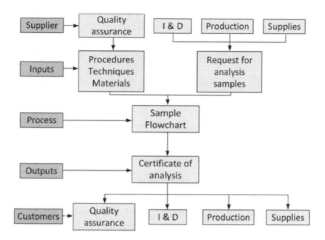

Fig. 2. SIPOC diagram for the sample analysis process of a pharmaceutical lab

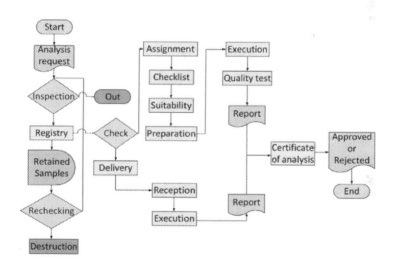

Fig. 3. Flowchart of the sample analysis process

was created for the scheduling, dissemination, and monitoring of production orders. To effectively identify the elements involved in the physicochemical analysis process, a SIPOC (refer to Fig. 2) and flow diagrams (refer to Fig. 3) were prepared.

After providing a conceptual model of the sample analysis process, the modelers identified the following process variables to be incorporated into the simulation model: Time between arrivals for each material type (raw material, solid, trace, sterile, non-sterile, supplies and semi-solid), processing time (raw material, solid, trace, sterile, non-sterile, supplies and semi-solid), lead-time of external suppliers and cost per analysis.

4.2   Input Data Analysis

After gathering the data related to the variables identified in Subsect. 4.1 and discarding the presence of outliers, a run test was initially performed to establish whether these variables were randomly sequenced. A summary of these tests is detailed in Table 1. In this case, all the variables were found to be independent since the p-values were greater than the significance level (0.05).

Table 1. Results of intra-dependence tests

Process variable	P-value	Conclusion
Time between arrivals for raw material	0.054	Random
Time between arrivals for solid material	0.205	Random
Time between arrivals for trace material	0.068	Random
Time between arrivals for non-sterile material	0.74	Random
Time between arrivals for semi-solid material	0.892	Random
Time between arrivals for sterile material	0.326	Random
Time between arrivals for supplies	0.838	Random
Lead-time of external suppliers	0.07	Random
Processing time for raw material	0.818	Random
Processing time for solid material	0.818	Random
Processing time for trace material	1	Random
Processing time for non-sterile material	0.107	Random
Processing time for semi-solid material	1	Random
Processing time for sterile material	1	Random
Processing time for inputs	1	Random

After finishing the intra-dependence analysis, a heterogeneity test was performed for each variable in order to detect sub-groups of data (refer to Table 2). In particular, a Kruskal-Wallis test detected that the *time between arrivals* and *processing time* should be modeled separately according to the type of material since the p-values were found to be lower than the significance level (non-homogeneous data).

Table 2. Results of homogeneity tests

Variable type	P-value	Conclusion
Time between arrivals	0.0001	Non-homogeneous
Processing time	0.0060	
Lead-time of external suppliers	0.0000	

Considering the randomness and heterogeneity of the process variables, probability distributions should be thus defined through Goodness-of-fit tests. In this case, p-values higher than the alpha level (0.05) provided good support for the probability assumptions. The stochastic expressions to be used for modeling the process variables in the simulation model are enlisted in Table 3.

Table 3. Results of Goodness-of-fit tests

Process variable	P-value	Stochastic expression
Time between arrivals for raw material	0.254	8 * BETA (0.554, 2.15) − 0.5
Time between arrivals for non-sterile material	0.326	LOGN (2.62, 3.56) − 0.5
Time between arrivals for trace material	0.093	29 * BETA (0.395, 5.12) − 0.5
Time between arrivals for semi-solid material	0.097	LOGN (2.67, 3.62) − 0.5
Time between arrivals for solid material	0.172	LOGN (1.63, 1.68) − 0.5
Time between arrivals for sterile material	0.106	WEIB(2.81, 0.533) − 0.5
Time between arrivals for supplies	0.077	51 * BETA (0.171, 0.688) − 0.5
Lead-time of external lab 1	0.118	UNIF (8.5, 22.5)
Lead-time of external lab 2	0.098	WEIB(13.7, 1.3) + 8.5
Lead-time of external lab 3	0.164	27 * BETA (0.509, 0.525) + 6.5
Lead-time of external lab 4	0.115	WEIB (9.18, 1.39) + 6.5
Processing time for raw material	0.237	783 * BETA (0.828, 0.592) + 429
Processing time for non-sterile material	0.803	360 * BETA (0.528, 0.459) + 480
Processing time for trace material	0.221	215 * (0.0438, 0.165) BETA + 22
Processing time for semi-solid material	0.623	BETA(0.339, 0.0805) * $1.21 * 10^{-3}$ + 003 + 482
Processing time for solid material	0.554	EXPO (314) + 117
Processing time for sterile material	0.187	UNIF (480, 840)
Processing time for supplies	0.256	UNIF (210, 408)

4.3   Creation and Validation of the DES Model

The simulation model (refer to Fig. 4) was designed with the aid of Arena 14.0® software whereas the basic process modules, the collected information and the conceptual model were simultaneously incorporated into the model. To ensure the reliability of the simulation results, we ran the model for a time period of 245 days with 8 h per day. In addition, 10 replications were executed to calculate the required sample size (n = 5) for adequately representing the system variability. To validate the model measure the current performance (productivity rate), 1250 analyzes/year (390 raw materials, 270 solid products, 200 traces, 150 non-sterile liquids, 160 semi-solids, 60 sterile materials and 20 samples for input analysis) was established as the theoretical quantity μ. Simulation results were later evaluated with a t student hypothesis test $(H_o : \mu = 1250 \ analyses | H_a : \mu \neq 1250 \ analyses)$ by using Minitab® software. A p-value = 0.887 and 95% IC [1199.1; 1307.8] evidenced that there is enough statistical evidence to affirm that the simulation model is a reliable representation of the physicochemical analysis laboratory under study. Hence, it can be used for further analysis, diagnosis, and pretest.

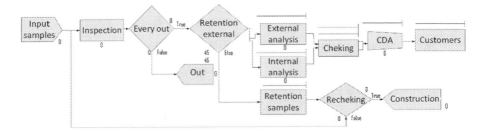

Fig. 4. Simulation model of the physicochemical analysis lab under analysis

4.4 Definition and Assessment of Improvement Scenarios

In spite of DES models provide a means to effectively pretest changes in manufacturing systems before implementation, little research work has been done to evaluate potential improvement scenarios [22]. Therefore, the present study aims to validate two proposed scenarios (refer to Table 4): (i) S1: Reallocation of 4 analysts in 3 work shifts (Analyst 1: 6 am – 2 pm; Analyst 2: 2 pm – 10 pm; Analyst 3: 10 pm – 6 pm; Analyst 4: 8 am – 12 m and 2 pm – 6 pm) and (ii) S2: Redistribution of functions (1 worker from the Maintenance Department is assigned to perform the machine setup which is currently executed by analysts who spend two hours a day during this process). However, the S1 is suggested to be implemented since it is cost-effective in terms of productivity rate evidenced by a significant difference between the scenarios (326 analyses – 29.87%). In addition, although the S1 investment is significantly higher than required in S2, its cost per additional analysis is found to be lower than S2. In addition, the proportion of tardy jobs in S1 is 0% whilst in S2 is 22.64% which demonstrates a superior performance of Scenario 1 over Scenario 2.

Table 4. Operational and economic analysis of potential improvement scenarios

Potential improvement scenario	Productivity rate (analysis)	Number of additional analysis	Improvement percentage	Investment (US$)	Cost per additional analysis (US$)
S1	1583	490	44,87	$1478.44	$3.02
S2	1257	164	15,00	$512.85	$3.12

5 Conclusions

Pharmaceutical manufacturing systems are complex to model due to the wide variety of pathways and activities that may derive from the drug nature. Therefore, it is highly suggested that the modelers work closely with the production managers and operational staff in order to ensure that the simulation models are statistically comparable to the real system so that potential improvement scenarios can be effectively pretested before implementation.

A critical aspect is the availability of high-quality datasets. In this regard, DES models will be thoroughly described depending on the available information. Of course, this ends up with affecting the reliability and robustness of the resulting decisions. Hence, it is relevant to count on the engagement of the pharmaceutical companies involved in the project with the goal of developing complete simulation models.

The proposed methodology enables production managers to create integrated models representing the pharmaceutical manufacturing systems. Nevertheless, it can be complemented with other techniques in order to provide more detailed models supporting further analysis on the process. For future work, it is intended to include interactions with other departments aiming at offering more focused improvement scenarios.

The intervention here described presented the use of DES models in a pharmaceutical analysis lab. Based on the outcomes, it can be concluded that S1 (44.87%) provides a better productivity rate than S2 (15.0%). This enables decision-makers to address the problem of insufficient drug supply and increases the competitiveness of pharmaceutical companies in international markets.

Acknowledgments. The authors would like to thank the support of INCOBRA Laboratories, a company from the pharmaceutical sector, where this study was implemented. Additionally, we fully appreciate the collaboration of Eng. Giuseppe Polifroni Avendaño who provided good support during this process.

References

1. Hernández, R.S., Miranda, P.P.: Una mirada a la industria farmacéutica en Colombia. Rev. FACCEA **4**(2), 107–115 (2014)
2. Laínez, J.M., Schaefer, E., Reklaitis, G.V.: Challenges and opportunities in enterprise-wide optimization in the pharmaceutical industry. Comput. Chem. Eng. **47**, 19–28 (2012)
3. Van Der Vorst, J.G., Tromp, S.O., Zee, D.J.V.D.: Simulation modelling for food supply chain redesign; integrated decision making on product quality, sustainability and logistics. Int. J. Prod. Res. **47**(23), 6611–6631 (2009)
4. AbouRizk, S., Halpin, D., Mohamed, Y., Hermann, U.: Research in modeling and simulation for improving construction engineering operations. J. Constr. Eng. Manag. **137**(10), 843–852 (2011)
5. Melouk, S.H., Freeman, N.K., Miller, D., Dunning, M.: Simulation optimization-based decision support tool for steel manufacturing. Int. J. Prod. Econ. **141**(1), 269–276 (2013)
6. Martinez, J.C.: Methodology for conducting discrete-event simulation studies in construction engineering and management. J. Constr. Eng. Manag. **136**(1), 3–16 (2009)
7. González, V., Echaveguren, T.: Exploring the environmental modeling of road construction operations using discrete-event simulation. Autom. Constr. **24**, 100–110 (2012)
8. Sharda, B., Akiya, N.: Selecting make-to-stock and postponement policies for different products in a chemical plant: a case study using discrete event simulation. Int. J. Prod. Econ. **136**(1), 161–171 (2012)
9. Cafaro, V.G., Cafaro, D.C., Méndez, C.A., Cerdá, J.: Oil-derivatives pipeline logistics using discrete-event simulation. In: Proceedings of the Winter Simulation Conference, pp. 2101–2113, December 2010

10. Johansson, B., Stahre, J., Berlin, J., Östergren, K., Sundström, B., Tillman, A.M.: Discrete event simulation with lifecycle assessment data at a juice manufacturing system. In: Proceedings of the 5th FOODSIM Conference, University College Dublin, Ireland (2008)

11. Parthanadee, P., Buddhakulsomsiri, J.: Simulation modeling and analysis for production scheduling using real-time dispatching rules: a case study in canned fruit industry. Comput. Electron. Agric. **70**(1), 245–255 (2010)

12. Geng, N., Jiang, Z.: A review on strategic capacity planning for the semiconductor manufacturing industry. Int. J. Prod. Res. **47**(13), 3639–3655 (2009)

13. Pool, A., Wijngaard, J., Van der Zee, D.J.: Lean planning in the semi-process industry, a case study. Int. J. Prod. Econ. **131**(1), 194–203 (2011)

14. Park, C.M., Seong, K.Y., Park, S.C., Wang, G.N., Han, K.H.: Simulation based control program verification in an automobile industry. In: The International Conference on Modeling Identification and Control, Innsbruck, Austria, February 2008

15. Steinemann, A., Taiber, J., Fadel, G., Wegener, K., Kunz, A.: Adapting discrete-event simulation tools to support tactical forecasting in the automotive industry. CoDesign **9**(3), 159–177 (2013)

16. The Discrete Event Simulation as a Fundamental technique in making high impact decisions. http://www.vaticgroup.com/perspectiva-logistica/ediciones-anteriores/simulacion-deeventos-discretos/

17. Rodríguez, J., Serrano, D., Monleón, T., Caroc, J.: Discrete-event simulation models in the economic evaluation of health technologies and health products. Gac. Sanit. **22**(2), 151–161 (2008)

18. Ortíz-Barrios, M., Jimenez-Delgado, G., De Avila-Villalobos, J.: A computer simulation approach to reduce appointment lead-time in outpatient perinatology departments: a case study in a maternal-child hospital. In: Siuly, S., Huang, Z., Aickelin, U., Zhou, R., Wang, H., Zhang, Y., Klimenko, S. (eds.) HIS 2017. LNCS, vol. 10594, pp. 32–39. Springer, Cham (2017). https://doi.org/10.1007/978-3-319-69182-4_4

19. Negahban, A., Smith, J.: Simulation for manufacturing system design and operation: literature review and analysis. J. Manuf. Syst. **33**, 241–261 (2014)

20. Zupan, H., Herakovic, N.: Production line balancing with discrete event simulation: a case Study. IFAC-Papers onLine **48**(3), 2305–2311 (2015). https://doi.org/10.1016/j.ifacol.2015.06.431

21. Ortíz-Barrios, M., López-Meza, P., Jimenez-Delgado, G.: Applying computer simulation modelling to minimizing appointment lead-time in elderly outpatient clinics: a case study. In: Ochoa, S.F., Singh, P., Bravo, J. (eds.) UCAmI 2017. LNCS, vol. 10586, pp. 323–329. Springer, Cham (2017). https://doi.org/10.1007/978-3-319-67585-5_34

22. Nuñez-Perez, N., Ortíz-Barrios, M., McClean, S., Salas-Navarro, K., Jimenez-Delgado, G., Castillo-Zea, A.: Discrete-event simulation to reduce waiting time in accident and emergency departments: a case study in a district general clinic. In: Ochoa, S.F., Singh, P., Bravo, J. (eds.) UCAmI 2017. LNCS, vol. 10586, pp. 352–363. Springer, Cham (2017). https://doi.org/10.1007/978-3-319-67585-5_37

23. Reynolds, M., Vasilakis, M., McLeod, N., Barber, A., Mounsey, S., Newton, A., Jacklin, A., Dean, B.: Using discrete event simulation to design a more efficient hospital pharmacy for outpatients. Health Care Manag. Sci. **14**(3), 223–236 (2011). https://doi.org/10.1007/s10729-011-9151-1

24. Van Merode, G., Hasman, A., Derks, J., Schoenmaker, B., Goldschmidt, H.: Advanced management facilities for clinical laboratories. Comput. Methods Programs Biomed. **50**, 195–205 (1996)

25. Goldschmidt, H., De Vries, J., Van Merode, G., Derks, J.: A workflow management tool for laboratory medicine. Lab. Autom. Inf. Manag. **33**, 183–197 (1998)

26. Akcay, A., Martagan, T.: Stochastic simulation under input uncertainty for contract-manufacturer selection in pharmaceutical industry, pp. 2292–2303 (2016). Electronic ISSN: 1558-4305

27. Sachidanandaa, M., Erkoyuncua, J., Steenstraa, D., Michalskaa, S.: Discrete event simulation modelling for dynamic decision making in biopharmaceutical manufacturing. Procedia CIRP **49**, 39–44 (2016)

28. Andrea Costigliola, A., Ataíde, F., Vieira, S., Sousa, J.: Simulation model of a quality control laboratory in pharmaceutical industry. IFAC-Papers onLine **50**(1), 9014–9019 (2017)

29. Ortiz Barrios, M.A., Escorcia Caballero, J., Sánchez Sánchez, F.: A methodology for the creation of integrated service networks in outpatient internal medicine. In: B, J., Hervás, R., Villarreal, V. (eds.) AmIHEALTH 2015. LNCS, vol. 9456, pp. 247–257. Springer, Cham (2015). https://doi.org/10.1007/978-3-319-26508-7_24

30. Ramírez, L.E., Medoza, F.D., Parody, A., Gonzalez, F., Castro, L.J., Jiménez, M.A.: Simulation model to find the slack time for schedule of the transit operations in off-peak time on the main terminal of massive transport system. Rev. ESPACIOS **38**(13), 1 (2017)

Architecture of an Object-Oriented Modeling Framework for Human Occupation

Manuel-Ignacio Balaguera[1]([✉]), María-Cristina Vargas[2],
Jenny-Paola Lis-Gutierrez[1], Amelec Viloria[3],
and Luz Elena Malagón[4]

[1] Fundación Universitaria Konrad Lorenz, Bogotá D.C, Colombia
{manueli.balagueraj,jenny.lis}@konradlorenz.edu.co
[2] Escuela Colombiana de Rehabilitación, Bogotá D.C., Colombia
tocupacional@ecr.edu.co
[3] Universidad de la Costa, Barranquilla, Colombia
aviloria7@cuc.edu.co
[4] Corporación Universitaria del Meta, Villavicencio, Colombia
luz.malagon@unimeta.edu.co

Abstract. The limitations of the actual theoretical structure of occupational science are discussed emphasizing on its implications when dealing with the stability and sustainability of social systems. By using a literature review focused on the time evolution and disciplinary distribution of the scientific production about human occupation, it is verified the insufficient production leading to the development of models that facilitate quantitative reasoning to support decision making. As an alternative, the architecture of an object-oriented framework is proposed. The framework is presented by using an UML (Unified Modeling Language) class diagram of a generic occupational system, including the class model of each system's component: attributes and behaviors. Finally, guidelines are given for the use of the models produced with the framework in simulating diverse occupation systems scenarios.

Keywords: Human occupation · Occupational science · Occupational system
Complexity · Complex system · Modeling framework
Object-oriented modeling

1 Introduction

Human occupation plays an essential role in the stability of the various social systems that can be considered: from small social systems such as a family to international systems, including the global social system [1, 2].

A particularly important scenario in which human occupation plays a transcendental role is that which occurs in post-conflict processes in which the interest, behavior and actions of a single person or a small group of people can trigger a collective destabilizing dynamics that propagates as emergent phenomena across several levels of social organization [3].

© Springer International Publishing AG, part of Springer Nature 2018
Y. Tan et al. (Eds.): ICSI 2018, LNCS 10942, pp. 452–460, 2018.
https://doi.org/10.1007/978-3-319-93818-9_43

Human occupation, considered as a system: a set of entities that in interaction acquire a global, temporary or permanent identity, has all the characteristics of a complex system [4]: (1) a system whose components are organized hierarchically at spatial levels, temporary dynamics levels and control levels, (2) a system in which emergent events and phenomena frequently occur, (3) a non-ergodic system with many possible metastable states whose probability does not depend only on their associated energies because they are composed by agents (autonomous entities) which obeys diverse control processes regulated by information structures, scales of value and principles that are learned, adapted and evolve.

The foregoing, added to the urgent need to forecast scenarios for the different social systems in economics, political science, education and in general the social sciences. In addition to the inadequacy of the reductionist paradigm for such purposes, justifies the great importance of progressing both, in updating the theoretical structures of human occupation as well as in the development of tools that allow the making of strategic decisions based on quantitative reasoning and not only heuristic and qualitative reasoning.

Figure 1 presents the result of a bibliometric exploration carried out in the SCO-PUS system with the historical evolution of the production registered by this system containing the expression "occupational science" since 1974, the year in which the first finding is recorded, up to the present. This exploration resulted in 653 articles using the term "occupational science" in any of the three fields: title, abstract or keywords, as a search criterion, while only 132 articles were reported for the search restricted to expression only in the title, which indicates a very low activity focused exclusively on aspects directly related to the theoretical structure of human occupation sciences.

On the other hand, Fig. 2 shows a contribution of 2% corresponding to 9 articles in the field of Engineering, but those 9 articles deal with human occupation in the area of Civil Engineering, presenting as a result a total absence of articles that deal with human occupation from the perspective of systems sciences, computer science or computer science.

As a consequence of the reductionist approach to science that prevailed during the period between the birth of Newtonian mechanics in the mid-eighteenth century, and the acceptance of global change in the late twentieth century, human and social sciences, including the science of occupation, remained almost outside the activities tending to build theoretical structures and tools for predictive or prognostic activities, remaining limited to make quantitative descriptions based on descriptive statistics and formulating occasionally and in an unsubstantiated way control and regulation policies under the assumption of that human and social systems behave in an analog way to physical systems following rhythmic dynamics governed by a few differential equations [5, 6].

Thanks to the appearance and accelerated progress of computing in the technical-scientific field, since the birth of Operations Research in the framework of the Second World War and the General Systems Theory at the end of the 40s century, the systemic paradigm of science has been consolidated to the point of giving rise to the crisis, revolution and consolidation of the science and engineering of Complex Systems [7, 8].

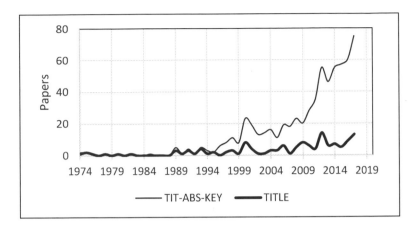

Fig. 1. Historical evolution of the literature on "occupation science" according to SCOPUS.

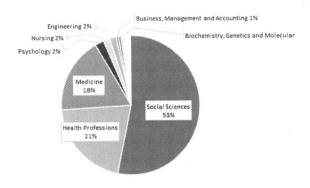

Fig. 2. Disciplinary distribution of the literature on "occupation science" according to SCOPUS.

Together with the science and engineering of complex systems whose fundamental elements will be briefly explained later, they have progressed in parallel with the computational methods for the modeling and simulation of complex systems, including the one proposed here, the Object Oriented [9], as well as Artificial Intelligence techniques [10, 11] that together allow us to tackle the adventure of creating digital versions of social systems for the exploration of possible dynamics according to different scenarios, thus allowing greater levels of awareness in the decision making on crucial aspects for all humanity, and naturally, in everything related to systems of human occupation [4].

2   Complex Systems

In reference to "reality" José Ortega y Gasset writes in his book "History as a system" the following: "Human life is a strange reality, of which the first thing to say is that it is the radical reality, in the sense that to her we have to refer all the others, since the other realities, effective or presumed, have one way or another to appear in it" [12].

An essential facet of human knowledge or of any other "intelligent system" is that this is the quintessential resource that allows it to act coherently in order to identify the univocal conditions that cause another entity on which it acts responds in a certain way, triggering a desired behavior [13].

In the other hand, an unchangeable fact inherent to human cognition is the impossibility of knowing reality or any of its scenarios in a single unit without fragmenting it into components. The first thing that we humans do when trying to know something, is to "analyze it" which means, "to decompose it in order to find the simplest and primary causes of its properties and behaviors". The problem arises when trying to assemble into a single system's model the component models obtained by studying the components in isolation. The reductionist paradigm of science is supported on the "superposition principle" which states that the value of a property corresponding to the whole system can be obtained by adding the values of the property corresponding to each one of system's components. This principle leads to a cornerstone of the reductionist science: linearity: "the whole is equivalent to the superposition of the parts".

Complexity science recognizes the imperative necessity of decomposing the system under study, however, the decomposition process is not based on the idea of the ultimate elementary component, "the atom", "elementary particle" or the "basic building block", instead, complexity science recognizes the hierarchical structure present in all complex systems. Their components are distributed along "organization levels" each one of them not reducible to a superposition of the lower level instances. Each level is an emergent phenomenon or simply, "an emergence" occurring as a consequence of criticality under ergodicity breaking, adaptation or evolution.

Operations research has become the standard alternative to deal with complex systems [14, 15]: it starts by accepting that complex problems (problems associated to complex systems) don't have just one solution which univocally states the "correct" action or set of actions leading to the desired situation. For a given "input scenario", when dealing with complex problems, there are many "output scenarios", some of them with long term stability but the greater part of solutions being highly unstable requiring continuous production of solutions in order to maintain sustainability, adaptation and evolution.

Operations research: the science of dealing with complex systems and problems uses a continuous lifecycle: problem setup, model development, determination of possible input scenarios and determination of desired, acceptable and unacceptable scenarios, simulations executions for each input scenario and decision-making.

The critical issue in order to choose a successful solution when dealing with a complex system is the step of model development, in particular when treating nonlinearity. If one solution produced an undesired and unexpected result, the most likely cause was the use of a model that was not a good representation for the real system because it used invalid hypotheses about the integrative interactions between the components of the real system giving account for its overall behavior.

Artificial intelligence and object-oriented modeling have become excellent alternatives for the development of complex systems models, facilitating the creation of low risk models, or, in the worst case, models with a known associated risk. Artificial intelligence brings to operations research a large amount of resources, concepts and methods to represent the components of a complex system, as well as to represent different integration schemes: networks theory, neural networks, agent based modeling, game theory, genetic algorithms, cellular automata, etc. while object-oriented Methods facilitate the computational integrative modeling coming from a high diversity of disciplines, modeling methods and paradigms, that is to say, object-oriented methods help to overcome ontological and epistemological heterogeneity.

3   Occupational Systems as Complex Systems

Figure 3 presents a UML (Unified Modeling Language) "class diagram" [9, 16–22] which visualize the architecture of "OccFram", the proposed modeling framework. A class diagram represents the classes present in a model and their relationships. A class is a category of objects with a common identity description in terms of attributes and behaviors. From a single class definition, it is possible generate any quantity (limited by the computer memory) of "class instances" or simply, "objects" individually distinguished from other objects of the same class by the actual values of their defining attributes.

The arrows connecting classes in the class diagram specify the type of association between two classes. Open arrows indicate "composition association", single open arrow is used if only one lower level object is a component of the higher class, for example, one "occupation system" includes only one "environment". Double open.

A closed arrow tip corresponds to an "inheritance association" indicating that the arrow origin class is a specialized class (or "sub-class") of the class where the arrow ends. As an example, Population, Community, Group and Person classes are all sub-classes of the Agent super-class. Due to paper space limitations, inheritance arrows may be replaced by writing the name of the super-class inside the sub-class box.

A very useful feature of class diagrams is the possibility to visualize the hierarchical nature of a system as in the case of an occupation system: it may be composed by a single population, which may be composed by a field of communities, a field of groups and a field of persons. A community may be composed by a field of groups and a field of persons and a group is composed by a field of persons.

As an example of the internal structure of a class, Fig. 4 presents the internal structure of the "Person" class. A class is composed by a set of properties whose values specified in an object determine the object's state and by a set of methods that represent the behaviors of any object defined by the class.

In the Agent class, the "character" property is a boolean variable indicating by its TRUE or FALSE value that the agent have or don't have a set of principles determining its decisions. The "compliance" property is a normalized real variable (with a minimum of zero and a maximum of one) that measures the agent's adherence to standards, regulations, and other requirements. "conformity" is a normalized variable whose value represents the satisfaction of the agent with the values of a chosen set of the agent's properties (for example the values of variables such as the assigned roles and tasks to the agent).

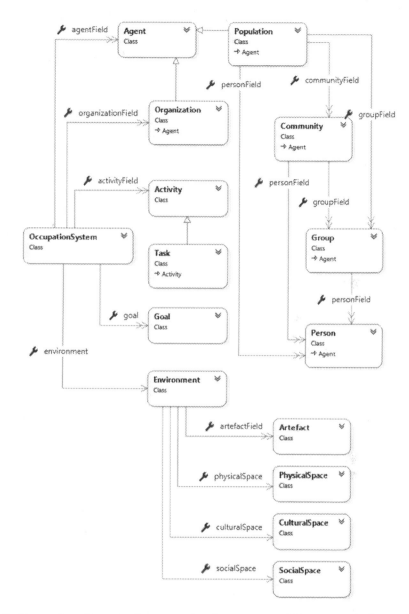

Fig. 3. Proposed architecture for occupational systems modeling arrow indicates that a higher-level object may be composed by a "field" of lower level objects, understanding by "field" a connected array of objects.

The "goal" variable may be an array of integers where each integer is an index labeling a given goal. In a similar way, the "option" variable is an array of integers where a given set of options is in correspondence to a given set of integer numbers. "rationality" property, a normalized variable, refers to the tendency of an agent to reproduce behaviors or to make decisions in agreement with a set of predefined rules

Fig. 4. Agent class model

or "principles". Finally, the "role" and "task" properties are arrays of string type or integer type where the value of each array's component codifies a specific role and task.

Each method in the agent's methods set is the codification of a procedure giving to an object the instructions necessary to perform a given behavior. The method called "Action_i" indicates that it is possible to define a set of behaviors by using the notation Action_1, Action_2,…etc. The method with the same name as the class, in this case the "Agent" method is called the "class constructor" and is the first executed method when creating an instance of the class. The constructor is the method where the initial values to the class properties are given.

One important fact about methods and in general about object-oriented modeling is that system dynamics occur only by two ways: object's "mutations" which occur via internal state modification by the action of "private" object's methods, while the interaction between objects in the system occurs by calling "public" methods which conform the object's interface.

As a sample of the possibilities offered by object-oriented methods in the task of quantitatively modeling occupational systems, it has been included in the Agent class definition, methods such as "Choose", "Compromise", "Decide", "Defect", which resemble anthropomorphic behaviors. One important task when modeling such behaviors is the appropriate selection of the data structures that the method will return or the data type of the property that a method will modify.

4 Further Work

It is important to remark that the computational structures presented in this work are simply seminal ideas elucidating the guidelines leading to the architectural design of a software framework that facilitates the construction of quantitative models of occupational systems. In order to choose which classes should be included in the framework and consequently in the models produced by using it, it is necessary a profound and detailed transdisciplinary work between researchers from the fields of occupational science and knowledge engineering. The same applies to the design of the chosen classes: their properties, methods and the data structures used as data types.

The mentioned transdisciplinary work also will be necessary in the tasks of develop a visualization system and in the selection of the cases of study where real occupational systems data will be compared with simulated data as part of the validation process.

In the present, our team is engaged in these tasks in order to produce the first version of OccFram, an object-oriented framework for the modeling of occupational systems having particularly in mind its use in social stability for post-conflict situations.

References

1. Gallagher, M., Muldoon, O., Pettigrew, J.: An integrative review of social and occupational factors influencing health and wellbeing. Front. Psychol. **6**, 1281 (2015)
2. Rees, M.: Our Final Hour: A Scientist's Warning: How Terror, Error, and Environmental Disaster Threaten Humankind's Future in This Century — on Earth and Beyond. Basic Books, New York (2003)
3. Peñas-Felizzola, O., Gómez-Galindo, A., Parra-Esquivel, E.: The role of occupational therapy in contexts of armed conflict and the post-conflict. Rev. Salud Pública **17**(4), 612–625 (2015)
4. Fogelberg, D., Frauwirth, S.: A complexity science approach to occupation: moving beyond the individual. J. Occup. Sci. **17**(3), 131–139 (2010)
5. Amozurrutia, J.A.: Complejidad y Ciencias Sociales. Universidad Autónoma de México, México D.F. (2012)
6. Johansen, O.: Introducción a la Teoría General de Sistemas. Limusa, Mexico D.F. (2007)
7. Lewin, R.: Complexity, Life at the Edge of Chaos. University of Chicago Press, Chicago (2000)
8. Mitchell, M.: Complexity: A Guided Tour. Oxford University Press, Santa Fe (2011)
9. Booch, G., Maksimchuk, R., Engle, M., Young, B., Conallen, J., Houston, K.: Object-Oriented Analysis and Design with Applications. Addison Wesley, Boston (2007)

10. Nakai, Y., Koyama, Y., Terano, T. (eds.): Agent-Based Approaches in Economic and Social Complex Systems VIII. Springer, New York (2013). https://doi.org/10.1007/978-4-431-55236-9
11. López-Paredes, A.: Ingeniería de Sistemas Sociales. Universidad de Valladolid, Valladolid (2004)
12. Gasset, J.O.Y.: History as a System and Other Essays Toward a Philosophy of History. W. W. Norton & Company, New York (1962)
13. Carsetti, A.: Epistemic Complexity and Knowledge Construction. Springer, Dordrecht (2013). https://doi.org/10.1007/978-94-007-6013-4
14. Anderson, P.: Complexity Theory and Organization Science. Organ. Sci. **10**, 216–232 (1999)
15. Nemiche, M.: Advances in Complex Societal, Environmental and Engineered Systems. Springer, New York (2017)
16. Parunak, H., Odell, J.: Representing social structures in UML. In: AOSE 2001, Montreal, Canada (2002)
17. Castellani, B., William, H.: Sociology and Complexity Science. Springer, Berlin (2009). https://doi.org/10.1007/978-3-540-88462-0
18. Forrester, J.W.: Counterintuitive behavior of social systems. Reason, 4–13 (1971)
19. Fritzson, P.: Principles of Object-Oriented Modeling and Simulation with Modelica 3.3: A Cyber-Physical Approach. Wiley-IEEE Press, Linköping (2014)
20. Rumbaugh, J., Jacobson, I., Booch, G.: The Unified Modeling Language Reference Manual. Addison Wesley Longman Inc., Cambridge (1999)
21. Slanina, F.: Essentials of Econophysics Modelling. Oxford University Press, Oxford (2014)
22. Viloria, A., Viviana Robayo, P.: Virtual network level of application composed IP networks connected with systems - (NETS Peer-to- Peer). Indian J. Sci. Technol. (2016). ISSN 0974-5645

A Building Energy Saving Software System Based on Configuration

Jinlong Chen[1,2], Qinghao Zeng[2], Hang Pan[2], Xianjun Chen[1(✉)],
and Rui Zhang[3]

[1] Guangxi Key Laboratory of Cryptography and Information Security,
Guilin University of Electronic Technology, Guilin 541004, Guangxi, China
hingini@126.com
[2] Key Laboratory of Intelligent Processing of Computer Image and Graphics,
Guilin University of Electronic Technology, Guilin 541004, Guangxi, China
[3] Guangxi Cooperative Innovation Center of Cloud Computing and Big Data,
Guilin University of Electronic Technology, Guilin 541004, Guangxi, China

Abstract. A design method of building energy saving software system based on configuration is proposed, it can meet the needs of large-scale building energy efficiency through this method. The software system utilizes the configuration design concept to realize the process monitoring, analysis and evaluation functions for large-scale building energy consumption. It can find abnormal energy consumption equipment within the building, and reduce the peak power consumption to achieve the purpose of building energy efficiency. This paper first introduces the process control software development based on the idea of configuration, the overall framework of the building energy-saving configuration software system and the design process of each module is described in detailed. The software design practice validates the availability and good scalability of process control software based on configuration ideas. This system meets the needs of large building energy consumption monitoring and building energy efficiency.

Keywords: Building energy saving · Intelligent management · Control system
Configuration software

1 Introduction

With the rapid development of our country's economy, building energy consumption, especially the problem of high energy consumption in state organs of office building and large public buildings has become increasingly prominent. Building energy consumption accounts for a large proportion of our country's energy consumption. To form the standardization management and assessment for public buildings and office buildings, and reduce building energy consumption, achieve building energy efficiency, so as to achieve the purpose of reducing costs, is a matter of urgency to be solved of far. The only way to effectively reduce the consumption of building energy, and truly achieve building energy is to take an effective way to monitor the consumption and use of internal energy in large buildings, and do real-time data acquisition, analysis and control of building energy consumption, to achieve intelligent energy management within the building.

© Springer International Publishing AG, part of Springer Nature 2018
Y. Tan et al. (Eds.): ICSI 2018, LNCS 10942, pp. 461–470, 2018.
https://doi.org/10.1007/978-3-319-93818-9_44

With the continuous improvement of the level of industrial automation [1], as well as the use of a large number of control equipment and process monitoring devices in the industrial, so that the traditional model and process for industrial control software development has been unable to meet the diverse needs of users. In the practice of traditional industrial control software development, once the control object was changes, you need to modify the source of the control system. It is because of the existence of such problems, the cycle and cost of software development was increased, and the scalability of the software is not high enough. The presence of the configuration effectively addresses the problem. The Configuration software [2, 3], also known as configuration monitoring system software, is used in industrial automation control, with the functions of industrial field real-time data acquisition, data monitoring and instruction control, provide users a software system that they can use it to rapidly construct a industrial integrated monitoring system, by combining the secondary development environment with the software operating environment. The dynamic picture and object-oriented coding way that provided by configuration software can help users to quickly build the automatic control system which satisfy their own needs.

Aiming at the demand of building energy saving, this paper presents a design method of building energy saving software system based on configuration. This system uses distributed control network technology to monitor the energy consumption of various buildings, with functions of data collection, storage, statistics and analysis, to provide effective means for large building energy monitoring, and to achieve effective energy conservation and improve the management level of building energy.

2   Overall Design of Building Energy Saving Configuration Software System

2.1   Principles for Achieving a Configuration Software

Configuration is any combination of modular. The main principles of general configuration system design are [4]:

(1) Encapsulation. We can encapsulate the common function and algorithm module in configure software by use the ideas of object-oriented, and provide interface for users. In the actual application, the user only needs to call the corresponding interface according to actual needs. The method of encapsulation makes the control software development process simple and clear. The procedures which developed by that method is easy to modify and maintain and has a certain degree of robustness.

(2) Scalable. For configuration software, when the device functions and user needs changed, it only needs to do a small amount of changes to complete the software update.

(3) Reuse. Based on the actual control process, the user can quickly complete a project with control process visualization, real-time data management and equipment monitoring using device drives, configuration screens, and general–purpose real-time databases provided by the configuration system. These components in design process are reusable and have good versatility.

The building energy saving software system based on the configuration method is a concrete realization of the configuration development mode. We use the platform/plug-in architecture, combined with object-oriented design method to complete the system structure, making the system more common and stable. According to the characteristics of building energy consumption monitoring, we encapsulated different equipment driver and equipment data acquisition method in the form of plug-in and integrated in the system. In this method, on the one hand, it facilitates the management of monitoring equipment, on the other hand it also improve the stability of the system. The configuration screen editing subsystem and the project file real-time runtime subsystem are also integrated into the system frame in the form of plug-ins by using the same encapsulation method. The real-time data obtained by the device is associated with the variables in the configuration system and the display of the picture in the real-time configuration is also related to the variables in the configuration system. The device data obtained from each device is associated with the content displayed on the visual configuration screen. The system will visually display the acquired real-time data and storage the data in the real-time database of the configuration system, so that the collected data can be further analyzed and utilized and it also provides a data foundation for the implementation of other functional modules in the configuration software.

2.2   The Function Module of Building Energy Saving Configuration Software

The function of this configuration software system is to carry out centralized monitoring, management and decentralized control of energy use such as power distribution, lighting, elevators and air conditioners in buildings, and find inefficient operation and abnormal energy consumption equipment through the overall monitor of the situation of internal equipment energy consumption in buildings to reduce the peak level of electricity, so as to achieve the ultimate goal of reducing energy consumption and building energy efficiency. The system consists of metering devices, data collectors and energy consumption data monitoring and management and other components. The configuration software provides a multi-device acquisition algorithm library and analysis tool for the development of building energy control software. It also has monitoring screen configuration, energy consumption equipment monitoring in real-time, and energy analysis and other functions. The function module of the configuration software is shown in Fig. 1.

(1) Engineering create and management module. This module implements the creation and management of project files. The project file includes the configuration process for the specific monitoring plan, and the user configuration parameters for the data acquisition module and other information. This module is also responsible for the start and run of the project files. Features include real-time acquisition of monitoring data and update the display of configuration screens.

(2) Graphical configuration module. This module constructs the equipment energy consumption monitoring and data acquisition process in the building in form of graphic configuration design according to the relevant modules of the equipment energy consumption collection library.

(3) Device management module. This module manages various device drivers and data acquisition algorithm components. It allows the user to configure the parameters of the various available devices according to the type of protocol supported by the device, read and write control and other operations.

(4) Data processing module. This module is responsible for data processing analysis and channel variable management. It provides functions include formula system, historical data query and data analysis and comparison.

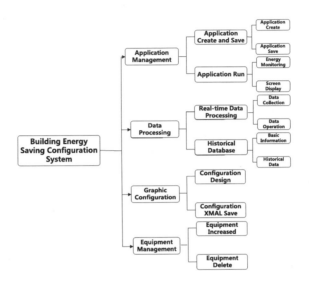

Fig. 1. Function module of the system

3   Detailed Design of Building Energy Saving Configuration Software System

The Building energy saving configuration software is composed of two parts, one is the framework of the main body to provide the basic function of the system, and the other part is plug-ins that encapsulates the specific device driver and control algorithm.

3.1   Design of Engineering Creation and Management Module

Project creation and management is one of the main functions of the configuration software system framework. The main task of the module is responsible for the creation of project documents, content analysis. The user will prompt to create a new project when using the configuration software for the first time and this project is related to the user's specific control tasks. The configuration software provides the configuration picture design window, and the user can use the picture components provided by the configuration software to design the content display screen during the control process and associate the data collected by system with the screen content through the variable association process. All of the above design content and configuration parameters will be saved in the form of project files. Once the project file is built, users can run the project file through the real-time running program provided by system. When the project is running successfully, the configuration screen will be displayed in real time. The process of creating and loading project files is shown in Fig. 2.

3.2   Design of Graphic Configuration Module

The graphical configuration module is one of the core functions of the configuration software and it is the graphical basis in the configuration software system. This module is an important part of the interface interaction between configuration software and user. The development of the graphical interface is based on the graphics engine provided by WPF. The entire graphics configuration module includes the graphics rending section, the property manager, the event manager, and the serialization of the view. The graphical configuration module is shown in Fig. 3.

The graphic drawing of the designer is based on the Canvas graphic board. Graphic drawing is container of the screen control element, we can use it to quickly locate and display the control elements in the screen. In actual use of Graphic Configuration Module, we can select the standard graphics control from the toolbar provided by system, and directly drag the control into the canvas through mouse drag and drop function, and then we can connect and combine these joined control elements into the real-time configuration screen through a certain way by use of function that provided by system.

The property Manager provides attribute management for all graphical controls. In the drawing process of the configuration screen, the properties of each graphic control can be set by the property manager. Users can bind different properties for design controls, such as height, width, visibility, margins, and shapes. When users configure the properties of all controls, they can bind to the channel variables provided by the configuration system, by this way, the display of this control is linked to the real-time data obtained by the system.

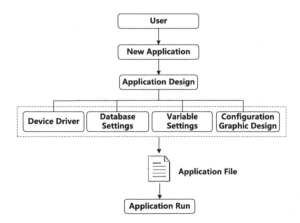

Fig. 2. The process of creating and loading project files

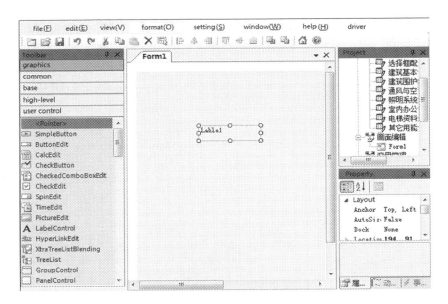

Fig. 3. The process of creating and loading project files

The event manager provides an event binding operation for a graphical control. For each of the graphical control the Graphical configuration design corresponding attributes, as well as provides a common event interface. The system design a series of corresponding operations for these events, such as the display of data reports, the opening and closing of the screen, and the preservation of data for different controls in the graphical configuration. Through the design interface, the user will add a specific event to the event list of control, and obtain a specific response to this event when user do the corresponding operation to trigger the event of the control in the run time of the system. Through event binding, the event manager combines the specific action response logic with the events of the control itself when the system is running, and achieves the exchange between real-time message and data in system.

When the secondary developer of the configuration system completed the drawing of configuration graphics interface, the graphic configuration converts all controls on the canvas and the position properties and mouse events of these controls into XAML languages [5], save as XAML file in screen name. The system saves the properties of each control in the designed graphical configuration as XAML tags in a certain way, and writes to the XMAL file together with the event binding and attributes settings of the control.

3.3   Design of Equipment Management Module

Building energy saving configuration software needs to control different energy consumption equipments. These intelligent instruments are produced by different manufactures. To enable these intelligent instruments from different manufacturers to complete communication with the control system in real-time, the problem of difference in communication protocol between devices need to be solved. Since each device has its own specific communication protocol, we can not only integrate several specific equipment communication algorithms in the system implementation process. The scalability of the system must be taken into account. The plug-in development approach effectively addresses this issue. The equipment communication module of our building configuration software system is developed by plug-in approach, to meet the needs of equipment updates and system modular management. The system main frame provides the interface required for the plug-in, and then we encapsulate frequently used device drivers and operations algorithms into the systems in form of plug-in.

The configuration software system framework provides the plug-in interface. The device driver and operation plug-in that is integrated into the system as a plug-in implements the interface provided by the framework. Framework of system communicates with device driver plug-in through the interface, and also achieves operations of plug-in load, delete and update by this way. At present our system supports ModBus protocol, DLT645 protocol and OMRON protocol. We designs and implements the corresponding protocol classes for each protocol, these classes contain methods for communicating with devices that support the protocol, and these methods are used for data exchange with device.

The software system defines "station" and "channel" for device data reading and writing. In our configuration system, each actual physical device corresponds to a "station". We define a "station" class as an abstract in the final implementation process. Each station provides the function of communication port or serial port on or off, communication parameter settings, and communication thread packaging. These above related functions are implemented in each station class. User calls the corresponding method in the class instance to implement the function provide by station. In addition to the "station" we use the channel to represent the type of data actually read. Each smart device has different registers. Each type of data is stored in different register. Each register correspond to the "channel". We also define the "channel class" as a concrete implementation in the system.

3.4   Design of Data Processing Module

The data processing module is also the core module in the configuration software. The data processing module in Building energy configuration software is divided into two parts: The first part is the input and storage of the initial static data. The data in this part is mainly some of the basic data of energy consumption equipment. The second part is the dynamic data generated during the operation of the system. This part of the data mainly includes the data collected by system from the equipment in the monitoring process and the operation result data calculated by the collected device data and basic data.

For basic information in Building energy saving configuration system, mainly composed of three functional modules: Building information, energy formula, energy consumption information. The building information mainly stores the basic structure of the building information and the ventilation and air conditioning, lighting systems, temperature, temperature monitoring system and other basic information within the building. The energy formula is mainly related to the energy formula, these formulas mainly include the specific professional mathematical formula and evaluation analysis model. The system uses these formulas to complete the statics, analysis and evaluation of building energy consumption. Energy consumption information is mainly detailed breakdown sub-item information in the energy consumption within the building. That information provide classification basis for the subsequent building energy monitoring.

The dynamic information generated during the operation of the system is mainly completed by system data acquisition, formula system and historical data query and comparison module. Data acquisition module obtains the real-time data stored in the device register. In order to achieve data acquisition from a device at a specific time interval, we have designed a timer in the data acquisition threads of each device in the system. The timer interval is 10 s. When the system starts monitoring, the timer is triggered and the timer starts counting, time events are generated every 10 s, the content of the event is to obtain the current monitoring data and store the data to the real-time database. When the system obtains the energy consumption information of the equipment, it can be used for calculation in formula system. The data obtained by the system is only a single type of data for each device. We can substitute these data into the energy formula and evaluation modules which obtained from basic information base, then our system can generate bills and energy consumption statistics statements. The system variable formula editing interface is shown in Fig. 4.

The system provides historical data query function for users to query the historical data. Users can set up different time periods or select multiple channels of the device, which will be displayed in an intuitive chart. The real-time comparison of the collected data is shown in Fig. 5.

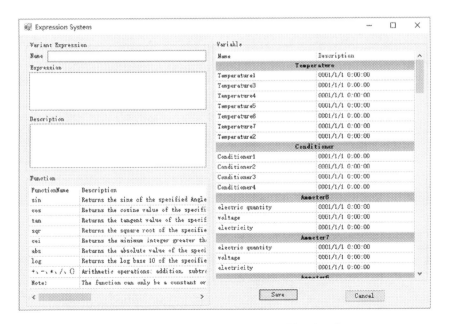

Fig. 4. The system variable formula editing interface

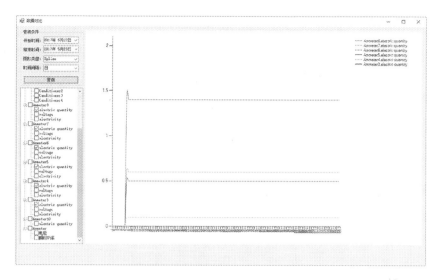

Fig. 5. The real-time comparison of the collected data

4 Conclusion

In this paper, the design of building energy saving software system based on the configuration for energy monitoring and energy saving in large buildings is proposed. This paper first introduces the idea of configuration in the process of industrial control software development. Building energy saving configuration software is a complete example of configuration ideas. Then introduced the overall structure of the building configure software and the detailed design process of each specific module. The software system design process includes plug-in/platform architecture ideas, and the use of object oriented design methods. It has been proved that the building energy-saving software system adopts the configuration way to make the system have better versatility and expansibility in building energy monitoring. The application of the system has successfully solved the problem of energy consumption monitoring in large buildings. This system provides a good solution for building energy saving.

Acknowledgments. This research work is supported by the grant of Guangxi science and technology development project (No: 1598018-6), the grant of Guangxi Key Laboratory of Cryptography & Information Security of Guilin University of Electronic Technology (No: GCIS201603), the grant of Guangxi Colleges and Universities Key Laboratory of Intelligent Processing of Computer Images and Graphics of Guilin University of Electronic Technology (No:GIIP201602), the grant of Innovation Project of GUET Graduate Education (2017YJCX55), and the grant of Guangxi Cooperative Innovation Center of Cloud Computing and Big Data of Guilin University of Electronic Technology (No: YD16E11).

References

1. Xu, Y.: Research and Implementation of Configuration Software System Based on WPF Framework, pp. 27–32. South University of Science and Technology (2013)
2. Wang, K.: The Design And Implementation of Configuration Software, pp. 1–5. Beijing University of Posts and Telecommunications, Beijing (2013)
3. Lian, J., Huang, X.H., Wang, W.Q.: Design and implementation of configuration software for aircraft engine control software. J. Measur. Control Technol. **31**(6), 115–119 (2012)
4. Yin, F., Ding, W.M.: Patterns research in the design of configuration software. J. Comput. Measur. Control **13**(3), 298–300 (2005)
5. Steven, G., Maarten, M.: The quality of the XML web. J. Serv. Agents World Wide Web **6** (12), 72–76 (2012)

Measures of Concentration and Stability: Two Pedagogical Tools for Industrial Organization Courses

Jenny-Paola Lis-Gutiérrez[1(✉)], Mercedes Gaitán-Angulo[2],
Linda Carolina Henao[3], Amelec Viloria[4], Doris Aguilera-Hernández[5],
and Rafael Portillo-Medina[4]

[1] Universidad Central, Bogotá, Colombia
jlisg@ucentral.edu.co
[2] Corporación Universitaria de Salamanca, Barranquilla, Colombia
m_gaitan689@cues.edu.co
[3] Corporación Universitaria Minuto de Dios, Bogotá, Colombia
linda.henao@uniminuto.edu
[4] Universidad de la Costa, Barranquilla, Colombia
{aviloria7, rportill3}@cuc.edu.co
[5] Corporación Universitaria del Meta, Villavicencio, Colombia
viceacademica@unimeta.edu.co

Abstract. This document describes two pedagogical tools developed for teaching applied microeconomics, specifically the issues related to concentration, dominance, stability and asymmetry of firms. The tools make a compilation of several concentration and stability indexes used in the literature since 1945. Among the benefits of the applications are the ease and agility to perform comparative analyzes of intersectorial and/or intertemporal type in a simple and agile way; and the use of unconventional concentration and stability measures.

Keywords: Measures of concentration · Market concentration
Concentration indexes · Stability indexes

1 Introduction

From the work of [1], which made an excellent compilation of the concentration measures available so far, there are numerous studies that have used different indices to analyze the industrial concentration in different scenarios. In the last three decades, progress has been made in the construction of other indices to study market instability and many of the traditional measures have been modified to analyze geographic or spatial concentration.

In 2013, [2] within the Economic Studies Group of the Superintendence of Industry and Commerce, he designed two applications that contained a compilation of various concentration and stability indexes used in the literature since 1945. This pedagogical tool allows automatic calculation, in the first application, 10 concentration indices, 3 of dominance and 2 of asymmetry, and the second 10 stability indicators based on basic information from market agents. The number of sectors that can be analyzed

© Springer International Publishing AG, part of Springer Nature 2018
Y. Tan et al. (Eds.): ICSI 2018, LNCS 10942, pp. 471–480, 2018.
https://doi.org/10.1007/978-3-319-93818-9_45

simultaneously is 7, and in each of them 100 signatures can be included. The two applications were updated in February 2015.

Since 2014, the applications have been used for a seminar on industrial organization in an undergraduate degree in Economics, and applied microeconomics courses in specialization and masters, in two Colombian universities. The objective is for students to be able to carry out market studies, understand the structure of different sectors and the warning signs when faced with behaviors or situations that may alter free competition.

2   About the Indicators

Several authors, including [1, 3, 4] proposed several criteria that should be met by the concentration measures and which are indicated below:

1. It must be easy to calculate and interpret.
2. It should be a one-dimensional measure, in other words, that can be calculated from a single variable.
3. It should be bounded between 0 and 1, which facilitates its comparability and interpretation.
4. It must be independent of the absolute size of the market.
5. Transfers between companies by spin-off or merger must have an effect on the concentration measure (merger condition).
6. According to the transfer principle, the concentration increases when the market share of some firm increases at the expense of another small one.
7. If the variable used for the elaboration of the index is multiplied by a scalar, the value of the index must also be affected in the same proportion (multiplied or divided by the scalar).
8. If all the companies are of equal size, the measure of concentration should be a decreasing function of the number of signatures and tend to $1/N$.
9. Given a number of companies, increasing the market share of a firm should lead to an increase in concentration and therefore in the index.
10. The entry of new signatures with a size below the average should be reflected in the reduction of the concentration (entry condition), the exit of signatures with this characteristic should result in an increase in concentration (exit condition).
11. The entry of large firms should increase the concentration and their output should reduce it.
12. The contribution of a company in the index must match its market share.

According to [5] there are two types of concentration measures, absolute and relative. The former use information on the number of signatures and the variance of the size of the signature. The second ones are also known as representations of inequality and only use the information of the variance of the size of the signatures.

There is a recurrent fact in the reviewed works, the IHH is the most used measure, followed by the concentration ratio. However, in several documents other indicators of market concentration and stability are used. Within the first group of works are the articles of [6], which compare the concentrations of the manufacturing industry with

Compustat data, which were prepared from the industrial census. The authors find that the results of concentration and profit margins are consistent with what is described by the theory (in industries with higher concentration, there is less competition and prices are higher). For their part, [7] they compare the concentration of the industry (with IHH and Cr4) and the profit margins considering two classifications: Standard Industry Classification (SIC) and Global Industry Classification Standard (GICS), between 2008 and 2009. They show that in the latter case, it is a better proxy for industrial concentration. [8] analyzed how direct foreign investment affects market concentration in the Turkish manufacturing industry, between 1989 and 2006, and measured with CR4 and IHH. These authors did not find any significant relationship between the variables used.

Within the second group of studies is the work of [9], who use the indexes of Hirschman-Herfildalh (IHH), Rosenbluth (RHT) and CR for cultural industries, between 2006 and 2008. The authors identify high levels of concentration in the subsectors. [10] use the Gini index, the concentration curve, the Hannah-Kay index family and the Rosenbluth index to study the degree of concentration of the Spanish hotel industry, between 2001 and 2006. In the work of [11] the concentration ratio, the Herfindahl-Hirschman indexes, the equivalent number of companies and the stability indicator are used, in order to analyze the degree of competitiveness of the Bolivian banking system. Its purpose was to determine if there was evidence of an oligopolistic market structure and to establish whether the entry of new financial entities into the banking system would be convenient from the perspective of the regulator. With respect to the banking sector, there is also the study of [12], in which the concentration ratio, the HHI, the Hall-Tideman and Rosenbluth indicators and the comprehensive industrial concentration index are used to analyze the structure of the banking market. [13–15] additionally employ the concentration ratio and the HHI in the banking structure, an indicator of competition. Following [13, 16] identifies that industries that make use of external financing perform better, in countries where banking concentration is high and competition is low. The H statistical of Panzar and Rosse, together with the HHI was used a year earlier by [17], applying it to 1,700 observations of banks in Latin America, between 1999 and 2006, these indicators were introduced in a panel and estimated by Generalized Method of moments (Generalized Method of Moments (GMM)). They identified that concentration rates and market share had little or no influence on interest rate margins, while the relationship between loans and assets seems to be associated with high margins.

Within the competition authorities that use indices that go beyond the IHH is [18]. This authority uses the Rosenbluth, Entropy and Volatility indices, in addition to the use of the IHH, C5 and C10, and applies it to the different branches of economic activity between 1999 and 2008. It also analyzes the correlation between the different indices used and proposes a matrix with three levels of volatility and concentration. The agency also proposes other indicators associated with business dynamics. The business branch, for example, allows to identify some activities in which there is a structure of large companies that have multiple establishments. Likewise, it allows to capture situations of horizontal concentration in some cases.

Two other indicators are structural branchization and dynamic branchization. [19] the index used the dominance index to analyze Mexican airlines. This indicator was used in Mexico by [20]. The author also compares the properties of the dominance index and the

IHH against the analysis of mergers. For their part, [21] they study the forestry industry in Spain and use for it the pidiche of Rosenbluth, Hannah-Kay and IHH, by industry and by autonomous community. From another perspective, [22] calculate concentration indexes (concentration ratio of k companies, the IHH, Theil's entropy index, the dominance and stability index), for the Chilean domestic wine market, considering the 2001 period and 2005 and the sales variable. [23] used the IHH, the concentration ratio and the Linda index to analyze the international audit market between 1997 and 2003. [24] used these same indicators to analyze the market concentration of cable television in the United States, identifying the promotion of an oligopoly of four firms.

3   Simulation

The idea of the two applications was derived from the work of [5] who used Excel to simulate the main concentration measures, however, this work only allowed calculations for 12 firms and 9 indicators, and its purpose was to illustrate the proposed axioms in the work of [3].

The concentration and stability indexes are presented in independent Excel applications, which will be available for free download in the Academic Studies section within the microsite of the Economic Studies Group of the Superintendence of Industry and Commerce (http://www.sic.gov.co/estudios-academicos-2013) or by request by email.

3.1   Simulation Concentration Indicators

The first simulation exercise is presented in the "Concentration index" application. The main purpose of the application, the way to contact the Economic Studies Group and the use license (creative commons) are indicated on the welcome screen. The second screen of the aforementioned application allows the user the following options (Fig. 1):

(a) Enter the data from which the participations of the firms will be obtained (maximum 100, in 7 different sectors) and the respective indexes. The information must be organized from highest to lowest.
(b) Include the value of α to calculate the Hannah-Key index.
(c) Delete all the information entered with the clean button.
(d) After including the data calculate the different indices selected the "Calculate" button.

Once the "Calculate" button is pressed, the results screen appears (Fig. 2). In the left part of it, the indices are calculated. On the right side the graphs of cumulative concentration for each of the seven sectors (Fig. 3).

3.2   Simulation of Stability Indicators

The second simulation is performed from an application called "Stability indexes". As in the previous simulation, the main purpose of the application, the way to contact the Economic Studies Group and the use license (creative commons) are indicated on the welcome screen (Fig. 4).

Fig. 1. Initial screen of the application. The original version in Spanish language is shown

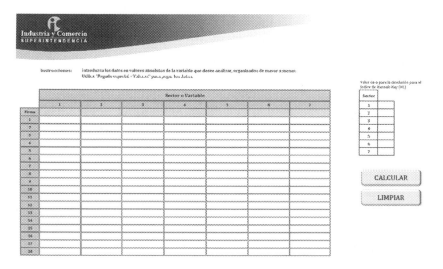

Fig. 2. Application data entry screen "Concentration indices". The original version in Spanish language is shown

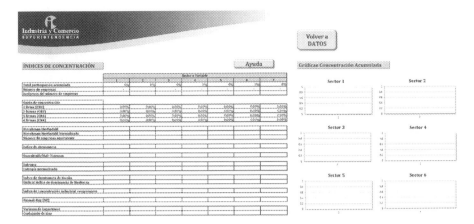

Fig. 3. Results screen of "Concentration indices". The original version in Spanish language is shown

Fig. 4. Initial screen of the application "Stability indexes". The original version in Spanish language is shown

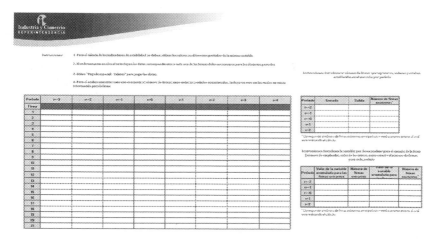

Fig. 5. Application data entry screen "Stability indexes". The original version in Spanish language is shown

In this tool, the user is asked the following (Fig. 5):

(a) Enter the data from which you want to obtain the participations of the signatures (maximum 100, for 8 periods) and the stability indexes. As in the first simulation, the information must be organized from highest to lowest.
(b) Enter data of incoming, outgoing, total and leader signatures for a sector, during 5 periods.
(c) Enter the values of the variable that you want to use to compare the size of the incoming firms versus the existing ones (for example, number of employees, value of assets, among others) for a sector, for 5 periods.
(d) Include the information of premises and firms, to analyze the branch in a geographical space, for 3 periods and 10 sectors.
(e) Delete all the information entered with the clean button f. After including the data calculate the different indices selected the "Calculate" button.

After pressing the "Calculate" button, the results screen appears (Fig. 6).

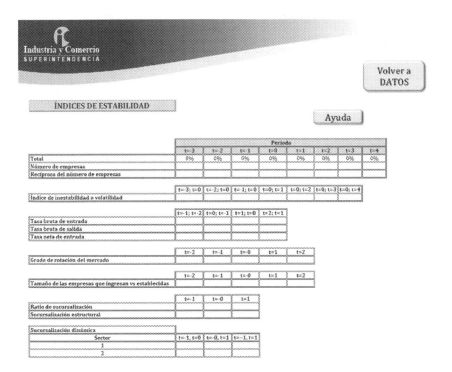

Fig. 6. Application results screen "Stability indexes". The original version in Spanish language is shown

4   Conclusions

In this document, two pedagogical tools were presented for the calculation of the concentration, symmetry, dominance and stability of various economic sectors, based on the indicators most frequently used in the literature and by the authorities that preserve free competition. While there are various measures of concentration and market stability alternatives to those commonly used in the literature. The use and interpretation of the alternative indexes must be associated to the criteria and judgment of the person applying them, according to the structure of the market, the type of product, the sector, among others.

Among the benefits of the proposed Excel application are the following: 1. It is an instrument that allows comparative analysis of intersectorial and/or intertemporal type in a simple and agile. 2. It incorporates into the analysis in research related to the protection of competition those measures of unconventional concentration and stability. 3. The applications serve as didactic material to illustrate the scope of the indicators proposed in the document and it is an input for the academic community interested in the topic of competence analysis and industrial organization. In future work, a similar application could be made for the stability and concentration indicators that have been modified and that were presented in the document. Special usefulness would have a study that prioritizes in the analysis of the specialization indexes and concentration and geographic diversification.

References

1. Curry, B., George, K.D.: Industrial concentration: a survey. J. Ind. Econ. **31**(3), 203–255 (1983)
2. Lis-Gutiérrez, J.P.: Market Concentration and Market Stability Measures: An Application for Excel (2013). http://dx.doi.org/10.2139/ssrn.2279769
3. Hannah, L., Kay, J.A.: Concentration in Modern Industry: Theory, Measurement and the UK Experience. Macmillan, London (1977)
4. Hall, M., Tideman, N.: Measures of concentration. J. Am. Stat. Assoc. **62**(317), 162–168 (1967)
5. Latreille, P., Mackley, J.: Using Excel to Illustrate Hannah and Kay's Concentration Axioms. Int. Rev. Econ. Educ. **10**, 117–127 (2010)
6. Ali, A., Klasa, S., Yeung, E.: The limitations of industry concentration measures constructed with compustat data: implications for finance research. Rev. Financ. Stud. **22**, 3839–3871 (2009)
7. Hrazdil, K., Zhang, R.: The importance of industry classification in estimating concentration ratios. Econ. Lett. **114**, 224–227 (2012)
8. Elmas, F., Degirmen, S.: Foreign direct investment and industrial concentration in the Turkish manufacturing system. Int. Res. J. Financ. Econ. **23**, 246–252 (2009)
9. Alonso Cifuentes, J.C., Ríos, A.M.: Concentración de la producción de las industrias culturales en Cali **27**(119), 99–121 (2011). http://www.icesi.edu.co/revistas/index.php/estudios_gerenciales/article/view/1060/pdf
10. Furió Blasco, E., Alonso Pérez, M.: Concentración y heterogeneidad en la industria hotelera (2009)
11. Gonzales Martínez, R.: Estructura de Mercado, Condiciones de Entrada y Número Óptimo de Bancos en el Sistema Bancario Boliviano: Una Aproximación de Indicadores de Concentración y Movilidad Intra-industrial (2008)
12. Bikker, J.A.: Competition and Efficiency in a Unified European Banking Market. Edward Elgar Publishing, Northampon (2004)
13. Hoxha, I.: The market structure of the banking sector and financially dependent manufacturing sectors. Int. Rev. Econ. Financ. **27**, 432–444 (2013)
14. Lis-Gutiérrez, J.P., Macias-Rojas, S., Gaitán-Angulo, M., Moros, A., Viloria, A.: Analysis of concentration, dominance and symmetry in bank deposits in Colombia. J. Eng. Appl. Sci. **12**, 2831–2834 (2017). https://doi.org/10.3923/jeasci.2017.2831.2834
15. Lis-Gutiérrez, J.P., Macias-Rojas, S.: Análisis Departamental de las Captaciones en el Sistema Financiero Colombiano. Estudios Económicos Sic - Superintendencia De Industria Y Comercio, Bogotá (2014)
16. Panzar, J.C., Rosse, J.N.: Testing for 'monopoly' equilibrium. J. Ind. Econ. **35**, 443–456 (1987)
17. Chortareas, G.E., Garza-García, J., Girardone, C.: Competition, efficiency and interest rate margins in Latin American banking. Int. Rev. Financ. Anal. **24**, 93–103 (2012)
18. Agencia de Defensa de la Competencia de Andalucía: Panorama de la Competencia en Andalucía. Consejería de Economía y Hacienda. Junta de Andalucía, Sevilla (2009)

19. Alba Iduñate, P.G.: El índice de dominancia y el análisis de competencia de las líneas aéreas mexicanas. Boletín Latinoamericano de Competencia **6**, 62–74 (1999)
20. Comisión Federal de Competencia: Resolución del 24 de julio de 1998 (1998)
21. Herruzo Martínez, A.C., Díaz Balteiro, L., Calvo Medina, X.: Concentración industrial y especialización regional de la industria forestal en España. In: Díaz Balteiro, L. (ed.) Caracterización de la Industrial Forestal en España. Aspectos Económicos y Ambientales, pp. 59–86. Fundación BBVA, Madrid (2008)
22. Lobos, G., Viviani, J.-L.: Estimation des indicateurs de concentration et d'instabilité dans l'industrie vitivinicole du Chili. Agroalimentaria **24**, 55–61 (2007)
23. Piot, C.: Concentration et competitive du marché de l'audit en France: Une étude longitudinale 1997-2003. Revue Finance Controle Strategie **11**(4), 31–63 (2008)
24. Perani, J.: Concentration et pouvoir de marché: la télévision par câble aux ÉtatsUnis entre 1984 et 1992. Réseaux **72–73**, 77–100 (1995)

Image Enhancement

The Analysis of Image Enhancement for Target Detection

Rui Zhang[1], Yongjun Jia[2], Lihui Shi[2], Hang Pan[3], Jinlong Chen[1,3], and Xianjun Chen[1,4(✉)]

[1] Guangxi Key Laboratory of Trusted Software,
Guilin University of Electronic Technology, Guilin 541004, Guangxi, China
hingini@126.com
[2] Beijing Institute of Special Electrometrical Technology, Beijing 100190, China
[3] Key Laboratory of Intelligent Processing of Computer Image and Graphics,
Guilin University of Electronic Technology, Guilin 541004, Guangxi, China
[4] Information Engineering School, Haikou College of Economics,
Haikou 571127, Hainan, China

Abstract. In the process of automatic detection and recognition based on image, the quality of the detected images affects the target detection and recognition results. To solve the problem of low contrast and high signal-to-noise ratio of the target image in the target detection process, this paper introduces two types of image detail enhancement algorithms which are widely used in recent years, including brightness contrast image enhancement algorithm and HSV color space based enhancement algorithm, and its impact on the target detection. Experiments show that the image detail enhancement can improve the overall and local contrast of the image, highlight the details of the image, and the enhanced image can effectively improve the number and accuracy of the target detection.

Keywords: Image enhancement · Brightness contrast · HSV color space
Target detection

1 Introduction

In the process of target detection and recognition based on static image, image is an important part of target detection and recognition. The quality of the target image to be detected directly affects the result of the target detection and recognition. In the process of image acquisition, the quality of the image will be degraded when there is a distance between the imaging system and the imaged object, the target features are not clear, and the background is an obvious environment such as clouds and deserts. In this case, the acquired images will have low contrast, narrow grayscale, uneven illumination, low quality in image features and high signal-to-noise ratio, which bring about great impact on target detection or recognition. Therefore, the study of image detail enhancement is of great significance to the subsequent detection and recognition of targets.

Image enhancement refers to highlighting the useful information in the image according to a specific requirement, removing or weakening the useless information, enlarging the difference between the features of different objects in the image, improving

© Springer International Publishing AG, part of Springer Nature 2018
Y. Tan et al. (Eds.): ICSI 2018, LNCS 10942, pp. 483–492, 2018.
https://doi.org/10.1007/978-3-319-93818-9_46

the image quality, and converting the original image information into a more suitable for human visual or easily handled by machines. It has a wide range of applications in medical imaging, remote sensing imaging, photography and other fields of image enhancement technology [1].

Image enhancement should pay attention to the following aspects: (1) Improve the image of the overall and local contrast, both to improve the overall image contrast and local image information. (2) While enhancing the image, if you can't effectively suppress the noise in the image, you should avoid the amplification of the noise and image quality decreased caused by that. (3) The enhanced image should have a good visual effect and consistent with the characteristics of human visual.

Commonly used image enhancement processing methods are mainly divided into spatial image enhancement and frequency domain image enhancement. Spatial enhancement refers to the directly processing on each pixel of an image. After processing, the position of the pixel remains unchanged, such as gray transformation, histogram equalization (HE), spatial smoothing and sharpening of the image. The frequency domain enhancement transforms the image into a frequency domain, and calculates the coefficients, and then transforms the original domain to the enhanced image, such as low-pass filter technology, high-pass filter technology, band-pass filter. Histogram equalization is a technique that uses the histogram to adjust the contrast of the image. The Histogram Equalization (HE) algorithm changes the probability density function (PDF) of the image gray level so as to satisfy the approximately uniform distribution to achieve the purpose of increasing the dynamic range of the image and improving the image contrast [2–4]. There are many improved algorithms based on the histogram equalization (HE) algorithm, such as the double histogram equalization (BBHE) algorithm [5], it solves the problem of uneven brightness in the enhanced image local area. The histogram equalization (LMHE) algorithm based on logarithm function mapping in [6] makes the enhanced image more in line with human visual characteristics. Wavelet transform image enhancement (WT) belongs to the frequency domain image enhancement algorithm. By decomposing an image into a low-frequency image and a high-frequency image, and enhancing different frequency, it achieved the purpose of enhancing the image details. The homomorphic filtering algorithm is also a frequency-domain image enhancement algorithm [7–9]. Based on the illumination-reflection model, the homomorphic filtering algorithm regards the image as a component of the brightness component and a reflection component. It achieves the enhancement by increasing the high frequency part and suppresses the low frequency part.

This paper introduces two image detail enhancement algorithms commonly used in recent years, including image detail enhancement algorithm based on brightness and contrast, image enhancement algorithm based on HSV color space. We use different objective and subjective evaluation methods to compare the results of different enhancement algorithms. At the same time, the effect of the enhanced image on target detection and recognition is also studied.

2   Image Detail Enhancement Algorithm

2.1   Image Detail Enhancement Algorithm Based on Brightness Contrast

The purpose of image enhancement is to emphasize the region of interest and improve the quality of visual perception of the image. Contrast and brightness are two important indicators that describe the quality of image perceived. Contrast is the difference between the highest and lowest brightness levels in the image. The larger the difference range is, the larger the contrast ratio is. Contrast is an important factor that affects the visual effect of the image. The larger the contrast is, the more vivid and colorful of the image. The smaller the contrast is, the less clear the image is. Contrast stretching is a practical and effective method for image enhancement. The main idea is to adjust the local or global contrast of the image to enhance the visual effect by compressing the brighter part and enhancing the dark part. The contrast stretch of image can be expressed as Eq. (1).

$$I_t(x, y) = \frac{d}{I_{max} \quad I_{min}} \times (I(x, y) - I_{min}) + I_0. \tag{1}$$

Where $I_t(x, y)$ is the new dynamic range image, d is the new dynamic range value, $I(x, y)$ is the original input image, I_{max} and I_{min} are the minimum and maximum luminance values of the input image, I_0 is the Offset value of the dynamic range image.

The above transformation is a global linear contrast stretch algorithm. This method is simple and more realistic, and the contrast is also more obvious after stretching. In practical work, in order to better adjust the image contrast, highlighting the image of interest in the target or brightness interval, you can also use segmental linear trans-formation method. The image brightness interval is divided into multiple segments, respectively, to do the above linear transformation and stretching. Taking a few seg-ments in the image brightness range, each adjacent segment can be stretched or compressed. The location of the segment and the parameters can be determined by the user according to the need to be processed. Linear or segmental linear stretch is the transformation of equal proportions to specify the luminance value of the pixel in the dynamic range. We can also change the brightness value of the original image by a non-linear function. The dynamic range of the entire brightness value is transformed in a non-linear manner, such as dark areas, bright areas for different proportions of expansion. It can produce a good effect in enhancement by this way. There are many ways to implement nonlinear stretching, such as logarithmic function, exponential function, histogram equalization and specification.

Because most of the natural images are concentrated in narrower intervals, the detail of the image is not clear enough. Histogram equalization can large the gray interval of the image and make the gray distribution evenly, so as to increase the contrast and improve the contrast. Histogram Equalization employs the Cumulative Distribution Function (CDF) to map the specified input brightness level to the output brightness level so that the output has an approximately uniform probability density function, and achieve the purpose of widening the dynamic range of the image. Simple histogram equalization enhancement is shown in Fig. 1 below.

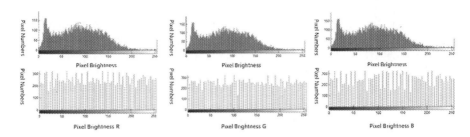

Fig. 1. Simple histogram enhance example

Each pixel value in the digital image is a manifestation of the image brightness level. The 8-bit grayscale image has only one channel, each pixel value in the image represents a different gray level, and is also the brightness value of the image. There are three channels in the color image, and the pixel values of each channel represent the brightness of the image at different pixel positions. Image brightness adjustment is shown in Eq. 2.

$$I_t(x,y) = \begin{cases} I(x,y)+v & 0 \le I+v \le 255 \\ 0 & I+v < 0 \\ 255 & I+v < 255 \end{cases}. \tag{2}$$

In the above formula, $I(x,y)$ represent the original input image. $I_t(x,y)$ is brightness adjusted image. $v \in [-255, 255]$. The brightness value of an image can be expressed as the sum of the original value of the pixel in the image and the adjustment increment. The maximum brightness is 255, that is, white, and the minimum brightness is 0, that is, black.

Contrast is a reflection of the difference in brightness levels between bright and dark areas of the image, Contrast adjustment of the image is to ensure that the average brightness of the same circumstances, to expand or reduce the difference between bright and dark spots. To ensure the value of average brightness unchanged before and after adjusting, the adjustment ratio for each point must be related to the difference between the pixel value of the point and the average brightness of the image. The contrast adjustment formula to keep the average brightness of the image unchanged is expressed as Eq. (3).

$$I_t(x,y) = I_v(x,y) + (I(x,y) - I_v(x,y)) \times (1+\alpha). \tag{3}$$

In the above formula, $I(x,y)$ represent the original input image. $I_t(x,y)$ is brightness adjusted image. $I_v(x,y)$ indicates the average brightness of the entire image. $\alpha \in [-1, 1]$ is the range of adjustment.

We use the following formula for both brightness and contrast adjustment.

$$\begin{cases} I_t(x, y) = [I(x, y) - 127.5 * (1 - \beta)] * K + 127.5 * (1 + \beta) \\ K = \tan\left(\frac{45 + 44*a}{180} * \pi\right) \end{cases} \quad (4)$$

In the above formula, $I(x, y)$ represent the original input image. $I_t(x, y)$ is brightness adjusted image. β is the brightness adjustment factor, the range is $[-1, 1]$, a is contrast adjustment factor, the range is $[-1, 1]$. When $\beta = 0$, $I_t(x, y) = [I(x, y) - 127.5] * K + 127.5$, only the contrast is adjusted. When $a = 0$, $I_t(x, y) = I(x, y) + 255 * \beta$, only the brightness is adjusted.

2.2 Image Detail Enhancement Algorithm Based on HSV Color Space

The HSV space was created by Smith in 1978, which nonlinearly converts the usual RGB three color models to the new color space model made by three channels, including Hue, Saturation and Brightness. The HSV color space is an intuitive color model. The color space not only removes the connection between the brightness component and the color information in the image, but also the hue and saturation components are closely related to the way people obtain the color. These features make the HSV color space be called an ideal algorithm for image processing algorithm which is based on color sensory characteristics of the human visual system.

HSV color space is decomposed and represented in different dimensions to represent different colors and is a mathematical representation of color. As shown in Fig. 2, the angle between the radius of the bottom of the cone and the $0°$ line represents the chromaticity H, the radius of the bottom of the cone represents the saturation S, and the height of the cone represents the brightness V, and their values range are $H \in [0°, 360°]$, $S \in [0, 1]$, $V \in [0, 1]$.

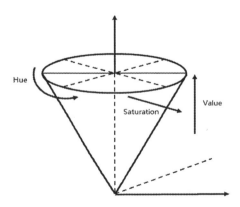

Fig. 2. HSV color space model

When converting from RGB space to HSV space, the values of the three channels of R, G and B are first normalized to [0, 1]. The minimum values of the three channels are n = min(R, G, B), N = max(R, G, B),D = N − n. Conversion process is shown below.

$$H = \begin{cases} 60° \times \left(\frac{G-B}{D} \, mod\, 6\right), & N = R \\ 60° \times \left(\frac{B-R}{D} + 2\right), & N = G \\ 60° \times \left(\frac{R-G}{D} + 4\right), & N = B \end{cases}. \tag{5}$$

$$S = \begin{cases} 0, & V = 0 \\ \frac{D}{V}, & else \end{cases}. \tag{6}$$

$$V = N. \tag{7}$$

The image detail enhancement algorithm based on HSV color space converts the image from RGB space to HSV color space, and adjusts the hue, saturation and value respectively in the HSV color space and then reconstructed image Component, convert the image from HSV color space to RGB space. Algorithm processing is shown in Fig 3.

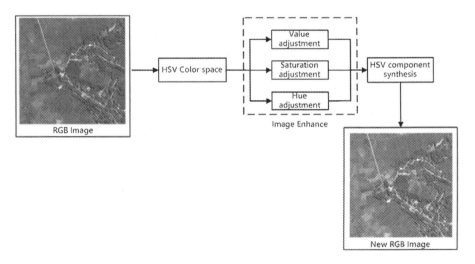

Fig. 3. Image enhancement algorithm flow based on HSV color space

3   Experimental Results and Evaluation Analysis

3.1   Image Enhancement Effect

Using the algorithms introduced in this paper, two groups of images are respectively tested for image enhancement algorithm. We selected two groups of images, the size of the first group of images is 747 × 716, and the second group of images is 743 × 723.

The enhancement of the two groups of images is respectively enhanced, as shown in Figs. 4 and 5.

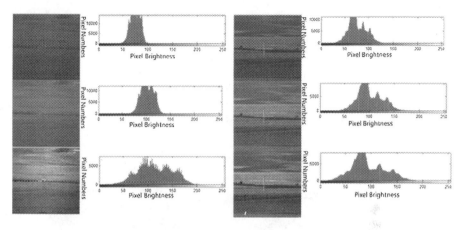

Fig. 4. The enhanced image and histogram, two groups, from top to bottom, followed by the original image, brightness adjustment, contrast adjustment

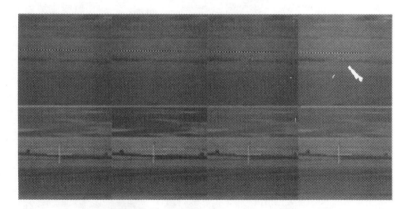

Fig. 5. HSV color space adjustment algorithm to obtain enhanced images, two groups, each from left to right in order for the hue adjustment, saturation adjustment, brightness adjustment

We can see that the brightness adjustment algorithm enhances the overall brightness of the image to achieve the purpose of image enhancement by increasing the pixel value overall. The contrast adjustment algorithm achieves the effect of image enhancement by increasing the dynamic range of the image and the contrast between pixels. Brightness adjustment algorithm based HSV Color space can enhance the vivid color of the image, making the image more full color, to a certain extent, enhance the contrast of the image to achieve an enhanced effect.

3.2   Effects of Image Enhancement on Target Detection

We use the enhanced optical and SAR images for targeted detection. It can be seen from the test that the contrast and brightness adjustment based on the SAR image can have a positive effect on the target detection and the adjustment of the HSV has no significant effect on the result. Test result is shown in Figs. 6 and 7.

From Fig. 6, it can be seen that in the target detection of the original SAR image (a), the target area is not obvious in many target areas due to the small details of the image, which leads to the fact that the detection result is not particularly good. Adjust the contrast of the image before target detection, the result of the test after the enhancement is shown in image (b), Image (b) is more prominent around the target, so the detection effect is more significant. To further adjust the brightness of the image (a), image (c) obtains more significant results.

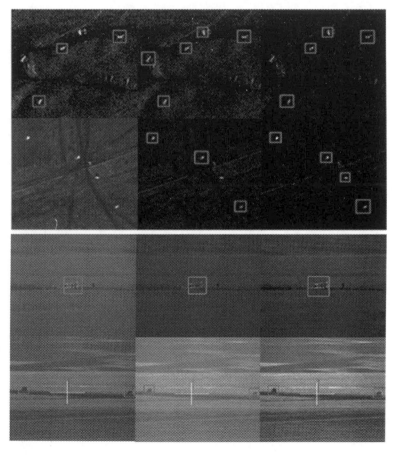

Fig. 6. Effect of contrast brightness adjustment on target detection, from left to right is (a) target detection of original image, (b) target detection of brightness enhancement image (c) target detection of both contrast and brightness enhancement image.

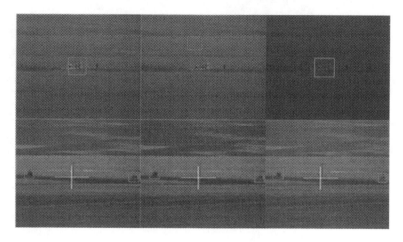

Fig. 7. Effect of HSV color space based enhancement on target detection

Table 1. Target detection before and after the image enhancement

Image enhancement method	Detection after the enhancement	Detection with origin
Bright adjustment	40	35
Contrast adjustment	38	35
Hue adjustment	36	35
Saturation adjustment	35	35
Value adjustment	34	35

We use another image in the data set that contains more targets for test, the following Table 1 the correct number of target detections before and after enhancement.

As can be seen from the table, the detection accuracy of the image can be increased by about 10% after contrast and brightness enhancement, but Saturation and chrominance enhancement have no significant effect on the target detection.

4 Conclusion

This paper introduces two image enhancement algorithms for target detection and recognition. By adjusting the contrast and brightness of the image, the dynamic range of the image brightness level can be enlarged, and the contrast of the image can be improved. We can also convert images to HSV color space to adjust and enhance the image's hue, saturation, and brightness. Experiments show that the enhancement of contrast and brightness of optical and SAR images can improve the efficiency of subsequent detection and recognition. Saturation and chrominance enhancement have no significant effect on target detection.

Acknowledgments. This research work is supported by the grant of Guangxi science and technology development project (No: AC16380124), the grant of Guangxi Science Foundation (No: 2017GXNSFAA198226), the grant of Guangxi Key Laboratory of Trusted Software of Guilin University of Electronic Technology (No: KX201601), the grant of Guangxi Colleges and Universities Key Laboratory of Intelligent Processing of Computer Images and Graphics of Guilin University of Electronic Technology (No: GIIP201602), and the grant of Innovation Project of GUET Graduate Education (2017YJCX55), the grant of Guangxi Colleges and Universities Key Laboratory of Intelligent Processing of Computer Images and Graphics (No. GIIP201602),the grant of Guangxi Key Laboratory of Trusted Software (No. kx201601), Guangxi Cooperative Innovation Center of cloud computing and Big Data, the grant of Guangxi Colleges and Universities Key Laboratory of cloud computing and complex systems (No. YD16E11), the grant of Guangxi Key Laboratory of cryptography and information security (GCIS201601, GCIS201602, GCIS201603).

References

1. Hao, Z.C., Wu, C., Yang, H., Zhu, M.: Image detail enhancement method based on multi-scale bilateral texture filter. J. Chin. Opt. **9**(4), 423–431 (2016)
2. Zimmerman, J.B., Pizer, S.M., Staab, E.V., et al.: An evaluation of the effectiveness of adaptive histogram equalization for contrast enhancement. J. IEEE Trans. Med. Imaging **7**(4), 304–312 (1988)
3. Wang, Q., Ward, R.: Fast image/video contrast enhancement based on WTHE. J. IEEE Trans. Consum. Electron. **53**(2), 757–764 (2007)
4. Yang, S., Oh, J.H., Park, Y.: Contrast enhancement using histogram equalization with bin underflow and bin overflow. In: Proceedings 2003 International Conference on Image Processing, Spain, pp. 881–884(2003)
5. Kim, Y.T.: Contrast enhancement using brightness preserving bi-histogram equalization. J. IEEE Trans. Cons. Electron. **43**(1), 1–8 (1997)
6. Kim, W.K., You, J.M., Jeong, J.: Contrast enhancement using histogram equalization based on logarithmic mapping. J. Opt. Eng. **51**(6), 1–10 (2012)
7. Fries, R., Modestino, J.: Image enhancement by stochastic homomorphic filtering. J. IEEE Trans. Acousties Speech Signal Process. **27**(6), 625–637 (1979)
8. Ein-Shoka, A.A., Kelash, H.M.: Enhancement of IR images using homomorphic filtering in fast discrete curvelet transform(FDCT). J. Int. J. Comput. Appl. **96**(8), 22–25 (2014)
9. Delac, K., Grgic, M., Kos, T.: Sub-image homomorphic filtering technique for improving facial identification under difficult illumination conditions. In: International Conference on Systems, Signals and Image Processing, Budapest, Hungary, pp. 95–98 (2006)

Image Filtering Enhancement

Zhen Guo[1,2], Hang Pan[1], Jinlong Chen[2], and Xianjun Chen[1,3(✉)]

[1] Guangxi Key Laboratory of Cryptography and Information Security,
Guilin University of Electronic Technology, Guilin 541004, Guangxi, China
hingini@126.com
[2] Key Laboratory of Intelligent Processing of Computer Image and Graphics,
Guilin University of Electronic Technology, Guilin 541004, Guangxi, China
[3] Information Engineering School, Haikou College of Economics,
Haikou 571127, Hainan, China

Abstract. With the development of science and technology, mankind has entered the information age. Image has become the main source of human access to information. However, in the actual process of image signal transmission, the loss and damage of data packet are inevitable due to the physical defects of the channel, which lead to a serious decline in the quality of the video stream. So it is necessary and even urgent now to do some research work on image enhancement technology. In this paper, the image enhancement algorithms that are commonly used, such as bilateral filtering algorithm, homomorphic filtering algorithm, are analyzed in image processing. In the design of the image enhancement, the best modeling and design schemes are chosen according to the comparison. The experimental results demonstrate that the bilateral filtering algorithm can effectively maintain the details of the image edges and make the image more smooth; the homomorphic filtering algorithm can effectively adjust the image gray range, so that the image details on the image area can be increased, and the algorithm can handle the image with inhomogeneous intensity. This work will lay a good foundation of further research.

Keywords: Image enhancement · Homomorphic filtering · Bilateral filtering

1 Introduction

With the advancement of technology and the increasing popularity of mobile terminals, people are increasingly demanding imaging systems, and they always hope to obtain high-resolution, high-definition images. However, the image quality is degraded due to various factors in the collection, transmission, compression, transformation and other processes [1]. For example, in different lighting environments, the brightness of the image may change; when the device is operated, jitter causes image shifting, etc., which may cause the details and textures in the image to be unclear. In practical applications, these problems will cause the readability of the image to decline, which also brings great difficulties to image processing methods such as image detection, feature information extraction and analysis [2]. In order to solve these problems, the image needs to be enhanced. Image enhancement process-ing is to enhance the useful information in the image. Its purpose is to extract the information hidden in the image or to improve the contrast of the image, to improve the quality and visual effect of the image, or to convert the image to be more suitable for human eye observation or machine Analyze the form of recognition to get more useful information from the image [3].

By adjusting the pixel gray value of the image, the degree of distortion of the image can be relieved to some extent. However, when dealing with some textures, borders, and other information, it is difficult to be effective, and it needs to be analyzed by using a near-field processing method. The image can be enhanced by adjusting the contrast between the pixel and the surrounding pixels in the image, which means that the filtering enhancement technique is required to be processed. By suppressing the low-frequency information by enhancing the high-frequency information by filtering, the details such as edges, lines, or textures where the gray value of the pixel greatly changes can be highlighted. For image applications, the overall or local characteristics of the image are purposefully emphasized, and the original unclear image becomes clear or emphasizes some interesting features. Extend the difference between different objects in the image and suppress uninteresting features to match the image with visual characteristics. Improving image quality enhances the effects of image interpretation and recognition for subsequent analysis and understanding of the image.

2   Image Enhancement Classification

Image enhancement can be divided into two categories: spatial domain and frequency domain.

2.1   Spatial Domain Filtering Enhancement

The spatial domain filtering technology has three kinds of consideration: (1) extracting edge information of original image. (2) the fuzzy component of the original image is weighted, and then superposed with the original image. (3) using a specified function, the original image is weighted so that the image is generated Sharpen or smooth effect. In the three operations, the space convolution technique is used, and the template is moved on the original image by the template, and the local operation is carried out block by block [4]. Assuming that the original image is $f(x, y)$, we can detect the edge information of the window by some way, $\nabla f(x, y)$, and then add it to the original image after weighted processing, and then:

$$g(\text{x,y}) = g(x, y) \pm K \cdot_\Delta f(x, y) \tag{1}$$

Where g(x, y) is the filtered image and K is a constant term.

There are already a variety of convolution filters available, such as sharpening (high pass) filters that help to highlight target contour and edge, line information, smoothing (low pass filters) to eliminate noise and excessive detail, non-linear mean filter. Various directional filters can enhance the different edges and streaks in the specified direction.

2.2   Frequency Domain Filtering Enhancement

Convolution theorem and Fourier transform are the basis of frequency domain filter enhancement. Which can be expressed as:

$$f(x, y) \xrightarrow{FFT} F(u, v) \rightarrow G(u, v) \xrightarrow{IFFT} f'(x, y) \qquad (2)$$

$$G(u, v) = F(u, v).H(u, v) \qquad (3)$$

Which $H(u, v)$ is a transfer function, its role is to suppress some frequencies in the Fourier transform but retain some other frequency, it is also known as the filter. Two types of filters are commonly used: one is a filter for attenuating high frequencies through high frequencies, called a "low-pass filter," and the other is a filter for attenuating low frequencies through high frequencies. It is a "high pass filter."

3   Image Enhancement Algorithm

3.1   Bilateral Filtering Algorithm Based on Spatial Domain

Bilateral filtering is an improvement over Gaussian filtering. Gauss filtering is a weighted average process of the whole image, and the value of each pixel is obtained by weighted averaging of other pixel values in the neighborhood itself. The specific process of Gauss filtering is to use a template or convolution to scan every pixel in the image, and use the weighted average gray value of pixels in the neighborhood to replace the value of the template center pixel. The Gauss filter only considers the proximity of the image space pixels. The following Fig. 1 is the effect of the parameters on the filtering effect in the Gauss filter [5].

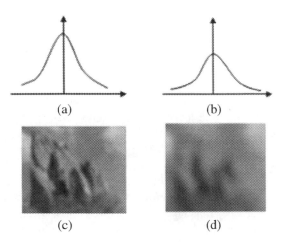

(a)   (b)

(c)   (d)

Fig. 1. Gaussian filter parameters: (a) α parameter value small, (b) α parameter value large, (c) Smoothness small, (d) Smoothness larger

$$GB[I]_\mathrm{p}= \sum_{q\in S} G_\delta(\|p - q\|)I_q \tag{4}$$

where α is the size of the sliding window. Compared with the Gaussian filter, the bilateral filter increases the effect of the gray value on the image, that is, if the pixel gray value of the neighborhood is closer to the gray value of the central pixel, the weight is added to the weight of the Gaussian filter relatively large weights. Conversely, if the grayscale difference is large, a small weight will be added to the position of the generated Gaussian template. Bilateral filtering is a kind of compromise which combines the image spatial proximity and the pixel similarity [6]. It takes the spatial information and the gray similarity into consideration to achieve the preserving edge from denoising. It has the characteristics of simple, non-iterative and local [7].

The pixel value g of the bilateral filter output (i, j) position depends on the weighted combination of the neighborhood pixel value f(k, l represents the neighbor-hood pixel position).

$$g(i,j) = \frac{\sum_{k,l} f(k,l) w(i,j,k,l)}{\sum_{k,l} w(i,j,k,l)} \tag{5}$$

$$w(i,j,k,l) = \exp\left(-\frac{(i-k)^2 + (j-l)^2}{2\sigma_d^2} - \frac{\|f(i,j) - f(k,l)\|^2}{2\sigma_d^2}\right) \tag{6}$$

The weight coefficient w(i, j, k, l) depends on the product of the domain kernel and the domain r, The following Fig. 3 (b) and (d) is the effect of bilateral filtering, in which the neighborhood diameter is 20, the value of the color space filter δ is 35, and the value of the filter δ in the coordinate space is 35.

Gaussian filter parameters are shown in Fig. 1.

3.2   Homomorphic Filtering Algorithm Based on Frequency Domain

Homomorphic filtering is an image processing method that combines frequency and spatial gray transform. It uses the illumination/reflectivity model of the image as the basis of frequency domain processing to improve the quality of the image by compressing the brightness range and enhancing the contrast. Due to the small changes in illumination can be seen as the low-frequency components of the image, while the reflectivity is the high-frequency components. By dealing with the effect of illuminance and reflectance on pixel gray value respectively, the image quality can be improved and the details of the shaded area can be revealed, which makes the image process more accords with the non-linear characteristic of the human eye to the brightness response and avoids the direct Distortion of Fourier transform processing [8]. Homomorphic filtering is a kind of frequency domain filtering. Its function is to adjust the gray range of the image and enhance the image detail of the dark area by eliminating the problem of uneven illumination on the image, without losing the image detail of the bright area [9]. The Illumination-Reflection model can be used to develop a frequency-domain process that changes the appearance of an image by simultaneously performing grayscale range compression and contrast enhancement.

The basic principle of homomorphic filtering is that the pixel gray value is regarded as the product of illumination and reflectivity, that is, the image $f(x, y)$ consists of the product of the illumination component $i(x, y)$ and the reflection component $r(x, y)$.

$$f(x, y) = i(x, y)r(x, y)$$
$$DFT[\ln f(x, y)] = DFT[\ln i(x, y)] + DFT[\ln r(x, y)] \quad (7)$$

The illumination component, $i(x, y)$, reflects the average brightness of the image. The data changes are usually flat. So the illumination component mainly occupies the low frequency region of the image spectrum. The reflection component reflects the dramatic changes in the image, such as isolated noise, $r(x, y)$ edge of target and background and other false edges and image details are included in the reflection component, thus constitute the high-frequency part of the spectrum image. Do Fourier transform of the image to get its corresponding frequency domain representation [10].

The low frequency part of the image logarithmic Fourier transform mainly corresponds to the illuminance component, and the high frequency part mainly corresponds to the reflection component [3, 11]. Design a frequency domain filter $H(u, v)$ logarithmic image frequency domain filtering. In order to suppress the low-frequency brightness component and enhance the high-frequency reflection component, the filter H should be a high-pass filter, but can not completely suppress the low-frequency component, only suitable suppression. Therefore, the homomorphic filter generally adopts the following form:

$$H(u, v) = (\gamma_H - \gamma_L)H_{hp}(u, v) + \gamma_L \quad (8)$$

which $\gamma_H < 1, \gamma_L > 1$ control the scope of the filter. H_{hp} usually high-pass filter, such as Gaussian high-pass filter, Butterworth high-pass filter, Laplacian filter. The filter function tends to attenuate the contribution of low frequency (illumination) while enhancing the contribution of high frequency reflection. The end result is simultaneous dynamic range compression and contrast enhancement. Figure 2 shows the cross section of the filter function.

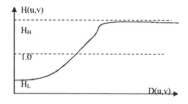

Fig. 2. Cross-sectional view of the filter function

4   Experimental Comparison

The bilateral filtering effect is shown in Fig. 3.

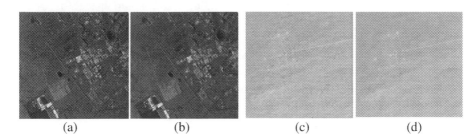

| (a) | (b) | (c) | (d) |

Fig. 3. Bilateral filtering effect, (a) and (c) is the original, (b) and (d) is the corresponding renderings.

It can be seen from Fig. 3(a) and (b) that the bilateral filter preserves the image edge details and other information well and smoothes the edge of the image. From Fig. 3(c) and (d), there is no obvious change before and after using the bilateral filter to process the image.

The homomorphic filter effect is shown in Fig. 4.

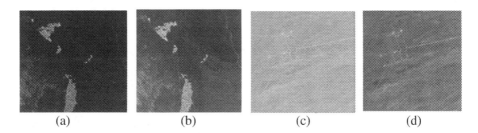

| (a) | (b) | (c) | (d) |

Fig. 4. The homomorphic filtering effect, (a) and (c) is the original, (b) and (d) is the corresponding renderings.

It can be seen from Fig. 4(a) and (b), the original image is unevenly illuminated. After the homomorphic filtering, the gray level of the image is adjusted to eliminate the problem of uneven illumination in the image and enhance the image detail of the dark area without losing the Image details. The detail of the image has been significantly enhanced, and in line with the characteristics of human visual observation. You can see from Fig. 4(c) and (d) image processing effect contrast is very obvious, the processed image to display the image invisible part, display the details of the image features, image processing is superior to the original.

5 Conclusion

With the method of image enhancement technology, we can extract image features effectively, and make it easier for everyone to understand and recognize. This paper is going to look into the different advantages between bilateral filtering algorithm and homomorphic filtering algorithm, based on those former studies on image processing. The experiment results show that bilateral filtering algorithm can effectively maintain the image edge details and make the image smoother; homomorphic filtering algorithm can effectively adjust the gray range for uneven shading image, the image area on the image details can be increased, and as far as possible to maintain the image details of bright region. Aiming at improving the effect of image enhancement, we will devote oneself to the development of image processing in the future ceaselessly.

Acknowledgments. This research work is supported by the grant of Guangxi science and technology development project (No: AC16380124), the grant of Guangxi Science Foundation (No:2017GXNSFAA198226),the grant of Guangxi Key Laboratory of Cryptography & Information Security of Guilin University of Electronic Technology (No: GCIS201604), the grant of Guangxi Colleges and Universities Key Laboratory of Intelligent Processing of Computer Images and Graphics of Guilin University of Electronic Technology (No:GIIP201602), and the grant of Innovation Project of GUET Graduate Education (2017YJCX55).Guangxi Key Laboratory of Trusted Software (No kx201601), Guangxi Cooperative Innovation Center of cloud computing and Big Data, Guangxi Colleges and Universities Key Laboratory of cloud computing and complex systems (No YD16E11), Guangxi Key Laboratory of cryptography and information security (GCIS201601, GCIS201602, GCIS201603).

References

1. Xiaochen, W.: Research on Image Quality Evaluation Based on Machine Learning. Tianjin University (2016)
2. Daoqing, S.: Image enhancement algorithm research. Wuhan University of Science and Technology (2007)
3. Chuxia, C.: Image filtering and edge detection and enhancement of technology of HeFei University of Technology (2009)
4. ZhiQun, Z., Li, C.: Application of retinex algorithm in satellite remote sensing image enhancement. J. Laser J. **37**(10), 106–110 (2016)
5. Junfeng, L.: Fast realization of bilateral filtering algorithm and its application in image processing. Southern Medical University (2013)
6. Rong, W.: Image enhancement algorithm. Yangtze University (2014)
7. Elad, M.: On the origin of the bilateral filter and ways to improve it. IEEE Press (2002)
8. Chun-ning, C., Yan-jie, W.: enhancement of image contrast by homomorphic filtering in frequency domain. J. Microcomput. Inf. **06**, 264–266 (2007)
9. Lin, M., Ning, Y.: An analysis of digital image enhancement algorithm. J. Transp. Sci. Technol. **13**(01), 122–125 (2011)
10. Bo, W.: Application of filtering algorithm in image enhancement. Comput. Simul. **30**(03), 364–367 (2013)
11. Chunxiang, L., Hongtong, L.: Real-time image enhancement algorithm. Chin. Opt. Appl. Opt. **2**(05), 395–401 (2009)

Random Forest Based Gesture Segmentation from Depth Image

Renjun Tang[1,2], Hang Pan[1], Xianjun Chen[1,3(✉)], and Jinlong Chen[2]

[1] Guangxi Key Laboratory of Trusted Software,
Guilin University of Electronic Technology, Guilin 541004, Guangxi, China
hingini@126.com
[2] Key Laboratory of Intelligent Processing of Computer Image and Graphics,
Guilin University of Electronic Technology, Guilin 541004, Guangxi, China
[3] Information Engineering School, Haikou College of Economics,
Haikou 571127, Hainan, China

Abstract. Gesture image segmentation is a challenge task due to the high degree of freedom of human gestures, large differences in shape and high flexibility, traditional pattern recognition and image processing methods are not effective in gesture detection. The traditional image segmentation based on the detection of skin color and the image of the depth image are limited by the effects of ambient light, skin color difference and image depth variation, resulting in unsatisfactory results. Therefore, we propose a hand gesture depth image segmentation method based on random forest. The method learns the gesture image feature representation of the depth image by supervising learning. Experiments show that the proposed method segments the gesture s' pixels from the backgrounds area of the depth image. The proposed method potential has widely usages in gesture tracking, gesture recognition and human computer interaction.

Keywords: Random forest · Gesture segmentation · Depth image

1 Introduction

Gesture is a kind of natural interaction, through it human beings can express interactive information of various meanings. In recent years, the pursuit of a more natural way of interaction is the trend of development in the field of human-computer interaction. Therefore, gesture interaction technology is also more and more people's attention. In the study of gesture interaction work, the most critical is the gesture image segmentation technology. Gesture Image Segmentation is to separate the part of the human gesture from the background of the image, which is the basis for further research on gesture recognition, gesture understanding and gesture tracking.

Gesture segmentation is a hugely challenging task. On the one hand, human gestures are in a high degree of freedom, flexibility and non-rigid body. The human hand has about 20–25 degrees of freedom [1], and each degree of freedom has about 1–3 dimensions. Conventional template matching, edge detection, skin color model and other image recognition algorithms are not able to completely separate all the gestures pixels from the background or other parts of the body. Such traditional image recognition algorithms require complex and complicated manual feature design. The artificial characteristics of light conditions, background complexity, random noise handling ability is weak. On the other hand, the existence of gesture occlusion deepens the difficulty of gesture segmentation. In the past, most research on gesture segmentation has centered around the color images captured by conventional RGB cameras. Gesture segmentation is not only sensitive to changes of illumination conditions and background interference, but also can only obtain the result of 2D plane segmentation. If the 3D image is to be reconstructed from the gesture pixels of the two-dimensional image, the need to carry out in-depth study of space coordinate transformation and three-dimensional reconstruction algorithm undoubtedly increases the difficulty and depth of the research work.

With the popularity of depth image sensing technology, it has become very convenient to use a depth camera to acquire a depth image. Recently, some researchers have done research on gesture image segmentation in depth images. Our proposed method based on random forest segmentation of the gesture image is applied to the depth image, and the part of the depth image belonging to the gesture pixel is separated from the background. Our method is mainly divided into three parts: (1) a training database for generating a gesture depth image based on RGB images; (2) a method for calculating pixel depths of gestures; and (3) training a random forest model for depth pixel classification. In summary, we trained random forest models to learn the characteristic representation of the depth pixel of the gesture and completed the segmentation of the gesture image on the depth image, which effectively solves the problem that the threshold of the skin color model is difficult to be adjusted on the RGB image. And it is not necessary to lock the distance between the gesture and the depth camera. This method can accomplish the task of gesture image segmentation well under various scenes.

2   Related Work

As the basic work of gesture recognition based on computer vision, gesture image segmentation plays an important role in human body detection methods. In the past ten years, gesture image segmentation, as the foundation of the new generation of human-computer interaction technology, And many researchers at home and abroad, many research institutes such as Royal Institute of Technology in Sweden, University of Ottawa in Canada, International Islamic University in Malaysia, Schengen State University and so on have made a great contribution to the work of gesture image segmentation [2–6], their research advances the development and progress of gesture image segmentation.

Due to the complexity of the gesture itself, the current gesture image segmentation methods mainly include feature-based detection methods, template matching-based methods, machine learning detection methods based on Adaboost, and video-based detection methods. As early as 2002, Lars et al. Proposed the detection of gesture based on multi-scale hierarchical color features. This method can extract the multi-scale color features and detect and track the position of the hand using the particle filter algorithm. The method can be Real-time gesture tracking detection, but the calculation is relatively large; Chen et al. proposed a combination of statistical analysis and syntax analysis of real-time gesture recognition method, which uses Harr features and AdaBoost trained classifier to detect gestures; Manresaye et al proposed a hand palmprint image from RGB space to HSL space, and then use the skin pixel probability statistical model for coarse palms segmentation, and achieved good detection [7]; Chen et al. proposed a based on the HMM (Hidden Markov Model) model is proposed. This method uses the gesture of two-color skin model and the background adaptive model to segment the gesture, and uses the Fourier descriptor to characterize the gesture outline, and then realizes the segmentation of the real-time gesture and the background [8] Stereoscopic video input method, by setting two or more imaginary points, the movement of the gesture Trace multi-directional data acquisition and analysis [9], but these methods cannot solve problems due to complex conditions that cause light pollution detected background low.

After Microsoft launched Kinect, a new type of somatosensory peripheral in 2010, it brought a wider range of ideas for gesture image segmentation based on depth images. Gesture segmentation can be achieved using different depth values between the gesture area and the background area. According to the human body each part has a closer depth value of this feature, each pixel in the depth image clustering, and finally using the gesture shape and other priori knowledge to extract gestures containing the clustering to achieve gesture image segmentation [10]. The method of combining the depth image and the color image is used to apply the frame difference method to the depth map [11]; Tang et al. Apply the skin color method to the depth image and change the RGB three-dimensional vector of each pixel to an RGBD four-dimensional (Where D represents the depth value) to segment the gesture area [12]. Di et al. Use the skin color algorithm and the threshold segmentation method based on the depth image to map the thresholded pixels into the color image. If the mapped Point corresponding to the color is retained, otherwise removed. Although the above method has made some achievements in gesture image segmentation, it still has some limitations in solving the dynamic changes of gestures and the change of illumination conditions. Inspired by the work in [13], this paper designs a random forest model. Each node in the model evaluates the depth pixel value of a given pixel, the relationship between the depth pixel value of the offset pixel and the depth threshold to determine whether the particular pixel belongs to the gesture.

3   Gesture Segmentation from Depth Images

The summarized process of the proposed method is shown in Fig. 1. The three main steps of the method will be described in detail below.

3.1   Gesture Marking Based on HSV Color Space

Color space is a mathematical representation of color that is decomposed and represented in different dimensions and is a mathematical representation of color. The Hue, Saturation, Value (HSV) color model is a color space created by AR Smith in 1978

Regardless of brightness and saturation, each color has a corresponding hue value in the HSV color space, so different colors can be split using the hue dimension in the HSV color space. Ambient lighting often changes so bright and saturated colors may

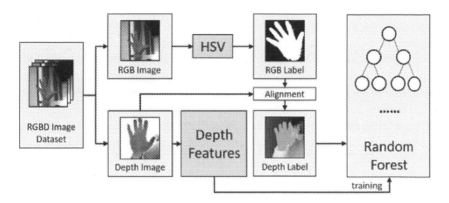

Fig. 1. The overall of gesture image pixels segmentation process.

change in brightness and saturation, but the hue generally does not change. So red color is chosen to mark gestures in RGB images, and further based on the H dimension in the HSV color space Red for segmentation.

First RGB normalization, then R, G, B ∈ [0,1], from the RGB space to HSV space transformation as follows:

$$V = \max(R, G, B). \tag{1}$$

$$S = \begin{cases} 0 & if\ V = 0 \\ \frac{V - \min(R,G,B)}{V} & else \end{cases}. \tag{2}$$

$$r = \frac{V - R}{V - \min(R, G, B)}, g = \frac{V - G}{V - \min(R, G, B)}, b = \frac{V - B}{V - \min(R, G, B)}. \tag{3}$$

In order to establish a good gesture marking model, the red-labeled gesture images in color images under various environmental conditions were further collected, and a total of 91 facial color regions of 91 pieces of hands were collected, totaling 5910513 pixels. After calculation and statistics, H values of most histograms are uniform and concentrated on the left about 120–180. From the equation of HSV to RGB space transformation, it can be seen that the H value distribution represents the color of the gesture mark in the range of 120–180, and for a very small amount of H value distributed in other areas, considering the extremely small probability density and the actual situation, it can be determined These H values are all noise. In order to make the selected threshold have a good anti-noise ability, the H threshold of skin color segmentation is selected from the experimental measurements to 126–168. Using this range, most of the gesture regions can be segmented and have good anti-noise performance.

3.2   Local Depth Shift Comparison Feature Extraction

The depth image is also called the distance image, and its pixels reflect the distance information between the target object and the camera. The depth image is not affected by light and environment changes and can directly reflect the three-dimensional information of the object, which greatly simplifies the three-dimensional reconstruction, recognition and positioning of the object. For the convenience of gesture recognition based on depth images, Shotton et al. Use the depth of field offset pixels as the feature. This feature utilizes the random distribution of offset pixels, that is, the three-dimensional information that reflects the local surface of the depth image, and links the different local spaces, Has a good recognition effect. On this basis, combined with the characteristics of the gesture, the local depth offset is used to compare features.

Local Area Acquisition. Due to the large scale of the image, if the feature extraction is performed on the entire image, the time complexity is high. Therefore, the HSV color space is first used to obtain the color region in RGB space, and the method based on convolution neural network classification [14] The determination of the color area of the gesture and the further reduction of the size of the image of the local area of the gesture. Finally, the depth image area corresponding to the RGB space is taken as the local area to be processed.

Feature Extraction. Assuming that the depth image is I and any pixel is $I(x, y)$, the following equation is used.

$$F_{(u,v)}(x, y) = I(x + \Delta u, y + \Delta v) - I(x, y). \tag{4}$$

Where: $I(x, y)$ is the depth value of the current pixel; u, v is the horizontal and vertical offset; Δ is the threshold and controls the offset distance; $F_{(u,v)}(x, y)$ Is the offset characteristic of the pixel. In the next section of this article, we detail how to train a random Forest Gesture Pixel Classifier using local depth-shift comparison features.

3.3   Training

Random forests consist of many decision trees. These decision trees are formed in a random way. There is no correlation between trees in a random forest. When the test data into the random forest, in fact, is to make each decision tree classification, and finally take all the decision tree that the most classification results of the type. Random Decision Forest has proven to be an efficient multi-class classifier. Random Decision Forests are a synthesis of all decision trees, each containing branches and leaf nodes. In order to realize the segmentation of the human hand and the background in the depth image, we adopt the random decision-making forest classifier to train the above-mentioned features. The trained classifier classifies the image by pixel.

Training the Random Forest. Random decision forest has been proved to be a fast and effective classifier. Each branch of each tree in the random forest is composed of a feature $F_{(u,v)}$ and a threshold ε, and the pixel p in image I are classified, Starting from the root node and iteratively evaluating it, comparing the left and right branches with ε thresholds, classifying them by $p_t(c|I, p)$ training at the leaf nodes of the tree t, and storing the label c beyond the gesture part. Average all the trees in the forest for final classification training (Fig. 2).

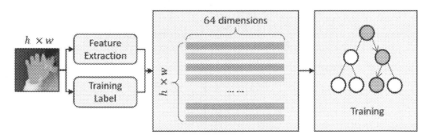

Fig. 2. The training process of random forest model. The gray squares represent the pixels marked as the background, and the green squares represent the pixels marked as gestures. (Color figure online)

Random Decision Forest Algorithm: Random Forest Each tree is trained on a different set of randomly selected sample images. Randomly select 2000 pixels in the acquired local gesture area as the training sample set D to ensure uniform distribution of the gesture parts, and further randomly select n features as training feature sets F for each pixel. Select the sample, after the feature. Each tree T in the forest is trained according to the following algorithm:

① Calculate the information gain $G(\emptyset)$ of each feature in the feature set F for the training sample set D, and select the feature F with the largest information gain;

$$G(\emptyset) = H(D) - \sum_{i=1}^{n} \frac{|D_i|}{|D|} H(D_i) \tag{5}$$

② If the information gain of F_g is less than the threshold ε, then T is a single-node tree, and the class C_k with the largest instance in the sample set D is used as the class label of this node to return T;

③ Otherwise, for each possible value f_i of F_g divide the sample set D into several non-empty sub-sets D_i according to $F_g = f_i$, and mark the class with the largest number of instances in D_i as a mark. And by the node and its child nodes constitute a tree T, return T;

④ For the i th sub-node, D_i is the training set and $\{F - F_g\}$ is the feature set. Recursively call 1–3 steps to obtain the subtree T_i and return T_i.

Testing the Random Forest. For the test sample, classify the current pixel P, starting at the root node of the tree, obtain the characteristics of the current pixel by using Eq. (6), and choose whether to be left or right based on the size of the threshold. For a tree T until it reaches the leaf node, the posterior distribution of the gesture part is stored $P(l|v)$. The final distribution is an average of these decision tree distributions.

$$P(l|v) = \frac{1}{N}\sum_{t}^{N} P_t(l|v).\tag{6}$$

N is the number of decision trees in a random forest. Gesture pixel markers can be obtained by the maximum posteriori probability:

$$l^* = argmax_l P(l|v).\tag{7}$$

4   Experiment

In order to study the influence of parameters such as number of training images, pixel feature dimension, number of decision trees and depth of decision tree on the performance of gesture image segmentation in random forest model, we designed a series of control experiments. The CPU of our experimental machine is the Intel i7 6700K. When training a random forest model, we only use the CPU for calculation. In order to facilitate visual observation and comparison, we randomized forest classification results of depth images into binary images. After random forest classifier model judged as pixels belonging to the gesture, the pixel value was set as 1. The white part of the result image. We choose nine training images outside the training set to experiment and fix each depth pixel eigenvector length of 64 dimensions, random forest model segmentation effect is shown in Fig. 3.

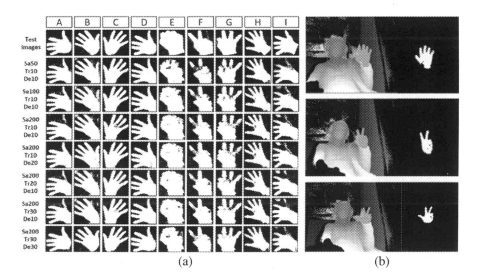

(a)   (b)

Fig. 3. (a) Show some experimental results, **Sa** represents the number of training images, **Tr** represents the number of decision trees in the random forest model, and **De** represents the depth of the decision tree. For the convenience of visual comparisons, we will zoom in on different areas of different sizes to the same size. (b) Real-time depth image gesture segmentation

Figure 3 cannot quantify the effect of gesture image segmentation. Therefore, we design Eq. (9) to evaluate the accuracy of the model. Equation (8) shows the degree of coincidence between the predicted image and the real labeled image.

$$Acc = \frac{\sum_u \sum_v I(u, v) \cdot G(u, v)}{\sum_u \sum_v G(u, v)}. \tag{8}$$

Here, $I(u, v)$ represents the prediction result image of the random forest classifier model, and its pixel value is given by Eq. (9). $G(u, v)$ represents the real marked test image, whose pixel value can be described as Eq. (9).

Table 1. The accuracy of random forest model gesture segmentation experiment. A to I correspond to 9 test images in Fig. 3.

Parameters			Accuracy									
Sa	Tr	De	A	B	C	D	E	F	G	H	I	Ave.
50	10	10	90.34	89.29	94.92	93.63	87.46	87.24	90.40	90.79	85.55	89.96
		20	96.59	97.44	**98.90**	98.08	85.03	86.03	89.56	91.20	86.16	92.11
		30	99.76	99.65	99.66	**99.95**	82.00	83.62	88.19	90.30	84.61	91.97
	20	10	90.74	90.08	**95.09**	93.80	86.99	87.39	90.24	91.65	84.51	90.05
		20	96.61	97.93	**98.88**	98.42	86.95	86.60	90.23	92.13	86.31	92.67
		30	96.63	97.78	**98.96**	97.83	84.83	83.58	89.47	91.95	85.62	91.85
	30	10	90.63	90.44	**94.70**	93.78	87.87	87.54	91.06	91.07	84.65	90.19
		20	96.65	97.91	**98.90**	98.13	86.14	87.36	90.44	92.61	86.25	92.71
		30	99.96	99.76	99.82	**99.97**	85.74	84.89	89.72	92.17	85.84	93.10
100	10	10	89.64	87.91	**94.51**	93.71	89.64	87.91	**94.51**	93.71	88.05	91.07
		20	95.37	96.59	**98.53**	97.22	88.61	87.81	90.78	92.60	87.41	92.77
		30	99.69	99.67	99.69	**99.83**	85.88	84.65	89.45	92.23	86.02	93.01
	20	10	90.03	88.40	**94.41**	93.83	90.60	88.55	89.68	90.99	84.11	90.07
		20	95.48	96.58	**98.57**	97.49	88.24	87.93	90.77	92.97	86.93	92.77
		30	**99.93**	99.77	99.76	**99.93**	87.95	87.63	89.88	92.67	87.45	93.89
	30	10	90.08	88.96	**94.80**	93.37	88.64	88.87	90.78	91.28	84.74	90.17
		20	95.41	96.55	**98.57**	97.37	87.98	88.30	90.74	93.44	87.38	92.86
		30	99.96	99.80	99.83	**99.97**	86.79	86.81	90.77	93.20	86.97	93.79
200	10	10	87.18	84.55	93.19	**93.54**	92.06	89.05	90.29	90.34	84.59	89.42
		20	94.48	95.25	**97.68**	96.87	88.46	83.23	93.92	93.24	87.04	92.24
		30	99.44	99.55	99.69	**99.73**	86.49	88.59	89.88	91.72	85.87	93.44
	20	10	88.29	83.80	**94.33**	93.60	93.11	89.88	90.85	90.93	83.91	89.86
		20	94.70	95.34	**97.83**	96.77	91.24	89.89	92.42	92.89	87.74	93.20
		30	99.56	99.43	99.74	**99.83**	89.88	89.86	91.84	92.74	86.60	94.39
	30	10	88.70	84.33	**93.77**	93.49	92.37	90.15	90.50	91.05	84.38	89.86
		20	94.89	95.34	**97.82**	97.03	90.58	90.67	92.43	93.24	88.36	93.37
		30	99.48	99.61	99.78	**99.81**	89.61	89.63	92.11	93.10	88.29	**94.60**

$$I(u, v) = \begin{cases} 1, & \text{If the pixel } I(u, v) \text{ is classified as a pixel of gesture.} \\ 0, & \text{else} \end{cases} \tag{9}$$

$$G(u, v) = \begin{cases} 1, & \text{if pixel } G(u, v) \text{ belongs to gesture.} \\ 0, & \text{else} \end{cases} \tag{10}$$

We use the nine test images in Fig. 3 for experiments and Eq. (8) to evaluate the predictions of the random forest model. The results of the experiments are shown in the following table.

From the data in Table 1, we can draw the following conclusions: 1. When the number of training images is the same, increasing the number and depth of trees in the random forest model can improve the accuracy of gesture segmentation, but the promotion effect is limited; 2. Increasing the number of training images can effectively improve the accuracy of gesture classification accuracy; 3. the quality of training image sets has a greater impact on the segmentation accuracy. According to our observation, our model performs better on the test images C and D because there are more images in the training image set similar to the test images C and D. However, there are fewer images similar to the test images E and I, so the accuracy of these two types of images is lower.

5   Summary

Gesture segmentation is an important foundation of gesture recognition, gesture understanding and gesture interaction. Its effect has a direct impact on the next step. In view of the unsatisfactory segmentation result caused by the inherent characteristics of high human hand gestures such as high degree of freedom, large shape difference and high flexibility, this paper presents a method for gesture segmentation from depth images based on random forest. Experiments show that the method has good accuracy and robustness. This method uses the rapid classification ability of random forest to classify the comparative characteristics of the depth-displacement of gestures, and realizes the segmentation of gestures and backgrounds. In order to improve the speed of segmentation, this paper first obtains the local area where the gesture is located, which is helpful to reduce the data processing capacity, meets the real-time requirement of human-hand segmentation, and achieves good experimental results. Although the proposed algorithm is robust to the large changes in the degrees of freedom of gestures, there are still some problems to be solved. For example, holding an object in the hand may result in a small number of pixel misclassifications because the depth of the object being held is similar to that of a finger. The next step will be to segment the depth information in the occlusion conditions may be wrong, further combined with the optical image of the color, texture segmentation, in order to achieve a more accurate gesture of the target.

Acknowledgments. This research work is supported by the grant of Guangxi science and technology development project (No: AC16380124), the grant of Guangxi Science Foundation (No: 2017GXNSFAA198226), the grant of Guangxi Key Laboratory of Trusted Software of Guilin University of Electronic Technology (No: KX201513), the grant of Guangxi Colleges and

Universities Key Laboratory of Intelligent Processing of Computer Images and Graphics of Guilin University of Electronic Technology (No: GIIP201602), and the grant of Innovation Project of GUET Graduate Education (2018YJCX43).

References

1. Erol, A., Bebis, G., Nicolescu, M., Boyle, R.D., Twombly, X.: Vision-based hand pose estimation: a review. Comput. Vis. Image Underst. **108**(1–2), 52–73 (2007)
2. Bretzner, L., Laptev, I., Lindeberg, T.: Hand gesture recognition using multi-scale colour features, hierarchical models and particle filtering. In: Proceedings of the Fifth IEEE International Conference on Automatic Face and Gesture Recognition, 2002, (pp. 423–428). IEEE (2002)
3. Chen, Q., Georganas, N.D., Petriu, E.M.: Real-time vision-based hand gesture recognition using haar-like features. In: Proceedings of the 2007 Instrumentation and Measurement Technology Conference. IMTC 2007, pp. 1–6. IEEE (2007)
4. Bilal, S., Akmeliawati, R., El Salami, M.J., Shafie, A.A.: A hybrid method using haar-like and skin-color algorithm for hand posture detection, recognition and tracking. In: 2010 International Conference on Mechatronics and Automation (ICMA), pp. 934–939. IEEE (2010)
5. Jo, Y.G., Lee, J.Y., Kang, H.: Segmentation tracking and recognition based on foreground-background absolute features, simplified SIFT, and particle filters. In: IEEE Congress on Evolutionary Computation, 2006. CEC 2006, pp. 1279–1284. IEEE (2006)
6. Hong, H., Zhu, X.: A human hand-image detection based on skin-color and circular degree. In: 10th ACIS International Conference on Software Engineering, Artificial Intelligences, Networking and Parallel/Distributed Computing, 2009. SNPD 2009, pp. 373–376. IEEE (2009)
7. Manresa, C., Varona, J., Mas, R., Perales, F.J.: Hand tracking and gesture recognition for human-computer interaction. ELCVIA Electron. Lett. Comput. Vis. Image Anal. **5**(3), 96–104 (2005)
8. Chen, F.S., Fu, C.M., Huang, C.L.: Hand gesture recognition using a real-time tracking method and hidden Markov models. Image Vis. Comput. **21**(8), 745–758 (2003)
9. Velloso, M.L.F., Carneiro, T.A., de Souza, F.J.: Unsupervised change detection using fuzzy entropy principle. In: Proceedings of the 2004 IEEE International Geoscience and Remote Sensing Symposium, 2004. IGARSS 2004, vol. 4, pp. 2550–2553. IEEE (2004)
10. Malassiotis, S., Aifanti, N., Strintzis, M.G.: A gesture recognition system using 3D data. In: Proceedings of the First International Symposium on 3D Data Processing Visualization and Transmission 2002, pp. 190–193. IEEE (2002)
11. Sohn, M.-K., Kim, D.-J., Kim, H.: Hand part classification using single depth images. In: Jawahar, C.V., Shan, S. (eds.) ACCV 2014. LNCS, vol. 9009, pp. 253–261. Springer, Cham (2015). https://doi.org/10.1007/978-3-319-16631-5_19
12. Tang, M.: Recognizing hand gestures with Microsoft's Kinect. Department of Electrical Engineering of Stanford University, Palo Alto (2011)
13. Tompson, J., Stein, M., Lecun, Y., Perlin, K.: Real-time continuous pose recovery of human hands using convolutional networks. ACM Trans. Graph. (ToG) **33**(5), 169 (2014)
14. Neverova, N., Wolf, C., Taylor, G.W., Nebout, F.: Hand segmentation with structured convolutional learning. In: Asian Conference on Computer Vision, pp. 687–702. Springer, Cham (2014)

Deep Learning

DL-GSA: A Deep Learning Metaheuristic Approach to Missing Data Imputation

Ayush Garg, Deepika Naryani, Garvit Aggarwal, and Swati Aggarwal$^{(\boxtimes)}$

Division of Computer Engineering, Netaji Subhas Institute of Technology,
University of Delhi, New Delhi, India
ayushgarg1804@gmail.com, naryanideepika10@gmail.com, gravity0905@gmail.com,
swati1178@gmail.com

Abstract. Incomplete data has emerged as a prominent problem in the fields of machine learning, big data and various other academic studies. Due to the surge in deep learning techniques for problem-solving, in this paper, authors have proposed a deep learning-metaheuristic approach to combat the problem of imputing missing data. The proposed approach (DL-GSA) makes use of the nature inspired metaheuristic, Gravitational search algorithm, in combination with a deep-autoencoder and performs better than existing methods in terms of both accuracy and time. Owing to these improvements, DL-GSA has wider applications in both time and accuracy sensitive areas like imputation of scientific and research datasets, data analysis, machine learning and big data.

Keywords: Autoencoder · Missing at random
Missing data imputation · Gravitational search algorithm
Missing completely at random

1   Introduction

In educational and psychological studies, data has been found missing at a rate of 15% to 20% [5]. Further, [16] surveyed quantitative studies in 11 journals from 1998–2004 and found that 36% of studies boasted of no missing data, 48% of them comprised of missing data, and about 16% cannot be determined. Such dominant presence of incomplete information in studies makes the induced results less specific, and their extensibility decreases hysterically. Missing data in datasets used in various fields like medicine, production, transport and law & order presents various challenges. Ignoring such cases might lead to the loss of information which in turn decreases statistical relevance of results. Hence, missing data imputation is a binding factor for accurate research results as well as careful data analysis.

It is imperative to know the categories in which missing data falls, before working on its imputation. There are three main mechanisms governing the relationship between the missing and observed values [13]. A variable is missing completely at random (MCAR) if the probability of it being missing is the same

© Springer International Publishing AG, part of Springer Nature 2018
Y. Tan et al. (Eds.): ICSI 2018, LNCS 10942, pp. 513–521, 2018.
https://doi.org/10.1007/978-3-319-93818-9_49

for all units. However, if data is missing at random (MAR), the cause of the missing data may have a relationship with the observed values of other variables. Data is missing not at random (MNAR) when the value of the variable that's missing is related to the reason why it is missing.

One of the earliest approaches to combat missing data dates back to 1977 when Dempster et al. [4] presented the EM algorithm, an iterative algorithm for efficiently predicting the missing data. In [18], the authors introduced a model of multiple imputation and categorized the missing patterns into three categories - MAR, MCAR and MNAR. More recently, researchers have investigated the applicability of several approaches which majorly revolve around neural networks, regression [2,14] and genetic algorithms [1,12,15].

An attempt has also been made to use swarm optimization algorithms combined with deep autoencoder network to impute missing values in high dimensional datasets [10,11]. In this paper, authors propose a novel method DL-GSA in which a deep autoencoder network is trained in combination with the GSA algorithm (DL-GSA) and its performance is compared to that of other similarly proposed schemes. From experimentation, it has been found that the recent best deep-learning hybrid approach [11] takes approximately two times the time required by the proposed approach and is less accurate.

2   Proposed Approach

2.1   Motivation

The deep learning hybrid techniques to impute missing data suffer from the shortcomings of either having a high estimation time, which is the time required to obtain accurate estimates for the missing data entries, or have a low accuracy of estimation of missing data. The objective of this research is to shorten the estimation time while improving accuracy to make the algorithm more useful for large datasets.

2.2   Background

The following sections briefly discuss the methods and techniques used in this paper.

Restricted Boltzmann Machine (RBM): RBM is an undirected network representing a probability distribution in a parameterized graphical model based upon Markov Random Field (MRF) [6]. It represents input data using m visible units $V = (V_1, ... V_m)$, and n hidden units $H = (H_1, ..., H_n)$. The features V have values $v \in [0,1]^{m+n}$, while the values of H, $h \in \{0,1\}^{m+n}$ [6]. The following equation depicts the energy function of Gibbs Distribution in scalar form:

$$E(v,h) = -\sum_{i=1}^{n}\sum_{j=1}^{m} w_{ij} h_i v_j - \sum_{j=1}^{m} b_j v_j - \sum_{i=1}^{n} c_i h_i. \qquad (1)$$

where b and c are the bias terms for the visible and hidden variables respectively and w_{ij} is a real valued weight between V_j and H_i.

To train RBM models, Contrastive Divergence algorithm utilises the observation that running a Markov chain for just a few steps can be sufficient for obtaining estimates of log-likelihood gradient [6].

Autoencoder (AE): An artificial neural network trained to replicate its input at the output layer is known as an autoencoder. It maps the input vector x to an encoded or hidden representation by using a mapping function [8] of the form

$$f_\theta(x) = \Phi(Wx + b). \tag{2}$$

where, θ comprises of W, which is the weight matrix and b, which is the vector of biases, and Φ is the activation function. The hidden representation is mapped to a reconstructed vector z [3] using

$$z = g_{\theta'}(y) = \Phi(W'y + b') \quad or \quad z = g_{\theta'}(y) = W'y + b'. \tag{3}$$

In the above given equation, θ' refers to a set of parameters consisting of the transpose of weight matrix and vector of biases obtained from the encoder before fine-tuning, and y is the hidden representation.

Gravitational Search Algorithm (GSA): GSA is a metaheuristic optimisation algorithm based on the law of gravity [17]. Each agent X_i of N agents defines a solution of d dimensions as

$$X_i = (x_{i1}, \ldots, x_{id}), \quad i = 1, 2, \ldots, N. \tag{4}$$

For each agent, mass is then calculated from its fitness value. At iteration t, the force acting $F_{id}(t)$ on i^{th} agent is:

$$F_{id}(t) = \sum_{j=1, j\neq i}^{N} \frac{rand_j G(t)(M_{pi}(t) \times M_{aj}(t))}{R_{ij}(t) + \varepsilon} (x_j^d(t) - x_i^d(t)). \tag{5}$$

where $rand_j$ is random number between $[0, 1]$, $Kbest$ is the set of best agent indices decreased linearly over the iterations to improve performance of GSA, $R_{ij}(t)$ is the euclidean distance:

$$R_{ij}(t) = \|X_i(t), X_j(t)\|_2. \tag{6}$$

According to the law of motion, acceleration,

$$a_{id}(t) = \frac{F_i^d(t)}{M_{ii}(t)}. \tag{7}$$

where M_{ii} is the inertial mass of ith agent. Velocity and new position of each agent's position is then computed as:

$$v_i^d(t+1) = rand_i \times v_i^d(t) + a_i^d(t), \tag{8}$$

$$x_i^d(t+1) = x_i^d(t) + v_i^d(t+1). \tag{9}$$

2.3   Proposed Approach: DL-GSA

Authors have proposed a model, DL-GSA, which combines a deep autoencoder network and a metaheuristic, the GSA algorithm, to approximate the missing data. An autoencoder has been used owing to its capability of reproducing the given input by projecting it to lower dimensions and hence learn the different covariances and correlations. The autoencoder network has a few layers representing the encoding section of the network and a second set of layers represent the decoding section. Restricted Boltzmann Machines or RBMs are stacked together to form the overall deep autoencoder network and these are pre-trained using Contrastive Divergence Algorithm [7]. The missing values in the input data are then estimated with the help of a nature inspired metaheuristic, the Gravitational Search algorithm, and the autoencoder loss has been used to calculate the fitness of agents in GSA. GSA helps to optimize the objective function (which is calculated using the trained network) and has been used to estimate the missing values.

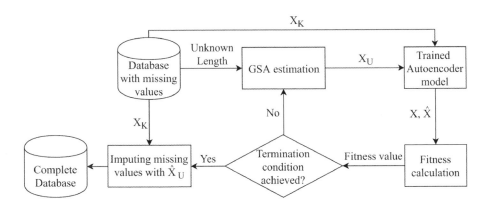

Fig. 1. Structure of DL-GSA model

Figure 1 illustrates the structure of the proposed DL-GSA model to impute missing values in a database. An input sample is fetched from the database and examined for missing values. The count of missing values is accepted by GSA as a parameter. The estimations made by GSA, X_U along with the set of known values, X_K are combined and fed as an input to the autoencoder. Subsequently, the reconstruction error is evaluated between the input and reconstruction $\hat{X}$. This error is utilized to compute the fitness of agents in GSA. If the termination condition is not satisfied, another estimation is produced by GSA. The termination criteria comprises of either the maximum permissible iterations (1000) being reached or convergence of the values generated by objective function during estimation. After termination, the solution corresponding to the most promising agent in GSA is used to impute the missing values in the input sample.

The input data sample X can be represented as

$$X = \{X_U, X_K\}. \tag{10}$$

where X_U and X_K denote the set of unknown values and known values respectively. X_U is calculated with the help of GSA. Since the output of a deep autoencoder should match the input, the fitness value [11] can be calculated by

$$\delta = \left(\begin{bmatrix} X_K \\ X_U \end{bmatrix} - f\left(\begin{Bmatrix} X_K \\ X_U \end{Bmatrix}, W, b \right) \right)^2. \tag{11}$$

where δ is the fitness value, f is the autoencoder function, and W and b are the weights and biases respectively.

3   Experiments

For imputation of missing data, the proposed algorithm improves over the deep learning-swarm technique, DL-CS [11], in terms of time as well as accuracy. Due to the proposed vectorized implementation, execution time per sample has been brought down from 2 h per sample to less than a minute per sample. In the following paragraphs, the experimental setup has been explained along with the results obtained.

In order to examine the performance of the model presented by the authors, the MNIST or Mixed National Institute of Standards and Technology [9] dataset has been used. It is a dataset of handwritten digits with 784 features which represent the different pixel values. The experiments have been carried out on a computer with Intel(R) Core(TM) i5-5200U CPU @2.20 GHz processor, 8.00 GB RAM, 64-bit Operating System running Windows 10 with vectorised implementation in Python 3.5.2 with NumPy.

The deep learning autoencoder network uses 784-1000-500-250-30-250-500-1000-784 layers [7]. Linear activation function has been used in the layer with 30 units, which is also known as the bottleneck layer. All other layers use sigmoidal activation function. To procure weights and biases, restricted Boltzmann machines or RBMs have been used along with the train dataset of 60,000 images for pretraining of the stacked network layers using the stochastic gradient descent or SGD algorithm. After training, the autoencoder has a mean squared error of 0.25% and 0.32% for train and test dataset respectively.

The dataset has then been used for simulation of MAR and MCAR data, and the missing pixel values in images are used to impute missing data. A binomial matrix of size $10,000 \times 784$, same as the test set, has been created consisting of zeros and ones and after adhering to the stated mechanisms and pattern, every occurence of one is replaced with NaN to simulate missing data. The authors then selected 100 samples randomly from this set with approximately 10% missing values per sample.

The number of agents used in both the algorithms under comparison are 40. For evaluation of the approach, metrics like mean squared error (MSE), correlation coefficient (r), root mean squared logarithmic error (RMSLE), and global deviation (GD) have been used.

Table 1. Metrics comparison of DL-GSA and DL-CS

Metric	DL-GSA	DL-CS
MSE	0.44%	0.56%
RMSLE	1.814%	2.09%
GD	$6.57E - 05$	$8.93E - 05$
r	0.9744	0.9658

4   Analysis and Results

As shown in Figs. 2, 3, 4 and 5, the proposed approach performs better than [11]. The samples, with the help of GSA, take half the time to converge per sample as compared to DL-CS [11] as shown in Fig. 4. Moreover, the proposed algorithm surpasses DL-CS's [11] performance with better accuracy as shown in Figs. 2, 3, 4 and 5 and Table 1.

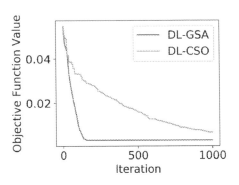

Fig. 2. Convergence graph of DL-GSA and DL-CS

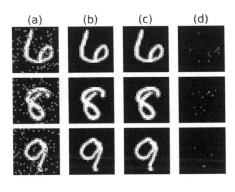

Fig. 3. Visualizations of 3 samples used by DL-GSA

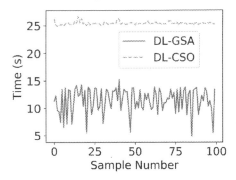

Fig. 4. Running time comparison of DL-GSA and DL-CS

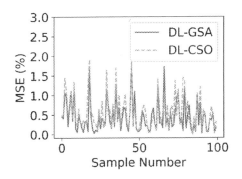

Fig. 5. Mean squared error comparison of DL-GSA and DL-CS

The mean squared error (MSE) yields a measure of deviation between the predicted and actual values (12). In Fig. 5, MSE values for various samples have been plotted for both the algorithms in comparison, DL-CS [11] and DL-GSA.

$$MSE = \frac{\sum_{i=1}^{n}(X_{U_i} - \hat{X}_{U_i})^2}{n}. \tag{12}$$

The root mean squared logarithmic error (13) and global deviation (14) are also used to assess the deviation between predicted and actual values.

$$RMSLE = \sqrt{\frac{\sum_{i=1}^{n}(log(X_{U_i} + 1) - log(\hat{X}_{U_i})^2}{n}}. \tag{13}$$

$$GD = \left(\frac{\sum_{i=1}^{n}(X_{U_i} - \hat{X}_{U_i})}{n}\right)^2. \tag{14}$$

The correlation coefficient (15) estimates the extent of agreement between the actual and estimated values. The value of this metric is in the range $[-1, 1]$ where $+1$ implies a total positive linear correlation while -1 implies total negative linear correlation.

$$r = \frac{\sum_{i=1}^{n}(X_{U_i} - \bar{X}_U)(\hat{X}_{U_i} - \bar{\hat{X}}_U)}{\sqrt{\sum_{i=1}^{n}(X_{U_i} - \bar{X}_U)^2 \sum_{i=1}^{n}(\hat{X}_{U_i} - \bar{\hat{X}}_U)^2}}. \tag{15}$$

In Eqs. (12)–(15), n denotes the number of missing values. X and $\hat{X}$ denote the actual test set values and the predicted values respectively. In Eq. (15), $\bar{X}_U$ denotes the mean of X_U. As shown in the Table 1, the proposed algorithm produces better results than DL-CS, which in turn performs better than DL-FA, MLP-GA, MLP-PSO and MLP-SA as shown in [11].

Visualizations of different samples have been shown in Fig. 3, where (a) highlights missing pixels in some of the samples used whereas (b) and (c) represent the original and imputed images. The difference between the original and imputed images is portrayed in column (d).

The time taken for samples by DL-GSA and DL-CS have been plotted in Fig. 4, which shows that the average time taken by DL-CS is 2.2 times more than that of DL-GSA. Figure 2 shows how the optimization function values are converging in case of both the algorithms. Hence, all the experiments carried out have demonstrated that DL-GSA is capable of imputing missing data with higher estimation accuracy while consuming lower time.

5   Conclusion

In this paper, authors have proposed a faster and more accurate approach to carry out missing data imputation. The technique makes use of an autoencoder in combination with the Gravitational Search Algorithm which is a nature inspired metaheuristic. On basis of the comparison shown in the Table 1, the proposed algorithm produces better results than DL-CS, which in turn performed better than DL-FA, MLP-GA, MLP-PSO and MLP-SA as shown in [11]. The comparison has been made in terms of various metrics such as mean squared error, correlation-coefficient, root mean squared logarithmic error and global deviation. DL-CS requires approximately two times the estimation time per sample as compared to DL-GSA. Hence, DL-GSA is a better choice in time as well as accuracy centered applications like big data, research and scientific datasets, and data analysis among others. Future works supplementing the proposed work would focus on generalizing the algorithm for different datasets.

References

1. Abdella, M., Marwala, T.: The use of genetic algorithms and neural networks to approximate missing data in database. In: 2005 IEEE 3rd International Conference on Computational Cybernetics, ICCC 2005, pp. 207–212. IEEE (2005)
2. Aydilek, I.B., Arslan, A.: A novel hybrid approach to estimating missing values in databases using k-nearest neighbors and neural networks. Int. J. Innovative Comput. Inf. Control 7(8), 4705–4717 (2012)
3. Bengio, Y., Courville, A., Vincent, P.: Representation learning: a review and new perspectives. IEEE Trans. Pattern Anal. Mach. Intell. 35(8), 1798–1828 (2013)
4. Dempster, A.P., Laird, N.M., Rubin, D.B.: Maximum likelihood from incomplete data via the EM algorithm. J. R. Stat. Soc. Ser. B (Methodol.) 39, 1–38 (1977)
5. Enders, C.K.: Using the expectation maximization algorithm to estimate coefficient alpha for scales with item-level missing data. Psychol. Meth. 8(3), 322 (2003)
6. Fischer, A., Igel, C.: An introduction to restricted boltzmann machines. In: Alvarez, L., Mejail, M., Gomez, L., Jacobo, J. (eds.) CIARP 2012. LNCS, vol. 7441, pp. 14–36. Springer, Heidelberg (2012). https://doi.org/10.1007/978-3-642-33275-3_2
7. Hinton, G.E., Osindero, S., Teh, Y.W.: A fast learning algorithm for deep belief nets. Neural Comput. 18(7), 1527–1554 (2006)
8. Isaacs, J.C.: Representational learning for sonar ATR. In: Proceedings SPIE. vol. 9072, p. 907203 (2014)
9. LeCun, Y., Cortes, C., Burges, C.J.: Mnist handwritten digit database. AT&T Labs (2010). http://yann.lecun.com/exdb/mnist2
10. Leke, C., Marwala, T.: Missing data estimation in high-dimensional datasets: a swarm intelligence-deep neural network approach. In: Tan, Y., Shi, Y., Niu, B. (eds.) ICSI 2016. Lecture Notes in Computer Science, vol. 9712. Springer, Cham (2016). https://doi.org/10.1007/978-3-319-41000-5_26
11. Leke, C., Ndjiongue, A.R., Twala, B., Marwala, T.: A deep learning-cuckoo search method for missing data estimation in high-dimensional datasets. In: Tan, Y., Takagi, H., Shi, Y. (eds.) ICSI 2017. LNCS, vol. 10385, pp. 561–572. Springer, Cham (2017). https://doi.org/10.1007/978-3-319-61824-1_61
12. Leke, C., Twala, B., Marwala, T.: Modeling of missing data prediction: computational intelligence and optimization algorithms. In: 2014 IEEE International Conference on Systems, Man and Cybernetics (SMC), pp. 1400–1404. IEEE (2014)
13. Little, R.J., Rubin, D.B.: Statistical Analysis With Missing Data. Wiley, New York (2014)

14. Marivate, V.N., Nelwamodo, F.V., Marwala, T.: Autoencoder, principal component analysis and support vector regression for data imputation. arXiv preprint arXiv:0709.2506 (2007)
15. Mistry, F.J., Nelwamondo, F.V., Marwala, T.: Missing data estimation using principle component analysis and autoassociative neural networks. J. Syst. Cybern. Inf. **7**(3), 72–79 (2009)
16. Peng, C.Y.J., Harwell, M., Liou, S.M., Ehman, L.H., et al.: Advances in missing data methods and implications for educational research. Real data analysis, pp. 31–78 (2006)
17. Rashedi, E., Nezamabadi-Pour, H., Saryazdi, S.: GSA: a gravitational search algorithm. Inf. Sci. **179**(13), 2232–2248 (2009)
18. Rja, L., Rubin, D.: Statistical analysis with missing data. Wiley, New York (1987)

Research on Question-Answering System Based on Deep Learning

Bo Song[1(✉)], Yue Zhuo[1], and Xiaomei Li[2]

[1] College of Software, Shenyang Normal University, Shenyang, Liaoning, China
songbo63@aliyun.com, 1993zhuoyue@sina.com
[2] Research Training Center of Basic Education,
Shenyang 110034, Liaoning, China

Abstract. With the continuous development of the network, Question-Answering system has become a way for people to get information quickly. The QA task aims to provide precise and quick answers to user questions from a collection of documents or a database. In this paper, we introduce an attention based deep learning model to match the question and answer sentence. The proposed model employs a bidirectional long-short term memory(BLSTM) to solve the problem of lack features. And we also use the attention mechanism which allows the question to focus on a certain part of the candidate answer. Finally, we evaluate our model and the results show that our approach outperforms the method of feature construction based on machine learning. And the attention mechanism improves the matching accuracy.

Keywords: Question-answering system · Deep learning · BLSTM
Attention mechanism

1 Introduction

The increasing knowledge accessible via internet affects our habits to query information and to obtain answers to our questions [1]. More and more people would like to use a search engine when they looking for information. However, these search engines return too many results, making it difficult for users to locate the desired information quickly and accurately. Ordinary users can only get links may contain the required information. For example, in the Baidu search: how to seek the perimeter of a square, when the relevant results will be found about 6,530,000. In addition, search engines are based on keyword matching. It's only focus on the syntax of statement, does not consider the semantics, which makes it difficult for users to accurately express the information need, and then impact the retrieval effect [2].

We need other tools such as question answering (QA) systems to respond to user queries with precise answer. Different from the search engine, QA system can not only ask questions in natural language, for the users to return the desired answer directly, rather than relevant web pages. A question answering system can be composed of three main tasks: analysis of the questions, information retrieval and answer extraction. Within an overall framework, such systems receive questions and return concise answers in natural language style.

© Springer International Publishing AG, part of Springer Nature 2018
Y. Tan et al. (Eds.): ICSI 2018, LNCS 10942, pp. 522–529, 2018.
https://doi.org/10.1007/978-3-319-93818-9_50

Recently, deep learning methods have been shown to be effective for many NLP tasks, such as sentence classification [3], machine translation [4–6], abstractive summarization [7] and paraphrase detection [8]. Compared with the traditional machine model, it has a more powerful ability to learn sentence semantics [9].

In this paper, we proposed a question answer matching method based on deep learning to solve the problem of lack of features and low accuracy due to artificial structural feature in machine learning. The proposed model employs a bidirectional long short-term memory (BLSTM) to learn the deep semantic features in the sentence and calculate the similarity distance of feature vectors. And then we add an attention mechanism into this model, which allows the question to focus on a certain part of the candidate answer. Finally, we evaluate our model and the results show that the combined deep neural network model is superior to the method of feature construction based on machine learning. Integrating our model improves the performance of our question answering system.

2   Related Work

2.1   About QA System

At present, some relatively mature question answering systems based on Web, such as START [10] and AnswerBus [11], have been developed. With the development of Internet technology, especially the semantic web, ontology is used as the source of knowledge, which can be used to understand the semantic meaning of irrelevant information. LASSO [12] uses the question classification technology, and sets up the corresponding processing strategy to each kind of question, raises the question analysis accuracy greatly. Its drawback is that the classification granularity is too coarse, so we can't get the answer to many questions. AQUA [12] is a QA system that can be used to search the academic field. It combines Natural Language Processing (NLP), Ontologies, Logic, and Information Retrieval technologies in a uniform framework.

According to the difference of the domain, the question answering system can be divided into the Specific Domain QA, the Open Domain QA, the Frequently Asked Question system. One of the common QA system is the Frequently Answering Question (FAQ)——to solve those questions seemingly simple, but higher frequency. FAQ is a QA system based on question-answer pairs. It has the advantages of high quality of questions and corresponding answers, but the number is relatively small in specific fields, which restricts its development. On the contrary, CQA (Community-based Question Answering), a new kind of data based on question-answer pairs, has more and more question-answer pairs but poor quality.

2.2   Several Methods About Question-Answering

When the FAQ base is built, we calculate the similarity of two questions. These two questions are the one entered by user and the other one in FAQ base. Then the two sentence similarity calculation methods are introduced.

TF-IDF

At present, the TF-IDF method is widely used in the field of information retrieval. It is a sentence similarity calculation method based on word feature. The main idea of TF-IDF is [14]: Each sentence consists of $T_1, T_2, \ldots, T_n$, and assign a weight value W to each entry T. Therefore, $T = <T_1, T_2, \ldots, T_n>$ can be used to express an interrogation. Also, others can be expressed in $T' = <T'_1, T'_2, \ldots, T'_n>$. The similarity values of the two sentences can be represented by their cosine values. The formula is as follows:

$$sim(T, T') = \frac{\sum_{i=1}^{n} T_i \cdot T'_i}{\sqrt{\sum_{i=1}^{n} T_i^2 \sum_{i=1}^{n} T'^2_i}} \tag{1}$$

It is a statistical method based on large scale corpus. The effect can be reflected only when the corpus reaches certain size. And there are some limitations, because it does not consider the semantic information in the context.

Sentence Similarity Computing Based on Semantic Dependency

The idea of this method is: the core verb is the central component of the whole sentence, and it not only isn't swayed by other ingredients, but can control other components of the sentence. The premise of this method is to get the dependencies between various components of the sentence in advance. It just considers those core verbs of the sentence and the pair counts of the words that depends on it. The pair count includes most of notional word [15]. The calculation formula is as follows:

$$sim(sen1, sen2) = \frac{\sum_{i=1}^{n} W_i}{Max\{PairCount1, PairCount2\}} \tag{2}$$

Here, $PairCount1$ is the number of valid pair count of sentence 1, and the $PairCount2$ is for sentence 2. $\sum_{i=1}^{n} W_i$ is the valid total weight of sentence 1 and sentence 2.

As we know, a sentence can be presented by many kinds of style, if we want to describe what a sentence means, we should dip into the semantic level and consider about the dependency structure. Therefore, the method that based on semantic dependency relationship analysis to compute sentence similarity is necessary [16].

Deep Learning Method——LSTM

Over the past few years, in the field of Natural Language Processing, deep learning has made outstanding achievements in the language modeling, machine translation, part-of-speech tagging, POS tagging, entity recognition, sentiment analysis, advertising recommendation and search sort, and so on. Among them, deep recurrent neural network(RNN) has made many remarkable achievements in Natural Language Processing, such as Machine Translation and question answering system. RNN has added memory function on the basis of traditional deep neural network (DNN), making it naturally have better ability to represent context semantics (Fig. 1).

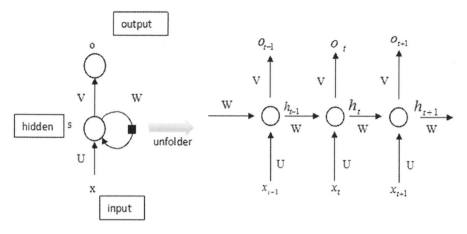

Fig. 1. Recurrent neural network model

LSTM (Long Short-Term Memory) improved RNN and solved the problem of long-term dependence. LSTM is a deep learning system that avoids the vanishing gradient problem. It is normally augmented by recurrent gates called "forget" gates [17]. Compared with RNN, the most important improvement is the addition of three gate controllers: input gate, output gate and forget gate [18]. The function of forget gate is to let recurrent neural network forget the useless information before. It will decide which part of memory needs to be forgotten based on the current input x_t, the state of last time c_{t-1} and the output of last time h_{t-1}. After recurrent neural network's "forgotten" the part of the state, it also needs to accept the latest memory from the current input. This process is completed by the "input gate". The "input gate" will decide which part will enter the current state of the moment be depend on x_t, c_{t-1} and h_{t-1}. The output gate will generate the output based on c_t, h_{t-1} and x_t.

$$i_t = \sigma(U_i \cdot x_i + W_i \cdot s_{t-1} + V_i \cdot c_{t-1}) \tag{3}$$

$$f_t = \sigma(U_f \cdot x_t + W_f \cdot s_{t-1} + V_f \cdot c_{t-1}) \tag{4}$$

$$o_t = \sigma(U_o \cdot x_t + W_o \cdot s_{t-1} + V_o \cdot c_t) \tag{5}$$

$$\tilde{c}_t = \tanh(U_c \cdot x_t + W_c \cdot s_{t-1}) \tag{6}$$

$$c_t = i_t \otimes \tilde{c}_t + f_t \otimes c_{t-1} \tag{7}$$

$$h_t = o_t \odot \tanh(c_t) \tag{8}$$

In the LSTM architecture, there are three gates (input i, forget f and output o), and a cell memory vector c. σ is the sigmoid function (Fig. 2).

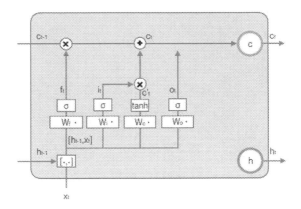

Fig. 2. LSTM model

3   Attention Based BLSTM Model

As mentioned above, LSTM just can forward pass. However, every element is influenced only by the previous elements. In question answering tasks, the future content can also be useful to the previous words [19]. The bidirectional LSTM(BLSTM) can efficiently make use of past words and future words. In this study, at each time, the input will be provided at the same time to the two LSTMs in the two directions, and the output is determined by the two LSTMs (Fig. 3).

The idea of the attention mechanism is that the attention of the human brain to different things is also different. It focuses on information in an auto weighted way [20] (Fig. 4).

Given a question Q, we first translate the question Q to a query q. Then we search for the candidate answers of the query. The answer candidate pool is defined as $A = \{a_1, a_2, \ldots, a_n\}$ for question Q (a_i is a candidate answer and n is the pool size). The goal is to find the best answer candidate a_i ($1 \leq i \leq n$). If the selected answer a_i is in the truth set of query q, query q is considered to be answered correctly; otherwise, it

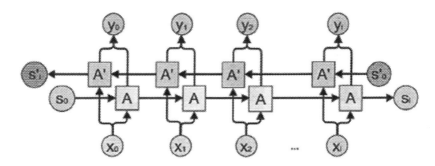

Fig. 3. BLSTM model

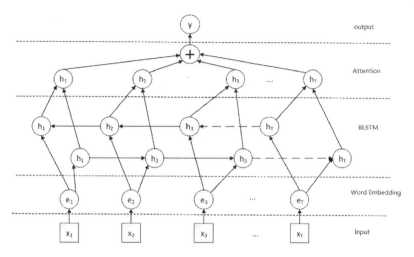

Fig. 4. Attention based BLSTM model

is answered incorrectly. In our study, the details are as follows. First, initialize the BLSTM model and transform the training set Q, A into Q', A'. Using gradient descent method to solve the model parameters in BLSTM and attention. And then the user's question q is divided and converted into a set of Word2vec vectors q'. For each word vector in q', the attention mechanism will produce a weighted representation γ.

$$M = \tanh(W_{am}h + W_{qm}o_q) \qquad (9)$$

$$\gamma = H \cdot soft \max(\omega^T M) \qquad (10)$$

Here, $H = [h_1, h_2, \ldots, h_N]$ represents the hidden vector. Where W_{am} and W_{qm} are attention parameters.

4   Experiments

In order to evaluate the model, we use the dataset NLPCC 2017 to conduct experiments. We use the standard metrics MAP (mean average precision) and MRR (mean reciprocal rank). MRR measures the rank of any correct answer and MAP examines the ranks of all the correct answers.

$$MAP = \frac{1}{n}\sum_{q=1}^{n} avg(P(q))rank(q) \qquad (11)$$

$$MRR = \frac{1}{n}\sum_{q=1}^{n} \frac{1}{rank(q)} \qquad (12)$$

Table 1. Experimental evaluation results.

Methods	MRR/%	MAP/%
RNN	67.91	61.33
LSTM	71.98	64.26
BLSTM + Attention	80.01	71.99

where $avg(P(q))$ is the average precision score of query q and $rank(q)$ is the ranking position of the first correct answer in the candidate answers. Table 1 shows the experimental results on the dataset.

As shown in Table 1, the LSTM model has a better performance than the RNN. Just because LSTM has a naturally stronger ability to learn long-range temporal dependency data. And the Attention based BLSTM can match questions and answers more effectively since the bidirectional LSTM can use both previous and future contexts and the attention mechanism can pay attention to key information in the answer and neglect the irrelevant part of the answer.

5   Conclusion

This paper presents a method for question answering using BLSTM model and attention mechanism. We test our model and the results show that our model is more effective compared to the traditional machine learning methods. In future investigations, we would like to evaluate the models for different tasks further and try to improve our model. At present, the corpus of Chinese question answering system is relatively inadequate. Besides collecting and labeling more corpus, we can also try to effectively integrate traditional feature extraction methods in deep learning model in the future.

Acknowledgments. Project supported by the Basic scientific research projects of colleges and universities in Liaoning Province (2017L317).

References

1. Abacha, A.B., Zweigenbaum, P.: MEANS: a medical question-answering system combining NLP techniques and semantic web technologies. J. Inf. Process. Manag. **51**(5), 570–594 (2015)
2. Mao, X.L., Li, X.M.: A survey on question and answering systems. J. Front. Comput. Sci. Technol. **06**(3), 193–207 (2012)
3. Kim, Y.: Convolutional Neural Networks for Sentence Classification. Eprint Arxiv (2014)
4. Bahdanau, D., Cho, K., Bengio, Y.: Neural Machine Translation by Jointly Learning to Align and Translate. Computer Science (2014)
5. Cho, K., Merrienboer, B.V., Gulcehre, C., et al.: Learning Phrase Representations using RNN Encoder-Decoder for Statistical Machine Translation. Computer Science (2014)
6. Sutskever, I., Vinyals, O., Le, Q.V.: Sequence to Sequence Learning with Neural Networks. In: NLPS (2014)

7. Rush, A.M., Chopra, S., Weston, J.: A Neural Attention Model for Abstractive Sentence Summarization. Computer Science (2015)
8. Iyyer, M., Boyd-Graber, J., Claudino, L., et al.: A neural network for factoid question answering over paragraphs. In: Conference on Empirical Methods in Natural Language Processing, NIPS (2014)
9. Hu, B., Lu, Z., Li, H., et al.: Convolutional neural network architectures for matching natural language sentences. In: Advances in neural information processing (2015)
10. START Natural Language Question Answering System. http://start.csail.mit.edu
11. Zheng, Z.: AnswerBus question answering system. In: International Conference on Human Language Technology Research. pp. 399–404. Morgan Kaufmann Publishers Inc. (2002)
12. Moldovan, D.I., Harabagiu, S.M., Goodrum, R.A., et al.: LASSO: a tool for surfing the answer net. In: National Institute of Standards and Technology (1999)
13. Vargas-Vera, M., Motta, E.: AQUA – ontology-based question answering system. In: Monroy, R., Arroyo-Figueroa, G., Sucar, L.E., Sossa, H. (eds.) MICAI 2004. LNCS (LNAI), vol. 2972, pp. 468–477. Springer, Heidelberg (2004). https://doi.org/10.1007/978-3-540-24694-7_48
14. Song, B., Zhuo, Y., Li, X.: A personalized intelligent tutoring system of primary mathematics based on perl. In: Tan, Y., Shi, Y., Li, L. (eds.) ICSI 2016. LNCS, vol. 9713, pp. 609–617. Springer, Cham (2016). https://doi.org/10.1007/978-3-319-41009-8_66
15. Zhang, W.: Chinese Question Answering System Technology and Application. Electronic Industry Press, Beijing (2016)
16. Li, J.N.: Research and Implementation of IT Domain Question Answering System. South China University of Technology (2015)
17. Gers, F.A., Schraudolph, N.N.: Learning precise timing with LSTM recurrent networks. JMLR.org (2003)
18. Graves, A.: Generating Sequences With Recurrent Neural Networks. Computer Science (2013)
19. Nie, Y.P., Han, Y., Huang, J.M., et al.: Attention-based encoder-decoder model for answer selection in question answering. J. Front. Inf. Technol. Electr. Eng. 18(4), 535–544 (2017)
20. Rong, G.H., Huang, Z.H.: Question answer matching method based on deep learning. J. Comput. Appl. 37(10), 286–2865 (2017)
21. Yin, W., Schütze, H., Xiang, B., et al.: ABCNN: Attention-Based Convolutional Neural Network for Modeling Sentence Pairs. Computer Science (2015)
22. Tan, M., Xiang, B., Zhou, B.: LSTM-based Deep Learning Models for non-factoid answer selection. Computer Science (2015)

A Deep Learning Model for Predicting Movie Box Office Based on Deep Belief Network

Wei Wang$^{(\boxtimes)}$, Jiapeng Xiu, Zhengqiu Yang, and Chen Liu

Beijing University of Posts and Telecommunications, Beijing, China
wangwei@goldensystem.cn

Abstract. For the limitation that Chinese movie box office forecasting accuracy is not high in the long-term prediction research, based on the research of the Chinese movie market, this paper proposes a long-term prediction model for movie box office based on the deep belief network. The new model improved the movie box office influence model of Barry, screened out the effective box office impact factor, normalized the quantitative factor and formed a measurement system which is suitable for the Chinese movie market. Based on this measurement system, the characteristics of the data set in the original space are transferred to the space with semantic features and a hierarchical feature representation by deep learning, thus the accuracy of box office prediction was improved. Experimental evaluation results show that, in view of the 439 movie data, the DBN prediction model of movie box office has better prediction performance, and has good application value in the field of film box office.

Keywords: Deep learning · Movie box office prediction · Deep belief network

1 Introduction

The research about movie box-office focuses on the influence factors of the box office, the long-term prediction of the box office and the short-term prediction of the box office. Among them, the study of the box office influence factors is the basis of box office study. Besides its own meaning, the study of the box office influence factors is also the cornerstone of long-term prediction and short-term prediction. Long-term forecasting refers to the general box office forecast of the film during the entire release period. Short term prediction refers to the box office value of a movie at a period of time. Long term prediction and short-term prediction are different in influencing characteristics and prediction methods, but short-term prediction is often more accurate than long-term prediction, and the influencing factors are changing every day, so when the time span extend, prediction accuracy tends to decrease. The significance of long-term prediction is that it can provide reliable reference for film production risk assessment, the decision-making of film making, the publicity before movie release, and film layout before movie release.

The study of long term movie box office prediction has a long history. It began in the United States first in the 40s of last century. During this period, researchers paid more attention to the research of movie content, excavated every factor that influenced the movie box office, and improved the influential factors to improve the box office. It

© Springer International Publishing AG, part of Springer Nature 2018
Y. Tan et al. (Eds.): ICSI 2018, LNCS 10942, pp. 530–541, 2018.
https://doi.org/10.1007/978-3-319-93818-9_51

is called "audience research" [1]. Later, Litman et al. [2] absorbed the achievements of "audience research". Based on the two factors: MAPP and Oscar awards, a regression model was used to get a model between movie rental income and movie box office influence factors.

Sharda and Delen [3] first proposed the box office prediction model using neural network method, and made breakthrough progress. But Barman et al. [7] use the type of film as a box office forecast, and use simple Boolean numeric values to represent the input and output results; in addition, the proposed neural network structure is too simple.

A multi-layer neural network for multiple input and multi output was proposed to establish a long-term prediction model by Zhang et al. [5]. Later, Zheng et al. [6] established a more suitable feature system for China's film market system, and established long-term box office forecasting model based on back propagation neural network, finally, obtained a better prediction result than Zhang et al. [5], but there is still a lot of room for progress.

For the limitation that Chinese movie box office forecasting accuracy is not high in the long-term prediction research, this paper presents a long-term box office forecasting model, which is based on the DBN, which is in line with the Chinese market. The experimental results of this paper prove that the model is more accurate than the previous box office prediction model.

2 Box Office Feature System

2.1 Feature Analysis

The selection of the feature of the film is closely related to the accuracy of the box office prediction. In order to construct a model which is more accord with the characteristics of China's film market and improve the prediction accuracy of box office, the paper divides the feature into three aspects: creativity, distribution and marketing. Among them, the creative component factors include: movie genre, IP, actor, director, production technology; the distribution factors include: the release schedule, the competition of the market, the number of market screens, the issuance capacity of the issuing company; The marketing part of the factors include: film awards, Internet word of mouth.

$$\text{Input} = \left\{ \begin{array}{l} \text{Genre}_i, \text{IP}, \text{Actor}_i, \text{Director}, \text{ProductionTech}_i, \text{Date}_i, \text{Screen}, \\ \text{ReleaseCapacity}, \text{Awards}, \text{Score}, \text{RatersNumber} \end{array} \right\}. \quad (1)$$

2.2 Feature Pretreatment

Movie Genre. According to the distribution of movie genre from 2015 to 2016 (see Fig. 1), action types and sci-fi films have taken a large part in the movie market. We also can know the types of Chinese films and the percentage of each type, so this article uses the following six main types of movies: comedy, thriller, love, drama, action, science fiction.

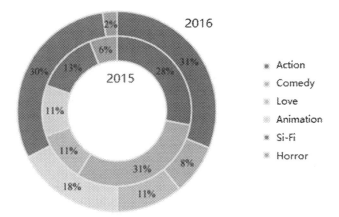

Fig. 1. 2015–2016 movie genre

A movie may contain more than one type, so if a movie contains a movie type, then value 1, or 0 (Table 1).

$$\text{Genre}_i \in \{0, 1\}, i \in [1, 6] \tag{2}$$

Table 1. The movie genre corresponds to variables

Variables	Genre	Variables	Genre
Genre_1	Comedy	Genre_4	Sci-fi
Genre_2	Thriller	Genre_5	Action
Genre_3	Love	Genre_6	Drama

IP. IP films include Internet IP dramas and previous movie sequels, and IP films have gained wide attention before the movie's release. If the movie is not an IP play, then the IP value is 0; If the movie is a sequel or a novel of the same name, or other literary form of the same name, the IP value is 1; If the IP drama is on the list of China's entertainment index, the IP value is 2.

$$\text{IP} \in \{0, 1, 2\} \tag{3}$$

Actor. There is no reference standard for the movie industry in China. To draw lessons from the United States Hollywood movie actor evaluation method, this paper USES actor history box office to represent actors to bring the business value of the film, starring actor's position in the ranking of the top four, so when calculating the actor's great influence on box office hours, using only the four main actors influence at the box office. So box office influence indicator of actor k is:

$$A_k = \left[\sum\nolimits_{j=1}^{m} u_{kj}b_j\right]/m \tag{4}$$

Where, k: the actor serial number; j: the movie to be taken by k and the movie's sort is j; m: the number of films which starred by the actor k; u_{kj}: the participation coefficient of movie j for actor k, which is defined as follows:

$$u_{kj} = \begin{cases} 1 - \frac{n-1}{10}, & n \in [1,2] \\ 0.5, & n \in (2,4] \end{cases} \tag{5}$$

In which, n is positive integer, which indicates the order of the actor i in the movie j. The actors have an order of magnitude larger, so the logarithmic method is used to reduce the order of magnitude:

$$Actor_i = lg(A_k) \tag{6}$$

In which, i indicates the sequence of the actors' performances of the movie, and k represents the serial number of actor i.

Director. The director's ability to move the film to the screen, as well as the chief executive, determines the quality of a film. Similar to the movie's box office influence, there is no uniform standard for domestic industry reviews of film directors. For the director's own box office appeal, he can perform at the average box office of the director. Then the box office appeal of director k can be defined as:

$$D_k = \left[\sum\nolimits_{j=1}^{m} b_{kj}\right]/m \tag{7}$$

Where: k represents the serial number of the director; j says the movie j which directed by director k; m says all the films made by director k, b_{kj} represent the total box office of the movie j. The influence of the director is larger, so the logarithmic method is used to reduce the order of magnitude:

$$Director = lg(D_k) \tag{8}$$

Where, k represents the director's serial number.

Production Technology. ProductionTech$_i$ describes the production technology of movie, in which, $i \in \{0,1,2\}$. ProductionTech$_0$ indicate 3D movies. If the movie is a 3D movie, the ProductionTech$_0$ value is 1, otherwise it is 0; ProductionTech$_1$ indicates the IMAX film, if the movie is IMAX, the ProductionTech$_1$ is 1, otherwise it is 0; ProductionTech$_2$ indicates 2D movies, if the movie is 2D, ProductionTech$_2$ is 1, otherwise it is 0.

$$ProductionTech_i \in \{0,1\}, i \in \{0,1,2\} \tag{9}$$

Release Date. Movie release dates also have a lot of influence on the box office, and the appropriate movie tickets for the appropriate release date tend to be higher. In this paper, the number of films in the corresponding schedule and the number of box office blockbusters in the film market will be referenced in the box office prediction index system established in this paper. According to the film in China mainland, before and after three days of holiday, this paper is divided into five a film screening slot (from April 27 to May 10th), summer (July 1 solstice) on September 1, National Day (Sept. 27 solstice October 10), New Year file (the first day to the fifteenth day of the first lunar month) and other sessions, a total of 5 classes.

$$Date_i \in \{0, 1\}, \quad i \in \{0, 1, 2, 3, 4\} \tag{10}$$

If the movie is in the May Day holiday, $Date_0$ values 1, otherwise value 0; If the movie is in the summer vacation, $Date_1$ values 1, otherwise the value is 0; If the movie is in National Day, $Date_2$ values 1, otherwise value 0; If the movie is in the Spring Festival period, $Date_3$ values 1, otherwise value 0; If the movie does not belong to any schedule, $Date_4$ values 1, otherwise value 0.

Screen Number. Movie screen data is an important standard for the development of the film industry, and the number of screens corresponding to the movie's release date can be calculated through the method of increasing technology. That is:

$$Screen = \begin{cases} S_y + (S_{y+1} - S_y)/12 * (m - 1), & y \in [2006, 2016] \\ S_y + \frac{S_y - S_{y-1}}{12} * (m - 1), & y > 2016 \end{cases} \tag{11}$$

Where: y means the year of the movie's release date, and m means the month of the movie's release, and S_y represents the total number of screens in the year of y.

Issuing Capacity of Company. The box-office success of a film is inseparable from the marketing promotion of the company online and offline, and the ability of marketing promotion is closely related to the distribution of the issuing company. In this paper, the distribution capacity of the issuing company is evaluated according to the market share of the company that issues the film.

$$ReleaseCapacity_i = Rc_{ij}/Rc_j \tag{12}$$

Where: i represents the serial number of the issuing company, j represents the year of issuance, Rc_j represents the total box office of the domestic drama in j year, and Rc_{ij} represents the total box office of the company of i in the year of j.

Movie Awards. The film's awards are recognized and accepted by most audiences in terms of quality and style, and winning the film before or during its release can also boost ticket sales. On the authority of the domestic film awards, this article selects famous and influential Chinese film industry's biggest five professional film awards, namely: China golden rooster, public movie hundred flowers awards, China ornamental column awards, Hong Kong film awards, and Taiwan's golden horse film.

$$Awards_i = m, m \in [0, 5] \tag{13}$$

Where, i: the serial number of the movie; m: the number of awards.

Internet Word of Mouth. The network word of mouth mainly uses professional film appraisal website score or social platform carries on individual evaluation two kinds of way, and the box office trend is closely related. This paper USES the combination of scoring and scoring Numbers as the reference standard of box office influence ability.

$$Score_i = m \tag{14}$$

$$RatersNumber_i = lg(n) \tag{15}$$

Where, i: the sequence number of the movie; m: the Douban score of the corresponding movie; n: the number of reviewer, the logarithm of 10.

Box-Office. Box-Office can be referred to as the film industry's GDP, the paper selects the movie box office as a prediction of the dependent variable. The order of magnitude of the box office is larger, so the logarithmic method is used to lower the order of magnitude:

$$R_i = lg(BoxOffice_i) \tag{16}$$

To sum up, the characteristics of the index system for larger orders of magnitude difference in the movie factor, data preprocessing is usually adopt the method of data to reduce the order of magnitude.

3   Prediction Model

Deep learning refers to the machine learning process based on the sample data through a certain training method to get the deep network structure containing multiple layers. DBN is a kind of classic two-way deep network of deep learning, which is widely used in image classification, speech recognition, and has strong classification and prediction ability. Therefore, this paper proposes a box office prediction model based on DBN.

3.1   Deep Belief Network

DBN is composed of several layers of restricted Boltzmann machine networks and a layer of back-propagation networks (see Fig. 2). A layer of matter on the network after learning the characteristics of the output as input of the next layer, so that each layer can better abstracts the characteristics of a layer, to extract data one by one. The BP network at the top is used as input for features extracted from RBM network for classification or prediction.

RBM consists of the visual layer V and the hidden layer H (see Fig. 2). The visual layer is used for input feature data, and the hidden layer is used for feature detectors. There is no connection between the visible layer and the nodes in the hidden layer, that

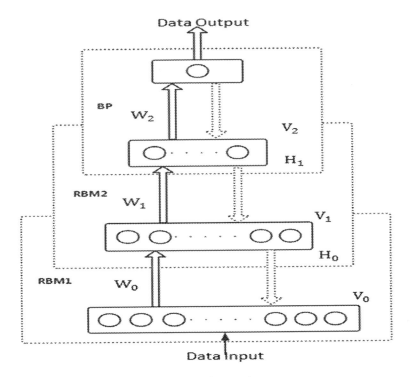

Fig. 2. Deep belief network structure

is, each node is independent of each other. The nodes of the hidden layer can only be evaluated at random 0 or 1, and the full probability distribution P(V, H) satisfies the Boltzmann distribution, and the conditional distribution can be determined by the full probability distribution $p(h|v)$ and $p(v|h)$. When the input v, through $p(h|v)$ can be hidden layer, hidden layer by h, by $p(v|h)$ can get visual layer again, by adjusting the parameters, makes the visible layers from hidden layer v_1 with the original visual layer v, or get another expression of hidden layer for visual. Therefore, the hidden layer can be used as a feature of the input data for the visual layer (Fig. 4).

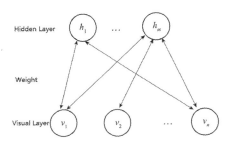

Fig. 3. RBM structure

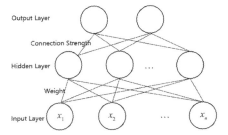

Fig. 4. BPNN structure

The joint distribution of RBM under a given model parameter (θ) is:

$$p(v, h; \theta) = \exp(-E(v, h; \theta))/Z \tag{17}$$

Where, $Z = \sum_v \sum_h \exp(-E(v, h; \theta))$ is normalized factor, energy function E is defined as:

$$E(v, h; \theta) = -\sum_{ij} W_{ij} v_i h_j - \sum_i b_i v_i - \sum a_j h_j \tag{18}$$

Where, i, j is the node; W_{ij} is the connection weight between the visual layer and the hidden layer. b_i and a_j are offset.

BP neural network consists of three layers of neurons, such as input layer, hidden layer and output layer, and its structure is shown in Figs. 2 and 3. The BP network in DBN can be understood as a classifier with supervisory learning.

In BP network, output of hidden layer nodes is:

$$O_j = f\left(\sum_i W_{ij} x_i - a_j\right), \tag{19}$$

and a_j is the neuron threshold. f is the excitation function, and the Sigmoid function is generally taken. Output node output is:

$$y_k = f\left(\sum_j T_{jk} O_j - b_k\right), \tag{20}$$

where b_k is the neuron threshold; T_{jk} is the connection strength between the hidden layer node and the output node.

3.2   Box Office Prediction Model Based on DBN

Model Structure. The DBN structure is determined by the number of RBM visual layer nodes, the number of outputs, the depth of the DBN (number of RBM network layers), and the number of hidden layer nodes in each layer.

The number of nodes of the first layer RBM visual layer is determined by the number of input sample characteristics. In this paper, the input characteristics of the box office prediction are 10, and the number of visual layer nodes of RBM is 25 according to the feature factor analysis of Sect. 2.1.

The depth of DBN has great influence on model performance. The research proves that if the number of RBM layers increases, the modeling capability of DBN is enhanced, and the hidden layer in the higher layer may excavate more abstract characteristics and improve the prediction performance of the network. However, too many layers can reduce the generalization ability of DBN.

Each hidden layer node number of DBN has some influence on the performance of the model, the number of nodes is too few, and the data information performance of the model is weak. If the number of nodes is too many, it is also easy to have the fitting phenomenon.

Model Training. The training of DBN model is divided into two steps.

Pre-training: unsupervised training separately matter network, each layer by unsupervised greed method step by step a weight training generated model, to ensure the feature vector map to different feature space, keep characteristic information as much as possible. The training process of RBM, in fact, is to find the probability distribution of the most training samples by determining the weights. That's to say, find a distribution, so you have the greatest chance of training samples in this distribution.

Adjustment: DBN last layer BP network, accept the output feature vector of RBM as input feature vector, and have supervised training classifier. Matter each layer network adjustment weights within itself, to ensure the optimum, the feature vector map layer and the characteristic of DBN vector map did not achieve the optimal, so the error of the BP network information top-down spread to every matter, fine-tuning the DBN network.

4   Experiment and Evaluation

4.1   Data Set Preparation

The data set is a domestic film released in China from January 2015 to June 2017, with a total of 439 films. According to the characteristics of the first part of the box office system, this paper analyses the demand for various indicators, using the python crawler public data access to the Internet to obtain the required data sets, this paper mainly includes the released China film association, the arts and other famous movie website in China. According to the target demand of box office characteristics system, the data is quantitatively processed, and Table 2 is the variable and cleaning standard in the measurement system for box office prediction model.

   The collected data needs to be cleaned, which can be divided into two steps: elimination of data and filling data. Training samples, test samples and prediction samples are selected for the data to be cleaned. In this paper, 300 data were randomly selected as training samples, 70 data were used as test samples, and 69 data was used as the forecast sample.

4.2   Evaluation Metrics

In this paper, the average absolute error of MAE and RMSE of RMSE are used as evaluation indexes. The calculation formula of the mean absolute error is as follows:

$$\text{MAE} = \frac{1}{n} \sum\nolimits_{i=1}^{n} |R_i - P_i| \tag{21}$$

Table 2. Variable and cleaning method

Input variable	Data cleaning	Input variable	Data cleaning
$Genre_1$	Eliminate the data	$ProductionTech_2$	Fill 0
$Genre_2$		$ProductionTech_3$	Fill 0
$Genre_3$		$Date_1$	Fill 0
$Genre_4$		$Date_2$	Fill 0
$Genre_5$		$Date_3$	Fill 0
$Genre_6$		$Date_4$	Fill 0
IP	Fill 0	$Date_5$	Fill 1
$Actor_1$	If missing more than three stars, eliminate the data; Otherwise, fill the mean	Screen	Fill the mean
$Actor_2$		ReleaseCapacity	Fill the mean
$Actor_3$		Awards	Fill 0
$Actor_4$		Score	Fill the mean
Director	Eliminate data	RatersNumber	Fill the mean
$ProductionTech_1$	Fill 1	BoxOffice	Eliminate the data

The calculation formula of the root mean square error is as follows:

$$RMSE = \frac{1}{n}\sqrt{\sum\nolimits_{i=1}^{n}(R_i - P_i)^2} \qquad (22)$$

Among them, n is the predicted number of samples; R_i and P_i are the actual values and predictive values of the box office values for test samples.

4.3   Determine the DBN Model Structure

In order to reasonably set the number of network depth and hidden layer nodes of DBN, this paper firstly studied the influence of DBN on the prediction performance of the model in {2, 3, 4} layer. The prediction performance is optimal when the number of DBN layer is 2 (see Fig. 5).

Secondly, this paper studies the influence of hidden layer nodes on the prediction performance of the model in the experiment. When the number of hidden layer nodes is 50, the performance of the box office prediction model is optimal (see Figs. 5, 6 and Table 3).

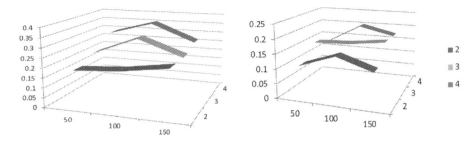

Fig. 5. MAE and RMSE value of different number of hidden layer

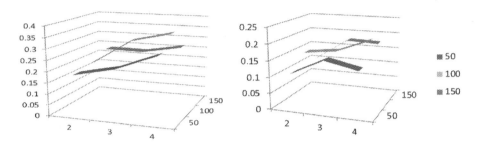

Fig. 6. MAE and RMSE value of different number nodes of hidden layer

Table 3. Comparison of different hidden layer and different number of hidden node

	50		100		150	
	MAE	RMSE	MAE	RMSE	MAE	RMSE
2	0.182	0.108	0.199	0.151	0.234	0.112
3	0.221	0.157	0.312	0.162	0.231	0.177
4	0.291	0.135	0.354	0.201	0.263	0.173

4.4   Comparison of Experimental Error

In order to verify the performance of the model, the DBN box office prediction model is compared with the optimal prediction results of BP neural network box office prediction model and BRP model on the same data set. The comparison results are shown in Fig. 7 (Table 4).

The best prediction performance of traditional BRP models is relatively poor. Comparing the performance of the back propagation neural network box office prediction model and the DBN box office prediction model, we can see that the DBN model still takes the lead and effectively improves the long-term prediction performance of the box office.

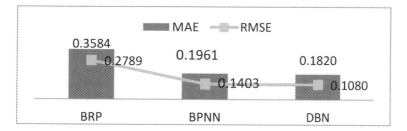

Fig. 7. MAE, RMSE comparison chart of BRP/BPNN/DBN

Table 4. MAE, RMSE value of BRP/BPNN/DBN

	BRP	BPNN	DBN
MAE	0.3584	0.1961	0.1820
RMSE	0.2789	0.1403	0.1080

References

1. Asheim, L.: Hollywood looks at its audience: a report of film audience research. J. Mark. Res. **20**(4), 453 (1951)
2. Litman, B.R., Kohl, L.S.: Predicting financial success of motion pictures: the '80s experience. J. Media Econ. **2**(2), 35–50 (1989)
3. Sharda, R., Delen, D.: Predicting box-office success of motion pictures with neural networks. Expert Syst. Appl. **30**(2), 243–254 (2006)
4. Barman, D., Chowdhury, N., Singha, R.K.: To predict possible profit/loss of a movie to be launched using MLP with back-propagation learning. In: International Conference on Communications, Devices and Intelligent Systems, pp. 322–325. IEEE (2012)
5. Zhang, L., Luo, J., Yang, S.: Forecasting box office revenue of movies with BP neural network. Expert Syst. Appl. **36**(3), 6580–6587 (2009)
6. Zheng, J., Zhou, S.: Modeling on box-office revenue prediction of movie based on neural network. J. Comput. Appl. **34**(3), 742–748 (2014)
7. Henry, M., Sharda, R.: Using neural networks to forecast box office success (2007)
8. Hinton, G.E., Osindero, S., Teh, Y.W.: A fast learning algorithm for deep belief nets. Neural Comput. **18**(7), 1527–1554 (2014)
9. Schmidhuber, J.: Deep learning in neural networks: an overview. Neural Netw. **61**, 85–117 (2015)
10. Glorot, X., Bordes, A., Bengio, Y.: Deep sparse rectifier neural networks. In: JMLR W&CP (2011)
11. Lecun, Y., Bengio, Y., Hinton, G.: Deep learning. Nature **521**(7553), 436–444 (2015)

A Deep-Layer Feature Selection Method Based on Deep Neural Networks

Chen Qiao$^{(\boxtimes)}$, Ke-Feng Sun, and Bin Li

School of Mathematics and Statistics, Xi'an Jiaotong University, Xi'an 710049, China
qiaochen@xjtu.edu.cn

Abstract. Inspired by the sparse mechanism of the biological nervous system, we propose a novel feature selection algorithm: features back-selection (FBS) method, which is based on the deep learning architecture. Compared with the existing feature selection method, this method is no longer a shallow layer approach, since it is from the global perspective, which traces back step by step to the original key feature sites of the raw data by the abstract features learned from the top of the deep neural networks. For MNIST data, the FBS method has quite well performance on searching for the original important pixels of the digit data. It shows that the FBS method not only can determine the relevant features for learning task with keeping a quite high prediction accuracy, but also can reduce the space of data storage as well as the computational complexity.

Keywords: Features back-selection · Deep neural networks
Deep-layer architecture · Key sites

1 Introduction

How to reduce the dimension of the large-scale high-dimensional (LSHD) data and effectively select the characteristic information which can describe the essential features of them are quite critical steps for dealing with them (Dzwinel and Wcislo 2015). One of the most commonly used dimensionality reduction methods is feature selection. By feature selection, those essential features that have the greatest contribution to distinguish different objects from the raw data can be identified. For the existing feature selection methods, most of them aim to achieve the structure of the data based on shallow models, that is, the feature selection process only performs on the representation of the original signal for the data, which will lead to the limitation on the understanding of the data quite locally, and the key effects of the important features in the global analysis will be missed. Searching for a method to obtain the deep expression of the layered abstract structure for the data, can help us to further achieve the crucial features of the original data in a global view.

On the other hand, for large-scale high-dimensional data, only those models with strong expression ability can fully explore the massive valuable information contained in the data. As a new learning paradigm in machine learning, deep

© Springer International Publishing AG, part of Springer Nature 2018
Y. Tan et al. (Eds.): ICSI 2018, LNCS 10942, pp. 542–551, 2018.
https://doi.org/10.1007/978-3-319-93818-9_52

learning can learn the layer-by-layer structure by greedy layer-wise training, and the neurons can obtain the multi-layer nonlinear expression of the data. Thus, deep learning has very strong ability of expressive stratification, and it can profoundly reveal the complex abstract information of the data. However, for deep learning, there are still a series of problems worth exploring. Currently, the deep learning methods are most used for abstract feature extraction and further for classification task, and there exists few research on using deep learning for feature selection. In this paper, we will use the depth and sparsity architecture of deep learning to obtain the key features of the original data, which can help us to explore the profound mechanism that the human brain can recognize different things, that is, how the human brain can find the most essential features from different data and thus discriminate them.

Based on one of the general used deep learning architecture, i.e., deep neural network (DNN), we will propose a new feature selection algorithm, i.e., the feature back-selection method. This method integrates the processes of target optimization function, search procedure as well as the evaluation method wholly. Compared with the shallow feature selection method, by this method, the understanding of the data is no longer limited locally, but through the global abstract analysis, one can find out the most important features of the original data.

By applying this method to practical problems, we have the following results. For the MNIST dataset, it is possible to successfully select the key pixels that can distinguish different types of handwritten digits. The experimental results show that with this method, under the premise of high classification accuracy (e.g., the average classification accuracy for two kinds of digits is 98.56% and for three kinds it is 97.80%), the very high compression rates can be guaranteed to ensure (the average space saving rate of two kinds is 92% and it is 83% for three kinds). That means, the important distinguish pixels of the handwritten digits are found by this method. From these experiments, it is shown that the features back-selection method can accurately identify the original important pixels of the digits data, and all of them are under the precondition of maintaining a quite high prediction accuracy. In addition, this method also greatly improves the spatial storage capacity of raw data, and guarantees the search speech of the important features to be rapider and the search speech process to be more stable.

2   The Structure of DNN

A deep belief network (DBN) is a generative graphical model, or alternatively a type of deep neural network, composed of multiple layers of hidden units (Hinton and Salakhutdinov 2006). When trained on a set of examples in an unsupervised way, a DBN can learn to reconstruct the probability distribution of its inputs. A DBN can be viewed as a composition of simple, unsupervised networks, i.e., restricted Boltzmann machines (RBMs), and uses a greedy unsupervised training method to learn the true distribution of the real data and further to perform feature extraction task (Hinton et al. 2012). Each RBM can find a compressed feature representation of the input data, and the last layer of the DBN provides abstract features of the raw data.

In an RBM, there are two layers: one is the visible input layer, and the other is a hidden layer. There are connections between the layers but no connection between units within each layer. Assume $v = (v_1, v_2, \cdots, v_{N_v})^T$ is the visible units, $h = (h_1, h_2, \cdots, h_{N_h})^T$ is the hidden units, $\alpha = (\alpha_1, \alpha_2, \cdots, \alpha_{N_v})^T$ is the bias of the the visible units, $\beta = (\beta_1, \beta_2, \cdots, \beta_{N_h})^T$ is the bias of the hidden units, and $W = \{W_{ij}\}_{N_v \times N_h}$ with each w_{ij} is the connection weight of v_i and h_j. A joint configuration, (v, h) of the visible and hidden units has an energy, which is given by

$$E(v, h) = -\sum_{i=1}^{N_v} \alpha_i v_i - \sum_{j=1}^{N_h} \beta_j h_j - \sum_{i=1}^{N_v} \sum_{j=1}^{N_h} v_i W_{ij} h_j$$

and the compact form of it is $E_\theta(v, h) := E(v, h) = -\alpha^T v - \beta^T h - v^T W h$, here $\theta = \{W, \alpha, \beta\}$ is the set of all parameters. Thus, we have the joint probability distribution of the state (v, h):

$$P_\theta(v, h) = \frac{1}{Z_\theta} e^{-E_\theta(v,h)} \tag{1}$$

in which $Z_\theta = \sum_{v,h} e^{-E_\theta(v,h)}$ is known as the partition function or normalizing constant. $P_\theta(v)$, the distribution of the observed data v_θ, is the marginal distribution of $P_\theta(v, h)$, and it is defined as $P_\theta(v) = \frac{1}{Z_\theta} \sum_h e^{-E_\theta(v,h)}$. $P_\theta(v)$ also has another name, i.e., likelihood function. Maximizing it is just the task of training an RBM. In other words, maximizing the likelihood function is equal to determining the parameters to fit the given training samples, i.e., to find a θ^*, such that

$$\theta^* = \arg \max_\Theta \mathcal{L}(\theta) \tag{2}$$

with $\mathcal{L}(\theta) = \log P_\theta(v)$. By maximizing the log-likelihood of input data, we obtain the parameters of an RBM, and this can be achieved by a very simple learning rule for performing stochastic steepest ascent in the log probability of the training data. The weights are updated by $\Delta W_{ij} = \epsilon \cdot \frac{\partial \mathcal{L}}{\partial W_{ij}} = \epsilon \cdot (\langle v_i h_j \rangle_{data} - \langle v_i h_j \rangle_{model})$, in which, ϵ is the learning rate, and $\langle \cdot \rangle$ is the operator of expectation with the corresponding distribution denoted by the subscript.

The absence of direct connections between hidden unites in an RBM makes it is quite easy to get an unbiased sample of $\langle v_i h_j \rangle_{data}$. While, obtaining an unbiased sample of $\langle v_i h_j \rangle_{model}$ is much more different. That is because, in order to calculate it, we should know Z_θ first, which is quite hard to do. It can be solved by starting from any random state of the visible unites and performing alternating Gibbs sampling. However, for Gibbs sampling, this does really take much time, especially when the number of features of the training samples are very large. A much faster learning using contrastive divergence (CD) was proposed by Hinton (Hinton 2002 and Hinton 2010). It starts by setting the states of the visible units to a training vector, and then it only needs a few steps to find the satisfactory states of all hidden units followed by a one step of CD procedure. Once binary states have been chosen for the hidden units, a so-called reconstruction is performed on each v_i. Then, the states of the hidden unites are updated again. The change in a weight is given by

$$\Delta W_{ij} = \epsilon \cdot (\langle v_i h_j \rangle_{data} - \langle v_i h_j \rangle_{recon}) \tag{3}$$

and similarly, the updates of the biases are

$$\Delta \alpha_i = \epsilon \cdot (\langle v_i \rangle_{data} - \langle v_i \rangle_{recon}) \tag{4}$$

$$\Delta \beta_j = \epsilon \cdot (\langle h_j \rangle_{data} - \langle h_j \rangle_{recon}) \tag{5}$$

Furthermore, in order to limit the quickly increasing bounds of the weights, the optimization function is modified to be

$$\max_{\Theta}\{\mathcal{L}(\Theta) - \frac{1}{2}\lambda_1 \|W\|_2^2\}$$

where $\| \cdot \|_2$ is the L_2 norm and λ_1 is the parameter to control the bound of W. The purpose of adding the regularization $\|W\|_2$ is to prevent overfitting. Thus, by using the gradient descent method, we can update the parameters in (3) based on (6)

$$\Delta W_{ij} = \epsilon \cdot (\langle v_i h_j \rangle_{data} - \langle v_i h_j \rangle_{recon}) - \lambda_1 W_{ij} \tag{6}$$

and remain the updating of α_i in (4) as well as β_j in (5).

Further, a decided layer is added on the top of the stacked RBMs, and a fine-tuning method is used for further tuning the parameters of the network. Such a whole network is just the DNN.

3 FBS: Features Back-Selection Algorithm Based on DNN

Mathematically, the feature selection method can be described as follows. For any raw data $X = (x_1, x_2, \cdots, x_N)^T$, we hope to select vector $\tilde{X} = (x_{R_1}, x_{R_2}, \cdots, x_{R_M})^T$, where each x_{R_i} $(i = 1, 2, \cdots, M)$ is the key feature chosen from $\{x_1, x_2, \cdots, x_N\}$ based on some rules R. The rule could be either of the following items. $\tilde{X}$ is the optimal choice with some evaluation indexes for classifiers; the feature subset has the lowest dimension for a given accuracy; the error rate of classifier would not be reduced by neither increase nor decrease in the number of features; the conditional probability distribution function for the data and that of the selected features remain the same.

In an RBM, for each hidden unit, it receives weighted signals from the visible layer by the synaptic connections between it and the visible units. The connections between each hidden unit and the visible layer are measured normally with the connection strength values (weights); generally speaking, these connections encode the memories we expect to have. The larger the absolute value of the connection weight is, the stronger the influence (strategic decision) of the corresponding visible unit makes on the hidden layer. Thus, it has a high probability that this position is a key site of the raw data. For the layer-wised network, i.e., DNN, it can be considered that there exists a positive relationship between the input and the weighting matrices of all layers.

In what follows, we propose a new feature selection method called features back-selection on DNN, to select the essential features/sites of the raw data. The whole process of the features back-selection is described as follows. First, during the learning step, a DNN is trained to obtain the probabilistic construction of the raw data. Then, the learned DNN is fine-tuned with back-propagation by using the label information of the training data. And further, we perform the features back-selection method on the fine-tuned DNN. For each RBM of the learned DNN, we select key sites of the current visible layer (i.e., the important sites of the current input data) by

$$I = \{i : |w_{ij}| \geq \alpha, \exists j \in \{1, \cdots, N_h\}\} \tag{7}$$

Where w_{ij} is the connection between visible unit i and hidden unit j, α is a given threshold and N_h is the number of units in the hidden layer. Model (7) is based on the understanding about neural networks that the larger the absolute value of w_{ij} is, the higher the influence of the i-th visible unit will be on the j-th hidden unit (current output unit). Thus, set I contains all those visible units (sites) which are responsible for the hidden units to be active in the current RBM. At last, based on model (7), we obtain the features back-selection method for the whole DNN. That is, we do feature selection from up to down on the DNN, and get the very important sites of the raw data. Each site can be considered as with a high probability to cause the output of the network to be activated and make a decision for prediction or judgment. The features back-selection method on DNN is provided in Algorithm 1.

Algorithm 1. The features back-selection method on DNN

Require: L, $w^{(l)}(l = L - 1, \cdots, 1)$, $\alpha^{(l)}(l = L - 1, \cdots, 1)$, $I^{(L)}$
Ensure: $I^{(1)}$
  1: **for** $l = L - 1 : -1 : 1$ **do**
  2:     $I^{(l)} = \{i : |w_{ij}^{(l)}| \geq \alpha^{(l)}, \exists j \in I^{(l+1)}\}$
  3:     $N^{(l)} = length(I^{(l)})$
  4: **end for**
  5: **return** $I^{(1)}, N^{(l)}(l = L, \cdots, 1)$

In which L is the amount of layers in DNN, $w^{(l)}$ is the connecting weight between layer $l+1$ and layer l. $\alpha^{(l)}$ is the threshold for key features/sites selection of layer l. $I^{(L)}$ is the set of units in the top layer of DNN. $I^{(l)}$ is such a set which contains key sites of the current layer l. Thus, by back-selection method, we can get these features (i.e., $I^{(1)}$) from the raw data which contribute most to data recognition.

The presented features back-selection method combines the tasks of establishing target optimization function, determining the search procedure and the evaluation method together. What is the most important, unlike the existing feature selection method, e.g., Lasso, Information Gain, Relief, Fisher Discriminant methods, mRMR and Chi Squares, this method is no longer a shallow method, and can help us to obtain the most important key features of the original data by tracing back the distinguishing features from the top layer.

4 Experiments on the MNIST Database

In this section, we use the MNIST database to show the validation of the features back-selection method. The MNIST database is a simple computer vision dataset, and it contains a training set of 60,000 examples, and a test set of 10,000 examples (LeCun and Cortes 2010). Each one is an image and is one of the 10 handwritten digits (from 0 to 9). All of the digits have been size-normalized and centered in a fixed-size image. Each image has a total of $28 * 28 = 784$ pixels, the 784-dimensional pixels are listed into a vector, so that each image is represented by a 784-dimensional vector. For every pixel, its value is between 0, which represents white, and 255, which represents black. Intermediate pixel values represent shades of gray.

In our experiments, the training set including 60,000 images are used to train the sparse DNN, and the test set (10,000 images) are used for testifying that if the obtained pixels by features back-selection method are the key pixels for recognition of different digits. The main purpose here is to get the important pixels of the 0–9 digit images for discriminating different digits.

We use a DNN which contains 5 layers, one is the visible layer, three are hidden layers, and the top one is the decision layer. Let $\alpha_k^{(l)} = c_k^{(l)} w_{mean}^{(l)}$ ($l = 1, \cdots, 4$) be the threshold of key features/sites selection with layer l for digit k, where $c_k^{(l)}$ is a coefficient and $w_{mean}^{(l)} = \frac{1}{N_v \cdot N_h} \sum_{i=1}^{N_v} \sum_{j=1}^{N_h} |w_{ij}^{(l)}|$. Denote

$$\alpha_k = (c_k^{(4)} w_{mean}^{(4)}, c_k^{(3)} w_{mean}^{(3)}, c_k^{(2)} w_{mean}^{(2)}, c_k^{(1)} w_{mean}^{(1)})^T$$

and $c_k = (c_k^{(4)}, c_k^{(3)}, c_k^{(2)}, c_k^{(1)})^T (k = 0, 1, \cdots, 9)$ for different digit k.

4.1 Key Pixels Back-Selection Results for Two Types of Digits

In this part, by using two types of digits to train the DNN, and based on Algorithm 1, we get the distinguishing pixels for two types of digits. In this way, the two types of digits are trained together, and the key pixels for each other are obtained separately.

For convenience, we denote the dimension of the original data as N_o, the dimension of the selected pixels as N_s, the classification accuracy rate of the raw testing data as AR_o, the classification accuracy rate for the testing data with selected key pixels as AR_s and the space saving rate as SR (i.e., $SR = 1 - N_s/N_o$). The classifier for the raw testing data as well as the same testing samples with selected key pixels is the softmax classifier adding on a DNN. We will show the performance of random selected two types digits.

(I) The performance for digits 5 and 6
The coefficient vectors are $c_5 = (5, 15, 19, 26)$ and $c_6 = (6, 14, 16, 29.2)$ for digits 5 and 6 (Table 1 and Fig. 1).

Table 1. Performance before and after pixels back-selection for digits 5 & 6

DIGIT	N_o	N_s	AR_o	AR_s	SR
5	784	50	0.9955	1	0.94
6	784	90	0.9948	0.9687	0.89

(a)   (b)

Fig. 1. Original VS. distinguishable images for digits 5 and 6

(II) The performance for digits 9 and 0
The coefficient vectors are $c_9 = (5, 10, 20, 25)$ and $c_0 = (5, 15, 17, 22)$ for digits 9 and 0 (Table 2 and Fig. 2).

Table 2. Performance before and after pixels back-selection for digits 9 & 0

DIGIT	N_o	N_s	AR_o	AR_s	SR
9	784	30	0.9980	1	0.96
0	784	57	0.9990	0.991	0.93

4.2   Key Pixels Back-Selection Results for Three Kinds of Digits

In this part, we train three kinds of digits at the same time, and get the distinguishing sites for each digit.

(I) The performance for digits 3, 4 and 6
Here, by cross validation, the coefficient vectors are chosen to be $c_3 = (6, 6, 8, 10)$, $c_4 = (4.5, 5.9, 6.3, 7.4)$ and $c_6 = (6, 5.5, 7, 15)$ for digits 3, 4 and 6, respectively (Table 3 and Fig. 3).

(a)   (b)

Fig. 2. Original VS. distinguishable images for digits 9 and 0

(II) The performance for digits 2, 5 and 8
The coefficient vectors are chosen respectively to be $c_2 = (7, 12, 15, 24)$, $c_5 = (10, 14, 14, 14)$ and $c_8 = (8, 10, 11, 27)$ for digit 2, 5 and 8, respectively (Table 4 and Fig. 4).

4.3   Average Performance

Let AVG-AR_o be the average classification accuracy rate (ACAR) of the raw testing data, AVG-AR_s be the ACAR of the testing data with selected sites, AVG-N_s be the average number of sites which are selected, and AVG-SR be the average space saving rate. The average performance for all two kinds of digits and the results for all three kinds of digits are summarized in the following table.

From the above experiments, we can see that by applying the features back-selection method, the key pixels which can identify different kinds of digits can be successfully picked out. Not only the very high space saving rates are achieved, but also the high recognition accuracy rates are still kept by this method. In addition, for some cases, the accuracy can even improve for the data with the selected pixels, which enhances the powerfulness of the features back-selection method. For example, the experiment for digit 1 and digit 2 shows that the average space saving rate for digit 2 reaches 96%, and the classification accuracy rises from 96.61% to 100%. From experiment for digits 0, 1 and 3, we get that the average space saving rate for digit 1 is 90%, and the corresponding classification accuracy increases to 100%. From Table 5, it is shown that for the case of two kinds of digits, the average space saving rate is almost 92%, i.e., the average

Table 3. Performance before and after pixels back-selection for digits 3, 4 and 6

DIGIT	N_o	N_s	AR_o	AR_s	SR
3	784	63	0.9980	0.9842	0.92
4	784	348	0.9959	0.9847	0.56
6	784	47	0.9979	0.9656	0.94

(a)   (b)   (c)

Fig. 3. Original VS. distinguishable images for digits 3, 4 and 6

Table 4. Performance before and after pixels back-selection for digits 2, 5 and 8

DIGIT	N_o	N_s	AR_o	AR_s	SR
2	784	196	0.9961	0.9622	0.75
5	784	101	0.9989	0.9910	0.87
8	784	202	0.9969	0.9374	0.74

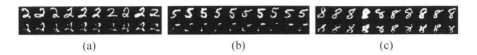

(a)   (b)   (c)

Fig. 4. Original VS. distinguishable images for digits 2, 5 and 8

Table 5. Average performance of FBS

Kinds of Digits	AVG-AR_o	AVG-AR_s	AVG-N_s	AVG-SR
2	0.9976	0.9856	63	0.92
3	0.9975	0.9780	138	0.83

compression ratio is a quite considerable number, 8%. The average classification accuracy rates keeps around 98%, with only a loss of nearly 1% in comparison with the average classification accuracy rates of the raw data. For the case of three kinds of digits, the space saving rate is nearly 83%, and the average classification accuracy rates still keeps around 97%, with only a accuracy loss of nearly 2%.

Although the MNIST digits are embedded in the 784-dimensional space, they are generally considered as occupying a lower dimensional subspace. Exploring the lower dimensional structure of the MNIST data is a quite interesting topic. During the past several years, some dimensionality reduction techniques are used for discussion the structure of MNIST digits. Among them, most of the approaches are based on the feature abstraction technique. Jiang et al. (2013) used the Principal Component Analysis (PCA) to preserve linear structure. Dzwinel and and Wcislo (2015) apply the multidimensional scaling (MDS) to preserve global geometry, and the t-Distributed Stochastic Neighbor Embedding (t-SNE) is tried to preserve topology (neighborhood structure) by Lee and Verleysen (2011) and Maaten and Hinton (2008). Hinton use the deep learning method to perform feature extraction, and the classification results of MNIST are shown and compared with the results of PCA (Hinton and Salakhutdinov 2006). One feature selection approach based on the genetic algorithm is used to select the feature subsets by introducing some specifical index to evaluate the subsets (Stefano 2014). Wang et al. (2015) discusses the feature selection results by using Lasso on MNIST dataset. Compared with the above feature abstraction methods, the deep learning approach used here can directly select the important key pixels of the raw MNIST digits. Furthermore, our results have better performance in the aspect of saving the storage space and improving the classification accuracy than the results provided by Stefano (2014) and Wang et al. (2015). The features back-selection method based on DNN provides a new view to gain some more distinct understanding on the MNIST data.

5   Conclusion

By exploring the correspondence between the weights of the DNN and the key features that can identify different data, a new feature selection method, i.e., features back-selection, is proposed. This method has shown quite powerful application in extracting the intrinsic characteristics of different digits. It's promised that the features back-selection method can be utilized directly to other fields, such as imaging analysis and accurate positioning in genes, and they are all in our current research.

Acknowledgment. This research was supported by NSFC Nos. 11471006 and 11101327, National Science and Technology Cooperation Program of China (No. 2015DFA81780), and the Fundamental Research Funds for the Central Universities (No. xjj2017126).

References

Dzwinel, W., Wcisło, R.: Very fast interactive visualization of large sets of high-dimensional data. Procedia Comput. Sci. **51**, 572–581 (2015)

Hinton, G.E., Salakhutdinov, R.R.: Reducing the dimensionality of data with neural networks. Science **313**(5786), 504–507 (2006)

Hinton, G.: training products of experts by minimizing contrastive divergence. Neural Comput. **14**, 1771–1800 (2002)

Hinton, G.E.: A practical guide to training restricted Boltzmann machines. Momentum **9**(1), 599–619 (2010)

LeCun, Y., Cortes, C.: MNIST Handwritten Digit Database (2010). http://yann.lecun.com/exdb/mnist

Jiang, B., Ding, C., Luo, B., et al.: Graph-Laplacian PCA: closed-form solution and robustness. CVPR **9**(4), 3492–3498 (2013)

Maaten, L., Hinton, G.: Visualizing data using t-SNE. J. Mach. Learn. Res. **9**, 2579–2605 (2008)

Lee, J.A., Verleysen, M.: Shift-invariant similarities circumvent distance concentration in stochastic neighbor embedding and variants. Procedia Comput. Sci. **4**(2), 538–547 (2011)

Stefano, C.D., Fontanella, F., Marrocco, C., et al.: A GA-based feature selection approach with an application to handwritten character recognition. Pattern Recognit. Lett. **35**(1), 130–141 (2014)

Hinton, G., Deng, L., Yu, D., et al.: Deep neural networks for acoustic modeling in speech recognition: the shared views of four research groups. Signal Process. Mag. IEEE **29**(6), 82–97 (2012)

Wang, J., Wonka, P., Ye, J.: Lasso screening rules via dual polytope projection. J. Mach. Learni. Res. **16**(1), 1063–1101 (2015)

Video Vehicle Detection and Recognition Based on MapReduce and Convolutional Neural Network

Mingsong Chen, Weiguang Wang$^{(\boxtimes)}$, Shi Dong, and Xinling Zhou

Guilin University of Electronic Technology, Guilin 541004, China
wwg_1121@163.com

Abstract. With the rapid growth of traffic video data, it is necessary to improve the computing power and accuracy of image processing. In this paper, a video vehicle detection and recognition system based on MapReduce and convolutional neural network is proposed to reduce the time-consume and improve the recognition accuracy in video analysis. First, a fast and reliable deep learning algorithm based on YOLOv2 is used to detect vehicle in real-time. And then the license plate recognition algorithm based on improved convolutional neural network is presented to recognize the license plate image extracted from the detected vehicle region. Finally, the Hadoop Video Processing Interface (HVPI) and MapReduce framework are combined to apply the video vehicle detection and recognition algorithms for parallel processing. Experimental results are presented to verify that the proposed scheme has advantages of high detection rate and high recognition accuracy, and strong ability of data processing in large-scale video data.

Keywords: YOLOv2 · MapReduce · Convolutional neural network
HVPI

1 Introduction

Vehicle detection and recognition plays an important role in traffic video analysis. It can be applied to many fields such as intelligent traffic control, autonomous driving, public safety and security. In the field of parallel computing, MapReduce is a major distributed computing framework, which can be used to analysis massive data.

Vehicle detection and license plate location often take a long time, resulting in poor real-time performance in video analysis. And the objects in the video frame often have problems of blurring and distortion, which leads to the low accuracy for license plate recognition. [1–3] presented different classification methods for vehicles, but the detection speed is hard to meet the real-time requirements. [5] proposed the YOLO9000 algorithm to optimize the model structure based on the YOLO [4]. [6] built a system that could perform multi-class multi-object tracking in real time using YOLOv2. [7–9] combined MSER with different classifier to locate characters, but there were some characters that can't be detected by MSER in complex environments. [10] grew seeds to locate other degraded candidate characters in text detection. [11]

© Springer International Publishing AG, part of Springer Nature 2018
Y. Tan et al. (Eds.): ICSI 2018, LNCS 10942, pp. 552–562, 2018.
https://doi.org/10.1007/978-3-319-93818-9_53

proposed a solution based on convolutional neural network to recognize the license plate characters. [12] used the linear support vector machines to identify the true license plate. [13, 14] recognized handwritten digits based on LeNet-5. [15] proposed the Hadoop Video Processing Interface to enable MapReduce to process video data.

In this paper, a video vehicle detection and recognition scheme based on MapReduce and convolutional neural network is presented. In order to improve the real-time performance of the system, YOLOv2 is applied to locate and extract the vehicle regions. MSER and BPNN are used to locate seed character component, and grow these seeds to locate other degraded candidate characters. And two improved CNN models are used to recognize license plate characters. In order to apply vehicle detection and recognition algorithm in processing large-scale video data. HVPI is used to parse traffic video data stored on HDFS into a series of images, and combined with vehicle detection and recognition algorithm to implement parallel computing of videos in MapReduce framework. This paper makes the following main contributions. (1) Apply YOLOv2 to detect and extract the vehicle region as the input of license plate recognition, it can reduce the time-consume of vehicle detection and recognition. And two improved CNN models based on LeNet-5 are used to enhance the accuracy. (2) A system of distributed video vehicle detection and recognition based MapReduce and convolutional neural network is proposed. It can provide stronger data processing capability for large-scale video data while maintaining the recognition accuracy.

This paper is organized as follows: In Sects. 2.1 and 2.2, the vehicle detection based on YOLOv2 and license plate recognition based on improved CNN are introduced. In Sect. 2.3, the structure of distributed video vehicle detection and recognition based on MapReduce is described. In Sect. 3, experiments are conducted to evaluate the performance. Finally the paper is concluded in Sect. 4.

2 System Model

The System mainly contains three parts: vehicle detection, license plate recognize and parallel computing based on MapReduce. First of all, the YOLOv2 network is introduced to convert multi-object classification problem into a single-object classification problem to detect vehicle in the traffic video. And then the improved CNN is presented to recognize the license plate characters from the detected region. Finally, vehicle detection and license plate recognition has been implemented on Hadoop cluster for parallel video processing.

2.1 Vehicle Detection

YOLOv2 is an improved model of YOLO without building complex network, and some techniques are used to improve the precision of object detection. There techniques include batch normalization, high resolution classifier, dimension clusters, and etc. Based on YOLOv2, this model has 22 convolutional layers and 5 pooling layers. YOLOv2 downsamples the input image by a factor of 32 to get an output feature map of $S \times S$. And each grid cell of output feature map predicts B bounding boxes. Each bounding box predicts 5 coordinates and C class probabilities. When $B = 5$, the network gives a good tradeoff between high recall and model complexity. So the number of filters in the last convolutional layer can be calculated as follows:$(B \times (5 + C))$. In order to use YOLOv2 for vehicle detection, each bounding box only predicts 1 class: $C = 1$, so the number of filters is set to 30 and the previous convolution and pooling layers used for feature extraction are kept unchanged. In order to achieve a higher video processing rate, Tiny YOLOv2 is modified in the same way and then compared with the performance of YOLOv2. Finally, pre-trained weights of the YOLOv2 network and DETRAC vehicle dataset are used to train the model.

2.2 Vehicle License Plate Recognition

License plate recognition algorithm is used to identify the license plate from the area of detected vehicle. An overview of the detection and recognition is shown in Fig. 1. License plate recognition algorithm is divided into two parts: license plate location and character recognition.

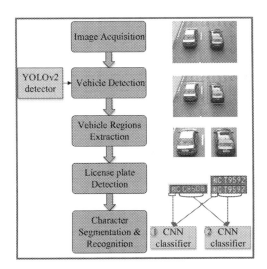

Fig. 1. An overview of vehicle detection and recognition

License Plate Location: The license plate location is realized based on MSER, seed growth and BP neural network.

MSER [7–9] and BPNN [7] are introduced to locate stable seed character component [10], which preserve the relatively completed characteristics of the license plate characters and have the high output probability of BPNN, and then these seeds are grown to locate other degraded candidate characters [10] according to BPNN classifier and the geometrical relationship of characters in standard license plates [8]. And the license plate classifier based on linear support vector machines [12] is used to identify the true license plate from the candidate regions. SVM classification model based on RBF kernel is trained by extracting the projection features of binarized image and the color features of HSV image. BP neural network model is trained by extracting the projection features of binarized image. The number of neurons in input layer is equal to the dimension of extracted feature vector, the number of neurons in output layer is equal to the number of categories of license plate characters.

Character Recognition Based on CNN: The LeNet-5 [13] model was originally used for recognizing handwritten 10 types of numbers. Chinese license plate consists of more complex character structure of Chinese and simpler character structure of non-Chinese. And in order to avoid misidentification between Chinese characters and non-Chinese characters, two CNN models are improved and trained respectively for two character structures with different complexity. The two improved network parameter lists are shown in the Tables 1 and 2.

The improved convolutional neural network consists of input layer, convolution layer, pooling layer, hidden layer and classification layer.

Table 1. Configuration of the improved model1 for Chinese characters, where k is the size of the kernel, s is stride, p is padding

Layer type	Parameters
Soft-max	31 classes
Fully connected	Number of neurons:31
Dropout	0.7
ReLU	
Fully connected	Number of neurons:500
Maxpooling	k:2 × 2, s:2
Convolution	Number of filters: 32, k:3 × 3, s:1, p:0
Maxpooling	k:2 × 2, s:2
ReLU	
Convolution	Number of filters: 64, k:7 × 7, s:1, p:0
Input	32 × 32 pixels gray-scale image

Table 2. Configuration of the improved model2 for non-Chinese characters, where k is the size of the kernel, s is stride, p is padding

Layer type	Parameters
Soft-max	34 classes
Fully connected	Number of neurons:34
Dropout	0.7
ReLU	
Fully connected	Number of neurons:500
Maxpooling	k:2 × 2, s:2
ReLU	
Convolution	Number of filters: 16, k:3 × 3, s:1, p:0
Input	32 × 32 pixels gray-scale image

The convolutional layer is mainly used for feature extraction. The convolution layer is convolved with a trainable convolution kernel, and then the output feature map is obtained through an activation function. In order to prevent vanishing gradient problem and accelerate network convergence, Rectified Linear Unit (ReLU) is used as the activation function.

$$x_j^l = f\left(\sum_{i \in M_j} x_i^{l-1} * k_{ij}^l + b_j^l\right) \tag{1}$$

$$f(x) = \max(0, x) \tag{2}$$

According to (1) and (2), the new feature map will be generated after convolution. Where x_j^l is the output feature map, x_i^{l-1} is the input feature map, b_j^l is biases, k_{ij}^l is the convolution kernel, $f(\cdot)$ is the activation function.

The pooling layer downsamples the input feature map to produce a new feature map.

$$x_j^l = f(\beta_j^l down(x_j^{l-1}) + b_j^l) \tag{3}$$

According to (3), every four pixels are divided into a group, and then taking the maximum value from each group to generate the new feature map. Where $down(\cdot)$ is the down-sampling function, and max-pooling configuration is used. $f(\cdot)$ is the ReLU function, β_j^l is the multiplicative bias of the l layer, b_j^l is the additive bias of the l layer.

The last layer of the network is the classification layer, which is responsible for the classification of the output characteristics of the hidden layer to obtain the probability of each classification result, the Soft-max classification structure is used in the classification layer.

$$x_i = \sum_j \beta_{ij} \times y_j + b_i \tag{4}$$

$$y_i = \frac{e^{x_i}}{\sum_{c=0}^{c-1} e^{x_c}} \tag{5}$$

According to (4) and (5), the classification probability of each neuron in the last layer can be calculate, where c is the number of neurons in the last layer, and there are 34 types of non-Chinese characters and 31 types of Chinese characters in the Chinese license plate. c is set to 31 and 34 respectively in the improved model1 and model2, y_i is the output probability of the neuron i in the last layer. x_i is the input of the neuron i, y_j is the output of the neuron j of the previous layer. β_{ij} is the multiplicative bias between the neuron i and the neuron j, b_i is the additive bias of the neuron i.

The structure of non-Chinese is relatively simple, so a set of convolutional layers and pooling layers are removed to simplify the network structure. In the same time the size of the convolution kernels is reduced to extract more types of features as supplements. And the Chinese characters are relatively complex, so more fine-grained features are extracted by reducing the size of the convolution kernel and increasing the number of convolution kernel. In order to avoid the situation of fitting during training and increase the anti-noise performance of the network, dropout is introduced at the input of hidden layer.

2.3   Hadoop Video Data Processing

Video data is an unstructured data type, Hadoop native Record Reader can't parse the input video data into the data type of <key, value>. Therefore, the Hadoop video processing interface (HVPI) is described to parse the input video data into a series of <key, value> and enable MapReduce to support the distributed computing for video data. HVPI [15] includes the VideoInputFormat class and the VideoRecordReader class, which use the video decoding library Xuggler to parses the input video data into a series of <key, value>. Key consists of the video name and frame id, and value is the frame data. Figure 2 shows the framework of video processing.

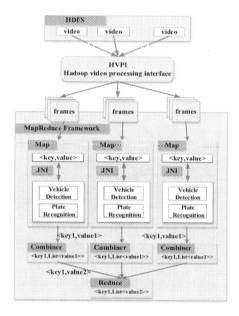

Fig. 2. The framework of video processing

The Map method is mainly used to detect the vehicle area and recognize the license plate from frame data. Since the underlying framework of Hadoop is written in Java, which is not efficient in complex image processing and the license plate recognition algorithm has high computational complexity. So this paper used C++ language combined with OpenCV to realize vehicle detection and license plate recognition algorithm, and then compiled algorithm into a dynamic link library that can be called on the Hadoop platform. The distributed image processing is realized by interacting with the dynamic link library through the JNI (Java Native Interface) in the Map function. This method can obtain high execution efficiency for the large-scale video data. The execution result of the Map function is used as the input of the Combiner function, which can reduce the amount of data transferred between Map and Reduce by merging and processing the Map results from the current logical block. Reduce function merges the output of all combiner function, and then generate vehicle recognition results <key1, List<value2>>, key1 is the license plate recognition result, value2 contains the video name and frame id.

3   Experiment and Analysis

3.1   Vehicle Detection and Recognition Test

The modified YOLOv2 networks are trained on DETRAC dataset. The number of data samples is 80000. The 85% of them is used as a training set and 15% as a test set. The trained models are tested on a single GeForce GTX 1060. Figure 3 shows the detecting result of Tiny YOLOv2 and YOLOv2 in different scenes.

From Fig. 3, it can be seen that YOLOv2 and Tiny YOLOv2 exhibit sufficient robustness of complicated illumination and high-density vehicles. From Table 3 and Fig. 4, they can achieve high precision when recall is less than 0.8, and Tiny YOLOv2 can meet the real-time detection.

Fig. 3. Detecting results in different scenes. (a)–(f) Tiny YOLOv2 detecting results; (g)–(l) YOLOv2 detecting results.

Table 3. The performance and speed of the above two detectors.

	Precision	Recall	AP	F1-score	FPS
Tiny YOLOv2	74.41%	85.49%	82.10%	0.80	31
YOLOv2	77.10%	91.32%	88.58%	0.84	13

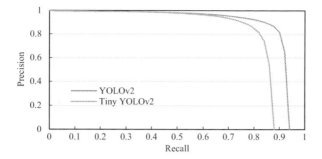

Fig. 4. Precision-Recall curve

The two improved CNN models and LeNet-5 are trained on our collected dataset. Before feeding features to convolution neural network, the samples are randomly scaled and rotated to augment data. The whole dataset of 700 character samples is divided into training set and test set, 600 for training and 100 for testing. Figure 5 shows the loss which varies with the number of iterations during the process of training improved models and LeNet-5.

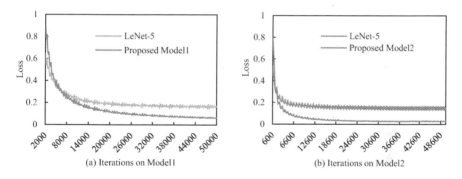

Fig. 5. The loss with iterations.

The two improved CNN models have lower loss than the LeNet-5 model. And 1000 license plate images are used to test accuracy, Table 4 shows the accuracy of different classifiers.

Table 4. Accuracy of different classifiers.

Classifier	Chinese characters	non-Chinese characters
BPNN	88.45%	91.34%
LeNet-5	91.76%	92.82%
Proposed models	97.66%	96.41%

3.2   Analysis of Computation Cost

The time-consume of the vehicle detection and license plate recognition is tested. Vehicle detection algorithm based on Tiny YOLOv2 processes images at 31 FPS on GeForce GTX 1060, and license plate recognition algorithm processes images at 2 FPS. The vehicle detection is used to extract the detected vehicle area to reduce the calculation area of license plate recognition. The time-consume of the license plate recognition is tested respectively on 500 completed images and extracted vehicle regions from 500 completed images. The average time-consume of the former is 0.5 s, and the latter is 0.17 s.

Video processing requires high computing power and consumes more time. The detection and recognition algorithms are combined with MapReduce to achieve parallel computing for video data stored on HDFS. This processing is carried out on a cluster of 3 data-nodes and 1 name-node. The number of videos uploaded to HDFS is used as a control variable. Each video is a 100 M traffic video, and Fig. 6 shows the time-consume which varies with the number of input videos.

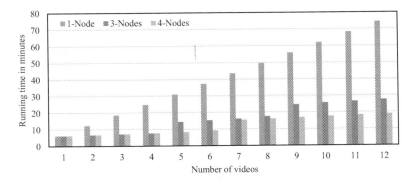

Fig. 6. The running time with different number of videos

Two containers are allocated to perform map tasks on each slave node. With the increase of the number of input videos, the stand-alone running time grows linearly, while more slave nodes can shorten the time-consume by parallel Map tasks. With the same number of videos, as the number of cluster nodes increases, the system consumes less time and shows better execution efficiency.

4   Conclusion and Future Work

In this paper, a video vehicle detection and recognition system based on MapReduce and convolutional neural network is proposed. Vehicle detection and recognition is designed based on YOLOv2 and CNN, and then implemented on MapReduce framework for parallel computing of videos. From the experiments, vehicle detection can achieve enough speed to process video data with competitive precision. The accuracy of model1 is 5.9% higher than LeNet-5 and the accuracy of model2 is 3.59% higher than LeNet-5. The calculation time for extracted vehicle area is 2/3 times lower than the time for processing the completed input image. And this scheme has higher efficiency in processing large-scale video data by increasing the number of cluster nodes. For future work, more efforts will be put into the improvement of the real-time performance of license plate recognition and the resource utilization of Hadoop clusters.

Acknowledgments. This work is supported by the National Natural Science Foundation of China (No. 61561014) and the Innovation Project of GUET Graduate Education (No. 2016YJCX93 & No. 2018YJCX29).

References

1. Lee, S.H., Bang, M.S., Jung, K.H.: An efficient selection of HOG feature for SVM classification of vehicle. In: IEEE International Symposium on Consumer Electronics, pp. 1–2 (2015)
2. Ren, S., He, K., Girshick, R.: Faster R-CNN: Towards real-time object detection with region proposal networks. In: Advances in Neural Information Processing Systems, pp. 91–99 (2015)
3. Fan, Q., Brown, L., Smith, J.: A closer look at Faster R-CNN for vehicle detection. In: IEEE Intelligent Vehicles Symposium, pp. 124–129 (2016)
4. Redmon, J., Divvala, S., Girshick, R.: You only look once: unified, real-time object detection. In: Proceedings of the IEEE Conference on Computer Vision and Pattern Recognition, pp. 779–788 (2016)
5. Redmon, J., Farhadi, A.: YOLO9000: Better, faster, stronger. CVPR (2017)
6. Jo, K.U., Im, J.H., Kim, J.: A real-time multi-class multi-object tracker using YOLOv2. In: IEEE International Conference on Signal and Image Processing Applications, pp. 507–511 (2017)
7. Hong, T., Gopalakrishnam, A.K.: License plate extraction and recognition of a Thai vehicle based on MSER and BPNN. In: IEEE International Conference on Knowledge and Smart Technology, pp. 48–53 (2015)
8. Gou, C., Wang, K., Yu, Z.: License plate recognition using MSER and HOG based on ELM. In: IEEE International Conference on Service Operations and Logistics, and Informatics, pp. 217–221 (2014)
9. Sung, M.C., Jun, B., Cho, H.: Scene text detection with robust character candidate extraction method. In: IEEE International Conference on Document Analysis and Recognition, pp. 426–430 (2015)
10. Xu, H., Su, F.: A robust hierarchical detection method for scene text based on convolutional neural networks. In: IEEE International Conference on Multimedia and Expo, pp. 1–6 (2015)
11. Liu, P., Li, G.H., Tu, D.: Low-quality license plate character recognition based on CNN. In: IEEE International Symposium on Computational Intelligence and Design, pp. 53–58 (2016)
12. Yuan, Y., Zou, W., Yong, Z.: A robust and efficient approach to license plate detection. IEEE Trans. Image Process. **26**(3), 1102–1114 (2017)
13. Lecun, Y., Bottou, L., Bengio, Y.: Gradient-based learning applied to document recognition. Proc. IEEE **86**(11), 2278–2324 (1998)

14. Yu, N., Jiao, P., Zheng, Y.: Handwritten digits recognition base on improved LeNet5. In: IEEE Control and Decision Conference, pp. 4871–4875 (2015)
15. Zhao, X., Ma, H., Zhang, H.: HVPI: extending hadoop to support video analytic applications. In: IEEE International Conference on Cloud Computing Computer Society, pp. 789–796 (2015)

A Uniform Approach for the Comparison of Opposition-Based Learning

Qingzheng Xu[1]([✉]), Heng Yang[1], Na Wang[1], Rong Fei[2], and Guohua Wu[3]

[1] College of Information and Communication,
National University of Defense Technology, Xi'an 710106, China
xuqingzheng@hotmail.com
[2] School of Computer Science and Engineering,
Xi'an University of Technology, Xi'an 710048, China
[3] College of Systems Engineering, National University of Defense Technology,
Changsha 410073, China

Abstract. Although remarkable progress has been made in the application of opposition-based learning in recent years, the complete theoretical comparison is seldom reported. In this paper, an evaluation function of opposition strategy is defined and then a uniform evaluation approach to compute the mean minimum Euclidean distance to the optimal solution is proposed for one dimensional case. Thus different opposition strategies can be compared easily by means of the mathematical expectation of these evaluation functions. Theoretical analysis and simulation experiments can support each other, and also show the effectiveness of this method for sampling problems.

Keywords: Opposition-Based learning · Performance comparison
Evaluation function · Uniform approach

1 Introduction

For intelligent algorithms inspired by nature behaviors or biological systems, the starting points are chosen randomly in the whole research space in many cases. According to the Principle of Insufficient Reason [1], without any prior knowledge about the problem, assuming "equal probability" for the location of the optimal solution can be seriously as a reasonable course of action [2]. If the starting points are exactly close to the optimal solution, the convergence process will be very fast. Thus looking simultaneously for a better candidate solution in both current and opposite directions may help us to solve science and engineering problems quickly and efficiently.

The main idea of Opposition-Based Learning (OBL) is, for finding a better candidate solution, an estimate and its corresponding opposite estimate are evaluated simultaneously and then the fitter one which is closer to the global optimum is maintained in next generation [3]. Since then, it has become a fast growing research field that has drawn increasing attention. For a detailed overview on state-of-the-art OBL research, we strongly recommend a recent review article by Xu [4].

© Springer International Publishing AG, part of Springer Nature 2018
Y. Tan et al. (Eds.): ICSI 2018, LNCS 10942, pp. 563–574, 2018.
https://doi.org/10.1007/978-3-319-93818-9_54

Since OBL was originally introduced in computational intelligence, its different variations have been proposed in the literature to accelerate convergence of meta-heuristic algorithms. Mathematical comparison between these variations is one of the most important research topics related to OBL. This paper belongs to this field. Our main contribution is an evaluation function and a uniform approach to compare the usefulness of different opposite strategies for one dimensional problem.

2 Fundamentals

2.1 OBL and Its Variations

Up to now, the variations of opposition-based learning include Quasi-Opposition-Based Learning (QOBL) [5], Quasi-Reflection Opposition-Based Learning (QROBL) [6], Center-based Sampling (CBS) [7], Generalized Opposition-Based Learning (GOBL) [8], Opposition-Based Learning using the Current Optimum (COOBL) [9] and Opposite-Center Learning (OCL) [10]. Note that the opposite point based on GOBL is dependent on a random number (k) and the opposite point based on COOBL may vary apparently along with the population evolution. Considering the nature of uncertainty, these two opposite strategies will not be discussed in this paper.

Let $p = (p_1, p_2, \ldots, p_D)$ be an arbitrary point in D-dimensional space, where $p_1, p_2, \ldots, p_D \in R$ and $p_i \in [a_i, b_i], \forall i \in \{1, 2, \ldots, D\}$. The opposite point $\breve{p}_o = (\breve{p}_{o1}, \breve{p}_{o2}, \ldots \breve{p}_{oD})$, quasi-opposite point $\breve{p}_{qo} = (\breve{p}_{qo1}, \breve{p}_{qo2}, \ldots, \breve{p}_{qoD})$, quasi-reflection point $\breve{p}_{qr} = (\breve{p}_{qr1}, \breve{p}_{qr2}, \ldots, \breve{p}_{qrD})$, center sampling-based opposite point $\breve{p}_{cb} = (\breve{p}_{cb1}, \breve{p}_{cb2}, \ldots, \breve{p}_{cbD})$ of p can be completely defined by its coordinates, respectively

$$\breve{p}_{oi} = a_i + b_i - p_i \tag{1}$$

$$\breve{p}_{qoi} = \text{rand}(c_i, \breve{p}_{oi}) \tag{2}$$

$$\breve{p}_{qri} = \text{rand}(p_i, c_i) \tag{3}$$

$$\breve{p}_{cbi} = \text{rand}(p_i, \breve{p}_{oi}) \tag{4}$$

where c_i is the center of the search interval $[a_i, b_i]$ and rand(MIN, MAX) is a random number (uniformly distributed) between MIN and MAX. Here, MIN can be equal to c_i or p_i, and MAX can be equal to $\breve{p}_{oi}$ or c_i.

General speaking, the opposite points generated by different opposite strategies have a shorter expected distance towards the global minimum than randomly generated ones. To further reduce the expected distance, opposite-center learning was proposed as following [10].

Let $p = (p_1, p_2, \ldots, p_D) \in R^D$ be a starting point and $x = (x_1, x_2, \ldots, x_D) \in R^D$ be the global optimal solution of an unknown optimization problem. Then the opposite-center point $\breve{p}_{oc}$ is defined by

$$\breve{p}_{oc} = \underset{\breve{p}}{\arg\min} \int_{x \in T} \|\breve{p} - x\| f(x) dx \tag{5}$$

where $T = \left\{ x : \|p - x\| > \|\breve{p} - x\| \right\}$ and $f(x)$ is the supposed probability distribution function (PDF) of variable X.

Therefore, $\breve{p}_{oc}$ by definition is recognized as the best opposite point theoretically, which leads to the minimal expected distance towards the global optimal solution. If the random variable X follows uniform distribution between a and b, we can obtain the exact analytical solution of opposite-center point [10]:

$$\breve{p}_{oc} = \begin{cases} \frac{p}{3} + \frac{2b}{3}, & a \leq p \leq \frac{a+b}{2} \\ \frac{p}{3} + \frac{2a}{3}, & \frac{a+b}{2} \leq p \leq b \end{cases} \tag{6}$$

2.2 Performance Comparison

In practise, we observe the significant difference among these opposition schemes as mentioned above, but we cannot determine intuitively the best and the worst strategies. Therefore we have to take the second best way. General speaking, the better opposition strategy has the larger probability of its opposite point being closer than another opposite point to the optimal solution under certain conditions.

Without loss of generality, we may assume that optimal solution x and candidate solution p have uniform distribution between 0 and 1. Then the expected probabilities of being closer than other opposite point (or random point) to the solution x are given as follows: (1) $E\left(\Pr\left(|\breve{p}_o - x| < |p - x| \right) \right) = \frac{1}{2}$, (2) $E\left(\Pr\left(|\breve{p}_{qo} - x| < |p - x| \right) \right) = \frac{9}{16}$, (3) $E\left(\Pr\left(|\breve{p}_{qr} - x| < |p - x| \right) \right) = \frac{11}{16}$, (4) $E\left(\Pr\left(|\breve{p}_{qo} - x| < |\breve{p}_o - x| \right) \right) = \frac{11}{16}$, (5) $E\left(\Pr\left(|\breve{p}_{qr} - x| < |\breve{p}_o - x| \right) \right) = \frac{9}{16}$, and (6) $E\left(\Pr\left(|\breve{p}_{qo} - x| < |\breve{p}_{qr} - x| \right) \right) = \frac{1}{2}$. See [6, 11] for details of these theoretical results.

While these preliminary results are encouraging for us, there exist some issues in applying this method. First, only two OBL schemes can be compared directly by this method. Second, the expected probability is only a relative value under a given assumption, not representing the real performance of each OBL scheme. For example, while QOBL may be superior than QROBL according to (4) and (5), these two schemes are equivalent according to (6). Third, these preliminary results described above have only involved three OBL schemes and random sampling, and other influential OBL strategies (such as CBS, GOBL and COOBL) are left. One possible explanation to this observation could be each theoretical result is deduced by a special way. As a result, we cannot derive the similar result for new OBL scheme (such as OCL proposed recently) using the previous method. Thus a uniform theoretical approach is required to measure and compare the quality of different opposition strategies.

3   Evaluation Function and Its Numerical Calculation

In order to compare OBL schemes, perhaps the first problem we face is that how to quantitatively evaluate them. Inspired by opposition-based optimization [3] and some comparison results proposed in [6, 11], an evaluation function can be defined as

$$g(x) = E\left(\min\left\{|p - x|, |\breve{p} - x|\right\}\right) = \int_{-\infty}^{\infty} \int_{-\infty}^{\infty} \min\left\{|p - x|, |\breve{p} - x|\right\} f(p, \breve{p}) dp d\breve{p} \quad (7)$$

in this paper. When given the variable X, it represents the mean minimum Euclidean distance from a point (or its opposite point) to an optimal solution.

Some examples of this evaluation function in one dimension are displayed in Fig. 1. The computation process is identical to that appearing in [12]: the locations of the optimal solution are successively fixed at [0.00, 0.01, 0.02, ..., 0.99, 1.00], and for each optimal solution 10^4 point pairs (a candidate point and its corresponding opposite point) are sampled with each scheme.

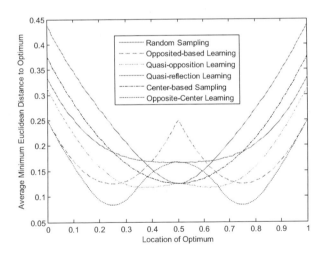

Fig. 1. Comparison of different sampling strategies in one dimension.

As seen from Fig. 1, five variations of OBL can be divided into three groups when compared with random sampling. (1) The original OBL is more desirable than random sampling, when the optimum is not near the center of the search interval. (2) On the contrary, QROBL and CBS are more undesirable than random sampling, when the optimum is near the center of the search interval. (3) Lastly, QOBL and OCL strategies outperform the random sampling clearly, no matter where the optimum is located in the search interval.

By careful observation, we find some preliminary and intuitive results as described previously. However this numerical calculation method may be impracticable and in some cases impossible to compare the well-known OBL schemes. For example, the relationship between OBL and QOBL is varying and ambiguous. When the optimum is near the center of the search interval, QOBL performs much better than OBL and it is quite opposite when the optimum is located at both the ends of the interval. Furthermore, the event probability and the extent of their differences are almost the same. Hence a uniform analysis approach to different opposite strategies is required in this case.

4   Theoretical Approach and Analysis Results

4.1   Theoretical Approach

We know from the definition that the evaluation function depends on three factors: the candidate point p, the OBL scheme and the optimal solution x of an optimization problem. As shown in Sect. 3, for each OBL scheme, if the optimal solution x is fixed, the evaluation function can be obtained by exhaustive candidate points. Along with this idea, the evaluation function $g(x)$ can represent the performance of OBL scheme in some ways. Clearly smaller the value of evaluation function is, the better the performance of OBL scheme is. In this section, in order to calculate the evaluation function, we provide a theoretical approach, which includes five steps as follows.

Step 1: According to the prior knowledge, the probability distributions of the candidate point p and its corresponding opposite point $\breve{p}$ are determined in advance. Otherwise, the uniform distribution is an alternative way.

Step 2: The whole space A is further divided into some areas A_i $(i = 1, 2, \ldots)$ based on the values of the candidate point p, its opposite point $\breve{p}$ and the optimal solution x. The following two steps are designed based on each one of these areas.

Step 3: Two absolute values $(|p - x|$ and $|\breve{p} - x|)$ are simplified under each special area A_i. Next the value of $\min\left\{|p - x|, |\breve{p} - x|\right\}$ can be obtained directly by an analytical method.

Step 4: The mathematical expectation is then calculated numerically over the given integration region A_i.

Step 5: The evaluation function over the whole space $(A = \underset{i}{\cup} A_i)$ can be obtained by summing these expectations over the individual region A_i.

4.2   A Calculation Example

To begin with, the evaluation function for QOBL scheme is presented in this section as an illustration to show the computation process.

As mentioned earlier, we assume that the candidate point p follows the uniform distribution between 0 and 1, that is $f(p) = \begin{cases} 1, & 0<p<1 \\ 0, & else \end{cases}$. According to Eq. 2, quasi-opposite point $\breve{p}$ is a random number between $1/2$ and $1 - p$. Thus when the candidate point p is located at left half space, $f(\breve{p}) = \begin{cases} \frac{1}{(1-p)-\frac{1}{2}}, & \frac{1}{2} < \breve{p} < 1-p \\ 0, & else \end{cases}$,

otherwise $f(\breve{p}) = \begin{cases} \frac{1}{\frac{1}{2}-(1-p)}, & 1-p < \breve{p} < \frac{1}{2} \\ 0, & else \end{cases}$. Note that, in this example, the candidate

point p and its quasi-opposite point $\breve{p}$ are independent of each other, which leads to $f(p,\breve{p}) = f(p) \cdot f(\breve{p})$.

In step 2, the whole space can be divided into 12 special cases based on the values of the optimum x, the candidate point p and its opposite point $\breve{p}$. It's evident that, for the first six cases, they must satisfy the following in equation: $0 < p < (p + \breve{p})/2 < 1/2 < \breve{p} < 1 - p < 1$. Similarly, for the latter six cases, they must satisfy the following inequation: $0 < 1 - p < \breve{p} < 1/2 < (p + \breve{p})/2 < p < 1$. The key goal of such division is to reduce two absolute values ($|p - x|$ and $|\breve{p} - x|$) in $g(x)$. Therefore for each case, the value of $\min\left\{|p - x|, |\breve{p} - x|\right\}$ can be calculated directly in step 3, and then the integration region (upper limit and lower limit of the integral variable) is determined as illustrated in Fig. 2. Thus we can discuss the evaluation function $g(x)$ as following.

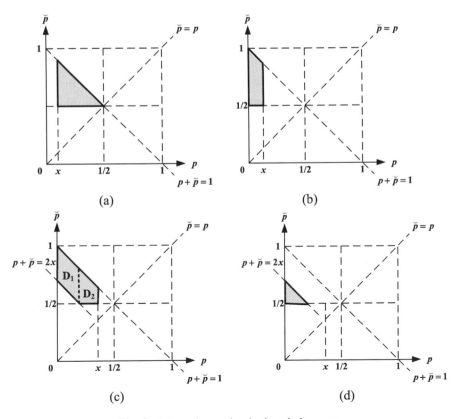

Fig. 2. Integration region in the whole space.

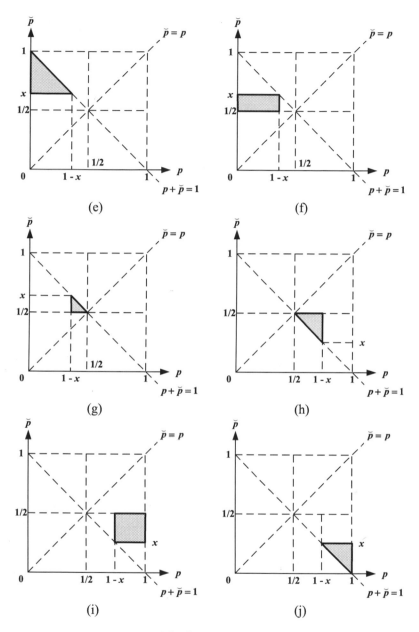

Fig. 2. (*continued*)

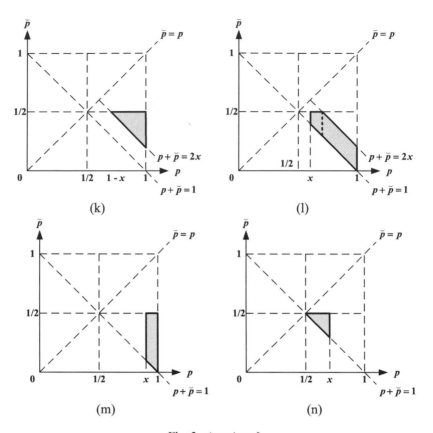

Fig. 2. (*continued*)

Case 1: We assume that $0 < x < p < (p + \breve{p})/2 < 1/2 < \breve{p} < 1-p < 1$. Hence,

$$g(x) = E\left(\min\left\{|p - x|, |\breve{p} - x|\right\}\right) = \int_{-\infty}^{\infty} \int_{-\infty}^{\infty} (p - x)f(p)f(\breve{p})dpd\breve{p}$$

we get   as illus-

$$= \int_{x}^{\frac{1}{2}} dp \int_{\frac{1}{2}}^{1-p} \frac{p - x}{-p + \frac{1}{2}} d\breve{p} = \frac{1}{2}(x - \frac{1}{2})^2$$

trated in Fig. 2(a).

Case 2: We assume that $0 < p < x < (p + \breve{p})/2 < 1/2 < \breve{p} < 1 - p < 1$. Hence, we get $g(x) = \int_{0}^{x} dp \int_{\frac{1}{2}}^{1-p} \frac{x-p}{\frac{1}{2}-p} d\breve{p} = \frac{1}{2}x^2$ if $0 < x < 1/4$ as illustrated in Fig. 2(b), and

$$g(x) = \int_{0}^{2x-\frac{1}{2}} dp \int_{2x-p}^{1-p} \frac{x - p}{\frac{1}{2} - p} d\breve{p} + \int_{2x-\frac{1}{2}}^{x} dp \int_{\frac{1}{2}}^{1-p} \frac{x - p}{\frac{1}{2} - p} d\breve{p}$$ if $1/4 < x < 1/2$ as illus-

$$= (1 - 2x)\left[(2x - \frac{1}{2}) + (\frac{1}{2} - x)\ln(1 - 2x)\right] + \frac{1}{2}(x - \frac{1}{2})^2$$

trated in Fig. 2(c).

Case 3: We assume that $0<p<(p+\breve{p})/2<x<1/2<\breve{p}<1-p<1$. Hence, we get $g(x) = 0$ if $0 < x < 1/4$, and $g(x) = \int_0^{2x-\frac{1}{2}} dp \int_{\frac{1}{2}}^{2x-p} \frac{\breve{p}-x}{\frac{1}{2}-p} d\breve{p} = (x - \frac{1}{4})^2$ if $1/4 < x < 1/2$ as illustrated in Fig. 2(d).

Case 4: We assume that $0<p<(p+\breve{p})/2<1/2<x<\breve{p}<1-p<1$. Hence, we get $g(x) = \int_0^{1-x} dp \int_x^{1-p} \frac{\breve{p}-x}{\frac{1}{2}-p} d\breve{p} = \frac{1}{4}(x - 1)(3x - 2) - \frac{1}{2}(x - \frac{1}{2})^2 \ln(2x - 1)$ as illustrated in Fig. 2(e).

Case 5: We assume that $0<p<(p+\breve{p})/2 < 1/2 < \breve{p} <x<1-p < 1$. Thence, we get $g(x) = \int_{\frac{1}{2}}^x d\breve{p} \int_0^{1-x} \frac{x-\breve{p}}{\frac{1}{2}-p} dp = -\frac{1}{2}(x - \frac{1}{2})^2 \ln(2x - 1)$ as illustrated in Fig. 2(f).

Case 6: We assume that $0 < p < (p + \breve{p})/2 < 1/2 < \breve{p} < 1-p < x < 1$. Hence, we get $g(x) = \int_{1-x}^{\frac{1}{2}} dp \int_{\frac{1}{2}}^{1-p} \frac{x-\breve{p}}{\frac{1}{2}-p} d\breve{p} = \frac{3}{4}(x - \frac{1}{2})^2$ as illustrated in Fig. 2(g).

Case 7: We assume that $0 < x < 1-p < \breve{p} < 1/2 < (p + \breve{p})/2 < p < 1$. Hence, we get $g(x) = \int_x^{\frac{1}{2}} d\breve{p} \int_{1-\breve{p}}^{1-x} \frac{p-x}{\frac{1}{2}-p} dp = \frac{3}{4}(x - \frac{1}{2})^2$ as illustrated in Fig. 2(h).

Case 8: We assume that $0 < 1-p < x < \breve{p} < 1/2 < (p + \breve{p})/2 < p < 1$. Hence, we get $g(x) = \int_x^{\frac{1}{2}} d\breve{p} \int_{1-x}^{1} \frac{\breve{p}-x}{p-\frac{1}{2}} dp = -\frac{1}{2}(x - \frac{1}{2})^2 \ln\frac{1}{1-2x}$ as illustrated in Fig. 2(i).

Case 9: We assume that $0 < 1-p < \breve{p} < x < 1/2 < (p + \breve{p})/2 < p < 1$. Hence, we get $g(x) = \int_{1-x}^{\frac{1}{2}} dp \int_{1-p}^{x} \frac{x-\breve{p}}{p-\frac{1}{2}} d\breve{p} = \frac{1}{4}x(3x - 1) + \frac{1}{2}(x - \frac{1}{2})^2 \ln\frac{1}{1-2x}$ as illustrated in Fig. 2(j).

Case 10: We assume that $0 < 1-p < \breve{p} < 1/2 < x < (p + \breve{p})/2 < p < 1$, we get $g(x) = 0$ if $3/4 < x < 1$, and $g(x) = \int_{2x-\frac{1}{2}}^{1} dp \int_{2x-p}^{\frac{1}{2}} \frac{x-\breve{p}}{p-\frac{1}{2}} d\breve{p} = (x - \frac{3}{4})^2$ if $1/2 < x < 3/4$ as illustrated in Fig. 2(k).

Case 11: We assume that $0 < 1-p < \breve{p} < 1/2 < (p + \breve{p})/2 < x < p < 1$. Hence, we get

$$g(x) = \int_x^{2x-\frac{1}{2}} \frac{p - x}{p - \frac{1}{2}} dp \int_{1-p}^{\frac{1}{2}} d\breve{p} + \int_{2x-\frac{1}{2}}^{1} \frac{p - x}{p - \frac{1}{2}} dp \int_{1-p}^{2x-p} d\breve{p}$$ if $1/2 < x < 3/4$ as

$$= (2x - 1)\left[(\frac{3}{2} - 2x) + (x - \frac{1}{2}) \ln 2(2x - 1)\right] + \frac{1}{2}(x - \frac{1}{2})^2$$

illustrated in Fig. 2(l), and $g(x) = \int_x^{1} \frac{p-x}{p-\frac{1}{2}} dp \int_{1-p}^{\frac{1}{2}} d\breve{p} = \frac{1}{2}(x - 1)^2$ if $3/4 < x < 1$ as illustrated in Fig. 2(m).

Case 12: We assume that $0 < 1-p < \breve{p} < 1/2 < (p + \breve{p})/2 < p < x < 1$. Hence, we get $g(x) = \int_{\frac{1}{2}}^x \frac{x-p}{p-\frac{1}{2}} dp \int_{1-p}^{\frac{1}{2}} d\breve{p} = \frac{1}{2}(x - \frac{1}{2})^2$ as illustrated in Fig. 2(n).

As a result, by summing these exceptions, we get the evaluation function

$$g(x) = \begin{cases} \frac{5}{2}x^2 - \frac{3}{2}x + \frac{5}{16} - (x - \frac{1}{2})^2 \ln(1 - 2x), & 0<x<\frac{1}{4} \\ \frac{1}{2}x(1 - x) + (x - \frac{1}{2})^2 \ln 4(1 - 2x), & \frac{1}{4}<x<\frac{1}{2} \\ \frac{1}{2}x(1 - x) + (x - \frac{1}{2})^2 \ln 4(2x - 1), & \frac{1}{2}<x<\frac{3}{4} \\ \frac{5}{2}x^2 - \frac{7}{2}x + \frac{21}{16} - (x - \frac{1}{2})^2 \ln(2x - 1), & \frac{3}{4}<x<1 \end{cases} \qquad (8)$$

4.3 Analysis Results

Taking the same approach with random sampling and other opposite strategies, their evaluation functions can also be calculated as following:

$$g(x) = \begin{cases} 2 \times \left(-\frac{2}{3}x^3 + x^2 - \frac{1}{2}x + \frac{1}{6}\right), & 0 < x < \frac{1}{2} \\ 2 \times \left(\frac{2}{3}x^3 - x^2 + \frac{1}{2}x\right), & \frac{1}{2} < x < 1 \end{cases} \text{ for random sampling,}$$

$$g(x) = \begin{cases} 2 \times \left(x^2 - \frac{1}{2}x + \frac{1}{8}\right), & 0 < x < \frac{1}{2} \\ 2 \times \left(x^2 - \frac{3}{2}x + \frac{5}{8}\right), & \frac{1}{2} < x < 1 \end{cases} \text{ for OBL,}$$

$$g(x) = \begin{cases} -\frac{1}{2}(x + \frac{1}{2})^2 + \frac{9}{16} + (x - \frac{1}{2})^2 \ln(1 - 2x), & 0 < x < \frac{1}{4} \\ \frac{5}{2}(x - \frac{1}{2})^2 + \frac{1}{8} - (x - \frac{1}{2})^2 \ln 4(1 - 2x), & \frac{1}{4} < x < \frac{1}{2} \\ \frac{5}{2}(x - \frac{1}{2})^2 + \frac{1}{8} - (x - \frac{1}{2})^2 \ln 4(2x - 1), & \frac{1}{2} < x < \frac{3}{4} \\ -\frac{1}{2}(x - \frac{3}{2})^2 + \frac{9}{16} + (x - \frac{1}{2})^2 \ln(2x - 1), & \frac{3}{4} < x < 1 \end{cases} \text{ for QROBL,}$$

$$g(x) = (x - \frac{1}{2})^2 + \frac{1}{8} \text{ for CBS, and}$$

$$g(x) = \begin{cases} (x - \frac{1}{2})^2, & 0 < x < \frac{1}{6}, \quad \frac{5}{6} < x < 1 \\ 4x^2 - 2x + \frac{1}{3}, & \frac{1}{6} < x < \frac{1}{3} \\ -2x^2 + 2x - \frac{1}{3}, & \frac{1}{3} < x < \frac{2}{3} \\ 4x^2 - 6x + \frac{7}{3}, & \frac{2}{3} < x < \frac{5}{6} \end{cases}$$

for OCL.

In our opinion, these theoretical results have two significant roles. Firstly, they can verify the previous numerical results, as shown in Fig. 1. Furthermore, their mathematical expectation $E(g(x))$ can be utilized to compare these sampling schemes in one dimensional case. For example, for random sampling,

$$E(g(x)) = \int_{-\infty}^{\infty} g(x)f(x)dx = \int_0^1 g(x)dx$$

$$= \int_0^{\frac{1}{2}} 2 \times \left(-\frac{2}{3}x^3 + x^2 - \frac{1}{2}x + \frac{1}{6}\right)dx + \int_{\frac{1}{2}}^1 2 \times \left(\frac{2}{3}x^3 - x^2 + \frac{1}{2}x\right)dx = \frac{5}{24}$$, where

$f(x) = 1, 0 < x < 1$. We suppose, once again, the global optimal solution x follows the uniform distribution between 0 and 1 for all sampling strategies in this section. Theoretical and simulation results are tabulated as Table 1.

Table 1. Mathematical expectation of the evaluation function for all sampling strategies.

Sampling strategy	Theoretical result	Simulation result	Relative error
Random sampling	0.2083 (5/24)	0.2025 ± 0.06222	2.78
OBL	0.1667 (1/6)	0.1647 ± 0.05074	1.20
QOBL	0.1667 (1/6)	0.1598 ± 0.05054	4.14
QROBL	0.25 (1/4, worst)	0.2401 ± 0.07724	3.96
CBS	0.2083 (5/24)	0.1948 ± 0.06363	6.48
OCL	0.1389 (5/36, best)	0.1354 ± 0.04242	2.52

It is observed from Table 1 that the theoretical results are very similar (the relative error is less than 6.5%) to the simulation experiments, which show the validity of the uniform analysis approach in this section. An interesting result is that, for all sampling strategies, the mathematical expectations by simulation experiments are always less than the theoretical results. Finding the reason behind this phenomenon is one of the directions we should work towards in near future. Furthermore, based on their mathematical expectations, all opposition strategies can be ranked easily: OCL (best) > OBL $\approx$ QOBL > random sampling $\approx$ CBS > QROBL (worst).

5 Conclusion

Inspired by opposition-based optimization and some primary comparison results, we proposed a novel evaluation function of opposition strategies in this paper. It is the mean minimum Euclidean distance from a point (or its opposite point) to the optimal solution. Thus different opposition strategies in one dimensional case can be compared easily by means of the mathematical expectation of these functions. Both theoretical analysis and simulation experiments indicate that, OCL scheme has the best performance for sampling problems, while QROBL has the worst performance among all tested schemes.

Note that although Euclidean distance is considered in our example, other choices (such as Manhattan distance and Chebyshev distance) are also allowed. Since meta-heuristic algorithms are generally employed for multidimensional problems, it is an urgent task for us to extend this approach in higher dimensions.

Acknowledgments. This work was supported in part by the National Natural Science Foundation of China (Nos. 61305083 and 61603404), Shaanxi Science and Technology Project (No. 2017CG-022) and Xi'an Science and Research Project (No. 2017080CG/RC043).

References

1. Bernoulli, J.: Ars conjectandi (The art of conjecture). Impensis Thurnisiorum, Basel, Switzerland (1713)
2. Papoulis, A., Pillai, S.: Probability, Random Variables, and Stochastic Processes. McGraw-Hill, New York (1965)
3. Tizhoosh, R.: Opposition-based learning: a new scheme for machine intelligence. In: International Conference on Computational Intelligence for Modelling, Control and Automation, and International Conference on Intelligent Agents, Web Technologies and Internet Commerce, Vienna, Austria, pp. 695–701 (2005)
4. Xu, Q.Z., Wang, L., Wang, N., Hei, X.H., Zhao, L.: A review of opposition-based learning from 2005 to 2012. Eng. Appl. Artif. Intell. **29**(1), 1–12 (2014)
5. Rahnamayan, S., Tizhoosh, H.R., Salama, M.M.A.: Quasi-oppositional differential evolution. In: IEEE Congress on Evolutionary Computation, Singapore, pp. 2229–2236 (2007)
6. Ergezer, M., Simon, D., Du, D.W.: Oppositional biogeography-based optimization. In: IEEE International Conference on Systems, Man and Cybernetics, San Antonio, USA, pp. 1009–1014 (2009)
7. Rahnamayan, S., Wang, G.G.: Center-based sampling for population-based algorithms. In: IEEE Congress on Evolutionary Computation, pp. 933–938. Trondheim, Norway (2009)

8. Wang, H., Wu, Z.J., Liu, Y., Wang, J., Jiang, D.Z., Chen, L.L.: Space transformation search: a new evolutionary technique. In: ACM/SIGEVO Summit on Genetic and Evolutionary Computation, Shanghai, China, pp. 537–544 (2009)
9. Xu, Q.Z., Wang, L., He, B.M., Wang, N.: Modified opposition-based differential evolution for function optimization. J. Comput. Inf. Syst. 7(5), 1582–1591 (2011)
10. Xu, H.P., Erdbrink, C.D., Krzhizhanovskaya, V.V.: How to speed up optimization? opposite-center learning and its application to differential evolution. Procedia Comput. Sci. 51(1), 805–814 (2015)
11. Ergezer, M., Simon, D.: Mathematical and experimental analyses of oppositional algorithms. IEEE Trans. Cybern. 44(11), 2178–2189 (2014)
12. Rahnamayan, S., Wang, G.G., Ventresca, M.: An intuitive distance-based explanation of opposition-based sampling. Appl. Soft Comput. 12(9), 2828–2839 (2012)

Author Index

Printed in the United States
By Bookmasters